To Nan, for 20 years

Contents at a Glance

Contents

About the Author

SCOT HILLIER is an independent consultant and Microsoft Most Valuable Professional (MVP) focused on creating solutions for information workers with SharePoint, Office, and related .NET technologies. He is the author of ten books on Microsoft technologies. When not writing about technology, Scot can often be found presenting to audiences ranging from developers to C-level executives. Scot is a former naval submarine officer and graduate of the Virginia Military Institute. Scot can be reached at scot@shillier.com. Support for his books can be found at http://www.sharepointstuff.com.

About the Technical Reviewer

■**SAHIL MALIK** (http://www.winsmarts.com) is a Microsoft MVP (C#), an INETA speaker, and the author of a best-selling ADO.NET 2.0 book. He is a consultant, a trainer, and a mentor in various Microsoft technologies. His talks are high-energy, highly charged, and highly rated. Sahil blogs about various technical topics at http://blah.winsmarts.com.

Acknowledgments

My relationship with Apress now spans three years and four books. Over the course of my career, I have written books for several houses, but none of them were as easy to work with. The Apress organization continues to have a great team that consistently produces quality books. I'd first like to acknowledge Gary Cornell and his leadership at Apress, which he is responsible for creating and building. I'd also like to thank Jim Sumser for managing my relationship with Apress prior to this work. Jonathan Hassell took over from Jim as lead editor for this book and assembled a first-class team. Leading off the team was the technical editor, Sahil Malik. Without exception I can say that Sahil is the single best technical editor I have ever worked with. His suggestions were detailed, pointed, and accurate. This book is better because of his efforts. Elizabeth Seymour was the project manager for the book and kept everything rolling along so we could meet our deadlines. Thanks also to Jennifer Whipple for her efforts in copy editing. A final thanks as well to Kelly Winquist for managing the production process.

Along with the Apress team, I'd also like to thank all of the Microsoft Most Valuable Professionals for SharePoint. This diverse group of people continues to be tremendously valuable in bringing key information, tips, and techniques to the development community. Throughout the writing process I shared thoughts with other MVPs, many of whom were writing their own books. We freely exchanged ideas and solutions that will ultimately make all of the SharePoint books better regardless of the author. Thanks everyone.

Every time I write a book, I am reminded of the importance of family. Writing late into the night, early in the morning, and on weekends definitely has an impact on everyone around you. I am fortunate to have such a wonderful family that supports me completely. Nan, we have known each other now for 26 years and have been married for 20. Everything I have ever accomplished I owe to your support. Thanks for being my best friend. Ashley, we are so proud of you; you are a blessing. We can't wait to see where life will take you, but we miss you, so come home sometimes! Matt, you are the son every parent wants; we continue to be amazed at your wisdom, grace, and talent.

Thanks to everyone.

Introduction

With SharePoint now in its third release, many developers and users are well familiar with its core functionality. However, this version of SharePoint is truly astonishing in its scope. Not only does this version have the familiar sites, documents, and lists, but it also supports vast new capabilities in content management, document management, records management, and business intelligence. Along with these capabilities, this version of SharePoint has many new ways to integrate data and create customized solutions. For me, the combination of business-oriented capabilities and advanced solution-development techniques has always been the basis of my enthusiasm for SharePoint. In fact, this is the perspective that I have tried to bring to this book; I want to combine business needs and technical skills to create solutions that truly impact business. You can be the judge of how well that vision has been reached.

Who This Book Is For

Many years ago, I asked a colleague what professional developers wanted in a book. He responded simply "Code they can steal." I have never forgotten this advice and it has been the foundation of every book I have written since. This book is therefore targeted squarely at the intermediate to advanced developer in a corporate environment with a pending SharePoint project. Readers do not have to have any prior experience with SharePoint to be successful with this book. However, readers should be well-versed in .NET development with C# to get the most out of the book. Furthermore, readers should be ready to make a commitment to this book. I have constructed the book with the intent that it be read cover to cover. I have also defined a development environment in Chapter 2 that I use throughout the book. The bottom line is that this book should be thought of as a technical training course as opposed to a reference manual. If you approach it that way, you will get the maximum benefit.

How This Book Is Organized

I began my technical career training professional developers in Visual Basic 3.0. As a result, my writing style and chapter organization reflect a training class. Each chapter in the book begins with an explanation of the appropriate foundational concepts followed by practical exercises to reinforce the explanation. A brief description of each chapter follows.

Chapter 1: SharePoint Business Solutions

This chapter is an overview of SharePoint solutions from a business perspective. Although this is a technical book, this chapter will help you understand and consider the environment into which your solutions will be deployed. This is some light reading before you get started.

Chapter 2: SharePoint Overview, Planning, and Installation

This chapter is the foundation for the entire book. In this chapter you will learn the planning and installation considerations for SharePoint. Additionally, you will set up a development environment that can be used throughout the book. You should not skip this chapter because its information is assumed throughout the rest of the book. Plan on spending a few days with this material to properly set up your SharePoint environment.

Chapter 3: SharePoint Fundamentals

This chapter provides an overview of the fundamental capabilities of SharePoint You'll use this information to get a fully functional SharePoint farm and create your first sites. You'll also learn about new capabilities in this version that specifically target weaknesses from previous versions of SharePoint.

Chapter 4: SharePoint Shared Services

This chapter completes the configuration of critical services within your SharePoint farm. You'll configure and use search, profiles, audiences, Excel Services, and the Business Data Catalog. This chapter is mandatory for anyone working with the Microsoft Office SharePoint Server (MOSS).

Chapter 5: SharePoint Content Development and Management

This chapter covers the new content management capabilities of SharePoint. You'll learn how to add new pages to sites and manage the deployment process. This chapter also shows you how to create and apply themes, master pages, and style sheets. If you want to customize the look of SharePoint, this chapter will show you how.

Chapter 6: SharePoint Document, Form, and Records Management

This chapter covers all of the integration points between SharePoint and documents, forms, and records. You'll learn the basics of metadata and how to interact with it. You'll also learn how to deploy forms in libraries and through the new InfoPath Forms Services technology. Finally, you'll set up a records library and apply retention policies to archived documents.

Chapter 7: SharePoint Custom Features and Workflows

Customization of SharePoint begins in earnest with this chapter. Here, you'll learn how to create your own custom features for adding items to menus, adding new administrative pages, making changes to the infrastructure, and receiving event notifications. This chapter also covers how to create workflow solutions with both the SharePoint Designer and Visual Studio.

Chapter 8: SharePoint Business Intelligence Solutions

This chapter focuses on creating dashboards within the new Report Center. You'll learn how to create scorecards with stoplights to represent key performance indicators (KPI) and how to integrate Excel spreadsheets to show data. This chapter also shows how to integrate SQL Analysis Services and SQL Reporting Services with SharePoint.

Chapter 9: SharePoint and Microsoft Office

This chapter covers all of the different ways to create solutions with Office 2007 products. You'll learn how to create add-ins for Office and make them part of a SharePoint solution. You'll also learn about the new open XML file formats and how they can be integrated with SharePoint.

Chapter 10: SharePoint Web Parts

This chapter provides complete coverage of creating and deploying web parts in SharePoint. You'll learn about the web part life cycle and how to code the new ASP.NET 2.0 web parts that are used by SharePoint. You'll also learn how to create web parts that can be connected together to act as filters. Finally, you'll learn to create solution files for deploying web parts to the SharePoint farm.

Chapter 11: Programming SharePoint Services

This chapter provides the fundamentals you'll need to get started programming against the SharePoint object model and web services. You'll learn the basics of accessing SharePoint programmatically and manipulating site information, user information, lists, and libraries. This chapter also covers the Microsoft Single Sign-On service.

Chapter 12: SharePoint Operations and Administration

This chapter provides all of the foundational information you will need to properly administer a SharePoint farm. You'll learn how to back up and restore a farm, get reports, and monitor the infrastructure. You'll also learn how to improve SharePoint performance with caching mechanisms.

CHAPTER 1

SharePoint Business Solutions

Although this book is packed full of solution examples and plenty of code, I've always thought it is important to frame the context of these solutions inside of the business environment they target. A successful SharePoint solution must take into account the overall direction Microsoft is going, the vertical marketplace in which your organization operates, and the willingness of end users to adopt new technologies. Therefore, I'll indulge in a little digression from my charter in this chapter. If you're just dying for some code, flip to the middle of the book and breathe deeply. Then come back and take a few minutes to read this chapter and think about the environment in which you are deploying SharePoint.

Before I begin a discussion of the details, I want to point out that the term *SharePoint* does not actually refer to any particular product or technology. Instead, it is an umbrella term that hangs over several products and technologies that have specific names. In general, however, most people use the term to mean any solution based on either Windows SharePoint Services (WSS) or the Microsoft Office SharePoint Server (MOSS). This is how I will use the term throughout the book, even though many Microsoft people frown on this usage.

The SharePoint Marketplace

The 2007 release of SharePoint and the Microsoft Office 2007 suite marks a significant milestone in the effort to create a single unified platform for information-based work. This is the third version of SharePoint products and technologies to be released by Microsoft, and it is substantially more powerful than any of its predecessors. Over the next three to five years the effect of this release will be felt by all organizations that have an infrastructure based on Microsoft technology.

As of this writing, the market for enterprise collaboration software is somewhere in the neighborhood of $1.5 billion and is projected to approach $2.5 billion by 2010. By all accounts, SharePoint products and technologies have the largest number of licensees in this market, with volume exceeding 30 million. However, these numbers don't tell the whole story because this release of SharePoint and Office clearly extend beyond the market for enterprise collaboration into areas such as content management and business intelligence.

WSS is at the core of SharePoint and can rightfully be considered enterprise collaboration software. However, MOSS goes well beyond this narrow definition. MOSS is a superset of WSS functionality and includes sophisticated publishing, business intelligence, and workflow capabilities. Using MOSS, organizations can not only create collaborative spaces, but can also deploy departmental intranets, public-facing Internet sites, business intelligence dashboards, formal workflow processes, and enterprise-wide search capabilities. My point is that Share-Point products and technologies—particularly MOSS—actually embody what were previously three or four separate products crossing three or four different market segments. This is why I believe that SharePoint products and technologies will have such a massive impact on organizations that choose to adopt them. Therefore, it is important to consider the people, systems, and processes into which SharePoint will be deployed. In the following sections, I present a loose framework for understanding the roles of people within a typical organization and the challenges they face, and how various SharePoint solutions may be applied.

Segmenting Information Workers

These days everyone talks about the "knowledge economy" and "information workers." These terms were used originally to acknowledge that many economies were moving away from traditional manufacturing toward the management of information. As globalization continues to take hold, however, we are realizing that everyone needs better management of information in order to compete effectively. In fact, we now see that most workers use information within the framework of a business process, regardless of their jobs. Everyone from the controller analyzing financial data to a repair crew with a work order on a wireless device is an information worker. When building solutions for these information workers, however, it is useful to segment them into three different groups so we can better understand their needs: transactors, professionals, and executives.

Transactors

Some information workers use a single line-of-business system all day long. This group is known as *transactors*. Transactors are front-line workers who often create or enter data into systems. For example, a designer using a computer-aided design (CAD) system to create a model is a transactor. The designer primarily uses the CAD system all day and creates new data used by the organization. Customer service representatives in a call center are also transactors. They primarily use a single system all day and enter new data about customers. Because other information workers rely on the new data produced by transactors, this data must be effectively integrated into any SharePoint solution so that it becomes available to support business processes.

Professionals

Professional information workers must access multiple line-of-business systems and may use any number of them throughout the day. They have access to customer data systems, product data systems, and financial systems. Their primary work environment, however, is usually the Microsoft Office suite. Professional information workers are generally sending e-mail, writing documents, or building spreadsheets. They often log in to a line-of-business system, but they do it primarily to retrieve information so they can continue to work in an Office product. The classic example of a professional information worker is the controller who logs into a financial system simply to copy data into an Excel spreadsheet for analysis. The goal is to create a financial model in Excel, but the data is in several different systems. In fact, many professional information workers have essentially become "human middleware" that glues together seemingly disparate information from multiple sources into a single document. Eliminating human middleware is one of the primary goals of any SharePoint solution.

Executives

Executives must monitor and adjust business processes based on key performance indicators (KPI). These KPIs tell the executive information worker whether the organization is healthy and functioning correctly. When KPIs indicate that a business process is not healthy, executives must be able to analyze information in order to adjust the business process. Delivering KPIs to executives in a way that supports managing organizational performance is a key part of any SharePoint solution.

Grouping Information Workers

Another useful way to think about information workers is in groups of various sizes. This means giving consideration to the needs of the individual all the way through the larger organization that includes partners and customers. This is because all information workers accomplish their tasks in concert with others. Therefore, any solution you create with SharePoint should properly address these groups.

Individuals

Understanding the needs and behaviors of individuals is perhaps the most important requirement for success in any project. Projects that fail do so most often because individual users fail to adopt the new system. Even if everyone believes the end users would be happier and more productive using the new systems, they often fail to change their habits. Because of this, it's appropriate to ask "What do individual users want?"

I think the short answer is a simple and repeatable way to get their jobs done. Most end users are not enamored with technology and see change as an impediment to their productivity, even if that change would eventually result in a better experience. Practically speaking, this means simplifying the virtual environment. Successful solutions will provide clean and obvious interfaces that end users can utilize to access the most important documents, information, and applications.

Although MOSS provides a specific type of site, called My Site, that is intended for individual productivity, adoption of this capability has been limited in my experience. Users overwhelmingly prefer Microsoft Outlook as their primary interface to the enterprise because e-mail is such an integral part of their day. To this end, Microsoft Outlook 2007 has many enhancements that make it a much stronger tool for individuals working with SharePoint products and technologies. I discuss these enhancements throughout the book.

Departmental Teams

As you move from the individual to a team, the dynamics of system adoption change. Because teamwork is done in a more public setting and under the guidance of a leader, it is easier to get a team to adopt new ways of working. Therefore, you have a better opportunity to make improvements.

Departmental teams typically consist of a small number of people (less than ten) working together to accomplish a goal. The goal is usually limited in scope and easily understood by the team. These types of teams typically struggle, however, with communications and collaboration. Task management and information sharing are the primary areas of need. This, of course, is a historical sweet spot for SharePoint.

Divisional Groups

At the divisional level, information workers tend to need broad categories of information that help them understand their roles in the larger organization. The type of functionality found here includes access to vital line-of-business systems, work processes such as purchasing, and information pertaining to related divisions. Additionally, management at this level becomes more complex and requires some form of electronic reporting. SharePoint solutions at this level often consist of document management, dashboard, and searching capabilities that aggregate information from many sources.

Enterprise

At the enterprise level, information workers are typically dealing with policies, practices, and regulations that govern their work. At this level, management communication and guidelines are critical to bind the various groups together. Furthermore, individual information workers do not spend much of their day working at this level. They might receive an e-mail from the corporate president or read a newsletter online. SharePoint solutions at this level often take the form of intranets.

Extended Enterprise

Reaching beyond the boundaries of the organization to involve partners, suppliers, and customers is becoming increasingly critical. This level includes marketing, sales, support, and shared processes with partners. While these things were possible with previous versions of SharePoint, the capability was not strong. With the latest release, MOSS can be used to create a complete public Internet site as well as a secure extranet site for customer or partner interaction.

Information Worker Challenges

Global competition, or *globalization*, is now the major economic force shaping business decisions. The traditional long-term relationship between companies and their employees is extinct. Companies are constantly looking for ways to make employees more productive in an increasingly competitive marketplace, cut costs, and improve productivity. For their part, employees are typically less loyal to their companies. Today's employees are just as likely to start their own businesses as they are to bring new ideas to their employer. At the same time, technology is creating an increasingly complex work environment. All of these factors combine to create special challenges for businesses and information workers around system complexity, information, processes, collaboration, access, and management.

The System Challenge

When the desktop metaphor was introduced, it offered a simplified mechanism for interacting with a new, complex, and often scary appliance—the personal computer. The success of the desktop metaphor was that it simplified interaction with a computer. Nontechnical people were not required to learn complex function key combinations in order to use the computer. This metaphor—and, above all, its simplifying effect—was responsible for the success of graphic operating systems.

Early on, of course, there were several operating systems from several vendors that used the desktop metaphor. Each of these—Apple, IBM, and Microsoft—were competing to dominate the personal computer market. As a result, vendors began to include more functionality in the operating systems. Instead of just a file explorer, computers were loaded with all kinds of applets for managing every aspect of the computer. Vendors even shipped the computer with simple games that became a standard part of the operating system.

Later, after Microsoft had established clear dominance with Windows, it used the operating system to compete against other companies that introduced new technologies. The most famous example of this is the fight over the Netscape browser. Ultimately, Microsoft was found guilty of using its operating system to unfairly compete against Netscape. However, the constant fear of a small rival suddenly taking over the marketplace has consistently driven Microsoft to add more and more features to its operating system. As a result, the typical desktop is now awash in functionality. You not only have every line-of-business application you need to do your daily job, but you also have CD players, DVD players, and games. You have three or four different document editors available to you. You have two or three ways to get e-mail. Applications have followed suit as well by adding more and more features, reports, and integration points. The desktop and the applications it hosts are complex all over again.

Along with mounting complexity, information workers are also faced with a lack of standards for application behavior and integration. The most obvious example of this problem can be seen in the use of passwords. Users are now forced to maintain upward of ten different sets of credentials to access all the client-server, browser-based, and Internet applications they need on a daily basis. Typically, each of these applications has different rules for password length and design. The result is that users are unable to remember all of their credentials without recording them somewhere, which threatens the entire network security system.

Not only must information workers manage several sets of their credentials, they also must have intimate knowledge of the data sources utilized by applications. A typical example of this intimate knowledge is when an application login screen prompts an information worker to select the database or domain he or she wants to access. This seemingly simple request actually forces an end user to understand the network topology of the organization. This is an unnecessary burden to place on an information worker. This same intimate knowledge is also required to access file servers, mapped network drives, and printers.

Considering the three categories of information workers reveals that most organizations are structured in a manner that only supports transactors. Because transactors work primarily with a single line-of-business system, they can easily log in to one system and be productive throughout the day. However, professionals and executives face a chaotic environment that actually works against them because they require information from multiple sources synthesized into documents and reports.

The Information Challenge

Because the information that professionals and executives need to support the organization is locked up in separate isolated systems, they tend to work around the systems by getting much of their information from other human beings. I find that most people will spend some time looking through systems for information, but they rapidly become frustrated and simply send an e-mail to the person they think is most likely to have a copy of the information. Typically an e-mail is sent with a query such as "Can you send me the link to that file again?" or "Do you have the latest document template?" The response to these queries is usually an e-mail with a hyperlink embedded or a document attached. The e-mail is then stored in the recipient's personal Outlook folder so he or she can use it again in the future. This situation results in information workers becoming what I call "human search engines."

I once worked with a company that hired a consulting organization to help it create formalized procedures for its information workers. The consultant that was leading the project did a great job identifying the processes, documenting the procedures, and creating the documents. Additionally, he created a special filing system on a network drive to store all of the procedures. The only problem was that no one understood the filing system except him. At the end of the project, the company was forced to hire the consultant as a full-time employee simply to help other people locate the various process documents. In fact, I can testify that this person has no other job than to receive requests for documents and respond by sending copies attached to e-mail. This is a true human search engine. How many of these do you have in your organization?

The Process Challenge

While many organizations have defined some level of business process, most organizations have no way to support it beyond attaching documents to e-mail. Professionals who are creating documents and spreadsheets typically need some form of review and approval, so they simply attach the document to an e-mail for routing. Recipients who are involved in the review and approval process have no formal mechanism for tracking comments or minding versions of the document, so they often respond by sending e-mail with suggested changes, comments, or observations. The document creator must subsequently synthesize all the mail into a set of changes and route the document again.

Nearly all organizations can force the processes to work, but the processes never improve. The people involved in the process will continue sending e-mail, attending meetings, and working late until the document is completed and approved. However, two problems result from this approach. The first problem is that the organization typically loses all of the historical knowledge generated in the process. This means that when a similar document is created, the organization cannot benefit from any previous work. The inefficient process is simply started all over again. The second problem is that the inefficient process delays the time to market. Organizations may miss critical deadlines, work overtime, or hire additional people as they wrestle with an unsupported, chaotic process.

The Collaboration Challenge

Increasingly, information workers are being asked to work on teams where the members are located in other geographies and time zones. However, most organizations have no means

beyond e-mail to facilitate the work of these virtual teams. Consequently, e-mail is functioning not only as a process engine, but also as a collaboration tool. You can see this in the dozens
of conversational e-mails you receive every day. A large part of all corporate e-mail traffic is
being used to facilitate collaboration, reach consensus, and make decisions.

More recently, many organizations have adopted some form of instant messaging system
to try and cut out the conversational e-mails clogging the system. Unfortunately, for most
information workers, however, this has become yet another task master demanding attention.
Because it is so easy to send an instant message, I often see desktops full of multiple conversations. Furthermore, many of these conversations are not urgent, but they constantly interrupt
the information worker with sounds and pop-up windows. The result is that low-level conversations actually get more attention because of the intrusive nature of instant messaging.

Just as organizations lose information when they use e-mail as a process engine, the
same thing happens when e-mail is used as a collaboration engine. Information is duplicated
in e-mail messages sent to multiple recipients, and no one really knows which copy is the
true working version. When comments come back from recipients, they must be placed back
in the original document by hand.

Along with facilitating collaboration, e-mail also serves most people as their global task
list. When I describe e-mail as a *global task list*, I am referring to the practice of keeping an
e-mail as a reminder to take an action. You might, for example, keep an e-mail from a customer as a reminder to follow up on a sales opportunity. It doesn't even matter if the e-mail
you keep has anything to do with the action you want to take. Keeping the e-mail makes you
think about the customer and reminds you to follow up.

People use their e-mail as a global task list because they have no other tool that shows
them all the tasks they have to perform for an organization. But this results in the average
professional information worker having dozens or even hundreds of e-mails in their inbox
with no organization or prioritization. Add your instant messages to that burden and you'll
do nothing except answer mail all day.

Along with e-mail, shared file systems are often routinely misused to facilitate collaboration. Nearly all organizations have some form of shared file system that is made available to
information workers for storing documents. In most cases, the information workers have
complete read/write access to these servers. They can create directories and save documents
at will. Unfortunately, once a file server is open to information workers, it quickly becomes a
chaotic mess.

Most file servers are exposed to information workers as mapped network drives. Information workers can access these drives directly from their own computers and are encour-
aged to store critical files on the drive so that they can be properly backed up. However, the
directory structure of these file servers is a nightmare. No one can remember where they are
supposed to create new directories and often don't remember where they have previously
stored a file. This results in different versions of the same file being stored in several directories with no one able to determine which one is the most recent.

The Access Challenge

Increasingly, information workers are working from locations other than the central company
headquarters. Workers today are highly mobile; they work from home, they work from the
road, and they work from other countries. They need constant access to systems even when
they are completely disconnected from a network. Information workers carry BlackBerry

devices, smart phones, and wireless computers. Partners and customers increasingly expect to be able to access appropriate information contained in your systems. All this means that solutions built for information workers must have a well-conceived access strategy that exposes information to the appropriate audience.

The Management Challenge

As if the complexity and variety of information systems were not enough, organizations are also faced with an explosion of data contained in these systems. A typical organization might have as many as eight customer databases crossing several isolated systems such as customer relationship management (CRM), enterprise resource planning (ERP), multiple spreadsheets, and documents. Each of these systems has a reporting mechanism to access the data, but there is generally no way to see all of the data together to create a single view of a customer, a supplier, or a partner. Consequently, organizations are forced to create manual systems to collect and analyze information.

Executive information workers need visibility into business processes in order to judge the health of the organization and make adjustments. This process of analyzing KPIs against goals followed by adjusting the business processes is known as *performance management*. Most executives really have no effective means beyond simple reports to manage the organizational performance. Furthermore, these reports are often nothing more than spreadsheets created by professional information workers who route them to executives via e-mail. As a result of this situation, many executives have simply given up trying to proactively manage organizational performance. Instead, they examine financial data and try to make strategic adjustments after the fact.

All of this is to say that the computing environment for most end users has become unbearably complicated. In this environment, end users are crying out for simplicity and consolidation. They need tools that give them a more personal view of enterprise resources to cut through the layers of complexity and make them more productive.

Stop for a moment and consider the role of Microsoft Outlook in most organizations. Microsoft Outlook is truly the workhorse of corporate America. Outlook is often the first application an end user opens at the beginning of the day and the last one closed at night. Why? The answer is because end users are trying to impose simplification by using Microsoft Outlook to access their enterprise resources.

Think about it. Your organization may have a document management system, but you generally get your documents as e-mail attachments. Your organization may have an enterprise reporting system, but you get your reports through e-mail as well. This is because end users do not want to use the document management client or wade through the hundreds of reports available in the enterprise reporting system. These systems are too painful to access and too complicated to use. What's more, the end user has probably forgotten her password for the document management system and isn't about to spend 30 minutes on the phone with the help desk to get it reset.

System complexity and variety, overwhelming amounts of data, and work-style challenges have all led end users to a frustrating relationship with their computers. They are begging for simplification, but each new effort rolled out by the IT department only seems to add to the problems. The key to solving this problem lies in creating a user experience that truly consolidates and simplifies.

The Regulatory Challenge

No one in business has to be told these days about the impact of regulations. This is espe-cially true if you are part of a public company, but it is increasingly true for everyone. Not only is compliance a necessity, but organizations must also be much more vigilant about identifying and maintaining records so that they are available for audit or discovery. This has become a significant problem in a world where e-mail is functioning as a process and collab-oration engine.

Most organizations have no effective way to understand what information is contained in their e-mail systems. Yet, estimates are that as much as 50% of all organizational knowl-edge now resides in e-mail inboxes and public folders. For organizations trying to comply with record retention regulations, this is an impossible situation. There is no way to know what e-mail is important, so many organizations simply save it all. This is a massive amount of information to store and will be nearly impossible to search later.

Understanding Business Scenarios

SharePoint products and technologies form a versatile set of building blocks that you can use to solve a variety of business problems. Unlike most technical solutions, however, a Share-Point implementation has the ability to transform the way in which an organization works. This is because SharePoint touches nearly all aspects of daily operations. SharePoint solutions can bring together information in the form of documents, forms, records, scheduling, com-munications, transactions, and reporting. This information can then be delivered to employees, partners, and customers.

Increasing Individual Productivity

Perhaps the most obvious and straightforward scenario involving a SharePoint deployment is the improvement of personal productivity for employees. I have already addressed in detail the system and data challenges that are facing users of the Windows desktop, but a productiv-ity solution based on SharePoint products and technologies can also be used to make relevant applications, documents, and data available to end users more quickly.

The typical end user spends a significant amount of time searching for documents and information each day. This is essentially lost productivity, while users browse document man-agement systems, reporting systems, or the Internet. Documents are easily lost on file servers because no standards for file taxonomy, naming, or version control are in use. What's more, business users are often frustrated by technical barriers such as mapped network drives or server names.

A SharePoint solution can bring immediate relief to this situation through the use of enterprise search capabilities. MOSS ships with an enterprise search feature that allows you to search nearly every information repository in your organization. This includes documents, people, databases, and web sites. Figure 1-1 shows a view of the Search center with results.

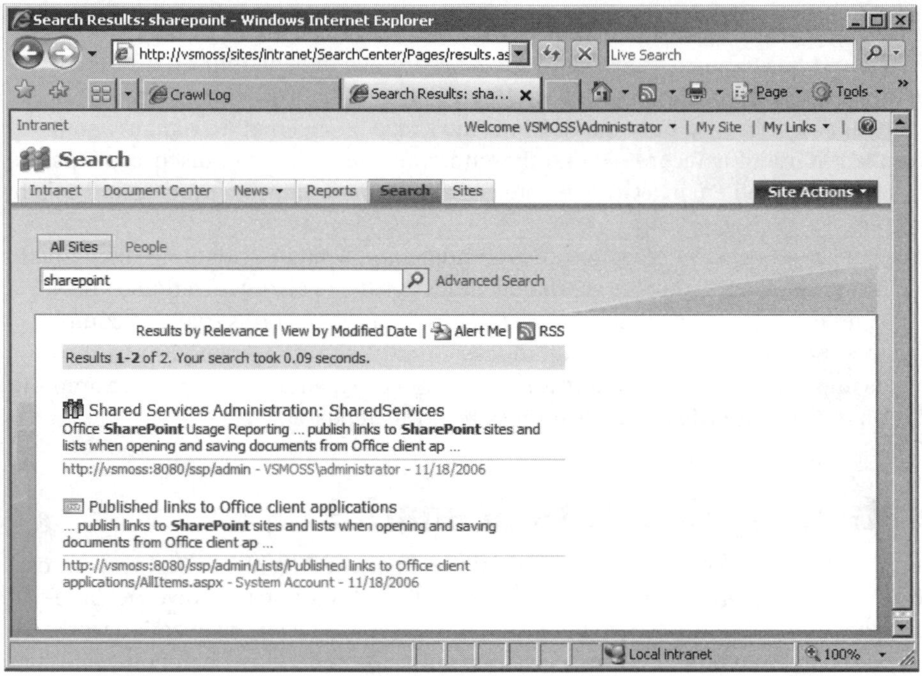

Figure 1-1. *Search center*

Increasing Team Productivity

Along with personal productivity solutions, SharePoint products and technologies can also create team productivity solutions. Increasingly, team productivity is a vital part of business success. Today, most organizations have some combination of formal teams and ad hoc teams. The formal teams are often fixed and departmentalized whereas the other teams may form spontaneously or for a limited time. SharePoint products and technologies support both kinds of teams.

Because formal teams are generally long-lived, a SharePoint solution may contain several fixed sites for these teams. These sites may be created during an initial rollout and then enhanced over time. For these types of teams, SharePoint supports both document and meeting workspaces where team members can collaborate even if they are not physically present. Along with meetings and documents, team members can also take advantage of threaded discussion forums that facilitate collaboration even if team members are not present in both time and place. Figure 1-2 shows a typical team site in WSS.

Ad hoc teams can benefit from the same collaborative features enjoyed by formal teams, but the sites that host these groups may be created on the fly. SPS is a truly decentralized model. The philosophy is intended to support team building and productivity from the boardroom to the company softball team. A collaborative solution focused on team building may give site-creation permissions to many individuals who can then easily create team sites from directly within the portal.

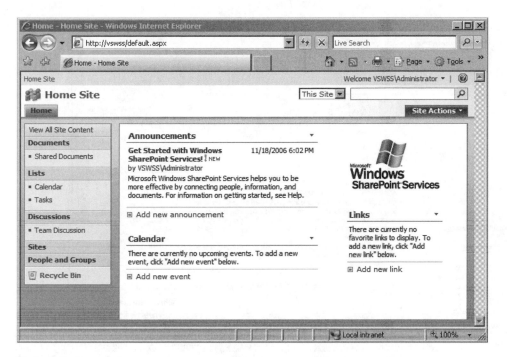

Figure 1-2. *A team site*

Increasing Divisional and Enterprise Productivity

At the division and enterprise level, SharePoint products and solutions can be used by management personnel to better understand performance and make adjustments. Figure 1-3 shows a management dashboard created in the Report Center. The Report Center is designed to be the single place in the enterprise that provides information on organizational performance.

Beyond performance management, SharePoint sites can also be used to improve communication within the organization. This can be accomplished by using SharePoint as the basis for the corporate intranet. In support of this role, MOSS also has special publishing capabilities that allow intranet—and Internet—content to be created, routed, approved, and published.

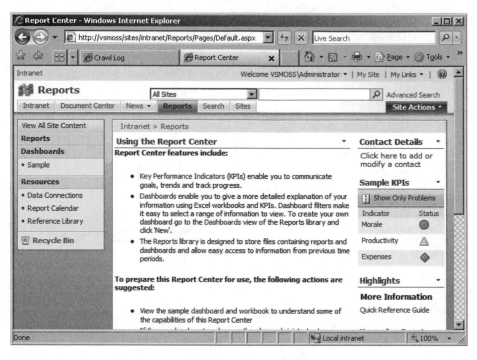

Figure 1-3. *Report Center*

Supporting Remote Workers

Increasingly, the concept of a central place where employees commute to perform work is fading. Organizations today have more telecommuters, distant offices, and mobile workers than ever before. For organizations, this has typically meant an increase in support costs. Remote workers often require high-end laptops, remote synchronization, wireless connectivity, and more client-side software. Using a SharePoint solution focused on remote workers, organizations can eliminate some of the maintenance required to support them.

Solutions built around SPS may be made accessible outside of an organization's firewall. Using this type of approach, an organization can make sites and services available to employees as long as they have an Internet connection. This means that telecommuters can easily access required resources with less software installed on their local machine. For mobile workers, such a solution can ease the burden of data synchronization by integrating such operations within the portal. Figure 1-4 shows a SharePoint solution running on a mobile device.

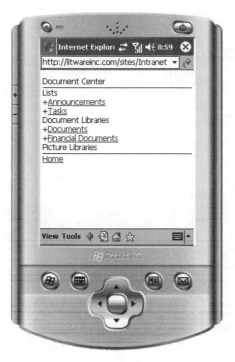

Figure 1-4. *A site on a mobile device*

Integrating with Partners and Customers

Because SharePoint solutions can be safely exposed outside the firewall, they make excellent platforms for integrating with customers and partners. SharePoint now supports forms-based authentication so that external users do not have to be members of the organization's domain in order to log in. This means that you can place an entire SharePoint site within the DMZ and safely publish information for partners and customers. Figure 1-5 shows a typical SharePoint login form.

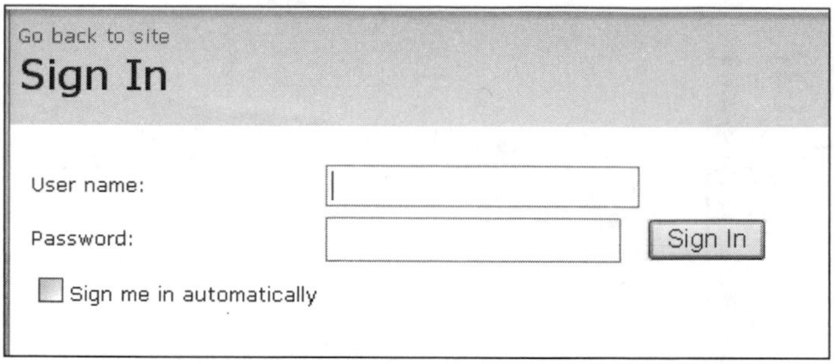

Figure 1-5. *Logging in to an extranet*

Complying with Regulations

Records management has become an increasing concern for organizations that need to comply with regulations. Identifying critical e-mail and documents, applying retention policies, and protecting documents from change are all key parts of a record management strategy. In this version, MOSS provides a record repository template that you can use to store and control key documents. Documents can be sent to the repository manually or as the result of a workflow process. When documents expire, they can be automatically deleted or initiate a workflow process. Figure 1-6 shows an example of the records repository in MOSS.

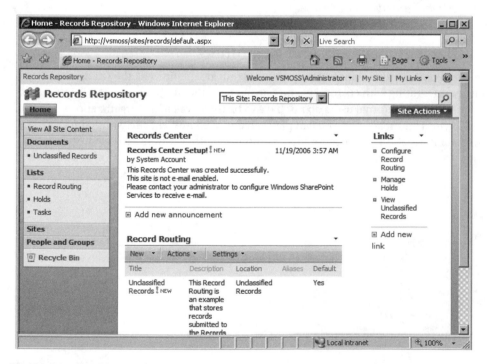

Figure 1-6. *Using a records repository*

Analysis and Design Considerations

SharePoint can be remarkably easy to install. In fact, if you follow the single-server deployment strategy, you can have SPS up and running in 45 minutes. However, that does not mean that it is simple to create an effective business solution using SharePoint products and technologies. The key to properly designing a SharePoint solution is to spend the required time to identify the business problem to be solved and the expected result. Once you understand the solution, you must document the roles, policies, and systems that constitute the solution. Finally, you must design a solution that incorporates all of the elements in a way that solves the original business problem.

Documenting the Business Vision

For as long as I have been involved in designing software solutions, teams have always agreed in principle that identifying the business problem and understanding the return on investment (ROI) are critical to the success of every project. However, I have rarely seen a team actually engage in these activities, and in the end, this often is a leading factor in the failure of a project.

Shortcutting required analysis is a fact of life in the information technology world, and it is driven equally by managers and engineers. On the management side, project sponsors are frequently unable to articulate the expected return from a technology project. When interviewed, managers are incapable of explaining the productivity increases or cost savings that are expected from a technology effort. Instead, they rely on a vague feeling that the mere presence of a tool, or portal, will surely help the organization be better.

On the technical side, most engineers are not trained to look at technology issues as essentially business problems. Instead they look at business issues as primarily technology problems. The typical technical thought process asks the following question: What data does the end user need? Then it asks this: What application provides that data? The solution then is to deploy the application that provides the data and declare the problem solved.

A solution based on SharePoint products and technologies is a web of solutions to a myriad of problems. Organizations considering such an implementation would do well to begin by interviewing key project sponsors to document the expected company benefit from such an effort. Sponsors should be clear about the expected productivity increases or cost savings associated with the effort. Use this exercise as a litmus test for the entire project. If a significant return cannot be envisioned for the project, it may not be worth the effort.

If the return is determined to warrant the project effort, the correct process is first to create a vision document. The vision document is the first deliverable of the project. This document articulates the business problem, proposed solution, and expected benefit. This document is the highest-level guidance for the project. It acts as the beacon to which the team is headed. In well-run projects, the vision is periodically revisited to ensure that no extraneous effort is expended and that the team is correctly implementing the vision and achieving the desired results.

Documenting Policies, Practices, and Regulations

Once the vision document is completed, the next step is to document the policies, practices, and regulations that will constrain the use of the solution. Policies, practices, and regulations act as boundary conditions for the solution. Successful projects exist within these boundaries while solving the original business problem.

Policies are restrictions placed on the organization by its management and articulated as simple statements. For example, the statement "company credit cards are not to be used for personal expenses" is a policy that restricts the use of a company credit card. Similarly, the statement "only port 80 will be open on the firewall" is also a policy. This policy restricts the use and configuration of the company infrastructure. Policies are not easily changed; therefore, a successful project must identify the policies that constrain it.

Practices are similar to policies in that they act as boundary conditions on the solution design. However, practices are more closely associated with the tactical processes used by the organization to do business. For example, the use of an approved vendor list to simplify the purchase process is a practice. Practices are less formal than policies, but they can easily be just as limiting on the final design.

Policies and practices exist at many levels in an organization. Some policies may apply to an entire organization whereas others may be specific to a single process. Initially, you should try to identify the policies and practices that are most likely to constrain the general use of a solution. As the effort matures, you will identify departmental processes constrained by additional policies, practices, and regulations. As a starting point, consider the following common areas where policies, practices, and regulations may affect the initial deployment: allowing external access, negotiating service-level agreements, accessing the application, managing content, and addressing regulatory requirements.

Allowing External Access

If external access will be allowed, then document the policies for authentication. Determine whether a simple username and password will be sufficient, or whether stronger measures will be required. Specifically, you should determine whether Secure Sockets Layer (SSL) and certificates will be required.

Along with system policies, determine whether users will be required to access the solution utilizing a two-factor authentication system such as RSA SecurID. SecurID tokens act as virtual ATM cards for the portal. In order to access the portal, users must possess the token and know a personal identification number (PIN). The passcode generated by the token changes every 60 seconds, so a user must be in possession of the token at the time of login. The PIN is a fixed set of numbers known only to the user. The combination of these two elements to complete a login request is the reason it is called *two-factor* authentication. When combined with SSL and certificates, such access schemes are exceedingly hard to hack.

In addition to considerations about personnel access, you should document policies for system deployments. Determine what parts of the system will be deployed behind the firewall or in a DMZ. All of these issues arise early in a development project and will affect the final design significantly.

Negotiating Service-Level Agreements

Based on the business vision, you should determine the expected availability for the solution. If the solution is functioning as little more than an intranet, perhaps no significant impact will occur if it goes down. On the other hand, some organizations are utilizing the portal as the primary workspace for employees. In this case, a formal service-level agreement should be negotiated for the system.

Along with a service-level agreement, the solution may have to be part of the disaster recovery/business continuity plan. Again, based on the business vision, determine whether the criticality of this system warrants a replicated site on the disaster recovery network. If so, make disaster recovery an integral part of the project plan. I have seen many organizations ignore this point and roll out a solution as "just a pilot." These same organizations turn around a few months later and realize they have a single point of failure in their system architecture and a gaping hole in their disaster recovery plan.

Accessing the Application

Determine the policies and practices you will use to provide application access. This includes both internal and external access along with the method of authentication. Additionally, the Microsoft vision of SharePoint incorporates tight integration with Office 2007. If this is in line with your company vision, you must evaluate your current Office deployment. Give thought to any planned upgrades and how you will handle installation and maintenance on the client machines.

Managing Content

Documents and other content are a significant part of a SharePoint solution. Therefore, organizations must document the policies and practices that determine how the content is created, posted, and managed. Determining the policies and practices surrounding content will have a lot to do with the culture of the organization. In its heart, SharePoint is a distributed solution. This means that it is structured to allow easy content creation and posting. Additionally, sites and subsites can be created without necessarily requiring centralized approval. Many organizations find this philosophy incompatible with the traditional centralized approach to information technology.

Administrators do have significant control over permissions granted to portal users; however, every organization will have to determine which people will be responsible for creating and maintaining content. This may be a formal system where each department has a content manager, or it may be a freewheeling approach that lets nearly anyone create a site on the fly and populate it with relevant content. In any case, you should consider these issues carefully before you begin designing the portal.

Addressing Regulatory Requirements

SharePoint solutions allow you to create and manage content through its entire life cycle. In order to properly design a solution, you should identify the content that must be retained for regulatory or historical purposes. For each type of content, you should gather the retention requirements and define what to do when the retention period ends.

Project and Design Documents

SharePoint products and technologies are best thought of as a solution platform. This means, however, that it is impossible to define exactly what constitutes a SharePoint solution and therefore what design deliverables are required. I have seen many SharePoint projects that are nothing more than installing WSS and turning a departmental team loose. While this approach may violate several planning and change principles, it certainly is not a project that requires layers of design documents.

On the other hand, I have also been part of unique projects that utilize forms, documents, search, and workflow to implement specific processes. In these projects, good documentation—specifically use cases—is invaluable. Furthermore, SharePoint solutions are iterative by nature; as users become more familiar with the environment, you end up fine-tuning your solution.

As a result, you must decide for each project how much documentation is needed. The danger here, however, is that it's just so easy to start customizing in SharePoint. While this is not necessarily a bad approach for small projects, it can also lead to a maintenance nightmare if entire departmental or enterprise solutions are approached in this way. Instead of customizing many sites individually, for example, creating a single site template that can be used over and over will be much more efficient.

Managing Change

During a presentation, a customer once asked me to describe the most difficult issue surrounding a SharePoint deployment. My answer was immediate. I responded "It's the same issue as every other project—managing the change for the end users." Change management is the process that helps end users adopt new ways of doing business, and it is never easy.

Despite its ability to affect the success of a project, change management is rarely considered in sufficient detail. In my experience, this is because the team is primarily concerned with correctly implementing the technical solution. What's more, technical teams really are not trained to help users through the change management process.

Successful change management is about educating and assisting end users. Every good project must involve some key elements to help end users adapt and be productive. Scheduling end-user training is an obvious first step, but it is rarely enough to ensure success. Instead, consider the entire group of end users and have a complete plan to manage the change.

Begin by mentally dividing the end users into three groups. The first group is the set of people who are excited about the project. This group can be a strong ally in your effort to bring others through the change process. The second group is the set of people who are neutral about the project. This group is waiting to see if the project will be successful before they get behind it. The last group is the set of people who are openly hostile toward the project. This group does not want to change and is typically very vocal about it.

Although the third group is the loudest and cries for the most attention, it should be largely ignored. Instead, I like to start a pilot with the first group. Don't worry about the traditional approach of piloting your project with a particular department. This approach is too narrow and invites people from all three groups into the pilot. This will surely result in someone from the third group declaring the project a disaster. Just locate the most enthusiastic people you can—regardless of department—and start a pilot.

Piloting with enthusiastic people guarantees good press. This means that the people in the second group—the ones who are waiting for success—will begin to hear good things about the project. This will result in more people from the second group becoming enthusiastic and joining the first group. Now you can expand your pilot to include more people. In this way, you can continue to build momentum for the project. This strategy can save you a lot of heartache when rolling out something with as much organizational impact as a portal.

CHAPTER 2

SharePoint Overview, Planning, and Installation

Before planning a SharePoint installation, you should have a strong understanding of the intended purpose. You should identify whether the installation will serve sites on the intranet, extranet, or Internet. You should also determine how many users and documents the system must support. Finally, you need to decide if the system is mission-critical or if downtime can be tolerated. In this chapter, I walk you through the major components of SharePoint and help you plan your installation. At the end of the chapter is a complete installation procedure you can use to create a development environment for use with this book.

Windows SharePoint Services

Windows SharePoint Services (WSS) is an application framework that is primarily designed to facilitate collaboration among teams through customizable web sites known as *team sites*. Team sites are secure, document-centric sites that provide a set of tools for sharing documents, tracking progress, and communicating with colleagues. Within a team site, document libraries provide basic document management capabilities. Task lists, contact lists, discussion forums, and calendars provide the means to coordinate and track associated work, which can be automated through workflow processes. All of these tools are managed through an administrative interface designed to allow groups to service themselves. Figure 2-1 shows a typical team site in WSS.

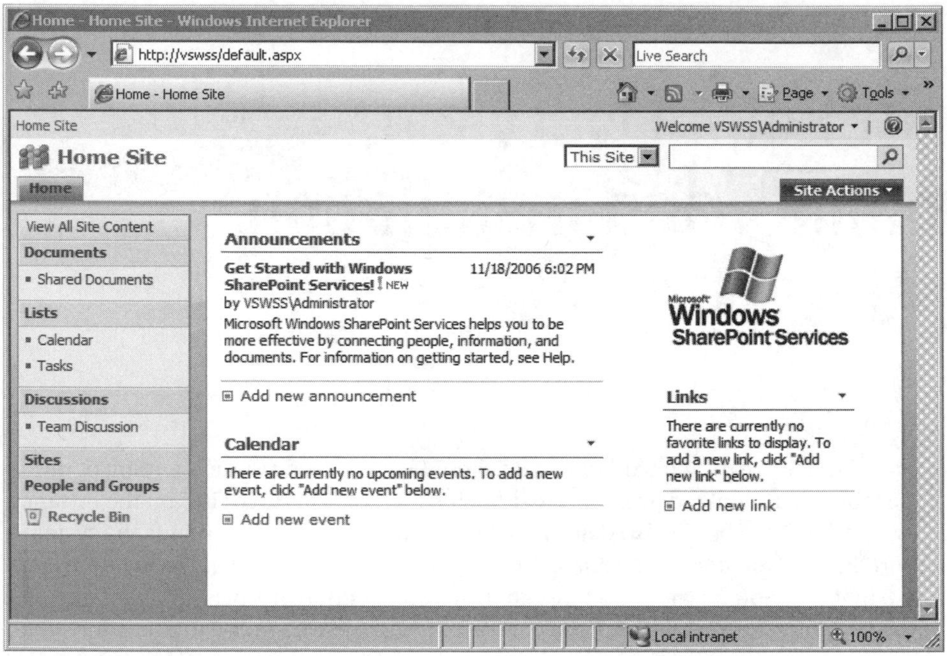

Figure 2-1. *A WSS team site*

Document Libraries

Every WSS team site you create may have one or more document library associated with it. A document library is like a mini document management system with check-in, checkout, version control, and approval capabilities built right in. Document libraries are intended to contain all of the documents that a team needs to accomplish a business function. These documents may be Office documents built into the Office suite or they may be non-Office documents such as Adobe Acrobat files, text files, e-mail, or even media assets. Just about any document may be stored in a document library. It is true, however, that there are several special integration points between Office documents and SharePoint that are not extended to other file types. I cover these special integration points throughout the book. Figure 2-2 shows a typical document library in a WSS team site.

Document libraries also support an event system that you can tap into programmatically. These events can call into .NET assemblies when new documents are placed in a library, modified, or deleted. This version of WSS also comes with its own workflow engine. Based on the Windows Workflow Foundation, the engine provides simple workflow processes such as document approval out of the box. Power users can develop more sophisticated workflows using the SharePoint Designer (formerly called Microsoft FrontPage) while developers can create custom workflows with Visual Studio 2005 and harness all the power of the .NET Framework.

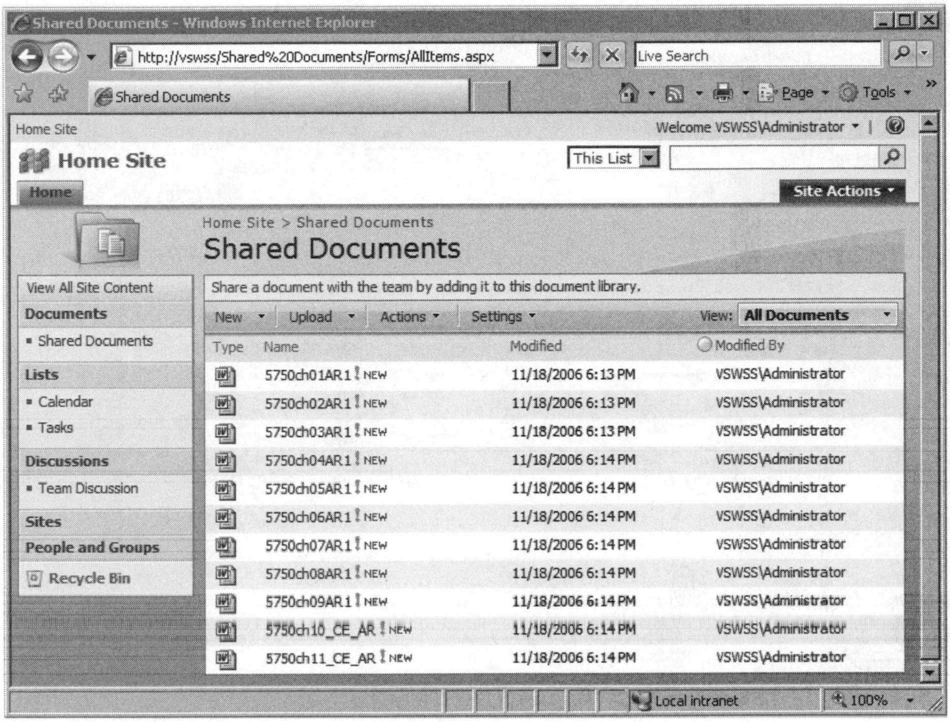

Figure 2-2. *A document library*

Lists

Teams really need more than just document information in order to accomplish a business purpose. For example, teams may need a task list, a list of contacts, or a calendar to facilitate and coordinate their efforts. This type of information all falls under a broad category in WSS simply called *lists*.

In the previous version of WSS, lists used a different underlying infrastructure than document libraries. In the 2007 version, lists and libraries are essentially the same thing to Share-Point, although they are seen by users as quite different. Lists in WSS can be lists of anything, but most often they take the form of information typically found in Microsoft Outlook. In fact, many list types can be synchronized with information contained in Outlook. For example, you can create a list of key contacts on a WSS team site and synchronize it with your contact list in Outlook. Just like document libraries, lists are also capable of raising events that you can trap in code. Lists can also participate in workflow processes. Figure 2-3 shows a typical task list in a WSS team site.

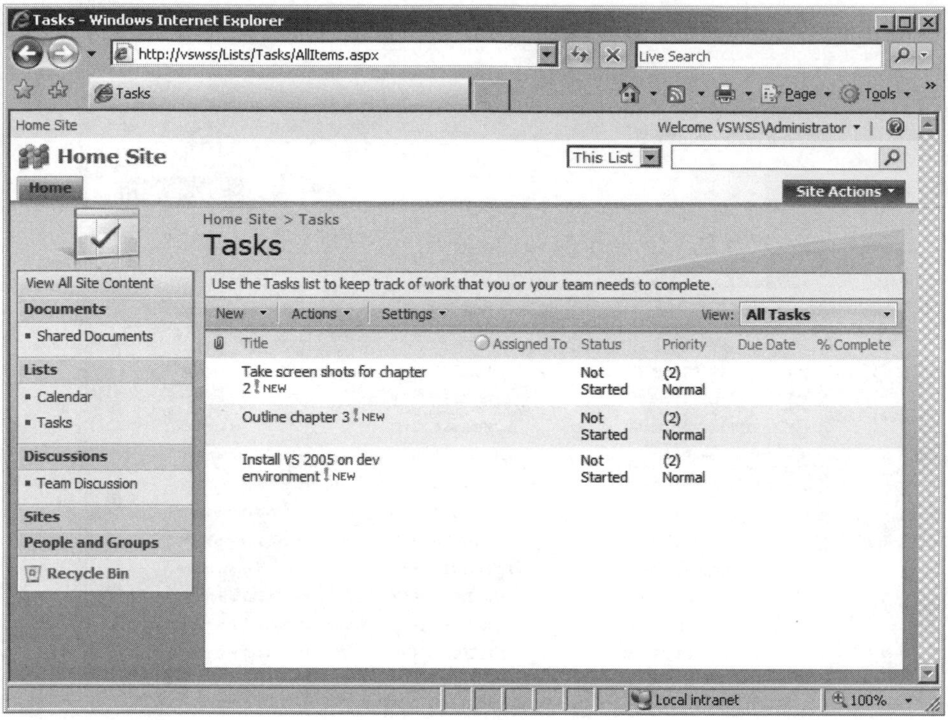

Figure 2-3. *A task list*

Web Parts and Custom Development

Along with documents and lists, teams may also need functionality that is not a part of Share-Point out of the box. Adding this functionality is accomplished using a SharePoint technology called *web parts.* Web parts are .NET assemblies that add customized functionality to a site where normally a developer might use ASP.NET code. This version of WSS utilizes ASP.NET 2.0 web parts, which are the same web parts you can use in your own custom ASP.NET applications. Additionally, this version has complete backward compatibility for web parts created in the 2003 version. I cover the various ways to customize SharePoint through code in the second half of this book.

The latest version of WSS is built on top of ASP.NET 2.0, so developers can take advantage of the .NET Framework 2.0. Furthermore, Microsoft has done away with the previous approach of using an ISAPI filter to intercept HTTP requests for processing by SharePoint. Instead, WSS now utilizes an `HttpModule` and an `HttpHandler` that are registered inside of the `web.config` file. This approach gives WSS more stability by ensuring that an ASP.NET context always exists before any custom code is run. The `HttpModule` and `HttpHandler` allow the incoming page request to be processed by WSS and the appropriate HTML is constructed on the fly for return to the calling client. The web pages you see in a WSS site do not actually exist on the web server. Instead they are constructed from a combination of page templates located on the file system and data contained in the Content Database. The Content Database is a SQL Server 2005 database that maintains all of the web page definitions, documents, lists, and security information. This means that SharePoint products and technologies require an associated SQL Server 2005 installation. It also means that all documents in document libraries are saved in the Content Database as binary large objects (BLOB).

Site Creation and Branding

In previous versions of WSS, it was very difficult to create a new type of site that differed dramatically from the out-of-the-box templates. To accomplish this task, you had to create a new site definition using an XML language known as the *Collaborative Application Markup Language (CAML)*. Even after these site definitions were created, branding the site remained challenging and was often accomplished by extensively modifying individual pages in Microsoft FrontPage.

WSS also introduces a new concept for deploying site functionality called a *Feature*. A *Feature*—with a capital *F*—is a modular approach to defining a site. Using this new capability, developers can create packages of web parts, workflows, or other customizations that may be turned on and off by site administrators. This approach allows Features to be reused across sites, which makes the WSS site infrastructure much more maintainable.

For controlling site styling, WSS now takes advantage of ASP.NET *master pages*. Master pages were introduced in ASP.NET 2.0 and provide a way for developers and designers to specify the basic look and feel of a site in just one place. The master page defines colors, styles, and visual elements—often called the *chrome*—that will appear on every page. It is now possible to brand a significant portion of a site by changing a single file.

In the past, many developers were reluctant to use Microsoft FrontPage for customizations because it would cause a site to become "unghosted." *Unghosting* refers to a situation in which an individual page is separated from its site definition. This separation could lead to strange behavior and performance issues in the previous versions of WSS. In the latest version of WSS, unghosted pages are now called *customized pages*, and modifying an uncustomized page in the SharePoint Designer will still cause it to become separated from its site definition. However, the performance issues have now been eliminated, and the SharePoint Designer will even allow you to revert a customized page back to its uncustomized state. While there are still good reasons to avoid customizing pages—such as when you are rolling out many sites with the same branding—the improvements in the SharePoint Designer make it a serious option for organizations that need a tool specifically for nonprogrammers and content creators.

Microsoft Office 2007

Microsoft Office 2007 is the most significant revision to the Office suite in ten years and is the result of countless hours of user testing by Microsoft. The entire user interface has been completely reworked around the central concept of a *ribbon*. The ribbon interface is designed to group functions together by activity. This approach is intended to make it easier for users to find commands that might have been buried deep in a menu tree in previous versions. Beginning and intermediate users of Office are likely to adopt the new interface quickly and become more productive as they discover new commands exposed on the ribbon. Advanced Office users, however, will probably react negatively to the new user interface because it is completely different, and familiar patterns of clicking will no longer work. In fact, I see this as the greatest obstacle to rolling out the new Office suite because advanced users with dozens of linked spreadsheets, for example, will have to relearn the interface before they can be productive again. Figure 2-4 shows the new ribbon interface in Word 2007.

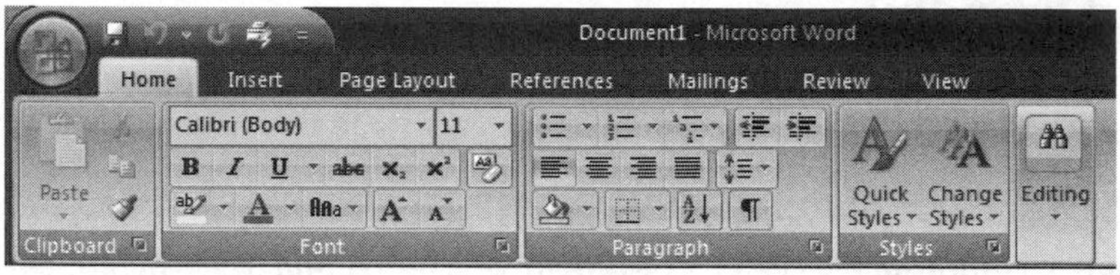

Figure 2-4. *The Office ribbon*

Document Panels

Just like Office 2003, Office 2007 is tightly integrated with SharePoint. Along with the ribbon interface, Microsoft has also changed the interface Office users see when working with SharePoint. The Shared Workspace available in Office 2003 still exists, but it has been replaced as the primary view into WSS team sites. Instead, users will now see two panels that appear beneath the ribbon interface called the Document Information Panel (DIP) and the Document Action Panel (DAP).

The DIP is a view of the metadata associated with the current document. The purpose of the DIP is to make metadata visible throughout the document editing process so that users can update the information as they determine the right values. The goal is to get better metadata through a nonmodal interface as opposed to the old approach of demanding all the metadata values when the document is saved to a library. Additionally, you can synchronize the DIP with the document so that metadata is filled in automatically as the document is created, or document text is automatically added when a user enters metadata. Figure 2-5 shows the DIP.

Properties: Document ▼			
Title:	Chapter Title:	Author:	Technical Reviewer:
SharePoint 2007: Building Solut	Overview and Installation	Scot Hillier	Jim Broaddus

Figure 2-5. *The Document Information Panel*

The DAP is a view of tasks associated with the document that apply to the current user. These tasks become visible when the document is associated with a workflow in SharePoint. These tasks can involve review, approval, content creation, or any other activity dictated by an associated workflow.

Working Offline, While Mobile, or With Peers

With this version of Office, Microsoft has made significant improvements in the offline capabilities of WSS. The primary tool for working with WSS data offline is Microsoft Outlook.

Outlook has the ability to synchronize with many different types of WSS data including lists, calendars, tasks, discussions, contacts, and document libraries. This means that users can, for example, take an entire document library offline, edit the documents, and then synchronize their changes later. Mobility has improved as well with the ability to create sites that specifically target mobile devices.

WSS sites are also enabled with Really Simple Syndication (RSS) and Outlook is equipped with an RSS reader. This means that end users can subscribe to SharePoint RSS feeds and collect all of the information in Outlook. However, RSS will not allow users to write data back to a WSS site. You can, however, send e-mail to lists in this version of WSS, which can include attachments that get saved into SharePoint.

With the acquisition of Groove Networks, Office now has the capability to support peer-to-peer integration with WSS sites and other users. Utilizing Microsoft Groove, end users can get documents from a WSS site and then take advantage of the peer-to-peer capabilities of Groove to share and edit the documents with others. Groove also makes an excellent offline solution with more capability than Microsoft Outlook alone. The capabilities of Groove are beyond the scope of this book, but they are worth investigating for those organizations where peer-to-peer capabilities may be beneficial.

Microsoft Office 2007 Suites

Microsoft Office 2007 is available in no less than eight different suites. The suites range from Microsoft Office Basic 2007—containing Word, Excel, and Outlook—to Microsoft Office Enterprise 2007, which contains all of the standard Office products plus Communicator and Groove support. In this book, I cover all of the advanced integration and development techniques with Office products; therefore, I assume that you have one of the advanced suites available. Specifically, you should have the Microsoft Office Ultimate 2007, Microsoft Office Professional Plus 2007, or Microsoft Office Enterprise 2007 suite. Information on all the suites can be obtained at http://office.microsoft.com.

Microsoft Office SharePoint Server

The Microsoft Office SharePoint Server (MOSS) is a significant new product with broad and deep capabilities designed to support a wide variety of enterprise functions to manage content, present business intelligence data, automate workflow processes, manage records, and build both public and private web sites. Although MOSS can be thought of as the next version of SharePoint Portal Server 2003 (SPS), it is really a completely new product. Its organizational structure and customization patterns are much different than those of SPS.

MOSS is based entirely on WSS technology and is a true superset of WSS functionality. Every enhancement you create in WSS will function identically in MOSS. This also means that the end user experience is consistent between MOSS and WSS. Navigation elements, styles, and site organization are the same whether you are in MOSS or WSS. This is a far cry from SPS, which often seems to have no relationship at all to WSS. For those who experienced SPS, you will find that the old Topic and Area structure has been eliminated in favor of a more flexible interface that can easily be changed.

Portal Features

Many of the portal features of MOSS will be familiar to anyone who has worked previously with SPS. Although the look and feel of MOSS more closely resembles the current version of WSS than the previous version of SPS, familiar capabilities of SPS such as Audiences, Profiles, My Site, and Single Sign-On (SSO) have been retained. These features differentiate a true organizational portal from a simple team collaboration site and should be thought of as one of the primary differences between MOSS and WSS.

Audiences in MOSS are used to target content at portal users. Within MOSS, you may define an audience based on user attributes such as membership in an Active Directory group. Then you may use that audience definition to show or hide content when a page is viewed.

MOSS user profiles allow you to define, search, and present metadata about portal users. Profiles draw information from Active Directory to provide basic information such as first name and last name, but you may also extend the metadata to include custom fields such as languages spoken or areas of expertise. Additionally, these custom fields can even be derived from other systems, for example like PeopleSoft. Once defined, profiles can be a search scope that allows users to locate people within the organization.

Along with their profile, every MOSS user can also be given their own personal site—called My Site. My Site functions as a personal workspace for MOSS users and allows them to organize their own documents and information. Through My Site, users may connect to colleagues, manage their profiles, and be alerted when key information changes somewhere in MOSS.

Although SSO services were available in SPS, my experience is that they were rarely used. In MOSS, however, SSO takes on new meaning, because it is used to facilitate access to several new features such as data in line-of-business systems. SSO allows you to specify a set of credentials for accessing a secondary system and then give those credentials an application name that may be invoked later by either a MOSS feature or your own custom code.

Enterprise Content Management

Enterprise Content Management (ECM) is a broad term that refers to managing the entire document life cycle from ideation through archival. This includes not only the same workflow capabilities I described earlier for WSS sites, but also the ability to archive these records and apply retention policies to them. Additionally, ECM encompasses web content management (WCM) to support the creation, approval, and deployment of web sites.

MOSS supports several different templates that allow organizations to create both public and private sites. One of those templates allows you to create a records repository that you can use to archive documents according to a document retention policy. Documents may be added to the records repository either manually from within a SharePoint document library, or automatically by associating a workflow with a retention policy. In the latter case, a document could, for example, be routed through a review process and then sent to the repository after it has reached a certain age. It might also be good to mention at this point that both WSS and MOSS have a recycle bin that works similarly to the Windows Recycle Bin and allows a single document to be recovered if it is inadvertently deleted.

Along with documents, MOSS also manages web content. Prior to the release of MOSS, the Microsoft Content Management Server (MCMS) was the primary way that organizations created, approved, and published web content. With the release of MOSS, MCMS is being retired. The major capabilities formerly in MCMS have been moved to MOSS. This includes creating page templates with content placeholders, implementing approval processes, and deploying pages in bulk from separate development environments to production environments. Figure 2-6 shows a typical MOSS page template in design mode with content being added to placeholders on the page.

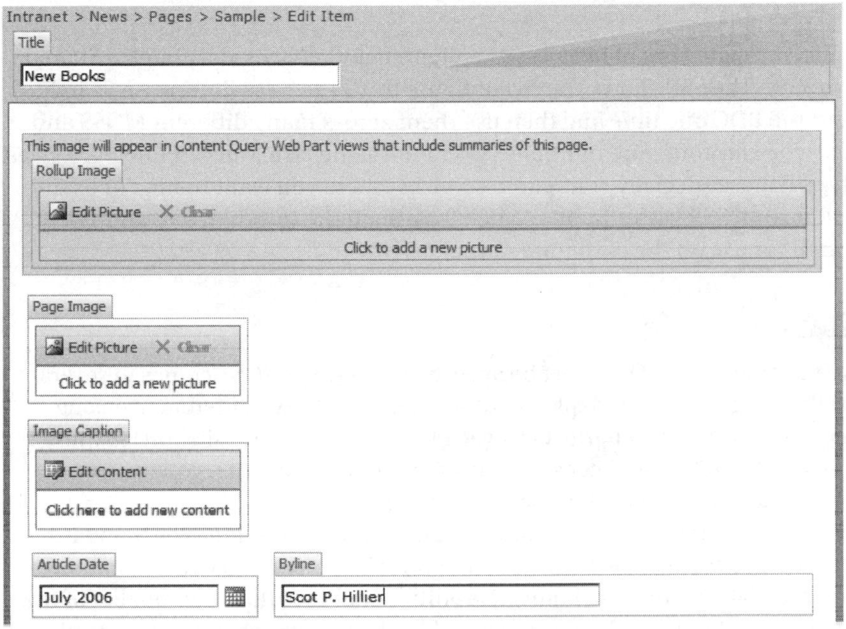

Figure 2-6. *Modifying page content*

Business Intelligence

Business intelligence represents a key area where MOSS brings many new capabilities that were unknown in previous versions of SharePoint. One of the MOSS templates available out of the box is a Report Center template designed to act as a hub for business intelligence data. While business intelligence capabilities can be utilized anywhere within MOSS, the Report Center template is specially designed to support report distribution and the creation of key performance indicator (KPI) dashboards. Reports can be delivered either by creating Excel spreadsheets or by designing reports in Microsoft Reporting Services. KPI dashboards can be created either by hand or by connecting them to a spreadsheet or an analysis cube built in SQL Server 2005.

Along with these features, MOSS also supports two new server-based versions of Office products: Excel Services and Office Forms Server. With these servers, you can distribute Excel spreadsheets and InfoPath forms to end users even when they do not have Excel or InfoPath installed. This means that spreadsheet-based reports and dashboards can be delivered over the web without exposing critical data or calculation formulas to users. It's also now possible to expose InfoPath forms over the web to traveling personnel, customers, and partners who might need to fill out a form but do not have the InfoPath client available.

Rounding out the business intelligence feature set is the Business Data Catalog (BDC). The BDC is a new no-code mechanism for exposing line-of-business data within MOSS. Using the BDC, you can define the data structure in back-end systems such as your customer relationship management (CRM) system or human resources database. This data may then be mapped into web parts for easy searching, displaying, and filtering.

Shared Services

Many of the advanced capabilities of MOSS are configured and delivered through a Shared Services Provider (SSP). The SSP allows you to configure things such as Enterprise Search, Excel Services, and the BDC one time and then use them across many different MOSS and WSS sites. Because you can configure multiple SSPs in the same farm, this architecture gives you the flexibility to expose specially configured services where you want them. For example, you may configure an SSP with a public search for use on the Internet, and another SSP with a private search for use on the corporate intranet.

MOSS Versions

While WSS is a free component, MOSS must be licensed separately. MOSS comes in several different versions that target different deployment scenarios and have different licensing requirements. Regardless of your scenario, however, every organization using MOSS must purchase the base MOSS 2007 server license. Along with the server license, you must also purchase the appropriate client access licenses (CAL) to meet your needs.

For general use, MOSS comes in a Standard and an Enterprise edition. The Standard edition gives you access to the basic set of MOSS functionality, including content management, workflow, and collaboration. The Enterprise edition includes the functionality of the Standard edition but adds the BDC, Excel Services, Office Forms Server, and more. Additional versions allow you to use MOSS solely for deploying Internet sites or separate features such as the Office Forms Server. In this book, I always assume that you have the MOSS 2007 Enterprise edition available.

Installation Considerations

Planning for a WSS or MOSS deployment is not trivial. There are many issues to consider as you try and decide exactly how much hardware and what configuration is necessary to support your end users. The Microsoft Office System technical library (http://technet2.microsoft.com/Office/en-us/library/3e3b8737-c6a3-4e2c-a35f-f0095d952b781033.mspx?mfr=true) is an excellent resource for performing detailed planning, and I will not try to repeat all of that information in this chapter. However, there are some fundamental considerations worth covering that will provide you a framework for deciding what type of deployment you will need.

User Capacity Planning

Whenever I discuss SharePoint infrastructure with customers, they almost immediately jump on user capacity. This is because we tend to think of systems in terms of how many people are going to use them. However, determining the actual number of people who can access a SharePoint infrastructure is based on so many variables as to be nearly meaningless. First of all, you must consider the usage profile. Light site usage for simple browsing might mean that you can support three to five times as many concurrent users as you can if people are performing heavy queries and displaying complicated data views. Performance will also be affected by whether the activity is distributed across the farm or concentrated in a single area. In any case, even a single-server deployment is good for several hundred concurrent users on a typical day with typical activity.

The total latency of a SharePoint farm is split about evenly between server-side processing and client-side processing. On the server, latency is affected by ASP.NET processing, trips to the database, and security trimming designed to remove all of the menu actions that are inappropriate for the current user. On the client side, latency is affected by client-side scripting and asynchronous processing (e.g., AJAX) as well as the quality of the client machine. The biggest impact on latency, however, is poorly designed custom web parts. When web parts make too many round trips to the database or exhaustively recurse the SharePoint object model, latency increases dramatically. Before deploying any new web part, you would be wise to profile its performance and address areas that will cause excessive latency.

Storage Capacity Planning

Storage capacity is a major planning point in any SharePoint deployment. Since all of the pages, lists, and documents are stored in SQL Server 2005, you must adequately size the disk space to support not only your initial needs, but also to allow for growth over a period of years. Start by considering any existing documents that you want to migrate to SharePoint. For these documents, plan on having disk storage equal to one and a half times the total size of the documents to be migrated. Additionally, you'll need another 30% for indexing the new content, and an additional 60% for the search server. Finally, you'll need to consider growth, including the number of versions that will be created. This is calculated by assuming an average document size multiplied by an average number of versions. Table 2-1 details the planning formulas and shows an example based on migrating 100GB of existing documents with an average file size of 1MB and planning for five years of growth.

Table 2-1. *Calculating Storage Requirements*

Item	Formula	Example
Existing documents	1.5 × file size	1.5 × 100GB = 150GB
Indexes	30% of document storage	150GB × .3 = 45GB
Search server	60% of document storage	150GB × .6 = 90GB
Growth	Average document size × average number of versions × documents created annually × years	1MB × 5 × 10,000 × 5 = 250GB

Access and Authentication Planning

SharePoint offers new capabilities that make it a much stronger choice for extranet and Internet applications than it was previously, with templates specifically designed to support applications both inside and outside the firewall. Because SharePoint now also supports several different authentication providers including NT LAN Manager (NTLM), Kerberos, and Forms authentication, you should give some thought to access and authentication to determine the best combination.

NTLM and Kerberos

Integrated Windows Authentication is the simplest form of authentication for browser applications where the end user has a Windows account. Whenever a user browses to a site that uses Integrated Windows Authentication, the browser sends a token to the server identifying the Windows account of the user. If the server can authenticate the user with this information, access is granted. If the server cannot authenticate the user, a login box appears prompting the user to enter credentials manually. Both NTLM and Kerberos are forms of Integrated Windows Authentication.

NTLM uses a challenge-response protocol to authenticate the client to the server. It begins when the client attempts to connect to a secure application. The server sends a challenge to the client, and the client responds with a hashed value that the server can use to validate the user and password. All of this is seamless to the end user who simply sees the requested web page open in the browser.

NTLM is simple, works well, and developers have often been able to ignore authentication concerns because it was essentially transparent. As security concerns have grown, however, the need for a more secure authentication provider has become increasingly obvious. This is where Kerberos comes in to the picture.

Kerberos is a ticket-based authentication protocol. When a client wants to access a secure application, it requests a ticket from the key distribution center (KDC), which is the server running Active Directory. The KDC then creates a ticket based on the user credentials stored in Active Directory. The ticket is then sent back to the client, which can only use the ticket if it has the correct password. Once the user is authenticated, the ticket is cached locally where it remains until it expires.

Kerberos has several advantages over NTLM that SharePoint developers should care about. First, Kerberos has much better performance than NTLM. Because Kerberos caches credentials, servers can respond more quickly than under NTLM. Kerberos is also more secure than NTLM because the client can essentially authenticate the server as well as have the server authenticate the client. The biggest reason for developers to care about Kerberos, however, is delegation.

Take a step back and consider the process of connecting to a WSS team site using NTLM authentication. We know that NTLM will successfully authenticate a user that has a Windows account and grant access to the team site, which will then appear in the browser. While most of the page content will appear correctly, what if a web part on that page displays information from a line-of-business system with its own separate database? The web part itself must also authenticate against this other database. What credentials does it use? In many cases, we want the web part to use the same credentials as the current user. In other words, we want the web part to *impersonate* the current user.

SharePoint sites are set up so that web parts will initially impersonate the user accessing them. The user credentials may subsequently be passed to any system residing on the same server as SharePoint or on a different server that requires only a single additional authentication. If the data source requires a second authentication—like when you access a web service, which subsequently accesses a database—the impersonation will fail. This is typically referred to as the "double-hop" issue.

Kerberos, on the other hand, supports impersonation across machines. This type of extended impersonation is known as *delegation*. If the end user were authenticating to the team site using Kerberos, the web part would successfully authenticate to the line-of-business database and information would appear in the page.

It's important to point out that Kerberos requires some additional configuration that can only be accomplished if you have rights to Active Directory. Additionally, there are other ways to solve the double-hop issue. Many developers, for example, utilize a SQL Server standard security account buried in a connection string that a web part uses to access the database. The MOSS SSO service can also be used to gain access to any system in the enterprise. The bottom line, however, is that Kerberos is superior to NTLM in several ways and you should utilize it where you can. In the exercise in this chapter, "Creating a Development Environment," I detail the steps necessary to set up and configure Kerberos.

Forms Authentication

One of the reasons that previous versions of SharePoint have not been ideal candidates for extranets is that they did not directly support forms-based authentication. Therefore, organizations would often have to create a separate domain for partners and customers where they could be assigned a Windows account for authentication. Under SharePoint 2007, however, you can now implement forms-based authentication and utilize a data store such as SQL Server to manage the accounts. I discuss setting up forms authentication in Chapter 3.

Limitations

SharePoint has several limitations that you should keep in mind as you are planning your deployment. Generally, the limits presented here are not hard limits, but exceeding them can cause performance degradation. The limits are typically quite large and you're unlikely to run into most of them, but it is possible. For example, you could easily exceed the recommended 2,000 documents per folder unless you plan your document migration accordingly.

When examining the SharePoint limits, you'll see references to several terms that are specific to SharePoint. In SharePoint, a *web application* refers to an Internet Information Server site that has been extended with SharePoint. Each web application may contain one or more site collection. A *site collection* is typically a complete intranet, extranet, or Internet implementation. A site collection is made up of one or more sites. A *site* is a dedicated section of the site collection for team collaboration, business intelligence reporting, records management, or the like. Sites contain lists and documents and may have subsites underneath them. Table 2-2 lists the SharePoint limits associated with these terms.

Table 2-2. *SharePoint Limitations*

Item	Limit
Number of site collections in a web application	50K
Number of sites in a site collection	250K
Number of subsites nested under a site	2K
Number of lists on a site	2K

Continued

Table 2-2. *Continued*

Item	Limit
Number of items in a list	10M
Number of documents in a library	2M
Number of documents in a folder	2K
Maximum document file size	2GB
Number of documents in an index	50M
Number of search scopes	1K
Number of user profiles	5M

Deployment Architectures

SharePoint may be deployed in several different architectural configurations from a single
server utilizing SQL Server Express to a multiserver farm with an active-passive SQL cluster.
The exact deployment architecture will be based on the number of users, storage requirements, and availability requirements. Small team-based installations may be able to use a
single server while large Internet presence sites will need a farm. Table 2-3 lists the various
configurations and their specifications based on an average corporate user with an average
amount of activity.

Table 2-3. *Deployment Architectures*

Configuration	Users	Sites	Documents	Index	Availability
Single server	500	1,000	10K	100K	Low
Small farm	5,000	Thousands	Tens of thousands	Hundreds of thousands	Low
Medium farm	100,000	Tens of thousands	Hundreds of thousands	Hundreds of thousands	High
Large farm	500,000	Tens of thousands	Millions	Millions	High

Single-Server Configuration

A single-server deployment of WSS or MOSS can be created on a server that has a 2.8GHz
processor with 2GB of RAM and a 100GB hard drive. In this scenario, you would utilize SQL
Server Express to create the required databases directly on the server without the need for
a separate installation of SQL Server 2005. This deployment is remarkably easy to set up by
simply running the WSS or MOSS installation and following the steps. However, this is the
least reliable configuration because everything obviously relies on the availability of a single
machine.

Small Farm Configuration

System performance can be improved by moving the database off of the single server and onto its own server. This requires a separate installation of SQL Server, but improves performance significantly because all database operations can happen on the separate server. However, this configuration is really no more reliable than the single-server configuration because it is still vulnerable to a single failure.

Medium Farm Configuration

True enterprise reliability begins with the medium farm configuration. In this configuration, the web front-end servers, application server, and database servers are separate. A typical configuration would have two front-end web servers, a single application server, and an active-passive SQL Server cluster. Generally, these servers are dual-processor machines with at least 4GB of RAM and upward of 200GB hard drives. Performance and reliability in this configuration are greatly enhanced by separating the required functions across machines.

Large Farm Configuration

The large farm configuration is a scaled-out version of the medium farm configuration. In the large farm, upward of four front-end web servers are used to handle hundreds of thousands of users. An application server and active-passive SQL Server cluster are employed in the same way as the medium farm configuration. This configuration is typical for a large Internet presence site.

Exercise 2.1. Creating a Development Environment

As discussed in this chapter, there are several different configurations you can use to set up a SharePoint environment. You can, for example, install WSS on a single server using the Express version of SQL Server and work many examples in the book. However, the exercises in this book assume that you have a certain development environment available when specifying the steps to follow. This means that if you create a development environment that differs significantly from the one described in this exercise, you may experience some difficulty getting certain examples to work. Furthermore, the examples and exercises will deal with features of both WSS and MOSS. Therefore, if you do not install the Enterprise edition of MOSS, you will not be able to work exercises that specifically require it. I have included setup instructions for WSS in this exercise because I recognize that many readers will have easy access to WSS while MOSS requires a separate license.

■**Tip** Even if you are not going to use the Enterprise edition of MOSS in your production environment, you can still get a trial version free for 180 days. The download and trial keys are available at `http://www.microsoft.com/downloads/details.aspx?FamilyID=2e6e5a9c-ebf6-4f7f-8467-f4de6bd6b831&DisplayLang=en`.

I have chosen to specify a development environment from scratch assuming you have no existing domain controller, e-mail server, or web server. My infrastructure will consist of three servers—a domain controller, a web server, and a database server—in a medium farm configuration. I have selected this configuration because it is not overly complex, but it will allow you to get a feeling for the farm installation process. The only difference between the infrastructure described here and a production environment is that I would normally include an application server in the farm for handling expensive operations such as indexing. In this exercise, all of the services will reside on the web server.

Additionally, I will utilize Kerberos authentication throughout the farm. You may choose to complete this exercise without using Kerberos; however, you may have some issues later with authenticating web parts or assemblies using NTLM. Generally, I recommend using Kerberos authentication whenever it is practical to do so. You will need to be a domain administrator to properly configure Kerberos authentication.

For maximum flexibility, I recommend creating the development environment using Microsoft Virtual Server 2005 virtual machines. *Virtual machines* allow you to create multiple operating system installations on a single hardware platform, which can be reconfigured to set up various scenarios. Using virtual machines, for example, would allow you to create a development environment that can easily switch between MOSS and WSS. In this exercise, I include the instructions for downloading and installing Microsoft Virtual Server 2005.

This exercise is not intended to walk you through an exhaustive screen-by-screen installation of the required software. Instead, I focus on special areas of the installation where you need to configure the software or take special care to ensure a correct installation. Generally, I assume that you have some idea of how to install Microsoft server products, but I will try to give enough guidance to keep you from going astray.

Prerequisites

In setting up the development environment, I use a single dual-processor server running Microsoft Virtual Server 2005. If you are using Microsoft Virtual Server 2005 to create your development environment, you must meet the minimum requirements to create and run virtual machines. In order to ensure that you have a trouble-free environment, I recommend that you install the software on a server-class machine with at least a 3GHz processor and at least 4GB of RAM (more is better).

If you are not using virtual machines, you must have servers that meet the minimum requirements for Windows 2003 operating systems, SQL Server, and SharePoint. Generally speaking, you should strive to have machines with at least a 3GHz processor and at least 2GB of RAM. Table 2-4 lists the virtual machines I created and the software installed on each.

When using virtual machines, I connect them to the required software through the use of an ISO file. An ISO file is a complete image of a CD-ROM or DVD, which can be mounted to a virtual machine. Once mounted, the ISO file appears as a CD or a DVD drive in the virtual machine. ISO files can be created using many popular disk-burning software titles such as Nero (http://www.nero.com), and are available directly through Microsoft subscription downloads for those readers with access to a software subscription.

Table 2-4. *Machine Configurations*

Machine	List of Software
VSPDC	Microsoft Windows Server 2003 R2, Active Directory, POP3 service
VSSQL	Microsoft Windows Server 2003 R2, SQL Server 2005
VSMOSS	Microsoft Windows Server 2003 R2, Microsoft .NET Framework 3.0, Microsoft Office SharePoint Server, Visual Studio 2005
VSWSS	Microsoft Windows Server 2003 R2, Microsoft .NET Framework 3.0, Microsoft Windows SharePoint Services, Visual Studio 2005
VSCLIENT	Microsoft Vista, Microsoft Office Ultimate 2007

Next, if you are using Microsoft Virtual Server 2005, proceed to the next section, "Section 1: Installing Virtual Server 2005." Otherwise, proceed to "Section 3: Creating the Domain Controller."

Section 1: Installing Virtual Server 2005

In this section, you'll download and install Microsoft Virtual Server 2005. Because you'll need several virtual machines for the development environment, my strategy will be to create one base operating system and then make copies of it for the other machines. This is possible because of the portable nature of the virtual hard drive (VHD) files used by Virtual Server. Before a base image can be copied, however, it must be processed using a utility called SYSPREP. SYSPREP guarantees unique identifiers for each of the operating systems you clone from the original base image.

Microsoft Virtual Server 2005 is available as a free download from Microsoft at http://www.microsoft.com/windowsserversystem/virtualserver/software/default.mspx. When you link to this address, you will be able to download the software after logging in using a Windows Live identity. The software is contained in a single self-extracting executable named SETUP.EXE. After downloading the software, simply run the executable and perform a complete install. Figure 2-7 shows the virtual machine management panel in Microsoft Virtual Server 2005. Once the software is installed, follow these steps to create the base machine image:

1. Log into the server where Microsoft Virtual Server 2005 is installed as a local administrator.

2. Select Start ➤ All Programs ➤ Microsoft Virtual Server ➤ Virtual Server Administration Website.

3. In Virtual Server Administration Website, select Virtual Machines ➤ Create.

4. On the Create Virtual Machine page, type **VSIMAGE** in the Virtual Machine Name field.

5. Specify a value in the Virtual Machine Memory.

6. Specify a size for a new Virtual Hard Disk.

7. Select External Network from the Virtual Network Adapter drop-down list.

8. Once the values are specified, click the Create button.

■**Tip** If possible, run your VHD files on separate disks. This will greatly improve performance.

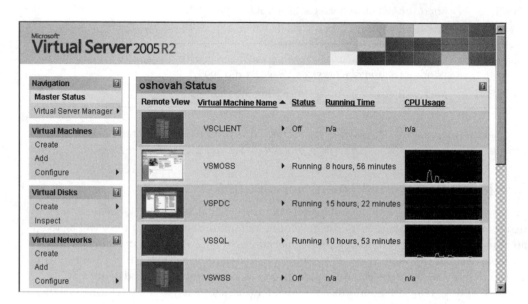

Figure 2-7. *Managing virtual machines*

Section 2: Creating the VPC Images

In this section, you will create the base virtual PC (VPC) image that you will use to create the other virtual machines. Creating this image is accomplished by installing the operating system onto a virtual machine and then preparing the image for cloning. Once created, we'll use this image in the rest of the exercise to make setup easier.

Getting Started

In this section, I walk through a moderately detailed procedure for setting up Windows 2003 Server. In subsequent sections, I simply direct you to copy the base image. To get started, boot the server using the Windows Server 2003 R2 CD-ROM.

Follow these steps to boot the virtual machine:

1. On the Virtual Server 2005 home page, select Configure ➤ VSIMAGE.

2. On the VSIMAGE Status page, click the CD/DVD link.

3. On the VSIMAGE CD/DVD Drive Properties page, specify the complete path to the ISO image for the Windows 2003 Server R2 software.

4. Click the OK button to return to the VSIMAGE Status page.

5. On the VSIMAGE Status page, select VSIMAGE ➤ Turn On.

Once the virtual machine is started, you may either click the screen thumbnail to view the session or utilize the Virtual Machine Remote Control Client to view the session. The Virtual Machine Remote Control Client is located in the Microsoft Virtual Server Program Group. I prefer to use the Virtual Machine Remote Control Client because it has a full-screen mode.

Formatting the Partition

When prompted during the installation, be sure to format the installation partition using the NTFS file format. SharePoint products require the NTFS file format.

■**Caution** The hard drive that you use to store your VHD files must also be formatted as NTFS. Many external USB hard drives are formatted as FAT32 by default.

Naming the Server

When prompted during installation, name this machine **VSIMAGE**. When you use this image to make copies later, you will change the copied machine name to match the entries in Table 2-4.

Skipping the Domain

When prompted during installation, do not join an existing domain because this server will be used as the base image. Later when you create the other servers, you will join them to a new domain.

Post-Setup Security

After the initial installation is complete, log on to the local machine as the system administrator. The Windows Server Post-Setup Security Updates page appears automatically. This page allows you to apply updates and configure automatic updates for the server. Once you have completed these tasks, click the Finish button.

Virtual Machine Additions

This is a good time to install the Virtual Machine Additions. These additions help improve the performance and stability of virtual machines. You can install them through the Virtual Server web interface under the Configurations section.

■**Note** Installing the Virtual Machine Additions can unmount the Windows 2003 Server installation disk. Verify that the installation disk is still available because you will need it for preparing the virtual image.

Creating an Answer File

Preparing the base virtual image for cloning is accomplished using a utility called SYSPREP. SYSPREP is available in the SUPPORT\TOOLS directory of the Windows 2003 installation disk. The utility, along with several other files, is contained in the file `DEPLOY.CAB`. In order to use SYSPREP, you must first create a configuration file known as an *answer file*. The answer file contains all of the information necessary to automate the operating system installation.

Follow these steps to create an answer file:

1. Locate `DEPLOY.CAB` in the SUPPORT\TOOLS directory of the Windows 2003 installation disk.

2. Double-click the `DEPLOY.CAB` file to view the contents in the File Explorer.

3. Create a new directory at `C:\Deploy` and extract all of the files from `DEPLOY.CAB` into the directory.

4. Execute the file `C:\Deploy\setupmgr.exe` to begin creating the answer file.

5. On the Welcome screen of the wizard, click the Next button.

6. On the New or Existing Answer File screen, select Create New and click the Next button.

7. On the Type of Setup screen, select Sysprep Setup and click the Next button.

8. On the Product screen, select the version of the Windows Server 2003 operating system you are using and click the Next button.

9. On the License Agreement screen, select Fully Automate the Installation and click the Next button.

10. On the Name and Organization screen, type in values and click the Next button.

11. On the Display Settings screen, accept the default settings and click the Next button.

12. On the Time Zone screen, select your time zone and click the Next button.

13. On the Product Key screen, enter your product key and click the Next button.

14. On the Licensing Mode screen, make any changes you want and click the Next button.

15. On the Computer Name screen, type **VSIMAGE** in the Computer Name field and click the Next button.

16. On the Administrator Password screen, enter a password and click the Next button.

17. On the Networking Components screen, select Typical Settings and click the Next button.

18. On the Workgroup or Domain screen, leave the machine in the workgroup and click the Next button.

19. On the Telephony screen, click the Next button.

20. On the Regional Settings screen, click the Next button.

21. On the Languages screen, click the Next button.

22. On the Install Printers screen, click the Next button.

23. On the Run Once screen, click the Next button.

24. On the Additional Commands screen, click the Next button.

25. On the Identification String screen, click the Finish button.

26. When finished, save the file to `C:\Deploy\sysprep.inf`.

Prepping the Operating System

Once the answer file is created, you can run the SYSPREP utility. The SYSPREP utility will prepare the image for cloning so that all subsequent copies have unique identifiers and will not conflict on the network. Once prepared, you must never start the base operating system image because it will undo all of the changes you make in this section.

Follow these steps to prepare the base image:

1. Close all of the open windows in VSIMAGE.

2. Open a command prompt and execute `C:\Deploy\SYSPREP.EXE`.

3. When the warning dialog appears, click the OK button.

4. In the System Preparation Tool dialog, check the box labeled Don't Reset Grace Period for Activation.

5. Ensure that the Shutdown Mode drop-down list is set to Shutdown.

6. Click the Reseal button.

7. When the warning dialog appears, click the OK button.

8. Wait until the system is prepared and shut down.

9. When the system is shut down, open the Virtual Server Administration web site.

10. On the Master Status page, select Remove from the fly-out menu associated with the VSIMAGE virtual machine.

Next, if you are going to have a separate domain controller for the development environment, proceed to "Section 3: Creating the Domain Controller." If you are going to join an existing domain, proceed to "Section 4: Creating the Database Server."

Section 3: Creating the Domain Controller

In this section, you will clone the base VPC image and create a domain controller. In my development environment, I use the VSPDC virtual machine as the domain controller. Although an Active Directory domain is not required for SharePoint to function, I assume its presence in this and many other exercises throughout the book.

Cloning the Base VPC

Once the base VPC image is prepared, it can be used to create as many images as you want. The basic process involves creating a new virtual machine without a hard drive and then attaching a copy of the prepared hard drive from the clone. When you first start the new image, it will subsequently be configured based on the options you selected in the answer file.

Follow these steps to create a new cloned image:

1. Log into the server where Microsoft Virtual Server 2005 is installed as a local administrator.

2. Select Start ➤ All Programs ➤ Microsoft Virtual Server ➤ Virtual Server Administration Website.

3. In Virtual Server Administration Website, select Virtual Machines ➤ Create.

4. On the Create Virtual Machine page, type **VSPDC** in the Virtual Machine Name field.

5. Specify a value in the Virtual Machine Memory.

6. Select the option Attach a Virtual Hard Disk Later.

7. Select External Network from the Virtual Network Adapter drop-down list.

8. Once the values are specified, click the Create button.

9. Open the File Explorer and copy the `VSIMAGE.VHD` file into the directory where the `VSPDC.VMC` file was created.

10. In Virtual Server Administration Website, select Configure ➤ VSPDC.

11. In the Configuration section, click the Hard Disks link.

12. Click the Add Disk button.

13. Specify the complete path to the `VSIMAGE.VHD` file you just copied and click the OK button.

14. On the VSPDC Status page, select VSPDC ➤ Turn On.

Configuring the Domain Controller

After you log in to the new virtual machine, you should immediately change the name to VSPDC. You should also configure the networking settings to a static IP address. Domain controllers function much better with static IP addresses.

After the new server starts up, the Manage Your Server applet will open automatically. This applet can be used to set up the server in various roles. Follow these steps to set up the server as a domain controller:

1. From the Manage Your Server applet, select the right-facing arrow to add or remove a role to the server.

2. On the Preliminary Steps screen, click the Next button.

3. On the Server Role screen, select Domain Controller (Active Directory) from the list of available roles and click the Next button.

4. On the Summary of Selections screen, click the Next button to start the Active Directory Wizard.

5. When the Active Directory Wizard starts, click the Next button.

6. On the Operating System Compatibility screen, click the Next button.

7. On the Domain Controller Type screen, make sure the Domain Controller for a New Domain option is selected and click the Next button.

8. On the Create New Domain screen, ensure the Domain in New Forest option is selected and click the Next button.

9. On the Install or Configure DNS screen, select No, Just Install and Configure DNS on This Computer and click the Next button.

10. On the New Domain Name screen, enter the name of a new domain (I use **domain.local** and will refer to it throughout the book) and click the Next button.

11. On the NetBIOS Domain Name screen, click the Next button.

12. On the Database and Log Folders screen, accept the default values by clicking the Next button.

13. On the Shared System Volume screen, click the Next button.

14. On the Permissions screen, accept the default selection by clicking the Next button.

15. On the Directory Services Restore Mode Administrator Password screen, enter a password and then click the Next button.

16. On the Summary screen, click the Next button.

17. When the Wizard completes, restart the server.

Setting Up the POP3 Service

In order to work with the many e-mail features of SharePoint, you will need an e-mail server with test accounts. Although you could certainly use Microsoft Exchange for this purpose, setting up a POP3 service uses significantly fewer resources, and SharePoint does not require Microsoft Exchange. Follow these steps to set up a POP3 service on the domain controller:

1. From the Manage Your Server applet, select the right-facing arrow to add or remove a role to the server.

2. On the Preliminary Steps screen, click the Next button.

3. On the Server Role screen, select Mail Server (POP3, SMTP) from the list of available roles and click the Next button.

4. On the Configure POP3 Service screen, enter the name of an e-mail domain (I use **domain.local** and will refer to it throughout the book) and click the Next button.

5. On the Summary of Selections screen, click the Next button to start the installation.

6. When the installation is complete, click the Finish button.

Adding Users and Groups to the Domain

After the domain controller is installed, you must add required users and groups to Active Directory. Whether you are setting up MOSS or WSS, several groups and accounts are required to run services and application pools. These groups and accounts do not need any special configuration because the installation process handles it for you. Table 2-5 describes the required accounts and indicates if they are required for a WSS or a MOSS installation.

Follow these steps to add the accounts:

1. Select Start ➤ Administrative Tools ➤ Active Directory Users and Computers.

2. In the Active Directory Users and Computers management console, expand the tree until the Users folder is visible.

3. Right-click the Users folder and select New ➤ User from the context menu.

4. In the New Object dialog, type the name of the account into the Full Name field and the User Logon name field.

5. Click the Next button.

6. On the next screen, give the account a password and uncheck the box titled User Must Change Password at Next Logon.

7. Check the boxes titled Password Never Expires and User Cannot Change Password.

8. Click the Next button.

9. Click the Finish button.

10. Repeat these steps to add each account.

11. When finished, add the SPAdmins group shown in Table 2-5.

■**Note** This is a good time to add some test users to Active Directory. These test accounts are useful for setting up various scenarios in SharePoint. When you add a new account, be sure to also set up a new mailbox for each account in the POP3 service.

Table 2-5. *Required Users and Groups*

Name	Group/Account	Description	WSS/MOSS
SPAdmins	Group	The SharePoint administrators security group	WSS/MOSS
SPConfigAcct	Account	The account used to connect to the Configuration database, run the administration application pool, and run the timer service	WSS/MOSS
SPContentPool	Account	The account used for the site collection application pool	WSS/MOSS
SPSearchAcct	Account	The account used to perform searches	WSS/MOSS
SPCrawlAcct	Account	The account used to crawl and index content	WSS/MOSS
SPSharedServicesPool	Account	The account used for the Shared Services application pool	MOSS only
SPSharedServicesAcct	Account	The account under which Shared Services run	MOSS only

■**Tip** Although SharePoint is supposed to grant all of the necessary permissions to your accounts, I have regularly seen DCOM errors in the System event log that indicate the application pool accounts were not given the required launch permissions for the IWAM Reg Admin Service component. After you complete the installation, check your System event log. If you see these errors, you can fix them by adding the SPContentPool and SPSharedServicesPool accounts to the launch permissions list of the IWAM Reg Admin Service component. The System event log message will give you the exact details to guide you in correcting the error.

Configuring Remote Desktop Administration

The Remote Desktop for Administration (RDA) is a handy way to access the domain controller when you are logged into another machine. This is especially helpful if you have created your development environment using separate machines. The RDA uses only about 2MB of memory and has little impact on processing power, so Microsoft recommends enabling it for every server.

The RDA is enabled from the System Properties dialog on the server. Clients attach to it using the Remote Desktop Connection applet. You can find the client applet on a Windows XP machine at Start ➤ All Programs ➤ Accessories ➤ Communications ➤ Remote Desktop Connection.

Follow these steps to enable the RDA:

1. Select Start ➤ Control Panel ➤ System to open the System Properties dialog.

2. Select the Remote tab.

3. Check the box titled Enable Remote Desktop on this Computer.

4. If you want to provide access for any other accounts besides the domain administrator, click the Select Remote Users button and add the accounts.

5. Click OK.

Next, if you are going to create a database server for the development environment, proceed to "Section 4: Creating the Database Server." Otherwise, proceed to either "Section 5: Installing Windows SharePoint Services" or "Section 6: Installing Microsoft Office SharePoint Server."

Section 4: Creating the Database Server

Follow the same steps as you did for creating the image for the domain controller. There are only two differences in the installation process. First, be sure to name this server VSSQL. Second, join the server to the domain that you created earlier.

Adding the Application Server Role

ASP.NET is required on the server where SQL Server 2005 will be installed in order to support Reporting Services. The SQL Server 2005 setup will automatically install the .NET Framework 2.0, but you must first configure the Application Server role.

Follow these steps to configure the server:

1. From the Manage Your Server applet, select the right-facing arrow to add or remove a role to the server.

2. On the Preliminary Steps screen, click the Next button.

3. On the Server Role screen, select Application Server (IIS, ASP.NET) from the list of available roles and click the Next button.

4. On the Application Server Options screen, leave both boxes unchecked and click the Next button.

5. On the Summary of Selections screen, click the Next button.

Installing SQL Server 2005

SQL Server 2005 is the back end for all SharePoint data. You can also use Analysis Services with SharePoint to create dashboards of KPIs. Additionally, you can use SQL Reporting Services to create reports that may be viewed in SharePoint. Having a fully functional set of SQL Server services will significantly enhance your SharePoint installation.

Follow these steps to install SQL Server 2005:

1. Mount the SQL Server 2005 ISO file or insert the setup disk to start the installation.

2. On the installation Start screen, click the link titled Server Components, Tools, Books Online, and Samples.

3. On the End User License Agreement screen, accept the agreement and click the Next button.

4. On the Installing Prerequisites screen, click the Install button.

5. When the prerequisites are installed, click the Next button.

6. On the Welcome screen of the installation wizard, click the Next button.

7. When the System Configuration Check appears, verify that your system has passed all of the checks and click the Next button.

8. On the Registration Information screen, enter your Product Key and click the Next button.

9. On the Components to Install screen, select to install SQL Server Database Services, Analysis Services, Reporting Services, and Workstation Components, Books Online, and Development Tools. Then click the Next button.

10. On the Instance Name screen, make sure the Default Instance option is selected and click the Next button.

11. On the Service Account screen, select the Use the Built-In System Account option.

12. Select Local System from the drop-down list of accounts and click the Next button.

13. On the Authentication Mode screen, ensure the Windows Authentication Mode option is selected and click the Next button.

14. On the Collation Settings screen, click the Next button.

15. On the Report Server Installation Options screen, select the option to Install the Default Configuration and click the Next button.

16. On the Error and Usage Report Settings screen, click the Next button.

17. On the Ready to Install screen, click the Install button.

Configuring SQL Server 2005 Surface Areas

When configuring a farm environment for MOSS, you must modify the SQL Server surface areas to support communication among the components. This is because SQL 2005 installs in a secure mode that you must open up. Follow these steps to configure SQL Server surface areas:

1. Select Start ➤ All Programs ➤ Microsoft SQL Server 2005 ➤ Configuration Tools ➤ SQL Server Surface Area Configuration.

2. In the SQL Server 2005 Surface Area Configuration window, click the link titled Surface Area Configuration for Services and Connections.

3. In the Surface Area Configuration for Services and Connections dialog, select Remote Connections from the tree control.

4. Select the option labeled Using Both TCP/IP and Named Pipes.

5. Click the OK button.

6. When the alert dialog appears, click the OK button.

7. Close the SQL Server Surface Area Configuration dialog.

8. Reboot the VSSQL server.

Next, proceed to "Section 5: Installing Windows SharePoint Services" or "Section 6: Installing Microsoft Office SharePoint Server."

Section 5: Installing Windows SharePoint Services

You can follow the steps in this section if you do not plan on deploying MOSS. If you are going to deploy MOSS, you can skip this section and move on to the MOSS deployment. Initially, you can follow the same steps as you did for creating the virtual server for the domain controller or database server. Name this server VSWSS and join the server to the domain that you created earlier.

Adding the Application Server Role

ASP.NET is required to run Windows SharePoint Services. In the next section, you will install the .NET Framework 2.0, but you must first configure the Application Server role. Follow these steps to configure the server:

1. From the Manage Your Server applet, select the right-facing arrow to add or remove a role to the server.

2. On the Preliminary Steps screen, click the Next button.

3. On the Server Role screen, select Application Server (IIS, ASP.NET) from the list of available roles and click the Next button.

4. On the Application Server Options screen, leave both boxes unchecked and click the Next button.

5. On the Summary of Selections screen, click the Next button.

Installing the .NET Framework 2.0

Windows SharePoint Services requires the .NET Framework 2.0. You can access and download the framework using Windows Update. Follow these steps to install the .NET Framework 2.0:

1. Launch the Microsoft .NET Framework Version 2.0 Redistributable Package DOTNETFX.EXE.

2. Follow the simple steps in the wizard to complete the installation.

3. When the installation completes, select Start ➤ Administrative Tools ➤ Internet Information Services (IIS) Manager.

4. In the IIS Manager applet, click the Web Service Extensions folder.

5. Select ASP.NET 2.0.50727 from the list of extensions and click the Allow button.

Installing the .NET Framework 3.0

Windows SharePoint Services requires the .NET Framework 3.0 for workflow support. You can access and download the framework using Windows Update. The installation is straightforward and requires no special considerations.

Installing WSS Software

Installing WSS on the server requires installation and then configuration. The installation is straightforward and only requires a few steps through a wizard interface. Configuration is performed after the software is installed.

Follow these steps to install Windows SharePoint Services:

1. Run SETUP.EXE for WSS v3.

2. On the License Agreement screen, accept the agreement and click the Continue button.

3. On the next screen, click the Advanced button.

4. On the Server Type tab, select the Web Front End option.

5. Click the Install Now button.

6. When the installation is complete, check the box to run the Configuration Wizard and click the Close button.

Configuring Authentication and Database Options

Configuring the basic WSS installation is done through a wizard interface. In the wizard, you will specify the database server and configuration database name. You will also select to use either NTLM or Kerberos as the authentication provider.

Follow these steps to configure WSS:

1. On the welcome screen, click the Next button.

2. In the warning dialog, click the Yes button to acknowledge that the listed services will be stopped.

3. On the Connect to a Server Farm screen, select No, I Want to Create a New Server Farm and click the Next button.

4. On the Configuration Database Settings screen, enter **VSSQL** in the Database Server field.

5. Enter **WSS_Config** in the Database Name field.

6. Enter **DOMAIN\SPConfigAcct** in the Username field.

7. Enter the password for the SPConfigAcct in the Password field.

8. Click the Next button.

9. On the Configure SharePoint Central Administration Web Application, select either NTLM or Kerberos as the authentication provider and click the Next button.

■Caution If you choose to use Kerberos authentication, further steps will be necessary to configure the authentication provider. Do not use Kerberos authentication if you do not have the ability to access and modify Active Directory.

10. On the completion screen, click the Next button to apply the configuration settings.

11. After closing the configuration wizard, the Central Administration site will open automatically. If prompted with a login dialog, enter the administrator credentials.

12. When prompted, add the Central Administration site to the list of trusted sites.

13. After the Central Administration site opens, close it until you have finished configuring security.

Turning Off Internet Explorer Enhanced Security

Windows Server 2003 installs Internet Explorer with Enhanced Security activated. Although this is a good default setting for production machines, it can and will prevent content from being rendered in SharePoint. You'll want to disable Enhanced Security in the development environment to make sure you have complete access to administrative functions.

Follow these steps to disable Internet Explorer Enhanced Security:

1. Select Start ➤ Control Panel ➤ Add or Remove Programs.

2. Click the Add/Remove Windows Components button on the Add/Remove Programs screen.

3. Uncheck the Internet Explorer Enhanced Security Configuration box.

4. Click the Next button.

Adding WSS to the List of Trusted Sites

You may find that when you access WSS sites that you are prompted for a username and password. You can eliminate this behavior by adding the VSWSS server to the list of trusted sites or the Local Intranet zone. In either case, you should also ensure that the browser settings are configured to automatically log the user on to the site.

Follow these steps to add the server to the list of trusted sites:

1. In the Internet Explorer, select Tools ➤ Internet Options.

2. On the Security tab, click the Trusted Sites icon.

3. Click the Sites button.

4. Clear the box titled Require Server Verification (https) for All Sites in this Zone.

5. Verify that `http://vswss` is in the Websites list. If not, add it to the list.

6. Click the Close button.

7. Click the Custom Level button.

8. In the Settings list, under User Authentication, select Automatic Logon with Current Username and Password.

9. Click the OK button.

10. Click the OK button to close the options dialog.

Configuring Kerberos Authentication

If you selected to use Kerberos as the authentication provider, you must perform additional configuration steps. The steps involve the definition of a Service Principal Name (SPN) for the application pool account. The SPN is used to authenticate the server to the client.

Follow these steps to configure Kerberos authentication:

1. Log in to VSPDC as a domain administrator.

2. Select Start ➤ Administrative Tools ➤ Active Directory Users and Computers.

3. In the Active Directory Users and Computers applet, click the Computers folder.

4. Right-click VSWSS and select Properties from the context menu.

5. On the General tab, check the box labeled Trust Computer for Delegation and then click the OK button.

6. Click the Users folder.

7. Right-click the SPConfigAcct account and select Properties from the context menu.

8. On the Account tab, check the box labeled Account is Trusted for Delegation and click the OK button.

9. Repeat steps 7 and 8 for the SPContentPool account.

10. Download the SPN tool from the following URL: http://www.microsoft.com/downloads/details.aspx?familyid=5fd831fd-ab77-46a3-9cfe-ff01d29e5c46&displaylang=en.

11. Create the SPN for the SPConfigAcct by running the following command:

   SETSPN –A HTTP/VSWSS.DOMAIN.LOCAL DOMAIN\SPConfigAcct

12. Repeat step 11 for the SPContentPool account.

Configuring WSS Components

Once you have the security settings properly configured, you can open the SharePoint Central Administration site on VSWSS by selecting Start ➤ Administrative Tools ➤ SharePoint 3.0 Administration. On the home page, you will see a task list of recommended actions you should take to configure WSS. Figure 2-8 shows the WSS Central Administration site. In this exercise, you will configure several items, but not all of the items in the task list. Several of these tasks will be configured later in the book where they are explained in more detail. The following sections will help you get the basic WSS configuration completed.

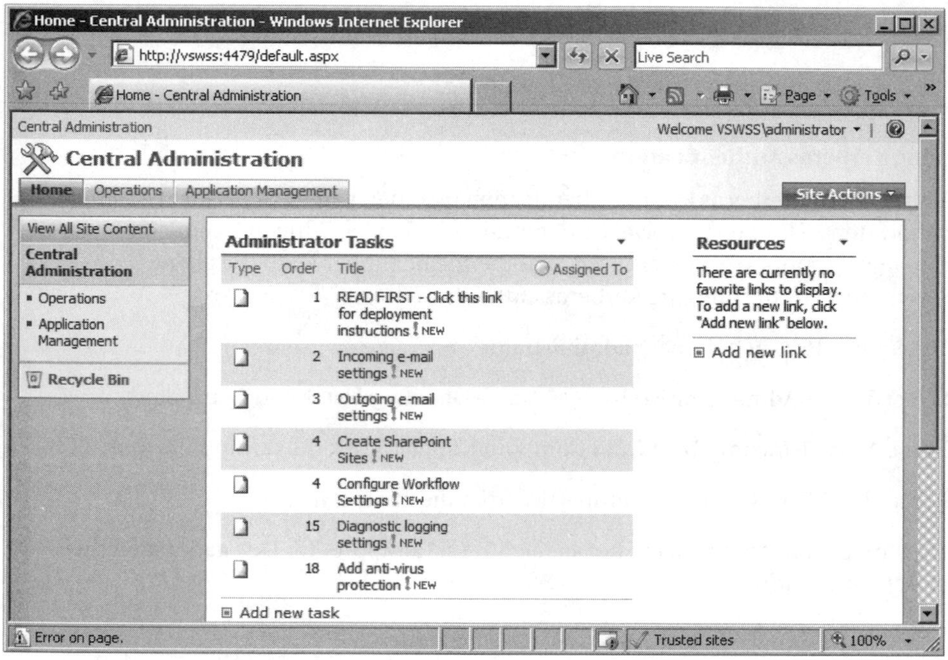

Figure 2-8. *WSS Central Administration*

Designating the SharePoint Administrators Group

Earlier in the exercise, you created a security group for the SharePoint administrators. At this point, only the account you used to install WSS can function as the administrator. By adding a group to the list of administrators you can easily grant others administration capabilities through Active Directory.

Follow these steps to designate an administrator group:

1. Select Start ➤ Administrative Tools ➤ SharePoint 3.0 Administration.

2. On the SharePoint Central Administration page, click the Operations tab.

3. Under the Security Configuration section, click the link titled Update Farm Administrator's Group.

4. On the People and Groups: Farm Administrators page, select New ➤ Add Users.

5. On the Add Users page, enter **DOMAIN\SPAdmins** in the Users field.

6. Click the OK button.

Starting the Search Service

The WSS Search Service is not running initially. In order to use search functions, you must configure the service with an appropriate account for searching and one for crawling. In this section, you will use the accounts you created earlier to configure the Search Service.

Follow these steps to configure the Search Service:

1. On the SharePoint Central Administration page, click the Operations tab.

2. In the Topology and Services section, click the link titled Services on Server.

3. On the Services on Server page, click the Start link next to the Windows SharePoint Services Search.

4. In the Service Account section, enter **DOMAIN\SPSearchAcct** in the User Name field.

5. Enter the account password in the Password field.

6. In the Content Access Account section, enter **DOMAIN\SPCrawlAcct** in the User Name field.

7. Enter the account password in the Password field.

8. Click the Start button.

Configuring Outgoing E-Mail

WSS uses an SMTP server to send alerts and messages to users. In this section, you will enter the e-mail settings for WSS. Follow these steps to configure the e-mail settings:

1. On the SharePoint Central Administration page, click the Operations tab.

2. In the Topology and Services section, click the link titled Outgoing E-mail Settings.

3. On the Outgoing E-Mail Settings page, enter **VSPDC** in the Outbound SMTP Server field.

4. Enter **administrator@domain.local** in the From Address field.

5. Enter **administrator@domain.local** in the Reply To field.

6. Click the OK button.

Creating a New Web Application and Site Collection

Once WSS is properly configured, you can finally create your first site. In this section, you will create a site collection based on the team site template. Follow these steps to create your first site:

1. On the SharePoint Central Administration page, click the Application Management tab.

2. On the Application Management page, click the link titled Create or Extend Web Application.

3. On the Create or Extend Web Application page, click the link titled Create a New Web Application.

4. On the Create a New Web Application page, select the option Use an Existing IIS Web Site.

5. Choose Default Web Site in the drop-down list.

6. Under the Authentication Provider, choose either Negotiate (Kerberos) or NTLM, depending upon the choice you made earlier.

7. In the Application Pool section, select Create a New Application Pool.

8. Enter **WSS_Pool** as the pool name.

9. Select the Configurable option for the application pool security account.

10. In the User Name field, enter **DOMAIN\SPContentPool**.

11. In the Password field, enter the account password.

12. In the Reset Internet Information Services section, select the option to Restart IIS Automatically.

13. In the Search Server section, select VSWSS from the drop-down list.

14. Click the OK button.

15. On the Application Created page, click the link titled Create Site Collection.

16. On the Create Site Collection page, enter **Home Site** in the Title field.

17. Use the drop-down list in the Web Site Address section and verify that just the single forward slash is selected. This will create the site at the root for the server.

18. Under the Primary Site Collection Administrator section, enter **DOMAIN\Administrator** in the User Name field.

19. Click the OK button to create the new site collection.

20. Once the Site Collection is created, return to the Application Management tab.

21. Click the link titled Policy for Web Application under the Application Security section.

22. On the Policy for Web Application page, click the Add Users button.

23. On the Add Users page, click the Next button.

24. Under the Choose Users section, enter any accounts that should have administrative control over the Site Collection. Be sure to include the DOMAIN\Administrator and VSWSS\Administrator accounts.

25. In the Choose Permissions section, check the box labeled Full Control.

26. Click the Finish button. You should now have full access to the new Site Collection.

Installing Visual Studio 2005 and SharePoint Designer

Throughout the book, I utilize Visual Studio 2005 and SharePoint Designer to customize SharePoint. For simplicity, you should install these products directly on the WSS server. There are no special considerations; simply install the products in a typical configuration.

Next, proceed to "Section 7: Creating a Test Client."

Section 6: Installing Microsoft Office SharePoint Server

Installing MOSS is the best way to experience the information, examples, and exercises in the book. MOSS has many components that are simply not available in WSS. This section will walk you through creating a MOSS installation for development. Start out cloning Windows 2003 Server just as you did on every other machine. Name this machine VSMOSS and join it to the domain you created earlier.

■**Caution** Always install MOSS using a domain account that is a local administrator on every machine in the farm. Never install MOSS as simply a local administrator on the SharePoint server. The MOSS installation automatically makes the installation account the administrator for shared services, and using a local account can cause you to be denied access to the farm later.

Adding the Application Server Role

ASP.NET is required to run MOSS. In the next section, you will install the .NET Framework 2.0, but you must first configure the Application Server role. Follow these steps to configure the server:

1. From the Manage Your Server applet, select the right-facing arrow to add or remove a role to the server.

2. On the Preliminary Steps screen, click the Next button.

3. On the Server Role screen, select Application Server (IIS, ASP.NET) from the list of available roles and click the Next button.

4. On the Application Server Options screen, leave both boxes unchecked and click the Next button.

5. On the Summary of Selections screen, click the Next button.

Installing the .NET Framework 2.0

MOSS requires the .NET Framework 2.0. You can access and download the framework using Windows Update. Follow these steps to install the .NET Framework 2.0:

1. Launch the Microsoft .NET Framework Version 2.0 Redistributable Package DOTNETFX.EXE.

2. Follow the simple steps in the wizard to complete the installation.

3. When the installation completes, select Start ➤ Administrative Tools ➤ Internet Information Services (IIS) Manager.

4. In the IIS Manager applet, click the Web Service Extensions folder.

5. Select ASP.NET 2.0.50727 from the list of extensions and click the Allow button.

Installing the .NET Framework 3.0

MOSS requires the .NET Framework 3.0 for workflow support. You can access and download the framework using Windows Update. The installation is straightforward and requires no special considerations.

Installing Microsoft Office SharePoint Server Software

Installing MOSS on the server requires installation and then configuration. The installation is straightforward and only requires a few steps through a wizard interface. Configuration is performed after the software is installed and is somewhat more complicated than the typical WSS installation.

Follow these steps to install MOSS:

1. Run SETUP.EXE for MOSS.

2. On the License Agreement screen, accept the agreement and click the Continue button.

3. On the next screen, click the Advanced button.

4. On the Server Type tab, select Complete.

5. Click the Install Now button.

6. When the installation is complete, check the box to run the Configuration Wizard and click the Close button.

Configuring Authentication and Database Options

Configuring the basic MOSS installation is done through a wizard interface. In the wizard, you will specify the database server and configuration database name. You will also select to use either NTLM or Kerberos as the authentication provider.

Follow these steps to configure MOSS:

1. On the welcome screen, click the Next button.

2. In the warning dialog, click the Yes button to acknowledge that the listed services will be stopped.

3. On the Connect to a Server Farm screen, select No, I Want to Create a New Server Farm and click the Next button.

4. On the Configuration Database Settings screen, enter **VSSQL** in the Database Server field.

5. Enter **MOSS_Config** in the Database Name field.

6. Enter **DOMAIN\SPConfigAcct** in the Username field.

7. Enter the password for the SPConfigAcct in the Password field.

8. Click the Next button.

9. On the Configure SharePoint Central Administration Web Application, select either NTLM or Kerberos as the authentication provider and click the Next button.

■**Note** If you choose to use Kerberos authentication, further steps will be necessary to configure the authentication provider. Do not use Kerberos authentication if you do not have the ability to access and modify Active Directory.

---

10. On the completion screen, click the Next button to apply the configuration settings.

11. After closing the configuration wizard, the Central Administration site will open automatically. If you are presented with a login dialog, use the administrator credentials.

12. When prompted, add the Central Administration site to the list of trusted sites.

13. After the Central Administration site opens, close it until you have finished configuring security.

Turning Off Internet Explorer Enhanced Security

Windows Server 2003 installs Internet Explorer with Enhanced Security activated. Although this is a good default setting for production machines, it can and will prevent content from being rendered in SharePoint. You'll want to disable Enhanced Security in the development environment to make sure you have complete access to administrative functions.

Follow these steps to disable Internet Explorer Enhanced Security:

1. Select Start ➤ Control Panel ➤ Add or Remove Programs.

2. Click the Add/Remove Windows Components button on the Add/Remove Programs screen.

3. Uncheck the Internet Explorer Enhanced Security Configuration box.

4. Click the Next button.

Adding MOSS to the List of Trusted Sites

You may find that when you access SharePoint sites that you are prompted for a username and password. You can eliminate this behavior by adding the VSMOSS server to the list of trusted sites or the Local Intranet zone. In either case, you should also ensure that the browser settings are configured to automatically log the user on to the site.

Follow these steps to add VSMOSS to the list of trusted sites:

1. In the Internet Explorer, select Tools ➤ Internet Options.

2. On the Security tab, click the Trusted Sites icon.

3. Click the Sites button.

4. Clear the box titled Require Server Verification (https) for All Sites in This Zone.

5. Verify that `http://vsmoss` is in the Websites list. If not, add it.

6. Click the Close button.

7. Click the Custom Level button.

8. In the Settings list, under User Authentication, select Automatic Logon with Current Username and Password.

9. Click the OK button.

10. Click the OK button to close the options dialog.

Configuring Kerberos Authentication

If you selected to use Kerberos as the authentication provider, you must perform additional configuration steps. The steps involve the definition of a Service Principal Name (SPN) for the application pool account. The SPN is used to authenticate the server to the client.

Follow these steps to configure Kerberos authentication:

1. Log in to the domain controller as a domain administrator.

2. Select Start ➤ Administrative Tools ➤ Active Directory Users and Computers.

3. In the Active Directory Users and Computers applet, click the Computers folder.

4. Right-click VSMOSS and select Properties from the context menu.

5. On the General tab, check the box labeled Trust Computer for Delegation and then click the OK button.

6. Click the Users folder.

7. Right-click the SPConfigAcct account and select Properties from the context menu.

8. On the Account tab, check the box labeled Account Is Trusted for Delegation and click the OK button.

9. Repeat steps 7 and 8 for the SPContentPool account.

10. Download the SPN tool from the following URL: `http://www.microsoft.com/downloads/details.aspx?familyid=5fd831fd-ab77-46a3-9cfe-ff01d29e5c46&displaylang=en`.

11. Create the SPN for the SPConfigAcct by running the following command:

    ```
    SETSPN -A HTTP/VSMOSS.DOMAIN.LOCAL DOMAIN\SPConfigAcct
    ```

12. Repeat step 11 for the SPContentPool, SPSharedServicesPool, and SPSharedServicesAcct accounts.

Configuring MOSS Components

Once you have the security settings properly configured, you can open the SharePoint Central Administration site on VSMOSS. On the home page, you will see a task list of recommended actions you should take to configure MOSS. Figure 2-9 shows the MOSS Central Administration site. In this exercise, you will configure several items, but not all of the items in the task list. Several of these tasks will be configured later in the book where they are explained in more detail. The following sections will help you get the basic MOSS configuration completed.

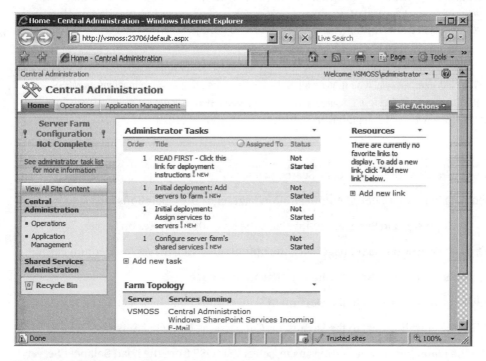

Figure 2-9. *MOSS Central Administration*

Designating the SharePoint Administrators Group

Earlier in the exercise, you created a security group for the SharePoint administrators. At this point, only the account you used to install MOSS can function as the administrator. By adding a group to the list of administrators you can easily grant others administration capabilities through Active Directory.

Follow these steps to designate an administrator group:

1. Select Start ➤ Administrative Tools ➤ SharePoint 3.0 Administration.

2. On the SharePoint Central Administration page, click the Operations tab.

3. Under the Security Configuration section, click the link titled Update Farm Administrator's Group.

4. On the People and Groups: Farm Administrators page, select New ➤ Add Users.

5. On the Add Users page, enter **DOMAIN\SPAdmins** in the Users field.

6. Click the OK button.

Starting Required Services

The MOSS Search Service is not running initially. In order to use search functions, you must configure the service with an appropriate account for searching and one for crawling. Additionally, you must start several other shared services that I will cover in Chapter 4. In this section, you will use the accounts you created earlier to configure the services.

■**Caution** In this exercise, you'll be running all of the farm services on the same machine as MOSS. Because many of these services are resource intensive, you would normally deploy these services to a separate application server for improved performance.

Follow these steps to configure the Search Service:

1. On the SharePoint Central Administration page, click the Operations tab.

2. In the Topology and Services section, click the link titled Services on Server.

3. On the Services on Server page, click the option titled Web Server for Medium Farm.

4. Click the Start link next to the Excel Calculation Services.

5. Click the Start link next to the Document Conversions Load Balancer Service.

6. Click the Start link next to the Document Conversions Launcher Service.

7. On the Launcher Service Settings page, select VSMOSS from the Load Balancer Server drop-down list.

8. Click the OK button.

9. Click the Start link next to Office SharePoint Server Search.

10. On the Office SharePoint Services Search Settings page, check the boxes labeled Use This Server for Indexing Content and Use This Server for Serving Search Queries.

11. Enter **administrator@domain.local** in the E-mail Address field.

12. In the Farm Search Service Account section, enter **DOMAIN\SPSearchAcct** in the User Name field.

13. Enter the account password in the Password field.

14. Click the Start button.

15. On the Services on Server page, click the Start link next to Windows SharePoint Services Search.

16. In the Service Account section, enter **DOMAIN\SPSearchAcct** in the User Name field.

17. Enter the account password in the Password field.

18. In the Content Access Account section, enter **DOMAIN\SPCrawlAcct** in the User Name field.

19. Enter the account password in the Password field.

20. Click the Start button.

Setting Up the Shared Services Provider

The Shared Services Provider hosts several services that can be used across web applications in the farm. Services such as search and user profiles typically only need to be created one time and then used by all sites. In this section, you will create a new web application for the Shared Services Provider. Follow these steps to set up the Shared Services Provider:

1. Select Start ➤ Administrative Tools ➤ SharePoint 3.0 Administration.

2. On the Application Management tab, under the Office SharePoint Server Shared Services section, click the link titled Create or Configure this Farm's Shared Services.

3. On the Manage This Farm's Shared Services page, click New SSP.

4. On the New Shared Services Provider page, click the link titled Create a New Web Application under the SSP Name field.

5. On the Create a New Web Application page, select the option Create a New IIS Web Site.

6. Enter **SharedServices – 8080** in the Description field.

7. Enter **8080** in the Port field.

8. Under the Authentication Provider, choose either Negotiate (Kerberos) or NTLM, depending upon the choice you made earlier.

9. In the Application Pool section, select Create a New Application Pool and enter **SSP_Pool** in the Application Pool Name field.

10. Select the Configurable option for the application pool security account.

11. In the User Name field, enter **DOMAIN\SPSharedServicesPool**.

12. In the Password field, enter the account password.

13. Select the option Restart IIS Automatically.

14. Click the OK button.

15. On the New Shared Services Provider page, click the link titled Create a New Web Application under the My Site Location section.

16. On the Create a New Web Application page, select the option Create a New IIS Web Site.

17. Enter **PersonalSites – 8081** in the Description field.

18. Enter **8081** in the Port field.

19. Under the Authentication Provider, choose either Negotiate (Kerberos) or NTLM, depending upon the choice you made earlier.

20. In the Application Pool section, select Use Existing Application Pool and choose SSP_Pool from the drop-down list.

21. Select Restart IIS Automatically.

22. Click the OK button.

23. On the New Shared Services Provider page, enter **Shared Services** in the SSP Name field.

24. Under the SSPService Credentials section, enter **DOMAIN\SPSharedServicesAcct** in the Username field.

25. Enter the account password in the Password field.

26. In the Index Server section, select VSMOSS from the Index Server drop-down list.

27. Click the OK button.

Configuring Outgoing E-Mail

Once the Shared Services are set up, you may return to the Central Administration pages to continue configuring additional components. In this exercise, you will configure an SMTP server for MOSS. MOSS uses an SMTP server to send alerts and messages to users. Follow these steps to configure the e-mail settings:

1. Click the Operations tab in SharePoint 3.0 Central Administration.

2. Click the link titled Outgoing E-Mail Settings under the Topology and Services section.

3. On the Outgoing E-Mail Settings page, enter **VSPDC** in the Outbound SMTP Server field.

4. Enter **administrator@domain.local** in the From Address field.

5. Enter **administrator@domain.local** in the Reply To field.

6. Click the OK button.

Creating a New Web Application and Site Collection

Once MOSS is properly configured, you can create a new web application and site collection. The site templates available to you include intranets, public web sites, wikis, and blogs. In this section, you will create a corporate intranet site. Follow these steps to create your first site:

1. Select Start ➤ Administrative Tools ➤ SharePoint 3.0 Central Administration.

2. On the Application Management tab, under the SharePoint Web Application Management section click the link titled Create or Extend Web Application.

3. On the Create or Extend Web Application page, click the link titled Create a New Web Application.

4. On the Create a New Web Application page, select the option Use an Existing IIS Web Site.

5. Choose Default Web Site in the drop-down list.

6. Under the Authentication Provider, choose either Negotiate (Kerberos) or NTLM, depending upon the choice you made earlier.

7. In the Application Pool section, select Create a New Application Pool.

8. Enter **Intranet_Pool** as the pool name.

9. Select the Configurable option for the application pool security account.

10. In the User Name field, enter **DOMAIN\SPContentPool**.

11. In the Password field, enter the account password.

12. In the Reset Internet Information Services section, select the option to Restart IIS Automatically.

13. Click the OK button.

14. On the Application Created page, click the link titled Create Site Collection.

15. On the Create Site Collection page, enter **Intranet** in the Title field.

16. In the Web Site Address section, select /sites/ from the drop-down list and enter **intranet** in the URL field.

17. Under the Template Selection section, click the Publishing tab and then select the Collaboration Portal template.

18. Under the Primary Site Collection Administrator section, enter **DOMAIN\ Administrator** in the User Name field.

19. Click the OK button to create the new site collection.

20. Once the site collection is created, return to the Application Management tab.

21. Click the link titled Policy for Web Application under the Application Security section.

22. On the Policy for Web Application page, click the Add Users button.

23. On the Add Users page, click the Next button.

24. Under the Choose Users section, enter any accounts that should have administrative control over the site collection. Be sure to include the DOMAIN\Administrator and VSMOSS\Administrator accounts so you can always access the site collection.

25. In the Choose Permissions section, check the box labeled Full Control.

26. Click the Finish button. You should now have full access to the new site collection.

Installing Visual Studio 2005 and SharePoint Designer

Throughout the book, I utilize Visual Studio 2005 and SharePoint Designer to customize MOSS. For simplicity, you should install these products directly on the MOSS server. There are no special considerations; simply install the products in a typical configuration.

Section 7: Creating a Test Client

In order to work with the examples in the book, you will need to create at least one client machine running Windows Vista or XP. While installing the operating system, you should name the client VSCLIENT and join the client machine to the domain you created earlier. Once joined to the domain, you should be able to view the site you created in SharePoint. Remember to add the SharePoint server to the list of trusted sites in order to avoid being prompted for credentials. After the operating system is installed, you will need to install Microsoft Office 2007. All of these setups are straightforward; you can simply use the typical installations.

CHAPTER 3

■ ■ ■

SharePoint Fundamentals

SharePoint 2007 is a significant product with many functional areas to master. Installing the software and creating a web application are only the beginning of the administrative and programming tasks you must perform to develop a professional site. These tasks include managing users, configuring authentications, and deploying functionality to the site. In this chapter, I cover the fundamental configurations, features, and functions that are required to get a site up and running.

Managing Users

Once you have created a web application and a site collection, you will want to give users permission to access the new site. Adding users is relatively straightforward. However, determining the permissions that should be granted to each user requires understanding and planning. When planning user permissions, you should consider what permissions you will make available to a web application and how to group those permissions for assignment to end users.

SharePoint defines 33 separate rights divided into three categories: *list permissions*, *site permissions*, and *personal permissions*. The list permissions determine whether a user can create new lists or manage list items within the site. The site permissions determine whether a user can change the content and appearance of various site aspects. The personal permissions allow the user to manage personal content. All of the available SharePoint rights are explained in the following three tables.

Table 3-1 shows list permissions and their descriptions.

Table 3-1. *List Permissions*

Right	Description
Manage Lists	Create and delete lists, add or remove columns in a list, and add or remove public views of a list.
Override Check Out	Discard or check in a document that is checked out to another user.
Add Items	Add items to lists, add documents to document libraries, and add web discussion comments.
Edit Items	Edit items in lists, edit documents in document libraries, edit web discussion comments in documents, and customize web part pages in document libraries.

Continued

Table 3-1. *Continued*

Right	Description
Delete Items	Delete items from a list, documents from a document library, and web discussion comments in documents.
View Items	View items in lists, documents in document libraries, and web discussion comments.
Approve Items	Approve a minor version of a list item or document.
Open Items	View the source of documents with server-side file handlers.
View Versions	View past versions of a list item or document.
Delete Versions	Delete past versions of a list item or document.
Create Alerts	Create e-mail alerts.
View Application Pages	View forms, views, and application pages. Enumerate lists.

Table 3-2 shows site permissions and their descriptions.

Table 3-2. *Site Permissions*

Right	Description
Manage Permissions	Create and change permission levels on the web site and assign permissions to users and groups.
View Usage Data	View reports on web site usage.
Create Subsites	Create subsites such as team sites, meeting workspace sites, and document workspace sites.
Manage Web Site	Grant the ability to perform all administration tasks for the web site as well as manage content and permissions.
Add and Customize Pages	Add, change, or delete HTML pages or web part pages, and edit the web site using a Windows SharePoint Services–compatible editor.
Apply Themes and Borders	Apply a theme or borders to the entire web site.
Apply Style Sheets	Apply a style sheet (CSS file) to the web site.
Create Groups	Create a group of users that can be used anywhere within the site collection.
Browse Directories	Enumerate files and folders in a web site using SharePoint Designer and WebDAV interfaces.
Use Self-Service Site Creation	Create a web site using self-service site creation.
View Pages	View pages in a web site.
Enumerate Permissions	Enumerate permissions on the web site, list, folder, document, or list item.
Browse User Information	View information about users of the web site.
Manage Alerts	Manage alerts for all users of the web site.
Use Remote Interfaces	Use SOAP, WebDAV, or SharePoint Designer interfaces to access the web site.

Right	Description
Use Client Integration Features	Use features that launch client applications. Without this permission, users will have to work on documents locally and upload their changes.
Open	Allow users to open a web site, list, or folder in order to access items inside that container.
Edit Personal User Information	Allow a user to change his or her own user information, such as adding a picture.

Table 3-3 shows the personal permissions and their descriptions.

Table 3-3. *Personal Permissions*

Right	Description
Manage Personal Views	Create, change, and delete personal views of lists.
Add/Remove Private Web Parts	Add or remove private web parts on a web part page.
Update Personal Web Parts	Update web parts to display personalized information.

SharePoint allows you to control which of these rights are available for assignment to a user in a web application; not all of them must be made available to every site. Depending upon the site template you use, several of the rights may already be available to your web application by default. However, you can change the available rights for any site as you require.

Follow these steps to view and modify the rights available in a web application:

1. Open the Central Administration site by selecting Start ➤ Administrative Tools ➤ SharePoint 3.0 Central Administration.

2. In the Central Administration site, click the Application Management tab.

3. Under the Application Security section, click the link titled User Permissions for Web Application.

4. On the User Permissions for Web Application Page, select the rights that will be available to the web application.

5. Click the Save button.

Understanding Permission Levels and SharePoint Groups

Although you can specifically control the availability of each of the individual SharePoint rights, you will never directly assign one of these rights to a user. Instead, SharePoint gives you a way to collect rights into *permission levels* and levels into *SharePoint groups*. You then assign a user to a group, which assigns all of the contained rights from the associated permission levels.

Levels and groups are defined and assigned by an administrator directly within the SharePoint site. If you have appropriate permissions within the site to perform administrative tasks, you will see the Site Actions menu on the page. Clicking this item causes a drop-down menu to appear with available administrative options. The Site Actions menu, along with just about everything else in SharePoint, is *security-trimmed*. This means that users will only see options and menus that are valid for their permission set. This is a big improvement over the previous version of SharePoint, which allowed users to click any menu item only to be denied access later when the system discovered they had insufficient rights.

Although there are several specific items on the drop-down menu, the easiest way to get started with site administration is to open the Site Settings page. The Site Settings page gives you access to a broad range of settings grouped together by category. In order to access the Site Settings page through the MOSS site you created in Chapter 2, click the Site Actions menu and select Site Settings ➤ Modify All Site Settings. In WSS, simply select Site Settings from the Site Actions drop-down menu. Figure 3-1 shows the drop-down menu with items available for an administrator in MOSS.

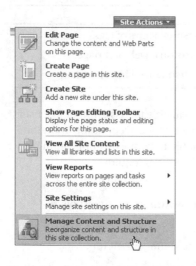

Figure 3-1. *Accessing site administration functions*

When you create a site collection within a web application, SharePoint provides you with several predefined permission levels and groups that you can use immediately to assign rights to users. From the Site Settings page, you can see the predefined groups by clicking the link titled Advanced Permissions under the Users and Permissions section. From the list, select Add ➤ New Users from the list toolbar to put users into the existing groups.

When you look at the list of available groups, you'll notice that they are associated with permission levels that have unfamiliar names. For example, the Hierarchy Managers group is associated with the permission levels Limited Access and Manage Hierarchy. When you first set up SharePoint, it can be difficult to know exactly what rights are being assigned to a user in these groups. Fortunately, you can access the definition for the permission levels by selecting Settings ➤ Permission Levels from the list toolbar. This brings up a page listing all of the defined permission levels. From this page, you can define your own permission levels or modify the existing ones. You cannot, however, modify the Full Control or Limited Access permission levels because SharePoint assumes their presence for things such as administrative tasks. Table 3-4 lists the rights and groups that exist by default in MOSS. WSS contains a subset of the MOSS groups.

Table 3-4. *Default Groups, Permission Levels, and Rights*

Right	Approvers	Designers	Hierarchy Managers	Members	Owners	Visitors	Quick Deploy Users	Restricted Readers
Manage	—	X	X	—	X	—	—	—
Override Check	X	X	X	—	X	—	—	—
Add Items	X	X	X	X	X	—	—	—
Edit Items	X	X	X	X	X	—	—	—
Delete Items	X	X	X	X	X	—	—	—
View Items	X	X	X	X	X	X	—	X
Approve Items	X	X	—	—	X	—	—	—
Open Items	X	X	X	X	X	X	—	X
View Versions	X	X	X	X	X	X	—	—
Delete Versions	X	X	X	X	X	—	—	—
Create Alerts	X	X	X	X	X	X	—	—
View Application Pages	X	X	X	X	X	X	—	—
Manage Permissions	—	—	X	—	X	—	—	—
View Usage Data	—	—	X	—	X	—	—	—
Create Subsites	—	—	X	—	X	—	—	—
Manage Web Site	—	—	X	—	X	—	—	—
Add and Customize Pages	—	X	—	—	X	—	—	—
Apply Themes and Borders	—	X	—	—	X	—	—	—
Apply Style Sheets	—	X	—	—	X	—	—	—
Create Groups	—	—	X	—	X	—	—	—
Browse Directories	X	X	X	X	X	—	—	—
Use Self-Service Site Creation	X	X	X	X	X	X	—	—
View Pages	X	X	X	X	X	X	—	X
Enumerate Permissions	—	—	X	—	X	—	—	—
Browse User Information	X	X	X	X	X	X	X	X
Manage Alerts	—	—	X	—	X	—	—	—
Use Remote Interfaces	X	X	X	X	X	X	X	X
Use Client Integration Features	X	X	X	X	X	X	X	X
Open	X	X	X	X	X	X	X	X

Continued

Table 3-4. *Continued*

Right	Approvers	Designers	Hierarchy Managers	Members	Owners	Visitors	Quick Deploy Users	Restricted Readers
Edit Personal User Information	X	X	X	X	X	—	—	—
Manage Personal Views	X	X	X	X	X	—	—	—
Add/Remove Private Web Parts	X	X	X	X	X	—	—	—
Update Personal Web Parts	X	X	X	X	X	—	—	—

Configuring Anonymous Access

Before you can configure a site to allow anonymous access, the associated web application must first have anonymous access enabled through Central Administration. If the web application is set through Central Administration to allow anonymous access, you can control what parts of your site are visible to anonymous users. If the central administrator has not enabled anonymous access for the web application, the functionality will not be visible.

Follow these steps to enable anonymous access for the web application:

1. Open the Central Administration site by selecting Start ➤ Administrative Tools ➤ SharePoint 3.0 Central Administration.

2. In the Central Administration site, click the Application Management tab.

3. Under the Application Security section, click the link titled Authentication Providers.

4. On the Authentication Providers page, make sure that the correct web application is selected. If not, drop the menu and select Change Web Application.

5. On the Authentication Providers page, click the Default Zone link.

6. On the Edit Authentication page, check the box labeled Enable Anonymous Access.

7. Click the Save button.

Once the web application is configured for anonymous access, you can return to the Permissions page. From the Permissions page, you can select Settings ➤ Anonymous Access to open the Anonymous Access Settings page. On this page, you may select to expose the entire site, all lists and libraries, or nothing at all. Additionally, you can control the visibility of an individual list or library through its permission settings. This combination of site-level and list-level configuration gives you a good deal of control over what parts of the site can be accessed anonymously.

Understanding Security Policies

Along with assigning rights to end users, you can also establish broader security policies for a web application. On the Application Management tab of the Central Administration site, you can click the link titled Policy for Web Application to set security policies. Using the Policy for Web Application page, you can change the policy for anonymous access, grant full control, or deny all access. These security policies override the rights that have been assigned through the Site Settings page so they should only be used when you want to grant a high-level of permission to an administrator or completely deny access to a set of users. You used this functionality in Chapter 2 to grant access rights to the administrator in the development environment. Additionally, these policies are set for a given zone, which determines whether they apply to users inside the firewall or outside. Zones are discussed in detail later in the section titled "Understanding Authentication Options."

Managing Site Structure

When you first create a web application and a site collection, you will notice that a default structure has been created for you based on the template you selected. You will likely want to modify the site structure significantly before making it accessible to end users. Modifying the structure, however, should not be done lightly. You should first begin by understanding all of the sites, pages, and lists that come with the template. Then you can move on to making changes. Figure 3-2 shows the home page of the site collection you created in Chapter 2, which contains a number of predefined sites, pages, and lists.

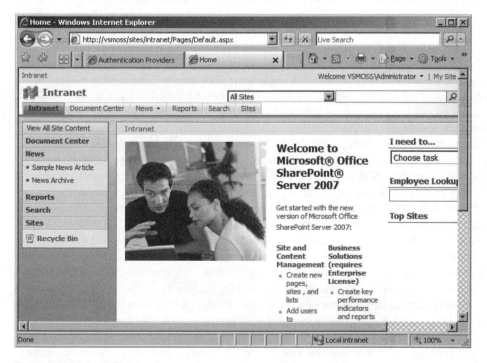

Figure 3-2. *A site collection home page*

The best way to understand the existing site collection structure is to examine it inside SharePoint using the Site Content and Structure explorer, which is only available within MOSS. This page presents a tree view of the entire site collection that you can navigate. Additionally, you can add and delete elements from the site collection directly from this one page. You can access the Site Content and Structure explorer by selecting Site Actions ➤ Manage Content and Structure from the MOSS home page.

Working with Sites

A *site collection* in SharePoint contains one or more sites. *Sites* within a site collection represent a security boundary and a way to group teams and functionality for a business purpose. When you create a site collection, SharePoint will define some initial sites based on the template that you selected. The sites that SharePoint creates are designed to support the audience for which the template was designed. In the case of the MOSS site collection you created in Chapter 2, SharePoint defined sites named Document Center, News, Reports, Search, and Sites. If you created a site collection in WSS, you'll only see a home page with no additional sites defined.

The Document Center site in MOSS is designed to act as a central repository for documents throughout the organization. This site seems to be an acknowledgement that many customers simply want to use SharePoint as a document management system without necessarily taking advantage of its many other features. In previous versions of SharePoint, it was difficult to create such a document management system because of limitations in the library metadata and available document templates. SharePoint 2007 has largely overcome these limitations; I discuss the document management features in detail in Chapter 6.

The News site is designed to support the creation and publishing of news articles for the organization. This site makes use of special article templates, content management, and publishing features that allow the creation and approval of content directly within SharePoint. Content management is a major area of new functionality within SharePoint 2007 that I cover in Chapter 5.

The Reports site is a site designed to function as a report center for all business intelligence information within an organization. Using this site, you may define data connections to external sources such as SQL databases, and utilize that data to create reports and dashboards. These reports and dashboards can be presented in a number of ways, including scorecards, Excel spreadsheets, and SQL Reporting Services reports. Business intelligence is another major area of functionality that I cover in detail in Chapter 8.

The Search site implements an enterprise search capability that allows you to search all of the content within MOSS as well as external content and even external databases. Search is greatly enhanced in this version of SharePoint, and the Search site has the ability to truly function across all enterprise systems. I cover search in Chapter 4.

The Sites site forms a site directory that lists and catalogs all of the sites within the collection. The Site Directory helps end users locate sites of interest and understand the structure of the collection. If you have appropriate permissions, you can also create a new site within the collection by clicking the Create Site link. The Create Site link is a shortcut to the site creation page, which can also be reached through the Site Settings page. Most administrators will use the Site Settings page for site creation because it is conveniently grouped with other administrative tasks and works the same in both MOSS and WSS.

To create a new site, follow these steps:

1. Open the home page of the intranet site you created in Chapter 2 (`http://vsmoss/sites/intranet`).

2. Select Site Settings ➤ Modify All Site Settings from the Site Actions drop-down menu.

3. Under the Site Administration section, click the link titled Sites and Workspaces.

4. On the Sites and Workspaces page, click the Create link.

5. On the New SharePoint Site page, enter **Softball Team** in the title field.

6. Enter **softball** in the URL field.

7. Under the Permissions section, select the option to Use Same Permissions as Parent Site.

8. Under the Template section, select to create a site based on the Team Site template.

9. Click the Create button.

When you create sites in WSS or MOSS, you may see some different options for configuring how the site is displayed in the navigation system or how it is categorized in the Site Directory. If you are using MOSS in particular, you will notice that you have options to specify a division and a region with which to associate the site. These are the same options available in the previous version of SharePoint Portal Server. These options are configurable and can even be eliminated altogether (which is good because I don't know of any organization that uses the default values). The key to altering these options lies in modifying the columns associated with the Sites list.

Follow these steps to modify the division and region options in MOSS:

1. Click the Sites tab in MOSS to open the Site Directory.

2. On the Site Directory page, click View All Site Content.

3. On the All Site Content page, click the Sites list.

4. On the Sites list page, select Settings ➤ List Settings from the drop-down menu on the list toolbar.

5. On the Customize Sites page, scroll down to the Columns section and click either the Division column or the Region column.

6. On the Change Column page, change the list of available options and click the OK button. Alternately, you could click the Delete button to eliminate the column.

Working with Lists

Lists represent a broad umbrella of functionality in SharePoint that encompasses everything from document management to scorecards. This is because at the lowest level, SharePoint manages groups of items as lists regardless of what the items are. For administrative purposes, however, SharePoint divides list functionality into four distinct categories: Libraries,

Communications, Tracking, and Custom lists. The Libraries category contains list types for managing documents. The Communications category contains list types for communicating with other people. The Tracking category contains list types for managing tasks, plans, and issues. The Custom category allows you to create a custom list to meet your own needs. In this section, I provide an overview of each list type.

Using Document Libraries

In many ways, libraries are the central feature of SharePoint. Nearly all site users will be involved with creating, retrieving, and sharing documents. You can create document libraries at any level in the site hierarchy and assign different permissions at the item or library level. This makes libraries useful for facilitating collaboration among organizational teams. What's more, you'll see in Chapters 6, 7, and 9 that document libraries are fully integrated with Microsoft Office 2007.

When a new site is created it often comes with predefined libraries. The softball site you created earlier uses the Team Site template, which comes with a document library suitable for managing all kinds of documents including Office documents, text documents, PDF documents, and others. In WSS, you can also elect to create a picture library, a form library, or a wiki library for managing images, InfoPath forms, and wiki pages, respectively. In MOSS, you can create additional types of libraries for managing documents in multiple languages, reports, data connections, and slide libraries of PowerPoint presentations.

When new documents are added to any library, a document profile is created based on the content type of the new document. A *content type* is a set of characteristics—such as a document template, workflow processes, and properties—that uniquely define a document. Content types allow you to manage multiple kinds of documents within a single library. This is a great improvement over the previous version of SharePoint, which was designed to support only a single document profile for every document in a library. I discuss content types in greater detail throughout the book.

Once documents are part of a library, users can take advantage of the document management features built into SharePoint. These document management features include check-in, checkout, version control, initiating workflows, editing properties, and publishing. You may restrict the ability of users to utilize the document management feature set based on their membership in a security group, as I described earlier in the section "Managing Users." In this version of SharePoint, you may control these permissions at the document level, whereas the previous version controls them at the library level. Access to the document management features of a library is accomplished through a drop-down list associated with each document. Figure 3-3 shows the drop-down list for a document in a library.

You can check out documents directly from the document library using the drop-down list. When a document is checked out, it is still listed in the document library and visible to site users, but the username of the person who checked it out is visible in the list. For each library, you may control whether to require a checkout before a document can be edited. If you do not require a checkout, the document can be opened in a read-only mode by other users.

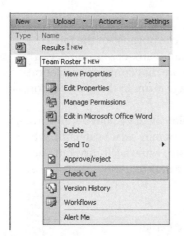

Figure 3-3. *Accessing document management functions*

Follow these steps to require checkout for a document library:

1. Open the home page of the softball team site you created earlier.

2. In the Quick Launch pane, click the link titled Shared Documents.

3. On the Shared Documents page, select Settings ➤ Document Library Settings from the drop-down menu on the list toolbar.

4. On the Customize Shared Documents page, click the link titled Versioning Settings.

5. On the Document Library Versioning Settings page, select the Yes option under the Require Check Out section.

Once changes are made to a document, it may be saved back to the library and checked in. Users can be granted the authority to cancel an existing checkout by another person. This action causes the document to be checked back in to the library immediately; however, all changes made to the document since it was checked out are lost. This feature is primarily used to recover a checked-out document when the holder is unavailable for some reason.

By default, the document library overwrites the old document version with the new version and does not keep any history. If you would like to keep version history, you must enable it from the Versioning Settings page. These settings allow you to specify whether you want to create major or minor versions and how many versions to retain. Once versioning is enabled, you can access the version history page from the drop-down menu associated with a document. This page will list all of the document versions and allow you to restore any of them as the current version.

Along with version control, you can also enable content approval for a document library. When document approval is enabled, new documents will not be visible to the general population of site users. Instead, the documents must be approved before they become generally available. Rejections and approvals are issued directly in the portal using the drop-down menu associated with each document.

Using Form Libraries

A *form library* can be thought of as a special document library. The purpose of the form library is to store XML-based forms created through Microsoft InfoPath. For example, you might create a form library in the human resources area of the site that contains a vacation request form, a 401(k) change form, or a health insurance change form. In this way, key forms are centralized and easily located.

Creating a form library can be done directly in the SharePoint site if you have appropriate permissions. Unlike document libraries, form libraries do not generally exist by default. When you create a form library, it is given a default form template for use with the library, but you will certainly want to modify it. As with any library, you can have multiple content types associated with the form library.

To create a form library, follow these steps:

1. Open the home page of the softball team site you created earlier.

2. Select Create from the Site Actions drop-down menu.

3. On the Create Page, click the Form Library link under the Libraries section.

4. In the Name field type **Team Forms**.

5. Click the Create button.

Once the form library is created, you can create and upload forms. Forms in InfoPath may be designed based on an existing template or a database schema or from scratch. All of the forms created with InfoPath are interactive with complete control sets such as list boxes, options, and text fields. Once the form is created, you can publish it to the form library.

Take these steps to publish a default InfoPath form:

1. Open Microsoft InfoPath 2007 on VSCLIENT.

2. In the Getting Started dialog, select Customize a Sample.

3. In the Customize a Sample window, double-click Sample – Travel Request.

4. In the Design Tasks window, select Publish Form Template.

5. When prompted, save the file to your desktop as `Travel.xsn`.

6. When the Publishing Wizard starts, select the publishing option To a SharePoint Server With or Without InfoPath Forms Services.

7. Click the Next button.

8. Type in the URL of the site you created earlier (e.g., **http://vsmoss/sites/intranet/softball**).

9. On the next screen of the wizard, uncheck the box labeled Enable This Form to Be Filled Out by Using a Browser.

10. Click the Next button.

11. On the next screen of the wizard, select the option to Update the Form Template in an Existing Document Library.

12. Select the Team Forms library and click the Next button.

13. On the next screen of the wizard, simply click the Next button.

14. On the next screen of the wizard, click the Publish button.

15. On the final screen of the wizard, check the box labeled Open This Document Library, and then click the Close button.

16. When the form library opens, you should be able to fill out the new form by selecting New ➤ New Document from the drop-down menu on the library toolbar.

Using Picture Libraries

Like form libraries, *picture libraries* are a special type of document library. These libraries are specifically intended to manage digital photography and images such as corporate logos and web site images. Although images can be stored in any document library, picture libraries have special features to view and use graphical content.

Uploading pictures into the library is similar to uploading any document or form and can be done using the Upload menu on the library toolbar. Once the images are uploaded, however, they may be presented in special views available only in the picture library. The images may also be edited with Microsoft Picture Manager or sent directly to any Office application for inclusion in a document.

Using Announcements

An *announcements list* is used to create a list of announcements with a title and a rich-text body. Announcements are simple list types that typically display the title and a few lines of the body on the home page of a site. Additionally, each item can be given an expiration date so that they are automatically hidden after a period of time.

Using Contacts

A *contact list* is used to track contact information about people. You can either type contact information directly into the list, or import the information from an address book. SharePoint contact lists can also be synchronized with Outlook contact lists by selecting Actions ➤ Connect to Outlook from the drop-down menu on the list toolbar.

Using Discussion Boards

Discussion boards are lists that can be used to start threaded discussions. *Threaded discussions* allow users to post topics and responses in a tree structure that keeps them together. Discussion boards are superior to e-mail threads when you want to preserve the discussion postings for reference.

Using Links

Link list items are hyperlinks to web pages of interest to a team or an organization. A blank list of links typically appears on any new site added to the portal. When users add links to the list, they provide the target URL and a description.

Using Calendars

Calendars are events associated with meetings, seminars, parties, and so on. When you create a new site, a blank calendar list typically appears on the home page. Users may enter new events directly from the home page and can also associate a document with the event. This is useful for linking directions or agendas with events. Calendars can be synchronized with Outlook by selecting Actions ➤ Connect to Outlook from the drop-down menu on the list toolbar.

Using Tasks

Task items form a to-do list for a team. When a new site is created, a blank task list is available. When you create a new task in the list, you may assign it to a team member. The list may then be viewed in summary to track all items for the team. Task lists can be synchronized with Outlook by selecting Actions ➤ Connect to Outlook from the drop-down menu on the list toolbar.

Using Project Tasks

Project task items are similar to normal task items except that they show the task list using a Gantt chart format. This list type is useful for creating mini project plans and tracking progress. Project task lists can be synchronized with Outlook by selecting Actions ➤ Connect to Outlook from the drop-down menu on the list toolbar. Figure 3-4 shows a picture of a Gantt chart displayed from a project task list.

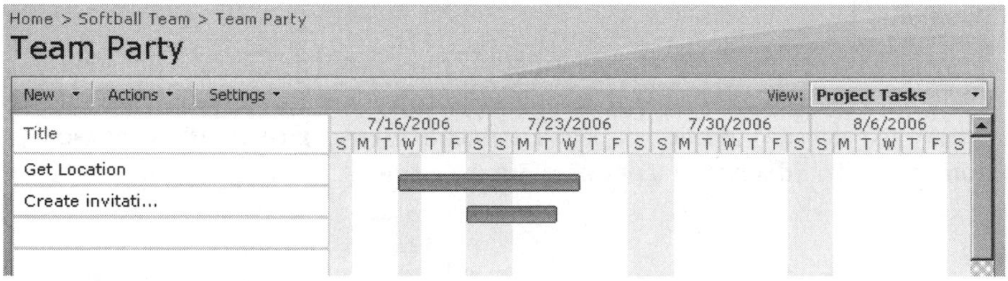

Figure 3-4. *A Gantt chart display*

Using Issues Tracking

Issue tracking lists are used to track problems for resolution. This list type is used like a simple help-desk application that assigns an identifier to each issue, a person to resolve it, and a due date. You can also associate other related issues together.

Using Surveys

Surveys provide a way to poll portal users for input on a subject. When a site is first created, it usually does not have a survey associated with it. Once created, surveys support a wide variety of response types from simple yes/no answers to free-form text. When the survey is filled out, you may display a number of simple reports to show the results. The list also supports branching logic for surveys, which allows you to present questions based on the response to previous questions.

Using Custom Lists

Custom lists in SharePoint allow you to create your own list with your own field definitions. You can create your custom list either in a standard list format or in a datasheet view. Additionally, you can import an existing Excel spreadsheet to create a custom list in SharePoint.

Configuring E-Mail–Enabled Lists

Along with using lists to manage documents and items, you can also configure them to receive e-mail. E-mail–enabled lists are given their own e-mail addresses. When they receive mail, the message can be stored and any attached documents can be saved. Configuring e-mail–enabled lists first requires that you set up the SMTP service on the server running MOSS.

Follow these steps to install and configure the SMTP service:

1. Log in to VSMOSS as an administrator.

2. Select Start ➤ Administrative Tools ➤ Configure Your Server Wizard.

3. In the Configure Your Server Wizard, click the Next button.

4. On the Preliminary Steps screen, click the Next button.

5. On the Server Role screen, select Mail Server (POP3, SMTP) and click the Next button.

6. On the Configure POP3 Service screen, enter **vsmoss.domain.local** in the E-Mail Domain Name field.

7. Click the Next button.

8. On the Summary of Selections screen, click the Next button.

9. When the SMTP service is installed, click the Finish button.

10. Open the IIS Manager by selecting Start ➤ Administrative Tools ➤ Internet Information Services Manager.

11. In the IIS Manager, right-click the Default SMTP Server and select Properties from the context menu.

12. In the Properties dialog, click the Access tab.

13. On the Access tab, click the Relay button.

14. On the Relay Restrictions screen, select the option to allow All Except the List Below and click the OK button.

15. Click the OK button.

Once the SMTP service is set up, you need to configure the general incoming e-mail settings for the farm. This is done through the Central Administration site. When you configure these settings, you can choose to simply relay incoming mail to the targeted list with no other frills, or you can choose to enable the directory management service (DMS). DMS is used to create mailing lists that you can use through Exchange and Outlook. This makes it easy to find addresses for lists in the same way that you find them for people.

Follow these steps to configure incoming e-mail settings:

1. Open the Central Administration site by selecting Start ➤ Administrative Tools ➤ SharePoint 3.0 Central Administration.

2. In the Central Administration site, click the Operations tab.

3. On the Operations page, click the link titled Incoming E-Mail Settings under the Topology and Services section.

4. On the Configure E-Mail Settings page, select the Yes option under the Enable Incoming E-Mail section.

5. Click the OK button.

Once the incoming e-mail settings are configured for the farm, you can finally enable an individual list to receive mail. Enabling a list is done through the settings associated with the list. In these settings, you specify the address to use for the list and options regarding the handling of attachments and the original mail message.

Follow these steps to e-mail–enable a list:

1. Open the home page of the softball team site you created earlier.

2. In the Quick Launch pane, click the link titled Shared Documents.

3. On the Shared Documents page, select Settings ➤ Document Library Settings from the drop-down menu on the list toolbar.

4. On the Customize Shared Documents page, click the Incoming E-Mail Settings Link.

5. On the Incoming E-Mail Settings page, select the Yes option under the Incoming E-Mail section.

6. Enter **softball** in the E-Mail Address field.

7. Click the Yes option under Save Original E-Mail.

8. Click the OK button.

9. Now try sending an e-mail to `softball@vsmoss.domain.local` and verify that the new e-mail appears in the list.

Working with Pages

When you first create a site, it is made up of only the home page. However, you can add additional pages to the site at any time by using the Create page. Although you can access the Create page from the Site Settings page, it is often easier to simply select Site Actions ➤ Create from within the site. From the Create page, you can select to either create a basic page or a web part page. A *basic page* allows you to create content using a standard web page, while a *web part page* allows you to design the page using web parts. Regardless of the type of page you create, all pages are stored within a document library. Therefore, you'll need to create a document library for storing pages.

Follow these steps to create a new page:

1. Open the home page of the softball team site you created earlier.

2. Select Create from the Site Actions drop-down menu.

3. On the Create page, click the Document Library link under the Libraries section.

4. On the New page, name the new document library **Basic Pages**.

5. In the Document Template drop-down list, select Basic Page.

6. Click the Create button.

7. When the Basic Pages library appears, click New ➤ New Document from the drop-down menu on the library toolbar.

8. On the New Basic Page, enter **SoftballRules** in the name field.

9. Click the Create button.

10. When the rich-text editor appears, type **Rule #1: Have Fun!**.

11. Try using various format tools in the dialog to make the text look interesting.

12. Click the Save button.

13. When the new page appears in the browser, copy the URL from the address bar so you can make a link to the new page.

14. Return to the home page of the softball site and locate the Links list.

15. Click the link titled Add New Link.

16. On the Add New Link page, paste the URL you copied earlier into the URL field.

17. Type **Softball Rules** in the description field.

18. Click the OK button, and you should now have a link from the home page to your new page.

Understanding Alerts and RSS Feeds

Alerts provide notification to a particular user when an item of interest has been added or updated within the portal. When a new alert is created, the user can define the areas of interest and set up how the notification will occur. An alert can be established for any list in SharePoint by selecting Actions ➤ Alert Me from the drop-down menu on the list toolbar. When you set up an alert, you can specify options regarding how you want to be alerted. You can ask for an e-mail immediately or have all alerts packaged and sent to you periodically. Figure 3-5 shows a typical alert received in Microsoft Outlook.

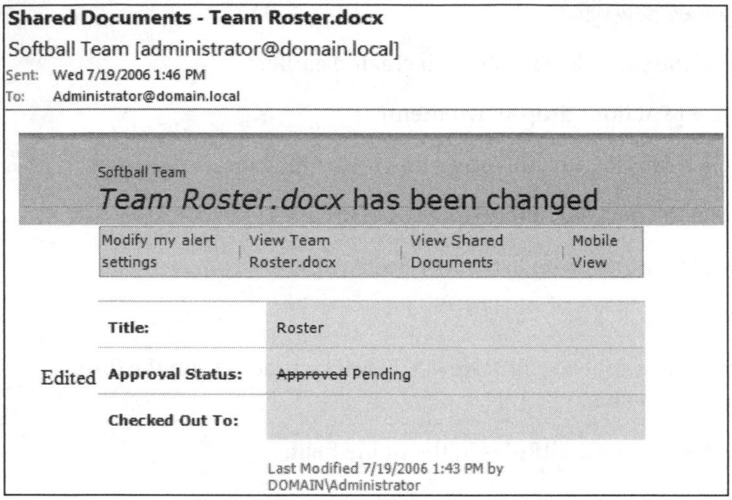

Shared Documents - Team Roster.docx

Softball Team [administrator@domain.local]

Sent: Wed 7/19/2006 1:46 PM
To: Administrator@domain.local

Softball Team

Team Roster.docx has been changed

| Modify my alert settings | View Team Roster.docx | View Shared Documents | Mobile View |

Title:	Roster
Edited **Approval Status:**	~~Approved~~ Pending
Checked Out To:	

Last Modified 7/19/2006 1:43 PM by
DOMAIN\Administrator

Figure 3-5. *A SharePoint alert*

Really Simple Syndication (RSS) is a mechanism for aggregating web content from multiple sources and displaying it in a reader. SharePoint 2007 now supports RSS feeds, which have long been available on the Internet and can make any SharePoint list a source for RSS. Additionally, Outlook 2007 contains an RSS reader that can collect the information from SharePoint lists and display it. You can establish an RSS feed for any SharePoint list by selecting Actions ➤ View RSS Feed from the drop-down menu on the list toolbar. Once established, the RSS feed appears in the folder list of Outlook 2007 and allows you to view list items. Figure 3-6 shows an RSS feed in Outlook 2007 based on the announcements list in the softball site you created earlier.

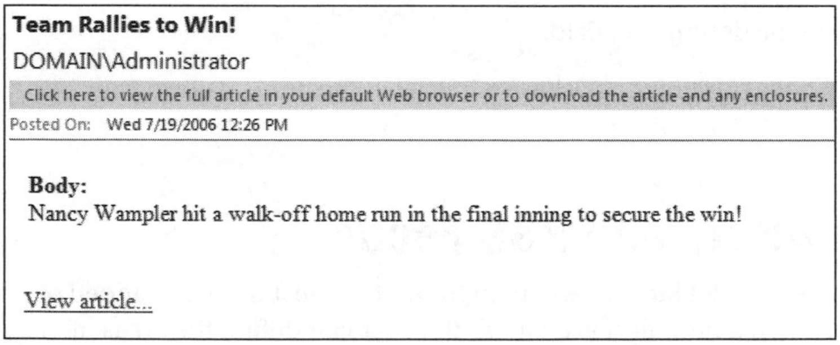

Team Rallies to Win!

DOMAIN\Administrator

Click here to view the full article in your default Web browser or to download the article and any enclosures.

Posted On: Wed 7/19/2006 12:26 PM

Body:
Nancy Wampler hit a walk-off home run in the final inning to secure the win!

View article...

Figure 3-6. *An RSS feed*

Understanding Features

In the previous version of SharePoint, a significant distinction exists between collaboration sites and portal sites. Microsoft saw these two types of sites as fundamentally different. As a result, different capabilities are built into them. For example, SharePoint Portal Server 2003 has the ability to hide content based on the current user's membership in a group known as an *audience*. However, Windows SharePoint Services Version 2 team sites do not have this capability. With this newest release of SharePoint, however, capabilities are packaged into *Features* that can be activated and deployed to any site in a collection. This means that every site in the collection can have a different combination of portal and collaboration capabilities as desired. While it's still true that MOSS has more Features than WSS, WSS sites can now use the MOSS Features when they are deployed together.

Features can be activated or deactivated at the farm, web application, and site level. You can see the list of available Features for the farm by clicking the link titled Manage Web Application Features on the Application Management tab of the Central Administration site. Similarly, you can access the available Features for a site by opening the Site Settings page and clicking the link titled Site Features. While some Features enable simple changes in a site, many of the listed Features represent significant areas of functionality that I describe in detail in later chapters. Figure 3-7 shows a typical list of Features associated with a site.

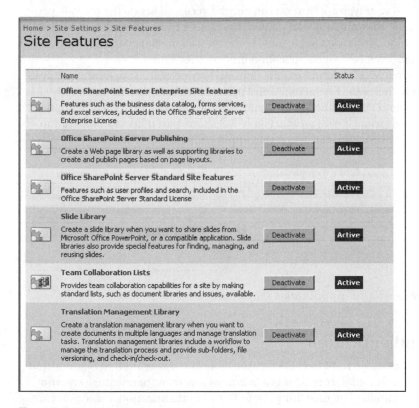

Figure 3-7. *Viewing Features*

Understanding Authentication Options

In Chapter 2, I discuss in detail how SharePoint utilizes Windows authentication in the form of NTLM or Kerberos and include detailed steps for enabling Kerberos. A SharePoint site always uses Windows authentication to start; however, you can change the authentication provider later to support authenticating users in a variety of ways. Typically, you will establish a new access *zone*, which is a configuration option representing an alternate access path, and associate an authentication mechanism with the new zone. Besides Windows authentication, you can configure web form authentication, web single sign-on authentication, or Active Directory Account Creation Mode.

Extending Web Applications

WSS and MOSS support a set of zones that allow you to establish different access methodologies to a single web application. Zones are an administrative category, which you use to specify a different URL for accessing the same web application. The value of this configuration is that you can establish different authentication methods for different zones while delivering the same content to each zone.

When you first create a new web application, it is always created in the *Default zone*. The Default zone is always set up to utilize Windows authentication either through NTLM or Kerberos as you specify. If your web application will only be accessed inside the firewall, you can simply use the Default zone and not worry about any further configuration. However, if you want to make the same content available outside the firewall or change the authentication method, you should *extend* the web application into another zone.

Extending a web application is done from the Central Administration pages on the Application Management tab. Under the SharePoint Web Application Management section, there is a link titled Create or Extend Web Application. Whenever you extend an existing web application, you can choose to associate it with a zone. Figure 3-8 shows part of the administration page where you can select to extend an existing web application into another zone.

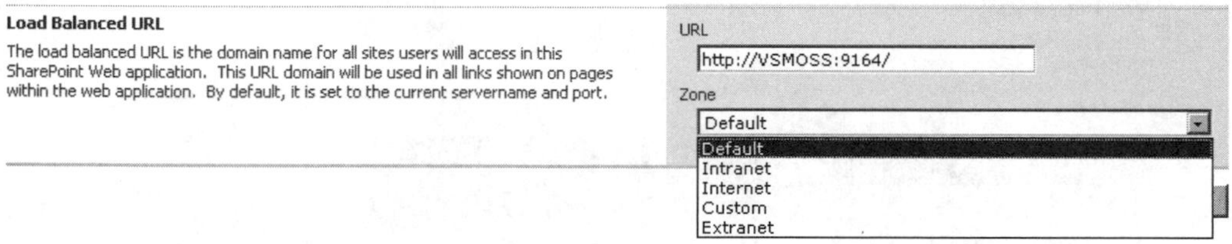

Figure 3-8. *Extending an existing web application into another zone*

Using Forms Authentication

Forms authentication uses a web form to collect a username and password that is submitted for verification against a credential store. This is a common way to authenticate users who are not members of the domain. The nice thing about Forms authentication is that you can use a SQL Server database or another Lightweight Directory Access Protocol (LDAP) source to authenticate the user. The data source you use is dictated by an authentication provider that is capable of authenticating users against the desired store. While you can use any authentication provider with SharePoint, common ones include `SqlMembershipProvider` for use with a SQL Server database; `ActiveDirectoryMembershipProvider` for use with Active Directory; and `LDAPMembershipProvider` for use with other LDAP sources such as Lotus Notes.

When you want to use Forms authentication, you must add a `connectionStrings` and a `membership` section to the `web.config` file of the web application. Additionally, you must add the same sections to the SharePoint Central Administration application so that permissions can be managed centrally. The exact syntax of the new sections varies, and you may have to perform some additional steps depending on what data store you will use. I cover the configuration details for key providers in the next few sections.

■Tip Save a backup copy of each web configuration file before you modify it. You may want to roll back your changes later.

Authentication with SqlMembershipProvider

One of the most common scenarios with Forms authentication employs a SQL Server database as the credential store. The SqlMembershipProvider is used to authenticate users against a SQL database when that database utilizes the same schema as a standard ASP.NET 2.0 application. When Visual Studio 2005 is installed, it automatically configures an instance of SQL Express to serve as a credential store for any ASP.NET 2.0 applications. If you want to use a SQL Server 2005 database instead, it must be configured with the appropriate schema. Creating a credential store in SQL Server 2005 that can be used with Forms authentication in SharePoint is done using the ASPNET_REGSQL.EXE utility.

Follow these steps to create a credential store in SQL Server 2005:

1. Log in to VSMOSS or VSWSS as a local administrator.

2. Open a command prompt window and change the directory to C:\WINDOWS\Microsoft.NET\Framework\v2.0.50727.

3. At the command prompt, run ASPNET_REGSQL.EXE.

4. On the Welcome screen of the wizard, click the Next button.

5. On the Select a Setup Option screen, select the option labeled Configure SQL Server for Application Services.

6. Click the Next button.

7. On the Select the Server and Database screen, enter **VSSQL** in the Server field.

8. Click the Next button.

9. On the Confirm Your Settings screen, click the Next button.

10. On the Finish Screen, click Next.

When using SQL Server 2005 as the credential store, you are not provided with a good interface for initially populating the database with usernames. If no names are initially in the database, no one can be designated as the site administrator for managing additional users. Therefore, you have to find a way to get at least one name into the database before enabling Forms authentication.

The best option for entering users is to simply use the web site configuration tools that ship with Visual Studio 2005. These tools are preconfigured to work with an instance of SQL

Express installed alongside Visual Studio. The strategy is to create an ASP.NET project and add a web configuration file that refers to the database you created earlier. Then you can configure the database directly from Visual Studio.

Follow these steps to edit the credential database with Visual Studio:

1. Log in to VSMOSS or VSWSS as a local administrator.

2. Start Visual Studio 2005.

3. In Visual Studio, select File ➤ New ➤ Web Site from the main menu.

4. In the New Web Site dialog, select to create a new ASP.NET Web Site.

5. In the Location drop-down list, select File System.

6. Click the OK button.

7. In the Solution Explorer, right-click the project and select Add New Item from the context menu.

8. In the Add New Item dialog, select Web Configuration File and click the Add button.

9. In the web configuration file, replace the `<connectionStrings/>` element with the following:

```
<connectionStrings>
  <remove name="LocalSqlServer" />
  <add name="LocalSqlServer"
  connectionString="Server=VSSQL;Database=aspnetdb;Integrated Security=SSPI;"
  providerName="System.Data.SqlClient" />
</connectionStrings>
```

10. Select Build ➤ Build Solution from the main menu.

11. After the project is built, select Website ➤ ASP.NET Configuration from the main menu to run the Web Site Administration Tool.

Tip If you have trouble running the Web Site Administration Tool, you can try creating your web site as an HTTP web site. I have seen some issues when file-based web sites and SharePoint are on the same machine.

---

12. In the Web Site Administration Tool, click the Security tab.

13. On the Security tab, click the link titled Select Authentication Type.

14. Click the option labeled From the Internet, and click the Done button.

15. On the Security tab, click the Create User link.

16. Fill in some information to create a user and click the Create button.

Once the credential store is created, you can add the new sections to the web.config files of the SharePoint sites. Remember, you must add the section to both the application you want to access and the Central Administration site. The configuration files are all located in subfolders in the path \Inetpub\wwwroot\wss\VirtualDirectories. Here you will find a subdirectory for each of the web applications you have created and the Central Administration site.

■**Note** SharePoint often uses port numbers to name the application subdirectories. This can make it hard to tell which site is associated with which directory. You can figure this out by examining the Local Path field in the site properties dialog in IIS Manager.

For each file, create a connectionStrings section immediately before the <system.web> tag and a membership section immediately following the <system.web> tag. The connectionStrings section defines a valid connection string to access the credential database. The membership section provides configuration information for the SqlMembershipProvider class to use the information in the credential store. Listing 3-1 shows example sections with the <system.web> tag visible between them. These entries are based on the database you created earlier.

Listing 3-1. *A Partial Web Configuration File*

```
<connectionStrings>
  <add name="DBService"
  connectionString="Server=VSSQL;Database=aspnetdb;Integrated Security=SSPI;"
  providerName="System.Data.SqlClient" />
</connectionStrings>
<system.web>
  <membership defaultProvider="DB">
    <providers>
      <add connectionStringName="DBService"
        enablePasswordRetrieval="false"
        enablePasswordReset="true"
        requiresQuestionAndAnswer="true"
        applicationName="/"
        requiresUniqueEmail="false"
        minRequiredPasswordLength="1"
        minRequiredNonalphanumericCharacters="0"
        passwordFormat="Clear"
        maxInvalidPasswordAttempts="5"
        passwordAttemptWindow="10"
        passwordStrengthRegularExpression=""
        name="DB"
        type="System.Web.Security.SqlMembershipProvider, ➥
          System.Web, Version=2.0.0.0, Culture=neutral, ➥
          PublicKeyToken=b03f5f7f11d50a3a" />
    </providers>
  </membership>
</system.web>
```

■**Note** Not all of the configuration elements associated with the `SqlMembershipProvider` are necessary for SharePoint. When you use Visual Studio to create the membership database, however, it creates
many of the configuration entries by default. You can learn more about the `SqlMembershipProvider`
options at `http://msdn2.microsoft.com/en-us/library/system.web.security.`
`sqlmembershipprovider.aspx`.

After the configuration files are updated, you are ready to enable Forms authentication. This is done through the Central Administration site. In the Central Administration
site, you will switch the provider for the extended web application from Windows to Forms
authentication.

Follow these steps to enable Forms authentication:

1. Open the Central Administration site by selecting Start ➤ Administrative Tools ➤
   SharePoint 3.0 Central Administration.

2. In the Central Administration site, click the Application Management tab.

3. Under the Application Security section, click the link titled Authentication Providers.

4. On the Authentication Providers page, locate the entry for the extended web application. It will be listed alongside the zone into which it was extended and will currently
   show that it is using Windows authentication.

5. Click the Windows Authentication link to change the provider.

6. On the Edit Authentication page, select the Forms option under Authentication Type.

7. In the Membership Provider Name field, type **DB**, which is the name of the provider as
   it appears in the web configuration file.

8. Click the Save button.

9. Click the Application Management tab.

10. Under the Application Security section, click the link titled Policy for Web Application.

11. If the correct web application is not already selected, drop down the web application
    selection list and click Change Web Application.

12. Click the Add Users button.

13. On the Add Users page, select the Custom zone where you extended the application
    earlier.

14. Click the Next button.

15. On the Add Users page, type the name of the user you entered into the credential
    database into the Users field and click the Check Names image button.

■**Note** If the Central Administration application cannot find the username you entered, it is very likely that the connection string contained in the configuration file is incorrect. You will generally not receive an error telling you this, but the vast majority of issues are related to the connection string.

---

16. Under the Choose Permissions section, check the box labeled Full Control – Has Full Control.

17. Click the Finish button.

Once the initial user has been given rights to the site you can open the site in a browser. You should see a login page where you can type the credentials you entered into the database earlier. Because you granted full control to this user, you can now use the Site Settings from within the site to add new users and give them rights.

Authentication with ActiveDirectoryMembershipProvider

The `ActiveDirectoryMembershipProvider` is an authentication provider for use with Active Directory. Using this provider, you can set up Forms authentication for users who have accounts within the domain. This type of authentication is good for creating extranet solutions where you want to provide a login screen rather than just popping up the ugly gray Windows authentication box. Exercise 3.1 at the end of this chapter uses the `ActiveDirectoryMembershipProvider` to create an extranet, so I will not cover it in detail here.

Authentication with LDAPMembershipProvider

MOSS ships with an additional authentication provider called `LDAPMembershipProvider`. The `LDAPMembershipProvider` allows you to authenticate users against other LDAP sources such as Lotus Notes. This provider is most useful for environments that are not using Active Directory—although it certainly could be used with Active Directory, which is LDAP-compliant. Like all of the other providers, the `LDAPMembershipProvider` requires you to make `connectionString` and `membership` entries in the web configuration file. Listing 3-2 shows an example configuration for the provider for the Active Directory you set up in Chapter 2.

Listing 3-2. *Configuring LDAP Authentication*

```
<membership defaultProvider="LDAP">
 <providers>
  <add name="LDAP"
    type="Microsoft.Office.Server.Security.LDAPMembershipProvider, ➥
      Microsoft.Office.Server, Version=12.0.0.0, Culture=neutral, ➥
      PublicKeyToken=71E9BCE111E9429C"
    server="VSPDC" port="389"
    useSSL="false" userDNAttribute="distinguishedName"
    userNameAttribute="sAMAccountName"
    userContainer="CN=Users,DC=domain,DC=local"
```

```
      userObjectClass="person"
      userFilter="(|(ObjectCategory=group)(ObjectClass=person))" scope="Subtree"
      otherRequiredUserAttributes="sn,givenname,cn" />
  </providers>
</membership>
```

Using Web Single Sign-On

In addition to the authentication providers already discussed, SharePoint also gives you the option to use a web single sign-on service for authentication. A web single sign-on service is a separate third-party service used to provide authentication across many disparate systems. Windows Live ID service is an example of a web single sign-on service. In addition to registering a provider in the web configuration file, these types of providers also require you to register an HTTP module with specific information about the provider. Web single sign-on providers are beyond the scope of this book.

Using Active Directory Account Creation Mode

The final authentication option available in SharePoint is a special account mode known as *Active Directory Account Creation (ADAC)*. This mode is intended for use by Internet service providers (ISPs) who support large constituencies that are not members of the hosting domain. In ADAC mode, users can self-register using e-mail addresses instead of domain accounts. In this way, an ISP can host Internet users without having to specifically add them to a domain.

It's important to note that ADAC is incompatible with the normal domain account mode. During the installation of WSS, you select the mode in which the farm will operate. After you make the selection, you cannot alter it. Throughout this book, I assume that SharePoint Services are operating in domain account mode.

Extending Web Applications Outside the Firewall

Once a new web application is created in SharePoint you can extend the web application onto another IIS site. Extending an existing web application to another IIS site allows you to create multiple access paths to the same web application. This is useful for setting up scenarios in which a web application will be accessed by one group of people inside the firewall and another group of people outside the firewall. Each time you extend a web application, you have the opportunity to change the authentication methods and URL mappings to suit the intended audience. Additionally, you can secure SharePoint sites using Secure Sockets Layer (SSL).

Working with Alternate Access Mappings

When you create a new web application in WSS or MOSS, it is configured by default to utilize internal server names and URLs. This means that a web application in the Default zone is not initially suitable for exposure outside the firewall. If you were to simply forward port 80 from your firewall to the internal IP address of the SharePoint server, you would discover that external users are redirected to the internal name of the server and access would fail. In order to make external access function correctly, you must provide an alternate access mapping that directs the incoming URL to the SharePoint web application. Incoming URLs are associated with a specific zone so you can limit the mapping to a given set of users.

Establishing alternate access maps is done through the Central Administration site on the Operations tab. Figure 3-9 shows a page from the Central Administration site with some mappings defined. Exercise 3.1 at the end of this chapter covers the steps necessary to create alternate mappings for an externally facing site.

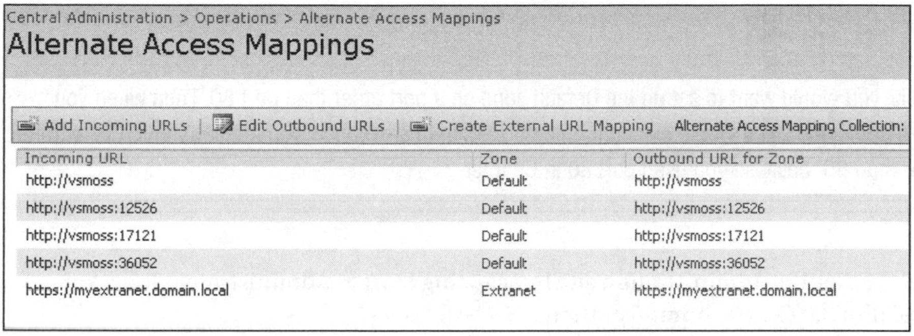

Figure 3-9. *Alternate access mappings*

Enabling Secure Sockets Layer

When you create or extend a web application, you will have the option to enable SSL. Enabling SSL provides an extra level of security based on certificates and encryption. In order to enable SSL for SharePoint, you must obtain and install a server certificate on any IIS web sites that will be accessed through SSL. Exercise 3.1 walks you through the process of creating a secure site with SSL enabled.

Exercise 3.1. Creating a Secure Internet Site

In the previous version of SharePoint, creating web sites that are accessible from outside the firewall is a challenge. Under SharePoint 2007, this capability is greatly improved through the use of zones, Forms authentication, and alternate access mappings. In this exercise, you will create a secure Internet site using several of these capabilities. This exercise assumes that you have set up the development environment described in Chapter 2 and will work with either WSS or MOSS. If your environment is different, you may have to modify some steps.

■**Note** If you have previously modified your SharePoint installation to use another Forms authentication provider—such as `SqlMembershipProvider`—while working through the chapter text, roll those changes back before you start this exercise.

Extending the Web Application

When you created your first web application in Chapter 2, it was created in the Default zone using Windows authentication. Generally speaking, it is a good idea to always use Windows authentication in conjunction with the Default zone so that users inside the firewall can access the web application. If you want to make the web application available outside the firewall, you should extend it into the Internet or Extranet zone. In this exercise, you will extend the existing web application into the Extranet zone in order to create a secure site.

Follow these steps to extend the existing web application into the Extranet zone:

■**Tip** Normally, you would want to set up the Default zone on a port other than port 80. Then when you extend the web application, you would extend it onto port 80. In this exercise, you are setting up the extranet on a port other than 80, because you used port 80 in Chapter 2.

---

1. Open the Central Administration site by selecting Start ➤ Administrative Tools ➤ SharePoint 3.0 Central Administration.

2. In the Central Administration site, click the Application Management tab.

3. Under the SharePoint Web Application Management section, click the link titled Create or Extend Web Application.

4. On the Create or Extend Web Application page, click the link titled Extend an Existing Web Application.

5. On the Extend Web Application to Another IIS Web Site page, drop down the Web Application selection list and click Change Web Application.

6. In the Select Web Application page, click the link for the web application that you set up in Chapter 2.

7. Under the IIS Web Site section, choose Create a New IIS Web Site.

8. In the Description field type **Extranet**, but leave the port number in parentheses as part of the name.

9. Under the Security Configuration section, choose Yes from the Use Secure Sockets Layer (SSL) option group.

10. Under the Load Balanced URL section, select Extranet from the Zone drop-down list.

11. Make note of the URL for the extended web application so you can access it later.

12. Click the OK button.

Creating an Alias

Creating an alias for your web site is a simple matter of making a new record entry in the Domain Name Service for the network. Creating an alias will allow you to use a name such as sharepoint.domain.local when accessing a web application. Although you will create your alias solely for internal use, you can create an alias for external use and map it to an IP address that will expose the portal on the Internet.

■**Note** Remember to add a new incoming URL entry to SharePoint when you utilize an external IP address. The steps for adding an incoming URL entry are covered earlier in this exercise.

Follow these steps to create an alias for the SharePoint server:

1. Log in to VSPDC as the domain administrator.

2. Select Start ➤ Administrative Tools ➤ DNS.

3. In the dnsmgmt dialog, expand the Forward Lookup Zones folder.

4. Right-click the domain.local folder and select New Alias (CNAME) from the pop-up menu.

5. In the New Resource Record dialog, type **extranet**.

6. Click the Browse button.

7. Double-click the VSPDC node.

8. Double-click the Forward Lookup folder.

9. Double-click the domain.local folder.

10. Select the VSWSS or the VSMOSS entry from the list as appropriate and click the OK button.

11. In the New Resource Record dialog, click the OK button.

Installing Certificate Services

Server certificates can be purchased commercially from a trusted source such as VeriSign, or you can create your own using Microsoft Certificate Services. In our exercise, we will install and utilize Microsoft Certificate Services. Making your own certificates is fine for testing and limited production use, but if you are going to allow access to the portal to a wide audience, you should consider getting a certificate from a trusted provider.

Adding the Application Server Role

IIS is required in order to make certificates available for download and distribution. Therefore, you must install IIS before installing Certificate Services. Follow these steps to configure VSPDC:

1. Log in to VSPDC as a domain administrator.

2. Start ➤ Administrative Tools ➤ Configure Your Server Wizard.

3. On the Preliminary Steps screen, click the Next button.

4. On the Server Role screen, select Application Server (IIS, ASP.NET) from the list of available roles and click the Next button.

5. On the Application Server Options screen, check the ASP.NET box and click the Next button.

6. On the Summary of Selections screen, click the Next button.

Adding Certificate Services

Once IIS is installed, you may proceed to add Certificate Services to the server. This will allow you to issue your own trusted certificates to SharePoint servers. Follow these steps to install Certificate Server:

1. Log in to VSPDC as a domain administrator.

2. Select Start ➤ Control Panel ➤ Add or Remove Programs.

3. In the Add or Remove Programs dialog, click the Add\Remove Windows Components button.

4. In the Windows Components dialog, check the Certificate Services box.

5. Respond to the warning dialog by clicking the Yes button.

6. Uncheck the Internet Explorer Enhanced Security Configuration box.

7. In the Windows Components dialog, click the Next button.

8. In the CA Type step, select Stand-Alone Root CA.

9. Click the Next button.

10. In the CA Identifying Information step, type **VSPDC** into the Common Name for This CA text box.

11. Click the Next button.

12. In the Certificate Database Settings step, accept the default values and click the Next button.

13. Click the Finish button to complete the operation.

Requesting a New Certificate

Creating a certificate begins by preparing a request using the virtual server that you want to secure. This server prepares a text file that may then be submitted to Certificate Services. In this exercise, you can create a request for either VSWSS or VSMOSS depending upon whether you installed WSS or MOSS in Chapter 2.

Follow these steps to prepare a request:

1. Log in to VSWSS or VSMOSS as a local administrator.

2. Open the Windows File Explorer.

3. Create a new directory named c:\certificates\sharepoint.

4. Select the c:\certificates directory, right-click it and select Sharing and Security from the pop-up menu.

5. On the Sharing tab, select Share This Folder.

6. Click the Permissions button.

7. Select Grant Everyone Full Control and click the OK button.

8. Press the OK button to close the directory properties dialog.

9. Select Start ➤ Administrative Tools ➤ Internet Information Services (IIS) Manager.

10. Open the Web Sites folder.

11. Right-click the Web Site node where the web application was extended into the Extranet zone and select properties from the pop-up menu.

12. On the Directory Security tab, click the Server Certificate button.

13. In the Web Server Certificate Wizard, click the Next button.

14. In the Server Certificate step, select the option to create a new certificate, and click the Next button.

15. In the Delayed or Immediate Request step, select the option to Prepare the Request Now, but Send It Later, and click the Next button.

16. In the Name and Security Settings step, leave the values as they are and click the Next button.

17. In the Organization Information step, type your company name in the Organization field and your company unit in the Organizational Unit field.

18. Click the Next button.

19. In the Your Site's Common Name step, type **VSWSS** or **VSWOSS** in the Common Name field as appropriate.

20. Click the Next button.

21. In the Geographical Information step, enter the appropriate information and click the Next button.

22. In the Certificate Request File Name step, click the Browse button.

23. In the Saves As dialog, navigate to the c:\certificates\sharepoint directory and click the Save button.

24. In the Certificate Request File Name step, click the Next button.

25. In the Request File Summary step, click the Next button.

26. Click the Finish button to complete the operation.

Creating a New Certificate

Once the request is prepared, you may use it to create a new certificate. Certificate Services uses the text file created under IIS to generate the certificate. The new certificate may then be installed on the SharePoint server.

Follow these steps to create the new server certificate:

1. Log in to VSPDC as the domain administrator.

2. Open the Internet Explorer and navigate to `http://vspdc/certsrv/default.asp`.

3. Click the Request a Certificate link.

4. Click the Advanced Certificate Request link.

5. Click the link to submit a certificate request by using a base-64–encoded CMC or PKCS #10 file, or submit a renewal request by using a base-64–encoded PKCS #7 file.

6. Open the certificate text file in Notepad that you previously saved at \\vswss\ certificates\sharepoint or \\vsmoss\certificates\sharepoint as appropriate.

7. Copy the entire contents of the certificate file and paste it into the Saved Request field.

8. Click the Submit button.

9. Select Start ➤ Administration Tools ➤ Certification Authority.

10. In the Certification Authority dialog, expand the tree and open the Pending Requests folder.

11. Locate the pending request, right-click it and select All Tasks ➤ Issue from the pop-up menu.

12. Open Internet Explorer and navigate to `http://vspdc/certsrv/default.asp`.

13. Click the link titled View the Status of a Pending Certificate Request.

14. Click the link for the pending certificate.

15. On the Certificate Issued page, click the Download Certificate link.

16. In the File Download dialog, click the Save button.

17. Save the file into the \certificates\sharepoint directory.

18. On the Certificate Issued page, click the Download Certificate Chain link.

19. In the File Download dialog, click the Save button.

20. Save the file into the \certificates\sharepoint directory.

Installing the New Certificate

Once the new certificate is created, you can install it on the SharePoint server. When using the Microsoft Certificate Services, you must install the certificate file with the P7B extension. This file will establish the appropriate trusts to ensure that you can view the web application.

To install the new certificate, do the following:

1. Log in to VSWSS or VSMOSS as the local administrator.

2. Select Start ➤ Administrative Tools ➤ Internet Information Services (IIS) Manager.

3. Expand the VSWSS or VSMOSS node as appropriate and open the Web Sites folder.

4. Right-click the Web Site node where web application was extended into the Extranet zone and select Properties from the context menu.

5. On the Directory Security tab, click the Server Certificate button.

6. In the Web Server Certificate wizard, press the Next button.

7. In the Pending Certificate Request step, select Process the Pending Request and Install the Certificate.

8. Press the Next button.

9. In the Process a Pending Request step, press the Browse button.

10. In the Open dialog, navigate to the \certificates\sharepoint directory and select the file with the P7B extension.

11. Click the Open button.

12. In the Process a Pending Request step, click the Next button.

13. In the SSL Port step, accept the default value and click the Next button.

14. In the Certificate Summary step, view the details and click the Next button.

15. Click the Finish button to complete the operation.

16. In the Default Web Site Properties dialog, click the View Certificate button.

17. In the Certificate dialog, verify that the certificate is valid by viewing the Certification Path tab.

18. Click the OK button.

19. In the Web Site Properties dialog, click the Edit button under the Secure Communications section.

20. In the Secure Communications dialog, check the Require Secure Channel box and click the OK button.

21. In the Web Site Properties dialog, click the OK button.

Configuring Forms Authentication

Forms authentication allows you to configure a SharePoint page as a login form instead of utilizing Windows authentication directly. SharePoint supports many different providers for authenticating users against other data stores such as SQL Server or an LDAP service. In this exercise, you will make use of the `ActiveDirectoryMembershipProvider` to configure Forms authentication against Active Directory. In this scenario, users will enter their Windows credentials into the login form to gain access to the secure site.

Follow these steps to set up Forms authentication:

1. Log in to VSWSS or VSMOSS as the local administrator.

2. Open the File Explorer and navigate to \Inetpub\wwwroot\wss\VirtualDirectories.

3. Under the VirtualDirectories folder, identify the subdirectory that is associated with your extranet site and the folder associated with the Central Administration site.

■**Note** Because the subdirectory names can be quite cryptic, it is often useful to open the properties dialog for a web site directly in the IIS Manager to determine which directory is associated with which site.

---

4. Open the `web.config` file for both the extranet site and the Central Administration site. The provider information must be added to both files.

5. Directly above the `<system.web>` tag in both files, add the following section to define a connection to Active Directory:

```
<connectionStrings>
  <add name="ADService"
  connectionString="LDAP://vspdc.domain.local/DC=domain,DC=local" />
</connectionStrings>
```

6. Directly underneath the `<system.web>` tag in both files, add the following section to utilize the `ActiveDirectoryMembershipProvider` as the authentication provider:

■**Note** Be sure to change the password in the following code to match your development environment.

```
<membership defaultProvider="AD">
  <providers>
    <add name="AD"
    type="System.Web.Security.ActiveDirectoryMembershipProvider, System.Web,
      Version=2.0.0.0, Culture=neutral, PublickeyToken=b03f5f7f11d50a3a"
      connectionStringName="ADService"
      connectionUsername="DOMAIN\Administrator"
      connectionPassword="P@ssw0rd"
      connectionProtection="None"
      attributeMapUsername="sAMAccountName" />
  </providers>
</membership>
```

7. Save and close both files.

8. Select Start ➤ Run. In the Run dialog, type **iisreset** and click the Open button.

9. Open the Central Administration site by selecting Start ➤ Administrative Tools ➤ SharePoint 3.0 Central Administration.

10. In the Central Administration site, click the Application Management tab.

11. Under the Application Security section, click the link titled Authentication Providers.

12. If the correct web application is not already selected, drop down the Web Application selection list and click Change Web Application. Then click the link for the initial web application that you set up in Chapter 2.

13. On the Authentication Providers page, click the Windows link associated with the Extranet zone.

14. On the Edit Authentication page, select Forms as the Authentication Type.

15. In the Membership Provider Name field, type **AD**, which is the name of the provider as it appears in the web.config file.

16. Click the Save button.

17. In the Central Administration site, click the Application Management tab.

18. Under the Application Security section, click the link titled Policy for Web Application.

19. If the correct web application is not already selected, drop down the Web Application selection list and click Change Web Application. Then click the link for the initial web application that you set up in Chapter 2.

20. Click the Add Users button.

21. On the Add Users page, select Extranet from the zone list.

22. Click the Next button.

23. On the Add Users page, type **Administrator** into the Users field and click the Check Names image button.

24. Under the Choose Permissions section, check the box labeled Full Control – Has Full Control.

25. Click the Finish button.

Adding a New Incoming URL

Whenever you use an alias or external IP address to access a SharePoint site, you must set up alternate access mappings or else the authentication will fail. This is because SharePoint will deliver URLs that reference internal server names by default. In this exercise, you need to add a new incoming URL because the project site uses an alias.

Follow these steps to specify an incoming URL:

1. Open the Central Administration site by selecting Start ➤ Administrative Tools ➤ SharePoint 3.0 Central Administration.

2. In the Central Administration site, click the Operations tab.

3. Under the Global Configuration section, click the link titled Alternate Access Mappings.

4. On the Alternate Access Mappings page, click the Add Internal URLs button.

5. On the Add Internal URLs page, drop down the Alternate Access Mapping Collection selection list and click Change Alternate Access Mapping Collection.

6. In the Select Alternate Access Mapping page, click the link for the initial web application that you set up in Chapter 2.

7. In the URL Protocol, Host, and Port field, enter **https://extranet.domain.local:[port]**.

8. In the Zone drop-down list, select Extranet.

9. Click the Save button.

10. On the Alternate Access Mappings page, click the Edit Public URLs button.

11. On the Edit Public Zone URLs page, enter **https://extranet.domain.local:[port]** in the Extranet field replacing the internal reference that SharePoint initially created.

12. Click the Save button.

Testing Secure Access

Once the certificate is installed on the SharePoint server, you are ready to utilize SSL. When users access the portal through SSL, they will initially see the certificate warning. They can subsequently install the certificate on their machines and trust your root authority. This will allow them to access the portal without acknowledging the certificate each time.

Follow these steps to test secure communications:

1. Log in to VSCLIENT as a portal end user.

2. Open Internet Explorer and navigate to `https://extranet.domain.local:[port]/` `sites/intranet/Pages/default.aspx`, which should correspond to the home page of the extended web application if you set up the environment in Chapter 2.

3. When the Security Alert dialog appears, click Yes.

4. When the login form appears, enter **Administrator** in the Username field along with the associated password and click the Sign In button. Figure 3-10 shows the login page.

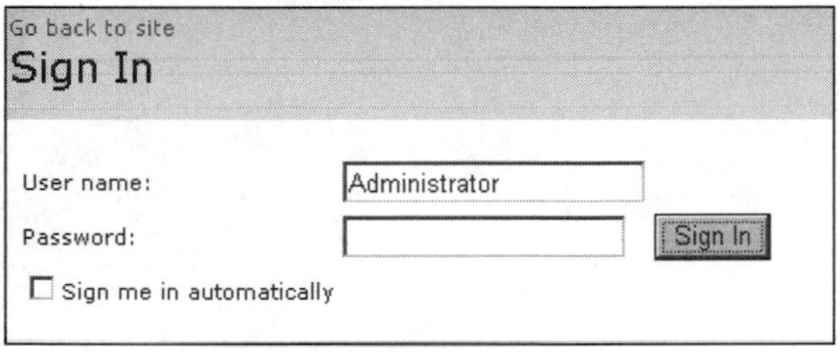

Figure 3-10. *Forms authentication on a secure site*

CHAPTER 4

■ ■ ■

SharePoint Shared Services

While a SharePoint farm gives you the ability to create many separate web applications, there are several services that you will not necessarily want to recreate for each new web application. The most obvious example of such a service is the Search Service. In many scenarios, it makes sense to set up the Search Service one time and then share it across several web applications. This is the concept behind the Shared Services Provider (SSP) in SharePoint.

An SSP provides not only a shared Search Service, but also *audiences, user profiles, personal sites, Excel Services*, and the *Business Data Catalog (BDC)*. Audiences allow you to target content at particular groups of users. The profile service allows you to track and share information about portal users. Personal sites give each user a private space to utilize. Excel Services makes spreadsheet information and calculations available as a web application, while the BDC allows you to integrate SharePoint sites with back-end line-of-business systems. I cover each of these services in detail throughout this chapter.

Creating and Managing Shared Services Providers

Creating an SSP is done through the Central Administration site in MOSS. While WSS sites can utilize an SSP, you cannot create one through WSS. Within a farm, you can configure zero or more SSPs, and MOSS will typically create one during the installation process. In fact, you already have one available if you set up the development environment described in Chapter 2.

Follow these steps to manage your SSP:

1. Log in to VSMOSS as a SharePoint administrator.

2. Select Start ➤ Administrative Tools ➤ SharePoint 3.0 Central Administration.

3. From the home page of the Central Administration site, click the Application Management tab.

4. On the Application Management tab, click the link titled Create or Configure This Farm's Shared Services.

On the Manage This Farm's Shared Services page, you'll see a list of all the SSPs that you have defined on your farm. Additionally, you'll see all of the web applications that are currently using those services. From this page, you can create a new SSP, change the associations with web applications, and recover an SSP from a backed-up database. Figure 4-1 shows the page with several web applications listed.

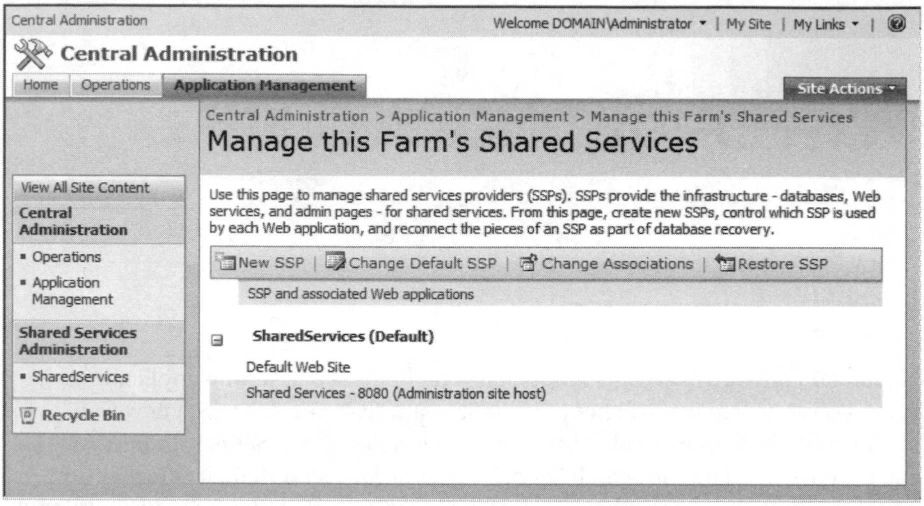

Figure 4-1. *Managing Shared Services*

When you create a new SSP, you get an administration site where you can configure and manage the Shared Services. You can access the administration site from the Manage This Farm's Shared Services page by clicking the appropriate link listed under Shared Services Administration. You can also hover over the name of the SSP in the list and select Open Shared Services Admin Site from the drop-down menu. In either case, you will be taken to the Shared Services Administration site shown in Figure 4-2.

■**Tip** If you should receive an "Access Denied" error, be sure your account has been given Full Control rights under the Policy for Web Application associated with the Shared Services web application.

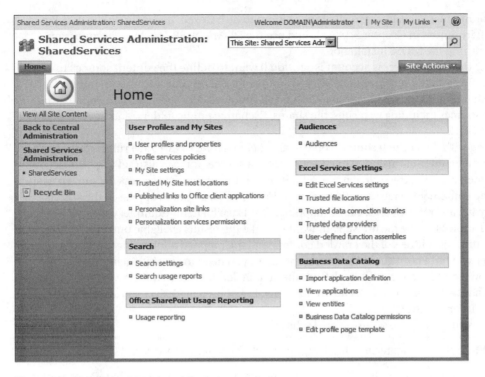

Figure 4-2. *The Shared Services Administration site*

Configuring Search

When you first installed MOSS, you started the Search Service, which is configured with the basic settings necessary to search web applications. However, you will want to spend some time adjusting the search configuration to control how content is indexed and delivered through the service. From the home page of the Shared Services Administration site, clicking the Search Settings link will take you to the Configure Search Settings page where you can refine the Search Service configuration.

■**Note** If you are just using WSS, you'll have a separate Search Service available to you. You can configure the service from the Central Administration web site. Click the link titled Services on This Server on the Operations tab. On the Services page, start the Windows SharePoint Services Search Service.

Crawling Content Sources

The crawl settings on the Configure Search Settings page determines what content is indexed by the Search Service. The first setting to check in this section is the default content access account. This account is the one that is used to crawl content and create an index. Therefore, the account must have access to all of the content to be indexed. If you set up the development environment in Chapter 2, you should use the DOMAIN\SPCrawlAcct account you created during the MOSS installation.

After the content access account is set, you'll want to define the content sources to be indexed. By default, MOSS creates a content source for SharePoint sites. If you only intend to search SharePoint content, this source may be all you need. However, you can define other content sources including web sites, file shares, Exchange public folders, and business data from the BDC.

Along with the content source, you can also define *crawl rules*. Crawl rules allow you to specify what content is included or excluded from a source. You can also set a special account to use when crawling the source if the default account does not have access for some reason.

If the content you crawl has a different address than you want to appear in the search results, you can create a server name mapping. This is useful if, for example, you crawl content using an address inside the firewall but want to make the results available outside the firewall. Simply enter the address of the crawled content and the mapped address for the search results.

After you have configured the content sources, you need to specify a schedule for the crawl. You won't get any results back from the Search Service until a full crawl of the content sources has been completed. Because a full crawl is resource intensive, you should try to schedule it for off-hours.

Follow these steps to set up a crawl schedule:

1. From the Configure Search settings page, click Content Sources and Crawl Schedules.

2. On the Manage Content Sources page, hover over the Local Office SharePoint Server Sites content source and select Edit from the drop-down menu.

3. On the Edit Content Source page, click the Create Schedule under the Full Crawl Schedule list.

4. In the Manage Schedules dialog, accept the default settings by simply clicking the OK button.

5. Check the box labeled Start Full Crawl of This Content Source.

6. Click the OK button.

Including File Types

When the Search Service creates a content index, it does not include all of the file types it encounters. This is because many file types might not make any sense in the search results. For example, EXE files are not included in the content index because they are not documents and might even contain a virus. While the out-of-the-box settings index most of the commonly used file types, not every file type you may want is included. In particular, most organizations want to include Adobe Acrobat portable document format (PDF) files in the search results, but they are not included by default.

In order to include other file types, you must first install the appropriate *IFilter*. IFilters are used to build indexes for specific document formats. Each file type that you want to include must have an installed IFilter before it can be part of the index. After you install the IFilter, you must then provide an image to represent the file within SharePoint and specifically tell the index to include the file type.

Follow these steps to include PDF files in your search results:

1. Log in to VSMOSS as a SharePoint administrator.

2. Open Internet Explorer and navigate to `http://www.adobe.com/support/downloads/thankyou.jsp?ftpID=2611&fileID=2457` to download the Adobe PDF IFilter v6.0.

3. Download and install the IFilter on VSMOSS. The installation is straightforward and requires no special considerations.

4. Open the Internet Explorer and navigate to `http://www.google.com`.

5. On the Google home page, click the Images link.

6. Type **ICPDF.GIF** in the search field and click the Search Images button.

7. In the search results, locate a 16-by-16 PDF icon image and click it.

8. On the Google Images page, click the link titled See Image Alone.

9. When the image appears alone in the browser, right-click the image and select Save Picture As from the content menu.

10. Save the image to `C:\Program Files\Common Files\Microsoft Shared\web server extensions\12\TEMPLATE\IMAGES`.

11. Open a copy of the File Explorer and locate the file `C:\Program Files\Common Files\Microsoft Shared\web server extensions\12\TEMPLATE\XML\DOCICON.XML`. Open this file in a text editor.

12. In the `DOCICON.XML` file, locate the `<ByExtension>` element. In this section, add the following code to specify the icon for use with PDF files:

    ```
    <Mapping Key="pdf" Value="icpdf.gif" />
    ```

13. Save and close `DOCICON.XML`.

14. On the Configure Search Settings page of the Shared Services Administration site, click the link titled File Types.

15. On the Manage File Types page, click the New File Type link.

16. On the Add File Type page, type **pdf** into the File Extension field and click the OK button.

17. Close the browser.

18. Select Start ➤ Run from the menu.

19. Type **iisreset** into the Open field and click the OK button.

Once you complete the previous steps, you should be able to add PDF documents to libraries and immediately see them associated with the appropriate icon. After the search index is rebuilt, you should also be able to return them in the search results. Of course, users will still need to have the Adobe Acrobat Reader installed to view the documents. For other file types, you can search the Internet for available third-party IFilters. It is even possible to create your own custom IFilter, although that topic is well beyond the scope of this book.

Understanding Search Scopes

While content sources define groups of documents to index, they may not correspond to groups of documents that users want to search. *Search scopes* allow you to define sets of documents from various content sources that should be searched together. Search scopes help users get better results by narrowing the search to items of interest.

Follow these steps to set up a new search scope:

1. From the Configure Search Settings page, click View Scopes.

2. On the View Scopes page, click New Scope.

3. On the Create Scope page, enter **Special Interest Groups** and click the OK button.

4. On the View Scopes page, locate the Special Interest Groups scope and click the Add Rules link.

5. On the Add Scope Rule page, select the Web Address option.

6. Enter the complete address to the softball site you created earlier in the Folder field (e.g., `http://vsmoss/sites/intranet/softball`).

7. Click the OK button.

8. On the Configure Search Settings page, click the Start Update Now link under the Shared Scopes section.

Once the search scope is created, it must be added to the search page in order to use it. Requiring a separate operation to make the scope visible allows you to control which web applications can use the scope. This ensures that only appropriate users make use of the scope.

Follow these steps to add the scope to the search page:

1. Open the home page to the MOSS intranet site you created in Chapter 2 (e.g., `http://vsmoss/sites/intranet/Pages/Default.aspx`).

2. Select Sites Settings ➤ Modify All Site Settings from the Site Actions drop-down menu.

3. On the Site Settings page, click the Search Scopes link under the Site Collection Administration section.

■Tip If you do not see the Search Scopes link, make sure that you are on the Site Settings page for the top-level site in the Site Collection.

---

4. On the View Scopes page, click the Search Dropdown link.

5. On the Edit Scope Display Group page, check the box next to the Special Interest Groups scope.

6. Click the OK button.

Using Keywords and Best Bets

Oftentimes organizations have important terms that are well-known by all of their members. These terms have definite meaning within an organization and are associated with certain documents. Therefore, when a user searches a particular term, you might want to ensure that it is always associated with the correct results. This is the purpose behind *keywords* and *best bets*.

Keywords allow you to define the terms that have special meaning in your organization. You can then associate those terms with a specific search result, or "best bet." The best bet results will appear at the top of the search results list whenever the keyword is used in a search. You can define keywords and best bets from the Site Settings page by clicking the Search Keywords link.

Reporting on Search Usage

One of the best ways to improve search results is to understand how users are searching. In order to support this, Shared Services provides a set of search usage reports for profiling search activity. You can access these reports from the home page of the Shared Services Administration site under the Search section.

Using Audiences

Although you will undoubtedly spend a significant amount of time deciding what content to display on which page, most users will be interested in only a subset of the information on a page. Furthermore, page real estate is often in short supply, especially if you want to limit the amount of scrolling required to view a page. With this in mind the Office SharePoint Standard Feature provides the ability to define *audiences*. Audiences in SharePoint are groups of users that share common interests and can be used to display or hide various content elements based on the audience membership of the current user.

Audiences can be defined based on various properties of user accounts in Active Directory. You can define an audience based on membership in an Active Directory group, position in the organizational structure, or other characteristics. Once defined, the audience must be compiled in order to make it available for use with web parts.

Follow these steps to define an audience:

1. Log in to VSPDC as a domain administrator.

2. Select Start ➤ Administrative Tools ➤ Active Directory Users and Computers.

3. In the Active Directory Users and Computers dialog, expand the tree underneath the DOMAIN.LOCAL node until the Users folder is visible.

4. Right-click the Users folder and select New ➤ Group from the context menu.

5. In the New Object – Group window, enter **Information Technology** in the Group Name field.

6. Click the OK button.

7. In the Active Directory Users and Computers dialog, right-click the Information Technology group and select properties from the context menu.

8. Click the Members tab and then the Add button.

9. In the Select Users, Contacts, or Computers window, add some users to the group.

10. Click OK to close the dialog when you are finished.

11. Log in to VSMOSS as a site administrator.

12. Open the Central Administration web site by selecting Start ➤ Administrative Tools ➤ SharePoint 3.0 Central Administration.

13. From the Central Administration home page, click the Application Management tab.

14. On the Application Management page, click the link titled Create or Configure This Farm's Shared Services.

15. In the Quick Launch area, click the link for the Shared Services Administration site.

16. On the Shared Services Administration home page, click the Audiences link.

17. On the Manage Audiences page, click the Create Audience link.

18. On the Create Audience page, type **Information Technology** in the Name field.

19. Click the OK button.

20. On the Add Audience Rule page, select the User option.

21. In the Operator drop-down list, select Member Of.

22. In the value field, type **Information Technology** and click the Check Names button.

23. Click the OK button.

24. On the Manage Audiences page, click the Start Compilation link, which will create the audience membership based on the rules you defined. Audiences will not have members until they are compiled.

Because audience membership can change over time, it's best to set up a compilation schedule. You can specify a compilation schedule by clicking the link on the Manage Audiences page. After that, the audience will always be available for use with web parts, documents, list items, and other content items in MOSS.

Using audiences to display or hide content is generally done as part of the configuration properties for an item. You can show or hide web parts in a page based on audience membership using the web parts property pane. Simply type the name of the audiences that you want to see the content. Figure 4-3 shows a Content Editor web part being targeted at the Information Technology audience.

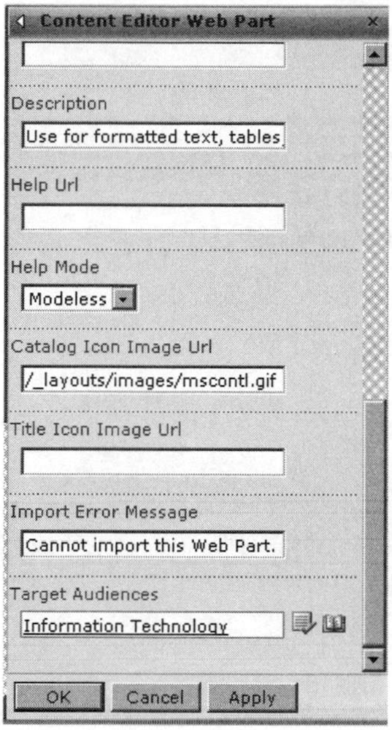

Figure 4-3. *Targeting content with audiences*

Understanding User Profiles

Members of a SharePoint site are not simply anonymous users who view web pages and read documents. Instead, users are active participants whose information is part of the overall content. In MOSS, the information about portal users is significantly enhanced through user profiles.

User profiles are created in a separate database that is populated by both manual data entry and importing data directly from Active Directory. Once created, the profile may be viewed after a search within the People scope or as the result of following a link associated with a person. Figure 4-4 shows a typical public profile page.

Setting up profiles requires you to configure an import connection to Active Directory. Typically, the import is scheduled to run daily using a specific account you assign to this task. As a best practice, you should define a new group in Active Directory for all accounts that will be imported and create a new account that SharePoint can use for reading Active Directory information.

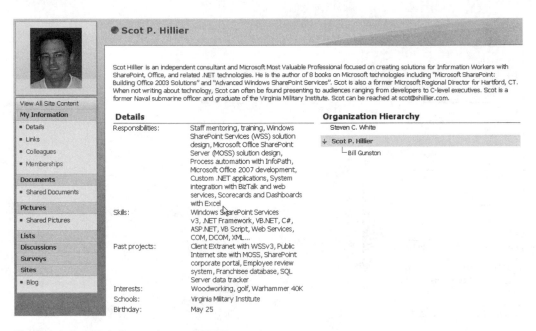

Figure 4-4. *Profile information on MOSS*

Follow these steps to create required groups and users:

1. Log in to VSPDC as a domain administrator.

2. Select Start ➤ Administrative Tools ➤ Active Directory Users and Computers.

3. In the Active Directory Users and Computers dialog, expand the tree underneath the DOMAIN.LOCAL node until the Users folder is visible.

4. Right-click the Users folder and select New ➤ User from the context menu.

5. In the New Object – User dialog, type **SPProfileImport** in both the Full Name and User Logon Name fields.

6. Click the Next button.

7. Uncheck the box labeled User Must Change Password at Next Logon.

8. Check the boxes labeled User Cannot Change Password and Password Never Expires.

9. Enter a password for the account and click the Next button.

10. Click the Finish button.

11. Right-click the Users folder and select New ➤ User from the context menu.

12. In the New Object – User dialog, enter some information for a new user account. The exact information does not matter, because you will disable this account later for testing purposes.

13. In the Active Directory Users and Computers dialog, right-click the new user you created and select properties from the context menu.

14. On the Account tab of the Properties dialog, check the box labeled Account Is Disabled.

15. Click the OK button.

16. Right-click the Users folder and select New ➤ Group from the context menu.

17. In the New Object – Group window, enter **Portal Profiles** in the Group Name field.

18. Click the OK button.

19. In the Active Directory Users and Computers dialog, right-click the Portal Users group and select Properties from the context menu.

20. Click the Members tab and then the Add button.

21. In the Select Users, Contacts, or Computers window, add the users who will have profiles in SharePoint including the disabled account.

22. Click OK to close the dialog when you are finished.

The simplest way to configure the profile import is to let SharePoint automatically detect the domain controller on the network. This simplifies the import configuration, but it doesn't make it foolproof. In most organizations, Active Directory is full of disabled accounts, service accounts, and test accounts that we don't want to import into the profile database. Therefore, you'll need to create a custom LDAP query to properly configure the import to exclude such accounts.

Creating a proper LDAP query from scratch can be a challenge so I like to use the command-line utility LDIFDE.EXE, which is part of the Windows operating system, to help me determine the correct query for importing accounts. LDIFDE.EXE creates, modifies, and deletes Active Directory objects. You can also use it to run LDAP queries and dump the results to a text file. In this way, you can see which users are returned from an LDAP query and make adjustments until you get the correct result set. Listing 4-1 shows sample output for a single user as it appears in LDIFDE.EXE.

Listing 4-1. *LDIFDE.EXE Sample Output*

```
dn: CN=Scot P. Hillier,CN=Users,DC=domain,DC=local
changetype: add
objectClass: top
objectClass: person
objectClass: organizationalPerson
objectClass: user
cn: Scot P. Hillier
sn: Hillier
givenName: Scot
initials: P
distinguishedName: CN=Scot P. Hillier,CN=Users,DC=domain,DC=local
```

```
instanceType: 4
whenCreated: 20051017174105.0Z
whenChanged: 20051017174908.0Z
displayName: Scot P. Hillier
uSNCreated: 13920
memberOf: CN=Portal Profiles,CN=Users,DC=domain,DC=local
uSNChanged: 13968
name: Scot P. Hillier
objectGUID:: xC6/b7NXnOak+PIEdCyh4Q==
userAccountControl: 66048
badPwdCount: 0
codePage: 0
countryCode: 0
badPasswordTime: 0
lastLogoff: 0
lastLogon: 0
pwdLastSet: 127740444656093750
primaryGroupID: 513
objectSid:: AQUAAAAAAUVAAAA+Tig7KBg3xJxhGmOUwQAAA==
accountExpires: 9223372036854775807
logonCount: 0
sAMAccountName: ScotHillier
sAMAccountType: 805306368
userPrincipalName: ScotHillier@domain.local
objectCategory: CN=Person,CN=Schema,CN=Configuration,DC=domain,DC=local
mail: ScotHillier@domain.local
```

In order to create the correct LDAP query for importing profiles, you should start by dumping all of the accounts from Active Directory into a text file. If you should happen to have thousands of accounts in your directory, start by dumping a single organizational unit or group. After dumping the accounts, examine the test file to locate the distinguished name (DN) that defines membership in the group you are targeting. Then use the DN to further refine the dump until you get what you want. You'll also want to add a special clause to the query to exclude all disabled accounts.

Follow these steps to create an LDAP query for importing profile information:

1. Log in to VSMOSS as a SharePoint administrator.

2. Select Start ➤ Run.

3. Type **ldifde -f c:\users.txt -r "(&(objectCategory=Person)(objectClass=User))"** into the Open field.

4. Click the OK button.

5. Open the file c:\users.txt in Notepad and verify that all of the accounts from Active Directory are returned.

6. Search the text file for one of the usernames that you included in the Portal Profiles group. This person should have at least one `memberOf` entry that looks like the following code. Copy this entry for use in the next step:

`memberOf: CN=Portal Profiles,CN=Users,DC=domain,DC=local`

7. Select Start ➤ Run.

8. Narrow the LDAP query to the Portal Profiles group by typing **ldifde -f c:\users.txt -r "(&(objectCategory=Person)(objectClass=User)(memberOf= CN=Portal Profiles, CN=Users,DC=domain,DC=local))"** into the Open field.

9. Open the file `c:\users.txt` in Notepad and verify that you are returning all of the members of the Portal Profiles group including the disabled account.

10. Select Start ➤ Run.

11. Exclude disabled accounts from the LDAP query typing **ldifde -f c:\users.txt -r "(&(objectCategory=Person)(objectClass=User)(memberOf= CN=Portal Profiles, CN=Users,DC=domain,DC=local) (!(userAccountControl:1.2.840.113556.1.4. 803:=2)))"** into the Open field.

12. Open the file `c:\users.txt` in Notepad and verify that you are returning only the enabled accounts from the Portal Profiles group.

Once you have created a query that returns only the accounts you want in the profile database, you are ready to configure the import. Profiles are managed as part of the Shared Services infrastructure, which is configured through a separate web site. After the import is configured, you can run a full import to populate the database.

Follow these steps to configure the profile import:

1. Log in to VSMOSS as a SharePoint administrator.

2. Open the Central Administration web site by selecting Start ➤ Administrative Tools ➤ SharePoint 3.0 Central Administration.

3. From the Central Administration home page, click the Application Management tab.

4. On the Application Management page, click the link titled Create or Configure This Farm's Shared Services.

5. On the Manage This Farm's Shared Services page, select Open Shared Services Admin Site from the drop-down menu.

6. On the Shared Services Administration home page, click the link titled User Profiles and Properties.

7. On the User Profiles and Properties page, click the link titled Configure Profile Import.

8. On the Configure Profile Import page, select the Custom Source option.

9. Under the Full Import Schedule section check the box labeled Schedule Full Import.

10. Click the OK button.

11. On the Import Connections page, click the link titled Create New Connection.

12. On the Add Connection page, type **domain.local** in the Domain Name field.

13. Click the option labeled Specify a Domain Controller.

14. Type **vspdc.domain.local** into the Domain Controller Name field.

15. In the Search Base field, type **DC=domain,DC=local**.

16. In the User Filter field, type **"(&(objectCategory=Person)(objectClass=User) (memberOf= CN=Portal Profiles,CN=Users,DC=domain,DC=local) (!(userAccountControl:1.2.840.113556.1.4.803:=2)))"**.

17. In the Authentication Information section, select the option labeled Specify an Account.

18. Enter **DOMAIN\SPProfileImport** into the Account Name field.

19. Enter the password for the account you defined earlier.

20. Click the OK button.

21. Click the Home tab in Shared Services Administration.

22. On the Shared Services Administration home page, click the link titled User Profiles and Properties.

23. On the User Profiles and Properties page, click the link titled Start Full Import.

24. After the Import is complete, click the link titled View User Profiles and verify that the appropriate profiles have been created.

The properties that make up the profile can be changed at any time from the User Profiles and Properties page. On this page, you can select to add a new property or view the existing ones. Properties may be explicitly tied to an Active Directory field or they can be filled in manually. Additionally, you can specify whether the end user has the ability to edit the field and control how it appears on his or her profile page.

Personalization with My Site

Along with all of the information, documents, and links you can present in MOSS, end users are also provided with a personal site known as My Site. My Site is easily accessed by clicking the associated link on the bar directly above the search box. A My Site is created for a user the first time it is accessed. Because a My Site is essentially created by the user without administrative permissions, you must enable self-service site creation in Shared Services before sites can be created. When first accessed, MOSS takes a moment to format the initial site and then prompts you to confirm the location using the message box shown in Figure 4-5.

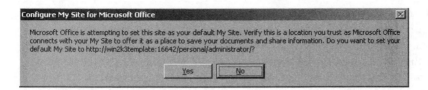

Figure 4-5. *Setting the default My Site*

Follow these steps to enable self-service site creation:

1. Log in to VSMOSS as a SharePoint administrator.

2. Open the Central Administration web site by selecting Start ➤ Administrative Tools ➤ SharePoint 3.0 Central Administration.

3. From the Central Administration home page, click the Application Management tab.

4. On the Application Management page, click the link titled Self-Service Site Management.

5. On the Self-Service Site Management page, make sure that the web application associated with Shared Services is selected.

6. Click the On option and then click the OK button.

Using My Site

My Site consists of two pages accessed through the My Home and My Profile tabs. The My Home page is intended as a personal workplace for the individual end user. The My Profile page, on the other hand, acts like a business card that can be accessed by other portal users. In fact, this is the page shown in Figure 4-4.

When My Site is first created, it shows a list of tasks with associated links to help you configure the site. One of the first things you should do is update your profile information. Clicking the link titled Describe Yourself will open the Edit Details page where you can enter information about yourself. For each field that you edit, you can also specify the visibility of the information. This allows you to determine whether information is seen by everyone or just selected groups.

You will notice that the profile items on My Site are a subset of the items available in the profile database. This is because the administrator determines which properties in the profile database can be edited by the end user directly and which ones will appear in the profile view of My Site. You can click the My Profile tab to see how your profile will appear to others. On this page, there is a drop-down list that gives you a preview of the page for various groups.

On the My Home page, you will notice a reference to My Calendar. My Calendar is a web part that you can connect to an Exchange server so that your calendar will be visible on My Site. To display your calendar, you must modify the properties of the web part. This will require end users to know the exact name of the Exchange server.

My Home also provides a web part called the Colleague Tracker for indicating your relationship to other users. The Colleague Tracker allows you to create a virtual social network that places you within the formal and informal organizational structure. You can not only associate yourself with your manager, but you can also show your relationship to colleagues with similar interests. Once you have established these relationships, you can then decide how to display them to other users. Showing these relationships can help other users locate people within the organization or find a person with expert knowledge in a certain area.

Clicking the link titled Identify the People You Know will take you to the My Colleagues page. Here you can choose to add new colleagues to your list. When you add colleagues, SharePoint tries to help by suggesting additions based on information such as group membership or shared managers.

My Home can also be a useful place to aggregate information from many sites. To support this type of personalized view, My Home includes a rolled-up view of both SharePoint sites and tasks. This view shows all of the documents and tasks from a site where you are a member. Figure 4-6 shows an aggregated view based on the softball site you created earlier.

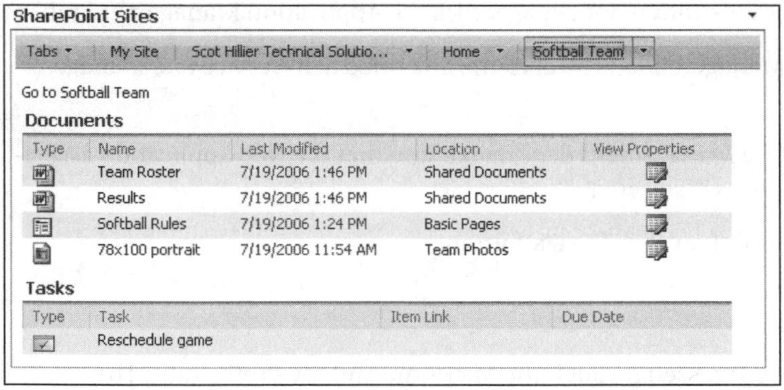

Figure 4-6. *Aggregating documents and tasks*

Customizing My Site

End users have full control over the items that appear on My Site. At any time, a user can customize My Site by clicking the link titled Add or Remove Web Parts. In this way, end users can make My Site a personalized workspace that shows them the information, documents, and links that they most care about. In addition to modifying the web parts that appear on My Site, users may also add new lists and pages directly by clicking the Create link under the Site Actions menu.

Although the administrator retains control over the appearance of the public view of My Site, end users can utilize the public view to share documents, sites, and links with other users. When documents and links are added to a list, the user may specify whether to show them on the public page. For example, the portal administrator may post a document describing the procedures to personalize My Site. This way, portal users can engage in self-service rather than sending all their questions directly to the portal administrator.

Publishing Links

Administrators can add pages to My Site through the Shared Services administration pages. Clicking the link titled Personalization Links allows you to add a new link that will appear as a tab on My Site. Additionally, you can target the links to an audience so the tabs only appear for certain users.

Using Excel Services

Excel Services is a new technology that ships as part of Shared Services and allows you to calculate and display Excel spreadsheets using MOSS without necessarily having a copy of Excel on the client machine. With Excel Services you can use spreadsheets to create dashboards within SharePoint or simply share a spreadsheet using the browser. Additionally, Excel Services has a calculation engine that supports calculating spreadsheets on the server in order to offload resource-intensive calculations. Excel Services consists of three components: the Excel Web Access web part, Excel Calculation Services, and Excel Web Services.

The Excel Web Access web part is used to display a spreadsheet as HTML within the browser. Once you properly configure Excel Services, you can drop this web part on any page and use it to render a spreadsheet. The web part is also used when a spreadsheet is viewed full-screen in the browser by a user that does not have Excel 2007 installed.

Excel Calculation Services performs server-side calculation, caching, and session management for spreadsheets. In the case where you have many users accessing complicated spreadsheets, Excel Calculation Services can be load balanced for improved performance. Excel Calculation Services is designed from the ground up to support calculations on millions of rows by scaling out as necessary.

Excel Web Services provide a programmatic interface to Excel Services. Using these web services, you can develop custom applications that use the calculation engine. This allows your applications to offload resource-intensive calculations to the server.

Configuring Excel Services

Performing the initial configuration of Excel Services is straightforward and is accomplished from the home page of the Shared Services Administration site. Under the Excel Service Settings section, click the link titled Edit Excel Services Settings. On the Excel Services Settings page, you will find options for managing resources and security. In many cases, the out-of-the-box settings will work fine, and you should work with Excel Services before deciding to make changes here.

While the basic settings are fine to get started, there is one configuration step you must perform before you can use Excel Services: you must designate at least one *trusted file location*. Trusted file locations are SharePoint sites, file folders, or web sites where you want to enable Excel Services. Spreadsheets can only be processed by Excel Services if they come from a trusted location.

Follow these steps to create a trusted location:

1. Log in to VSMOSS as a SharePoint administrator.

2. Open the home page of the MOSS intranet site you created in Chapter 2 (e.g., `http://vsmoss/sites/intranet/Pages/Default.aspx`).

3. Click the Document Center tab.

4. On the Document Center page, select Create from the Site Actions drop-down menu.

5. On the Create page, click the Document Library list.

6. On the New page, type **Spreadsheets** into the Name field.

7. Select Microsoft Office Excel Spreadsheet from the Document Template list.

8. Click the Create button.

9. When the Spreadsheets library opens, copy the URL of the library (e.g., `http://vsmoss/sites/intranet/Docs/Spreadsheets`).

10. Select Start ➤ Administrative Tools ➤ SharePoint 3.0 Central Administration.

11. From the home page of the Central Administration site, click the Application Management tab.

12. On the Application Management tab, click the link titled Create or Configure This Farm's Shared Services.

13. On the Manage This Farm's Shared Services page, click the link to open the Shared Services Administration site.

14. On the Home page of the Shared Services Administration site, click the Trusted File Locations link.

15. On the Excel Services Trusted File Locations page, click Add Trusted File Location.

16. Paste the address of the Spreadsheets library into the Address field.

17. Click the OK button.

Once the trusted file location is defined, you can create spreadsheets for use with Excel Services. While Excel Services allows you to share spreadsheets, you cannot create a spreadsheet using Excel Services. Excel 2007 must still be used for authoring spreadsheets. After you create the spreadsheet in Excel 2007, you can then make it available through the trusted library.

Follow these steps to create and share a spreadsheet:

1. Log in to VSCLIENT and select Start ➤ All Programs ➤ Microsoft Office ➤ Microsoft Office Excel 2007.

2. Select File ➤ New by clicking the Office button in the upper left corner of Excel 2007.

3. In the New Workbook dialog, select a workbook template that has some data in it already. I used the Sales Report template from Office Online.

4. Download the template if necessary and click the Create button.

5. Once the spreadsheet is visible in Excel, select File ➤ Publish ➤ Excel Services by clicking the Office icon in the upper left corner of Excel 2007.

6. In the Save As dialog, paste the address of the trusted Spreadsheets library you created earlier along with an appropriate name for the spreadsheet (e.g., `http://vsmoss/ sites/intranet/Docs/Spreadsheets/Sales report.xlsx`).

7. Click the Save button.

After a spreadsheet is published to Excel Services, it will open in the browser automatically. You can also return to the document library and open the spreadsheet in either the web browser or Excel 2007 using the drop-down menu associated with the document. You'll also notice on that same menu an option to open a *snapshot* in Excel 2007. A snapshot is just a copy of the data in the spreadsheet without any of the underlying formulas. If you restrict a user's permission on the spreadsheet to just viewing the item, they will only be able to open a snapshot.

Although it is fairly simple to get started with Excel Services, not all of your existing spreadsheets will work. Excel Services does not, for example, support macros. Essentially, anything that cannot be rendered in HTML will have difficulty. The following lists some of the Excel features that are not supported by Excel Services:

- ActiveX controls

- Add-ins

- Clip art and word art

- Information Rights Management (IRM)

- Linked spreadsheets

- Query tables, SharePoint lists, web queries, and text queries

- Smart documents

- Smart Tags

- Visual Basic for Applications (VBA)

Using Parameters in Excel Services

Along with publishing spreadsheet data, you can also enable a level of interactivity through the use of *parameters*. Parameters allow you to specify cells within the published spreadsheet where a user can enter values. This allows a user to make use of the formulas in a spreadsheet without exposing it. This can be important when the formula is proprietary or you simply want to make a calculation available through the browser.

Follow these steps to create a spreadsheet that has parameters:

1. Log in to VSCLIENT and select Start ➤ All Programs ➤ Microsoft Office ➤ Microsoft Office Excel 2007.

2. Enter **Fahrenheit** in cell A1.

3. Enter **Celsius** in cell B1.

4. In cell B2 enter the formula =**(100/180)*(A2-32)**.

5. Right-click cell A2 and select Name a Range from the context menu.

6. In the New Name dialog, accept the name Fahrenheit by clicking the OK button.

7. Select File ➤ Publish ➤ Excel Services by clicking the Office icon in the upper left corner of Excel 2007.

8. In the Save As dialog, click the Excel Services Options button.

9. In the Show tab, select Sheets from the drop-down list.

10. Check the box next to Sheet1.

11. On the Parameters tab, click the Add button.

12. In the Add Parameters dialog, check the box next to the Fahrenheit parameter.

13. Click the OK button.

14. In the Excel Services Options dialog, click the OK button.

15. In the Save As dialog, paste the address of the trusted Spreadsheets library you created earlier along with an appropriate name for the spreadsheet (e.g., `http://vsmoss/sites/intranet/Docs/Spreadsheets/Temperature Calculator.xlsx`).

16. Click the Save button.

After you save the sheet, it will open in the browser. You should now be able to enter a new value for the Fahrenheit parameter and see the resulting Celsius calculation. Figure 4-7 shows a picture of the spreadsheet.

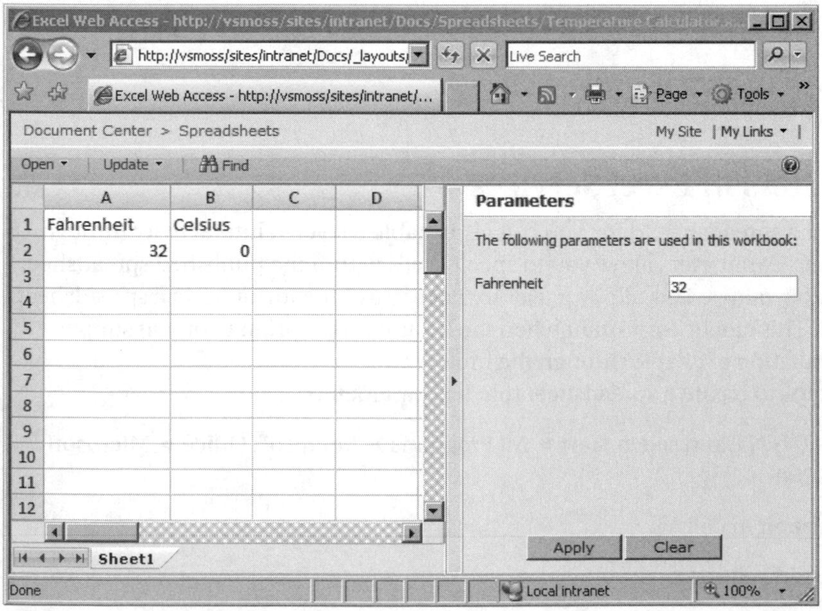

Figure 4-7. *Using parameters with Excel Services*

Using Data Connections

Excel spreadsheets are often used to view and manipulate data from external systems. This data can be imported into a spreadsheet through the use of a data connection. Data connections are not new to Excel 2007, but SharePoint now provides a better way to manage them in the form of a data connection library so that they are available across the enterprise.

A *data connection library* is similar to any library you create in SharePoint, but it is intended to hold Office Data Connection (ODC) files that define connections to external data sources. These ODC files are created in Excel and can then be reused in different spreadsheets or even in InfoPath forms, which I discuss in Chapter 6.

You can create and manage data connections by clicking the Data tab in Excel. To create a new data connection, click From Other Sources to start the data connection wizard. The wizard will walk you through the process of defining a connection, which you can then save as an ODC file to the data connection library.

Follow these steps to create a data connection:

1. Log in to VSCLIENT and open the home page of the intranet site you created in Chapter 2 (e.g., http://vsmoss/sites/intranet/Pages/Default.aspx).

2. Click the Document Center tab.

3. On the Document Center page, select Create from the Site Actions drop-down menu.

4. On the Create page, click the Data Connection Library link.

5. On the New page, type **Data Connections** in the Name field.

6. Select None from the Document Template list.

7. Click the Create button.

8. In the File Explorer, navigate to My Documents\My Data Sources.

9. Double-click the file named +NewSQLServerConenction.odc. This will start Excel 2007.

10. If you receive a warning that data connections are blocked, click the Enable button.

11. When the data connection wizard starts, enter **VSSQL\OFFICESERVERS** in the Server Name field.

12. Click the Next button.

13. On the Select Database and Table screen, select WSS_Content from the drop-down list.

14. Select the Webs table from the list and click the Next button.

15. Name the new data source **SharePointContent.odc** and click the Finish button.

16. Return to the data connections library.

17. Click the Upload button on the toolbar.

18. On the Upload page, click the Browse button.

19. In the Choose File dialog, navigate to My Document/My Data Sources, select the SharePoint Content.odc file, and click the Open button.

20. On the Upload page, click the OK button.

21. On the Data Connections page, click the Check In button.

22. Select Approve/Reject from the drop-down list associated with the new data connection file.

23. On the Approve page, select Approved and click the OK button. You can now close the Excel spreadsheet. You do not need to save it because you just used it to create the new data connection.

Using Excel Web Services

Once you have created and published a spreadsheet to Excel Services, you may access the cells and formulas through Excel Web Services. Excel Web Services is accessed through the server where the Shared Services reside. You can make use of the services in the development environment by setting a reference to them in Visual Studio at the following address: `http://vsmoss/_vti_bin/excelservice.asmx`.

Once you have a reference to Excel Web Services, you can call the `OpenWorkbook` method to access any spreadsheet published to Excel Services. This method takes the path to the workbook as an argument and returns a session identifier that you can use to perform operations on the workbook. The `GetCell` and `SetCell` methods allow you to read and write to the spreadsheet while the `Calculate` method calculates all the formulas in the workbook. Exercise 4.1 at the end of this chapter contains a complete exercise utilizing Excel Web Services.

Creating User-Defined Functions

Along with using Excel Services in your own applications, you can conversely provide assemblies that Excel Services can use. These custom assemblies are known as *user-defined functions (UDF)* and are called from an Excel spreadsheet in much the same way as a built-in function. The only difference is that UDFs are only available to workbooks that are published through Excel Services. Using UDFs, you can create custom functions that perform calculations and even access other data stores. The results are then returned to the spreadsheet for display in a cell.

UDFs are created as .NET assemblies that are decorated with special attributes. These attributes are found in the library `Microsoft.Excel.Server.Udf`. You can access this library from Visual Studio by setting a reference to the assembly `C:\Program Files\Common Files\Microsoft Shared\ web server extensions\12\ISAPI\Microsoft.Excel.Server.Udf.dll`. Once you have the reference set, you can add a directive for the library using the following code:

```
Using Microsoft.Office.excel.Server.Udf;
```

When you create a UDF, you typically define a function that accepts arguments and returns a value for display in a cell. This is elementary programming with the exception that you must decorate the class with the `UdfClass` attribute and the method with the `UdfMethod` attribute. Listing 4-2 shows a simple class definition with a function for rolling a six-sided die.

Listing 4-2. *A User-Defined Function*

```
using System;
using System.Collections.Generic;
using System.Text;

using Microsoft.Office.Excel.Server.Udf;

namespace UDFDice
{
    [UdfClass]
    public class Dice
    {
        [UdfMethod]
        public Int32 Roll()
        {
            Random r = new Random();
            return (Int32)((r.NextDouble() * 5) + 1);

        }
    }
}
```

Once you compile the assembly, you can save it to a file location or give it a strong name and place it in the Global Assembly Cache (GAC). Then you must make an entry in the user-defined functions list on the Shared Services Administration site that points to the new assembly. This is done by opening the list of user-defined assemblies using the link under the Excel Services Settings section. Once the new assembly is referenced in the list, you must specifically allow the use of user-defined functions from the trusted location page that you worked with earlier. When these configuration steps are complete, you can call the function from a spreadsheet cell. Just remember that the function will not work until you publish the spreadsheet to Excel Services.

Integrating the Business Data Catalog

The BDC is one of the Shared Services that allows you to integrate back-end line-of-business systems with SharePoint. Using the BDC, you can pull data from other databases or services and have that information appear in lists, web parts, search results, user profiles, and your own custom applications. Significantly, this integration requires no formal coding; instead, you describe the data source using an XML metadata file, and then the BDC performs all of the operations necessary to use the data in SharePoint. Figure 4-8 shows a conceptual drawing of the BDC architecture.

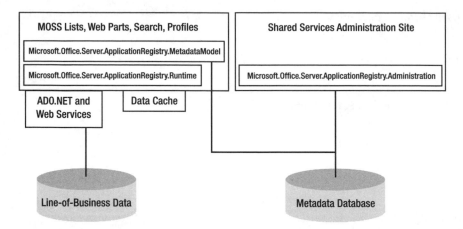

Figure 4-8. *The BDC architecture*

The heart of the BDC is the *metadata database*. The metadata database contains the XML used to describe the interface to a target data source. Creating this XML is the primary development task necessary to enable the BDC. Once created, the XML is uploaded using the Shared Services Administration site and is stored in the metadata database where it is available to every site in the SharePoint farm.

In order to provide a standard interface to the metadata, the BDC abstracts the metadata through a set of objects. These objects are part of the MOSS assembly `Microsoft.SharePoint.Portal.dll` and are contained in the libraries `Microsoft.Office.Server.ApplicationRegistry.MetadataModel` and `Microsoft.Office.Server.ApplicationRegistry.Runtime`. These libraries are the primary interface used by MOSS to access the target data and execute the commands defined by the metadata. Having this layer of abstraction is what permits integration of back-end systems without using any code, because the object libraries simply use ADO.NET or web services to perform all operations defined by the metadata.

The BDC infrastructure uses a data cache to hold metadata to minimize trips to the metadata database. This architecture improves BDC performance by making metadata available to SharePoint from the cache. Once per minute, the BDC infrastructure will check to see if any changes have occurred to the metadata and reload any objects that have changed.

Understanding Metadata

Although the BDC is advertised as a "no-code" solution, creating the required XML metadata by hand may leave you longing to write code instead. As of this writing, there are several publicly available tools under development that purport to create BDC metadata, but most of these tools are still buggy and lack the features necessary to create a wide variety of BDC solutions. Therefore, I will show you how to create a metadata file for the BDC from scratch.

Listing 4-3 shows a complete file that I will use throughout this discussion. The file is used to integrate the BDC with a simple SQL Server 2005 database containing a single table. The database is named CRM and contains a table called Names. The Names table is made up of a primary key integer and several text fields with information such as first name, last name, and address. This example should give you all the fundamental knowledge you need to get started with the BDC.

■Note When creating metadata, open a new XML file in Visual Studio and set the `SchemaLocation` property to `C:\Program Files\Microsoft Office Servers\12.0\Bin\BDCMetaData.xsd`. This will activate IntelliSense for the metadata schema and make it easier to create the file.

Listing 4-3. *A Complete BDC Metadata File*

```
<?xml version="1.0" encoding="utf-8" standalone="yes"?>

<LobSystem xmlns:xsi="http://www.w3.org/2001/XMLSchema-instance"
 xsi:schemaLocation=
 "http://schemas.microsoft.com/office/2006/03/BusinessDataCatalog BDCMetadata.xsd"
 SystemUtility=
 "Microsoft.Office.Server.ApplicationRegistry.SystemSpecific.Db.DbSystemUtility,
 Microsoft.SharePoint.Portal, Version=12.0.0.0, Culture=neutral,
 PublicKeyToken=71e9bce111e9429c"
 ConnectionManager=
 "Microsoft.Office.Server.ApplicationRegistry.SystemSpecific.Db.DbConnectionManager,
 Microsoft.SharePoint.Portal, Version=12.0.0.0, Culture=neutral,
 PublicKeyToken=71e9bce111e9429c"
 EntityInstance=
 "Microsoft.Office.Server.ApplicationRegistry.SystemSpecific.Db.DbEntityInstance,
 Microsoft.SharePoint.Portal, Version=12.0.0.0, Culture=neutral,
 PublicKeyToken=71e9bce111e9429c" Version="1.0.0.0" Name="MiniCRM"
 xmlns="http://schemas.microsoft.com/office/2006/03/BusinessDataCatalog">

    <Properties>
      <Property Name="WildcardCharacter" Type="System.String">%</Property>
    </Properties>

  <LobSystemInstances>
    <LobSystemInstance Name="ContactInfo">
      <Properties>
        <Property Name="AuthenticationMode"
          Type="System.String">PassThrough</Property>
        <Property Name="DatabaseAccessProvider"
          Type="System.String">SqlServer</Property>
        <Property Name="RdbConnection Data Source"
          Type="System.String">VSSQL</Property>
        <Property Name="RdbConnection Initial Catalog"
          Type="System.String">CRM</Property>
```

```
            <Property Name="RdbConnection Integrated Security"
               Type="System.String">SSPI</Property>
            <Property Name="NumberOfConnections" Type="System.Int32">-1</Property>
         </Properties>
      </LobSystemInstance>
   </LobSystemInstances>

   <Entities>
      <Entity EstimatedInstanceCount="10000" Name="Customer">

         <Identifiers>
            <Identifier Name="CustomerID" TypeName="System.Int32" />
         </Identifiers>

         <Methods>
            <Method Name="FindCustomers">

               <Properties>
                  <Property Name="Title" Type="System.String">LastName</Property>
                  <Property Name="RdbCommandType" Type="System.Data.CommandType,
                     System.Data, Version=2.0.0.0, Culture=neutral,
                     PublicKeyToken=b77a5c561934e089">Text</Property>
                  <Property Name="RdbCommandText" Type="System.String">
                     SELECT * FROM Names WHERE Lastname LIKE @LastName</Property>
               </Properties>

               <FilterDescriptors>
                  <FilterDescriptor Type="Wildcard" Name="LastName"/>
               </FilterDescriptors>

               <Parameters>
                  <Parameter Direction="In" Name="@LastName">
                     <TypeDescriptor TypeName="System.String, mscorlib, Version=2.0.0.0,
                        Culture=neutral, PublicKeyToken=b77a5c561934e089"
                        Name="LastName" AssociatedFilter="LastName" />
                  </Parameter>
                  <Parameter Direction="Return"
                     TypeReflectorTypeName=
   "Microsoft.Office.Server.ApplicationRegistry.SystemSpecific.Db.DbTypeReflector"
      Name="Customers">
                        <TypeDescriptor TypeName="System.Data.IDataReader, System.Data,
                           Version=2.0.0.0, Culture=neutral, PublicKeyToken=b77a5c561934e089"
                           IsCollection="true" Name="CustomerDataReader">
                           <TypeDescriptors>
                              <TypeDescriptor TypeName="System.Data.IDataRecord, System.Data,
                                 Version=2.0.0.0, Culture=neutral,
                                 PublicKeyToken=b77a5c561934e089" Name="CustomerDataRecord">
```

```xml
        <TypeDescriptors>
          <TypeDescriptor TypeName="System.Int32, mscorlib,
            Version=2.0.0.0, Culture=neutral,
            PublicKeyToken=b77a5c561934e089" Name="ID"
            IdentifierName="CustomerID" />
          <TypeDescriptor TypeName="System.String, mscorlib,
            Version=2.0.0.0, Culture=neutral,
            PublicKeyToken=b77a5c561934e089" Name="FirstName" />
          <TypeDescriptor TypeName="System.String, mscorlib,
            Version=2.0.0.0, Culture=neutral,
            PublicKeyToken=b77a5c561934e089" Name="LastName" />
          <TypeDescriptor TypeName="System.String, mscorlib,
            Version=2.0.0.0, Culture=neutral,
            PublicKeyToken=b77a5c561934e089" Name="Title" />
          <TypeDescriptor TypeName="System.String, mscorlib,
            Version=2.0.0.0, Culture=neutral,
            PublicKeyToken=b77a5c561934e089" Name="Company" />
          <TypeDescriptor TypeName="System.String, mscorlib,
            Version=2.0.0.0, Culture=neutral,
            PublicKeyToken=b77a5c561934e089" Name="Address1" />
          <TypeDescriptor TypeName="System.String, mscorlib,
             Version=2.0.0.0, Culture=neutral,
             PublicKeyToken=b77a5c561934e089" Name="Address2" />
          <TypeDescriptor TypeName="System.String, mscorlib,
            Version=2.0.0.0, Culture=neutral,
            PublicKeyToken=b77a5c561934e089" Name="City" />
          <TypeDescriptor TypeName="System.String, mscorlib,
            Version=2.0.0.0, Culture=neutral,
            PublicKeyToken=b77a5c561934e089" Name="State" />
          <TypeDescriptor TypeName="System.String, mscorlib,
            Version=2.0.0.0, Culture=neutral,
            PublicKeyToken=b77a5c561934e089" Name="Zip" />
          <TypeDescriptor TypeName="System.String, mscorlib,
            Version=2.0.0.0, Culture=neutral,
            PublicKeyToken=b77a5c561934e089" Name="Phone" />
          <TypeDescriptor TypeName="System.String, mscorlib,
            Version=2.0.0.0, Culture=neutral,
            PublicKeyToken=b77a5c561934e089" Name="Fax" />
          <TypeDescriptor TypeName="System.String, mscorlib,
            Version=2.0.0.0, Culture=neutral,
            PublicKeyToken=b77a5c561934e089" Name="EMail" />
        </TypeDescriptors>
      </TypeDescriptor>
    </TypeDescriptors>
  </TypeDescriptor>
  </Parameter>
</Parameters>
```

```xml
        <MethodInstances>
          <MethodInstance Type="Finder" ReturnParameterName="Customers"
            ReturnTypeDescriptorName="CustomerDataReader"
            ReturnTypeDescriptorLevel="0" Name="FindCustomersInstance" />
        </MethodInstances>
      </Method>

      <Method Name="FindCustomer">

        <Properties>
          <Property Name="Title" Type="System.String">ID</Property>
          <Property Name="RdbCommandType" Type="System.Data.CommandType,
            System.Data, Version=2.0.0.0, Culture=neutral,
            PublicKeyToken=b77a5c561934e089">Text</Property>
          <Property Name="RdbCommandText" Type="System.String">
            SELECT * FROM Names WHERE ID=@ID</Property>
        </Properties>

        <FilterDescriptors>
          <FilterDescriptor Type="Comparison" Name="ID"/>
        </FilterDescriptors>

        <Parameters>
          <Parameter Direction="In" Name="@ID">
            <TypeDescriptor TypeName="System.Int32, mscorlib, Version=2.0.0.0,
              Culture=neutral, PublicKeyToken=b77a5c561934e089"
              Name="ID" AssociatedFilter="ID" IdentifierName="CustomerID" />
          </Parameter>
          <Parameter Direction="Return"
            TypeReflectorTypeName=
"Microsoft.Office.Server.ApplicationRegistry.SystemSpecific.Db.DbTypeReflector"
Name="Customer">
            <TypeDescriptor TypeName="System.Data.IDataReader, System.Data,
            Version=2.0.0.0, Culture=neutral, PublicKeyToken=b77a5c561934e089"
            IsCollection="true" Name="CustomerDataReader">
              <TypeDescriptors>
                <TypeDescriptor TypeName="System.Data.IDataRecord, System.Data,
                  Version=2.0.0.0, Culture=neutral,
                  PublicKeyToken=b77a5c561934e089" Name="CustomerDataRecord">
                  <TypeDescriptors>
                    <TypeDescriptor TypeName="System.Int32, mscorlib,
                      Version=2.0.0.0, Culture=neutral,
                      PublicKeyToken=b77a5c561934e089" Name="ID"
                      IdentifierName="CustomerID" />
                    <TypeDescriptor TypeName="System.String, mscorlib,
                    Version=2.0.0.0, Culture=neutral,
                    PublicKeyToken=b77a5c561934e089" Name="FirstName" />
```

```
                    <TypeDescriptor TypeName="System.String, mscorlib,
                      Version=2.0.0.0, Culture=neutral,
                      PublicKeyToken=b77a5c561934e089" Name="LastName" />
                    <TypeDescriptor TypeName="System.String, mscorlib,
                      Version=2.0.0.0, Culture=neutral,
                      PublicKeyToken=b77a5c561934e089" Name="Title" />
                    <TypeDescriptor TypeName="System.String, mscorlib,
                      Version=2.0.0.0, Culture=neutral,
                      PublicKeyToken=b77a5c561934e089" Name="Company" />
                    <TypeDescriptor TypeName="System.String, mscorlib,
                      Version=2.0.0.0, Culture=neutral,
                      PublicKeyToken=b77a5c561934e089" Name="Address1" />
                    <TypeDescriptor TypeName="System.String, mscorlib,
                      Version=2.0.0.0, Culture=neutral,
                      PublicKeyToken=b77a5c561934e089" Name="Address2" />
                    <TypeDescriptor TypeName="System.String, mscorlib,
                      Version=2.0.0.0, Culture=neutral,
                      PublicKeyToken=b77a5c561934e089" Name="City" />
                    <TypeDescriptor TypeName="System.String, mscorlib,
                      Version=2.0.0.0, Culture=neutral,
                        PublicKeyToken=b77a5c561934e089" Name="State" />
                    <TypeDescriptor TypeName="System.String, mscorlib,
                      Version=2.0.0.0, Culture=neutral,
                        PublicKeyToken=b77a5c561934e089" Name="Zip" />
                    <TypeDescriptor TypeName="System.String, mscorlib,
                      Version=2.0.0.0, Culture=neutral,
                      PublicKeyToken=b77a5c561934e089" Name="Phone" />
                    <TypeDescriptor TypeName="System.String, mscorlib,
                      Version=2.0.0.0, Culture=neutral,
                      PublicKeyToken=b77a5c561934e089" Name="Fax" />
                    <TypeDescriptor TypeName="System.String, mscorlib,
                      Version=2.0.0.0, Culture=neutral,
                      PublicKeyToken=b77a5c561934e089" Name="EMail" />
                  </TypeDescriptors>
                </TypeDescriptor>
              </TypeDescriptors>
            </TypeDescriptor>
          </Parameter>
        </Parameters>

        <MethodInstances>
          <MethodInstance Type="SpecificFinder" ReturnParameterName="Customer"
            ReturnTypeDescriptorName="CustomerDataReader"
            ReturnTypeDescriptorLevel="0" Name="FindCustomerInstance" />
        </MethodInstances>
```

```
            </Method>
          </Methods>
        </Entity>
      </Entities>
    </LobSystem>
```

Authoring the LobSystem Element

The LobSystem element describes the external data source you want to access with the BDC. It is the outermost element in the file. Most of the attributes associated with this element are boilerplate, but the Name and Version attributes should be set by you to give the system a unique name and track the metadata version you are using. Listing 4-4 shows the LobSystem attribute with the extraneous parts removed and the key attributes bolded.

Listing 4-4. *The LobSystem Element*

```
<LobSystem xmlns:xsi=...
 xsi:schemaLocation=...
SystemUtility=...
ConnectionManager=...
EntityInstance=...Version="1.0.0.0" Name="MiniCRM"
```

The LobSystem attribute has several child elements defined in the schema, but we are most interested in the LobSystemInstances and the Properties elements. The LobSystemInstances element is used to contain the connection information for the data source, while the Properties element in this example simply defines the wildcard character that BDC should use when searching for partial strings. Since this data source is a SQL Server database, I define the wildcard to be a percent sign. Listing 4-5 shows how the wildcard character is defined.

Listing 4-5. *The Properties Element*

```
<Properties>
  <Property Name="WildcardCharacter" Type="System.String">%</Property>
</Properties>
```

Authoring the LobSystemInstance Element

The LobSystemInstance element is a child of the LobSystemInstances element and is used primarily to provide connection information to BDC. BDC may connect to either a database or a web service. Using Property elements, you can define what data source BDC should connect with and how to make the connection. Listing 4-6 shows the elements necessary to connect to a SQL Server database. Each of these elements should be customized for your specific database.

Listing 4-6. *Using Property Elements to Connect to a Data Source*

```
<LobSystemInstances>
  <LobSystemInstance Name="ContactInfo">
    <Properties>
      <Property Name="AuthenticationMode"
        Type="System.String">PassThrough</Property>
      <Property Name="DatabaseAccessProvider"
        Type="System.String">SqlServer</Property>
      <Property Name="RdbConnection Data Source"
        Type="System.String">VSSQL</Property>
      <Property Name="RdbConnection Initial Catalog"
        Type="System.String">CRM</Property>
      <Property Name="RdbConnection Integrated Security"
        Type="System.String">SSPI</Property>
      <Property Name="NumberOfConnections" Type="System.Int32">-1</Property>
    </Properties>
  </LobSystemInstance>
</LobSystemInstances>
```

The `AuthenticationMode` property is used to specify what credentials the BDC should use when accessing the data source. Setting this value to `PassThrough` uses the application pool identity under which the BDC is running, unless you are using Kerberos authentication, in which case the BDC uses the identity of the SharePoint user. Setting this value to `RevertToSelf` forces the BDC to use the credentials from the application pool, but this can also cause problems later when you try to integrate the BDC with search, because it may not have sufficient privileges to crawl BDC data. Setting this value to `WindowsCredentials` causes the BDC to use credentials from the Single Sign-On (SSO) system. I discuss SSO in Chapter 11. Setting this value to `Credentials` also uses SSO, but for access to a web service.

The next few properties are specific to database access and are used to build a connection string to the target data. The `DatabaseAccessProvider` property is used to specify what provider to use with the target data source. You can set this property to `SqlServer`, `OleDb`, `Oracle`, or `Odbc`. The `RdbConnection Data Source` property is used to specify the name of the server where the database is located, while the `RdbConnection Initial Catalog` property is used to specify the name of the database within the server. The `RdbConnection Integrated Security` property specifies to use Windows authentication.

Authoring Entities

Perhaps the most arduous part of creating BDC metadata is authoring *entities*. Entities represent business objects for which you want to display information. Customers, orders, parts, and suppliers are all examples of business objects that you might define for the BDC. In my example, I have defined a single entity named Customer. When you define an entity, you must provide explicit detail about the database fields and queries you want the BDC to execute. This is painstaking work that begins by defining the entity name and a unique identifier. Listing 4-7 shows how the entity definition is started.

Listing 4-7. *Using an Entity Element to Define a Business Object*

```
<Entities>
  <Entity EstimatedInstanceCount="10000" Name="Customer">
    <Identifiers>
      <Identifier Name="CustomerID" TypeName="System.Int32" />
    </Identifiers>
```

The Entity element is used to specify the name of the entity and approximately how many entities exist in the data source. The Name attribute should be unique across entities. The BDC uses the EstimatedInstanceCount attribute to make decisions about how to display entity information in SharePoint.

The Identifier element is used to specify a unique identifier for the entity. This is essentially a primary key and will be associated later with the primary key field from the database. The BDC uses this field when presenting information to automatically display detailed information for an entity through special BDC web parts.

Authoring Methods

Method elements are used by the BDC to define the SQL queries that should be executed to return data from the database. In most cases, you will need to define a query that returns groups of records based on a LIKE clause as well as a query that returns exact records based on a primary key value. These two queries help set up the basic BDC functionality that allows you to return a list of entities and then click to see the detail for a specific entity. Listing 4-8 shows two fragments that define methods. The first defines a query that will return multiple customers, while the second returns a specific customer based on a primary key.

Listing 4-8. *Using Method Elements to Define Queries*

```
<Methods>
  <Method Name="FindCustomers">
    <Properties>
      <Property Name="Title" Type="System.String">LastName</Property>
      <Property Name="RdbCommandType...>Text</Property>
      <Property Name="RdbCommandText...>
        SELECT * FROM Names WHERE Lastname LIKE @LastName
      </Property>
    </Properties>
    <FilterDescriptors>
      <FilterDescriptor Type="Wildcard" Name="LastName"/>
    </FilterDescriptors>

  <Method Name="FindCustomer">
    <Properties>
      <Property Name="Title" Type="System.String">ID</Property>
      <Property Name=" RdbCommandType...>Text</Property>
      <Property Name=" RdbCommandText...>
        SELECT * FROM Names WHERE ID=@ID</Property>
```

```
    </Properties>
    <FilterDescriptors>
      <FilterDescriptor Type="Comparison" Name="ID"/>
    </FilterDescriptors>
```

The Name attribute of the Method element should be unique and representative of the query to run. In my example, the first method named FindCustomers is used to return a set of customers based on a wildcard search. The second method returns a specific customer based on a primary key. The Title property is used to specify the field that should be used by default to represent the entity in some BDC displays. The RdbCommandText property is used to define the query to run. Notice the difference between the SQL statements in each method and how they return either a set of records or a specific record. This functionality is further defined by the FilterDescriptor element, which is set to either Wildcard or Comparison and then given a name so it can be referenced later by query parameters.

Authoring Parameters

Parameter elements are used to define the values that are sent into the query and the fields that are returned. Both of the methods I define in the metadata have input and output parameters. The input parameter is either a partial last name to use in a wildcard search or an integer value used to return an exact customer based on the primary key. The return values, on the other hand, are identical for both methods because I always want the same fields returned. Listing 4-9 shows the two input parameters and the common output parameters for the methods.

Listing 4-9. *Using Parameter Elements*

```
<Parameters>
  <Parameter Direction="In" Name="@ID">
    <TypeDescriptor TypeName=...
     Name="ID" AssociatedFilter="ID"
     IdentifierName="CustomerID" />
  </Parameter>

<Parameters>
  <Parameter Direction="In" Name="@LastName">
    <TypeDescriptor TypeName=...
      Name="LastName"
      AssociatedFilter="LastName" />
  </Parameter>

  <Parameter Direction="Return"
    TypeReflectorTypeName=... Name="Customer">
    <TypeDescriptor TypeName=... IsCollection="true" Name="CustomerDataReader">
      <TypeDescriptors>
        <TypeDescriptor TypeName... Name="CustomerDataRecord">
          <TypeDescriptors>
            <TypeDescriptor TypeName=... Name="ID" IdentifierName="CustomerID" />
```

```
            <TypeDescriptor TypeName=... Name="FirstName" />
            <TypeDescriptor TypeName=... Name="LastName" />
            <TypeDescriptor TypeName=... Name="Title" />
            <TypeDescriptor TypeName=... Name="Company" />
            <TypeDescriptor TypeName=... Name="Address1" />
            <TypeDescriptor TypeName=... Name="Address2" />
            <TypeDescriptor TypeName=... Name="City" />
            <TypeDescriptor TypeName=... Name="State" />
            <TypeDescriptor TypeName=... Name="Zip" />
            <TypeDescriptor TypeName=... Name="Phone" />
            <TypeDescriptor TypeName=... Name="Fax" />
            <TypeDescriptor TypeName=... Name="EMail" />
          </TypeDescriptors>
        </TypeDescriptor>
      </TypeDescriptors>
    </TypeDescriptor>
  </Parameter>
</Parameters>
```

Notice that each of the input parameters in the listing references the name of the `FilterDescriptor` defined earlier. This reference is how the BDC knows whether to apply the wildcard to the parameter before executing the query. Also notice that when the primary key field is used, it references the identifier created earlier. This tells the BDC that the parameter is a unique identifier. The return parameters are simply the data fields that will be returned from the query.

Uploading the Application Definition

Once the metadata is complete, it may be uploaded to the BDC as a new application definition. Application definitions are uploaded from the Shared Services Administration site by clicking the Add Application link under the Business Data Catalog section. When the metadata is uploaded, the BDC will check it for errors and notify you if the XML is not correct. Once the application is uploaded, you may choose to view the definition where you should see any entities you have defined. Figure 4-9 shows the example application in Shared Services.

Tip The example used here is targeted at SQL 2005 databases. If you wish to connect to web services or other types of databases, you should reference the examples in the MOSS SDK. For the most part, it is only a matter of using different elements in the application definition.

After viewing the application, you should click each entity you have defined. Clicking the entity will bring you to a page that shows the *field names* that will be returned, the *filters* you have available, and any defined *actions*. Field names will be used to create lists and views in SharePoint. Filters represent available wildcard search methods you defined. Actions are used to connect an item from a list to a detail view. Figure 4-10 shows the example Customer entity in Shared Services.

Figure 4-9. *Viewing an application definition*

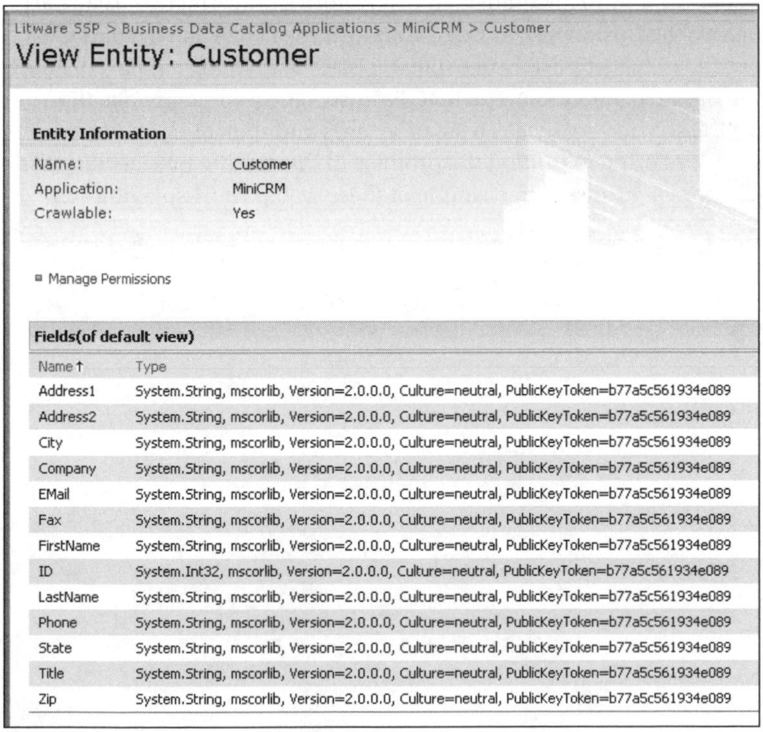

Figure 4-10. *Viewing an entity*

For each entity you define, you should configure the available actions. By default, the BDC defines an action called View Profile. Clicking this action will allow you to define what happens when it is invoked by an end user. On the Edit Action page, you can assign a parameter to use when displaying details about the entity. This is always the unique identifier you define in the metadata. In this example, I set the parameter to the ID field of the customer. Figure 4-11 shows the parameter setting in Shared Services.

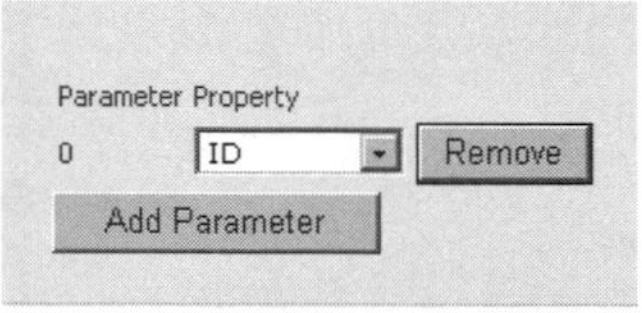

Figure 4-11. *Setting the action parameter*

Using BDC Information

Once the metadata is uploaded and configured, you are ready to use it in MOSS. MOSS ships with several web parts that know how to integrate with BDC information. The two basic parts are the Business Data List and the Business Data Item. The Business Data List web part displays the results of wildcard searches in a list form while the BDC Data Item web part displays an individual record based on the primary key. The BDC list also allows you to invoke the actions you define in the BDC so you can display a list of records and then click on one to display the details. These web parts bring to fruition the promise of integrating line-of-business systems with SharePoint. Figure 4-12 shows an example of these web parts displaying customer data.

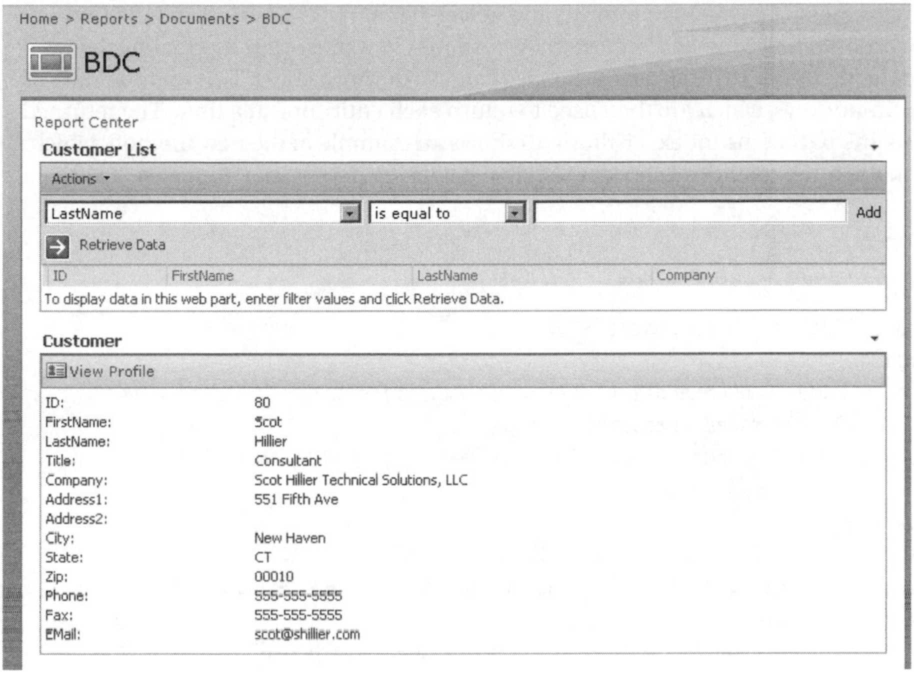

Home > Reports > Documents > BDC

BDC

Report Center

Customer List   ▾

Actions ▾

| LastName | ▾ | is equal to | ▾ | | Add |

→ Retrieve Data

ID	FirstName	LastName	Company

To display data in this web part, enter filter values and click Retrieve Data.

Customer   ▾

View Profile

ID:	80
FirstName:	Scot
LastName:	Hillier
Title:	Consultant
Company:	Scot Hillier Technical Solutions, LLC
Address1:	551 Fifth Ave
Address2:	
City:	New Haven
State:	CT
Zip:	00010
Phone:	555-555-5555
Fax:	555-555-5555
EMail:	scot@shillier.com

Figure 4-12. *Displaying BDC data with web parts*

Follow these steps to use the Business Data List web part:

1. Open the home page of the MOSS intranet site you created in Chapter 2 (e.g., http://vsmoss/sites/intranet/Pages/Default.aspx).

2. Select Edit Page from the Site Actions menu.

3. When the page enters edit mode, click the Add a Web Part link for any zone.

4. In the Add Web Parts dialog, check the box for the Business Data List and click the Add button.

5. When the Business Data List is added to the page, click the link titled Open the Tool Pane.

6. Click the Browser button next to the Type field at the top of the Tool Pane.

7. In the Business Data Type Picker dialog, select the ContactInfo entry and click the OK button.

8. Click the OK button in the tool pane.

9. In the Business Data List web part, click the Edit View link.

10. Select the fields you want to display and select the Title option for the field that represents the primary key for the data. This will allow you to create a detail action for the items in the list.

11. Click the OK button.

In addition to displaying BDC information in web parts, you can also search BDC information. In order to make the BDC information available, you must start by creating a new method in the metadata that the Search Service can use during a crawl. This method returns all of the primary keys, which are then used to return each entity one at a time. The returned entities become part of the index. Listing 4-10 shows an example of the new method, which is similar to the other methods I show in Listing 4-8. I have removed parts to make it easier to read.

Listing 4-10. *A Method to Support Indexing BDC Data*

```
<Method Name="CustomerIDErumerator">
  <Properties>
    <Property Name="RdbCommandText" Type="System.String">
      SELECT ID FROM Names</Property>
    <Property Name="RdbCommandType" Type="System.String">Text</Property>
  </Properties>
  <Parameters>
    <Parameter Name="CustomerIDs" Direction="Return">
      <TypeDescriptor TypeName=... IsCollection="true" Name="CustomerDataReader">
        <TypeDescriptors>
          <TypeDescriptor TypeName=... Name="CustomerDataRecord">
            <TypeDescriptors>
              <TypeDescriptor TypeName="System.Int32"
                IdentifierName="CustomerID" Name="ID">
                <LocalizedDisplayNames>
                  <LocalizedDisplayName LCID="1033">ID</LocalizedDisplayName>
                </LocalizedDisplayNames>
              </TypeDescriptor>
            </TypeDescriptors>
          </TypeDescriptor>
        </TypeDescriptors>
      </TypeDescriptor>
    </Parameter>
  </Parameters>
  <MethodInstances>
    <MethodInstance Name="CustomerIDEnumeratorInstance"
      Type="IdEnumerator" ReturnParameterName="CustomerIDs" />
  </MethodInstances>
</Method>
```

Once the metadata is updated, you can proceed to create a new search content source and scope based on the metadata as I described in the section "Configuring Search." Additionally, you must be sure to give the account that will crawl the BDC permission to access the data source. This can be done through the BDC Permissions link in Shared Services. If you have trouble with this, or any part of BDC configuration, be sure to look at the event log. The files often have good descriptions of BDC errors.

Exercise 4.1. Custom Solutions with Excel Services

Excel Services allows you to publish spreadsheets that can be viewed in a browser. Once the spreadsheet is published, however, you can also access it programmatically through web services. In this exercise, you will create a mileage calculator spreadsheet to determine the reimbursement for mileage traveled in a personal car. After creating the sheet, you will make a Windows application that uses Excel Services to calculate the reimbursement on the server and return the value to the application.

Trusting a Document Library

Before you can publish a spreadsheet to Excel Services, you must define trusted locations for documents. Trusted locations can come from SharePoint sites, other web sites, or file folders. In this exercise, you will create a document library to contain all of the published calculators for the company.

Follow these steps to create the trusted library:

1. Log in to VSMOSS as a SharePoint administrator.

2. Open the home page of the MOSS intranet site you created in Chapter 2 (e.g., `http://vsmoss/sites/intranet/Pages/Default.aspx`).

3. Click the Document Center tab.

4. On the Document Center page, select Create from the Site Actions drop-down menu.

5. On the Create page, click the Document Library list.

6. On the New page, type **Expense Calculators** into the Name field.

7. Select Microsoft Office Excel Spreadsheet from the Document Template list.

8. Click the Create button.

9. When the Expense Calculators library opens, copy the URL of the library (e.g., `http://vsmoss/sites/intranet/Docs/Expense%20Calculators`).

10. Select Start ➤ Administrative Tools ➤ SharePoint 3.0 Central Administration.

11. From the home page of the Central Administration site, click the Application Management tab.

12. On the Application Management tab, click the link titled Create or Configure This Farm's Shared Services.

13. On the Manage This Farm's Shared Services page, click the link to open the Shared Services Administration site.

14. On the home page of the Shared Services Administration site, click the Trusted File Locations link.

15. On the Excel Services Trusted File Locations page, click Add Trusted File Location.

16. Paste the address of the Expense Calculators library into the Address field.

17. Click the OK button.

Creating the Mileage Calculator Spreadsheet

Once the trusted library is defined, you can create spreadsheets and publish them to Excel Services. In this section you will create a simple spreadsheet that allows you to define a reimbursement rate for each mile and a place to enter miles traveled. When you publish the spreadsheet, you will define a parameter so that the spreadsheet can be used directly from the browser to calculate reimbursements if desired.

Follow these steps to create and publish the spreadsheet:

1. Start Excel 2007.

2. Enter **Mileage** in cell A1.

3. Enter **Rate** in cell B1.

4. Enter **Reimbursement** in cell C1.

5. Enter **0** in cell A2.

6. Enter **.445** in cell B2.

7. In cell C2 enter the formula **=(A2*B2)**.

8. Right-click cell A2 and select Name a Range from the context menu.

9. In the New Name dialog, accept the name Mileage by clicking the OK button.

10. Select File ➤ Publish ➤ Excel Services by clicking the Office icon in the upper left corner of Excel 2007.

11. In the Save As dialog, click the Excel Services Options button.

12. In the Show tab, select Sheets from the drop-down list.

13. Check the box next to Sheet1.

14. On the Parameters tab, click the Add button.

15. In the Add Parameters dialog, check the box next to the Mileage parameter.

16. Click the OK button.

17. In the Excel Services Options dialog, click the OK button.

18. In the Save As dialog, paste the address of the trusted Spreadsheets library you created earlier along with an appropriate name for the spreadsheet (e.g., `http://vsmoss/ sites/intranet/Docs/Expense%20Calculators /Mileage Calculator.xlsx`).

19. Click the Save button.

Creating the New Project

In this section, you will create a simple application that works with Excel Services. Although the published spreadsheet may be used directly, you can also call it from a web service and take advantage of the server-side calculation engine of Excel Services. This allows you to utilize complex or proprietary calculations in applications.

For this example, you will create a Windows application. The application will allow you to enter a value for mileage traveled and it will return the current reimbursement rate and the value of the reimbursement. Because the calculation is all done on the server, the reimbursement rate may be changed at any time and the application does not have to be modified.

Follow these steps to create the application:

1. Start Visual Studio 2005.

2. In Visual Studio 2005, select File ➤ New ➤ Project from the main menu.

3. In the New Project dialog, click the Visual C# node in the Project Types list.

4. In the Templates list, select Windows Application.

5. Type **MileageCalculator** in the Name field.

6. Click the OK button.

7. When the new project is created, drop a NumericUpDown control, two Label controls, and a Button control onto Form1.

8. Name the new controls `mileage`, `rate`, `reimbursement`, and `submit`, respectively.

9. Change the Text property of the button to **Calculate**. Your form should now appear as shown in Figure 4-13.

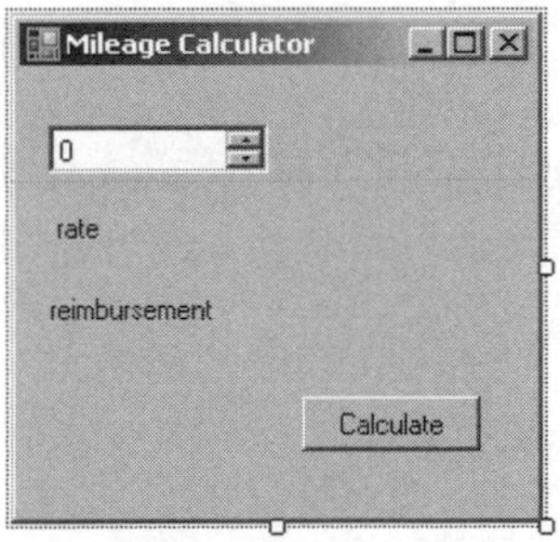

Figure 4-13. *The Windows form user interface*

Coding the Application

Calling a spreadsheet in Excel Services is done through a web services interface that allows you to read and write cells as well as calculate all the formulas in the sheet. After setting a reference to the web service, you will have access to several properties and methods for working with the spreadsheet. In this exercise, all of the code will be run when a button is clicked.

Follow these steps to code the application:

1. In Visual Studio 2005, select Project ➤ Add Web Reference.

2. In the Add Web Reference dialog, type **http://vsmoss/_vti_bin/excelservice.asmx** in the URL field.

3. Click the Go button.

4. After the web service is successfully located, type **ExcelWebServices** in the Web Reference Name field.

5. Click the Add Reference button.

6. Select Form1 in the Solution Explorer and then click the View Code button.

7. Add the following statements to reference the required namespaces:

```
using MileageCalculator.ExcelWebServices;
using System.Web.Services.Protocols;
```

8. Add the code from Listing 4-11 to pass the mileage to the spreadsheet, calculate the reimbursement, and return the value.

Listing 4-11. *Reimbursement Calculator*

```
private void submit_Click(object sender, EventArgs e)
{
    ExcelService calcSheet = new ExcelService();
    Status[] outStatus;
    RangeCoordinates rangeCoordinates = new RangeCoordinates();
    string sheetName = "Sheet1";
    string targetWorkbookPath =

"http://win2k3template/Docs/Expense%20Calculators/Mileage%20Calculator.xlsx";
    calcSheet.Credentials = System.Net.CredentialCache.DefaultCredentials;

    try
    {
        string id = calcSheet.OpenWorkbook(
          targetWorkbookPath, "en-US", "en-US", out outStatus);

        object rateCell = calcSheet.GetCell(
          id, sheetName, 1, 1, true, out outStatus);
        calcSheet.SetCell(id, sheetName, 1, 0, mileage.Value);
        calcSheet.Calculate(id, sheetName, rangeCoordinates);
        object reimbursementCell = calcSheet.GetCell(
          id, sheetName, 1, 2, true, out outStatus);
```

```
            rate.Text = rateCell.ToString();
            reimbursement.Text = reimbursementCell.ToString();

            calcSheet.CloseWorkbook(id);
        }
        catch (Exception x)
        {
            MessageBox.Show(x.Message);
        }

    }
```

Once you have the application coded, you should be able to run it directly from Visual Studio. When the form appears, enter a value for the mileage traveled and click the button. The application should return the current reimbursement rate and the total reimbursement for the travel.

CHAPTER 5

■■■

SharePoint Content Development and Management

Although the default installation of WSS and MOSS are acceptable for general-purpose usage, you will undoubtedly want to customize the appearance and behavior of sites to match your organization's branding and expectations. SharePoint supports customizing sites in several different ways. You can make many changes to the look and feel of a site directly through the site administration pages, or using the SharePoint Designer for more extensive control. Additionally, MOSS supports a publishing feature that enables professional content management capabilities for managing page creation, approval, and deployment. In this chapter, I cover all of the various ways to change the appearance, behavior, and content of sites.

Understanding Site Collection Templates

Developing content in SharePoint begins by creating a site collection geared toward your needs. As you saw in Chapter 2, when you create a site collection, you must choose a template upon which to base the new site collection. The templates that appear on the Create Site Collection page are different depending on whether you are using MOSS or WSS. Generally, you'll find that WSS ships with collaboration templates designed to support teams. MOSS, on the other hand, ships with templates for use in a wide variety of applications within an organization. The MOSS templates include not only team collaboration templates, but also enterprise templates for creating document management systems, records management systems, and Internet sites. Table 5-1 lists all of the available templates in both WSS and MOSS.

Table 5-1. *Site Collection Templates*

Name	Category	MOSS/WSS	Description
Blank Site	Collaboration	MOSS/WSS	A blank site with a single page
Blog	Collaboration	MOSS/WSS	A site for creating a web log that allows posts and comments
Document Workspace	Collaboration	MOSS/WSS	A site for creating a document with input from multiple people
Team Site	Collaboration	MOSS/WSS	A general collaboration site for multiple people to work on a project

Continued

Table 5-1. *Continued*

Name	Category	MOSS/WSS	Description
Wiki Site	Collaboration	MOSS/WSS	A site that allows users to share knowledge by editing web pages directly
Basic Meeting Workspace	Meetings	MOSS/WSS	A site with the fundamental tools required to plan, organize, and execute a meeting
Blank Meeting Workspace	Meetings	MOSS/WSS	A blank meeting site that can be customized
Decision Meeting Workspace	Meetings	MOSS/WSS	A site for supporting and tracking decisions made during a meeting
Multipage Meeting Workspace	Meetings	MOSS/WSS	A site with multiple pages for organizing more complex meetings
Social Meeting Workspace	Meetings	MOSS/WSS	A site to support the planning and execution of social events
Document Center	Enterprise	MOSS only	A site that functions like a centralized document management system
Records Center	Enterprise	MOSS only	A site that can be used as a records management repository
Report Center	Enterprise	MOSS only	A site for creating and delivering dashboards, scorecards, and reports
Search Center	Enterprise	MOSS only	A site for creating an enterprise search capability
Search Center with Tabs	Enterprise	MOSS only	A site for creating an enterprise search capability that can be customized to add new sources
Site Directory	Enterprise	MOSS only	A site that can be used to list and categorize key sites
My Site Host	Enterprise	MOSS only	A template for hosting all of the personal sites in an organization
Collaboration Portal	Publishing	MOSS only	A site for creating a corporate intranet
Publishing Portal	Publishing	MOSS only	A template for creating an Internet site or a corporate portal with complete content management facilities

In this chapter, I cover content development for both WSS and MOSS sites. Therefore, you'll need to create a new web application where you can work on content. Later, you'll create a more complex Internet site, but for now you'll start with a plain blank site.

Follow these steps to create a blank site:

1. Log in to VSMOSS or VSWSS as a SharePoint administrator.

2. Select Start ➤ Administrative Tools ➤ SharePoint 3.0 Central Administration.

3. On the Application Management tab, under the SharePoint Web Application Management section, click the link titled Create or Extend a Web Application.

4. On the Create or Extend a Web Application page, click the link titled Create a New Web Application.

5. On the Create a New Web Application page, select the option to Create a New IIS Web Site.

6. In the Description field, type **Content**.

7. In the Application Pool section, select Create a New Application Pool.

8. Enter **Content_Pool** as the pool name.

9. Select the Configurable option for the application pool security account.

10. In the User Name field, enter **DOMAIN\SPContentPool**.

11. In the Password field, enter the account password.

12. In the Reset Internet Information Services section, select the option to Restart IIS Automatically.

13. Click the OK button.

14. On the Application Created page, click the link titled Create Site Collection.

15. On the Create Site Collection page, enter **Blank Site** in the Title field.

16. Under the Primary Site Collection Administrator section, enter **DOMAIN\Administrator** in the User Name field.

17. Under the Template Selection section, click the Collaboration tab, and then select the Blank Site.

18. Click the OK button to create the new site collection. When the site collection is created, open it in a separate copy of the browser.

Adding and Editing Pages

After you create a new site in WSS or MOSS, you will undoubtedly want to start adding pages and content to the site. While some of the MOSS templates have sophisticated publishing tools that I cover in the section titled "Using the Publishing Feature," the basic templates, such as Team Site and Blank Site, use the Create page to add new pages. You can reach the Create page by selecting Create from the Site Actions menu.

On the Create page, you have links that allow you to create either a Basic Page or a Web Part Page. A *Basic Page* is a page that contains text and graphics, while a *Web Part Page* contains special placeholders, called *web part zones*, where you can add web parts. Regardless of which type of page you create, SharePoint will ask you to select a document library where the page will be stored. In most cases, you will not have a suitable document library available, so I recommend that you create two of them before adding new pages.

Follow these steps to create libraries:

1. From the home page of the blank site you created earlier, select Create from the Site Actions menu.

2. On the Create page, click the Document Library link.

3. On the New page, enter **Basic Pages** in the Name field.

4. Under the option Display This Document Library on the Quick Launch Bar, select No.

5. Select Basic Page from the Document Template list.

6. Click the Create button.

7. When the new library is complete, select Create from the Site Actions menu.

8. On the Create page, click the Document Library link.

9. On the New page, enter **Web Part Pages** in the Name field.

10. Under the option Display This Document Library on the Quick Launch Bar, select No.

11. Select Web Part Page from the Document Template list.

12. Click the Create button.

Once the new document libraries are created, you can choose to add new pages to your site by either using the Create page or by going directly to the document library and selecting New. Adding content to the Basic Page is done through a rich-text editing interface that allows you to add text, images, and tables to the page. This is a pretty simple interface that can be used by any nontechnical content owner to quickly create or edit a page. Figure 5-1 shows the editor with shameless content from my web site.

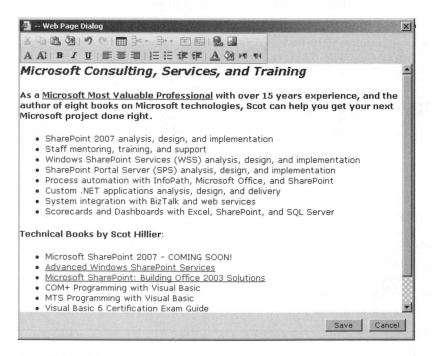

Figure 5-1. *Editing a Basic Page*

Using Web Parts

When you create a Web Part Page, you can select from various layouts with zones for web parts. Adding content to the Web Part Page is done by clicking the Add a Web Part link that appears at the top of each zone. When you click this link, SharePoint displays a dialog that allows you to select one or more web parts for the zone. Adding multiple web parts to a zone simply stacks them vertically within the zone. You can also drag the web parts between zones once they're on the page. Figure 5-2 shows the Add Web Parts dialog.

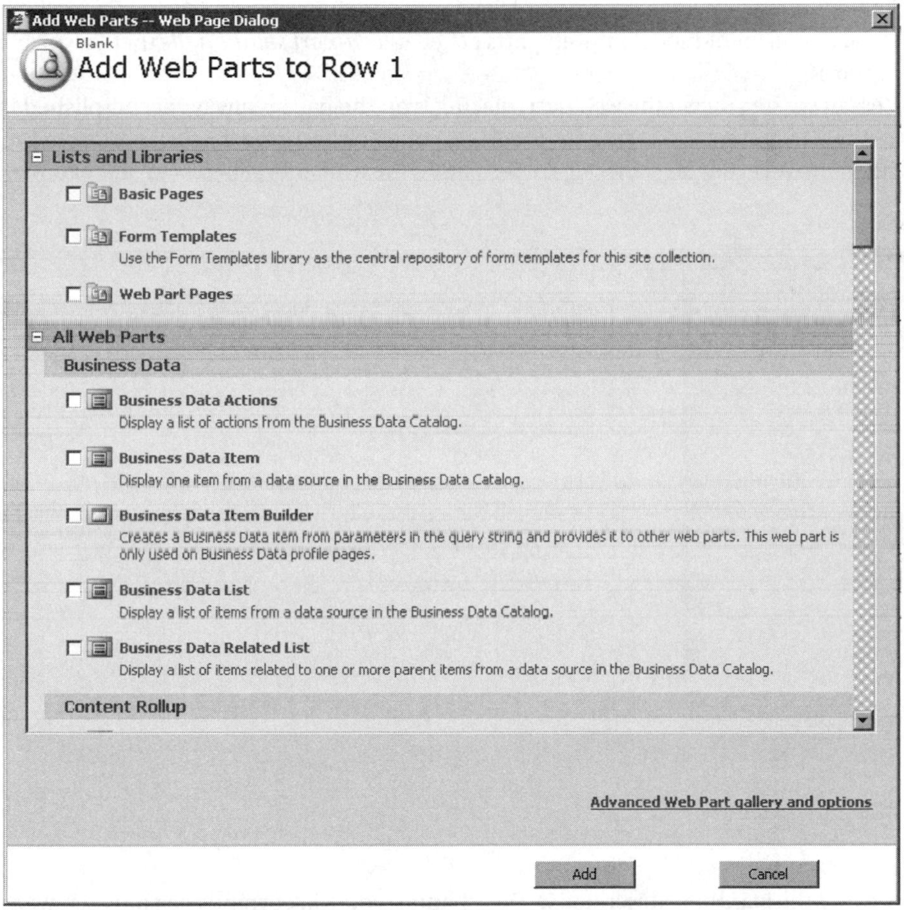

Figure 5-2. *Adding web parts*

If you click the link at the bottom of the Add Web Parts dialog, you will open the Web Parts Gallery pane, which allows access to all available web parts on the farm. There are three differ-ent galleries, which are essentially catalogs of web parts from which you can choose. The available galleries are Closed Web Parts, [site name] Gallery, and Server Gallery.

The Closed Web Parts Gallery contains all of the web parts that are available specifically to the web page that is being modified. Closed web parts still execute as part of the page, but their output is not rendered. If you close a web part, the web part disappears from the page and becomes available in the Closed Web Parts Gallery. Once it is in the gallery, it may be moved back to the page by dragging it from the gallery and onto the page.

The [site name] Gallery is named after the site where the current page is located. If your site is named Board of Directors, the [site name] Gallery will be named Board of Directors Gallery. This gallery contains the bulk of the general-purpose web parts that may be used throughout the current site. In Chapter 10, you will add your own custom web parts to this gallery.

The Server Gallery is a gallery intended for enterprise deployments of SharePoint. In these cases, the Server Gallery acts as an enterprise-level repository for web parts. Using this gallery entails a special deployment model for web parts called a *web-part solution file* that I also cover in Chapter 10.

Regardless of where you get the web part, placing it on the page is always accomplished in the same manner. To move a web part onto the page, you click and drag the web part from the selected gallery into an available zone. Figure 5-3 shows the available galleries in SharePoint.

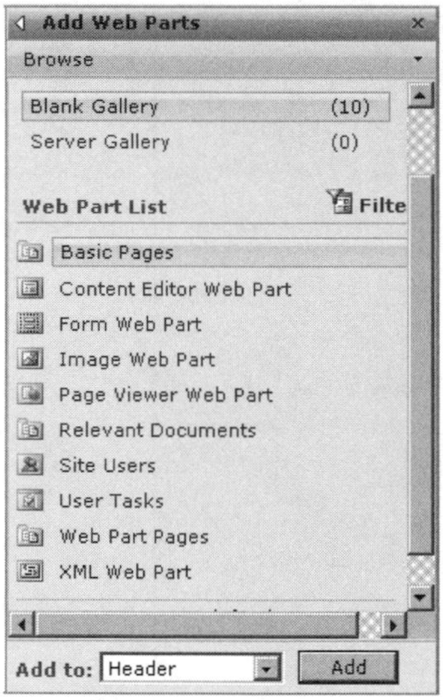

Figure 5-3. *Web part galleries*

If you created the blank site described in this chapter, you will currently see only ten web parts in the [site name] Gallery. This is because the Blank Site template only enables some of the basic web parts. Don't be fooled by this short list; there are many web parts available to you in SharePoint, and this book will cover several of them in the chapters where they are most useful. Table 5-2 lists the web parts found in the Blank Site template and explains their functions.

Table 5-2. *Blank Template Web Parts*

Web Part	Description
Basic Pages and Web Part Pages	These are the document libraries for holding web pages. All document libraries that you create will appear in the [site name] Gallery.
Content Editor	This web part allows you to add rich text, HTML, or script to a site.
Form	This web part is used to create an HTML form that can use script to communicate with other web parts.
Image	This web part is used to place images on a page.
Page Viewer	This web part provides an IFRAME viewer to other web content.
Relevant Documents	This web part is used to display documents from the site that are important to the current user.
Site Users	This web part displays a list of the site members and their status.
User Tasks	This web part shows all of the tasks assigned to the current user.
XML	This web part is used to add XML data and transform it with XSL.

Connecting Web Parts

Although web parts are useful for displaying information, links, and lists, so far we have only seen them acting as islands of information. The content presented by multiple web parts on a page may be related, but the web parts are unaware of the related information. With connected web parts, however, you can relate multiple web parts.

Connecting web parts is done when a Web Part Page is in edit mode. You enter edit mode by selecting Edit Page from the Site Actions menu. Once in edit mode, you may use the drop-down menu associated with the web part. If the web part supports connecting with another web part on the page, you will see a Connections menu item. You may then select the web part with which to connect.

When a connection is established, SharePoint will prompt you to select the data column on which to base the connection. This is like performing a crude outer join in a SQL statement; the web parts must share a common piece of data that allows a connection. As an example, I created a connection between two Contacts List web parts. The first list shows a view of available technology experts and their area of expertise. This web part is then connected to a second list that shows the contact information for the selected expert. I cover how to create your own connectable web parts in Chapter 10. Figure 5-4 shows the resulting master-detail relationship between the web parts.

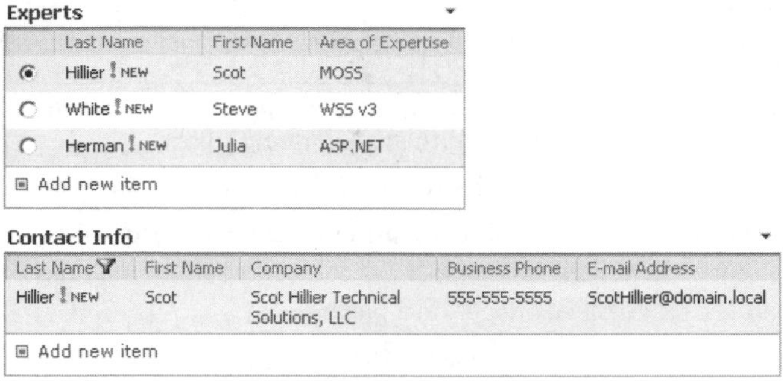

Figure 5-4. *Connecting web parts*

Modifying the Site Look and Feel

Once you add some pages and content to a new site, you will want to change the appearance and navigation of the site. Although I discuss several ways to alter the look and feel of a site throughout this chapter, the easiest way to get started is with the built-in options found inside SharePoint itself. You can change many navigation and appearance elements within a site simply by making configuration choices in the site administration pages. You can also change colors and styles with built-in options or by modifying some existing files.

Customizing Site Navigation

By default, both WSS and MOSS have a simple navigation system that uses tabs across the top to access sites along with a Quick Launch area on the left-hand side to access content elements within a site. Using the built-in configuration settings of WSS and MOSS, you can make some changes to the way this information is presented in the site collection. Although these changes are not radical, they can be helpful in many applications.

During the site creation process, you can specify whether a subsite in the collection should appear as a tab in the parent site. You can also choose whether the tabs appear as navigation elements on the child site. After the subsite is created, you can subsequently click the Top Link Bar hyperlink under the Look and Feel section of the Site Settings to modify the tabs.

You can use the Tree View link under the Look and Feel section of the Site Settings to enable a tree view navigation system as well as hide the Quick Launch navigation area. Additionally, you can click the Quick Launch link under the Look and Feel section of the Site Settings to change what information appears in the Quick Launch area and how it is ordered. Again, none of these changes are extreme, but they are simple to implement.

Clicking the link titled Title, Description, and Icon will allow you to change these elements for a site. When using a new logo, you will typically create a new image library to store the logo and then reference that image when making the change. This is a simple way to provide some consistent branding to your sites.

Using Themes and Styles

You can achieve some additional customization by selecting a new theme for the site collection. This is done by clicking the Site Theme link in the Look and Feel section. SharePoint offers several themes that you can select with various color palettes. Ideally, you would want to be able to select a theme that closely matches your organization's color scheme. Although, a complete match is unlikely, you can usually find something passable for internal sites. Later in this chapter, I discuss how you can create your own themes.

If you don't use one of the available themes to customize your site, SharePoint still makes use of some thematic elements simply to create the default look. In particular, SharePoint makes use of style sheets to control the layouts, fonts, and colors you see in a site. The main style sheet, CORE.CSS, controls the appearance of many elements in a site. Therefore, customizing CORE.CSS will have an immediate and global impact on the look and feel of all sites in the farm.

Customizing CORE.CSS can be challenging, however, because there are a huge number of classes defined in this style sheet and no good reference to help you determine what elements to modify. Over the last couple of years, some tools have emerged to help developers identify the classes associated with elements in a web page, but the best one is the Internet Explorer Developer toolbar, which you can download from Microsoft. This tool loads into Internet Explorer and exposes a tremendous amount of information about the page being rendered in the browser. You can use this tool to identify the style classes associated with an element and modify that element in the style sheet.

Keep in mind that modifying CORE.CSS will make changes to every site in your farm. So be certain that you intend to make global changes before proceeding. A better approach, however, is to leave the CORE.CSS file alone and override styles instead. SharePoint provides a mechanism for specifying alternate style sheets that will override the core styles. I discuss alternate style sheets in the section titled "Using an Alternate Style Sheet" later in the chapter.

In cases where these changes do not provide enough control, you may want to make your own theme. You can do this from scratch or by customizing an existing theme. Then you can save the theme and make it available to all sites. SharePoint keeps all of the predefined themes in the folder \Program Files\Common Files\Microsoft Shared\web server extensions\12\TEMPLATE\THEMES. Once created, the new theme is made available to SharePoint sites by making a new entry in the SPTHEME.XML file located in \Program Files\Common Files\Microsoft Shared\web server extensions\12\TEMPLATE\LAYOUTS\1033.

Customizing with the SharePoint Designer

Although Basic Pages and Web Part Pages offer you a quick way to get content into your site, you will likely find them too limiting. In my experience, organizations want much more control over the look and feel of the site. This is where the SharePoint Designer comes into play. The SharePoint Designer gives you a complete editing environment where you can significantly customize your pages.

You can open a SharePoint site directly in the SharePoint Designer by selecting File ➤ Open Site. In the Open Site dialog, you simply provide the URL to the site and click the Open button. When you open the site, the SharePoint Designer displays a folder list view that shows all of the sites, libraries, and lists defined in the site. If you have previously created the Basic Pages and Web Part Pages libraries, you will see them in the folder list along with any pages you have already created.

From the folder list, you can right-click a file and select Open from the context menu. When the page opens, you will see that many of the elements are exposed for editing. You'll see, for example, that you could easily type directly into a Basic Page to edit its content.

However, not everything you see is available for editing. What you are allowed to edit is a combination of SharePoint Designer settings and SharePoint page structure that I will unravel throughout this chapter.

Understanding Contributor Mode

As soon as you start to edit content in the SharePoint Designer, you'll have to deal with Contributor Mode. *Contributor Mode* is a limited-function mode that allows administrators to control which editing commands are available based on the author's membership in a Contributor Group. Contributor Mode is enabled by default for SharePoint sites and only administrators can change the settings.

Contributor Mode is closely linked with SharePoint permission levels. For the SharePoint Permission levels Full Control, Design, and Contribute, the SharePoint Designer defines the groups Site Manager, Web Designers, and Content Authors, respectively. When you first open a site in the SharePoint Designer, your ability to edit pages will likely be restricted by the Contributor Settings for your group. If you select Task Panes ➤ Contributor from the main menu, you'll be able to see your group membership, as shown in Figure 5-5.

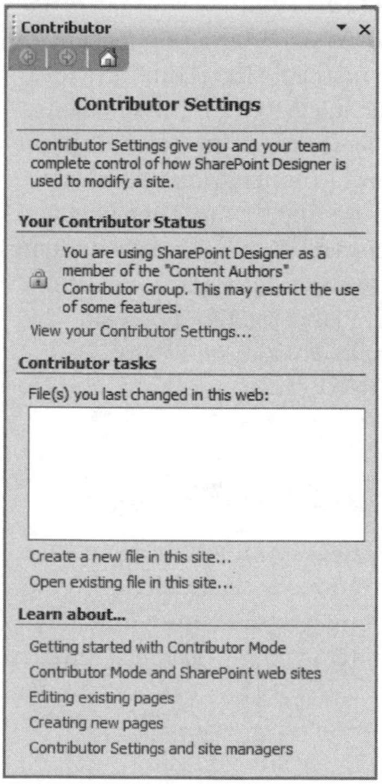

Figure 5-5. *Contributor Settings pane*

If you are a site administrator for the site that is opened in the SharePoint Designer, you can make changes to the Contributor Settings. This is accomplished by selecting Site ➤ Contributor Settings, which opens the Contributor Settings dialog. You can also enable or disable Contributor Mode for the entire site from this dialog.

If you disable Contributor Mode, anyone who is able to open a site in the SharePoint Designer will have the ability to make changes to any part of a page. This may be fine if you have a limited number of people making site customizations. Contributor Mode is really designed for teams of people who are all responsible for providing various content elements. In this situation, you may not want someone to have full access to the editing functions because they could accidentally change content that they should otherwise not have access to.

If you choose to use Contributor Mode, you do not necessarily have to do anything in the SharePoint Designer. Because Contributor groups are linked with SharePoint permission levels, you would simply add new users to the SharePoint site and assign them an appropriate permission level. This level would dictate their editing capabilities in the SharePoint Designer as I indicated previously. If, however, someone opens a site and he does not have any permission levels that map to a Contributor Group, he is automatically given the restrictions associated with the Content Authors group. This is because the Content Authors group has the least functionality in the SharePoint Designer. This often results in the interesting situation in which you could be a SharePoint farm administrator with little ability to edit a site because you were never specifically assigned a permission level.

As you'll see in the section "Using the Publishing Feature," much of the content that appears in a SharePoint page is contained in a content placeholder. Placeholders define text, image, and layout areas where content can reside on a page. When Contributor Mode is enabled, authors are restricted to editing the content in these placeholders only. This is how you can keep them from accidentally changing the underlying structure of a site. While it's tempting to simply turn Contributor Mode off, it will save you a lot of headaches when others are editing content. I've seen many pages destroyed by business users who were editing content in the previous version of SharePoint using Microsoft FrontPage with no restrictions.

Adding a New Page

When a site is open in the SharePoint Designer, you can add different elements including HTML, Active Server Pages, style sheets, lists, libraries, XML files, and many others. You can also customize existing elements that you made from the Create page in SharePoint. As a best practice, I generally prefer to add elements from within SharePoint and then customize them within the SharePoint Designer. This practice helps to ensure that the fundamental relationships between content elements are retained. However, there are times when adding content directly from the SharePoint Designer makes sense, such as when a large team of people is working on Internet-facing pages. It all depends on exactly what you are trying to accomplish.

Adding a page to an existing web site is a simple matter of selecting File ➤ New from the main menu. If you hover over the New menu item, a submenu will fly out, offering you some basic choices. If you click the New menu item, the New dialog will open with a complete collection of elements you can add to the site.

Once the new page is added, you may start designing it. Before you start creating sites that integrate directly with SharePoint Services, I'll start by reviewing some of the Basic Page–creation tools in the SharePoint Designer. These tools will be useful later when you are working with more complicated pages.

When starting a new page, many web designers will create a prototype page using a graphics program such as Adobe Photoshop. Then they cut the image apart to create the graphics for the new page. This is especially helpful if you have an existing web site and are trying to make the new page match that look and feel. You can get help with this effort by making use of a tracing image in the SharePoint Designer.

Tracing images allow you to take a JPEG, GIF, PNG, or BMP file and use it like tracing paper to help with the layout and design of a page. In order to set a tracing image, you must have the page in design view, which is controlled by a set of buttons underneath the page. Once in design view, the tracing image is set by selecting View ➤ Tracing Image ➤ Configure from the SharePoint Designer menu. When you configure the tracing image, you select the file to act as the image, its position on the page, and its opacity. Figure 5-6 shows a tracing image of the Apress web site.

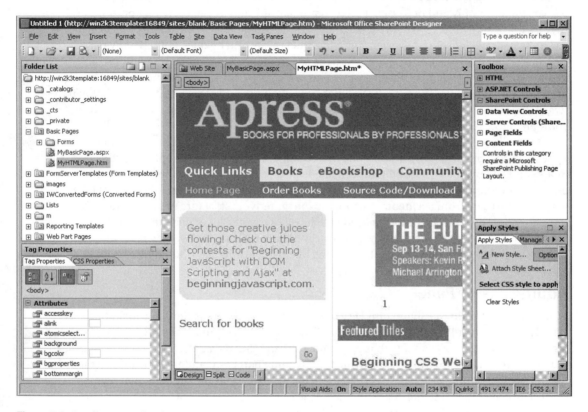

Figure 5-6. *Setting a tracing image*

Once you have a tracing image in place, you will want to construct the layout of the page to define the areas where content will be placed. The SharePoint Designer allows you to set up multiple complex regions for content using layout tables. *Layout tables* are similar to any HTML table, but they are specifically intended to help lay out content regions on the page. Inserting a layout table into a page is done by using the layout table task pane, which can be opened by selecting Table ➤ Layout Tables and Cells.

Within the task pane, you can choose to create your own layout tables or use the predefined layouts in the pane. Generally, the predefined layouts are sufficient because several different kinds are available. Even if these are not exactly what you want, you can modify the layouts once they are applied to the page.

To utilize layout tables and cells, take these steps:

1. Select Start ➤ Programs ➤ Microsoft Office ➤ Microsoft Office SharePoint Designer 2007 to open the SharePoint Designer.

2. From the main menu, select File ➤ Open Site.

3. In the Open Site dialog, type the address of the blank site you created earlier (e.g., **http://vsmoss:[port]**) and click Open.

4. When the site opens, make sure the folder list is visible by selecting Task Panes ➤ Folder List from the main menu.

5. Using the folder list, examine the sites, lists, and libraries defined in the site.

6. Add a new ASPX page to the site by selecting New ➤ ASPX from the main menu.

7. Open the Layout Tables and Cells task pane by selecting Table ➤ Layout Tables.

8. In the Layout Tables and Cells task pane, click a new layout from the Table Layout section with a top title row that spans the entire page and a navigation column that spans the left side of the page.

9. Click your mouse inside the top row.

10. In the Layout Tables and Cells task pane, click the Insert Layout Cell link.

11. In the Insert Layout Cell dialog, accept the default values and click OK to insert the new cell.

12. When the new cell appears, right-click it and select Cell Properties from the context menu.

13. In the Cell Properties dialog, change the Background Color drop-down list to Blue and click the OK button.

14. Click the sizing handle and make the cell fill the entire available area within the layout table.

15. Place additional cells in the layout so that the page has a blue title area and a blue navigation area.

Once the initial layout is complete, adding text is a simple matter of typing directly into the cells. You can format the font style directly from the editor using the same approach as you would in Microsoft Word. For images, you may either place the image directly in a cell or make use of layers to position images. Layers are floating frames that can be positioned anywhere on the page. You can add a new layer from the Format menu. Once added, you can drag the layer around the page and position it exactly where you want it. Using the layouts and layers, you can rapidly put a page together over a tracing image.

Working with Data Sources

Once you have an idea of how to use the basic layout tools, you will want to be able to add content more interesting than just text and graphics. The SharePoint Designer in conjunction with WSS supports the ability to create XML data sources that you can use in your web pages. This capability allows you to connect directly with SQL databases, XML files, SharePoint lists, and other sources to display dynamic data sets of information in tabular formats. Using the SharePoint Designer, you can display this data without ever writing code.

The key to using dynamic data sets in your web pages is to make use of the Data Source Library and the Data View web part. The *Data Source Library* acts as an agent for mapping access to any number of data sources that can provide XML data sets. The *Data View web part* is the component that displays those data sets on the page.

When the Data View web part is displaying an XML data set, it has the ability to format the data set based on the eXtensible Stylesheet Language Transform (XSLT). This means that you can use the SharePoint Designer editor to format columns, colors, and styles for a data set. You can also use a conditional format to change the style of a data cell when it reaches certain parameters. In this way, you can call attention to outlying data in the set.

Using XML data sets begins with the Data Source Library. You can access the Data Source Library by selecting Data View ➤ Insert Data View from the main menu in the SharePoint Designer. The library lists all of the available XML data sources. If you have an existing Share-Point site open in the SharePoint Designer, you'll notice that all of the lists and libraries in the site are available for use as data sources. In addition to these sources, you'll also see support for database connections, XML files, server-side scripts, web services, and the Business Data Catalog. Figure 5-7 shows an example of the Data Source Library.

Figure 5-7. *The Data Source Library*

When using the Data Source Library, you are not limited to the lists and libraries associated with the site that is currently open. You can either create new lists and libraries directly or utilize lists and libraries from other sites within the portal structure. If you click either the Create New SharePoint List or the Create New Document Library link, you will open a dialog that allows you to add a new list, library, or survey to the Data Source Library. If you instead want to add an element from another site, you can click the Connect to Another Library link to add a new source. From this link, you can add a reference to another SharePoint site, which will import all of the data sources defined for that site.

If the data source you want to use is not a SharePoint element already, you will have to spend some time setting up the source before it can be used. Most of the data sources are set up in a similar fashion that begins by clicking the link just below the data source type you want to use.

To add a database connection, follow these steps:

1. Place your cursor in the main body of the page you created earlier.

2. From the SharePoint Designer main menu, select Data View ➤ Insert Data View to open the Data Source Library pane.

3. In the Data Source Library, expand the Database Connections node.

4. Click the Connect to a Database link just beneath the node to open the Data Source Properties dialog.

5. Click the General tab, and name the connection Site Map.

6. On the Source tab, click the Configure Database Connection button.

7. In the Configure Database Connection dialog, check the box labeled Use Custom Connection String and click the Edit button.

8. In the Connection String dialog, enter **Integrated Security=SSPI ;Persist Security Info=False;Data Source=VSSQL;**.

9. Click the OK button.

10. Click Next.

11. On the next step, select a database and table from the list (I used the Names database from the Business Data Catalog examples in Chapter 4).

12. Click Finish.

13. On the Source tab, click Fields.

14. In the Displayed Fields dialog, remove any fields you do not want displayed and click OK.

15. On the Source tab, click Sort.

16. In the Sort dialog, select Sort the Fields By and click OK.

17. In the Data Source Properties dialog, click OK to complete the definition of the new data source.

When using a database connection as a data source, it is generally not a good idea to save the credentials directly in the database connection. Instead you can use Windows authentication to verify access credentials at the time the data is accessed in the web site. However, if you go down this path, you will have to set up credentials in the database for each user. A better mechanism for authentication is to use the Microsoft Single Sign-On

(SSO) service. This service allows you to set up a master set of credentials just for accessing such data sources. I cover the setup and usage of SSO in Chapter 11.

Once the data source is defined, adding it to the page is a simple matter of dragging the source from the catalog to the page. Once you drop the data source onto the page, the SharePoint Designer adds the server-side code necessary to access the data source and display the data. Because the page now contains server-side code, you may be prompted to rename the page to contain an ASPX extension. The ASPX extension is required for the page to be recognized as containing server-side code.

Working with Data Views

Once the data set is visible on the page, you can make changes to the presentation directly in the page. Changing font styles, font sizes, and column header names can be done using the same techniques as in a word processor. A drop-down menu also becomes available in the upper right corner of the table. This drop-down menu gives you the ability to sort and filter the data as well as change the presentation style. From this menu, you can also apply conditional formatting to call out values in the data set that need attention.

Although data views can stand alone on a page like a report, they also have the ability to interact with other data sources. For example, you can have one data view that displays names and another data view that displays contact information. Selecting a name from the first data view causes the contact information to show in the second data view. This is the same concept of connecting web parts that you saw when you modified pages directly in SharePoint.

You can connect two data views by selecting Web Part Connections from the drop-down menu associated with either of the views. The SharePoint Designer responds by running a wizard that helps you make the connection. The wizard walks you through the process of selecting the fields to connect and the behavior for each part. The wizard also allows you to select a connection with a web part that is on a different page.

Understanding the Impact of Customization

The templates that you can select from when creating a new site collection all come from site definitions. A *site definition* is a collection of pages and content specified using an XML markup language called the Collaborative Application Markup Language (CAML). I discuss CAML in some detail in Chapter 11, but for now I focus on the relationship between site definitions and pages in SharePoint. SharePoint uses site definitions to efficiently manage pages by saving the site definition once and then using it many times. For example, all of the sites you create that use the standard Team Site template share a single set of page definitions. These page definitions are loaded into memory when the site is accessed and subsequently used to render the site content. The pages that are created in memory based on the template are referred to as *uncustomized* pages.

Whenever a page is customized in the SharePoint Designer, it is saved to the SharePoint content database as a new unique page. Customized pages are separate from the site definition initially used to create them. This means that the customized site pages are no longer generated in memory from the initial template. While the SharePoint Designer makes it easy to customize pages, customizations can cause problems because they may not be properly updated whenever a service pack or security update is applied to the original site definition in SharePoint.

For many developers, the only acceptable way to modify a SharePoint site is to modify the site definition itself. While this is always a valid technical approach, it is much more difficult to modify pages using XML markup than with the SharePoint Designer. Additionally, you cannot take advantage of features such as Contributor Mode to ensure that customizations are done correctly. In my opinion, you should create site definitions only when you truly need a new template that does not exist in SharePoint already or are planning on using the definition to create many sites. Content changes are best done either directly in the SharePoint Designer or by making use of the publishing features discussed in the section "Using the Publishing Feature."

■Note For those familiar with previous versions of SharePoint, you may have heard customized pages referred to as *unghosted* pages. Rather than refer to pages as *ghosted* or *unghosted*, Microsoft now prefers *customized* and *uncustomized*. Furthermore, you may have also been aware that unghosted pages could cause performance problems in SharePoint sites. Microsoft now assures us that customizing pages in the SharePoint Designer will have no significant performance impact, because customized pages are now efficiently parsed.

Whenever you perform an operation in the SharePoint Designer that will customize a page and separate it from its site definition, you will receive a warning dialog. Additionally, the SharePoint Designer will mark the page with an information icon in the Folder List indicating that the page has been customized. Figure 5-8 shows the Folder List in the SharePoint Designer with a customized page highlighted. If you want, you can also discard the customizations and revert the page back to its original definition by right-clicking the page and selecting Revert to Page Template from the context menu. You can even discard the customizations for an entire site by clicking the link titled Rest to Site Definition located on the Site Settings page in SharePoint.

Figure 5-8. *Identifying customized pages*

Along with icons in the Folder List, the SharePoint Designer also provides a set of reports you can use to identify special pages. For example, you can select Site ➤ Reports ➤ Shared Content ➤ Site Template Pages to get a listing of all pages that indicate whether they have been customized. You can also run reports to detect site problems or show site usage.

Saving Customized Templates

Whenever you create a new site, SharePoint uses predefined templates to simplify the creation of the new elements for the site. You have already seen the list of templates in use several times. Although WSS and MOSS come with several templates already defined, you can create your own templates and then make them available to others for use. These new templates can be created directly in the browser and saved through the WSS or MOSS interface.

Creating Site Templates

SharePoint defines a site collection as the top-level site and all of the sites beneath it in the hierarchy. You have already seen that permissions granted at the top of a site collection are inherited by sites lower in the collection. Using the same organizational structure, SharePoint maintains a Site Template Gallery for each site collection. A new site template can be created and added to the gallery by administrators.

Site templates may be created outside of SharePoint using an authoring tool such as the SharePoint Designer, but the simplest way to create a template is to use an existing site within the portal framework. Creating a template from an existing site is done through the Site Settings page for the site you want to save. Simply select the link titled Save Site as Template from the Look and Feel section on the Site Settings page. Generally, you will save only the structure of a site as a template; however, SharePoint does allow you the option of saving content along with the structure. Site templates are always saved as files with an STP extension.

■**Note** It's important to realize that site templates saved as STP files are always considered customized sites as long as they haven't been edited with the SharePoint Designer prior to be being saved as a template. They are never related to any site definition within SharePoint. This is essentially the same situation as if you had created every page in the template by hand in the SharePoint Designer; however, it's much easier to create a template as an STP file than to customize an entire site.

Once you have created saved templates for a site collection, you can go back and manage the templates. Accessing the set of templates for a site collection is done through the Site Settings page associated with the top-level site. The Site Templates Gallery is a library of all the available templates for the site collection. You will not see any site definitions in this library, only template files with an STP extension.

Once you have several templates available for the site collection, you can control their availability to subsites in the collection. Clicking the Site Templates link on the Site Settings page allows you to configure which templates are available to subsites in the collection.

Creating List Templates

Just as you can create site templates from existing sites, SharePoint allows you to create list templates from existing lists. A *list template* consists of the site columns that you define for the list and any views you define. Just like site templates, you also have the option of saving the list content as part of the template. Saving a list as a template is done from the List Settings page, which can be accessed by selecting Settings ➤ List Settings from the toolbar of any list.

Using the Publishing Feature

While previous versions of SharePoint can be used as public Internet sites, they were never really designed with that purpose in mind. Chief among the limitations of previous versions is a complete lack of content management capabilities. Specifically, previous versions have no way to create page templates for different content, do not significantly separate content development from content publishing, and have only a simple mechanism for approving content.

The reason that previous versions of SharePoint have weak content management capabilities is probably because Microsoft Content Management Server (MCMS) already provides a structure for templating, authoring, and publishing web content; Microsoft saw SharePoint as primarily an intranet solution. That's all changed now because the web content management (WCM) features included with MOSS are a direct replacement for MCMS. Microsoft has already announced that there will be no new versions of MCMS, which means that organizations with MCMS infrastructures must eventually migrate to MOSS.

WCM consists of features that provide content publishing, page templates, document conversion from print to web, and multilanguage support. In this section, I focus specifically on the capabilities of the Office SharePoint Server Publishing Feature, which allows you to create and publish web content. I should point out before beginning a detailed discussion of WCM that content management is not limited to Internet sites. WCM is simply a set of features that provide the capability to implement content management within a site. You certainly could use it for an intranet or even a simple collaboration site. It is important to note, however, that WCM is strictly a MOSS feature. You will not find it in the list of available features for WSS.

Creating a Public Internet Site

While many content management capabilities are certainly useful in team sites, the most likely scenario for content management involves the enterprise. Therefore, I will assume for the rest of the chapter that you are using MOSS. To support the discussion, I'll use an Internet web site created on the VSMOSS server.

Follow these steps to create an Internet site:

1. Log in to VSMOSS as a SharePoint administrator.

2. Select Start ➤ Administrative Tools ➤ SharePoint 3.0 Central Administration.

3. On the Application Management tab, under the SharePoint Web Application Management section, click the link titled Create or Extend a Web Application.

4. On the Create or Extend a Web Application page, click the link titled Create a New Web Application.

5. On the Create a New Web Application page, select the option to Create a New IIS Web Site.

6. In the Description field, type **Internet**.

7. In the Application Pool section, select Create a New Application Pool.

8. Enter **Internet_Pool** as the pool name.

9. Select the Configurable option for the application pool security account.

10. In the User Name field, enter **DOMAIN\SPContentPool**.

11. In the Password field, enter the account password.

12. In the Reset Internet Information Services section, select the option to Restart IIS Automatically.

13. Click the OK button.

14. On the Application Created page, click the link titled Create a New Site Collection.

15. On the Create Site Collection page, enter **APress** in the Title field.

16. Under the Template Selection section, click the Publishing tab, and then select the Publishing Portal template.

17. Under the Primary Site Collection Administrator section, enter **DOMAIN\ Administrator** in the User Name field.

18. Click the OK button to create the new site collection. When the site collection is created, open it in a separate copy of the browser.

When creating a public Internet site, you may want to set it up so that you can author content on it from inside the firewall. One way to do this is to configure it so that it is accessible from two different zones. Typically the Default zone is accessible through Windows authentication while the Internet zone is accessible anonymously. With this configuration, you can use the Default zone for managing content and the Internet zone for presenting it. This is not the only possible authoring configuration; I discuss a more formal content deployment scenario in the section titled "Using Content Deployment."

Follow these steps to extend the web application into the Internet zone:

1. In the Central Administration site, click the Application Management tab.

2. Under the SharePoint Web Application Management section, click the link titled Create or Extend Web Application.

3. On the Create or Extend Web Application page, click the link titled Extend an Existing Web Application.

4. On the Extend Web Application to Another IIS Web Site page, drop down the Web Application selection list and click Change Web Application.

5. In the Select Web Application page, click the link for the Internet Web Application that you created.

6. Under the IIS Web Site section, choose to Create a New IIS Web Site.

7. In the Description field type **Public Internet**, but leave the port number in parentheses as part of the name.

8. Under the Load Balanced URL section, select Internet from the Zone drop-down list.

9. Make note of the URL for the extended web application so you can access it later.

10. Click the OK button.

Once the web application is extended, you will want to enable anonymous access to the new site collection. Enabling anonymous access requires that you first allow it for the site collection using Central Administration and then designate what portions of the Internet site will support anonymous access. In this way, you can create an Internet site that has both public and private areas.

Follow these steps to enable anonymous access:

1. Click the Application Management tab in the Central Administration web site.

2. Under the Application Security section, click the Authentication Providers link.

3. On the Authentication Providers page, make sure that your new web application is shown in the drop-down. If not, use the drop-down to change the selection.

4. Click the Windows link for the Internet zone of your web application.

5. On the Edit Authentication page, check the box labeled Enable Anonymous Access and click the Save button.

6. Click the Application Management tab in the Central Administration web site.

7. Under the Application Security section, click the link titled Policy for Web Application.

8. On the Policy for Web Application page, make sure that your new web application is shown in the drop-down. If not, use the drop-down to change the selection.

9. Click the Add Users link.

10. On the Add Users page, make sure All Zones is selected and click the Next button.

11. Enter **DOMAIN\Administrator** in the Users box and check the Full Control permission to grant the administrator access to both the Default and Internet zones.

12. Click the Finish button.

13. Now open the home page of the public Internet site you extended on the Internet zone and click the link titled Enable Anonymous Access.

■**Caution** Be sure that you open the Internet site using the URL for the extended application. Remember, you want anonymous access to the Internet zone and Windows access to the Default zone. I find it useful to save a link in the Favorites list named for the zone (e.g., Apress Default Zone and Apress Internet Zone).

---

14. On the Change Anonymous Access Settings page, select the option labeled Entire Web Site and click the OK button.

Once you have completed the previous steps you will be able to author content on the Default zone and access it anonymously on the Internet zone. While these steps are good for investigating MOSS, you will probably want to ensure the Internet zone is on port 80 in a production environment. Usually, I create the Default zone on a different port (e.g., 8080) and then extend the web application into port 80 as the Internet zone.

Another real-world consideration is the fact that Internet sites are often isolated in the DMZ and may not be accessible from the Windows domain. In this case, I make use of the content deployment capabilities of MOSS to push content from a staging server to production. I discuss content deployment in the section titled "Using Content Deployment" later in the chapter.

Creating and Approving Pages

Once you have a site created, you may begin adding content to it. Typically, you begin the process by adding new pages to the site. Adding a page requires the Manage Web Site right and is accomplished by selecting Create Page from the Site Actions menu. When you select to create a new page for an Internet site, MOSS displays a list of page layouts for the site. Page layouts are templates that define content structure for a page and are always associated with a content type. As I discussed in Chapter 3, a content type contains a document template, data columns, workflows, and other information that completely defines a document. The publishing feature of MOSS uses a single root content type for publishing called Page. All of the page layouts inherit from this base. Figure 5-9 shows the list of available page layouts for the Internet site.

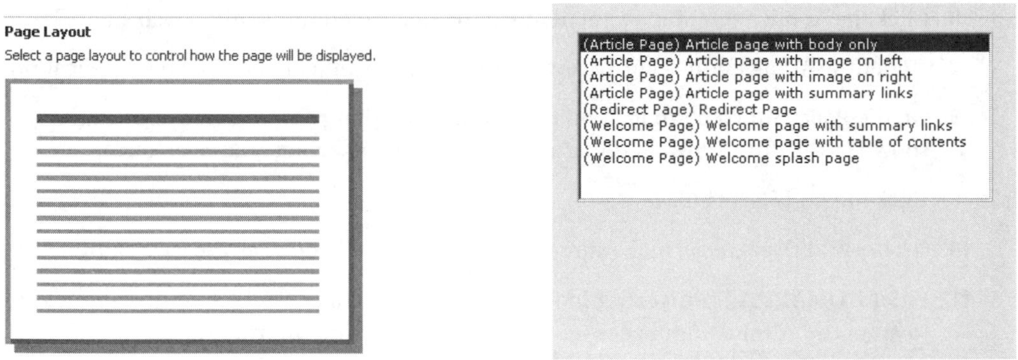

Figure 5-9. *Available page layouts*

You can get a better understanding of the content types behind the page layouts by viewing their definitions in MOSS. Content types can be accessed from the Site Settings page by clicking the link titled Site Content Types. This link displays the Site Content Type Gallery, which lists all of the available content types for web pages, documents, and lists. The page layouts for the Internet site are located under the Page Layout Content Types section of the gallery. These content types define the document template and columns for the page layouts. This information determines how the page appears in MOSS and makes it available in the page layouts list. Figure 5-10 shows part of the content type definition for the Article Page layout.

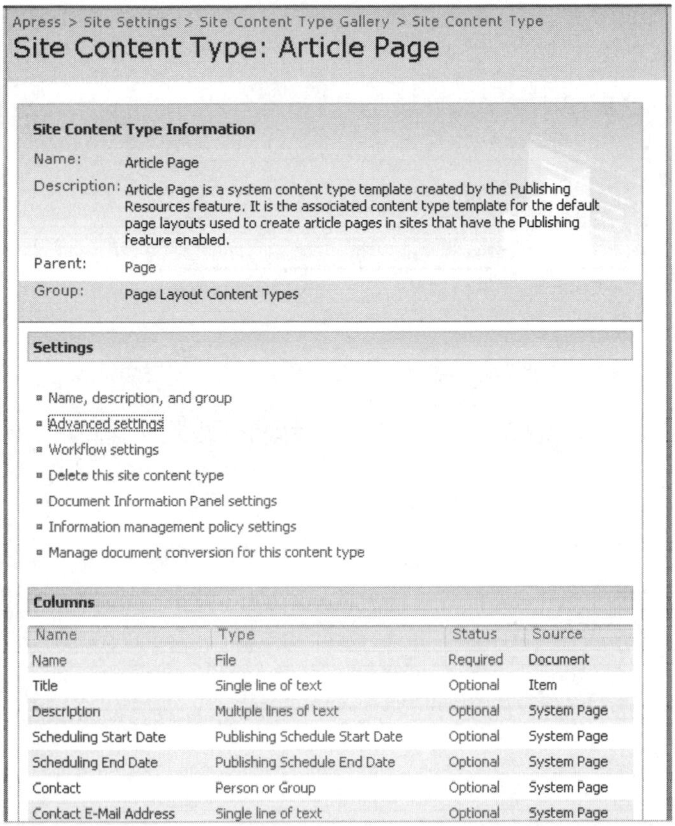

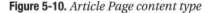

Apress > Site Settings > Site Content Type Gallery > Site Content Type

Site Content Type: Article Page

Site Content Type Information

Name: Article Page

Description: Article Page is a system content type template created by the Publishing Resources feature. It is the associated content type template for the default page layouts used to create article pages in sites that have the Publishing feature enabled.

Parent: Page

Group: Page Layout Content Types

Settings

- Name, description, and group
- Advanced settings
- Workflow settings
- Delete this site content type
- Document Information Panel settings
- Information management policy settings
- Manage document conversion for this content type

Columns

Name	Type	Status	Source
Name	File	Required	Document
Title	Single line of text	Optional	Item
Description	Multiple lines of text	Optional	System Page
Scheduling Start Date	Publishing Schedule Start Date	Optional	System Page
Scheduling End Date	Publishing Schedule End Date	Optional	System Page
Contact	Person or Group	Optional	System Page
Contact E-Mail Address	Single line of text	Optional	System Page

Figure 5-10. *Article Page content type*

When you create a new page, it is initially displayed in edit mode. In the body of the page, SharePoint displays field controls, which are used to add content to the page. Field controls hold values for columns associated with the content type. If you create a new Article Page, for example, it has field controls for Title, Rollup Image, Page Image, Article Date, Byline, Image Caption, and Page Content. If you examine the complete content type definition for an Article Page, you'll see that it has columns defined with the same names. Figure 5-11 shows an Article Page in edit mode.

Each of the field controls in a page layout can support different types of content, including images, text, groups, audiences, links, HTML, and more. When the page is in edit mode, each field control offers a different interface to help you properly configure the content. For example, field controls tied to images present an interface that allows you to select an image, provide alternate text, and specify hyperlinking behavior. To complete a page, simply work inside each field control to provide the needed content.

When working with a page in edit mode, SharePoint displays the page editing toolbar at the top. Once you've finished editing the page, you can use the page editing toolbar to allow other editors to view your work, save the page, or submit the page for approval. Figure 5-12 shows the page editing toolbar.

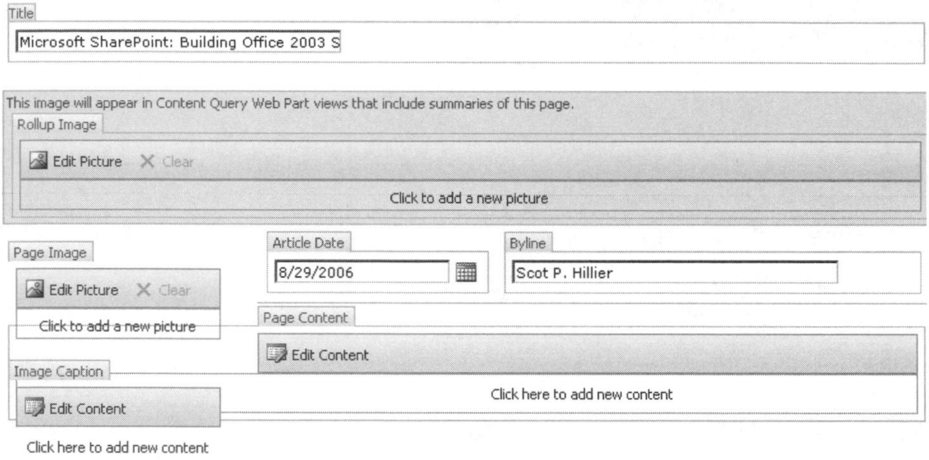

Title

Microsoft SharePoint: Building Office 2003 S

This image will appear in Content Query Web Part views that include summaries of this page.

Rollup Image

🖼 Edit Picture   ✕ Clear

Click to add a new picture

Page Image	Article Date	Byline
🖼 Edit Picture ✕ Clear	8/29/2006 📅	Scot P. Hillier

Click to add a new picture

Page Content

🖼 Edit Content

Click here to add new content

Image Caption

🖼 Edit Content

Click here to add new content

Figure 5-11. *Article Page in edit mode*

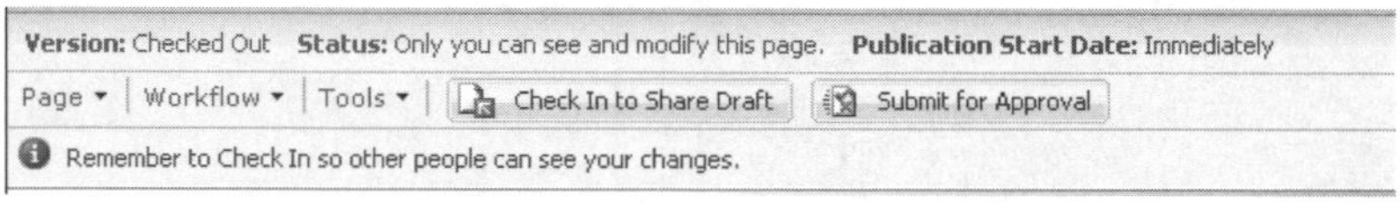

Version: Checked Out   **Status:** Only you can see and modify this page.   **Publication Start Date:** Immediately

Page ▾ | Workflow ▾ | Tools ▾ | 🖳 Check In to Share Draft | 🖳 Submit for Approval

ⓘ Remember to Check In so other people can see your changes.

Figure 5-12. *The page editing toolbar*

Clicking the button labeled Check In to Share Draft checks the new page in and allows other editors who have permission to review it. When a page is checked in, another editor may check out and alter the page by clicking the Edit Page button. MOSS automatically increments the minor version number of the page and displays it with a Draft status as each subsequent checkout, edit, check-in cycle is performed. When saved, the new page is stored in a document library named Pages that is fully accessible from within MOSS.

Most of the pages you create for a site will have other content elements such as images. In MOSS, individual content elements must be approved before they can appear in a published page. Content such as images is typically approved separately within the library where it resides and then used within pages.

Follow these steps to upload and approve an image:

1. Go to the home page of the Internet site you created earlier using the Default zone.

2. Select View All Site Content from the Site Actions menu.

3. On the All Site Content page, click the Images library.

4. In the Images Library, click Upload on the toolbar.

5. On the Upload Document: Images page, click the Browse button.

6. Using the Choose File dialog, locate an image to upload and then click the Open button.

7. On the Upload Document: Images page, click the OK button.

8. On the Edit Item page, give your image a title and click the Check In button.

9. On the Document Library page, note that the image now appears with an Approval Status of Draft.

10. Using the drop-down menu associated with the file name, select Publish a Major Version.

11. On the Publish a Major Version page, click the OK button.

12. On the Document Library page, note that the image now appears with an Approval Status of Pending.

13. Using the drop-down menu associated with the file name, select Approve/Reject.

14. On the Approve/Reject page, select Approved and click the OK button.

15. On the Document Library page, note that the image now appears with an Approval Status of Approved.

Once the page editing process is complete, you can click the Submit for Approval button. Submitting the page for approval starts a simple serial workflow process that allows you to route the page to a list of people one at a time. While the page is being routed for approval, you can also run a check of the content to make sure there aren't any unapproved content items used on the page.

Using an Alternate Style Sheet

Earlier in the chapter, I described how you could edit existing style sheets such as CORE.CSS to make changes to the appearance of sites. The drawback with this approach, of course, is that the changes made at this level are global. If you have the publishing feature installed, however, you can utilize an alternate style sheet that will override the styles found in CORE.CSS. Furthermore, each site collection can have its own alternate style sheet, which means that your changes do not have to be global. You can specify an alternate style sheet by clicking the Master Page link on the Site Settings page, which will take you to a page where you can enter a URL to the alternate style sheet.

Understanding Master Pages and Page Layouts

Master pages and *page layouts* are the two main components used by SharePoint to control the navigation, branding, and content of a site. The purpose of a master page is to provide a consistent navigation and page layout structure that is independent of the content on the page. The purpose of a page layout is to provide the content that appears within the page. Together, master pages and page layouts dictate the look and feel of a SharePoint site.

Editing the Default Master Page

Whenever you create a new site in SharePoint, a master page named default.master is created for the site and stored in the Master Page Gallery. This master page defines many of the navigational and branding elements that appear around a page. These elements are sometimes referred to as the *chrome* of the page, and changing them in the master page has a wide-ranging impact on a site.

Follow these steps to edit the master page:

1. Go to the home page of the Internet site you created earlier using the Default zone (e.g., `http://vsmoss:[port]`).

2. Select Site Settings ➤ Modify All Site Settings from the Site Actions menu.

3. On the Site Settings page, click the Master Page and Page Layout Gallery link under the Galleries section.

4. In the Master Page Gallery, select Check Out from the drop-down menu associated with the `default.master` file.

5. Select Edit in Microsoft SharePoint Designer from the drop-down menu associated with the `default.master` file.

6. When the master page opens, right-click the image near the site name and select Properties from the context menu.

7. In the tag Properties window, change the `ImageURL` property to point to the approved image you uploaded earlier (e.g., `/sites/apress/PublishingImages/Apress_Small.jpg`).

■**Note** If you have an image taller than 25 pixels, it will likely be too large for a nice appearance. Therefore, you might want to edit an image and publish it again before using it. For this example, I created a small Apress logo from images on the web site.

---

8. Select File ➤ Save All from the main menu.

9. When you receive the notice that you are customizing a page in the site template, click the Yes button.

10. Close the SharePoint Designer.

11. Return to the Master Page Gallery and select Check In from the drop-down menu associated with the `default.master` file.

12. On the Check In page, click the OK button.

13. Select Publish a Major Version from the drop-down menu associated with the `default.master` file.

14. On the Publish Major Version page, click the OK button.

15. Select Approve/Reject from the drop-down menu associated with the `default.master` file.

16. On the Approve/Reject page, select Approved and click the OK button.

17. The Master Gallery page should now have the new image similar to Figure 5-13.

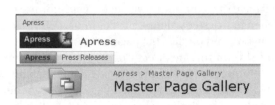

Figure 5-13. *A changed master page*

While changing the default.master page has resulted in a new image appearing, if you navigate to other pages you might notice that the new image is not present. For example, simply select View All Site Content from the Site Actions menu and you will see that the old image is still in use. This is because not all of the pages in the site use the default.master page to generate their chrome. Many of the pages use what is called the *application master page* instead.

The application master page is a global master page that is used across all site collections. It is located at \Program Files\Common Files\Microsoft Shared\web server extensions\12\ TEMPLATE\LAYOUTS. If you want, you can edit this page in Visual Studio or Notepad by opening it directly from the file system. The problem, however, is that these changes will affect every site collection in SharePoint. This means that you are left with a terrible choice when it comes to site branding. If you don't edit the application master, some pages will not appear with a consistent look and feel. If you do edit the application master, every site will get the change and may cause inconsistencies as well.

The problem is even worse than you might expect because SharePoint actually has several master pages that it uses beyond the default and application master. A search of the LAYOUTS directory for master pages on VSMOSS reveals more than 20 master pages. Some of these pages are associated with particular templates, while others are used for administration pages. In any case, you can see that SharePoint's use of master pages is less than optimal.

One way to solve the problems with multiple master files is to create a new LAYOUTS directory for each web application. To do this, you simply create a new directory under the TEMPLATE directory, for example LAYOUTS2, and then change the Local Path property in the Internet Information Server console for the virtual LAYOUTS directory to point to the new folder. Copy all of the contents from the original LAYOUTS directory to the new one and then you'll have a separate application master file just for that web application.

■**Caution** When editing any file located in the LAYOUTS directory, do not use the SharePoint Designer. The SharePoint Designer is not intended to edit the pages and will corrupt files opened directly from the LAYOUTS directory. For best results, I edit these files in Visual Studio or Notepad instead. In any case, be sure to save a backup copy of the file before making any changes.

Creating New Page Layouts

In the section "Using the Publishing Feature," I discuss creating new pages for a site and show the list of available page layouts. It is unlikely, however, that the available page layouts will work in most situations. Therefore, you'll have to create your own page layouts for use on the site. Creating a page layout is accomplished in five steps: define site columns, define a content type, create a page layout, edit the page layout, and publish the page layout.

As I mentioned already, page layout field controls are directly related to site columns. Therefore, you'll have to create new site columns for each of the separate content elements you want in a page layout. If, for example, you are creating a product page, you might define site columns such as Product Name or Product Description. These columns can then be used later to hold specific product information.

Creating new site columns is done from the Site Columns Gallery, which is accessible from the Site Settings page. From the Site Columns Gallery, you can click the Create button and define a new column. When you define a new site column you can select from any of the data types shown in Table 5-3.

Table 5-3. *Site Column Types*

Data Type	MOSS/WSS	Description
Single Line of Text	MOSS/WSS	A single line of text
Multiple Lines of Text	MOSS/WSS	Many lines of text
Choice	MOSS/WSS	A predefined list of choices
Number	MOSS/WSS	A specified minimum, maximum, and number of decimal places
Currency	MOSS/WSS	Money in a specified currency format
Date/Time	MOSS/WSS	A date or date/time formatted value
Lookup	MOSS/WSS	A value obtained from a list on the site
Boolean	MOSS/WSS	A yes or no value appearing as a check box
People	MOSS/WSS	A person or group based on SharePoint membership
URL	MOSS/WSS	A hyperlink or an image link
Calculated	MOSS/WSS	A computed value based on other fields
HTML	MOSS only	HTML content specifically for content management
Image	MOSS only	A picture specifically for content management
Hyperlink	MOSS only	A link specifically for content management
Summary	MOSS only	A column providing summary links
Business Data	MOSS only	A column for use with the Business Data Catalog
Audience	MOSS only	A column that targets specific audiences

After defining the site columns, you must then define a new content type that uses these columns. Defining a new content type is done from the Site Content Type Gallery, which is accessible from the Site Settings page. From the Site Content Type Gallery, you can click the Create button and define a new content type. The key to making a content type that works correctly with the WCM feature is to inherit from the existing page content type. After that, simply add the site columns you created to the new content type.

Once the content type is created, you can go on to create the new page layout. Creating a new page layout is done from the Master Page and Page Layout Gallery, which is accessible from the Site Settings page. From the Master Page and Page Layout Gallery, you can select New ➤ Page Layout from the toolbar. When you create the new page layout, you'll be asked to associate it with a content type. Here you would simply select the content type you created earlier.

After the new page layout is created, you must specifically add field controls to the page so that content editors can use them to create new pages. Field controls are added using the SharePoint Designer, and you can open the page layout for editing in the SharePoint Designer by using the drop-down menu associated with the file. Alternately, you can open the entire site in the SharePoint Designer and locate the page layout in the Master Page Gallery located at catalogs\masterpage.

Depending upon your exact role on the site, you may need to make changes to the Contributor Settings. In order to change the settings, select Site ➤ Contributor Settings, which will open a dialog. In the dialog, you can give groups the ability to edit certain content. Additionally, you can simply disable the settings to allow all content to be edited. In any case, if you have trouble making changes to the page layout, it is likely the result of restricted permissions.

If you have appropriate permissions, you can double-click the new page layout and it will open for editing. By selecting Task Panes ➤ Toolbox, you can open a window that shows all of the different components that you can add to the page. The field controls appear in the SharePoint Controls section under the Content Fields node. Using the toolbox, you can right-click any of the content fields and select Insert from the context menu to add them to the page layout, as shown in Figure 5-14.

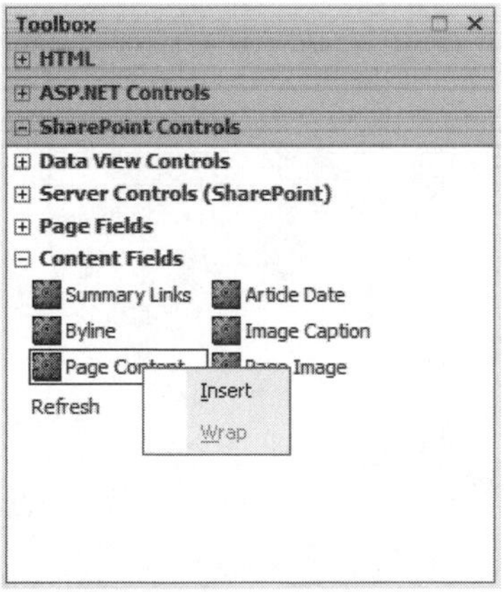

Figure 5-14. *Adding field controls*

Once the new page layout is completed, you must make it available to content editors. This is done by checking in the page layout, publishing it, and approving it. This process is largely the same as for any item in SharePoint. Once approved, the new page layout will be available on the site when a user selects Create Page from the Site Actions menu. If you are interested in a detailed examination of creating new page layouts, the Exercise at the end of the chapter will walk you through the entire process.

Creating New Master Pages

In addition to the default and application master pages, you may also associate page layouts with custom master pages. For example, many of the pages in the Publishing Portal template use the TopNavFlyouts master page. This master page was designed to be the foundation for all of the public content pages that appear on the site. Creating a custom master page gives you the most control over the look and feel of a site. If you are using SharePoint to create a public Internet site, you will definitely want to create a set of custom master pages. This is really the only way to achieve the level of design control needed for most Internet projects.

Unfortunately, there is no way in SharePoint to start with a blank slate and design your site. This is because both SharePoint and the WCM feature assume a certain infrastructure is in place when processing master pages and page layouts. Furthermore, there is no "Blank WCM Site" template that gives you everything you need for your own custom master page. This is a terrible shortcoming in my opinion, but we can compensate by developing our own blank master page that meets just the minimum requirements of the SharePoint infrastructure. Listing 5-1 shows a complete master page, available in the MOSS SDK, that you can use as the basis for your own custom look and feel.

Listing 5-1. *A Minimal Master Page*

```
<%@ Master language="C#" %>
<!DOCTYPE html PUBLIC "-//W3C//DTD HTML 4.01 Transitional//EN"
"http://www.w3.org/TR/html4/loose.dtd">
<%@ Import Namespace="Microsoft.SharePoint" %>
<%@ Register Tagprefix="SPSWC"
Namespace="Microsoft.SharePoint.Portal.WebControls"
Assembly="Microsoft.SharePoint.Portal, ,➡
        Version=12.0.0.0,➡
        Culture=neutral,➡
        PublicKeyToken=71e9bce111e9429c" %>
<%@ Register Tagprefix="SharePoint"
Namespace="Microsoft.SharePoint.WebControls"
Assembly="Microsoft.SharePoint,➡
        Version=12.0.0.0,➡
        Culture=neutral,➡
        PublicKeyToken=71e9bce111e9429c" %>
<%@ Register Tagprefix="WebPartPages"
Namespace="Microsoft.SharePoint.WebPartPages"
Assembly="Microsoft.SharePoint,➡
        Version=12.0.0.0,➡
        Culture=neutral,➡
        PublicKeyToken=71e9bce111e9429c" %>
<%@ Register Tagprefix="PublishingWebControls"
Namespace="Microsoft.SharePoint.Publishing.WebControls"
Assembly="Microsoft.SharePoint.Publishing,➡
        Version=12.0.0.0,➡
        Culture=neutral,➡
        PublicKeyToken=71e9bce111e9429c" %>
```

```
<%@ Register Tagprefix="PublishingNavigation"
Namespace="Microsoft.SharePoint.Publishing.Navigation",➥
Assembly="Microsoft.SharePoint.Publishing,➥
          Version=12.0.0.0,➥
          Culture=neutral,➥
          PublicKeyToken=71e9bce111e9429c" %>
<%@ Register TagPrefix="wssuc" TagName="Welcome"
    src="~/_controltemplates/Welcome.ascx" %>
<%@ Register TagPrefix="wssuc" TagName="DesignModeConsole"
    src="~/_controltemplates/DesignModeConsole.ascx" %>
<%@ Register TagPrefix="PublishingVariations",
    TagName="VariationsLabelMenu"
    src="~/_controltemplates/VariationsLabelMenu.ascx" %>
<%@ Register Tagprefix="PublishingConsole" TagName="Console"
    src="~/_controltemplates/PublishingConsole.ascx" %>
<%@ Register TagPrefix="PublishingSiteAction" TagName="SiteActionMenu"
    src="~/_controltemplates/PublishingActionMenu.ascx" %>

<html>
<WebPartPages:SPWebPartManager runat="server"/>
<SharePoint:RobotsMetaTag runat="server"/>


<head runat="server">
<asp:ContentPlaceHolder runat="server" id="head">
<title>
<asp:ContentPlaceHolder id="PlaceHolderPageTitle" runat="server" />
</title>
</asp:ContentPlaceHolder>
<Sharepoint:CssLink runat="server"/>
<asp:ContentPlaceHolder id="PlaceHolderAdditionalPageHead"
runat="server" />
</head>


<body onload="javascript:_spBodyOnLoadWrapper();">

<form runat="server" onsubmit="return _spFormOnSubmitWrapper();">
  <wssuc:Welcome id="explitLogout" runat="server"/>

  <PublishingSiteAction:SiteActionMenu runat="server"/>
  <PublishingWebControls:AuthoringContainer id="authoringcontrols"
   runat="server">
    <PublishingConsole:Console runat="server" />
  </PublishingWebControls:AuthoringContainer>

  <asp:ContentPlaceHolder id="PlaceHolderMain" runat="server" />
```

```
<asp:Panel visible="false" runat="server">
  <asp:ContentPlaceHolder id="PlaceHolderSearchArea"
   runat="server"/>
  <asp:ContentPlaceHolder id="PlaceHolderTitleBreadcrumb"
   runat="server"/>
  <asp:ContentPlaceHolder id="PlaceHolderPageTitleInTitleArea"
   runat="server"/>
  <asp:ContentPlaceHolder id="PlaceHolderLeftNavBar"
   runat="server"/>
  <asp:ContentPlaceHolder ID="PlaceHolderPageImage" runat="server"/>
  <asp:ContentPlaceHolder ID="PlaceHolderBodyLeftBorder"
   runat="server"/>
  <asp:ContentPlaceHolder ID="PlaceHolderNavSpacer" runat="server"/>
  <asp:ContentPlaceHolder ID="PlaceHolderTitleLeftBorder"
   runat="server"/>
  <asp:ContentPlaceHolder ID="PlaceHolderTitleAreaSeparator"
   runat="server"/>
  <asp:ContentPlaceHolder ID="PlaceHolderMiniConsole"
   runat="server"/>
  <asp:ContentPlaceHolder id="PlaceHolderCalendarNavigator"
   runat ="server" />
  <asp:ContentPlaceHolder id="PlaceHolderLeftActions"
   runat ="server"/>
  <asp:ContentPlaceHolder id="PlaceHolderPageDescription"
   runat ="server"/>
  <asp:ContentPlaceHolder id="PlaceHolderBodyAreaClass"
   runat ="server"/>
  <asp:ContentPlaceHolder id="PlaceHolderTitleAreaClass"
   runat ="server"/>
</asp:Panel>

</form>
</body>
</html>
```

The minimal master page consists of Imports and Register statements for referencing SharePoint assemblies that are required by the WSS or WCM infrastructure. The body of the master page contains server-side controls that interact with the WSS or WCM infrastructure. Each of these controls is responsible for generating part of the page within a SharePoint site. The following sections describe key tags in the master page in the order they appear.

WebPartPages:SPWebPartManager

WebPartPages:SPWebPartManager is the server control that implements the web part infrastructure. You'll find this control on every page in a SharePoint site. Without this control, web parts cannot be used on the page.

asp:ContentPlaceHolder

The server control `asp:ContentPlaceHolder` generates content for the page. In a typical page, there are several of these controls that are used to hold everything from text to user controls. Earlier when you created a page layout, you used the `PlaceHolderMain` placeholder to render the body of the page.

It's important to note that a master page must support all of the content holders referenced by a page layout. If a page layout has content holders defined in it that are not available in the master page, you will see errors on the page when it renders. The master page defined in Listing 5-1 is designed to be a starting point that contains the minimally required tags, but you will likely have to add additional content placeholders if you wish to replace an existing master page in a SharePoint site. Table 5-4 shows the placeholders from Listing 5-1 and describes their purpose.

Table 5-4. *Content Placeholders*

Placeholder	Purpose
PlaceHolderSearchArea	Defines the search box
PlaceHolderTitleBreadcrumb	Defines the main breadcrumb on the page
PlaceHolderPageTitleInTitleArea	Defines the title at the top of the page
PlaceHolderLeftNavBar	Defines the area on the far left of the page
PlaceHolderPageImage	Defines the page icon in the upper left corner
PlaceHolderBodyLeftBorder	Defines the left border of the main page
PlaceHolderNavSpacer	Defines the width of the left navigation area
PlaceHolderTitleLeftBorder	Defines the left border of the title area
PlaceHolderTitleAreaSeparator	Defines shadows for the title area
PlaceHolderMiniConsole	Defines an area for page-level commands such as exiting edit mode
PlaceHolderCalendarNavigator	Defines a date picker for a calendar view
PlaceHolderLeftActions	Defines the bottom of the left navigation area
PlaceHolderPageDescription	Defines the page description area
PlaceHolderBodyAreaClass	Defines additional body styles
PlaceHolderTitleAreaClass	Defines additional title styles

While content placeholders are most obviously used for text and graphics, they can also be used to render controls. The best example of this capability is the `SharePoint:DelegateControl`. This control is often used in conjunction with placeholders to display user controls on a page. In fact, SharePoint uses this capability extensively to render things such as the search box. The following code from the `default.master` page shows how the search box is displayed using a combination of the `PlaceHolderSearchArea` placeholder and the `DelegateControl`:

```
<asp:ContentPlaceHolder id="PlaceHolderSearchArea" runat="server">
<SharePoint:DelegateControl runat="server" ControlId="SmallSearchInputBox" />
</asp:ContentPlaceHolder>
```

The DelegateControl has a ControlId attribute that references the class name of a user control located in C:\Program Files\Common Files\Microsoft Shared\web server extensions\ 12\TEMPLATE\CONTROL TEMPLATES. If you examine the contents of this directory, you will see that there are many user controls available. Unfortunately at this writing, there is very little documentation on these controls. The best way to learn about them is to examine the default.master page, review the control file itself, and experiment with test code.

SharePoint:CssLink

The server control SharePoint:CssLink is responsible for generating the links between the page and the required style sheets. This link is created by using a link tag in the page. The following code shows an example of the output generated by the SharePoint:CssLink control:

```
<link rel="stylesheet" type="text/css" href="/_layouts/1033/styles/core.css"/>
```

PublishingWebControls:AuthoringContainer

The server control PublishingWebControls:AuthoringContainer is a container for the controls PublishingSiteAction:SiteActionMenu and PublishingConsole:Console. The PublishingSiteAction:SiteActionMenu server control is an enhanced Site Actions menu that is enabled by the WCM feature. The PublishingConsole:Console is used to generate the toolbar for the publishing process. All of these controls are required by the WCM feature.

Enabling Site Variations

If you are creating content that must be presented in different languages, you'll want to enable *site variations*. Site variations allow you to centralize the management of multilingual content and then propagate it to other sites. Site variations essentially set up parallel site collections that are synchronized with a master collection. When a change is made to the master collection, the content is copied to all the variations. Setting up site variations is relatively straightforward for a publishing site.

Follow these steps to set up site variations:

1. Go to the home page of the Internet site you created earlier using the Default zone.

2. Select Site Settings ➤ Modify All Site Settings from the Site Actions menu.

3. On the Site Settings page, click the Variations link under the Site Collection Administration section.

4. On the Variation Settings page, type a forward slash into the Location field.

5. Click the OK button.

6. On the Site Settings page, click the Variation Labels link under the Site Collection Administration section.

7. On the Variation Labels page, click the New Label button.

8. On the Create Variation Label page, enter **English (en-us)** in the Label Name field.

9. Enter **English** in the Display Name field.

10. Select English (United States) from the Locale drop-down list.

11. Select the option labeled Publishing Site and All Pages.

12. Check the box labeled Set This Variation to Be the Source Variation.

13. Select Publishing Site from the drop-down list labeled Select the Publishing Site Template You Want to Use.

14. Click the OK button.

15. On the Variation Labels page, click the New Label button.

16. On the Create Variation Label page, enter **Italian (it-IT)** in the Label Name field.

17. Enter **Italian** in the Display Name field.

18. Select Italian (Italy) from the Local drop-down list.

19. Select the option labeled Publishing Site and All Pages.

20. Click the OK button.

21. On the Variation Labels page, click the Create Hierarchies button.

Once the hierarchy creation is complete, you will have a subsite created for each of the labels you defined. These subsite structures allow you to have identical structures with localized content. Now when you make changes to the source label, they'll be propagated to the other labels you defined.

Using Content Deployment

Content deployment is a capability used to move content from one SharePoint site collection to another. Using content deployment, you can move content between site collections in the same farm or across farms. This capability allows you to create staging servers where you can develop and test solutions before deploying them into production.

Configuring content deployment is done through the Central Administration site. A content deployment section is located on the Operations tab and contains all of the functionality you need to set up paths and jobs. Paths form relationships between site collections so that one can act as a source and the other as a destination. Jobs define the actual content that will be deployed from the source to the destination.

Before creating paths and jobs, however, you must enable content deployment on the farm. This is done by clicking the Content Deployment Settings link on the Operations tab of the Central Administration site. On the Content Deployment Settings page, you must select the option to accept incoming content deployment jobs. You can also specify the servers to handle the incoming and outgoing jobs as well as whether connections must be made using the HTTPS protocol.

Once the farm is configured to allow content deployment, you can set up paths between site collections. This is accomplished by clicking the Content Deployment Paths and Jobs link. Here you can create a new path that defines a source and destination site collection.

Once the path is created, you can set up a job to move the content. The job can be set up to deploy an entire site collection or just selected sites. You can also set up the job to run on a schedule or to execute manually later. Lastly, you can configure the job to send an e-mail each time it runs.

Exercise 5.1. Web Content Management

In this exercise, you will create a new site that uses WCM to create a custom look and publish custom pages. The site will be an IT training site with custom page layouts to describe training courses offered internally to employees. I'll keep this site very simple to emphasize the process you should follow to create a custom look and feel that can differ radically from the standard SharePoint appearance. You'll then be able to use this same technique to create specific sites and page layouts for your own purposes.

Creating a New Site

When creating your own custom sites, you can either choose to modify the master pages and page layouts that are provided out of the box in templates, or create your own from scratch. In this exercise, you'll use a blank site and create new content that is not tied to an existing layout. The process of creating a new web application and site collection should be familiar to you by now.

Follow these steps to create a new site:

1. Log in to VSMOSS as a SharePoint administrator.

2. Select Start ➤ Administrative Tools ➤ SharePoint 3.0 Central Administration.

3. On the Application Management tab, under the SharePoint Web Application Management section, click the link titled Create or Extend a Web Application.

4. On the Create or Extend a Web Application page, click the link titled Create a New Web Application.

5. On the Create a New Web Application page, select the option to Create a New IIS Web Site.

6. In the Description field, type **Departmental** and make note of the port number that the new web application will use.

7. In the Application Pool section, select Create a New Application Pool.

8. Enter **Departmental_Pool** as the pool name.

9. Select the Configurable option for the application pool security account.

10. In the User Name field, enter **DOMAIN\SPContentPool**.

11. In the Password field, enter the account password.

12. In the Reset Internet Information Services section, select the option to Restart IIS Automatically.

13. Click the OK button.

14. On the Application Created page, click the link titled Create a New Site Collection.

15. On the Create Site Collection page, enter **IT Training** in the Title field.

16. Under the Primary Site Collection Administrator section, enter **DOMAIN\Administrator** in the User Name field.

17. Under the Template Selection section, click the Collaboration tab, and then select the Blank Site.

18. Click the OK button to create the new site collection. When the site collection is created, open it in a separate copy of the browser. You might also want to add a Favorites link in the browser so that you can get back to the site easily.

Activating and Configuring the Publishing Feature

Although the Blank Site template is available in both WSS and MOSS, I want to use the publishing feature of MOSS to enable the management of web content. Therefore, you will enable the Office SharePoint Server Publishing Feature on the blank site. Once enabled, you will be able to create custom page layouts for the site.

Follow these steps to activate the publishing feature:

1. From the home page of the IT training site, select Site Settings from the Site Actions menu.

2. On the Site Settings page, click the Site Collection Features list under the Site Collection Administration section.

3. On the Site Collection Features page, click the Activate button associated with the Office SharePoint Server Publishing Infrastructure Feature.

4. Return to the Site Settings page.

5. On the Site Settings page, click the Site Features link under the Site Administration section.

6. On the Site Features page, click the Activate button associated with the Office SharePoint Server Publishing Feature.

7. Save the code from Listing 5-2 as a file named `training.master`.

Listing 5-2. *training.master*

```
<%@ Master language="C#" %>
<!DOCTYPE html PUBLIC "-//W3C//DTD HTML 4.01 Transitional//EN"
 "http://www.w3.org/TR/html4/loose.dtd">
<%@ Import Namespace="Microsoft.SharePoint" %>
<%@ Register Tagprefix="SPSWC"
Namespace="Microsoft.SharePoint.Portal.WebControls"
```

```
        Assembly="Microsoft.SharePoint.Portal,➡
                Version=12.0.0.0,➡
                Culture=neutral,➡
                PublicKeyToken=71e9bce111e9429c" %>
<%@ Register Tagprefix="SharePoint"
Namespace="Microsoft.SharePoint.WebControls" Assembly="Microsoft.SharePoint,➡
                Version=12.0.0.0,➡
                Culture=neutral,➡
                PublicKeyToken=71e9bce111e9429c" %>
<%@ Register Tagprefix="WebPartPages"
Namespace="Microsoft.SharePoint.WebPartPages"➡
Assembly="Microsoft.SharePoint,➡
                Version=12.0.0.0,➡
                Culture=neutral,➡
                PublicKeyToken=71e9bce111e9429c" %>
<%@ Register Tagprefix="PublishingWebControls"
Namespace="Microsoft.SharePoint.Publishing.WebControls"
Assembly="Microsoft.SharePoint.Publishing,➡
                Version=12.0.0.0,➡
                Culture=neutral,➡
                PublicKeyToken=71e9bce111e9429c" %>
<%@ Register Tagprefix="PublishingNavigation"
Namespace="Microsoft.SharePoint.Publishing.Navigation"
Assembly="Microsoft.SharePoint.Publishing,➡
                Version=12.0.0.0,➡
                Culture=neutral,➡
                PublicKeyToken=71e9bce111e9429c" %>
<%@ Register TagPrefix="wssuc" TagName="Welcome"
        src="~/_controltemplates/Welcome.ascx" %>
<%@ Register TagPrefix="wssuc" TagName="DesignModeConsole"
        src="~/_controltemplates/DesignModeConsole.ascx" %>
<%@ Register TagPrefix="PublishingVariations"
        TagName="VariationsLabelMenu"
        src="~/_controltemplates/VariationsLabelMenu.ascx" %>
<%@ Register TagPrefix="PublishingConsole" TagName="Console"
        src="~/_controltemplates/PublishingConsole.ascx" %>
<%@ Register TagPrefix="PublishingSiteAction" TagName="SiteActionMenu"
        src="~/_controltemplates/PublishingActionMenu.ascx" %>

<html>
<WebPartPages:SPWebPartManager runat="server"/>
<SharePoint:RobotsMetaTag runat="server"/>
```

```
<head runat="server">
<asp:ContentPlaceHolder runat="server" id="head">
<title>
<asp:ContentPlaceHolder id="PlaceHolderPageTitle" runat="server" />
</title>
</asp:ContentPlaceHolder>
<Sharepoint:CssLink runat="server"/>
<asp:ContentPlaceHolder id="PlaceHolderAdditionalPageHead"
 runat="server" />
</head>


<body onload="javascript:_spBodyOnLoadWrapper();">

<form runat="server" onsubmit="return _spFormOnSubmitWrapper();">

  <table border="0">
    <tr>
      <td><asp:ContentPlaceHolder id="PlaceHolderPageTitleInTitleArea"
          runat="server"/></td>
      <td><wssuc:Welcome id="explitLogout" runat="server"/></td>
      <td><PublishingSiteAction:SiteActionMenu runat="server"/></td>
    </tr>
    <tr>
      <td colspan="3">
        <PublishingWebControls:AuthoringContainer
         id="authoringcontrols" runat="server">
          <PublishingConsole:Console runat="server" />
        </PublishingWebControls:AuthoringContainer>
      </td>
    </tr>
    <tr>
      <td colspan="3">
        <br/>
        <asp:ContentPlaceHolder id="PlaceHolderMain" runat="server" />
        <p><asp:ContentPlaceHolder id="PlaceHolderSearchArea"
            runat="server"/></p>
        <p><asp:ContentPlaceHolder id="PlaceHolderLeftNavBar"
            runat="server"/></p>
        <p><asp:ContentPlaceHolder ID="PlaceHolderPageImage"
            runat="server"/></p>
        <p><asp:ContentPlaceHolder ID="PlaceHolderBodyLeftBorder"
            runat="server"/></p>
        <p><asp:ContentPlaceHolder ID="PlaceHolderNavSpacer"
            runat="server"/></p>
```

```
        <p><asp:ContentPlaceHolder ID="PlaceHolderTitleLeftBorder"
            runat="server"/></p>
        <p><asp:ContentPlaceHolder ID="PlaceHolderTitleAreaSeparator"
            runat="server"/></p>
        <p><asp:ContentPlaceHolder ID="PlaceHolderMiniConsole"
            runat="server"/></p>
        <p><asp:ContentPlaceHolder id="PlaceHolderCalendarNavigator"
            runat ="server" /></p>
        <p><asp:ContentPlaceHolder id="PlaceHolderLeftActions"
            runat ="server"/></p>
        <p><asp:ContentPlaceHolder id="PlaceHolderPageDescription"
            runat ="server"/></p>
        <p><asp:ContentPlaceHolder id="PlaceHolderBodyAreaClass"
            runat ="server"/></p>
        <p><asp:ContentPlaceHolder id="PlaceHolderTitleAreaClass"
            runat ="server"/></p>
      </td>
    </tr>
  </table>

</form>
</body>
</html>
```

8. In the IT training site, select Site Settings ➤ Modify All Site Settings from the Site Actions menu.

Note Take note that the Site Actions menu has changed now due to the activation of the publishing feature.

---

9. On the Site Settings page, click the link titled Master Page and Page Layout Gallery under the Galleries section.

10. In the Master Page Gallery, click the Upload button.

11. On the Upload Master Page page, click the Browse button to open the Choose File dialog.

12. In the Choose File dialog, locate the `training.master` file and click the Open button.

13. On the Upload Master Page page, click the OK button.

14. On the Master Page Gallery page, select Publishing Master Page from the Content Type drop-down list and click the Check In button.

15. In the Master Page Gallery, locate the `training.master` file and select Publish a Major Version from the drop-down menu.

16. On the Publish Major Version page, click the OK button.

17. In the Master Page Gallery, locate the `training.master` file and select Approve/Reject from the drop-down menu.

18. On the Approve/Reject page, select Approved and click the OK button.

19. Select Site Settings ➤ Modify All Site Settings from the Site Actions menu.

20. On the Site Settings Page, click the Site Master Page Settings link under the Look and Feel section.

21. On the Site Master Page Settings page, select the `training.master` file from the Site Master Page drop-down list and click the OK button.

Creating a New Welcome Page

Now that the WCM features are available, you can use them to create a new page. A page layout already exists for creating a welcome page for the site. In this section, you will use the existing page layout to create a new welcome page for the training site.

Follow these steps to create a new welcome page:

1. In the IT training site, select Create Page from the Site Actions menu.

2. On the Create Page, enter **IT Training Home** in the Title field.

3. Enter **home** in the URL Name field.

4. Select (Welcome Page) Welcome Page with Table of Contents from the Page Layout list.

5. Click the Create button.

6. When the new welcome page appears in edit mode, click the button labeled Check In to Save Draft.

Note The page should be a fairly plain page indicating the influence of the training master page. You should also see that the Site Actions menu has changed position to the left side of the page.

---

7. From the new Welcome page, select Site Settings ➤ Modify All Site Settings from the Site Actions menu.

8. On the Site Settings page, click the Welcome Page link under the Look and Feel section.

9. On the Site Welcome Page page, click the Browse button.

10. Locate the `home.aspx` page in the Pages library and click the OK button.

11. On the Site Welcome Page page, click the OK button. The `home.aspx` page should now be the default page for the site.

Defining Site Columns

Page layouts are a key facet of content management within MOSS and are used to create specific types of web pages that have placeholders for content. Once created, page layouts make it easy for content owners to create new pages for a site, publish them, and route them for approval. The individual content elements that appear in a page layout are derived from site columns. When you create a page layout, you can use any of the site columns already defined or define your own. In this exercise, you will define several custom site columns that are specific to the course description page layout you will make later.

Follow these steps to create the custom site columns:

1. Select Site Settings ➤ Modify All Site Settings from the Site Actions menu.

2. On the Site Settings page, click the Site Columns link under the Galleries section.

3. On the Site Column Gallery page, click the Create button.

4. On the New Site Column page, enter **Course Name** in the Column Name field.

5. Under the Group section, select the New Group option and type **Course Page Layout** in the text field.

6. Click the OK button.

7. Repeat steps 3 through 6 to create columns as defined in Table 5-5.

Table 5-5. *Custom Columns*

Name	Type	Details
Course Description	Multiple lines of text	No support for rich text
Course Level	Choice	Choice values of 100, 200, 300
Course Outline	Publishing HTML	—

Defining the Content Type

Page layouts have a direct relationship to a content type defined within the site. The *content type* is a collection of site columns, a page template, workflows, and other information that determines the appearance and behavior of a page layout. In this exercise, you will create a new content type that derives from the existing Page content type. Inheriting the Page content type allows the new page layout to function correctly within the MOSS content management feature.

Follow these steps to create the new content type:

1. Select Site Settings ➤ Modify All Site Settings from the Site Actions menu.

2. On the Site Settings page, click the Site Content Types link under the Galleries section.

3. On the Site Content Type Gallery page, click the Create button.

4. On the New Site Content Type page, enter **Course Page** in the Name field.

5. Select Publishing Content Types from the list labeled Select Parent Content Type From.

6. Select Page from the list labeled Parent Content Type.

7. Select Custom Content Types from the list labeled Existing Group.

8. Click the OK button.

9. On the Site Content Type page, click the link titled Add from Existing Site Columns.

10. On the Add Columns to Site Content Type page, select Course Page Layout from the list labeled Select Columns From.

11. Move all of the columns from the Available Columns list to the Columns to Add list.

12. Click the OK button.

Creating the Page Layout

Page layouts are stored in the Master Page and Page Layout Gallery. From this gallery, you can create a new page layout and associate it with a content type. This process makes the site columns that are defined for the content type available to the page layout as field controls that you can place on the page with the SharePoint Designer.

Follow these steps to create the new page layout:

1. Select Site Settings ➤ Modify All Site Settings from the Site Actions menu.

2. On the Site Settings page, click the Master Page and Page Layout Gallery link under the Galleries section.

3. In the Master Page Gallery, select New ➤ Page Layout from the toolbar.

4. On the New Page Layout page, select Custom Content Types from the list labeled Content Type Group.

5. Select Course Page from the list labeled Content Type Name.

6. Type **CoursePage** in the URL Name field.

7. Type **Course Page** in the Title field.

8. Give the page layout a description.

9. Click the OK button.

Editing the Page Layout

Once you have created the new page layout, you must open it in the SharePoint Designer so that you can add the desired field controls. The site columns you define as part of the content type become available in the SharePoint Designer as field controls that you can place on the page layout. In this exercise, you'll place field controls for the columns that define a course description page.

Follow these steps to edit the page layout:

1. Open the SharePoint Designer by selecting Start ➤ All Programs ➤ Microsoft Office ➤ Microsoft Office SharePoint Designer 2007.

2. In the SharePoint Designer, select File ➤ Open Site from the main menu.

3. In the Open Site dialog, type the training site (e.g., **http://VSMOSS:20716/sites/itt**).

4. Select Site ➤ Contributor Settings.

5. In the Contributor Settings dialog, click the Advanced button.

6. Click the Disable Contributor Settings button.

7. Click the OK button.

8. In the Folder list, expand the _catalogs folder. Then expand the master page folder.

■**Note** If the Folder List pane is not visible, select Task Panes ➤ Folder List from the main menu.

---

9. If the `CoursePage.aspx` page is not already checked out, right-click the `CoursePage.aspx` file and select Check Out from the context menu.

10. Double-click the `CoursePage.aspx` file to open it for editing in the SharePoint Designer.

11. In the toolbox, expand the SharePoint Controls section.

■**Note** If the Toolbox is not visible, select Task Panes ➤ Toolbox from the main menu.

---

12. In the SharePoint Controls section, expand the Content Fields node. You should now see the custom columns you added earlier.

13. Right-click the Course Name field in the Toolbox and select Insert from the context menu.

14. Repeat the step to insert all of the fields into the Page Layout.

15. After the fields are added, click File ➤ Save from the main menu.

16. Exit the SharePoint Designer.

■**Tip** You can use just about any element available in the SharePoint Designer to create your page layout including layout tables, web part zones, and data views. Don't be shy about experimenting with the content; you can always undo your changes.

Publishing the Page Layout

Once the page layout is created, you must publish and approve it so that it becomes available for content authors. This process is essentially the same as publishing any item in MOSS. First the document is checked in, then it is published, and finally it is approved.

Follow these steps to make the new page layout available for use:

1. Go to the home page of the training site.

2. Select Manage Content and Structure from the Site Actions menu.

3. On the Site Content and Structure page, select Open Link in New Window from the drop-down menu associated with the Master Page Gallery.

4. In the Master Page Gallery, select Check In from the drop-down menu associated with the `CoursePage.aspx` file.

5. On the Check In page, click the OK button.

6. In the Master Page Gallery, select Publish a Major Version from the drop-down menu associated with the `CoursePage.aspx` file.

7. On the Publish Major Version page, click the OK button.

8. In the Master Page Gallery, select Approve/Reject from the drop-down menu associated with the `CoursePage.aspx` file.

9. On the Approve/Reject page, select Approved and click the OK button.

Using the Page Layout

Once the page layout is published and approved, content authors may use it to create new pages. This is done in the normal way by selecting the Create Page item from the Site Actions menu. After the page is created, the field controls may be edited.

Follow these steps to create a new page:

1. Go to the home page of the training site.

2. Select Create Page from the Site Actions menu.

3. On the Create Page page, enter **SharePoint Development** in the Title field.

4. Select Course Page from the list of page layouts.

5. Click the Create button.

6. When the page opens in edit mode, enter information into the fields of the page layout to create a new course description. Figure 5-15 shows how the new page should look.

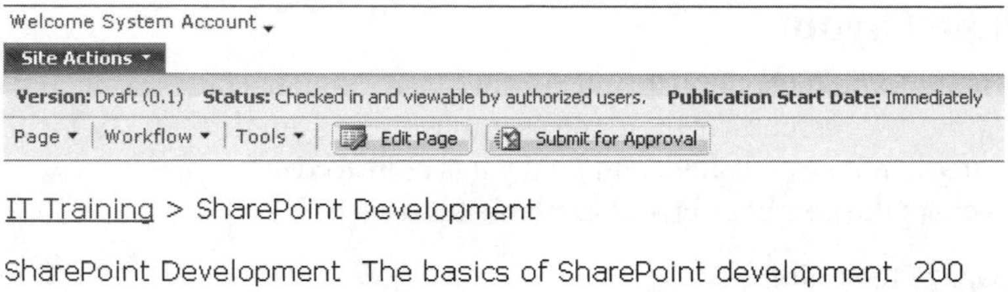

Welcome System Account ▾

Site Actions ▾

Version: Draft (0.1)   **Status:** Checked in and viewable by authorized users.   **Publication Start Date:** Immediately

Page ▾ | Workflow ▾ | Tools ▾ | ▣ Edit Page | ▣ Submit for Approval

IT Training > SharePoint Development

SharePoint Development   The basics of SharePoint development   200

Figure 5-15. *A new custom page layout*

■ ■ ■

CHAPTER 6

SharePoint Document, Form, and Records Management

Throughout the book, I have used document libraries in various examples and worked with some of the functionality. However, we have not yet investigated documents, forms, records, and libraries in detail. In this chapter, we will take a detailed look at the functionality in Share-Point for managing documents, forms, and records. After reading this chapter, you should have a strong understanding of the complete document life cycle from creation through archival and some good ideas for customizing the capabilities to meet your own needs.

Working with Content Types, Lists, and Libraries

Several times throughout the book, I have mentioned and used site content types. In the previous chapter, for example, you used them extensively to create page layouts for a site. By now, you probably think of a *content type* as a reusable document definition; however, content types can also define list items and folders. Furthermore, content types can be based on other content types to form an inheritance tree, and when the parent is updated the changes can be pushed down to the child. As you learn more, you'll see that a content type is a lot like a programming class that defines the information structure for a SharePoint site.

Both WSS and MOSS ship with a base set of content types that are listed in the Content Types Gallery, which is accessible from the Site Settings page. As you might expect, however, MOSS has more defined content types than WSS. This is because many MOSS features, such as the publishing feature discussed in the previous chapter, require additional content types such as the Page Layout. Table 6-1 lists the base content types that are common to both WSS and MOSS, their parent content type, a description, and whether the content type is visible in the Content Types Gallery. Content types that are not visible are typically for system use only.

Table 6-1. *Base Content Types*

Content Type	Parent Content Type	Description	Visible
System	—	The root of the content type tree	No
Item	System	Represents any item in a list or library	Yes
Document	Item	Represents any type of document	Yes
Form	Document	Represents an InfoPath form	No

Continued

Table 6-1. *Continued*

Content Type	Parent Content Type	Description	Visible
Picture	Document	Represents an image file	Yes
UntypedDocument	Document	Represents any generic file type	Yes
MasterPage	Document	Represents a master page	Yes
WikiDocument	Document	Represents a page in a wiki	Yes
BasicPage	Document	Represents a basic web page	Yes
WebPartPage	BasicPage	Represents a web part page	Yes
LinkToDocument	Document	Represents a link to a document in a different location	Yes
DublinCoreName	Document	Represents the Dublin Core metadata set, which is an open standard for metadata (see http://www.dublincore.org for more information)	Yes
Event	Item	Represents an event item in a list	Yes
Issues	Item	Represents an issue item in a list	Yes
Announcement	Item	Represents an announcement item in a list	Yes
Link	Item	Represents a link item in a list	Yes
Contact	Item	Represents a contact item in a list	Yes
Message	Item	Represents a message item in a list	
Task	Item	Represents a task item in a list	Yes
WorkflowTask	Task	Represents a task assigned by a workflow process	No
AdminTask	Task	Represents an administrative task assigned to an administrator	No
WorkflowHistory	Item	Represents a historical entry recording a workflow milestone	No
BlogPost	Item	Represents a blog post	Yes
BlogComment	Item	Represents a blog comment	Yes
FarEastContact	Item	Represents a personal or business contact in the Far East	Yes
Folder	Item	Represents a folder in a list	Yes
RootOfList	Folder	Represents the root folder of a list	Yes
Discussion	Folder	Represents a topic in a discussion list	Yes

When starting any new SharePoint project, it is important to decide what new content types you must create in order to support your information structure. While all content types ultimately inherit from the System content type, typically your content types will inherit from one of the lower-level content types listed in Table 6-1. You might, for example, define content types for common documents such as expense reports or vacation requests and base them on the Document content type.

Designing content types can be a significant effort because they can contain definitions for many different elements. Content types can contain defined metadata fields, document templates, workflows, and custom Document Information Panels (DIP). I cover metadata and templates in this section. I cover workflows in Chapter 7 and custom DIPs in Chapter 9.

Before you define any new content type, it is a good idea to determine all of the elements that it will contain; however, nothing stops you from updating a content type after it is defined. For this chapter, I'll create a content type to represent a software specification document and then modify it to contain additional elements.

Follow these steps to create a new content type:

1. Log in to the home page of the intranet site you created in Chapter 2 (e.g., `http://vsmoss/sites/intranet/Pages/default.aspx`).

2. Select Site Settings ➤ Modify All Site Settings from the Site Actions menu.

3. On the Site Settings page, select Site Content Types from under the Galleries section.

4. On the Site Content Type Gallery page, click the Create button.

5. On the New Site Content Type page, enter **Software Specification** in the Name field.

6. Select Document Content Types from the drop-down list labeled Select Parent Content Type From.

7. Select Dublin Core Columns from the drop-down list labeled Parent Content Type. This will give you a nice set of document-centric columns.

8. Under the Group section, select the New Group option and enter **Custom Software Documents** in the text field.

9. Click the OK button.

Understanding Site and List Columns

The metadata for a content type can consist of either site columns or list columns. *Site columns* are reusable columns that are defined at the site level and may be used by any list in a child site. *List columns* are defined at the list level and may only be used by the list where they are defined. When you create a new content type, it will inherit the site and list column definitions from its parent. You can also add any of the previously defined site columns that are available. Finally, you can define your own new columns and add them to the content type. As you can see, it is important to determine what metadata fields you will need to properly support your information structure before you begin creating content types.

When you create a new column, you assign it a name and select a data type. SharePoint offers you many different types, from simple text and lists to full HTML. Depending on the type, you may also have to specify additional information to complete the column definition. When you create new columns, they may also be grouped together under a custom heading so that they are easier to find later. As an example, I'll create some site columns to use with the software specification document.

Follow these steps to define the site columns:

1. Log in to the home page of the intranet site you created in Chapter 2 (e.g., `http://vsmoss/sites/intranet/Pages/default.aspx`).

2. Select Site Settings ➤ Modify All Site Settings from the Site Actions menu.

3. On the Site Settings page, select Site Columns from under the Galleries section.

4. On the Site Column Gallery page, click the Create link.

5. On the New Site Column page, enter **Application** in the Column Name field and leave the column type as Single Line of Text.

6. Under the group section, select the New Group option and enter **Software Specification Columns** in the text field. This new group will contain the new site columns and make them easier to find.

7. Select the option to require that the column contain information.

8. Click the OK button.

9. On the Site Column Gallery page, click the Create link.

10. On the New Site Column page, enter **Developer** in the Column Name field.

11. Select the Person or Group type for this column definition.

12. Select the option to put the site column into the existing Software Specification Columns group.

13. Click the OK button.

14. On the Site Column Gallery page, drop the Show Group list and select Software Specification Columns. You should only see your new columns now.

15. Select Site Settings ➤ Modify All Site Settings from the Site Actions menu.

16. On the Site Settings page, select Site Content Types from under the Galleries section.

17. On the Site Content Type Gallery page, drop the Show Group list and select Custom Software Documents.

18. Click the Software Specification content type link.

19. On the Site Content Type page, click the link titled Add from Existing Site Columns.

20. On the Add Columns to Site Content Type page, select Software Specification Columns from the drop-down list labeled Select Columns From.

21. Select all of the available columns and click the Add button.

22. Click the OK button.

Working with Views

Site and list columns play a critical role in SharePoint. Not only are they used to classify information, but they can also be used to create views that sort and filter lists. Additionally, they can be indexed to speed the display of lists within the browser. Creating a view of a list is done in this version of SharePoint in much the same way as in the previous version. The existing views are listed on the Customize page, which is accessible from the list by selecting Settings ➤ List Settings from the toolbar. From the Customize page, you may choose to edit an existing view or create your own new view. When you create a new view, you may choose the Standard View, Datasheet View, Calendar View, Gantt View, or Access View.

Creating a Standard View of a list results in a columnar display of the list that may be sorted, filtered, and grouped. Creating a Datasheet View of a list results in a tabular display that allows editing of all data in a single web page and includes a fly-out task pane that provides quick links to editing tools. Calendar Views require that one column in the list be a date/time dimension so that a calendar can be created using the list data. Gantt Views of a list create a Gantt chart view, but they require a list to have columns that can be mapped to Title, Start Date, and Due Date fields. An Access View is used to link a SharePoint list with a Microsoft Access 2007 database, which allows you to use Access to create reports and views.

Using List Data in Microsoft Access

SharePoint lists can be used in Microsoft Access 2007 in two key ways: list data can be imported into Access databases or lists can be linked to an Access database. Selecting Actions ➤ Open with Access from the toolbar of a list opens a dialog that allows you to select whether to export or link the list data. Additionally, you can create a new Access database or select an existing one to use as the target for the data.

Linking a SharePoint list to an Access database is similar to creating a new Access View for a list. The difference is that creating an Access View will automatically prompt you to create a new view for the list, whereas simply linking the list just creates a new database and you have to create any new views manually. In both cases, the term *view* really refers to either a form or a report created in the Access database.

After you create forms and reports in the new database, you may publish the database to a SharePoint library so the forms and reports can be viewed by end users. This is accomplished by clicking the Publish to SharePoint Site button inside of Microsoft Access. Figure 6-1 shows the button as it appears in the Document Action Panel of Access.

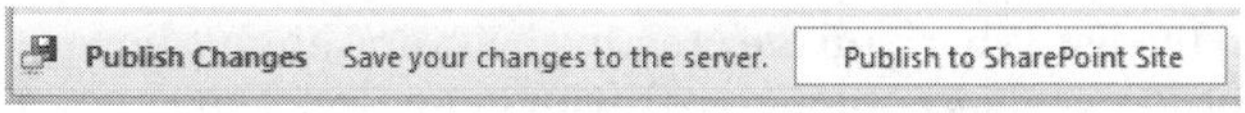

Figure 6-1. *Publishing an Access database to SharePoint*

Once published, users can open the Access database directly from the document library. Once opened, they may use the forms and reports as they would for any Access application. They may even take the entire database offline and synchronize their changes later. Figure 6-2 shows the SharePoint Lists group and the Work Offline button.

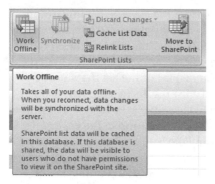

Figure 6-2. *Working offline with Microsoft Access*

Using List Data in Microsoft Excel

SharePoint lists are used in Excel spreadsheets by exporting the list. Selecting Actions ➤ Export to Spreadsheet creates a new workbook with a data connection to the list. Once the workbook is created, you are free to edit the data in the spreadsheet and save it anywhere you like.

You should note, however, that the data connection operates in only one direction. This means that you can refresh your workbook data from the list by clicking the Refresh button in the Workbook Connections dialog. However, you cannot push the changes you made in the spreadsheet back to the SharePoint list. While this was possible under Excel 2003 and SharePoint 2003, it is not possible in the 2007 versions. This behavior is potentially dangerous because changes made to the spreadsheet data manually can easily be overwritten by refreshing the data connection. To avoid this, you may want to remove the data connection from the workbook.

Using New Content Types

All document libraries and lists in SharePoint utilize content types. The content types help determine the columns that appear in the library, the types of new items you can create in a list, and the workflows associated with the list. When you are creating a list or a library, however, you are not given the opportunity to associate content types with it. Instead, you are either given a default content type (for lists) or asked to select a document template (for libraries). In order to change the content types associated with a list or a library, you must explicitly enable management of content types.

Enabling content type management for any list or library is done from the Customize page. On the Customize page, click the Advanced Settings link where you can select the option to allow management of content types. Figure 6-3 shows the option.

Figure 6-3. *Enabling content type management*

Once you enable content type management, you can add new content types to the list. When a new content type is added to the list, all of the columns defined in the content type are copied to the list. Note that lists and libraries never use site columns directly. Instead, the site columns associated with the content type are copied as list columns. Any changes made to a list column will not be reflected upward into the site column. In fact, you can never push changes up from any child content type or column to a parent. However, you can push changes down. Whenever you make a change to a site content type or site column, you can select an option to update all of the associated children.

Adding content types to a list or a library is also done through the Customize page. Once content type management is enabled, you will see the default content type on this page. For document libraries, it will be the Document content type. For other lists, it will be the content type for the default list item such as Event or Task. On this page, you can add new content types from the gallery and change the order in which they appear on the New button in the list toolbar.

Follow these steps to add a content type:

1. On the Customize page, click the link titled Add from Existing Site Content Types.

2. On the Add Content Types page, select Custom Software Documents from the drop-down list labeled Select Site Content Types From.

3. In the Available Site Content Types list, select Software Specification and click the Add button.

4. Click the OK button. Figure 6-4 shows the Customize page with the Software Specification content type added to a library.

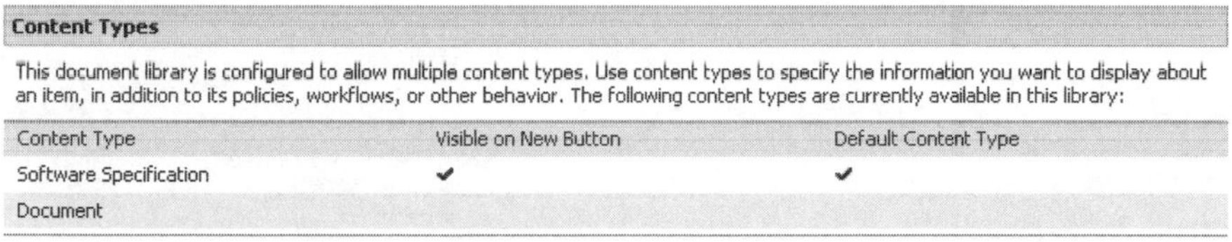

Content Types

This document library is configured to allow multiple content types. Use content types to specify the information you want to display about an item, in addition to its policies, workflows, or other behavior. The following content types are currently available in this library:

Content Type	Visible on New Button	Default Content Type
Software Specification	✔	✔
Document		

Figure 6-4. *Adding a new content type*

Once you add a content type to a library, you will be able to make new documents based on that type. Therefore, you'll want to define a document template that users will see when they create a new document of that type. Adding a document template to the content type is done by accessing the content type through the Content Types Gallery. When you are viewing the content type definition, click the Advanced Settings link and you will be able to upload a new document template to associate with the content type. Figure 6-5 shows the upload function.

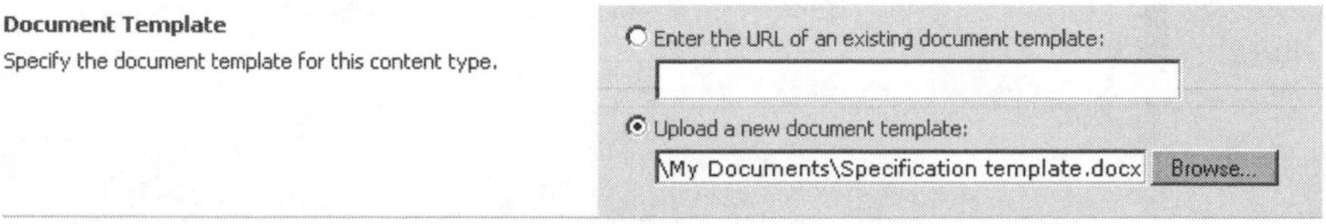

Document Template

Specify the document template for this content type.

○ Enter the URL of an existing document template:

◉ Upload a new document template:

\My Documents\Specification template.docx [Browse...]

Figure 6-5. *Uploading a document template*

Configuring Document Library Enhancements

Document libraries in SharePoint 2007 have some nice improvements over earlier versions. Some of these improvements, such as the recycle bin, I have mentioned previously. In this section, I review the new capabilities in more detail. These capabilities include new versioning settings, document policy settings, the recycle bin, item-level security, and item-level audience targeting.

Configuring Versioning Settings

As with any document management system, you would expect SharePoint libraries to have check-in, checkout, and version control capabilities. In this version, however, these capabilities are improved. From the Customize page, you can configure these functions by clicking the Versioning Settings link. On the Versioning Settings page, you can turn on versioning for a list or a library. You can also specify whether to version only major versions or both major and minor versions. Creating minor versions allows you to have draft versions that are only visible to selected individuals. These options give you a rudimentary process for creating, reviewing, and approving documents without the use of a workflow. Figure 6-6 shows the versioning settings.

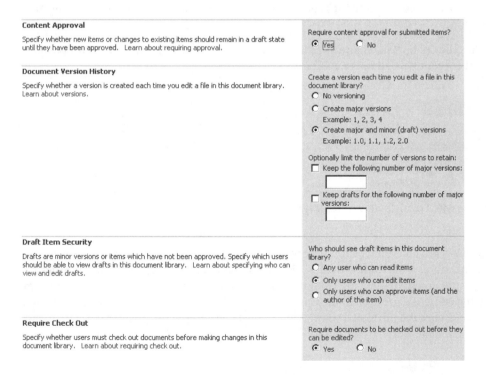

Figure 6-6. *Versioning settings*

Configuring Policy Settings

Document policies allow you to configure document labels, auditing, expiration dates, and bar codes for each content type used by the library. *Document labels* define text that will appear when the document is printed to help track its source and key information. *Auditing* allows you to track key documents events and changes along with the identity of the person who initiated the event. *Expiration dates* allow you to delete a document or initiate a work-flow after a given period of time. *Bar codes* allow you to generate a bar code for the document for tracking.

Take these steps to configure policies:

1. Browse to any document library you have created.

2. On the toolbar, select Settings ➤ Document Library Settings.

3. On the Customize page, click the link titled Information Management Policy Settings.

4. On the Information Policy Settings page, click the content type to manage.

5. Select the option to Define a Policy and click the OK button.

6. In the Administrative Description field, type **A test of all policies**.

7. In the Policy Statement field, type **Important document must be tracked and preserved**.

8. Check the Enable Labels box.

9. Check the box labeled Prompt Users to Insert a Label Before Saving or Printing.

10. In the Label Format field, enter **{Title} is Important** to label the document with its title and a message.

11. Check the Enable Auditing box.

12. Check all of the available auditing options.

13. Check the Enable Expiration box.

14. Enter **5** years in the time period field to set an expiration period.

15. Select the option to Perform This Action and select Delete from the drop-down list.

16. Check the Enable Bar Codes option.

17. Check the box labeled Prompt Users to Insert a Bar Code Before Saving or Printing.

18. Click the OK button.

Now you can return to the document library and create a new document. Enter some text in the document and then save it. When you try to save it, you should be prompted to add a label to the document and a bar code. Additionally, you should see the policy state-ment appear within Word to let you know that policies have been defined for the document. Your policy should also be auditing your actions as you work with the document, and you can run a report.

Follow these steps to run an audit report:

1. Go to the Site Settings page for the top-level site in the collection.

2. Click the Audit Log Reports link.

3. On the View Auditing Reports page, click the Content Modifications link.

4. In the File Download dialog, click the Open button. A new report should be generated for you in Excel.

Managing the Recycle Bin

Adding a recycle bin for SharePoint libraries was perhaps the most requested enhancement from the previous version. That's because there was no simple way to recover a deleted file in the previous version of SharePoint. Instead, administrators would have to completely recover a site from backup and retrieve the lost file by hand. With the recycle bin, users can recover their own files.

The recycle bin is actually a *two-stage bin*. This means that even if a user deletes the file from the library and the recycle bin, it will still be available in an administrator recycle bin. The end user recycle bin is located at the site level. The administrator's recycle bin is at the site collection level. At this level, administrators have a special view that shows the items that were deleted from other bins.

Administrators can set the time that a deleted file will remain in the recycle bin and the storage quota of the second stage bin so that old files do not take up space unnecessarily. This allows you to set a policy for users that deleted files can't be recovered after a given period.

Follow these steps to configure the recycle bin:

1. Log in to the Central Administration web site.

2. Click the Application Management tab.

3. Under the SharePoint Web Application Management section, click the link titled Web Application General Settings.

4. On the Web Application General Settings page, set the time period for automatic deletion of items in the recycle bin and the quota for the second-stage bin.

5. Click the OK button.

Managing Item-Level Security and Audiences

Along with the recycle bin, item-level security was another high-priority request from Share-Point users. In the previous version of SharePoint, security could only be set at the library level. In this version, you may use the drop-down menu for an item and select Manage Permissions to set the security just for that item.

Along with permissions, you can also manage the visibility of an item through audiences. In order to associate a document with an audience, you must first enable audiences for the library as a whole, which is done from the Customize page by clicking the Audience Targeting Settings link. Once audiences are enabled for the library, each individual item will have a Target Audiences property that you can set.

Configuring Column Indexing

Indexing a column is intended to improve the performance when displaying a view. You can index any column in the list directly from the Customize page by clicking the Indexed Column link. However, you should note that indexing a column will not remove the soft 2,000-item limit for a view. Indexing only increases the speed at which those items are displayed. Therefore, while a list or library may contain a virtually unlimited number of items, you should only create views that return 2,000 items or less.

■**Note** Quite often a large part of a SharePoint 2007 project involves the migration of documents and content from previous versions of SharePoint or other document management systems such as Documentum and Livelink. Moving tens or hundreds of thousands of documents into SharePoint is impossible without some kind of automated tool set. My favorite tool for this job is the Tzunami Deployer. For more information, visit http://www.tzunami.com.

Working with InfoPath and Form Libraries

In Chapter 3, I introduced you to the concept of a form library. *Form libraries* are special libraries designed to store Microsoft InfoPath forms. These forms can be used for any business function that is forms-based, from reserving a conference room to requesting travel. InfoPath 2007 has several improvements that make it an even better fit with this version of SharePoint. These enhancements include support for template parts that let you create reusable sections, template importing for converting Word and Excel documents into forms, and a managed code development environment. Additionally, if you deploy MOSS, you no longer need Microsoft InfoPath on your desktop because MOSS contains a forms server for delivering highly functional InfoPath forms as HTML. Because there is a lot to cover in this section, I will assume that you already have some familiarity with InfoPath so that I can focus just on new capabilities. However, I have included Exercise 6.1 at the end of the chapter so you can see in detail how an InfoPath application works within SharePoint.

Creating Template Parts

Creating a template part is a new capability of InfoPath 2007 that lets you build reusable sections for forms. With this capability, you can create a library of template parts for use in form design. This makes it easier to create new forms using the template parts as a starting point. As a best practice, you should start by creating a content type to represent template parts within SharePoint. After you create a content type, you can create a library to store them.

Follow these steps to create a content type:

1. Log in to VSCLIENT as a SharePoint administrator.

2. Log in to the home page of the intranet site you created in Chapter 2 (e.g., http://vsmoss/sites/intranet/Pages/default.aspx).

3. Select Site Settings ➤ Modify All Site Settings from the Site Actions menu.

4. On the Site Settings page, select Site Content Types from under the Galleries section.

5. On the Site Content Type Gallery page, click the Create button.

6. On the New Site Content Type page, enter **Template Part** in the Name field.

7. Select Document Content Types from the drop-down list labeled Select Parent Content Type From.

8. Select Form from the drop-down list labeled Parent Content Type.

9. Under the Group section, select the Existing Group option and select Document Content Types.

10. Click the OK button.

11. Select Start ➤ All Programs ➤ Microsoft Office ➤ Microsoft Office InfoPath 2007.

12. In the Getting Started dialog, click Design a Form Template.

13. In the Design a Form Template dialog, select the Template Part option.

14. Select Blank from the List View labeled Based On.

15. Click the OK button.

16. Select File ➤ Save from the main menu.

17. Save the blank template part to your desktop as `BlankPart.xtp`. You are going to use this as the template for the content type you created earlier.

18. Return to the home page of the intranet site.

19. Select Site Settings ➤ Modify All Site Settings from the Site Actions menu.

20. On the Site Settings page, select Site Content Types from under the Galleries section.

21. Click the link for the Template Part content type.

22. On the Site Content Type page, click the Advanced Settings link.

23. On the Advanced Settings page, select the option to Upload a New Document Template.

24. Click the Browse button.

25. In the Choose File dialog, select the `BlankPart.xtp` file and click the Open button.

26. On the Site Content Type page, click the OK button.

Once you have created a new content type with a blank template part, you can use it in a library. Creating a template parts library is a good idea because it allows template parts to be accessed by form designers throughout the enterprise. This approach saves a lot of time and ensures consistency across all forms.

Follow these steps to create a template parts library:

1. Click the Document Center tab.

2. Click the link titled View All Site Content in the Quick Launch area of the Document Center.

3. On the All Site Content page, click the Create link.

4. On the Create page, click the Form Library link.

5. On the New page, type **Template Parts** in the Name field.

6. Click the Create button.

7. In the Template Parts library, select Settings ➤ Form Library Settings from the toolbar.

8. On the Customize page, click the Advanced Settings link.

9. On the Form Library Advanced Settings page, select the Yes option to allow management of content types.

10. Click the OK button.

11. On the Customize page, click the link titled Add From Existing Content Types.

12. On the Add Content Types page, select the Template Part content type from the list labeled Available Site Content Types and click the Add button.

13. Click the OK button.

After you have created a library to store template parts, you can create new template parts from Microsoft InfoPath. Using this approach, you can build up a library of reusable parts. As an example, I'll build a reusable part that contains basic customer information.

Follow these steps to create a template part:

1. Log in to VSCLIENT.

2. Select Start ➤ All Programs ➤ Microsoft Office ➤ Microsoft Office InfoPath 2007.

3. In the Getting Started dialog, click Design a Form Template.

4. In the Design a Form Template dialog, select the Template Part option.

5. Select Blank from the List View labeled Based On.

6. Click the OK button.

7. In the Design Tasks pane, click the Layout link.

8. Drag the Table with Title layout from the Layout Pane to the form surface.

9. Click in the cell labeled Click to Add a Title and enter **Customer Information**.

10. Click in the cell labeled Click to add Form Content.

11. Select Table ➤ Insert ➤ Layout Table from the menu.

12. In the Insert Table dialog, set the number of columns to **2** and the number of rows to **3**.

13. Click the OK button.

14. In the Layout pane, click the Design Tasks link.

15. In the Design Tasks pane, click the Controls link.

16. Drag Text Box controls to each of the three cells in the right-hand column of the layout table.

17. In the left-hand column, type **Name** in the first row.

18. Type **Address** in the second row.

19. Type **City, State, Zip** in the third row.

20. Select File ➤ Save from the main menu.

21. In the Save As dialog, enter **CustomerInformation.xtp** and save it to the Template Parts library you created earlier.

22. Select File ➤ Design a Form Template from the main menu to start designing a new form.

23. In the Design a Form Template dialog, select blank from the List View labeled Based On and click the OK button.

24. In the Design Tasks pane, click the Controls link.

25. In the Controls Pane, click the link titled Add or Remove Custom Controls.

26. In the Add or Remove Custom Controls dialog, click the Add button.

27. In the Add Custom Control Wizard, select Template Part and click the Next button.

28. On the next screen, click the Browse button.

29. In the Browse dialog, browse to the Template Parts library you created earlier.

30. Select the CustomerInformation Template Part and click the Open button.

31. In the Add Custom Control Wizard, click the Finish button.

32. When the template part is added, close the wizard.

33. In the Add or Remove Custom Controls dialog, click the OK button to close it.

34. Locate the CustomerInformation Template Part in the Controls Pane and drag it onto the new blank form. Figure 6-7 shows the final template part.

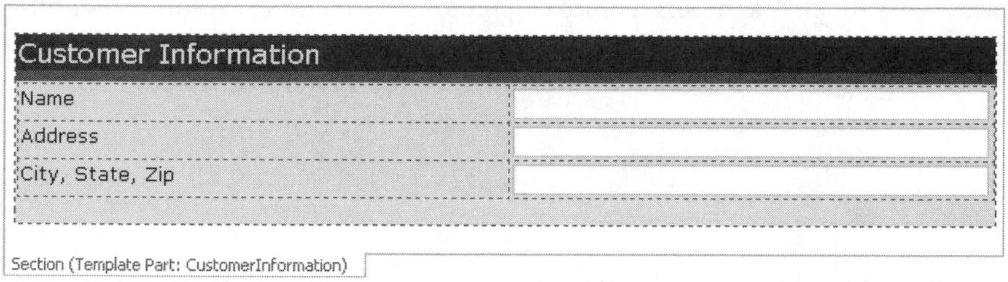

Figure 6-7. *Creating a template part*

While creating template parts is a good way to build up a library of components for form development, they do have limitations. Template parts do not have all of the functionality of an InfoPath form, and that can be a bit frustrating. For example, you can't write any script or managed code behind a template part. The following is a complete list of functionality not available to template parts:

- Template parts cannot use ActiveX controls.

- Template parts cannot use background images.

- Template parts cannot use color schemes.

- Template parts cannot use data connections for submitting data, but receiving data is supported.

- Template parts cannot use Information Rights Management (IRM) restrictions.

- Template parts cannot use script and managed code. I cover managed code development later in this section.

- Template parts cannot be published.

- Template parts cannot be exported.

- Template parts cannot have multiple views, read-only views, default views, or print views.

- Template parts cannot have digital signatures, custom task panes, security levels, or custom save/open behaviors.

Importing Word and Excel Documents

Many organizations have moved away from paper-based forms and made a significant investment in electronic forms. These electronic forms may be Word documents, Excel spreadsheets, Adobe forms, or other formats. Because of this investment, it has not been a simple matter for them to implement InfoPath forms. InfoPath 2007, however, includes a template import feature specifically designed to migrate electronic forms to InfoPath.

Out of the box, InfoPath 2007's import feature can handle Word and Excel forms. For other form types, InfoPath provides a set of interfaces for creating your own importer. Creating your own importer is beyond the scope of this book; interested readers should check out the InfoPath 2007 SDK.

Follow these steps to import a Word document:

1. Log in to VSCLIENT.

2. Select Start ➤ All Programs ➤ Microsoft Office ➤ Microsoft Office Word 2007.

3. Click the Office Button in the upper left-hand corner of Word and select New from the menu.

4. In the New Document dialog, select Forms from the Templates list under the Microsoft Office Online category.

5. When the forms categories appear, click Business.

6. Select any of the available business forms. I selected Petty Cash Reimbursement Request.

7. Click the Download button.

8. When the new form appears, click the disk icon on the top toolbar in Word to save the file.

9. In the Save As dialog, navigate to your desktop.

10. Enter **FormTemplate.docx** in the File Name field and click the Save button.

11. If Word displays a compatibility warning regarding the new file format, simply click the OK button. I cover the new Office file formats in detail in Chapter 9.

12. Exit Word.

13. Select Start ➤ All Programs ➤ Microsoft Office ➤ Microsoft Office InfoPath 2007.

14. In the Getting Started dialog, click the link titled Import a Form.

15. In the Import Wizard, select InfoPath Importer for Word Documents and click the Next button.

16. On the next screen, click the Browse button.

17. In the Import form dialog, navigate to your desktop.

18. Select the `FormTemplate.docx` file and click the Open button.

19. In the Import Wizard, click the Finish button.

After the form is imported, the Import Wizard will notify you if there were any issues converting the form. When it discovers issues, the wizard will refer you to the Design Checker to investigate the issues. The Design Checker is a new feature of InfoPath 2007 that assists you in not only importing forms but also making forms that are compatible for different deployment scenarios. I discuss using the Design Checker for deployment scenarios a little later in this section, but for now you can review any issues with the import using the

Design Checker, which will appear after you close the Import Wizard. Figure 6-8 shows the Design Checker in my environment after the import.

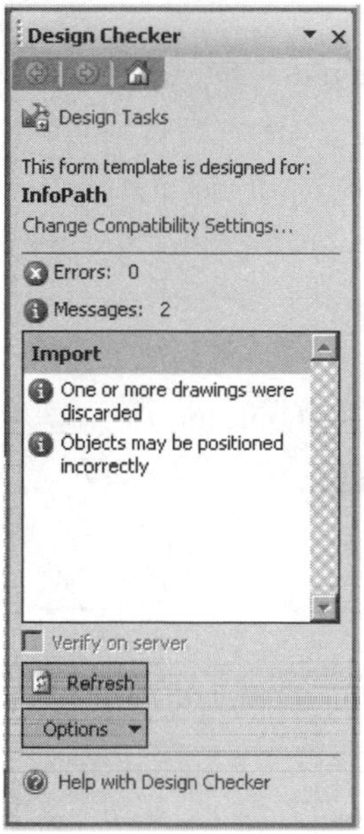

Figure 6-8. *The Design Checker*

Using Data Connection Libraries

InfoPath forms often use data connections to databases, web services, and other sources to retrieve information such as lookup lists. In the past, these connections were always defined as part of the InfoPath form. In InfoPath 2007, however, you can use a SharePoint data connection library to store connection information that may be used across the entire organization. These are the same data connection libraries that I discuss in Chapter 4 in relation to Excel Services, except the file format is different. Excel Services utilizes Office Data Connection (ODC) files, whereas InfoPath utilizes Universal Data Connection (UDC) files.

Selecting Tools ➤ Data Connections brings up the Data Connections dialog. This dialog lists all the available data connections you can use. To add a new one, simply click the Add button to start the data connection wizard. Using this wizard, you create, receive, and submit connections within the form. After they are created, you can then convert these connections into UDC files for future use.

If you created the data connection library in Chapter 4, you can follow these steps to create a UDC file in InfoPath:

1. Log in to VSCLIENT.

2. Select Start ➤ All Programs ➤ Microsoft Office ➤ Microsoft InfoPath 2007.

3. In the Getting Started dialog, click the Design a Form Template link.

4. In the Design a Form template dialog, select the Blank form and click the OK button.

5. Select Tools ➤ Data Connections from the main menu.

6. In the Data Connections dialog, click the Add button.

7. In the data connection wizard, select to Create a New Connection to Receive Data and click the Next button.

8. On the next screen, select to Receive Data from a SharePoint Library or List and click the Next button.

9. On the next screen, enter the address for your Document Center (e.g., `http://vsmoss/sites/intranet/docs`) and click the Next button.

10. On the next screen, select the Documents library and click the Next button.

11. On the next screen, select just the Title field and click the Next button.

12. On the next screen, click the Next button.

13. On the last screen, click the Finish button.

14. In the Data Connections dialog, click the Convert button to convert the data connection to a UDC file.

15. In the Convert Data Connections dialog, click the Browse button.

16. In the Browse dialog, navigate to the data connection library you created in Chapter 4 (e.g., `http://vsmoss/sites/intranet/docs/Data%20Connections`) and click the Save button.

17. In the Convert Data Connections dialog, click the OK button.

18. In the Data Connections dialog, click the Close button. The new UDC file is now saved to the data connection library.

Developing with Visual Studio Tools for Applications

Over the past nine years or so, Microsoft has supported Office developers with a built-in development environment known as Visual Basic for Applications (VBA). VBA was intended to be a simplified development environment for creating macro functionality within Office products. Typically, developers would detect events such as document creation and then exercise the Word or Excel object model to provide customized functionality such as data imports.

While VBA applications worked fine for a number of applications, VBA was created when the component object model (COM) standard was the prevailing technology for Microsoft development. As we all know COM has been steadily replaced by the .NET standard for development, but Microsoft Office continues to lag behind. Unfortunately for Word and Excel, this will remain the case in Office 2007; however, InfoPath has a new development environment known as Visual Studio Tools for Applications (VSTA) that finally brings managed code development to the Office suite.

■**Note** For those familiar with managed code development in Office using Visual Studio Tools for Office (VSTO), VSTA is not a replacement. VSTA is really intended to become the next generation of macro development environments within Office products. I cover VSTO development in Chapter 9. (As an interesting sidebar, how exactly do you pronounce VSTA? It can't possibly be "Vista"!)

VSTA is not installed by default when you install Microsoft Office 2007; it is an advanced installation option. To install VSTA, launch the Office 2007 installation disk and select to Add or Remove Features. You'll then be able to locate the VSTA installation under the Microsoft InfoPath options. Figure 6-9 shows the VSTA installation location.

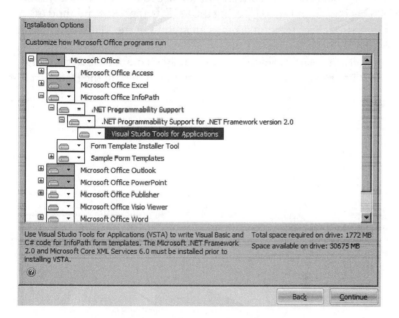

Figure 6-9. *Installing VSTA*

Once you have VSTA installed, you'll want to set your programming language in InfoPath to use C#. This is done by selecting Tools ➤ Options from the main menu. In the Options dialog, click the Design tab. On this tab, you will see language selection lists. Once the language is set, you can access the programming environment by selecting Tools ➤ Programming ➤ Microsoft Visual Studio Tools for Applications. Additionally, the Programming menu lists several key event handlers that you can add for the form or any control just by selecting them. Simply select the form or control in the designer and then choose the event you want to add from the Programming menu. This gives you a simple mechanism for generating the correct function signatures.

Writing VSTA code in InfoPath is a familiar experience for anyone who has used Visual Studio before. You can set references to .NET assemblies and utilize any of the classes contained in the .NET Framework. However, there are a couple of areas where development is unique to InfoPath. These areas concern accessing elements in the InfoPath form and managing trust levels.

Accessing Form Elements

Whenever you write VSTA code, you will almost always want to manipulate the field values in the form. Field values are accessed through the XPathNavigator class, which is used to reference the form's data source. The following code shows how to reference the form's data with the XPathNavigator class:

```
XPathNavigator data = this.MainDataSource.CreateNavigator();
```

Once you have a reference to the form's data source, you can use XPath to access any individual element on the form. This is accomplished by using the SelectSingleNode method of the XPathNavigator. The SelectSingleNode method takes as an argument the XPath that references the target element. Figuring out the correct XPath string necessary to access a given element can be tricky. Fortunately, you can retrieve the XPath for an element directly from the Data Source pane in InfoPath. Figure 6-10 shows the Copy XPath menu item in the Data Source pane.

Figure 6-10. *Retrieving the XPath for an element*

Once you have the XPath for a target element, you can paste it in to the code and use it to retrieve the target element as an XPathNavigator object. Using this object, you can read the element through the Value property or set its value through the SetValue method. Listing 6-1 shows a simple example of setting the username element in a form to the username of the person filling out the form.

Note Accessing the WindowsIdentity object requires that the InfoPath form operate with full trust. I discuss managing trust in the next section.

Listing 6-1. *Setting Element Values in VSTA*

```
using Microsoft.Office.InfoPath;
using System;
using System.Xml;
using System.Xml.XPath;
using System.Security.Principal;

namespace Travel
{
    public partial class FormCode
    {

        public void InternalStartup()
        {
            EventManager.FormEvents.Loading +=
              new LoadingEventHandler(FormEvents_Loading);
        }

        public void FormEvents_Loading(object sender, LoadingEventArgs e)
        {
            //Get a reference to the User Name element
            XPathNavigator data = this.MainDataSource.CreateNavigator();
            XPathNavigator element =
              data.SelectSingleNode(
              "/my:travelRequest/my:username", this.NamespaceManager);

            //Show user name
            WindowsIdentity identity = WindowsIdentity.GetCurrent();
            element.SetValue(identity.Name);

        }
    }
}
```

■**Tip** While the previous code is a simple example to use here, InfoPath 2007 now has a new `userName()` function to retrieve the current username.

The best thing about VSTA is that all of the code is part of the InfoPath form. This means that you do not have to deal with separate assemblies that must be distributed to clients. You also do not have to configure client-side code access security (CAS) settings as was necessary in previous versions of InfoPath. You do, however, have to manage the trust level of the form.

Managing Form Trust

InfoPath forms can operate at three different trust levels: Restricted, Domain, and Full Trust. *Restricted* forms are not allowed to access any data that resides outside the form itself. *Domain* forms can access data that comes from within the same domain as the form. *Full Trust* forms have no restrictions on the operations that they can perform.

By default, InfoPath is set to automatically select the appropriate security level for your forms. This typically means that forms operate with Domain trust. Domain trust is appropriate for most of the operations you will perform in a form. Some forms, however, may need an increased trust level to function correctly. Such is the case for the code in Listing 6-1, which tries to use the `WindowsIdentity` class to access information about the current user. If you want the form to operate with a different trust level, you must set it manually.

You can change the trust level of a form by selecting Tools ➤ Form Options from the main menu. This will open the Form Options dialog. Selecting Security and Trust from the category list displays the Security Level information shown in Figure 6-11.

In order to change the form's trust level, you must not only select the Full Trust security level, but you must also sign the form template with a digital certificate. If you have an appropriate digital certificate available, you simply check the box labeled Sign This Form Template, click the Select Certificate button, and pick a certificate. If you do not have a certificate available, you can make one by clicking the Create Certificate button.

If you deploy a form that performs operations that require full trust and you do not properly modify the form's trust level, you will receive typical security error messages from the .NET Framework. If, on the other hand, you sign the form with a certificate you created yourself, the end user will receive a message indicating that the certificate is not from a trusted source. In this case, the user can choose to trust the form, but you had better make this clear to end users before they receive the message shown in Figure 6-12.

After you finish creating your forms, you will want to publish them using the Publishing Wizard so they can be used by others. In Chapter 3, I showed you how to create a form library in SharePoint and publish a form to it. Beyond simply publishing a form, however, you can also use the Publishing Wizard to deploy your form and associate it with a new content type. You can then use the content type in multiple libraries throughout a site.

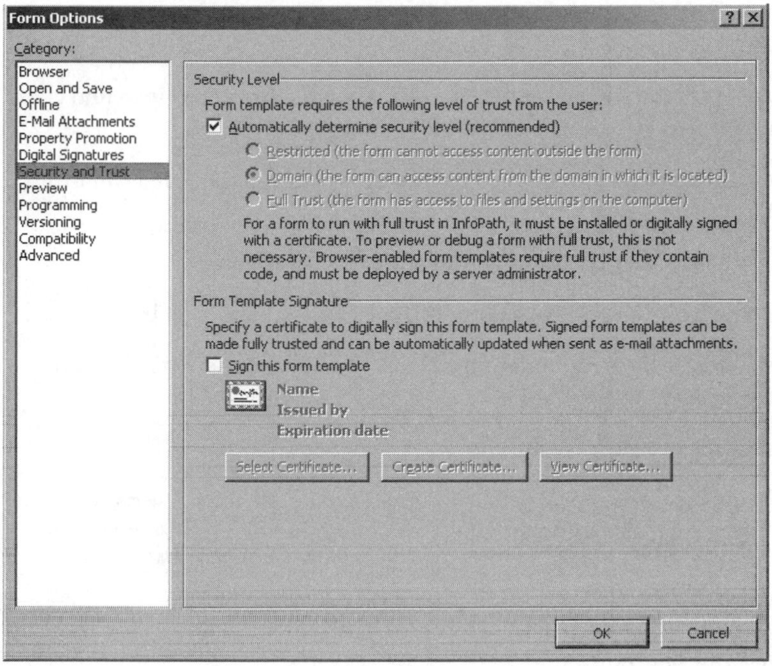

Figure 6-11. *Accessing security information*

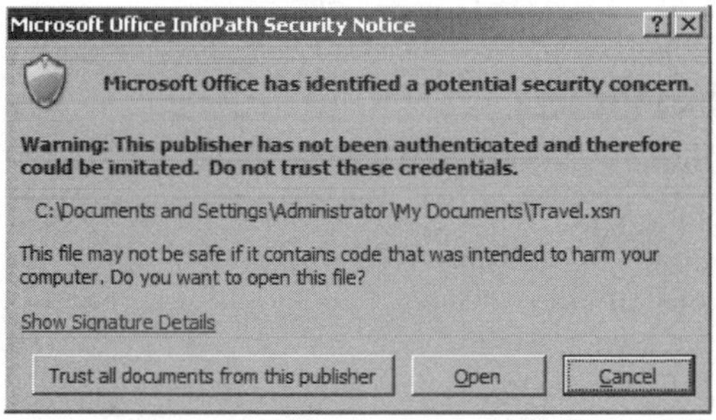

Figure 6-12. *InfoPath security warning*

Follow these steps to create a new content type:

1. Log in to VSCLIENT as a SharePoint administrator.

2. Select Start ➤ All Programs ➤ Microsoft Office ➤ Microsoft Office InfoPath 2007.

3. In the Getting Started dialog, double-click Sample – Expense Report.

4. In the Design Tasks pane, click the link titled Publish Form Template.

5. In the Save As dialog, select an appropriate place to save the form and click the Save button.

6. In the Publishing Wizard, select to publish the form to a SharePoint server and click the Next button.

7. In the next screen, enter the address of the SharePoint server, **http://vsmoss**, and click the Next button.

8. In the next screen, uncheck the box labeled Enabled This Form to Be Filled Out by Using a Browser.

9. Select the option labeled Site Content Type and click the Next button.

10. On the Next screen, select Create a New Content Type and click the Next button.

11. On the next screen, name the new content type **Expense Report** and click the Next button.

12. On the next screen, click the Browse button.

13. In the Browse dialog, locate the Form Server Templates folder at `http://vsmoss`. This is a special folder for storing form templates. I discuss it in more detail later in this section.

14. Name the new form **ExpenseReport.xsn** and click the Save button.

15. In the wizard, click the Next button.

16. On the next screen, click the Next button.

17. On the next screen, click the Publish button.

Understanding InfoPath Forms Services

While InfoPath is a good tool for creating forms, almost the instant it was released, customers began to request a way to fill out forms without having the InfoPath client installed. There are many scenarios, such as personnel on the road, or clients without access to InfoPath, where a zero-footprint form is useful. Microsoft's response to this need was to create InfoPath Forms Services.

InfoPath Forms Services allows you to take InfoPath forms and render them as HTML in a browser. InfoPath Forms Services is technically a separate product from SharePoint, however, MOSS ships with it. The server is set up automatically for you during the MOSS installation process.

Before you can begin using forms in the browser, you must make sure that InfoPath Forms Services is enabled at the farm and site level. You can access the configuration settings for InfoPath Forms Services from the Central Administration site. On the Application tab, you will find a section dedicated to InfoPath Forms Services. Here you can click the link titled Configure InfoPath Forms Services. This link will open a configuration page where you can enable services for the farm.

After you have enabled services for the farm, you must activate the Office SharePoint Server Enterprise Site Collection Features for each site collection where you want to use InfoPath Forms Services. Additionally, you must activate the Office SharePoint Server Enterprise Site Features for each site where you want to use InfoPath Forms Services. Note that

there are features at both the site collection and the site level that must be activated for
InfoPath Forms Services to work correctly.

Designing for InfoPath Forms Services

Most of what you know about creating forms in InfoPath also applies to forms that target
InfoPath Forms Services. However, there are many InfoPath features that can't be duplicated
in a browser, such as master-detail views. Therefore, when you create a form for use with
InfoPath Forms Services, it will always be limited to a subset of features that are available to
InfoPath as a whole. As of this writing there is not a definitive list of lost InfoPath functionality;
however, you can use the Design Checker to help ensure compatibility.

   The Design Checker is available as a link in the Design Tasks pane in InfoPath. Clicking
this link opens the Design Checker task pane, which shows errors and messages for the current form. Before you can get any meaningful information, however, you must change the
compatibility settings for the form to indicate that you are targeting InfoPath Forms Services.
Clicking the link titled Change Compatibility Settings opens the Form Options dialog where
you can check a box to indicate the form should be browser-enabled. You should also provide
the path to VSMOSS so that InfoPath Forms Services can verify compatibility. Figure 6-13
shows the browser compatibility options.

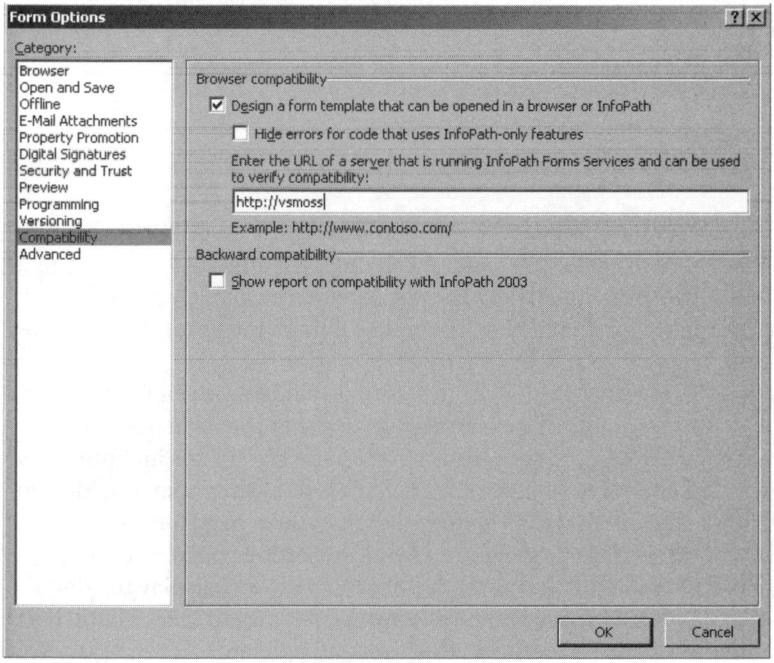

Figure 6-13. *Changing browser compatibility*

   Once you have changed the compatibility settings, the Design Checker will begin to display errors and messages regarding your form. Each error or message will show not only in the
Design Checker task pane, but also in the form or dialog box where the issue can be addressed.

Furthermore, the Design Checker provides hyperlinks that will take you to each issue so that you can fix them. Figure 6-14 shows the Design Checker with an error message in the task pane and the same error flagged on the form.

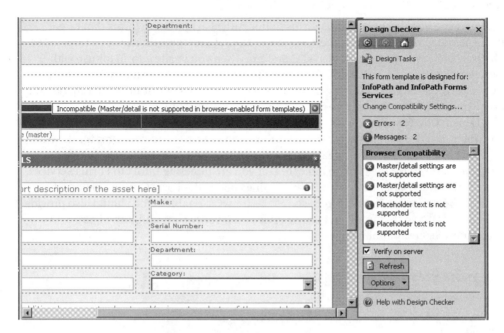

Figure 6-14. *The Design Checker*

After you have created a browser-compatible form, you will be able to publish the form to a form library in SharePoint. Here again, you can publish the form directly to a library or as a content type. If you publish the form directly to a library, it will be available immediately. If you publish the form as a content type, you'll need to create a library and associate the content type with the library so it can be used.

After you have created a form library with your new form available, you can create a new form using the toolbar and fill it out. However, you'll notice that the form does not initially open in the browser as you would expect. This is because the library has an option you can set to specify the preferred client for the form. The default is to always open the form in InfoPath if it is available. This setting is accessible from the Customize page for the form library by clicking the Advanced Settings link. On the Advanced Settings page, you can change the Browser-Enabled Documents setting for the library to always display the document as a web page. Because the setting never mentions forms, it's easy to miss. Figure 6-15 shows the correct configuration to display forms in the browser by default.

Browser-enabled Documents

Specify how to display documents that are enabled for opening both in a browser and a client application. If the client application is unavailable, these documents will always be displayed as Web pages in the browser.

Opening browser-enabled documents

○ Open in the client application
● Display as a Web page

Figure 6-15. *Displaying forms in the browser by default*

Deploying Centrally Managed Forms

When forms require full trust, they may not be published directly from InfoPath to a form library. Instead, fully trusted forms must first be uploaded into a central management store where they can be reviewed by a SharePoint farm administrator. Once reviewed, these forms are deployed from a central store to selected web applications where they can be made available to libraries or act as templates for content types.

In order to deploy a fully trusted form, you must first use the Publishing Wizard to prepare the form. As part of preparing the form, InfoPath publishes it to a network location of your choosing so that it can be accessed by the SharePoint administrator. Figure 6-16 shows the Publishing Wizard set to prepare a form for administrator approval.

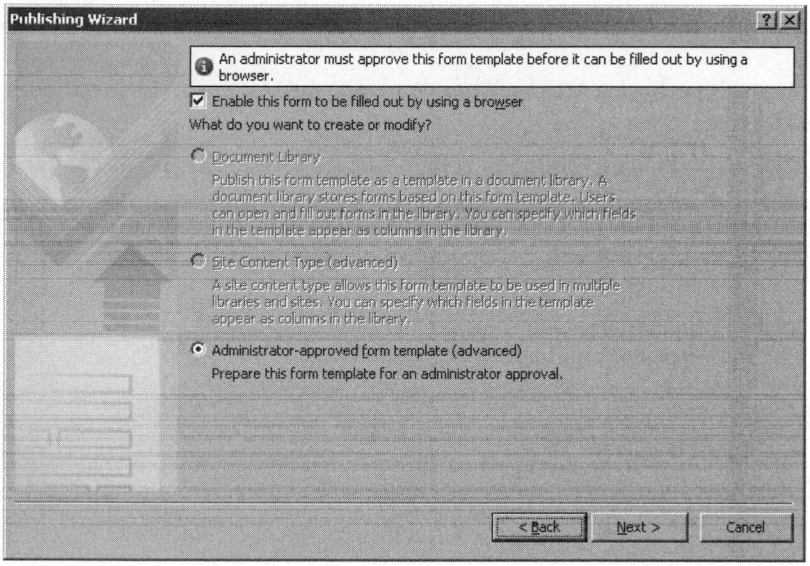

Figure 6-16. *Preparing a fully trusted form for approval*

Once the form is prepared, it may be uploaded to the central repository. This is accomplished through the Central Administration web site. On the Application Management tab, under the InfoPath Forms Services section, click the link titled Manage Form Templates. This will display the forms stored in the central repository and allow you to upload new forms. During the upload process, you can even have the form validated for errors before it is added to the repository.

After the form is added to the central repository, you may use the drop-down menu associated with the form to make it available to a site collection on the farm. Selecting Activate to a Site Collection from the menu will bring up a page where you can select the site collection where the form will be deployed. Clicking the OK button deploys the form into a library named FormServer Templates. This library is not visible from within SharePoint, but you can see it if you open the site in the SharePoint Designer. The point, however, is that once it's deployed, you can reference it as a template for a content type within the site collection.

Using the Document Conversions Service

The Document Conversions Service in MOSS allows you to convert between different types of documents within a library. For example, you can easily convert from a Word document to a web page using the out-of-the-box capabilities. Initially, this service is disabled on the farm because it is potentially an expensive operation, depending upon what documents are being converted. Therefore, you'll have to do a little configuration to get it running.

Follow these steps to configure the Document Conversions Service:

1. Log in to the Central Administration site as a farm administrator.

2. In the Central Administration site, click the Operations tab.

3. On the Operations tab, click the link titled Services on Server under the Topology and Services section.

4. On the Services on Server page, click the Start link next to the Document Conversions Load Balancer Service.

5. On the Services on Server page, click the Start link next to the Document Conversions Launcher Service.

6. On the Launcher Service Settings page, select the Load Balancer server as VSMOSS.

7. Click the OK button.

8. Click the Application Management tab.

9. Click the link titled Document Conversions under the External Service Connections section.

10. On the Configure Document Conversions page, make sure that the web application reflects the intranet site collection you created in Chapter 2. If not, use the drop-down menu to change the web application.

11. Select the Yes option under Enable Document Conversion for This Site.

12. Note the available document conversions that ship with MOSS are listed on the page, then click the OK button.

Once the Document Conversions Service is up and running, it's a simple matter to convert documents. Navigate to any document library you created earlier in the book that contains Word documents. You should now find that a conversion option is available from the drop-down menu associated with the document. When you select this menu item, you will be taken to a page where you can specify the name for the converted file, where it will be located, and who to notify. It's important to note that the target site must have the publishing feature I discuss in Chapter 5 activated in order to receive the new document. Figure 6-17 shows the new menu item for converting a Word document.

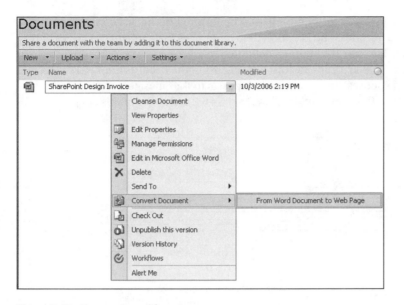

Figure 6-17. *Converting a document*

Understanding Records Management

The records management capabilities in MOSS allow you to create a repository to retain business documents that are necessary for regulatory compliance, business continuity, or historical interest. You can associate a records repository with a web application so that documents may be moved into the repository either manually or automatically as part of a workflow process. Access to the records repository may be closely controlled to ensure that key records are not altered or deleted. Additionally, you may establish policies for the records that ensure they are retained for a defined period of time.

You begin the process of creating a repository by creating a new site collection based on the Records Center template. After the repository is created, you can configure a connection between it and any web application through the Central Administration site. On the Application Management tab, click the Records Center link under the External Service Connection section. This link will open a configuration page where you can define the connection. The repository will utilize the OfficialFile web service to copy documents from production libraries to the Records Center. Therefore, the connection entry must properly reference the web service for the system to work. Generally, you need to provide the address of the root of the Records Center followed by the reference to the web service. An example is displayed on the configuration page to help you out, and Exercise 6.2 at the end of this chapter is a complete walk-through using the Records Center template. Once the connection is properly configured, you should see a new menu item associated with documents in libraries that allows you to send them to the repository.

When the repository site is created, it has a single document library named Unclassified Records and two lists named Record Routing and Holds. If you send a document to the repository at this point, the record will always end up in the Unclassified Records library. If you want to sort the records into different libraries, you must add additional libraries to the site and make appropriate entries in the Record Routing list. The Record Routing list contains entries that map content types to libraries. The Location field references the name of the target library in the repository and the Aliases field contains a delimited set of content type names. Figure 6-18 shows a sample New Item screen for the Record Routing list in the Records Center. This entry maps the content types Expenses, Proposals, and Forecasts to the Sales Records library in the Records Center. You will use this screen in detail in Exercise 6.2 at the end of this chapter.

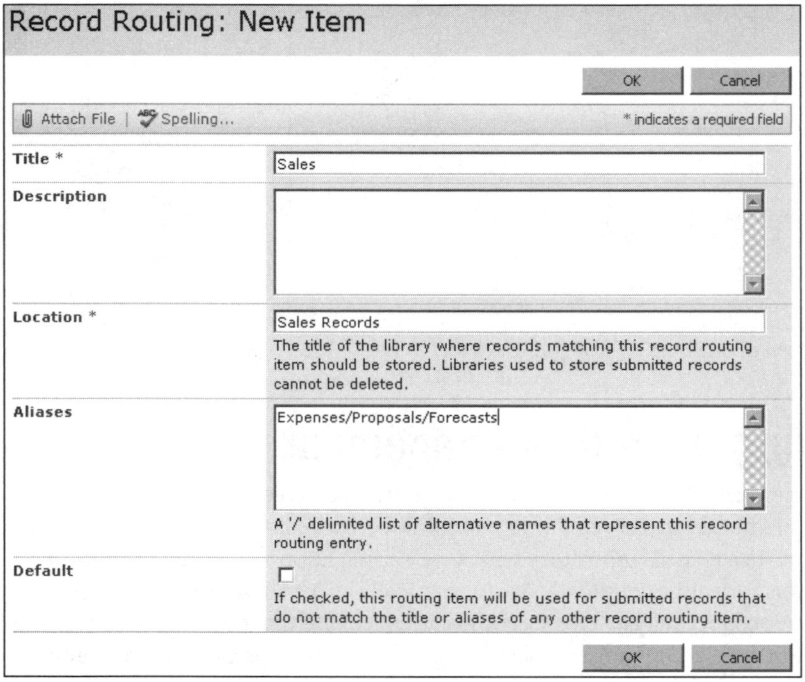

Figure 6-18. *Routing records in the Records Center*

The Holds list is used to place records on hold so that they cannot be deleted or changed. In order to place a record on hold, you must first add a hold to the Holds list. The hold can be named anything such as "Discovery" or "Audit." Once they are created, you can then place a record on hold by selecting Manage Holds from the drop-down menu associated with the record. If anyone tries to delete or change the record while it's on hold, they will receive an error message.

Exercise 6.1. InfoPath and SharePoint

While InfoPath is technically a separate product from SharePoint, it plays a critical supporting role. Many of the pages you see in SharePoint—such as content type metadata—are actually InfoPath forms hosted by SharePoint. Furthermore, InfoPath forms can be used to create complete applications that run within SharePoint. In this exercise, you will create an InfoPath application for submitting and tracking customer issues.

Prerequisites

Before you begin this exercise, you should have read through the InfoPath information in this chapter. Additionally, you should have created the Template Parts library from the "Creating Template Parts" section earlier in this chapter and built the sample template part for entering customer information. This exercise will make use of this template part to create a form for customer issues.

Creating a Customer Issues Site

For this exercise, you will create a new site for tracking customer issues. This site will have a form library that will contain the form for tracking issues. Therefore, you'll need to create this site before building the form.

Follow these steps to create the new site:

1. Log in to VSMOSS as a SharePoint administrator.

2. Open the home page of the intranet site you created in Chapter 2 (e.g., `http://vsmoss/sites/intranet/Pages/Default.aspx`).

3. Click the Sites tab to open the Site Directory.

4. In the Site Directory, click the Create Site link.

5. On the New SharePoint Site page, enter **Customer Issues** in the Title field.

6. Enter **CustomerIssues** in the URL Name field.

7. Select Blank Site from the template list.

8. Click the Create button.

The form that you'll create will contain a list that will allow you to categorize the customer issue. This list will be maintained in the SharePoint site so that it can be edited when necessary. You will subsequently utilize the list in your form by using a data connection.

Follow these steps to create the new list:

1. In the Customer Issues site, click the Lists link in the Quick Launch area.

2. On the All Site Content page, click the Create link.

3. On the Create page, click Custom List.

4. On the New page, enter **Issue Categories** in the Name field.

5. Click the Create button.

6. On the Issue Categories page, click the New button.

7. On the New Item page, enter **Product Defect** in the Title field and click the OK button.

8. Repeat steps 6 and 7 to add the following categories to the list: **Missing Parts**, **Wrong Item**, and **Damaged Item**.

Creating the Customer Issues Form

The Customer Issues form will utilize several of the new features of InfoPath and SharePoint. You will use template parts to help create the form, the Issue Categories list as a data source, a form library for saving the forms, and a simple workflow to route the issue for review. Once the forms are saved, you'll use library views to analyze the data.

Follow these steps to create the InfoPath form:

1. Log in to VSCLIENT as a SharePoint administrator.

2. Select Start ➤ All Programs ➤ Microsoft Office ➤ Microsoft Office InfoPath.

3. In the Getting Started dialog, click the link titled Design a Form Template.

4. In the Design a Form template dialog, select the Blank template and click the OK button.

5. In the Design Tasks pane, click the Controls link.

6. In the Controls pane, locate the CustomerInformation template part that you created earlier in this chapter.

7. Drag the CustomerInformation template part from the Controls pane to the blank form.

Creating the Data Connection

The CustomerInformation template part acts as the header for the new form. The body of the form will have the description of the problem and allow the user to select a category. The category will be driven by the Issue Categories list you created earlier.

Follow these steps to create the data connection:

1. Select Tools ➤ Data Connections from the main menu.

2. In the Data Connections dialog, click the Add button.

3. In the data connection wizard, select to create a new data connection to receive data.

4. Click the Next button.

5. On the Select Data Source screen, select to receive data from a SharePoint List and click the Next button.

6. On the SharePoint Site details screen, enter the complete URL to the home page of the Customer Issues site you created earlier (e.g., `http://vsmoss/intranet/sites/SiteDirectory/CustomerIssues`) and click the Next button.

7. Select the Issue Categories list and click the Next button.

8. Select just the Title field from the available fields and click the Next button.

9. Check the box to Store a Copy of the Data in the Form Template and click the Next button.

10. Click the Finish button.

11. In the Data Connection dialog, click the Close button. Note that you could choose to convert the data connection at this point and save it into a data connection library as I discuss in the section titled "Using Data Connection Libraries."

Creating the Form Body

Once the data connection is created, you can use it to populate a list in the Customer Issues form. The category list along with a text area will make up the body of the form. The form can then be published to the Customer Issues site for use.

Follow these steps to complete the form:

1. In the Controls pane, click the Design Tasks link.

2. In the Design Tasks pane, click the Layout link.

3. In the Layout pane, drag the Table with Title layout onto the form and drop it.

4. In the heading area labeled Click to Add a title, enter **Issue Details**.

5. Click inside the cell labeled Click to Add Form Content.

6. Select Table ➤ Insert ➤ Layout Table from the main menu.

7. Enter **2** columns and **2** rows in the Insert Table dialog and click the OK button.

8. In the Layout pane, click the Design Tasks link.

9. In the Design Tasks pane, click the Controls link.

10. Drag a Drop-Down List Box control to the upper right cell in the Issue Details table.

11. Right-click the Drop-Down List Box and select Drop-Down List Box Properties from the context menu.

12. In the List Box Entries section, select the option to Look Up Values from an External Data Source.

13. Click the Select XPath button.

14. In the Select a Field or Group dialog, expand the field nodes and select the Title field.

15. Click the OK button.

16. In the Drop-Down List Box Properties dialog, click the OK button.

17. Drag a Rich Text Box control from the Controls pane to the lower right-hand cell in the Issue Details table.

18. Type the text **Category** in the upper left-hand cell of the Issue Details table.

19. Type the text **Description** in the lower left-hand cell of the Issue Details table.

20. Right-click each control on the form and open the Properties dialogs one by one. For each control, change the field name to the value shown in Table 6-2. Figure 6-19 shows the final form.

Table 6-2. *Field Names*

Control Label	Field Name
Name	Name
Address	Address
City, State, Zip	CityStateZip
Category	Category
Description	Description

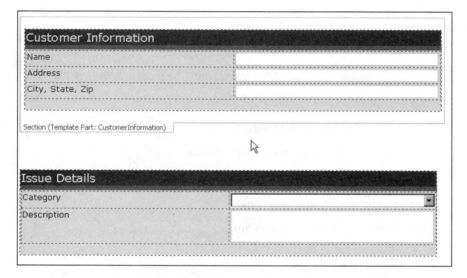

Figure 6-19. *The Customer Issues form*

Publishing the Form

Once the form is completed you are ready to publish it to the site. In our scenario, you want the form to be accessible over the web. Therefore, you will publish the form so that it can be delivered via InfoPath Form Services. This means that you must run the Design Checker and publish the form to be delivered across the web.

Follow these steps to publish the form:

1. In the Controls pane, click the Design Tasks link.

2. In the Design Tasks pane, click the Design Checker link.

3. In the Design Checker pane, click the Change Compatibility Settings link.

4. In the Form Options dialog, check the box labeled Design a Form Template That Can Be Opened in a Browser or InfoPath.

5. Enter **http://vsmoss** in the InfoPath Services URL field.

6. Click the OK button. After the Design Checker runs, you should have a single error telling you that the selected rich-text formatting options are not supported.

7. Right-click the Rich Text Box on the form and select Rich Text Box Properties from the context menu.

8. In the Rich Text Box Properties dialog, click the Display tab.

9. Uncheck the box labeled Embedded Images and click the OK button.

10. In the Design Checker pane, click the Refresh button. The error should now be resolved.

11. Select File ➤ Save from the main menu.

12. In the Save As dialog, enter **CustomerIssue.xsn** and click the Save button. It is not important where you save the form at this point because it will ultimately be published to the Customer Issues site.

13. Select File ➤ Publish from the main menu.

14. In the Publishing Wizard, select to publish the form to a SharePoint Server and click the Next button.

15. On the next screen, enter the complete URL to the home page of the Customer Issues site (e.g., `http://vsmoss/sites/intranet/SiteDirectory/CustomerIssues`) and click the Next button.

16. On the next screen, be sure that the box is checked to enable the form to be filled out with a browser and select the option to publish the form to a document library.

17. Click the Next button.

18. On the next screen, select to create a new document library and click the Next button.

19. On the next screen, enter **Customer Issue Forms** in the Name field and click the Next button.

20. On the next screen, click the Add button to select fields that will be displayed as columns in the document library.

21. In the Select a Field or Group dialog, select the Name field and click the OK button.

22. Repeat the previous step to add the Category field. When the fields are added, click the Next button.

23. Click the Publish button.

Configuring the Form Library

Once the form is published, it is available for use. However, you want to configure the new library so that it delivers the form through the browser by default. Additionally, you are going to use a built-in workflow to route the form for review.

Follow these steps to configure the library:

1. Open the Customer Issues site in the browser.

2. Click the new Customer Issues forms library link in the Quick Launch area.

3. In the Customer Issues forms library, select Settings ➤ Form Library Settings from the toolbar.

4. On the Customize page, click the Advanced Settings link.

5. On the Advanced Settings page, select the option labeled Display as Web Page to force the form to open in a browser by default.

6. Click the OK button.

7. On the Customize page, click the Workflow Settings link.

8. On the Add a Workflow page, select the Approval workflow from the Workflow Template list.

9. Enter **Approve Resolution** in the Name field.

10. Click the Next button.

11. On the Customize Workflow page, accept the default settings by clicking the OK button.

Using the New Form

Once the new form is published and the library is properly configured, you are ready to use the form. You should now be able to fill out the form with customer information and details about the problem. The category list should also be populated from the SharePoint list you created earlier. Additionally, you should be able to route the form for approval when the issue is resolved.

Follow these steps to fill out a form:

1. Navigate to the Customer Issues library.

2. Click the New button on the toolbar.

3. When the form opens in the browser, enter some data for the customer information.

4. Enter a problem description and select a category from the drop-down list.

5. Click the Save link.

6. When prompted, give the file a name and click the Save link.

7. Return to the Customer Issues forms library and verify that your new form is saved. You may have to refresh the browser if the form is not listed in the library.

8. Note that the Name and Category fields are visible. These fields can be used to sort and filter the view.

9. Using the drop-down list associated with your new form, select Workflows.

10. On the Workflows page, click the Approve Resolution workflow link.

11. On the Start page, enter the account you are using for the approver and click the Start button.

12. Return to the Customer Issues forms library and verify that the form now shows an In Progress status for the workflow.

13. Select Edit in Microsoft InfoPath from the drop-down menu associated with the new form.

14. When the form opens in InfoPath, you should be notified that you have a new task to complete. Click the Edit This Task button in the Document Action Panel.

15. In the task dialog, click the Approve button.

16. Select File ➤ Save from the main menu and close InfoPath. The form should now show an Approved status in the library.

Exercise 6.2. Document and Records Management

Combining document and records management within MOSS allows organizations to control the entire life cycle of a document. Team sites and document workspaces can be used to create and collaborate around documents. Created documents can be approved using built-in workflows or custom workflows, which I cover in Chapter 7. Documents that must be archived can then be saved as records in a repository. In this exercise, you will create new content types for important financial records and a records repository to store them in. After you finish this exercise, you should be able to plan out your own document and records management system.

Prerequisites

Before getting started with this exercise, it's important to note that you must have MOSS available to complete it. Records management is a MOSS capability and is implemented through a special web service and site template. WSS alone simply doesn't have the functionality.

Another thing you'll want to do before you get started is to download some document templates from the Microsoft Office site. In this exercise, you will create both an Invoice and Purchase Order content type so you'll need templates for them. I simply went to http:// office.microsoft.com and searched for templates that I could use. Then I saved the templates for later.

Defining Site Columns

All document and records management revolves around the definition of content types. Therefore, you will create several for this exercise. Content types begin with the definition of site columns that can be used for metadata. In this section, you will create some site columns that can be used later in a content type definition.

Follow these steps to create the site columns:

1. Log in to the home page of the intranet site you created in Chapter 2.

2. Select Site Settings ➤ Modify All Site Settings from the Site Actions menu.

3. On the Site Settings page, select Site Columns from under the Galleries section.

4. On the Site Column Gallery page, click the Create link.

5. On the New Site Column page, enter **Client Name** in the Column Name field.

6. Under the group section, select the New Group option and enter **Custom Financial Columns** in the text field.

7. Select the option to require that the column contain information.

8. Click the OK button.

9. On the Site Column Gallery page, click the Create link.

10. On the New Site Column page, enter **Department Name** in the Column Name field.

11. Select the Choice option for the field type.

12. Under the group section, select the Existing Group option and choose **Custom Financial Columns** from the drop-down list.

13. Select the option to require that the column contain information.

14. Add the following choices to the list: **Administration**, **Information Services**, **Facilities**, **Operations**, **Sales**, and **Marketing**.

15. Click the OK button.

16. On the Site Column Gallery page, click the Create link.

17. On the New Site Column page, enter **Amount** in the Column Name field.

18. Select the Currency option for the field type.

19. Under the Group section, select the Existing Group option and choose Custom Financial Columns from the drop-down list.

20. Select the option to require that the column contain information.

21. Click the OK button.

Defining Site Content Types

Content types bring together site columns, templates, and workflows to define a document. In this section, you will use the site columns defined earlier to help create several content types. You will also associate the templates you downloaded at the beginning of the exercise with these content types.

Follow these steps to create the content types:

1. Return to the intranet home page.

2. Select Site Settings ➤ Modify All Site Settings from the Site Actions menu.

3. On the Site Settings page, select Site Content Types from under the Galleries section.

4. On the Site Content Type Gallery page, click the Create button.

5. On the New Site Content Type page, enter **Financial Document** in the Name field.

6. Select Document Content Types from the drop-down list labeled Select Parent Content Type From.

7. Select Document from the drop-down list labeled Parent Content Type.

8. Under the Group section, select the New Group option and enter **Custom Financial Documents** in the text field.

9. Click the OK button.

10. On the Site Content Type page, under the Columns section, click the link titled Add from Existing Site Columns.

11. On the Add Columns to Site Content Type page, select Custom Financial Columns from the drop-down list labeled Select Columns From.

12. Select all of the available columns and click the Add button.

13. Click the OK button.

14. Return to the Site Content Type Gallery page and click the Create button.

15. On the New Site Content Type page, enter **Invoice** in the Name field.

16. Select Custom Financial Documents from the drop-down list labeled Select Parent Content Type From.

17. Select Financial Document from the drop-down list labeled Parent Content Type.

18. Under the Group section, select Custom Financial Documents from the Existing Group list.

19. Click the OK button.

20. On the Site Content Type page, click the Advanced Settings link.

21. On the Advanced Settings page, select the option to Upload a New Document Template and click the Browse button.

22. Upload the Invoice template you downloaded earlier.

23. Click the OK button.

24. Return to the Site Content Type Gallery page and click the Create button.

25. On the New Site Content Type page, enter **Purchase Order** in the Name field.

26. Select Custom Financial Documents from the drop-down list labeled Select Parent Content Type From.

27. Select Financial Document from the drop-down list labeled Parent Content Type.

28. Under the Group section, select Custom Financial Documents from the Existing Group list.

29. Click the OK button.

30. On the Site Content Type page, click the Advanced Settings link.

31. On the Advanced Settings page, select the option to Upload a New Document Template and click the Browse button.

32. Upload the Purchase Order template you saved earlier.

33. Click the OK button.

Creating the Document Library

Once the content types are created, they may be associated with a document library. In this exercise, you'll create a document library for the financial documents and configure it to use the content types you defined. Once configured, you can use the library to create new financial documents.

Follow these steps to create the new document library:

1. Click the Document Center tab on the intranet site.

2. Select Create from the Site Actions menu.

3. On the Create page, click Document Library.

4. On the New page, enter **Financial Documents** in the Name field.

5. Select Microsoft Office Word Document as the document template.

6. Click the Create button.

7. In the Financial Documents library, select Settings ➤ Document Library Settings from the toolbar.

8. On the Customize Financial Documents page, click the Advanced Settings link.

9. On the Advanced Settings page, select the option to Allow Management of Content Types.

10. Click the OK button.

11. On the Customize Financial Documents page, under the Content Types section, click the link titled Add from Existing Site Content Types.

12. On the Add Content Types page, select Custom Financial Documents from the drop-down list labeled Select Site Content Types From.

13. Select the Invoice and Purchase Order Content Types and click the Add button.

14. Click the OK button.

15. On the Customize Financial Documents page, under the Content Types section, click the Document Content Type.

16. On the List Content Type page, click the link titled Delete This Content Type.

17. Click the Document Center tab.

Creating the Records Repository

The *records repository* is where important documents will be archived. The repository is created using the Records Center template. Once created, you can associate the repository with a site collection so that documents may be sent to the repository directly from a document library.

Follow these steps to create the records repository:

1. Log in to VSMOSS as a SharePoint administrator.

2. Select Start ➤ Administrative Tools ➤ SharePoint 3.0 Central Administration.

3. On the Application Management tab, under the SharePoint Site Management section, click the link titled Create a Site Collection.

4. On the Create Site Collection page, ensure that the Web Application drop-down is referencing the web application where your intranet site is located. If not, drop the list and select the correct web application.

5. Enter **Records Repository** in the Title field.

6. Enter **records** in the Web Site Address field.

7. Under the Template Selection section, click the Enterprise tab, and then select the Records Center template.

8. Under the Primary Site Collection Administrator section, enter **DOMAIN\ Administrator** in the User Name field.

9. Click the OK button to create the new site collection. When the site collection is created, open it in a separate copy of the browser.

10. Return to the Application Management tab in the Central Administration web site and click the Records Center link under the External Service Connections section.

11. On the Configure Connection to Records Center page, select the option to Connect to a Records Center.

12. In the URL field, type the address of the records repository site followed by a reference to the Official File web service (e.g., **http://vsmoss/sites/records/_vti_bin/ officialfile.asmx**).

13. Type **Records Repository** in the Display Name field.

14. Click the OK button.

Configuring the Records Repository

There are several configuration tasks that must be performed when a new records repository is created. Specifically, you must configure the repository to recognize content types and route them to the correct archive within the site. Additionally, you should set up retention policies so documents are automatically processed after they expire.

Follow these steps to configure the records repository:

1. Navigate to the home page of the records repository site.

2. Select Create from the Site Actions menu.

3. On the Create page, click the Document Library link.

4. On the New page, enter **Financial Records** in the Name field.

5. Select Microsoft Office Word Document from the Document Template drop-down list.

6. Click the Create button.

7. In the Quick Launch area, click the Records Routing link.

8. In the Records Routing list, click the New button.

9. On the Records Routing: New Item page, enter **Financial Documents** in the Title field.

10. Enter **Financial Records** in the Location field.

11. Enter **Invoice/Purchase Order** in the Aliases field.

12. Click the OK button.

13. In the Quick Launch area, click the Financial Records link.

14. In the Financial Records library, click Settings ➤ Document Library Settings on the toolbar.

15. On the Customize Financial Records page, click the link titled Information Management Policy Settings.

16. On the Information Management Policy Settings page, select the option to Define a Policy and click the OK button.

17. On the Edit Policy page, check the box labeled Enable Expiration.

18. Select the option labeled A Time Period Based on the Item's Properties.

19. Enter **5** years for the expiration.

20. Select Delete in the Perform This Action drop-down list.

21. Click the OK button.

Archiving a Document

Once the repository is configured, you may begin sending documents to it. Documents can be sent to the repository directly from an enabled document library. In this section, you'll make a new document and send it to the repository.

Follow these steps to archive a document:

1. Click the Document Center tab on the intranet site.

2. In the Quick Launch area, click the Financial Documents link.

3. In the Financial Documents library, drop the New menu and verify that both the Invoice and Purchase Order content types are listed.

4. Select the Invoice content type.

5. When the document opens in Word, fill in the properties.

6. Select File ➤ Save Form and save the document back to the Financial Documents library.

7. Close Word and return to the Financial Documents library.

8. Using the drop-down menu associated with the document, select Send To ➤ Records Repository.

9. After the document has been sent to the repository, open the home page of the records repository site.

10. Click the Financial Records library link and verify that the document was correctly archived.

Creating a Hold Category

Once documents are in the repository, they may be put on hold. *Holds* help ensure that a document is not altered or destroyed during an important time period such as audit or discovery. In this section, you will place an archived document on hold for a tax audit.

Follow these steps to set up a hold:

1. In the Quick Launch area of the Records Repository site, click the Holds link.

2. In the Holds list, click the New button on the toolbar.

3. On the Holds: New Item page, enter **Tax Audit** in the Title field.

4. Click the OK button.

5. In the Quick Launch area of the Records Repository site, click the Financial Records link.

6. Locate the archived document, and using the drop-down list, select Manage Holds.

7. On the Item Hold Status page, select the Add to Hold option and choose Tax Audit from the Holds list.

8. Click the Save button.

9. Locate the archived document and using the drop-down list, select Delete.

10. Verify that you receive an error message indicating that the document cannot be deleted while on hold.

CHAPTER 7

■■■

SharePoint Custom Features and Workflows

Features are the backbone of SharePoint development because every custom development project can—and really should—be deployed as a feature. Features give tremendous control over SharePoint configurations and capabilities at the administrator level. This means that developers can create features and then turn them over to SharePoint administrators without having to get involved repeatedly in small configuration changes.

Workflow is a specialized feature that deserves extra attention because of the power it brings to SharePoint. Workflows allow you to start a series of operations manually or automatically in response to activity in a list. Workflows can be used for simple approval processes or complex system integration. In this chapter I cover all of the different ways to create features from simple hyperlink additions on a page to full-blown customized workflows.

Building Custom Features

In Chapter 3, I introduced the concept of features and defined it as a way to package capabilities that could be deployed to any site. Throughout the book, you have activated various features of SharePoint to enable new functionality within sites. Activating some features, such as publishing, causes major changes in the way that a site behaves. Other features, such as the slide library, add a single atomic piece of functionality. This capability to affect large or small changes makes the idea of creating custom features compelling, and you should think of features as the best practice for deploying any customization from a single web part to complete solutions.

Understanding the Feature Architecture

A SharePoint farm has a straightforward way to keep track of the available features. Each feature on the farm is given a folder in the path C:\Program File\Common Files\Microsoft Shared\web server extensions\12\TEMPLATE\FEATURES, and the name of the folder is considered to be the name of the feature. The feature folder must contain a file named `Feature.xml`, which defines the basic information about a feature. Listing 7-1 shows the `Feature.xml` file for the data connection library feature.

Listing 7-1. *A Sample Feature.xml File*

```xml
<?xml version="1.0" encoding="utf-8" ?>
<!-- Copyright (c) Microsoft Corporation. All rights reserved. -->
<Feature xmlns="http://schemas.microsoft.com/sharepoint/"
    Id="00BFEA71-DBD7-4F72-B8CB-DA7AC0440130"
    DefaultResourceFile="core"
    Title="Data Connections Feature"
    Hidden="TRUE"
    SolutionId="7ED6CD55-B479-4EB7-A529-E99A24C10BD3"
    Version="12.0.0.0"
    Scope="Web">
    <ElementManifests>
        <ElementManifest Location="ListTemplates\DataConnectionLibrary.xml" />
    </ElementManifests>
</Feature>
```

The Feature element is the highest level element in the definition and is required to have a unique identifier and a scope level. The unique identifier is simply a GUID. The scope identifier can be any of the values Farm, WebApplication, Site, or Web and is used to determine the list on which the feature will appear. Table 7-1 lists all of the attributes for the Feature element.

Table 7-1. *Feature Element Attributes*

Attribute	Required	Value	Description
ActiveOnDefault	No	True or False	Determines whether the feature is active by default when a new web application is created. The default value is True.
AlwaysForceInstall	No	True or False	Determines whether the feature installation process will proceed even if the feature is already installed. I discuss the feature installation process throughout this section. The default value is False.
AutoActivateIn CentralAdmin	No	True or False	Determines whether the feature is activated by default in the Central Administration site. The default value is False.
Creator	No	Text	Identifies the feature creator. This element is optional.
DefaultResourceFile	No	Text	Determines the name of a resource file for your feature. The search path for the resource file is C:\Program File\Common Files\Microsoft Shared\web server extensions\12\TEMPLATE\FEATURES\{Feature}\Resources.
Description	No	Text	Describes of the feature that will appear on the Feature list in SharePoint.
Hidden	No	True or False	Determines whether the feature is visible on the Feature list. If it is not visible, it can only be activated using the command-line utility STSADM.EXE –o ActivateFeature –name {Feature}. The default value is False.

Attribute	Required	Value	Description
Id	Yes	Text	Provides a unique identifier for the feature. Typically, this must be a GUID without the curly braces.
ImageUrl	No	Text	Associates an image file with a feature. The image appears in the Feature list alongside the feature description.
ImageUrlAltText	No	Text	Provides alternate text for the feature image.
ReceiverAssembly	No	Strong name	Identifies the strong name of an assembly that will receive activation and deactivation events for the feature. I cover receiver assemblies in the section of this chapter titled "Understanding Feature Receivers."
ReceiverClass	No	Class name	Identifies the class name of the class that will receive activation and deactivation events for the feature.
RequireResources	No	True or False	Indicates whether supporting resources are required for this feature. The default value is False.
Scope	Yes	Farm, WebApplication, Site, Web	Determines on what list the feature appears and therefore at what scope it can be activated.
SolutionId	No	GUID	Specifies the solution to which the feature belongs. I cover creating solutions in Chapter 10.
Title	No	Text	Specifies the title of the feature as it appears in SharePoint.
Version	No	Text	Specifies the version number in n.n.n.n format.

Along with attributes, there are several child elements that can be contained within the Feature element. These include the ActivationDependencies, Properties, and ElementManifests elements. The ActivationDependencies element allows you to establish dependencies between features so that a child feature must be activated before a parent feature. The Properties element allows you to define custom key/value pairs that your feature can access for configuration purposes. The ElementManifests element allows you to specify a file where additional Feature elements are defined.

Of the available elements, you will make the most use of the ElementManifests element. The ElementManifests element contains any number of ElementManifest or ElementFile elements that always have a Location attribute pointing to a manifest file. This manifest file contains information that lets you add new actions to SharePoint menus, add new pages to a site, add new list types to a site, use custom controls, and receive list events. Because the content of the manifest file can vary greatly between features, I'll show you examples of all of these customizations throughout the chapter. Listing 7-2 shows an example manifest file for the data connection library feature.

Listing 7-2. *Defining a Data Connection Library*

```xml
<?xml version="1.0" encoding="utf-8"?>
<Elements xmlns="http://schemas.microsoft.com/sharepoint/">
    <ListTemplate
        Name="datasrcs"
        Type="110"
        BaseType="1"
        Hidden="TRUE"
        HiddenList="TRUE"
        OnQuickLaunch="FALSE"
        SecurityBits="11"
        DisplayName="$Resources:core,datasourcesList;"
        Description="$Resources:core,datasourcesList_Desc;"
        Image="/_layouts/images/itdl.gif"
        DocumentTemplate="100"/>
</Elements>
```

Adding Actions to Menus and Toolbars

Creating a feature that adds an item to a menu or a toolbar can be very simple. In fact, you can create such a feature with no code and two simple XML files. As an example, I'll create a feature that adds an item to the Site Actions menu that lets you access the Apress site in order to download the code for this book. I'll call my new feature CodeDownload. Figure 7-1 shows the activated feature on the Site Actions menu.

Figure 7-1. *Adding an item to the Site Actions menu*

You begin the creation of a feature by constructing a Feature.xml file. I typically start a new project in Visual Studio just to keep things organized, but it's not a requirement until you build features that include custom assemblies. Once the project is created, I just add an XML file to it named Feature.xml.

■**Tip** Whenever you are creating feature files, associate the wss.xsd schema file with your XML in order to activate IntelliSense in Visual Studio. You can do this by setting the Schemas property of the XML file to C:\Program File\Common Files\Microsoft Shared\web server extensions\12\TEMPLATE\XML\wss.xsd.

As I stated earlier, the only required attributes of the Feature element are Id and Scope. However, you'll typically want a few more attributes such as Title and Description. Additionally, my feature will reference an ElementManifest file named Elements.xml that will contain the definition for my new menu item. For the unique identifier, simply generate a GUID in Visual Studio by selecting Tools ➤ Create GUID from the main menu. Listing 7-3 shows the complete Feature.xml file for the CodeDownload feature.

Listing 7-3. *The Feature.xml File for CodeDownload*

```
<?xml version="1.0" encoding="utf-8" ?>
<Feature xmlns="http://schemas.microsoft.com/sharepoint/"
    Id="BAF0C4A7-C707-47d2-809B-8130BC344048"
    Scope="Site"
    Title="Download Book Code"
    Description="A feature to open the code download page on Apress."
>
  <ElementManifests>
    <ElementManifest Location="Elements.xml" />
  </ElementManifests>
</Feature>
```

As I noted earlier, the contents of the manifest file vary depending upon the exact functionality you want to create. When adding menu and tool bar items, you'll utilize the CustomAction element in the manifest file. Each CustomAction element defines a single new entry on a menu or a toolbar. Listing 7-4 shows how I use the CustomAction element to define a new item on the Site Actions menu.

Listing 7-4. *Defining a Custom Action*

```
<Elements xmlns="http://schemas.microsoft.com/sharepoint/">
  <CustomAction
    Id=" 175B270F-239E-4955-97CB-94227E5DAA17"
    GroupId="SiteActions"
    Location="Microsoft.SharePoint.StandardMenu"
    Sequence="1000"
    Title="Download Book Code"
    Description="This action takes you to the Apress code download page."
    ImageUrl="_layouts/images/apress.jpg">
    <UrlAction Url="http://www.apress.com/book/download.html"/>
  </CustomAction>
</Elements>
```

The CustomAction element has two key attributes, GroupId and Location, that specify the menu or toolbar where a new item will be added. When you set these attributes, you have to use special values that are recognized by the Microsoft.SharePoint.WebControls. FeaturemenuTemplate object, which builds the menu. Admittedly there's a little "magic word" development going on. If you use the values properly, however, you can add an item to menus and toolbars in many useful places. Table 7-2 shows the complete list of possible values for the GroupId and Location attributes.

Table 7-2. *Locations and Group IDs*

Area	Location	GroupID
Display form toolbar	DisplayFormToolbar	N/A
Edit form toolbar	EditFormToolbar	N/A
New form toolbar	NewFormToolbar	N/A
List view toolbar	ViewToolbar	N/A
List item menu	EditControlBlock N/A	
Library/List New menu	Microsoft.SharePoint.StandardMenu	NewMenu
Library/List Actions menu	Microsoft.SharePoint.StandardMenu	ActionsMenu
Library/List Settings menu	Microsoft.SharePoint.StandardMenu	SettingsMenu
Library Upload menu	Microsoft.SharePoint.StandardMenu	UploadMenu
Site Actions menu	Microsoft.SharePoint.StandardMenu	SiteActions
Site Settings page, Site collection administration links	Microsoft.SharePoint.SiteSettings	SiteCollectionAdmin
Site Settings page, Site administration links	Microsoft.SharePoint.SiteSettings	SiteAdministration
Site Settings page, Galleries links	Microsoft.SharePoint.SiteSettings	Galleries
Site Settings page, Look and feel links	Microsoft.SharePoint.SiteSettings	Customization
Site Settings page, Users and permissions links	Microsoft.SharePoint.SiteSettings	UsersAndPermissions
Site Actions menu for surveys	Microsoft.SharePoint.StandardMenu	ActionsMenuForSurvey
Site Settings page, links for surveys	Microsoft.SharePoint.SiteSettings	SettingsMenuForSurvey
Content type settings links	Microsoft.SharePoint.ContentTypeSettings	N/A
Central Administration Operations page	Microsoft.SharePoint.Administration.Operations	N/A
Central Administration Application Management page	Microsoft.SharePoint.Administration.ApplicationManagement	N/A

Along with the GroupId and Location attributes, I have used the Id, Sequence, Title, Description, and ImageUrl attributes. I have also made use of the UrlAction element. The Id attribute is a GUID that uniquely identifies the new item. The Sequence is a relative value that determines the location of the new item. Setting it to a large value guarantees that it will appear as the last item. The Title is the only required attribute and specifies the text that will appear on the item. The Description is text describing the item, and the ImageUrl is a site-relative path to an image to use on the item. Finally, the UrlAction element specifies the address associated with the new item.

Once the two XML files were completed, I copied them both into a folder under the path C:\Program File\Common Files\Microsoft Shared\web server extensions\12\TEMPLATE\

FEATURES\CodeDownload. I also copied the graphic for the menu item to C:\Program File\Common Files\Microsoft Shared\web server extensions\12\TEMPLATE\Images. Once the files are copied into the appropriate location, you can run the STSADM.EXE utility to install the feature.

STSADM.EXE is located at C:\Program Files\Common Files\Microsoft Shared\web server extensions\12\bin\stsadm.exe. This administrative utility is used for many command-line operations. In fact, you can get a complete listing of the operations just by executing the utility with no arguments. In our case, we want to install the feature that is accomplished with the following arguments:

```
STSADM.EXE -o installfeature -filename  CodeDownload\feature.xml -force
```

Once the new feature is installed, you must reset Internet Information Server to make the feature available. Keep in mind that the feature will not be activated yet; you must go to the features list at the scope level you specified and click the Activate button. In this example, the scope was set to Site level (which actually means site collection). Figure 7-2 shows the new feature available in the site collections Features list.

Figure 7-2. *Activating a custom feature*

Using Custom Action Pages

In the CodeDownload feature, I simply used a public web site as the target in the UrlAction element. However, you can also use your own ASPX pages as a target. If you do this, you can respond to the user by presenting a custom page in the site, executing code, or both. As an example of this technique, I built a feature called ContentTypeHierarchy that shows a listing of all of content types in a hierarchy. This feature is useful because the standard list of content types doesn't show hidden types or a hierarchical listing. Figure 7-3 shows a partial image of the hierarchical listing.

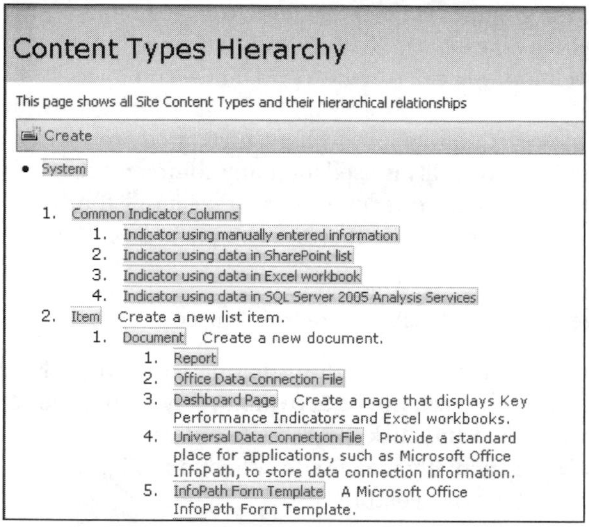

Content Types Hierarchy

This page shows all Site Content Types and their hierarchical relationships

💾 Create

- System

  1. Common Indicator Columns
     1. Indicator using manually entered information
     2. Indicator using data in SharePoint list
     3. Indicator using data in Excel workbook
     4. Indicator using data in SQL Server 2005 Analysis Services
  2. Item   Create a new list item.
     1. Document   Create a new document.
        1. Report
        2. Office Data Connection File
        3. Dashboard Page   Create a page that displays Key
           Performance Indicators and Excel workbooks.
        4. Universal Data Connection File   Provide a standard
           place for applications, such as Microsoft Office
           InfoPath, to store data connection information.
        5. InfoPath Form Template   A Microsoft Office
           InfoPath Form Template.

Figure 7-3. *Showing content types in a hierarchy*

For this feature, I built a standard Feature.xml file and manifest file that adds a new link to the Site Settings Galleries section. My new hierarchical view appears directly above the link for the standard view. Listing 7-5 shows the Feature.xml file, and Listing 7-6 shows the manifest file.

Listing 7-5. *The ContentTypeHierarchy Feature.xml File*

```xml
<?xml version="1.0" encoding="utf-8" ?>
<Feature xmlns="http://schemas.microsoft.com/sharepoint/"
  Id="2D9921AE-D263-4e2b-B4F7-ABDD6223C8B0"
  Scope="Site"
  Title="Content Type Hierarchy"
  Description="Shows the hierarchical relationship between content types."
  >
 <ElementManifests>
    <ElementManifest Location="Elements.xml" />
 </ElementManifests>
</Feature>
```

Listing 7-6. *The ContentTypeHierarchy Manifest File*

```xml
<Elements xmlns="http://schemas.microsoft.com/sharepoint/">
  <CustomAction
    Id="77C52F5D-D5C3-46a1-96EA-2B6B434564C2"
    GroupId="Galleries"
    Location="Microsoft.SharePoint.SiteSettings"
    Sequence="0"
    Title="Site Content Types Hierarchy"
```

```
         Description="Displays a hierarchy of site content types.">
         <UrlAction Url="_layouts/ContentTypeHierarchy.aspx"/>
      </CustomAction>
</Elements>
```

The key part of the feature that is new is the reference to the ASP.NET page
ContentTypeHierarchy.aspx. This is a custom page that will open when the link is clicked in
the Site Settings page. Inside this page, I build the hierarchical list of content types by using
the SharePoint object model. I discuss the object model in more detail in Chapter 11, but for
now this will help give you a good understanding of how features can interact with SharePoint
sites. Listing 7-7 shows the complete code for the ContentTypeHierarchy.aspx page.

Listing 7-7. *The ContentTypeHierarchy.aspx Page*

```
<%@ Page Language="C#" MasterPageFile="~/_layouts/application.master"%>
<%@ Assembly Name="Microsoft.SharePoint, Version=12.0.0.0, Culture=neutral,
    PublicKeyToken=71e9bce111e9429c"%>
<%@ Import Namespace="Microsoft.SharePoint" %>
<%@ Import Namespace="Microsoft.SharePoint.WebControls" %>
<%@ Register TagPrefix="wssuc" TagName="ToolBar"
    src="~/_controltemplates/ToolBar.ascx" %>
<%@ Register TagPrefix="wssuc" TagName="ToolBarButton"
    src="~/_controltemplates/ToolBarButton.ascx" %>

<asp:Content ID="Content2" runat="server"
    ContentPlaceHolderID="PlaceHolderPageTitleInTitleArea">
Content Types Hierarchy
</asp:Content>

<asp:Content ID="Content3" runat="server"
    ContentPlaceHolderID="PlaceHolderPageDescription">
This page shows all Site Content Types and their hierarchical relationships
</asp:Content>

<asp:Content ID="Content4" runat="server" ContentPlaceHolderID="PlaceHolderMain" >

  <TABLE border="0" width="100%" cellspacing="0" cellpadding="0">
  <TR>
    <TD ID="mngfieldToobar">
      <wssuc:ToolBar id="onetidMngFieldTB" runat="server">
      <Template_Buttons>
          <wssuc:ToolBarButton runat="server"
          Text="<%$Resources:wss,multipages_createbutton_text%>"
          id="idAddField"
          ToolTip="<%$Resources:wss,mngctype_create_alt%>"
          NavigateUrl="ctypenew.aspx" ImageUrl="/_layouts/images/newitem.gif"
          AccessKey="C" />
        </Template_Buttons>
```

```
        </wssuc:ToolBar>
    </TD>
  </TR>
  </TABLE>

<%

    //System Content Type is the root
    SPSite site = SPControl.GetContextSite(Context);
    SPContentTypeCollection types = site.OpenWeb().ContentTypes;
    SPContentTypeId id = types[0].Id;
    Response.Write("<table style='font-size:10pt' border='0'" +
      " cellpadding='2' width='50%'><tr><td>");
    Response.Write("<li><a class='ms-topnav'" +
    " href=\"/_layouts/ManageContentType.aspx?ctype=" +
    types[0].Id.ToString() + "\">" + types[0].Name +
    "</a><span class='ms-webpartpagedescription'>" + types[0].Description +
    "</span></li>");
    ShowChildren(id);
    Response.Write("</ol></td></tr></table>");

%>

</asp:Content>

<script runat="server">

    public void ShowChildren(SPContentTypeId id)
    {
        SPSite site = SPControl.GetContextSite(Context);
        SPContentTypeCollection types = site.RootWeb.ContentTypes;

        Response.Write("<ol>");

        foreach (SPContentType type in types)
        {
            if (type.Parent.Id == id && type.Parent.Id != type.Id)
            {
                Response.Write("<li><a class='ms-topnav'" +
                " href=\"/_layouts/ManageContentType.aspx?ctype=" +
                type.Id.ToString() + "\">" + type.Name +
                "</a><span class='ms-webpartpagedescription'>" +
                type.Description + "</span></li>");
                ShowChildren(type.Id);
            }
        }
    }
```

```
    Response.Write("</ol>");

  }

</script>
```

The first thing to note about Listing 7-7 is that it is written in the "old school" ASP style. It uses delimiters to place code directly in the ASPX page. Pages in the LAYOUTS directory can have inline code, while pages in the content database cannot have code added to them at all. Generally, I simply create these files directly in Visual Studio and deploy them to the LAYOUTS directory.

The next thing to point out about Listing 7-7 is that it uses placeholders to display content. As I discussed in Chapter 5, the master page provides the content placeholders and the page itself uses them to position content on the page. In this example, I am using the PlaceHolderPageTitleInTitleArea, PlaceHolderPageDescription, and PlaceHolderMain placeholders to display the page title, description, and body, respectively.

Finally, you'll notice that the ASPX page makes use of some user controls written as ASCX files. These controls are standard ones that SharePoint supplies to generate buttons and toolbars. I am using them in the page to recreate the same toolbar that is found in the standard Content Types Gallery. However, you could certainly use your own.

Using Tokens to Retrieve Information

When you write features, you quite often need to know about the site or item that is active when your menu item is clicked. For these scenarios, SharePoint supports a set of tokens you can use in your manifest file to represent sites and items. These tokens allow you to retrieve relevant URLs and item identifiers that can be used within your code. Normally, you would use the tokens as part of a query string (e.g., <UrlAction Url="/layouts/myPage. aspx?Item={ItemUrl}" />) and then extract the value in your ASP.NET code. Table 7-3 lists the available tokens and their functions. Additionally, Chapter 9 includes a complete exercise that uses this technique.

Table 7-3. *Manifest Tokens*

Token	Description
{ItemId}	ID of a list item that you can use with the SharePoint object model.
{ItemUrl}	URL of the document item being acted upon. Not valid for list items.
{ListId}	GUID of the list where the action occurred.
{RecurrenceId}	Recurrence index of the item.
~site	Site-relative link.
~sitecollection	Site collection-relative link.
{SiteUrl}	URL of the site where the action occurred.

Adding New Files to a Site

Another common scenario where features are useful is when you want to add new files to a site. The files that you add to a site using a feature can take many forms including web pages, master pages, and document templates. Since many of the elements in a SharePoint site are simply files, this opens up a lot of interesting possibilities. In order to add a new file using a feature, you make use of the Module element in combination with the File element through the manifest file. These two elements specify the new files to be added and where they should be added.

The Module element contains a Name attribute for the set of files to be added. The Url attribute designates the address of where the files should be placed. This address can either refer to a library or some other location on the site. The File element also contains a Url attribute that specifies a feature-relative path to the file that will be added. As an example, the following code shows how to add two new master pages to the master page catalog:

```
<Elements xmlns="http://schemas.microsoft.com/sharepoint/">
  <Module Name="MasterPages" List="116" Url="_catalogs/masterpage">
    <File Url="training.master" Type="GhostableInLibrary" />
    <File Url="minimal.master" Type="GhostableInLibrary" />
  </Module>
</Elements>
```

The target location for the new file is designated by the Url attribute of the Module element. If the target location is a document library, the Type attribute of the File element must be set to GhostableInLibrary. Furthermore the List attribute of the Module element must specify the type of list being targeted. This value is a number that represents the list type. Table 7-4 shows the different values for the List attribute and the corresponding list type.

Table 7-4. *List Attribute Values*

Value	Description
100	Generic list
101	Document library
102	Survey
103	Links list
104	Announcements list
105	Contacts list
106	Events list
107	Tasks list
108	Discussion board
109	Picture library
110	Data sources
111	Site Template Gallery
113	Web Part Gallery
114	List Template Gallery
115	Form library

Value	Description
116	Publishing library
120	Custom list
200	Meeting Series list
201	Meeting Agenda list
202	Meeting Attendees list
204	Meeting Decisions list
207	Meeting Objectives list
210	Meeting text box
211	Meeting Things to Bring list
212	Meeting Workspace Pages list
300	Portal Sites list
1100	Issue tracking
2002	Personal document library
2003	Private document library

If the target location is not a library, the Type attribute of the File element must be set to Ghostable. This essentially means that you are adding web pages to the site. The File element may further specify a Name attribute for the page when it is added. If a Name attribute is specified, the page will be customized and no longer connected to the original template. If the Name attribute is not specified, the page is uncustomized and will reflect any changes made later to the original file. The following code shows an example of adding new pages where the page templates are in a subfolder named Pages:

```
<Elements xmlns="http://schemas.microsoft.com/sharepoint/">
  <Module Path="Pages" Url="" >
    <File Url="welcome.aspx" Type="Ghostable" />
    <File Url="news.aspx" Type="Ghostable" />
    <File Url="news.aspx" Name="newsletter.aspx" Type="Ghostable" />
  </Module>
</Elements>
```

Understanding Feature Receivers

In many ways, activating a feature is similar to installing and managing software applications on a Windows desktop. Activating a feature is sort of like an installation process that makes changes to the system, and the Features list in SharePoint is similar to the Add/Remove Programs list in Windows. I point this out because, just like a good installation program, your feature should be mindful of the system changes it makes so that they can be undone during deactivation. While action links are removed automatically during deactivation, many other modifications, such as lists and pages, are not.

Consider the previous example that uses the File element to add new pages to a site during activation. You might initially think that these pages would be removed during deactivation, but they are not. Often the only way for your feature to undo its modifications is to receive notification that the feature is deactivating and respond with some custom code. You can receive feature events by creating a special assembly and associating it with your feature. These assemblies are called *feature receivers*.

Coding Feature Receivers

As an example of a feature receiver, I'll create a feature that changes the site master page from the default to the minimal master page I presented in Chapter 5. For this feature, I want the site to use the minimal page when the feature is activated, but I want the site to revert to the default master when the feature is deactivated. Therefore, I'll need a way to receive notification when my feature is activating or deactivating.

Creating a class to receive feature events is accomplished by inheriting from `Microsoft.SharePoint.SPFeatureReceiver`. This class has four methods that you must override: `FeatureInstalled`, `FeatureActivated`, `FeatureDeactivating`, and `FeatureUninstalling`. The `FeatureInstalled` method is called after the feature installation is complete. The `FeatureActivated` method is called after the feature is activated. The `FeatureDeactivating` method is called before the feature is deactivated, and the `FeatureUninstalling` method is called before the feature is uninstalled. Using these methods, you can take action at the appropriate time to make changes or roll them back.

In my example, I will use the `FeatureActivated` method to change the master page to the minimal master and the `FeatureDeactivating` method to change it back. Once again, I'll use the SharePoint object model to make these changes. Specifically, I will change the `MasterUrl` and `CustomMasterUrl` properties of the `SPWeb` object.

The `MasterUrl` and `CustomMasterUrl` are special properties that affect many pages within a SharePoint site. These properties are referenced in site ASPX pages using the special tokens `~masterurl/default.master` and `~masterurl/custom.default`, which act as placeholders for the properties. You can see these tokens when you look at a site ASPX page, such as `Default.aspx`, in the SharePoint Designer. Initially, both of these tokens are set to reference the `default.master` page in the Master Pages catalog, located at _catalogs/masterpage/default.master. However, they can be changed through code in response to an activate or a deactivate event. Listing 7-8 shows how to change the master page to the minimal master page that I describe in Chapter 5.

■**Note** Along with the dynamic tokens `~masterurl/default.master` and `~masterurl/custom.default`, SharePoint also supports the static tokens `~site/default.master` and `~sitecollection/default.master`. These tokens reference the `default.master` page for the site and site collection, respectively.

Listing 7-8. *Receiving Feature Events*

```
using System;
using System.Collections.Generic;
using System.Text;
using Microsoft.SharePoint;
using System.Diagnostics;
```

```
namespace MinimalMaster
{
  class Receiver:SPFeatureReceiver
  {
    public override void FeatureActivated(SPFeatureReceiverProperties properties)
    {
      try
      {
        SPWeb site = (SPWeb)properties.Feature.Parent;
        site.MasterUrl = site.ServerRelativeUrl +
        "/_catalogs/masterpage/minimal.master";
        site.CustomMasterUrl = site.ServerRelativeUrl +
        "/_catalogs/masterpage/minimal.master";
        site.Update();
      }
      catch (SPException x)
      {
        logMessage(x.Message, EventLogEntryType.Error);
      }
      catch(Exception x)
      {
          logMessage(x.Message, EventLogEntryType.Error);
      }
  }

  public override void FeatureDeactivating(SPFeatureReceiverProperties properties)
  {
    try
    {
      SPWeb site = (SPWeb)properties.Feature.Parent;
      site.MasterUrl = site.ServerRelativeUrl +
      "/_catalogs/masterpage/default.master";
      site.CustomMasterUrl = site.ServerRelativeUrl +
      "/_catalogs/masterpage/default.master";
      site.Update();
    }
    catch (SPException x)
    {
      logMessage(x.Message, EventLogEntryType.Error);
    }
    catch (Exception x)
    {
      logMessage(x.Message, EventLogEntryType.Error);
    }
  }
```

```
public override void FeatureInstalled(SPFeatureReceiverProperties properties)
{
  logMessage("MinimalMaster Feature installed",EventLogEntryType.SuccessAudit);
}

public override void FeatureUninstalling(SPFeatureReceiverProperties properties)
{
  logMessage("MinimalMaster Feature uninstalling", EventLogEntryType.Information);
}

private void logMessage(string message,EventLogEntryType type)
{
  if(!EventLog.SourceExists("SharePoint Features"))
    EventLog.CreateEventSource("SharePoint Features","Application");
  EventLog.WriteEntry("SharePoint Features",message,type);
 }
 }
}
```

A feature receiver must be installed in the Global Assembly Cache (GAC) in order to work. Therefore, you'll need to provide a strong name for the assembly and install it in the GAC. You can create a new strong name for the assembly directly from the Signing tab of the Properties dialog for your C# project. In this dialog, you can elect to create a new key file or use an existing one.

■**Tip** During development, I prefer to use the same key file because then the `PublicKeyToken` doesn't change. It makes it easier to create the `Feature.xml` file, which must reference the assembly's `PublicKeyToken`.

Creating the Feature.xml and Manifest Files

Just like any feature you create, you must have an associated `Feature.xml` file saved in a subdirectory under the FEATURES directory. When creating a feature that will utilize a receiver, you must include the `ReceiverAssembly` and `ReceiverClass` attributes of the `Feature` element. The `ReceiverAssembly` attribute specifies the complete strong name of the feature receiver. The `ReceiverClass` attribute specifies the class that inherits from `SPFeatureReceiver`. Listing 7-9 shows the feature file for my example.

Listing 7-9. *A Feature File That References a Receiver*

```
<?xml version="1.0" encoding="utf-8" ?>
<Feature xmlns="http://schemas.microsoft.com/sharepoint/"
  Id="142C1ADB-C56E-4fa2-AC5E-C947390BE659"
  Scope="Web"
```

```
  Title="Minimal Master Page"
  Description="Sets the master page to minimal.master."
  ActivateOnDefault="false"
  AlwaysForceInstall="true"
  Version="1.0.0.0"
  ReceiverAssembly=
  "MinimalMaster, Version=1.0.0.0, Culture=neutral, PublicKeyToken=689f1d0ba493bcce"
  ReceiverClass="MinimalMaster.Receiver"
  >
  <ElementManifests>
    <ElementManifest Location="Elements.xml" />
  </ElementManifests>
</Feature>
```

The strong name of the feature receiver is a combination of the namespace, version, culture, and PublicKeyToken associated with the assembly. The namespace is designated within the code of Listing 7-8. The version and culture information are typically found in the AssemblyInfo file of the project. However, the culture information is often not supplied so it is simply specified as neutral. The PublicKeyToken is a truncated version of the public key found in the key file. You can obtain the PublicKeyToken for an assembly by using the strong name tool with the following syntax:

```
sn.exe -T myassembly.dll
```

For my example to work, I also need to create a manifest file that will load the minimal master page into the Master Page catalog. I presented similar code earlier in the chapter, but I'll include it here so that the example is complete. The following code shows the manifest file for the example:

```
<Elements xmlns="http://schemas.microsoft.com/sharepoint/">
  <Module Name="MinimalMaster" List="116" Url="_catalogs/masterpage">
    <File Url="minimal.master" Type="GhostableInLibrary"/>
  </Module>
</Elements>
```

Receiving Site, List, and Item Events

In the previous version of SharePoint you could only receive events from document libraries, but this version is capable of handling a wide range of events. Events are handled by creating receiver assemblies that inherit from one of SharePoint's event classes. Once you create an event receiver, it may then be deployed as a feature. Table 7-5 lists the handled events and the associated event class, and when each event is triggered.

Table 7-5. *Site, List, and Item Events*

Event	Event Class	Description
SiteDeleted	SPWebEventReceiver	Fires after a site collection has been deleted
SiteDeleting	SPWebEventReceiver	Fires just before a site collection is deleted
WebDeleted	SPWebEventReceiver	Fires after a site has been deleted
WebDeleting	SPWebEventReceiver	Fires just before a site has been deleted
WebMoved	SPWebEventReceiver	Fires after a site has been moved
WebMoving	SPWebEventReceiver	Fires just before a site is moved
FieldAdded	SPListEventReceiver	Fires after a new field is added to the list
FieldAdding	SPListEventReceiver	Fires just before a pending new field is added to the list
FieldDeleted	SPListEventReceiver	Fires after a field is deleted from the list
FieldDeleting	SPListEventReceiver	Fires just before a field is deleted from the list
FieldUpdated	SPListEventReceiver	Fires after a field is updated
FieldUpdating	SPListEventReceiver	Fires just before a field is updated
ItemAdded	SPItemEventReceiver	Fires after a new item is added to the list
ItemAdding	SPItemEventReceiver	Fires just before a pending new item is added to the list
ItemDeleted	SPItemEventReceiver	Fires after an item is deleted from the list
ItemDeleting	SPItemEventReceiver	Fires just before an item is deleted from the list
ItemUpdated	SPItemEventReceiver	Fires after a list item is updated
ItemUpdating	SPItemEventReceiver	Fires just before a list item is updated
ItemAttachmentAdded	SPItemEventReceiver	Fires after an attachment is added to a list item
ItemAttachmentAdding	SPItemEventReceiver	Fires just before a pending attachment is added to a list item
ItemAttachmentDeleted	SPItemEventReceiver	Fires after an attachment is deleted from a list item
ItemAttachmentDeleting	SPItemEventReceiver	Fires just before an attachment is deleted from a list item
ItemCheckedIn	SPItemEventReceiver	Fires after an item is checked in
ItemCheckedOut	SPItemEventReceiver	Fires after an item is checked out
ItemCheckingOut	SPItemEventReceiver	Fires just before an item is checked out
ItemUncheckedOut	SPItemEventReceiver	Fires after an item checkout has been canceled
ItemUncheckingOut	SPItemEventReceiver	Fires just before an item checkout has been cancelled
ItemFileConverted	SPItemEventReceiver	Fires after a document conversion has taken place
ItemFileMove	SPItemEventReceiver	Fires after a file has been moved
ItemFileMoving	SPItemEventReceiver	Fires just before a file has been moved
EmailReceived	SPEmailEventReceiver	Fires after an e-mail–enabled list receives a new e-mail

■**Note** SharePoint still supports the old model of registering event receivers for document libraries through the object model. However, you will not find any page in this version of SharePoint for configuring these event handlers. They can only be configured by using the SharePoint object model.

Coding the Event Receiver

Creating a class to trap one of the events listed in Table 7-5 is fairly straightforward. All you have to do is inherit from the appropriate SharePoint receiver class and code the actions you want to take. As an example, I'll create a receiver that can be used with an Announcements list. My example will add the phrase "For Internal Use Only" to any new announcements added to the list. The idea here is that these are internal team announcements, which are inappropriate to share with customers or partners. Additionally, I'll prevent these items from being deleted once they are added to the list. Listing 7-10 shows the code for implementing the class.

Listing 7-10. *Trapping List Item Events*

```
using System;
using System.Collections.Generic;
using System.Text;
using Microsoft.SharePoint;

namespace AnnouncementHandler
{
    public class Processor:SPItemEventReceiver
    {
        public override void ItemAdding(SPItemEventProperties properties)
        {
            properties.AfterProperties["Body"]+= "\n **For internal use only **\n";
        }

        public override void ItemDeleting(SPItemEventProperties properties)
        {
            properties.Cancel = true;
            properties.ErrorMessage="Items cannot be deleted from this list.";
        }
    }
}
```

Each of the events listed in Table 7-5 has an associated Properties object that gets passed in to the event methods. The SPWebEventProperties class contains information about a site before and after an event. The SPListEventProperties class contains information about a list before and after an event. The SPItemEventProperties class contains information about a list item before and after an event.

In Listing 7-10, you can see that the Body item in the AfterProperties collection of the announcement is altered to append the disclaimer notice. The AfterProperties contain the values that the item will have after the event is complete. You can also access BeforeProperties that have the field values that exist before the event runs. Using the before and after properties to get and set information is used extensively in event programming.

Another common programming task is to stop the deletion of an item. This is accomplished by setting the Cancel property to true. You can also see that in Listing 7-10, I set the ErrorMessage property. The error message will be displayed on a full page if someone tries to delete an item.

Creating the Manifest File

When you create an event receiver, you'll need to create a Feature.xml file in the same way as I have presented throughout this chapter. However, you'll also need to use some new elements in the manifest file. Listing 7-11 shows the manifest file for my example.

Listing 7-11. *An Event Manifest File*

```xml
<Elements xmlns="http://schemas.microsoft.com/sharepoint/">
  <Receivers ListTemplateId="104">
    <Receiver>
      <Name>AnnouncementAddHandler</Name>
      <Type>ItemAdding</Type>
      <SequenceNumber>1000</SequenceNumber>
      <Assembly>AnnouncementHandler, Version=1.0.0.0, Culture=neutral,
        PublicKeyToken=689f1d0ba493bcce</Assembly>
      <Class>AnnouncementHandler.Processor</Class>
      </Receiver>
    <Receiver>
      <Name>AnnouncementDeleteHandler</Name>
      <Type>ItemDeleting</Type>
      <SequenceNumber>2000</SequenceNumber>
      <Assembly>AnnouncementHandler, Version=1.0.0.0, Culture=neutral,
      PublicKeyToken=689f1d0ba493bcce</Assembly>
      <Class>AnnouncementHandler.Processor</Class>
    </Receiver>
  </Receivers>
</Elements>
```

The Receivers element contains a Receiver element for each type of event that you want to receive. The Receivers element has a Name attribute that must be unique for each receiver. The Type attribute designates the kind of event to be received. The SequenceNumber attribute specifies the relative order in which the processing will occur. The Assembly and Class attributes designate the custom assembly and class that will handle the event. Once you have created the Feature.xml file, manifest, and assembly, you can deploy them just like any other feature. Figure 7-4 shows an example of the feature in use.

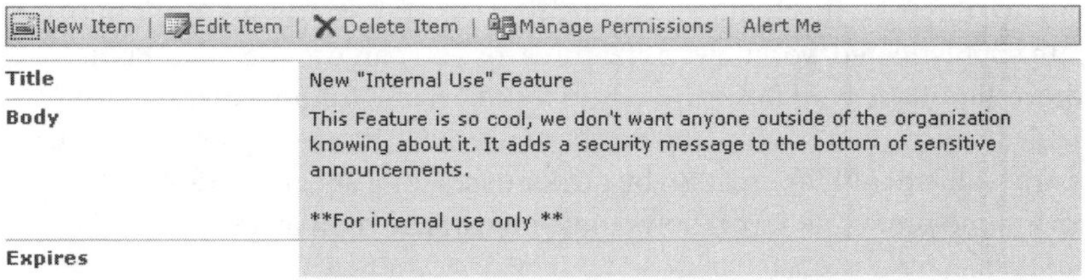

New Item	Edit Item	✗ Delete Item	Manage Permissions	Alert Me

Title	New "Internal Use" Feature
Body	This Feature is so cool, we don't want anyone outside of the organization knowing about it. It adds a security message to the bottom of sensitive announcements. **For internal use only **
Expires	

Figure 7-4. *The "Internal Use" Feature*

Building and Using Workflows

One of the major new functional additions to SharePoint is its support for workflow. More exactly, SharePoint supports a particular implementation of *human workflow*. A human workflow is one that requires the interaction of a person to move from step to step. If a document is routed serially to three people, for example, it cannot go to the second person until the first one has completed a review. This stands in contrast to *system workflow*, which can execute a series of operations without human interaction.

The implementation of human workflow in SharePoint is actually quite simplistic. A SharePoint workflow interacts with humans by assigning tasks and waiting. When the task is marked as completed, the workflow continues to the next step. Therefore, a SharePoint workflow will always have a task list associated with it. Figure 7-5 shows a typical task assignment associated with a workflow.

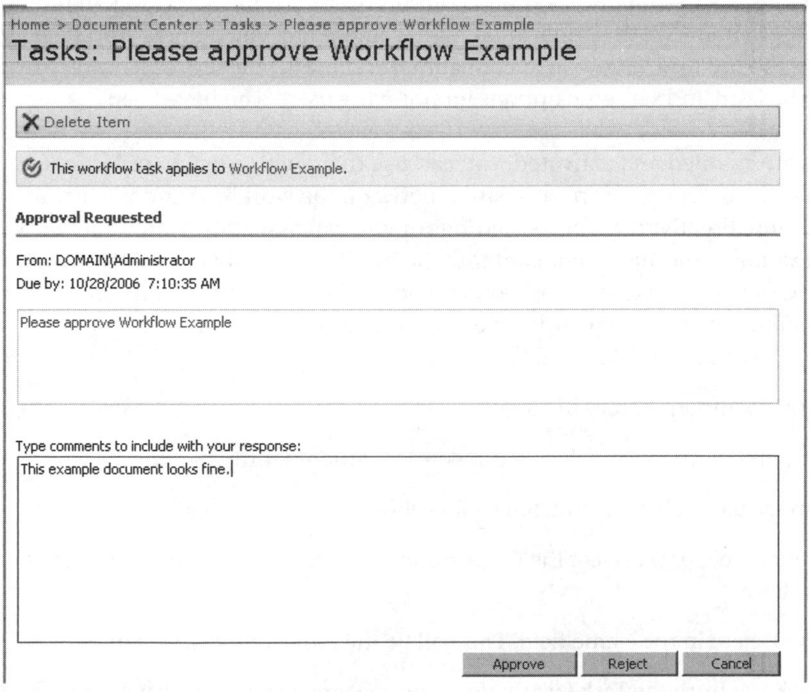

Home > Document Center > Tasks > Please approve Workflow Example

Tasks: Please approve Workflow Example

✗ Delete Item

✓ This workflow task applies to Workflow Example.

Approval Requested

From: DOMAIN\Administrator
Due by: 10/28/2006 7:10:35 AM

Please approve Workflow Example

Type comments to include with your response:

This example document looks fine.

| Approve | Reject | Cancel |

Figure 7-5. *SharePoint workflows are based on task assignments.*

SharePoint offers two different mechanisms for creating custom workflows. You can use Visual Studio to create sophisticated workflows as features, or you can use the SharePoint Designer to create more simplistic workflows directly in a site. Visual Studio workflows are intended to be reusable features that have all the power of the .NET Framework. SharePoint Designer workflows are really meant for creation by power users for a specific site. Additionally, MOSS comes with some predefined workflows that you can use right away.

Using Built-In Workflows

If you are using MOSS, you will have several built-in workflows available to you out of the box. These workflows, just like the custom one you will create in the exercise at the end of this chapter, are deployed as features that must be activated before they can be used. All of the built-in workflows are activated from the Site Collection Features page. As of this writing, MOSS supports the following workflows out of the box:

- *Collect Signatures*: A workflow to gather electronic signatures

- *Disposition Approval*: A workflow that is used to determine whether to delete or retain an expired document

- *Collect Feedback*: A workflow for collecting feedback from document reviewers

- *Approval*: A workflow for obtaining document approval from reviewers

- *Three-State*: A workflow for tracking list items

In addition to activating the various workflow features, you must also enable lists to support workflows. Enabling lists to support workflows is accomplished at the farm level. In the Central Administration web site, on the Application Management tab, you'll find a Workflow Settings link. Clicking this link will allow you to configure workflow for the farm. Here you can enable workflow for the farm and set some options for notifying users who have been assigned tasks.

Once workflows are enabled and activated, you can use them with a list. In order to use a workflow with a list, you must create an association between the workflow and the list. You can create an association directly from the list settings or you can associate a workflow with a content type. For example, the Document content type in MOSS already has the Approval, Collect Feedback, and Collect Signatures workflows associated with it. This means that any library using the Document content type will have these workflows available.

Follow these steps to create a workflow association:

1. Navigate to any document library in VSMOSS.

2. On the Document Library page, select Settings ➤ Document Library Settings.

3. On the Customize page, click the link titled Workflow Settings.

4. On the Add a Workflow page, select the Disposition Approval workflow from the list of available workflows.

5. Type **Retain or Delete** in the Name field. This will be the name of the association.

6. Select New Task List from the Task List section. This will create a new task list for assignments associated with this workflow.

7. Select New History List from the History List section. This will create a new list used to track workflow milestones for auditing and reporting.

8. Leave the option checked to allow manual initiation of a workflow, but note that you can automatically start workflows as well.

9. Click the OK button.

Once the association is made, you can initiate the workflow manually from the drop-down menu attached to any document in the library. Selecting the Workflows menu item brings up a page that lists the associated workflows and lets you choose to initiate one. When you start the workflow, you should see that a new task is created and assigned to a person. If you open the document in Microsoft Word, you should also see that the task appears in the Document Action Panel.

Follow these steps to complete the workflow:

1. Navigate to the Retain or Delete Tasks list.

2. Using the drop-down menu associated with the task item, select Edit Item.

3. Select the option labeled Do Not Delete This Item.

4. Add some comments in the text area.

5. Click the OK button.

6. Navigate back to the document library and note that the workflow is marked as completed.

As a workflow proceeds, different tasks will be assigned to different users depending upon the exact design of the workflow. All of these tasks will collect on the associated task list where they can be reviewed. Additionally, the workflow maintains a history list that allows you to run reports. These reports are created as Excel spreadsheets and can be accessed directly from SharePoint.

Follow these steps to view a history report:

1. Navigate to the Document Library where you created the Retain or Delete association.

2. On the Document Library page, select Settings ➤ Document Library Settings.

3. On the Customize page, click the link titled Workflow Settings.

4. On the Change Workflow Settings page, click the link titled View Workflow Reports.

5. On the View Workflow Reports page, click the Activity Duration Report link under the Retain or Delete workflow.

Creating Custom Workflows in Visual Studio

The built-in workflows are useful for many scenarios, but they are relatively unsophisticated. In order to create more complicated workflows, you will have to turn to Visual Studio. Creating workflows in Visual Studio, however, is not a trivial exercise. A custom workflow involves several domains of knowledge, including the .NET Framework 3.0, InfoPath form development, and feature development. A complete detailed discussion of custom workflow would require a separate book, but I provide an overview in this section so that you can begin creating your own. I have also included a complete exercise at the end of the chapter to get you started.

■**Note** Apress has in fact published a separate book on workflow: *Workflow in the 2007 Microsoft Office System* by David Mann.

Working in Visual Studio

The basis for all workflow in SharePoint is the Windows Workflow Foundation (WF). WF is a workflow engine and set of programming classes for building workflows (both human and system) on the Windows platform. It is important to understand that WF is not a part of SharePoint. WF is actually part of the operating system and is installed as a component of the .NET Framework 3.0. WF has an in-process engine that loads *activities* for execution. Activities represent the steps in the workflow to be executed. When you create a workflow, you actually create the activities to be executed.

WF provides a programming namespace System.Workflow with a set of classes that can be used in Visual Studio 2005 for creating workflows. In theory, you can create a custom workflow by simply building an assembly that utilizes the classes in this namespace. However, you would never want to actually create a workflow in this manner. Instead, Microsoft has provided several additional layers of abstraction that make developing workflows easier.

The first layer of abstraction is the Microsoft Visual Studio 2005 Extensions for Windows Workflow Foundation. The extensions are required for designing workflows in Visual Studio 2005. You can download the extensions from the Microsoft site at http://www.microsoft.com/downloads/details.aspx?FamilyId=5D61409E-1FA3-48CF-8023-E8F38E709BA6&displaylang=en. When you install them, you will see that new workflow projects have been added to Visual Studio as shown in Figure 7-6.

Even though you have added the workflow extensions to Visual Studio and could certainly start a new project, you'll also want to install the SharePoint template projects before getting started. The template workflow projects are part of the Enterprise Content Management Starter Kit, which also provides white papers and tools specifically targeting SharePoint workflow development. The starter kit installs as part of the MOSS SDK and it gives you specific projects for SharePoint workflows as shown in Figure 7-7. Once these templates are installed, you are ready to start developing workflows in Visual Studio 2005.

■**Tip** If you install the Enterprise Content Management Starter Kit, but do not see the appropriate project templates in Visual Studio, try executing devenv.exe /setup from the command line. This command will force Visual Studio to rebuild the project template listings.

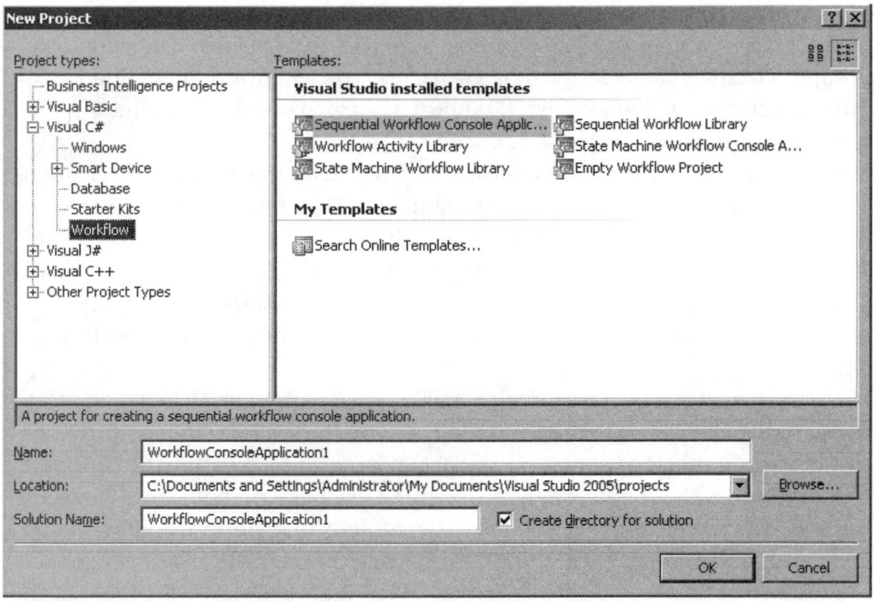

Figure 7-6. *Adding workflow project types to Visual Studio 2005*

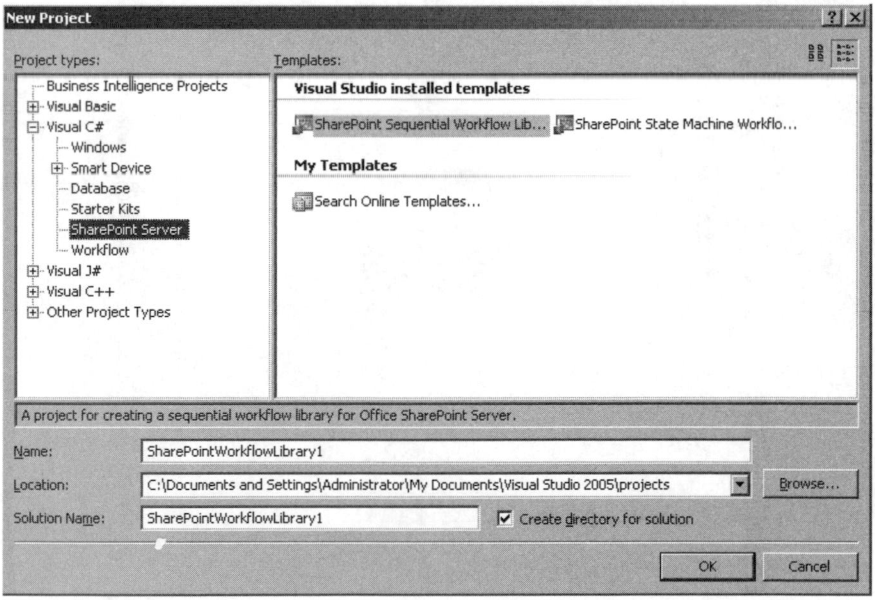

Figure 7-7. *Adding SharePoint workflow templates to Visual Studio 2005*

A workflow is a set of activities put together to represent a process. The activities are atomic units of work that execute in an order designed to model the real steps that people in an organization might execute. As the designer of a workflow, you can utilize predefined activities or create your own custom activities. First, I'll show you how to use the predefined activities, and later I'll show you how to build a custom activity.

When you create a new workflow project in Visual Studio, you may select from the sequential workflow template or the state machine workflow template. The *sequential workflow* is a series of steps that occur in serial or parallel. The *state machine workflow* determines the next step in a workflow based on the current state. Creating a workflow project will give you a new class that inherits from either System.Workflow.Activities.SequentialWorkflowActivity or System.Workflow.Activities.StateMachineWorkflowActivity, depending upon the project template you use.

Workflow classes in Visual Studio have a designer associated with them to help you create the workflow. The designer allows you to drag and drop activity shapes from the toolbox that represent sequential steps or machine states. Then you can write code to define the actions that should occur for a sequential step or when the machine reaches a certain state. There are a tremendous number of activity controls available in the toolbox to support workflow including loops, branches, and states. Each one of these controls requires some level of configuration, and many require associated code to function correctly. Figure 7-8 shows the toolbox and designer in a typical workflow project and Table 7-6 describes the available activities.

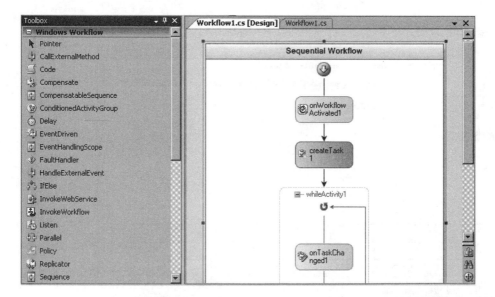

Figure 7-8. *Using the Workflow Designer*

Table 7-6. *Workflow Activities*

Activity	Description
Code	An activity that executes custom code
Compensate	An activity used within an exception-handling activity
ConditionedActivity Group	A set of activities executed under certain conditions
Delay	An activity that waits for a time period
EventDriven	An activity used to specify an event that should be listened for
ExceptionHandler	An activity that contains error-handling operations
IfElse	An activity containing other activities that will execute if a condition is True
InvokeWebService	An activity that calls a web service
InvokeWorkflow	An activity that starts another workflow
Listen	An activity that waits for an event to occur
Parallel	An activity that contains other activities that will execute in parallel
Replicator	An activity that executes multiple instances of contained activities
SelectData	An activity that receives a data class from the host process
Sequence	An activity that contains other activities that will execute in sequence
SetState	An activity that changes the state of a workflow
State	An activity that defines workflow state
StateInitialization	An activity that occurs when a state is initialized in the workflow
Suspend	An activity that pauses the workflow
Terminate	An activity that ends the workflow
Throw	An activity that throws an exception
TransactionalContext	An activity that contains other activities that are grouped into a transaction
UpdateData	An activity that sends a data class to the host process
WaitForData	An activity that waits for a data class from the host
WaitForQuery	An activity that receives a request for a data class
WebServiceReceive	An activity that waits for a web service call
WebServiceResponse	An activity that responds to a web service
While	An activity containing other activities that will execute while a condition is True

Configuring activities in the Workflow Designer generally involves setting property values that fall into one of two major categories: correlation tokens or members. *Correlation tokens* are placeholders you create that will be filled in by the workflow engine when an instance of your workflow starts. These tokens can have any name you want, but certain activities must share the same token in order for the workflow engine to track and manage the workflow instances. For example, controls that all deal with the life of a task item will share a single correlation token to indicate that they are all associated with the same task item.

Members are either variables or property code structures that maintain the state of the workflow. For example, if you are assigning a new task in a workflow, the CreateTask activity shown in Figure 7-8 will require you to define a member for tracking the unique identifier of the created task. You may also have members to track the values of the fields associated with the tasks. The Workflow Designer provides an interface for defining and tracking members and will automatically generate the required code in your project. You'll get a chance to use these interfaces in the exercise at the end of the chapter.

Once you have configured the activities, you can write code to run when each step of the process is executed. Each activity has methods associated with it that can be automatically generated in your project. In the designer, you can right-click any control and select Generate Handlers from the context menu. This will stub out the available methods for the activities in your code.

Creating InfoPath Forms

Along with creating the workflow, you must also create a series of InfoPath forms or ASPX files in order to use the workflow in SharePoint. The forms or pages are used to provide an interface to initiate a workflow or complete an assigned task. In this chapter, you'll make use of InfoPath forms for this purpose. These InfoPath forms must be fully trusted, compliant with InfoPath Forms Services, and contain fields for use inside of the workflow you create in Visual Studio. You have already seen examples of these forms when you used the built-in MOSS workflows. Figure 7-9 shows an example of such a form seen when the Approval workflow is started.

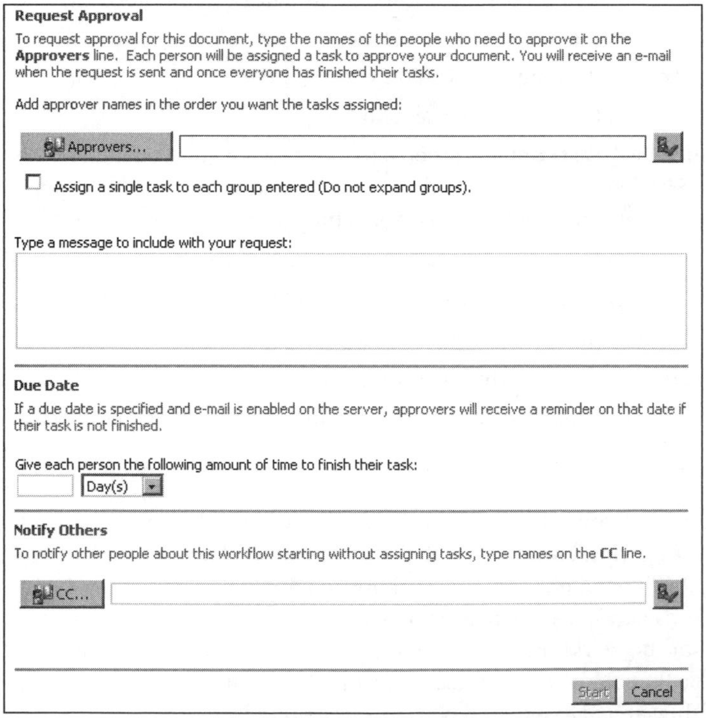

Figure 7-9. *InfoPath forms are used to gather workflow data.*

Deploying Workflows

After the workflow project is created in Visual Studio and the required InfoPath forms are built, you may deploy the workflow to SharePoint. As I mentioned previously, workflows are deployed as features that must be activated before they can be used. Therefore, you'll need to create a Feature.xml file and a manifest file. The feature must also deploy the InfoPath forms, and the workflow assembly must have a strong name and be installed in the GAC.

The Feature.xml file references the workflow engine by designating the assembly Microsoft.Office.Workflow.Feature as the ReceiverAssembly. The manifest file subsequently references your custom assembly and InfoPath forms. At run time, the WF engine loads your assembly and feeds the data from the InfoPath forms into the workflow. Again, the best way to get familiar with this entire process is to work the exercise at the end of this chapter.

Creating Workflows in SharePoint Designer

Unlike the workflows created in Visual Studio, SharePoint Designer workflows are not deployed as features and cannot be used across multiple lists or with content types. When you use the SharePoint Designer to create workflows, you must bind the workflow directly to a specific list. The SharePoint Designer provides a limited set of activities that can be used safely by a power user to create a workflow. The workflow steps are saved directly to the associated site and are compiled by SharePoint when it is run. As a developer, you can also create custom activities and make them available in the SharePoint Designer. I cover creating custom activities in the section of this chapter titled "Creating Custom Activities."

To begin creating a workflow with the SharePoint Designer, you must first open a site. Once the site is open, you may select New ➤ Workflow from the main menu. The Workflow Designer will then start. The Workflow Designer is a moderately sophisticated wizard that leads you step by step through the process of creating a workflow, but each step has many controls and options. When the Workflow Designer first starts, you will be asked to select a list to bind to the workflow. Figure 7-10 shows a new workflow for approving InfoPath travel forms.

When you create a new workflow, you can also specify initiation parameters and variables. Initiation parameters will be provided by the user when the workflow starts. If the workflow is started automatically, you can specify default values that will be used instead. Variables are used by the workflow to track values between steps. This is just a simple state management system so that one step can set a value that is retrieved by another. The Initiation and Variables buttons shown in Figure 7-10 open dialogs for adding initiation parameters or variables, respectively.

The heart of the Workflow Designer is the step creation interface. Using this interface, you can design a series of steps for the workflow. Each step consists of a condition and an action. If the condition evaluates as True, the action is executed. You may have as many steps containing as many condition/action sets as you need to define the workflow. Figure 7-11 shows a simple step checking to see whether the request is out of date.

Once you have completed designing the workflow, you can check it for errors by clicking the Check Workflow button. If your workflow has no errors, you simply save it and it is ready to use. You can initiate the workflow directly from the list in the same way as you did for any other workflow. If you have defined initiation parameters, the user will be prompted to enter them before the workflow starts.

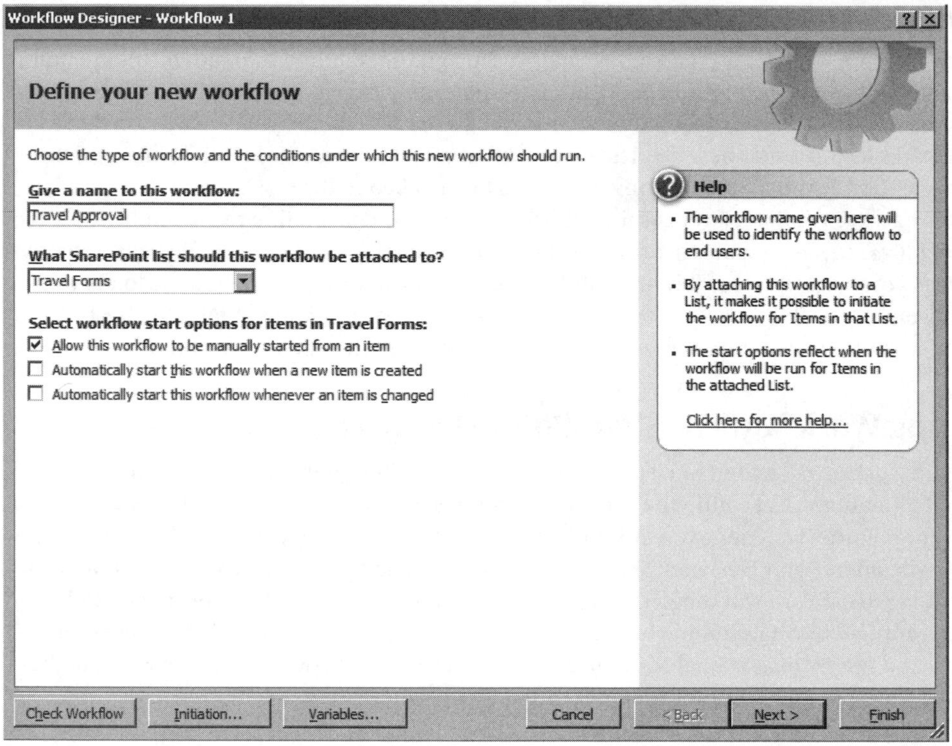

Figure 7-10. *Binding a workflow to a list*

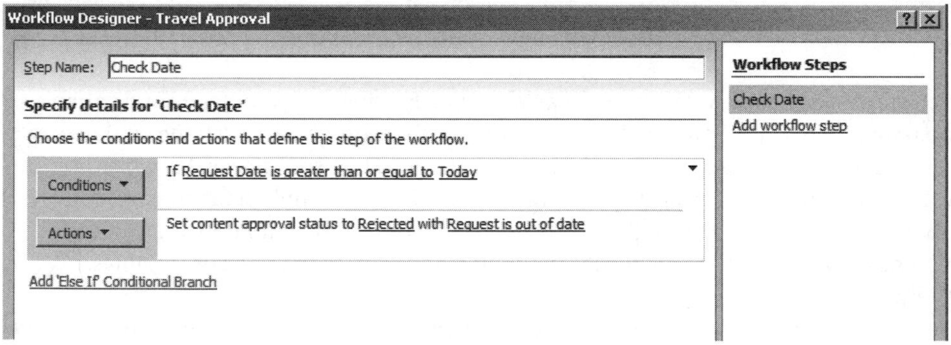

Figure 7-11. *A workflow step*

Creating Custom Activities

Throughout this chapter, I have shown you how to use the predefined activities in Visual Studio and the SharePoint Designer to create and deploy workflows. While there are many predefined activities to use in your workflows, you will undoubtedly want to create your own custom activities to handle special situations. This will be particularly true if you are supporting power users who are creating workflows in the SharePoint Designer because they cannot write any custom code in their workflows. In this section, I briefly walk you through the process of creating a custom activity. Again, this topic is a large one and a detailed examination is beyond the scope of this book. However, I'll present the basics here to get you started.

Coding a Custom Activity

A custom activity is created in Visual Studio by inheriting from the base activity class `System.Workflow.ComponentModel.Activity` or any predefined activity. As an example, I have created an activity that simply writes a message to the event log. The complete code for my activity is shown in Listing 7-12.

Listing 7-12. *The LogActivity Class*

```
using System;
using System.ComponentModel;
using System.ComponentModel.Design;
using System.Workflow.ComponentModel;
using System.Workflow.ComponentModel.Compiler;
using System.Workflow.ComponentModel.Design;
using System.Diagnostics;
using System.Drawing;

namespace CustomActivities
{
  [Designer(typeof(ActivityDesigner), typeof(IDesigner)),
  ToolboxItem(typeof(ActivityToolboxItem)),
  Description("Logging Activity"),
  ActivityValidator(typeof(LogActivityValidator))]
  public sealed class LogActivity : Activity
  {
    //Name of the Log
    public static DependencyProperty LogNameProperty =
    DependencyProperty.Register("LogName", typeof(string), typeof(LogActivity));

    public string LogName
    {
      get { return ((string)(base.GetValue(LogActivity.LogNameProperty)));}
      set { base.SetValue(LogActivity.LogNameProperty, value); }
    }

    //Message Property
    public static DependencyProperty MessageProperty =
    DependencyProperty.Register("Message", typeof(string), typeof(LogActivity));

    public string Message
    {
      get { return ((string)(base.GetValue(LogActivity.MessageProperty)));}
      set { base.SetValue(LogActivity.MessageProperty, value);}
    }
```

```
    //Entry Type
    public static DependencyProperty EntryTypeProperty =
DependencyProperty.Register("EntryType", typeof(string),typeof(LogActivity));

    public string EntryType
    {
      get { return ((string)(base.GetValue(LogActivity.EntryTypeProperty))); }
      set { base.SetValue(LogActivity.EntryTypeProperty, value);}
    }

    protected override ActivityExecutionStatus
      Execute(ActivityExecutionContext executionContext)
    {
      if (!EventLog.SourceExists(LogName))
        EventLog.CreateEventSource(LogName, "Application");

      switch (EntryType)
      {
        case "Error":
          EventLog.WriteEntry(LogName, Message, EventLogEntryType.Error);
          break;
        case "Failure":
          EventLog.WriteEntry(LogName, Message, EventLogEntryType.FailureAudit);
          break;
        case "Information":
          EventLog.WriteEntry(LogName, Message, EventLogEntryType.Information);
          break;
        case "Success":
          EventLog.WriteEntry(LogName, Message, EventLogEntryType.SuccessAudit);
          break;
        case "Warning":
          EventLog.WriteEntry(LogName, Message, EventLogEntryType.Warning);
          break;
      }

      return ActivityExecutionStatus.Closed;
    }
}

public class LogActivityValidator : ActivityValidator
{
  public override ValidationErrorCollection
    ValidateProperties(ValidationManager manager, object obj)
  {
    ValidationErrorCollection errors = new ValidationErrorCollection();
    LogActivity activity = obj as LogActivity;
```

```
      if (activity == null)
        errors.Add(new ValidationError("Not a valid activity.", 1));
      else
      {
        if (activity.LogName == null)
          errors.Add(new ValidationError("Not a valid log name.", 2));
        if (activity.Message == null)
          errors.Add(new ValidationError("Not a valid message.", 3));
        if (activity.EntryType == null)
          errors.Add(new ValidationError("Not a valid entry type.", 4));
      }
      return errors;
    }
  }
}
```

When you define the new activity class, you must add attributes to the class that specify the appearance of the activity in the Visual Studio environment and the name of the class that will handle validation for the activity. In my example, I use the System.Workflow.ComponentModel. Design.ActivityDesigner class to define the appearance of my activity, and the custom class LogActivityValidator for validation. The ActivityDesigner class will give my activity the default appearance and behavior of a standard activity in the Visual Studio environment. My custom LogActivityValidator class inherits from System.Workflow.ComponentModel.Compiler. ActivityValidator, which allows me to override the ValidateProperties method and check the values of the activity properties.

I designed my activity to support three properties: LogName, Message, and EntryType. These three properties correspond to the three arguments required to make an entry using the WriteEntry method of the System.Diagnostics.EventLog class. Creating properties for an activity is done by coding standard property structures for access methods. However, the member variable that stores the property value is coded as a System.Workflow. ComponentModel.DependencyProperty type. Coding the member variables in this way exposes it to the Visual Studio and SharePoint Designer environments so that people who use the activity can configure it at design time just like any other activity. Additionally, you use the SetValue and GetValue methods of the base Activity class to manage the member variable value instead of setting it directly.

Once you have the class created, you must give it a strong name and install it in the GAC. At this point, it is ready for use. In Visual Studio, you may simply right-click the toolbox inside of a workflow project and select Choose Items from the context menu. This will allow you to select the new activity and add it to the toolbox. Figure 7-12 shows my custom activity in a workflow project.

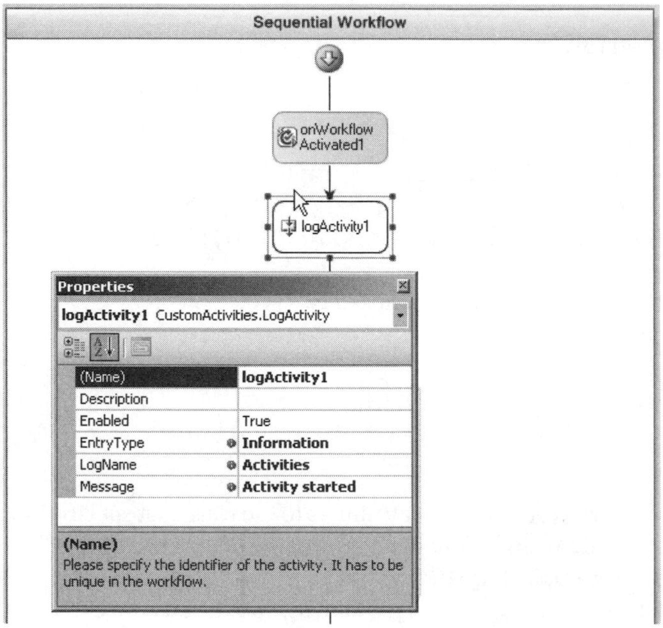

Figure 7-12. *The LogActivity in Visual Studio*

Using Custom Activities in the SharePoint Designer

If you wish to use the new activity in the SharePoint Designer, you'll also have to create a file with an `.ACTIONS` extension that describes the activity and how to represent it in the Workflow Designer. This is because the Workflow Designer does not use property sheets like Visual Studio. As you have seen already, it uses sentences and hyperlinks for configuration. Listing 7-13 shows the complete `CUSTOM.ACTIONS` file for my activity.

■**Note** Be sure to change the strong name in Listing 7-13 to match your assembly. Also, In order for the activity to work in the SharePoint Designer, you must also make an entry in the `AuthorizedTypes` section 0.

Listing 7-13. *The CUSTOM.ACTIONS File*

```
<?xml version="1.0" encoding="utf-8" ?>
<WorkflowInfo>
  <Actions Sequential="then" Parallel="and">
    <Action Name="Log an Event" ClassName="CustomActivities.LogActivity"
      Assembly="CustomActivities, Version=1.0.0.0, Culture=neutral,
```

```
   <Parameters>
     <Parameter Name="Message" Type="System.String, mscorlib" Direction="In" />
     <Parameter Name="LogName" Type="System.String, mscorlib" Direction="In" />
     <Parameter Name="EntryType" Type="System.String, mscorlib" Direction="In" />
   </Parameters>
   <RuleDesigner Sentence="Log %1 in %2 as %3">
     <FieldBind  Id="1" Field="Message"
      DesignerType="TextArea" Text="this message"/>
     <FieldBind  Id="2" Field="LogName"
     DesignerType="TextArea" Text="this log"/>
     <FieldBind  Id="3" Field="EntryType"
     DesignerType="DropDown" Text="this event type">
       <Option Name="Information" Value="Information"/>
       <Option Name="Success" Value="Success"/>
       <Option Name="Warning" Value="Warning"/>
       <Option Name="Error" Value="Error"/>
       <Option Name="Failure" Value="Failure"/>
     </FieldBind>
   </RuleDesigner>
  </Action>
 </Actions>
</WorkflowInfo>
```

The Actions element is simply a container for Action elements that define the activity and its appearance. The Action element defines the assembly that contains the custom activity, the list types that can use it, and the category it will appear under in the Workflow Designer.

The Parameters element contains a Parameter element for each of the properties defined in the custom activity. The Parameter element defines the data type of the property and whether it is an input or an output value. In this case, all three parameters are strings that are input during the workflow design process.

The RuleDesigner element contains multiple FieldBind elements that map property values in the activity to Parameter elements. The FieldBind elements also define the DesignerType that determines the type of user interface associated with each parameter. In my example, the Message and LogName properties will display a text box while the EntryType property will display a pick list.

The Sentence attribute defines the sentence that will appear in the Workflow Designer and has placeholders for the property values. In my case %1 will map to the Message, %2 will map to the LogName, and %3 will map to the EntryType.

Once you have completed the ACTIONS file, it needs to be saved into the directory C:\Program Files\Common Files\Microsoft Shared\web server extensions\12\TEMPLATE\ 1033\Workflow alongside the WSS.ACTIONS file that defines the basic activities for the Workflow Designer. Once the file is copied, you must reset Internet Information Server to see the changes. Then you can start the SharePoint Designer and create a new workflow. The new activity will be available under the category you defined in the ACTIONS file. In my example, the new activity is located under the Logging category. Figure 7-13 shows my new activity in the Workflow Designer.

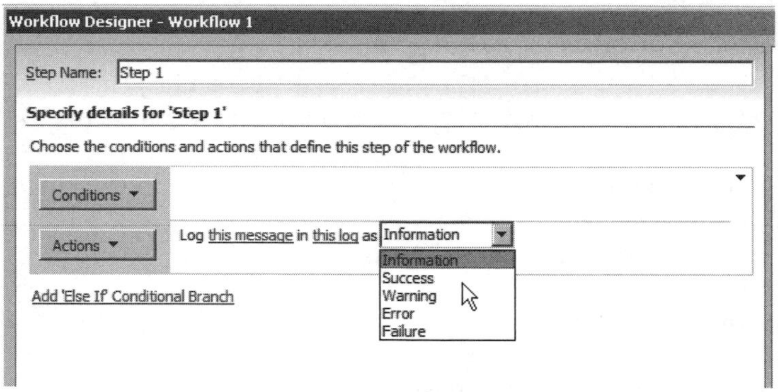

Figure 7-13. *The LogActivity in the Workflow Designer*

Considering Workflow Options

Now that I have reviewed the various options for creating workflows, it's appropriate to put them into perspective. It's important to understand exactly what WF brings to SharePoint and where it falls short. Planning for workflows should be done carefully and with consideration for the impact the various choices will have on the organization.

The built-in workflows that ship with MOSS are rather simplistic implementations that allow serial/parallel approval. The user who is starting the workflow can specify the reviewers and initiate the process. MOSS will assign tasks to each reviewer and track the progress of the workflow.

The good thing about MOSS workflows is that they are simple to use and available right away. For many organizations, these workflows can act as a good replacement for the normal process of attaching a document to an e-mail and sending it out to many people. In fact, this is a great place to start, because the people in any organization are going to take a long time to adapt to the use of workflow for daily tasks. These simple workflows will become important change catalysts over the first year of SharePoint adoption.

As workflow adoption progresses, it is likely that someone at the departmental level will get interested and want to do more. A nontechnical power user will realize what can be done with the SharePoint Designer, and they will dive in. This is certainly true for FrontPage when it is used in conjunction with SharePoint Portal Server, and I expect to see the same thing happen with the SharePoint Designer when used in conjunction with this version of SharePoint.

The good and bad things about SharePoint Designer workflows are the same as the good and bad things about the SharePoint Designer itself. Power users can initially do a lot without involving IT, and this will seem like a good thing. Just like FrontPage before it, however, this can become a nightmare. As power users get in trouble with the SharePoint Designer, they will increasingly rely on technical people to help them out. Then when IT does get involved, they'll often discover that the power users have not organized their projects well, have utilized nonstandard approaches, and have generally created a rat's nest.

I am certainly seeing a lot of excitement among developers with regard to developing workflows in Visual Studio. For many, this represents a brand-new domain of knowledge that will be fun to master and provide a much needed break from creating yet another ASP.NET database application. However, developing workflows for SharePoint in Visual Studio is not easy. In order to make it happen, you need strong skills in InfoPath, SharePoint feature development, SharePoint object model programming, the Visual Studio Workflow control set, and C#. The current process for creating SharePoint workflows is complicated and requires many seemingly arbitrary configuration steps.

The good thing about Visual Studio workflow development is that it gives you complete control over the solution. The bad thing is that it will take a highly skilled developer to pull it off. It will be difficult to design workflows so that they are fully configurable by the end user.

Another consideration is the use of third-party engines. At this point, all of the major vendors have announced that their next versions will be based on WF and fully support SharePoint 2007. Without a doubt, the design environments, deployment tools, and reporting capabilities will be vastly superior to what can be achieved in Visual Studio alone. Therefore, an assessment of these tools is critical for any organization that requires workflow beyond what the SharePoint Designer can provide.

■**Note** My favorite workflow engine for SharePoint remains K2.net. This is a highly functional engine that has significant capability and is much easier to use than the Visual Studio templates. You can find out more at `http://www.k2workflow.com`.

Exercise 7.1. Building an Employee Performance Review Workflow

In this exercise, you will create a complete human workflow for automating the employee performance review process. You will create InfoPath forms, a workflow assembly, and a feature. This workflow could be used with an associated InfoPath form, Word document, or even a list to assign and track the steps necessary to complete the review process. In this exercise, you'll create a Contact list of employees and use the workflow to schedule their performance reviews. Please note this exercise requires the Enterprise version of MOSS to complete. WSS cannot utilize InfoPath forms in the workflow.

Creating the InfoPath Workflow Forms

Before you can start creating the workflow in Visual Studio, you need to create the InfoPath forms that will support the workflow in SharePoint. A SharePoint workflow requires three separate InfoPath forms: the association form, the initiation form, and the action form. The *association form* is displayed to the user when the workflow is first associated with a list. The *initiation form* is displayed to the user when the workflow is launched. The *action form* is displayed when a user completes an assigned task. Over the next few sections, you will create all three of these forms.

Creating the Workflow Association Form

The association form allows users to specify key information when a workflow is first associated with a list. In this exercise, you will specify information about the manager who will be performing the performance reviews. The assumption here is that you will create separate lists for each manager that will use the workflow.

Follow these steps to create the association form:

1. Start Microsoft InfoPath.

2. In the Getting Started dialog, click the link titled Design a Form Template.

3. In the Design a Form Template dialog, select a Blank template and click the OK button to start with a blank form.

4. When the blank form opens, click the Data Source link in the Design Tasks pane.

5. Right-click the myFields node and select Properties from the context menu.

6. Rename the node **flowFields** in the Name text box and click the OK button.

7. Right-click the flowFields node and select Add.

8. In the Add Field or Group dialog, type **managerUsername** in the Name field and click the OK button.

9. Right-click the flowFields node and select Add.

10. In the Add Field or Group dialog, type **managerFullname** in the Name field and click the OK button.

11. Right-click the flowFields node and select Add.

12. In the Add Field or Group dialog, type **reviewType** in the Name field and click the OK button.

13. Right-click the flowFields node and select Add.

14. In the Add Field or Group dialog, type **reviewComments** in the Name field and click the OK button.

15. Click on the Design Tasks link at the top of the Data Source pane.

16. Click the Layout link in the Design Tasks pane.

17. Drag the Custom Table layout onto the blank form.

18. In the Insert table dialog, enter **1** in the Columns field and **3** in the Rows field, and click the OK button.

19. Click the Design Tasks link at the top of the Layout pane.

20. Click the Controls link in the Design Tasks pane.

21. Uncheck the box labeled Automatically Create Data Source.

22. Drag a text box from the Controls pane and drop it in the top cell of the table.

23. In the Text Box Binding dialog, select the managerUsername field and click the OK button.

24. Drag a text box from the Controls pane and drop it in the middle cell of the table.

25. In the Text Box Binding dialog, select the managerFullname field and click the OK button.

26. Drag a button from the Controls pane and drop it in the bottom cell of the table.

27. Right-click the button and select Button Properties from the context menu.

28. Enter **Done** in the Label field.

29. Click the Rules button.

30. In the Rules dialog, click the Add button.

31. In the Rules dialog, click the Add Action button.

32. In the Action dialog, select Submit Using a Data Connection from the drop-down list.

33. Click the Add button.

34. In the data connection wizard, select to Create a New Connection to Submit Data and click the Next button.

35. On the next screen select the option to submit the data to The Hosting Environment. This will ensure that the contents of the form are submitted back to the SharePoint workflow process.

36. Click the Next button.

37. On the next screen, name the connection **Association** and click the Finish button.

38. In the Action dialog, click the OK button.

39. In the Rules dialog, click the Add Action button.

40. Select Close the Form from the drop-down list.

41. Uncheck the box labeled If Changes Have Not Been Saved, Prompt the User to Save.

42. Click the OK button.

43. In the Rule dialog, click the OK button.

44. In the Rules dialog, click the OK button.

45. In the Button Properties dialog, click the OK button.

46. Save the form to an appropriate place for safekeeping such as `AssocForm.xsn`. You'll move the form later, so you just need a temporary location for now. Figure 7-14 shows the completed form.

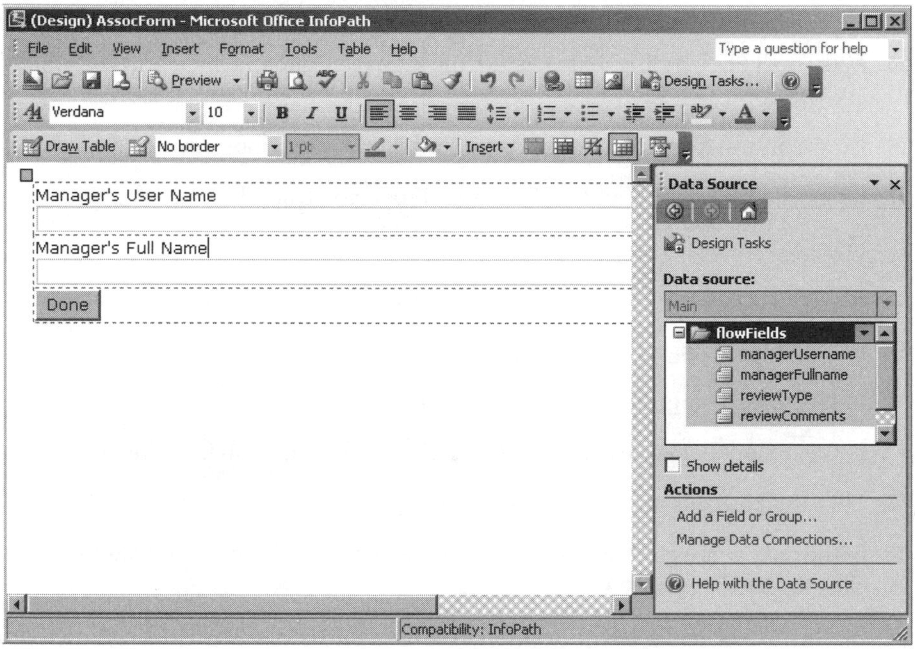

Figure 7-14. *The workflow association form*

Creating the Workflow Initiation Form

The initiation form allows users to specify key information when a workflow instance is first started. In this exercise, you will specify information about the type of performance review and add any relevant comments. Because the initiation form uses the same data source as the association form, you'll create the initiation form by modifying the association form.

Follow these steps to create the initiation form:

1. Open AssocForm.xsn in Design mode in InfoPath 2007 if it is not already open.

2. Select File ➤ Save As from the main menu.

3. In the Save As dialog, change the form name to **InitForm.xsn** and click the Save button. This ensures that the data elements and namespace for the initiation form exactly match those of the association form. This allows the forms to share data values.

4. Remove the text box controls for the managerUsername and managerFullname fields from the form. Do not delete the button.

5. Click the Design Tasks link at the top of the task pane.

6. Click the Controls link in the Design Tasks pane.

7. Uncheck the box labeled Automatically Create Data Source.

8. Drag a text box from the Controls pane and drop it in the top cell of the table.

9. In the Text Box Binding dialog, select the reviewType field and click the OK button.

10. Drag a text box from the Controls pane and drop it in the middle cell of the table.

11. In the Text Box Binding dialog, select the reviewComments field and click the OK button.

12. Save the initiation form. Figure 7-15 shows the final initiation form.

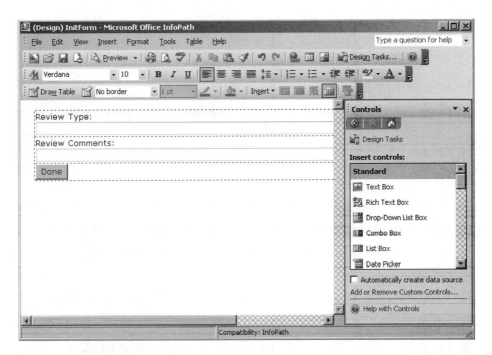

Figure 7-15. *The workflow initiation form*

Creating the Workflow Action Form

The action form is presented to the user when he or she has a task to perform in the workflow. In this exercise, the form is simply used to record the completion of the task. In more complicated workflows, the form could support different views for different user roles along with supporting fields.

Follow these steps to create the action form:

1. Start Microsoft InfoPath.

2. In the Getting Started dialog, click the link titled Design a Form Template.

3. In the Design a Form Template dialog, select a Blank template and click the OK button.

4. When the blank form opens, click the Data Source link in the Design Tasks pane.

5. Right-click the myFields node and select Properties from the context menu.

6. Rename the node **actionFields** in the Name text box and click the OK button.

7. Right-click the actionFields node and select Add.

8. In the Add Field or Group dialog, type **reviewCompleted** in the Name field.

9. Select True/False (Boolean) from the Data Type drop-down list and click the OK button.

10. Right-click the actionFields node and select Add.

11. In the Add Field or Group dialog, type **reviewNotes** in the Name field and click the OK button.

12. Click the Design Tasks link at the top of the Data Source pane.

13. Click the Layout link in the Design Tasks pane.

14. Drag the Custom Table layout onto the blank form.

15. In the Insert Table dialog, enter **1** in the Columns field and **3** in the Rows field, and click the OK button.

16. Click the Design Tasks link at the top of the Layout pane.

17. Click the Controls link in the Design Tasks pane.

18. Uncheck the box labeled Automatically Create Data Source.

19. Drag a check box from the Controls pane and drop it in the top cell of the table.

20. In the Check Box Binding dialog, select the reviewCompleted field and click the OK button.

21. Drag a text box from the Controls pane and drop it in the bottom cell of the table.

22. In the Text Box Binding dialog, select the reviewNotes field and click the OK button.

23. Drag a button from the Controls pane and drop it in the bottom cell.

24. Right-click the button and select Button Properties from the context menu.

25. Enter **Done** in the Label field.

26. Click the Rules button.

27. In the Rules dialog, click the Add button.

28. In the Rules dialog, click the Add Action button.

29. In the Action dialog, select Submit Using a Data Connection from the drop-down list.

30. Click the Add button.

31. In the data connection wizard, select to create a new data connection to submit data and click the Next button.

32. On the next screen, select the option to submit the data To the Hosting Environment so the form will be submitted back to the SharePoint workflow process.

33. Click the Next button.

34. Name the connection **Action** and click the Finish button.

35. In the Action dialog, click the OK button.

36. In the Rules dialog, click the Add Action button.

37. Select Close the Form from the drop-down list.

38. Uncheck the box labeled If Changes Have Not Been Saved, Prompt the User to Save.

39. Click the OK button.

40. In the Rule dialog, click the OK button.

41. In the Rules dialog, click the OK button.

42. In the Button Properties dialog, click the OK button.

43. Save the form to an appropriate place for safekeeping such as `ActionForm.xsn`. Figure 7-16 shows the completed workflow action form.

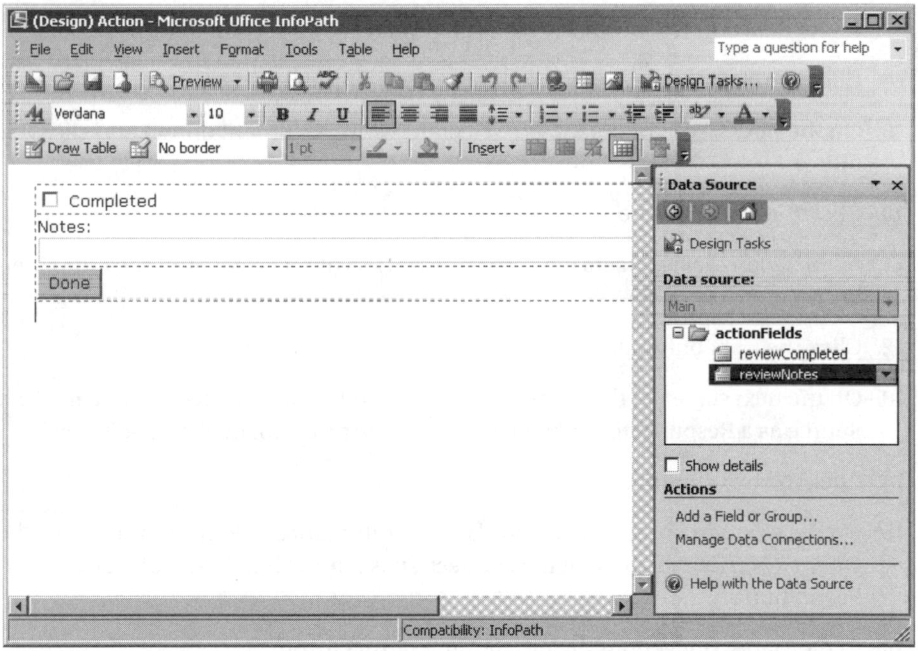

Figure 7-16. *The workflow action form*

Adding the Item Schema

When the action form is presented to the user, we will need to populate it with the data used in the association and initiation forms. In order to do this, we must create a schema that represents the incoming data and attach it to the action form as a secondary data source. This will allow the form to properly display the information. The process for defining the secondary data source requires you to create a very specific XML file and then attach it to the form. The format of this file is dictated by the workflow infrastructure.

Follow these steps to create and attach the schema:

1. Open a copy of Notepad and enter the following code. This code defines the fields that are available from the association and initiation forms:

```
<z:row xmlns:z="#RowsetSchema" ows_managerUsername="" ows_managerFullname=""
 ows_reviewType="" ows_reviewComments="" />
```

2. Save the file as `ItemMetadata.xml` to an appropriate location. You will only need this file temporarily while you define the secondary data source, but the file must be named `ItemMetadata.xml`.

3. Open `ActionForm.xsn` in design mode if it's not already open.

4. In the Design Tasks pane, click the Data Source link.

5. Click the Manage Data Connections link.

6. In the Data Connections dialog, click the Add button.

7. In the data connection wizard, select to Create a Connection to Receive Data.

8. Click the Next button.

9. On the next screen of the wizard, select the XML Document option and click the Next button.

10. Click the Browse button.

11. In the Open dialog, locate the `ItemMetadata.xml` file, select it, and click the Open button.

12. Click the Next button.

13. On the next screen of the wizard, ensure that the option labeled Include the Data Source as a Resource File in the Form Template or Template Part is selected.

14. Click the Next button.

15. On the next screen, ensure the box labeled Automatically Retrieve Data When Form Is Opened is checked and that the connection is named ItemMetadata. Then click the Finish button.

16. In the Data Connections dialog, click the Close button.

17. In the Action form, right-click the ReviewNotes text box and select Properties from the context menu.

18. Click the formula (fx) button under the Default Value section.

19. In the Insert Formula dialog, click the Insert Field or Group button.

20. In the Select a Field or Group dialog, select ItemMetadata (secondary) from the drop-down list.

21. Select the ows_reviewComments node and click the OK button.

22. In the Insert Formula dialog, click the OK button.

23. In the Field or Group Properties dialog, click the OK button.

24. Save the form and close InfoPath.

Creating the Workflow Project

The Visual Studio project you create for a workflow implements all of the functionality required to automate a process. In this exercise, you will simply be assigning a task to the manager to perform the employee review. Although you have the full power of the .NET Framework to use in your workflow, task assignment is a fundamental part of SharePoint workflows. Remember that human workflows in SharePoint typically assign tasks to users and then wait for them to be marked as complete.

Follow these steps to create the workflow project:

1. Start Visual Studio 2005.

2. From the main menu, select File ➤ New Project.

3. In the New Project dialog, click on SharePoint Server in the Project Types tree.

4. Select SharePoint Sequential Workflow Library in the Templates window.

5. Enter **ReviewFlow** in the Name field and pick a suitable location to develop the project.

6. Click the OK button.

7. When the project is created, save it and close Visual Studio. You must perform a few additional steps with the InfoPath forms before you can proceed to code the project.

Publishing the Forms

Once you have created the workflow project, you must publish the workflow forms to the project directory. This is required to support the deployment of the forms as part of the workflow feature you will create. This will allow you to deploy the forms along with the workflow assembly.

Follow these steps to publish the forms:

1. Open the form `AssocForm.xsn` in design mode in InfoPath.

2. In the Design Tasks pane, click the Design Checker link.

3. In the Design Checker pane, click the Change Compatibility Settings link.

4. In the Form Options dialog, check the box labeled Design a Form Template That Can Be Opened in a Browser or in InfoPath.

5. Enter the URL of a server running InfoPath Forms Services (e.g., `http://vsmoss`) that can be used to validate the form design.

6. Click the Security and Trust Category.

7. Uncheck the box labeled Automatically Determine Security Level.

8. Select the Full Trust option.

9. Check the box labeled Sign This Form Template.

10. Click the Create Certificate button.

11. Click OK to acknowledge the message regarding self-signed certificates.

12. Click the OK button.

13. In the Design Checker pane, click the Design Tasks link.

14. In the Design Tasks pane, click the Publish Form Template link.

15. In the first step of the Publishing Wizard, select to publish the form to a network location and click the Next button.

16. In the next step, click the Browse button.

17. In the Browse dialog, locate the directory where the file `Workflow1.cs` resides. This is the folder where the workflow project was created. The workflow forms must be published here.

18. Enter **AssocForm.xsn** in the File Name field and click the OK button.

19. In the Publishing Wizard, click the Next button.

20. In the next screen, clear the alternate access path and click the Next button. The workflow forms must only be accessed through the workflow process in SharePoint.

21. On the final screen, click the Publish button.

22. Close the wizard.

23. Repeat steps 1 through 10 to publish the `InitForm.xsn` and the `ActionForm.xsn`, only you should use the certificate you already created to sign the form instead of creating a new one.

Developing the Project

Developing the workflow project is a combination of placing activities on the workflow design canvas and writing code behind them. Each activity you place on the canvas must be configured using various properties and then associated with a method in the code. In this project, you use the activities and code to receive information from the initialization form and create a new task.

Follow these steps to get started:

1. Open the ReviewFlow project in Visual Studio 2005.

2. In the Solution Explorer, right-click `Workflow1.cs` and select View Designer from the context menu.

3. Right-click the WorkflowActivated1 activity and select Generate Handlers from the context menu. This will create the handler that runs when the workflow is started. You will code this later.

4. In the Solution Explorer, right-click `Workflow1.cs` and select View Designer from the context menu to display the design canvas again.

5. Right-click the Toolbox in Visual Studio and select Choose Items.

6. In the Choose Toolbox Items dialog, click the .NET Framework Components tab.

7. Select the CompleteTask, CreateTask, and OnTaskChanged workflow activities. These are the activities that you will use to create and assign a new task for the workflow.

8. Click the OK button to add these activities to the toolbox.

The CreateTask Activity

This workflow begins by creating a task and assigning values to it. Creating the task is done by using the CreateTask activity. This activity must be configured so that it is properly managed by the workflow activity and has a unique identifier and a mechanism for accessing the fields in the task item. In this section, you will use the CreateTask activity to create the new task item:

1. Drag a CreateTask activity from the toolbox and drop it on the node just below the onWorkflowActivated1 activity.

2. Right-click createTask1 and select Properties from the context menu.

3. In the Properties window, set the `CorrelationToken` property to **taskToken** and hit the Enter key. This token is used to keep track of the particular task item in the workflow as multiple instances of the workflow are run by SharePoint. This token must be shared by all activities involved with the task item.

4. In the Properties window, set the `OwnerActivityName` to **Workflow1**. This field can be found directly below the `CorrelationToken` property you set earlier. This is the name of the workflow class that was created for your project. Assigning the task to this activity ensures that the lifetime of the process components is properly managed.

5. In the Properties window, click the ellipses associated with the `TaskId` property.

6. In the Bind dialog, click the Bind to a New Member tab.

7. On the Bind to a New Member tab, select the Create Field option. This will create a simple member variable in your code. The `taskId` variable will uniquely identify the task you are creating.

8. Enter **taskId** in the New Member Name field and click the OK button.

9. In the Properties window, click the ellipses associated with the `TaskProperties` property.

10. In the Bind dialog, click the Bind to a New Member tab.

11. On the Bind to a New Member tab, select the Create Field option. This will create a simple member variable in your code. The `taskProperties` variable will contain information about the task that is created.

12. Enter **taskProperties** in the New Member Name field and click the OK button.

13. On the design canvas, right-click the CreateTask activity and select Generate Handlers from the context menu. This will create a new method that runs when the task is created. You will code this later. Figure 7-17 shows the Workflow Designer as it should appear at this point with the key property values visible. Check your work carefully against this image to avoid issues later.

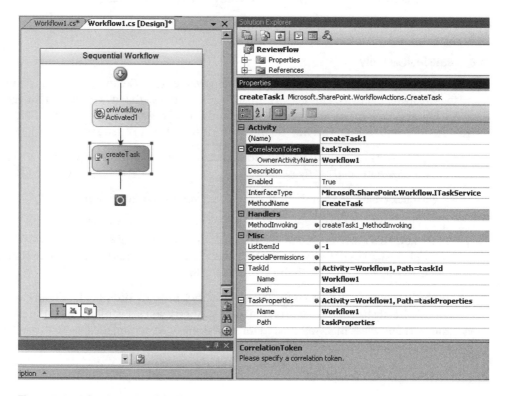

Figure 7-17. *The CreateTask activity*

The While Activity

Once the task is assigned, the workflow must wait until the user completes it. The While activity establishes a loop that checks the task to see if it is complete before continuing. The While activity will contain an OnTaskChanged activity that you will use to check the task to see if it is completed after it has been changed.

Follow these steps to wait for the task to complete:

1. Drag a While activity from the toolbox and drop it on the node just below the createTask1 activity.

2. Right-click the While activity and select Properties from the context menu.

3. In the Properties window, set the `Condition` property named `DynamicUpdateCondition` to `CodeCondition`. This will allow you to specify a variable in code that will be used to determine whether the task is completed.

4. Expand the `DynamicUpdateCondition` property and type **notComplete** in the field and hit the Enter key. This will create a method you can use to determine whether the task is completed. You'll code this method later.

5. Click the Workflow1.cs [Design] tab to return to the design canvas.

6. Drag an OnTaskChanged activity from the toolbox and drop it on the While activity.

7. Right-click the onTaskChanged1 activity and select Properties from the context menu.

8. In the Properties window, set the `CorrelationToken` property to **taskToken**.

9. In the Properties window, click the ellipses associated with the `AfterProperties` property.

10. In the Bind dialog, click the Bind to a New Member tab.

11. Enter **afterProperties** in the New Member Name field.

12. Select the Create Field option to create a member variable that will allow you to access the values of the task item after it has been changed.

13. Click the OK button.

14. In the Properties window, click the ellipses associated with the `BeforeProperties` property.

15. In the Bind dialog, click the Bind to a New Member tab.

16. Enter **beforeProperties** in the New Member Name field.

17. Select the Create Field option to create a member variable that will allow you to access the values of the task item before it has been changed.

18. Click the OK button.

19. In the Properties window, click the ellipses associated with the `TaskId` property.

20. In the Bind dialog, click the Bind to an Existing Member tab.

21. Select taskId from the list and click the OK button.

22. On the design canvas, right-click the OnTaskChanged activity and select Generate Handlers from the context menu. This will create a new method that runs when the task is changed. You will code this later. Figure 7-18 shows the Workflow Designer as it should appear at this point with the key property values visible. Check your work carefully against this image to avoid issues later.

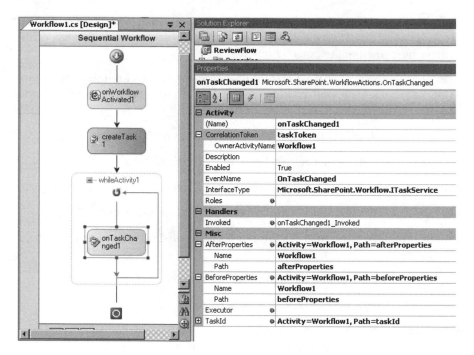

Figure 7-18. *The While activity*

The CompleteTask Activity

The CompleteTask activity is used to take action after the task is completed. Using this activity would allow you to initiate further steps in the process or interact with other systems. In this exercise, you'll simply add the activity to complete the workflow.

Follow these steps to add the CompleteTask activity:

1. Drag a CompleteTask activity from the toolbox and drop it just below the While activity.

2. Right-click the CompleteTask activity and select Properties from the context menu.

3. In the Properties window, set the CorrelationToken property to **taskToken**.

4. In the Properties window, click the ellipses associated with the TaskId property.

5. In the Bind dialog, click the Bind to an Existing Member tab.

6. Select taskId from the list and click the OK button.

7. On the design canvas, right-click the TaskComplete activity and select Generate Handlers from the context menu. This will create a new method that runs when the task is completed. You will code this later. Figure 7-19 shows the Workflow Designer as it should appear.

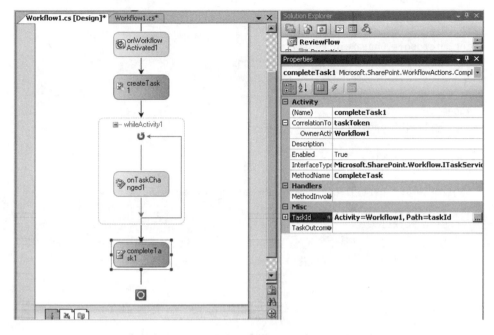

Figure 7-19. *The CompleteTask activity*

Coding the Project

Once you have finished configuring the activities on the designer, you are ready to code the workflow. Coding the workflow involves retrieving the initialization data, settings task properties, and waiting for the task to complete. I have provided the complete solution code in Listing 7-14 for reference. You should add the bolded sections to your code. I discuss the key parts of the code in the following sections.

Listing 7-14. *The Complete Workflow Code*

```
//Included in template
using System;
using System.ComponentModel;
using System.ComponentModel.Design;
using System.Collections;
using System.Drawing;
using System.Workflow.ComponentModel.Compiler;
using System.Workflow.ComponentModel.Serialization;
using System.Workflow.ComponentModel;
using System.Workflow.ComponentModel.Design;
using System.Workflow.Runtime;
using System.Workflow.Activities;
using System.Workflow.Activities.Rules;
using System.Xml.Serialization;
```

```csharp
using System.Xml;
using Microsoft.SharePoint;
using Microsoft.SharePoint.Workflow;
using Microsoft.SharePoint.WorkflowActions;
using Microsoft.Office.Workflow.Utility;

//Added
using System.Diagnostics;

namespace ReviewFlow
{
  public sealed partial class Workflow1: SequentialWorkflowActivity
  {
    public Workflow1()
    {
      InitializeComponent();
    }

    //Workflow activated
    public Guid workflowId = default(System.Guid);
    public string managerUsername = default(string);
    public string managerFullname = default(string);
    public string reviewType = default(string);
    public string reviewComments = default(string);

    public Microsoft.SharePoint.Workflow.SPWorkflowActivationProperties
    workflowProperties = new
      Microsoft.SharePoint.Workflow.SPWorkflowActivationProperties();

    private void onWorkflowActivated1_Invoked(
      object sender, ExternalDataEventArgs e)
    {
      try
      {
        //Save the identifier for the workflow
        workflowId = workflowProperties.WorkflowId;

        // InitiationData comes from the initialization form
        XmlDocument document = new XmlDocument();
        document.LoadXml(workflowProperties.InitiationData);

        XmlNamespaceManager ns = new XmlNamespaceManager(document.NameTable);
        ns.AddNamespace("my",
    "http://schemas.microsoft.com/office/infopath/2003/myXSD/2006-10-25T13:38:03");
                managerUsername =
      document.SelectSingleNode("/my:flowFields/my:managerUsername", ns).InnerText;
                managerFullname =
```

```
        document.SelectSingleNode("/my:flowFields/my:managerFullname", ns).InnerText;
            reviewType =
    document.SelectSingleNode("/my:flowFields/my:reviewType", ns).InnerText;
            reviewComments =
    document.SelectSingleNode("/my:flowFields/my:reviewComments", ns).InnerText;
    }
    catch (Exception x)
    {
      logMessage(x.Message, EventLogEntryType.Error);
    }
}


//Task Created
public Guid taskId = default(System.Guid);
public SPWorkflowTaskProperties taskProperties = new
  Microsoft.SharePoint.Workflow.SPWorkflowTaskProperties();

private void createTask1_MethodInvoking(object sender, EventArgs e)
{
    try
    {
      // Create unique task ID
      taskId = Guid.NewGuid();

      //Set task properties
      taskProperties.AssignedTo = managerUsername;
      taskProperties.Description = reviewComments + "/n";
      taskProperties.Title = "Perform employee review [" + reviewType + "]";

      //Populate the action form using the secondary data source
      taskProperties.ExtendedProperties["reviewComments"] = reviewComments;
    }
    catch (Exception x)
    {
      logMessage(x.Message, EventLogEntryType.Error);
    }

}


//Looping
private bool complete = false;
private void notComplete(object sender, ConditionalEventArgs e)
{
  e.Result = !complete;
}
```

```csharp
//Task Changed
public SPWorkflowTaskProperties afterProperties = new
  Microsoft.SharePoint.Workflow.SPWorkflowTaskProperties();
public SPWorkflowTaskProperties beforeProperties = new
  Microsoft.SharePoint.Workflow.SPWorkflowTaskProperties();

private void onTaskChanged1_Invoked(object sender, ExternalDataEventArgs e)
{
  try
  {
    complete =
    bool.Parse(afterProperties.ExtendedProperties["reviewCompleted"].ToString());
  }
  catch (Exception x)
  {
    logMessage(x.Message, EventLogEntryType.Error);
  }
}

//Task Completed
private void completeTask1_MethodInvoking(object sender, EventArgs e)
{
  try
  {
    afterProperties.Description +=
      afterProperties.ExtendedProperties["reviewNotes"].ToString();
    afterProperties.PercentComplete = 100;
  }
  catch (Exception x)
  {
    logMessage(x.Message, EventLogEntryType.Error);
  }
}

//Logging
private void logMessage(string message, EventLogEntryType type)
{
  if (!EventLog.SourceExists("SharePoint Workflow"))
    EventLog.CreateEventSource("SharePoint Workflow", "Application");
  EventLog.WriteEntry("SharePoint Workflow", message, type);
}
  }
}
```

Coding onWorkflowActivated1_Invoked

This method runs when the workflow is started. The `InitiationData` property of the `workflowProperties` object contains the XML data from the initialization form. Therefore, you can load this into an `XmlDocument` object and retrieve all of the values from the form. In this exercise, you simply store these values in variables for later use.

When you code this part of the solution, be sure to use the correct namespace and XPath values. Yours may be different than what is shown in Listing 7-14. You can get the XPath for any field by right-clicking it in the task pane in InfoPath and selecting Copy XPath from the context menu. I demonstrate this technique in detail in Chapter 6. In order to get the namespace for the form, select Properties from the same menu and click the Details tab on the Properties dialog.

You should also notice that I have placed error handling in all of the routines. If an error occurs, I log it to the Application event log. This technique can save you hours of painful debugging.

Coding createTask1_MethodInvoking

This method runs when a new task needs to be created. In this case, you are simply setting the values for the task item. Additionally, you use the `ExtendedProperties` collection to access the action form. Since the action form is associated with the task item, the extended properties will let you read or write to the form fields.

Coding the Loop

The `notComplete` method runs whenever the loop needs to check and see if it should continue or break. This code simply returns the opposite of the reviewCompleted field. This field is saved to a member variable in the `TaskChanged1_MethodInvoked` method.

Coding completeTask1_MethodInvoking

This method runs when the task is completed. In this code, the task is updated with the notes from the review. It is also set to be 100% complete. After this code runs, the workflow will show that it is completed in SharePoint.

Building the Project

Building the project is a matter of signing the assembly and building it. When you sign the assembly, be sure to record the `PublicKeyToken` for use in the `Feature.xml` file. Remember, you can obtain the `PublicKeyToken` for any assembly using the strong-name utility sn.exe with the –T option.

Deploying the Workflow

The workflow must be deployed as a feature. Therefore, you must create a `Feature.xml` and manifest file. The workflow project template provides a `Feature.xml` file and a manifest file named `Workflow.xml`. You can use these as starting points for creating the files. Additionally, Microsoft has provided a set of snippets that you can use to create the `Feature.xml` and `Workflow.xml` files. Although these snippets should be available after the MOSS SDK is installed, they never seem to be.

Follow these steps to get the snippets working:

1. Open `Feature.xml` in Visual Studio.

2. Press Ctrl ➤ K ➤ B to open the Code Snippets Manager.

3. In the Code Snippets Manager dialog, select XML from the Language drop-down list.

4. Click the Add button to search for the workflow snippets.

5. In the Code Snippets Directory dialog, navigate to C:\Program Files\Microsoft Visual Studio 8\Xml\1033\Snippets\SharePoint Server Workflow.

6. Click the Open button.

7. In the Code Snippets Manager, click the OK button.

8. In the `Feature.xml` file, right-click the body of the document and select Insert Snippet from the context menu.

9. Select SharePoint Server Workflow ➤ Feature XML Code from the snippet menu. The basic code for a `Feature.xml` file will be inserted.

The `Feature.xml` file is similar to ones that I discuss earlier in the chapter. The `ReceiverAssembly` and `ReceiverClass` attributes are used to reference the workflow infrastructure and are always the same. The `ElementManifests` element references the manifest for the feature, but also includes a separate `ElementFile` element for each of the three forms that you must deploy. Additionally, `Property` elements are used to register the InfoPath forms in the central form repository and designate them as appropriate for use with workflows. In the Solution Explorer, open the `Feature.xml` file and replace all of the code with the code in listing 7-15.

Listing 7-15. *The Feature.xml File*

```
<?xml version="1.0" encoding="utf-8"?>
<Feature  Id="53FF8395-A83A-4bfd-922C-E11412E0919A"
  Title="Review Process Workflow"
  Description="Automated review process"
  Version="1.0.0.0"
  Scope="Site"
  ReceiverAssembly="Microsoft.Office.Workflow.Feature, Version=12.0.0.0,
    Culture=neutral, PublicKeyToken=71e9bce111e9429c"
  ReceiverClass="Microsoft.Office.Workflow.Feature.WorkflowFeatureReceiver"
  xmlns="http://schemas.microsoft.com/sharepoint/">
<ElementManifests>
  <ElementManifest Location="workflow.xml" />
  <ElementFile Location="AssocForm.xsn"/>
  <ElementFile Location="InitForm.xsn"/>
  <ElementFile Location="Actionform.xsn"/>
</ElementManifests>
```

```
<Properties>
  <Property Key="GloballyAvailable" Value="true" />
  <Property Key="RegisterForms" Value="*.xsn" />
</Properties>
</Feature>
```

The `Workflow.xml` file is also similar to ones that you have created before. The
`AssociationUrl`, `InstantiationUrl`, and `ModificationUrl` attributes refer to the pages that
will host your InfoPath forms in the workflow. Additionally, there are specific identifiers
included in the `MetaData` section for each form. These are the unique identifiers assigned by
InfoPath and they can be retrieved by opening the form in design mode and selecting File ➤
Properties from the menu. In the Solution Explorer, open the `Workflow.xml` file and replace
all of the code with the code in listing 7-16, being sure to use your form identifiers and the
correct `PublicKeyToken` for your assembly.

Listing 7-16. *The Workflow.xml File*

```
<?xml version="1.0" encoding="utf-8" ?>
<Elements xmlns="http://schemas.microsoft.com/sharepoint/">
<Workflow
  Name="Review Process Workflow"
  Description="Automated review process"
  Id="8A5252A3-D1B2-4aff-A5BF-9D91D2BF7D67"
  CodeBesideClass="ReviewFlow.Workflow1"
  CodeBesideAssembly="ReviewFlow, Version=1.0.0.0, Culture=neutral,
     PublicKeyToken=689f1d0ba493bcce"
  TaskListContentTypeId="0x01080100C9C9515DE4E24001905074F980F93160"
  AssociationUrl="_layouts/CstWrkflIP.aspx"
  InstantiationUrl="_layouts/IniWrkflIP.aspx"
  ModificationUrl="_layouts/ModWrkflIP.aspx">
  <Categories/>
  <MetaData>
    <Association_FormURN>
    urn:schemas-microsoft-com:office:infopath:AssocForm:-myXSD-2006-10-25T13-38-03
    </Association_FormURN>
    <Instantiation_FormURN>
    urn:schemas-microsoft-com:office:infopath:InitForm:-myXSD-2006-10-25T13-38-03
    </Instantiation_FormURN>
    <Task0_FormURN>
    urn:schemas-microsoft-com:office:infopath:ActionForm:-myXSD-2006-10-26T11-03-06
    </Task0_FormURN>
    <StatusPageUrl>_layouts/WrkStat.aspx</StatusPageUrl>
  </MetaData>
</Workflow>
</Elements>
```

Once you have the files created, you can deploy the feature in the standard way. Copy all
of the InfoPath form files, `Feature.xml`, and `Workflow.xml` to a directory named ReviewFlow

underneath the FEATURES directory. Install the `ReviewFlow.dll` assembly in the GAC and use STSADM.EXE to install the new feature. The workflow project template also has a postbuild batch file you can use to perform these steps automatically. If you want to use this batch file, you should refer to the instructions inside the file, which is named `PostBuildActions.bat`.

■**Tip** If you have errors and need to redeploy the workflow, deactivate and uninstall the workflow completely. Then make your changes and try again. Never force a workflow to install over an existing installation because it can cause issues with the InfoPath form versioning that may prevent the workflow from executing.

Using the Workflow

Once the workflow is activated, you may use it with a list. For this exercise, you will use it with a Contacts list, but you could just as easily use it with an InfoPath form or a Word document. Open the site where you activated the workflow and create a new Contacts list named **Employees** and add some items. Once you have done this, you can associate the workflow with the list.

Follow these steps to use the workflow:

1. On the Employees page, select Settings ➤ List Settings.

2. On the Customize page, click the link titled Workflow Settings.

3. On the Add a Workflow page, select the Review Process Workflow from the list of available workflows.

4. Type **Employee Review Workflow** in the Name field. This will be the name of the association.

5. Select New Task List from the Task List section. This will create a new task list for assignments associated with this workflow.

6. Select New History List from the History List section. This will create a new list used to track workflow milestones for auditing and reporting.

7. Leave the option checked to allow manual initiation of a workflow.

8. Click the OK button.

Once the association is completed, you should be able to start a performance review for a person on the Employees list. Verify that your initialization form appears and that a new task is created. Then complete the task and verify it works as expected. Be sure to check the event log for any errors.

CHAPTER 8

SharePoint Business Intelligence Solutions

Microsoft's business intelligence (BI) offering has been evolving over the past few years with several products playing a role. SQL Server 2005 contains a database engine, an analysis services engine, and a report services engine, while Excel 2007 has been enhanced to support up to 2 million rows of data. Other products such as PerformancePoint Server 2007 and recently acquired ProClarity offer scorecarding and analytics. All in all, it is an offering that often feels cobbled together out of available pieces. Worst of all, there has never been a single centralized view of BI data in the Microsoft world. Excel spreadsheets might be e-mailed to users while reports are viewed through a web site and data is accessed through custom applications.

The role of SharePoint in this environment is to act as the front end to various business intelligence sources. While SharePoint is far from a complete BI solution, it does bring some focus that can help make better use of the Microsoft BI offering. In this chapter, I examine the use of SharePoint for interacting with business intelligence data and help you understand how it works with some key Microsoft BI products. Note that while I present information that can be used in both MOSS and WSS, most of the capabilities discussed here require MOSS. Therefore, I'll assume you have access to MOSS throughout the chapter.

Understanding Report Center

The home for all BI data within MOSS is the Report Center. You may create a Report Center as a separate site collection using the available template or utilize the one that is created as part of the Collaboration Portal. If you set up the development environment detailed in Chapter 2, you already have a Report Center available. Figure 8-1 shows a Report Center home page with several modifications already made.

The primary role of the Report Center is to allow the creation and display of dashboards. *Dashboards* in the Report Center are pages that consist of scorecards and reports. *Scorecards* are lists that display quantitative measures of organizational performance called *key performance indicators (KPIs)*. *Reports* are Excel spreadsheets delivered through Excel Services. Both scorecards and reports may act as front ends for a variety of data sources. Therefore, dashboards provide a centralized mechanism for viewing business intelligence data.

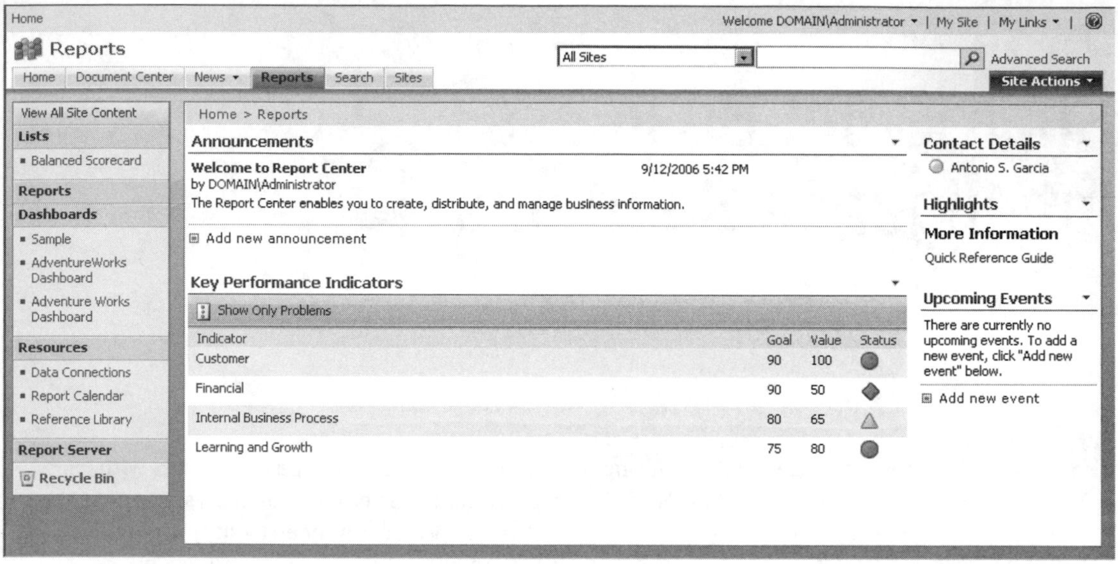

Figure 8-1. *The Report Center*

Follow these steps to create a new dashboard:

1. Log in to VSMOSS as a site administrator.

2. Click the Reports tab to view the Report Center.

3. Click the Dashboards link in the Quick Launch area.

4. In the Reports Library, select New ➤ Dashboard Page from the toolbar.

5. In the File Name field, enter **Performance**.

6. In the Page Title field, enter **Organizational Performance**.

7. In the Layout list, select One Column Vertical Layout.

8. Select the option labeled Create a KPI List for Me Automatically.

9. Click the OK button. This will give you an empty dashboard that you can populate through the rest of the chapter.

Using Scorecards

Scorecards are a mechanism for displaying data designed to support decision making at the executive level. The scorecards in the Report Center are really just custom lists that support three key fields: KPI Value, KPI Goal Threshold, and KPI Warning Threshold. The KPI Value field is a numeric measurement for a KPI. This measurement can be anything that the organization thinks is important such as sales, profit, and so on. The KPI Goal Threshold is typically the minimum value at which the goal can be considered to have been met. For example, an annual sales goal of 100 million may have a threshold value of 90 million. The KPI Warning Threshold is the value at which any further decline indicates the goal has not been met.

The scorecards you create in the Report Center use the KPI Value, KPI Goal Threshold, and KPI Warning Threshold to associate a green, yellow, or red icon with the KPI. These icons together are called the *stop light* and are used as a visual indicator for the KPI.

Follow these steps to create some KPIs:

1. On the Organizational Performance dashboard, select New ➤ Indicator Using Manually Entered Information.

2. In the Name field, type **Customer Satisfaction**.

3. In the Value field, type **82**.

4. In the field labeled Display When Has Met or Exceeded Goal, type **85**.

5. In the field labeled Display When Has Met or Exceeded Warning, type **70**.

6. Click the OK button.

7. Repeat the previous steps to add all of the KPIs listed in Table 8-1.

Table 8-1. *Sample KPIs*

Name	Value	Goal	Warning
Customer Satisfaction	82	85	70
Financial Performance	85	90	80
Internal Processes	90	80	70
Learning and Growth	50	70	60

When you create the KPIs, you'll notice that all of the values must be numeric, but there are no units associated with the values. Furthermore, you cannot make any changes to the data types in the KPI list without breaking the underlying mechanism that determines what icons to display. This means that scorecards should indicate something about the values in the name of the KPI (e.g., Customer Satisfaction Survey Rating) for it to make sense to the end user.

Another problem with the Report Center scorecards is that KPIs cannot have child KPIs. *Child KPIs* are important for creating aggregated measures that are appropriate for a given user. For example, the head of marketing may be interested in the aggregated results of marketing expenditures while regional managers may only want to see their individual data. In fact, most organizations have policies that prevent individuals from viewing performance data not directly related to their role. The workaround for most of these issues lies in creating multiple scorecards and making use of more sophisticated data sources such as SharePoint lists, Excel spreadsheets, and SQL Analysis Services. I discuss dashboard data sources in the section titled "Understanding Data Source Options."

Using Reports

The Report Center has a Reports Library, which holds Excel spreadsheets suitable for use with Excel Services. You can create a new spreadsheet directly from the Reports Library and use it in a dashboard. Furthermore, the Report Center has a data connection library where you can store all of your Office Data Connection files so that spreadsheets can access external data sources. I discuss Excel Services and Office Data Connections in detail in Chapter 4, so I will not repeat the information here. I'll just focus on using the spreadsheets within a dashboard.

Follow these steps to use a spreadsheet in your dashboard:

1. In the Report Center, click the Reports link in the Quick Launch area.

2. In the Reports Library, select New ➤ Report from the toolbar.

3. In the Name field, type **Customers**.

4. In the Title field, type **Customer Information**.

5. Click the OK button.

6. When the Customers report appears in the library, select Edit in Microsoft Excel from the drop-down list associated with the report.

7. In Excel 2007, click the Data tab.

8. In the Data tab, click the From Access button in the Get External Data group.

9. In the Select Data Source dialog, navigate to C:\Program Files\Microsoft Office\ OFFICE 12\1033.

10. Select the FPNWIND.MDB database and click the Open button.

11. In the Select Table dialog, select the Customers table and click the OK button.

12. In the Import Data dialog, click the OK button.

13. In the spreadsheet, click the black down arrow next to the formula box (fx) and select Table_FPNWIND to select all of the data imported from the query. Figure 8-2 shows the spreadsheet with the table selected.

14. Click the Design tab in the ribbon.

15. Click the Unlink button to unlink the query from the data. This is necessary because this particular type of external query definition is not supported by Excel Services.

16. When prompted, click the OK button to remove the link.

17. Save the spreadsheet and exit Excel.

18. Click the link for the Organizational Performance dashboard in the Quick Launch area.

19. In the Select a Workbook section, click the link titled Click Here to Open the Tool Pane.

20. In the Tool Pane, click the ellipsis associated with the Workbook field.

21. In the Select a Link dialog, double-click the Reports Library.

22. Select the Customers report and click the OK button.

23. In the Tool Pane, click the OK button to close it.

24. In the Content management toolbar, click the Publish button. Figure 8-3 shows the final dashboard.

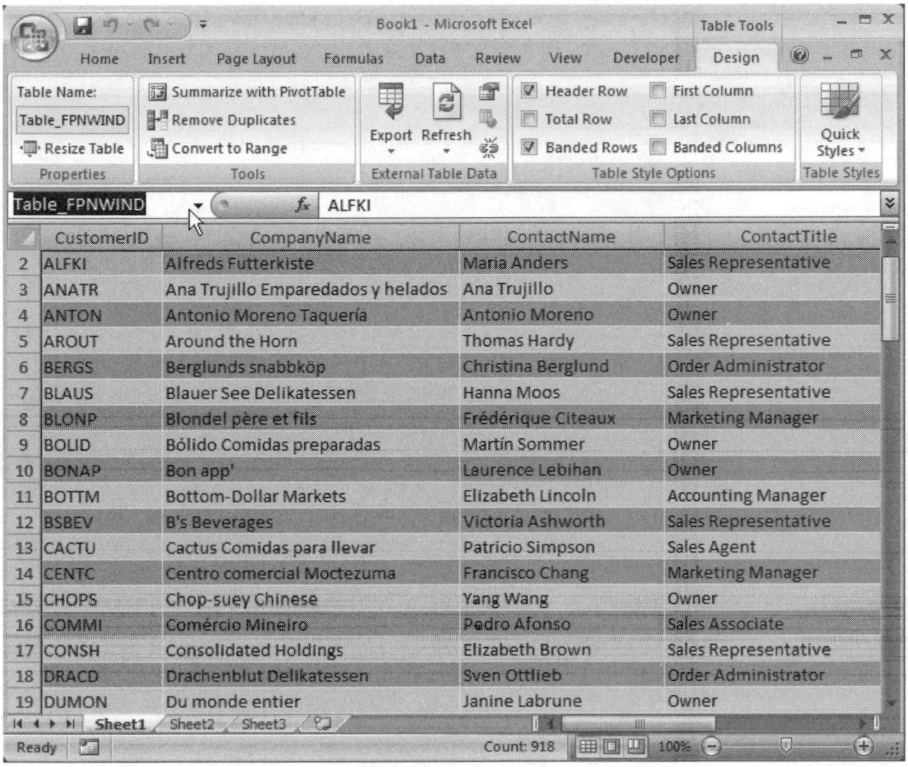

CustomerID	CompanyName	ContactName	ContactTitle
ALFKI	Alfreds Futterkiste	Maria Anders	Sales Representative
ANATR	Ana Trujillo Emparedados y helados	Ana Trujillo	Owner
ANTON	Antonio Moreno Taquería	Antonio Moreno	Owner
AROUT	Around the Horn	Thomas Hardy	Sales Representative
BERGS	Berglunds snabbköp	Christina Berglund	Order Administrator
BLAUS	Blauer See Delikatessen	Hanna Moos	Sales Representative
BLONP	Blondel père et fils	Frédérique Citeaux	Marketing Manager
BOLID	Bólido Comidas preparadas	Martín Sommer	Owner
BONAP	Bon app'	Laurence Lebihan	Owner
BOTTM	Bottom-Dollar Markets	Elizabeth Lincoln	Accounting Manager
BSBEV	B's Beverages	Victoria Ashworth	Sales Representative
CACTU	Cactus Comidas para llevar	Patricio Simpson	Sales Agent
CENTC	Centro comercial Moctezuma	Francisco Chang	Marketing Manager
CHOPS	Chop-suey Chinese	Yang Wang	Owner
COMMI	Comércio Mineiro	Pedro Afonso	Sales Associate
CONSH	Consolidated Holdings	Elizabeth Brown	Sales Representative
DRACD	Drachenblut Delikatessen	Sven Ottlieb	Order Administrator
DUMON	Du monde entier	Janine Labrune	Owner

Figure 8-2. *Selecting the Table_FPNWIND data*

■Note If you receive an access denied error, you will have to add the Reports Library as a trusted location using the setup outlined in Chapter 4.

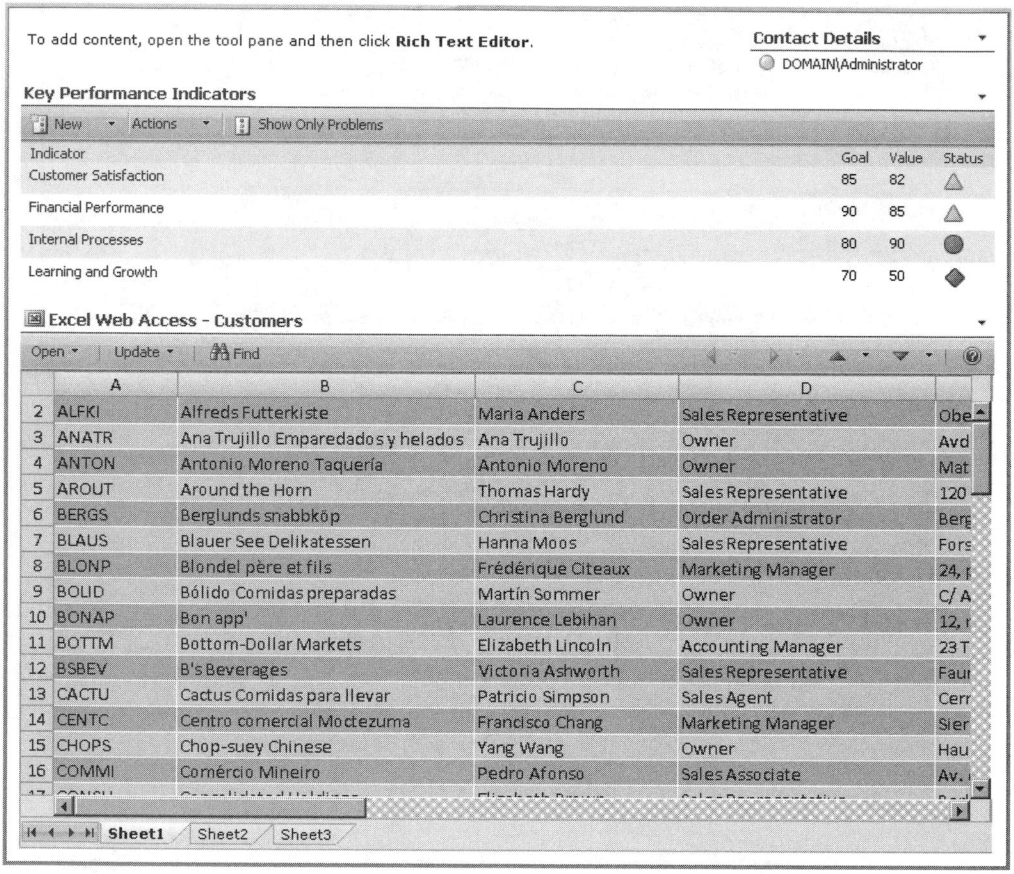

Figure 8-3. *A sample dashboard*

Understanding Data Source Options

Dashboards in the Report Center may utilize many different data sources for both scorecards and reports. Besides manual data, scorecards may use SharePoint lists, Excel spreadsheets, and Analysis Services cubes. Reports in the form of Excel Services spreadsheets may use SharePoint lists, databases, and cubes. In this section, I review the various data sources and how to use them within scorecards and reports.

Using SharePoint Lists as Data Sources

When you use a SharePoint list as a data source, you start by creating views in the list that filter the data in ways that you want to show it. As an example, I created a list with sales data from multiple regions. I then created several views that show the data for different regions. Figure 8-4 shows a view of the example sales data from the Central region.

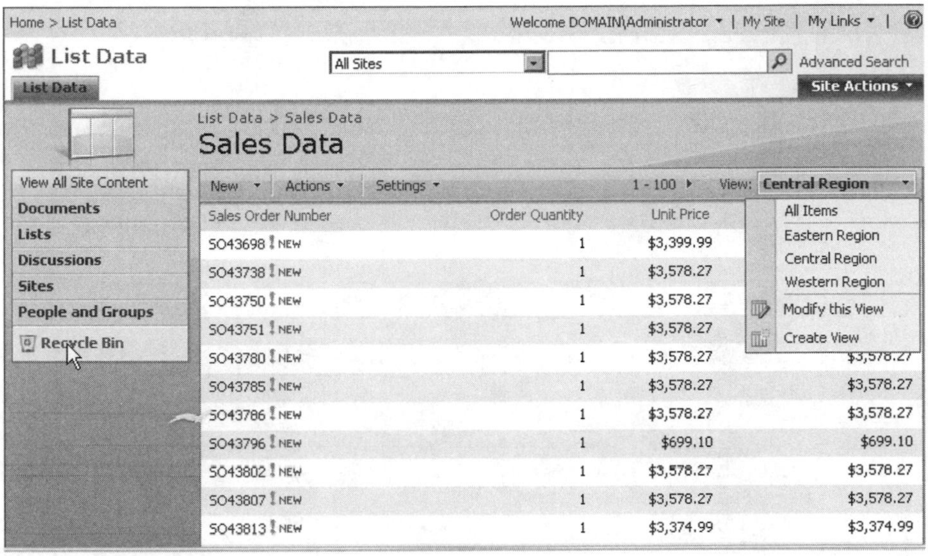

Figure 8-4. *Sample sales data in a SharePoint list*

Once the list is filtered into views, you can use the list in a scorecard to create more specific KPIs. From a scorecard, you select New ➤ Indicator Using Data in a SharePoint List. When you define the KPI, you may select from any list in the web application; it does not have to reside in the same site as long as you have permission to access the data. After you select a list, you may select a view to use and then an operation to perform. For example, I totaled all of the sales numbers in the list to create a total sales KPI for each region.

In order to use list data in a spreadsheet, you must export it. In order to export the data, select Actions ➤ Export to Spreadsheet from the list toolbar. When you export the list data to an Excel spreadsheet, a connection is made between the spreadsheet and the list. Unfortunately, Excel Services does not support rendering spreadsheets that have such connections. Therefore, you'll have to unlink the sheet from the list before you use it. This is done in the same manner as shown in Figure 8-2. In the spreadsheet, click the black down arrow next to the formula box (fx) and select the query object to select all of the data imported from the query. Then simply click the Unlink button in the Design tab. After you save the spreadsheet, you can add it to a dashboard from the Reports Library. Figure 8-5 shows a dashboard that uses a SharePoint list as a source for both the scorecard and the report.

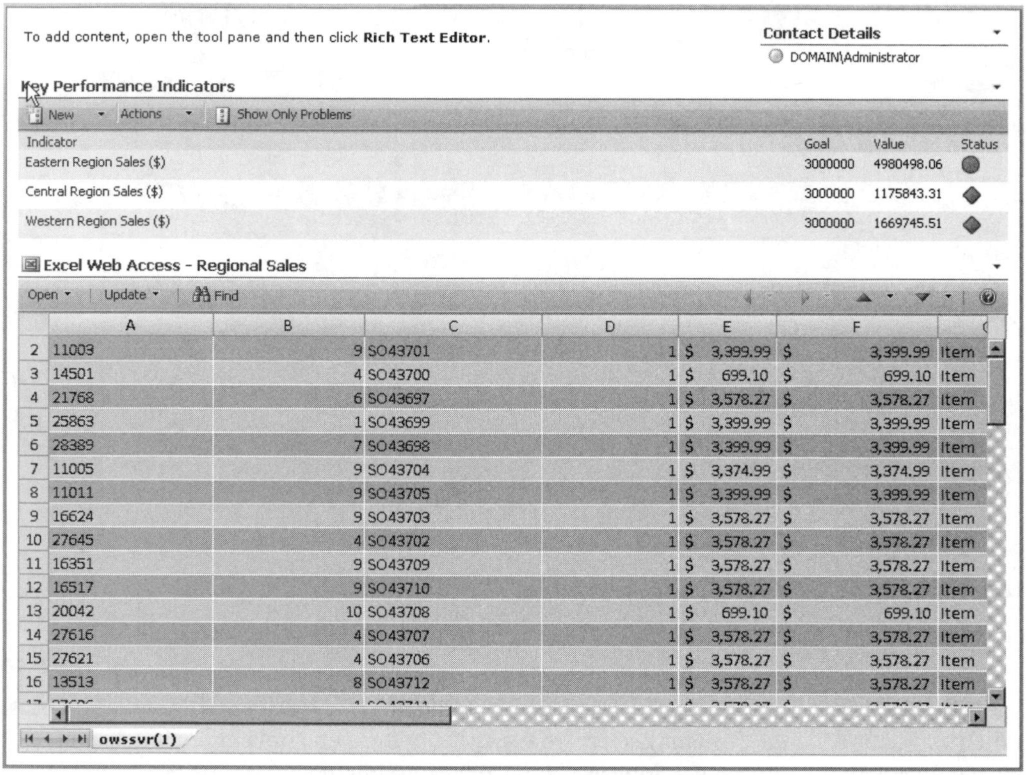

Figure 8-5. *Creating a dashboard from a SharePoint list*

Using Spreadsheets as Data Sources

Excel spreadsheets deployed via Excel Services can be used as a data source for scorecards. You create a new KPI from a spreadsheet by selecting New ➤ Indicator Using Data in Excel Workbook. After you select a workbook, you can view the data and select cells for the value, goal, and warning levels. This is done through a pick dialog.

When you select a cell, you may choose to use the value as it appears in the spreadsheet or you may create a simple formula. For example, you can multiply a cell by a value to create a threshold value. You can also simply type fixed values in for the thresholds. Figure 8-6 shows the cell picker interface with a cell selected and some values added by hand.

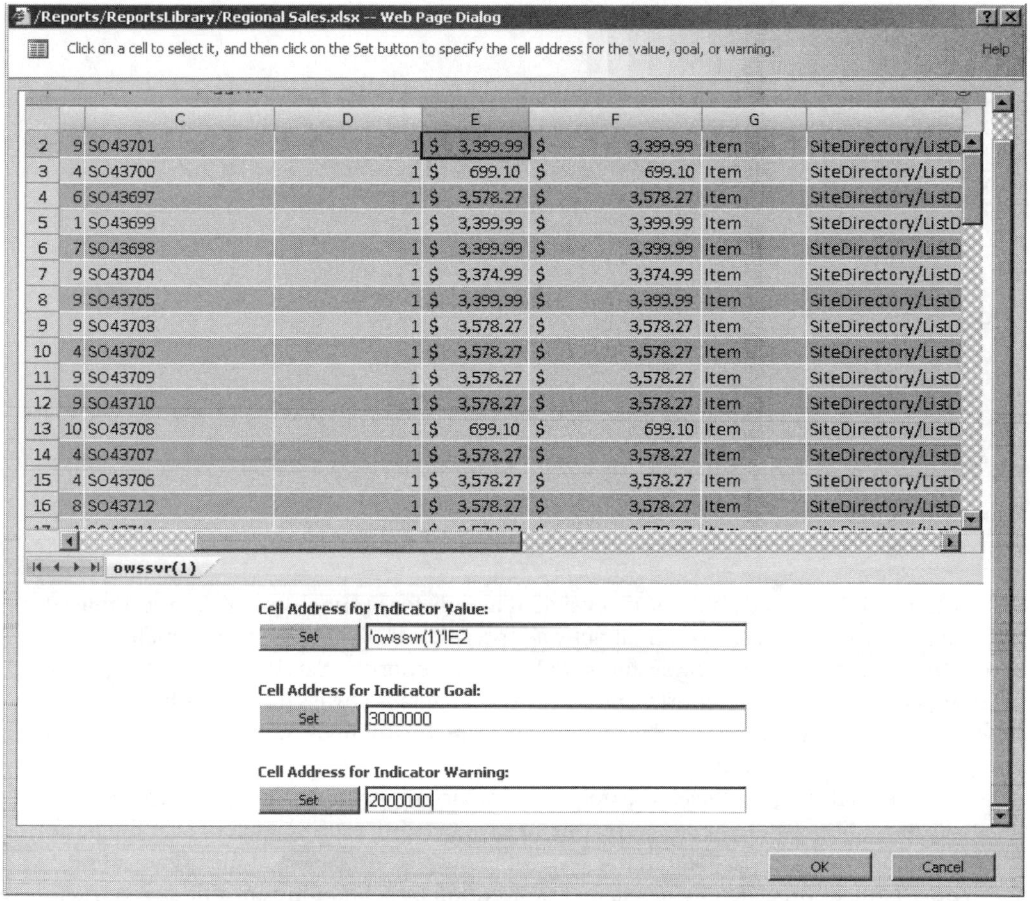

Figure 8-6. *Picking cells from an Excel spreadsheet*

Using Cubes as Data Sources

Both scorecards and reports may use cubes as a data source. Cubes are data structures that are optimized for queries and analysis. These data structures are built from data warehouses that bring together relational data from many different databases. In this section, I explain how to create a cube and use it with scorecards and reports.

Understanding Data Warehouses

Creating a cube always begins with understanding the data found in your organization's business systems. These systems utilize relational databases to store information, and this is a concept that is well-understood. If you are reading this book, you have probably written many applications that use relational databases. The key point of emphasis here, however, is that these relational databases are designed for optimal data storage. Figure 8-7 shows a classic relational database diagram from a customer relationship management (CRM) system representing the relationships between an organization's sales opportunities, customer companies, customer contacts, and the organization's employee working the deal.

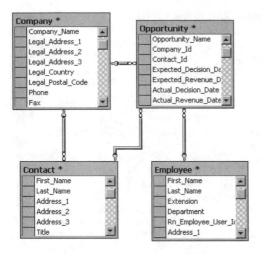

Figure 8-7. *A relational database diagram*

Although relational databases are designed mainly for optimal storage, the vast majority of organizations regularly use them directly as enterprise reporting sources. Initially, this seems to make sense. Reporting systems such as SQL Reporting Services can connect directly to these databases and run reports, and the available data is always up to date because the report is run directly against the transactional system. Invariably, however, challenges arise with this approach for several reasons.

Because relational databases are not optimized for reporting, running enterprise reports against transactional systems can have a significant performance impact. In fact, the performance degradation can be so great that it affects the internal processes of the organization.

The organization generally reacts to this situation by scheduling enterprise reports to run at night. This seems like a good idea because the information workers can use the system by day and the enterprise reporting infrastructure can use the system by night. This solution may work initially, but as reporting needs grow so does the processing time required for the reports. In many cases, this leads to a situation in which reports are still running when the workday begins.

The solution to the reporting problem rests in creating a *data warehouse*. A data warehouse is a separate database created from one or many systems, and it is optimized for enterprise reporting. Although data warehouses can be quite complicated and incorporate many data sources, the concept is pretty simple. While relational databases are optimized for storage with no repeating data, data warehouses purposely repeat data to make it easier to generate reports. Furthermore, because the data warehouse is separate from the business system, reports can be run any time of the day.

The process of creating a data warehouse begins by moving data from target systems into a new database called a *staging area*. The purpose of the staging area is to join data from different systems into a single set of tables and to reconcile the data from the various systems. Reconciling the data—or *cleansing* the data—is required because different systems may have different formats, conflicting data, or incorrect values. The process of moving the data from the business systems to the staging area is known as *extract, transform, and load (ETL)*.

Once the data is cleaned, it is then moved from the staging area into the data warehouse. The value of the data warehouse rests in its table structure. Instead of a relational structure, data warehouses utilize a *fact table*. A fact table can be thought of as a view that joins many relational tables together to focus on a certain area. For example, if we want to run reports about the sales opportunities shown in Figure 8-7, we might create a fact table of opportunities that joins together the four tables in a single view. This fact table would contain the value of every sales opportunity as a row, along with the primary keys for the other tables of interest.

The primary keys contained in a fact table are said to be the *dimensions* of the table, while the values contained in the fact table are called *measures*. Dimensions are used to create views of the measures in your reports. The fact table I describe, for example, would allow us to create a report that shows sales opportunity dollar values by employee. This report is a classic pipeline report used by all sales organizations.

In a data warehouse, the dimensions in the fact table are joined to tables that contain the actual values for the dimensions. This database structure results in a centralized fact table joined with many dimension tables. The resulting structure is called a *star schema* because the database diagram resembles a star. Figure 8-8 shows a star schema.

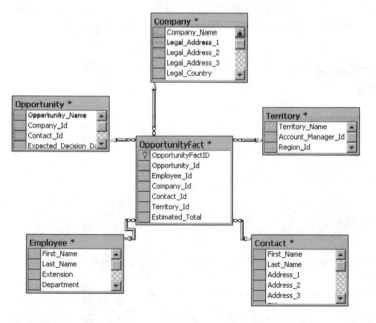

Figure 8-8. *A star schema*

Understanding Cubes

A data warehouse is an excellent structure for use with enterprise reporting tools such as SQL Reporting Services; however, reporting represents only one part of an organization's business intelligence needs. Along with classic reporting, organizations need a way for information workers and senior management to analyze performance data. Analysis involves more than just static reporting, because it allows people to answer questions by dynamically manipulating performance data.

As an example, consider what happens when an executive receives a report that quarterly earnings have dropped by 20 percent. The natural reaction is to ask why earnings are down. If an organization has no analysis capability, the IT department is left writing report after report, trying to create a view of the data that will provide an answer. With the analysis capability embodied in a cube, data may be directly manipulated to provide different views without writing a single report.

A cube is built using the star schema of the data warehouse as a starting point. SQL Analysis Services transforms the data warehouse into a cube. Just like a data warehouse, the cube will have facts, measures, and dimensions. The difference between the data warehouse and the cube is that the cube will be optimized for analysis so that different views can be created on the fly without running a new report.

In order to create a cube, you must have SQL Server 2005 Analysis Services available. If you created the development environment described in Chapter 2, you installed Analysis Services on the VSSQL machine. Along with Analysis Services, you also installed the SQL Server Business Intelligence Studio. The Business Intelligence Studio uses many of the same visual elements that are found in Visual Studio 2005, but the environment is specifically designed for the development of Business Intelligence projects such as cubes and reports. If you create a new project in Business Intelligence Studio, you'll see many of the familiar project types from Visual Studio along with the special Business Intelligence projects shown in Figure 8-9.

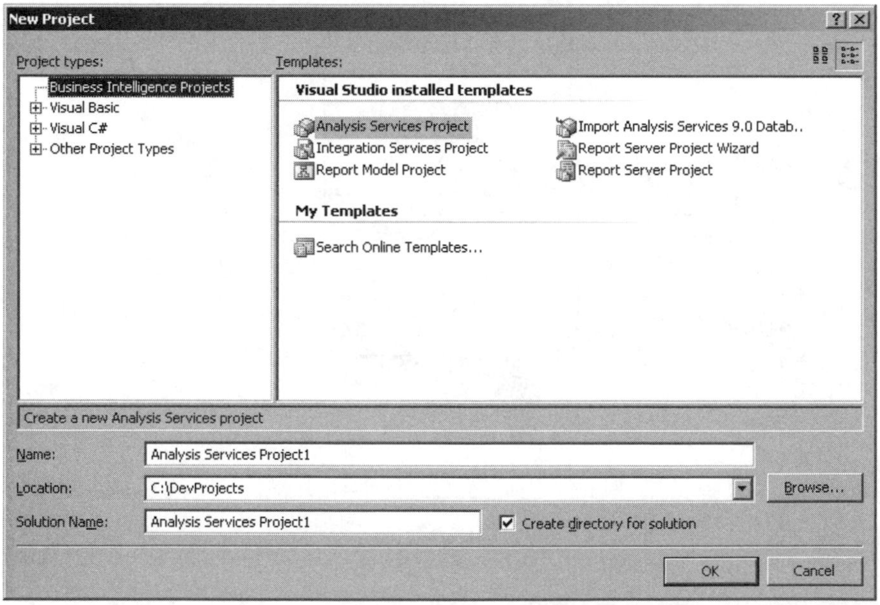

Figure 8-9. *Creating a new Business Intelligence project*

After you create a new Analysis Services project, Business Intelligence Studio creates a series of folders in the Solution Explorer. These folders represent the steps in a process for creating a cube. This process involves defining the data source to use, a view of that source, and then the cube. In each case, you can perform the required steps by right-clicking the appropriate folder and selecting New from the context menu. Figure 8-10 shows the folder set that is created.

Figure 8-10. *Folders in an Analysis Services project*

The first step is to connect to the data warehouse where the facts and dimensions are located. This is done by creating a new data source in the Data Sources folder. Creating a new data source simply allows you to specify a database connection. Ideally, this database would be a data warehouse, but it can actually be any database.

The next step is to define a view of the database to use when making the cube. The view is used to focus the cube just on the data of interest. Ideally, this view would have a single fact and several dimensions just like Figure 8-8. Most data warehouses have many facts and dimensions, so creating a view allows you to simplify the data.

The final step is to create the cube. Analysis Services provides a wizard for creating cubes that can detect facts and dimensions. You can run the wizard by right-clicking the Cubes folder and selecting New Cube from the context menu. You can then work your way through the wizard to ensure that the correct facts and dimensions are identified. Once the cube is built, you may deploy it to Analysis Services where it is ready to be used in scorecards and reports.

Using Cube Data

The best way to make use of a cube through SharePoint is to first define an Office Data Connection file and save it in the data connection library in the Report Center. Creating an Office Data Connection file can be done directly through Excel 2007 and then uploaded into SharePoint. The files are typically saved with an ODC extension and are located in the My Documents\My Data Sources folder. Figure 8-11 shows the Data tab in Excel with choices for different data sources.

Once an Office Data Connection file is uploaded to the data connection library in the Report Center, you may add a KPI based on the cube data by selecting New ➤ Indicator Using Data in SQL Server 2005 Analysis Services. When you create the new KPI, you will be able to browse the data connection library for data sources from which you can select a measure.

In order to use the cube data in a spreadsheet, you can create a new report by selecting New ➤ Report from the Reports Library. After the report is created, you can open it in Excel and click the Connections button on the Data ribbon to use the Office Data Connection file you saved earlier. At the end of this chapter, you will find a complete exercise that builds a cube and uses it to create a dashboard with a scorecard and a report.

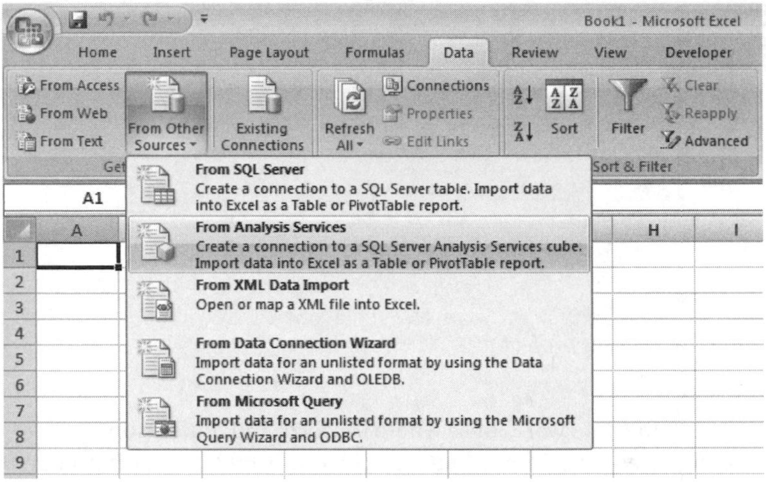

Figure 8-11. *Connecting to data sources in Excel 2007*

Integrating SQL Reporting Services

No discussion of BI would be complete without including SQL Reporting Services. SQL Reporting Services is the mechanism for creating, deploying, and consuming enterprise reports. If you set up the development environment outlined in Chapter 2, you already have SQL Reporting Services installed on VSSQL. As a starting point, I like to add this link directly to the Quick Launch area of the Report Center for easy access.

Follow these steps to add a link to the Quick Launch area:

1. Log in to VSMOSS as a site administrator and open the intranet site.

2. Click the Report Center tab.

3. Select Site Settings ➤ Modify Navigation from the Site Actions menu.

4. On the Site Navigation Settings page, click the Add Heading link.

5. In the Navigation Heading dialog, enter **Report Server** in the Title field.

6. Enter **http://VSSQL/Reports/Pages/Folder.aspx** in the URL field.

7. Click the OK button.

8. On the Site Navigation Settings page, click the OK button.

SQL Reporting Services reports are created in the Business Intelligence Studio. Creating reports can range from a very simple wizard-based process to a complex project containing rules and logic. The subject of SQL Reporting Services is the topic of many books and I cannot cover it in detail here. However, you can create a simple report for use with SharePoint.

Follow these steps to create a report:

1. Log in to VSSQL as an administrator.

2. Select Start ➤ All Programs ➤ Microsoft SQL Server 2005 ➤ SQL Server Business Intelligence Development Studio.

3. In Business Intelligence Studio, select File ➤ New ➤ Project.

4. In the New Project dialog, select Business Intelligence Projects from the Project Types tree.

5. Select Report Server Project Wizard from the Templates list.

6. Name the project **SharePointReport**.

7. Click the OK button.

8. When the Report Wizard starts, click the Next button.

9. On the Select Data Source screen, select the New Data Source option.

10. Name the data source **MOSS.**

11. Click the Edit button.

12. Type **VSSQL** in the Server Name drop-down list.

13. Type **WSS_Content** in the Database Name field.

14. Click the OK button.

15. In the Report Wizard, click the Next button.

16. Type **SELECT FullUrl, Title FROM Webs** in the Query String field.

■**Caution** Accessing the SharePoint content database directly is potentially dangerous because you could destroy critical data. Generally, it's fine to read these databases but not write to them.

---

17. On the Select a Report Type screen, click Finish.

18. On the Completing the Wizard screen, type **Webs** in the Report Name field.

19. Click the Finish button.

20. When the report is created, select Build ➤ Deploy from the main menu.

21. Log in to VSMOSS as a site administrator.

22. Click the Report Center tab.

23. Click the Report Server link you created earlier. Figure 8-12 shows the final report as it appears on a test server.

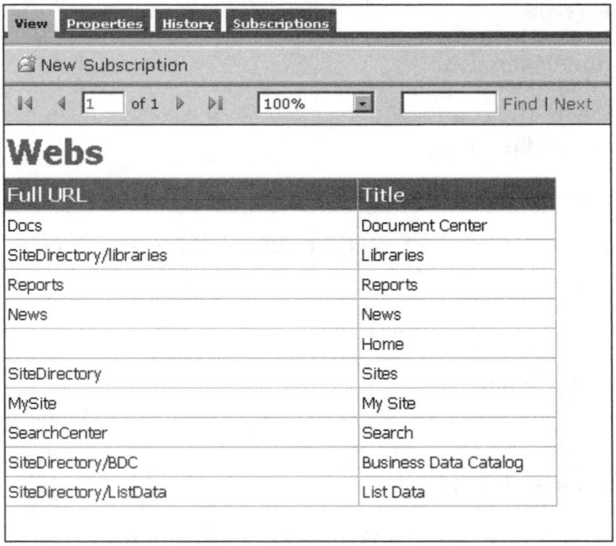

Figure 8-12. *Viewing a report*

Reporting Services Web Parts

Initially, you may think that SQL Reporting Services should be tightly integrated with the Report Center. After all, the Report Center is supposed to be the single location for all BI information. Unfortunately, at this writing there is little integration. Microsoft does have grand integration plans that will emerge along with SQL Server 2005 Service Pack 2, but for now we are limited to using some web parts that were designed for the previous version of SharePoint.

Because SharePoint 2007 has backward-compatibility support, we can use the web parts originally intended for SharePoint 2003 to browse reports and display them. One web part, called Report Explorer, displays a list of all reports in Reporting Services. Another web part, called Report Viewer, displays a single report. In order to install these web parts, we'll have to follow a process that worked in SharePoint 2003. This process involves installing a cabinet file using the STSADM.EXE command-line utility. I discuss SharePoint 2007 web parts in detail in Chapter 10, but I'll assume you have enough knowledge of web parts under SharePoint 2003 to follow this installation.

Follow these steps to install the Reporting Services web parts:

1. Log in to VSSQL as an administrator.

2. In the File Explorer, navigate to C:\Program Files\Microsoft SQL Server\90\Tools\ Reporting Services\SharePoint. The web parts and supporting files are located here in a single CAB file.

3. Right-click the SharePoint folder and select Sharing and Security from the context menu.

4. Select the option to Share This Folder and click the OK button. You will access this folder from VSMOSS to install the web parts.

5. Log in to VSMOSS as a SharePoint administrator.

6. In the File Explorer, select Tools ➤ Map Network Drive.

7. In the Map Network Drive dialog, enter **\\VSSQL\SharePoint** in the Folder field and click the Finish button.

8. Navigate to the mapped drive, right-click the RSWebParts.cab file and copy it to the root of the C: drive so you can access it easily.

9. Open a command window and navigate the directory C:\Program Files\Common Files\Microsoft Shared\web server extensions\12\bin.

10. Execute the following command line to install the web parts. Be sure that the url parameter is correct for your installation:

    ```
    STSADM.EXE -o addwppack -filename C:\RSWebParts.cab
    -url http://vsmoss/sites/intranet
    ```

11. Open the intranet site and click the Report Center tab.

12. Select Edit Page from the Site Actions menu.

13. Click the Add a Web Part link in any zone.

14. In the Add Web Parts dialog, select the Report Explorer web part.

15. Select Modify Web Part from the Edit menu associated with the Report Explorer web part.

16. Enter **http://VSSQL/Reports/Pages/Folder.aspx** in the Report Manager URL field.

17. Click the OK button.

18. Click the Publish button to publish the modified page. You should now see the Report Explorer web part in the Report Center. Figure 8-13 shows the Report Explorer with several reports.

Report Explorer				▼
Home			🖺 Report Builder	
Type	Name↓	Subscription	Description	When Run
📁	Adventure !NEW			
📁	Data Sources !NEW			
📁	SharePoint Report !NEW			

Figure 8-13. *The Report Explorer*

SQL Server 2005 Service Pack 2

SQL Server 2005 Service Pack 2 promises to bring much tighter integration between SharePoint and Reporting Services. At this writing, no preview of the integration was available, but published reports indicate that after installing SP2 you will be able to configure Report Services in SharePoint Integration Mode. This mode will enable publishing, viewing, and managing reports through SharePoint. Unfortunately, there will be no migration path for existing report servers. Only new instances can integrate with SharePoint.

Reports will be published into SharePoint libraries and will have associated metadata like any content type. Additionally, versioning and workflow can be used with the reports. SharePoint will manage all of the security, and the report creation tools will be updated to work inside SharePoint. Some functionality such as subscriptions and scheduling will still reside in the report server. Plans seem to call for tight integration with the Report Center and web parts. Reports can be made part of any dashboard and web parts can be used to filter the data displayed in a report. By the time you read this book, a preview, or even a release, of SP2 will likely be available.

Exercise 8.1. Creating a Dashboard

Dashboards in MOSS allow you to use a variety of data sources and presentation methods to display reports, information, and KPIs on a single page. These data sources can include SQL Server Analysis Services cubes, Excel spreadsheets, SharePoint lists, and manually entered values. In this exercise, you will create a dashboard that displays information from a cube presented in an Excel spreadsheet and a scorecard.

Installing the AdventureWorks Data Warehouse

In this exercise, you will be creating a cube with data from the AdventureWorks database. However, you will not use the AdventureWorks database directly. Instead, you will use a data warehouse based on the AdventureWorks database. A sample data warehouse is available from the Microsoft site that you can use for this exercise.

Follow these steps to install the AdventureWorks data warehouse:

1. Log in to VSSQL as an administrator.

2. Open the browser and navigate to `http://go.microsoft.com/fwlink/?linkid=31046`.

3. Run the `AdventureWorksBI.msi` file.

4. Select Start ➤ All Programs ➤ Microsoft SQL Server 2005 ➤ SQL Server Management Studio.

5. Connect to the default instance of SQL Server running on VSSQL.

6. In SQL Server Management Studio, right-click the Databases folder and select Attach from the context menu.

7. In the Attach Databases dialog, click the Add button.

8. In the Locate Database Files dialog, select the `AdventureWorksDW_Data.mdf` file and click the OK button.

9. In the Attach Databases dialog, click the OK button.

10. Close SQL Server Management Studio.

Building and Deploying a Cube

Once the AdventureWorks data warehouse is installed, you are ready to make a cube. The cube is created using the SQL Server Business Intelligence Development Studio, which is a development environment based on Visual Studio 2005. In this environment, you will make a new project, connect to the data warehouse, define a cube, and deploy it to Analysis Services.

Follow these steps to get started:

1. Log in to VSSQL as a local administrator.

2. Select Start ➤ All Programs ➤ Microsoft SQL Server 2005 ➤ SQL Server Business Intelligence Development Studio.

3. In the SQL Server Business Intelligence Development Studio, select File ➤ New ➤ Project from the main menu.

4. In the New Project dialog, select Business Intelligence Projects from the Project Types list.

5. Select Analysis Services project from the Templates list view.

6. Name the new project **AWCube** and click the OK button.

7. In the Solution Explorer, right-click the Data Sources folder and select New Data Source from the context menu.

Creating a New Data Source

After the new project is created, you can connect to the AdventureWorks data warehouse. Creating a data source will allow the cube to be built based on the dimensions and facts contained in the data warehouse. You will also specify in this section what credentials to use when Analysis Services connects to the data warehouse.

Follow these steps to define a new data source:

1. When the Data Source wizard starts, click the Next button on the welcome screen.

2. On the Select How to Define the Connection screen, select the option labeled Create a Data Source Based on an Existing or New Connection.

3. Click the New button.

4. In the Connection Manager dialog, select VSSQL from the Server Name drop-down list.

5. Select AdventureWorksDW from the database drop-down list.

6. Click the OK button in the Connection Manager dialog.

7. Click the Next button in the Data Source wizard.

8. On the Impersonation Information screen, select the option labeled Use the Service Account and click the Next button. This will use the service account to connect to the data warehouse.

9. On the Completing the Wizard screen, click the Finish button.

Creating a New Data Source View

A data source view is a single view of selected information in the data warehouse. This single view will be used to create the cube. The view will contain dimensions and facts that will be part of the cube.

Follow these steps to define a new data source view:

1. In the Solution Explorer, right-click the Data Source Views folder and select New Data Source View from the context menu.

2. When the Data Source View wizard starts, click the Next button.

3. On the Select a Data Source screen, ensure AdventureWorksDW is selected and click the Next button.

4. On the Select Tables and View screen, double-click the dbo.DimCustomer, dbo.DimGeography, dbo.DimProduct, dbo.DimTime, and dbo.FactInterrnetSales to move them to the Included Objects list. Figure 8-14 shows how the dialog should appear.

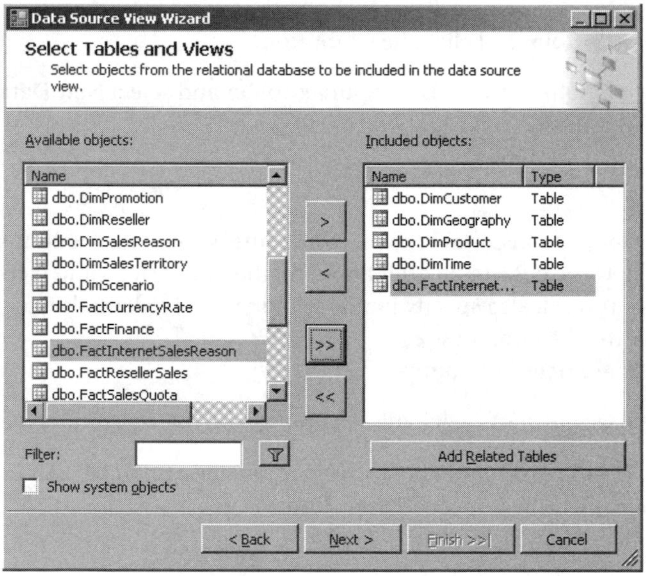

Figure 8-14. *Selecting tables and views*

5. On the Select Tables and Views screen, click the Next button.

6. On the Completing the Wizard screen, click the Finish button.

7. In the Tables list, right-click the DimCustomer table and select Properties from the context menu.

8. Enter **Customer** in the FriendlyName property.

9. In the Tables list, right-click the DimGeography table and select Properties from the context menu.

10. Enter **Geography** in the FriendlyName property.

11. In the Tables list, right-click the DimProduct table and select Properties from the context menu.

12. Enter **Product** in the FriendlyName property.

13. In the Tables list, right-click the DimTime table and select Properties from the context menu.

14. Enter **Time** in the FriendlyName property.

15. In the Tables list, right-click the FactInternetSales table and select Properties from the context menu.

16. Enter **Internet Sales** in the FriendlyName property.

Creating the Cube

The cube is created from the data view definition. Creating the cube is fairly simple when using the Cube wizard in the development environment. After the cube is defined, it can be deployed to Analysis Services where it will be ready for use in spreadsheets and scorecards.

Follow these steps to create a cube:

1. In the Solution Explorer, right-click the Cubes folder and select New Cube from the context menu.

2. When the Cube wizard starts, click the Next button on the welcome screen.

3. On the Select Build Method screen, accept the default settings by clicking the Next button.

4. On the Select Data Source View screen, select the view you created earlier and click the Next button. This will cause the wizard to scan for fact and dimension tables contained in the data warehouse.

5. On the Detecting Fact and Dimension Tables screen, click the Next button.

6. On the Identify Fact and Dimension Tables screen, select Time from the drop-down list labeled Time Dimension table.

7. Click the Next button.

8. On the Select Time Periods screen, map the Time Property Name column to the Time Table column according to Table 8-2.

Table 8-2. *Time Mappings*

Time Property Name	Time Table Column
Year	CalendarYear
Half Year	CalendarSemester
Quarter	CalendarQuarter
Month	EnglishMonthName
Date	FullDateAlternateKey

9. On the Select Time Periods screen, click the Next button.

10. On the Select Measures screen, clear the Promotion Key, Currency Key, Sales Territory Key, and Revision Number, because these are not actually measures you want to use in your cube. Figure 8-15 shows the selected measures.

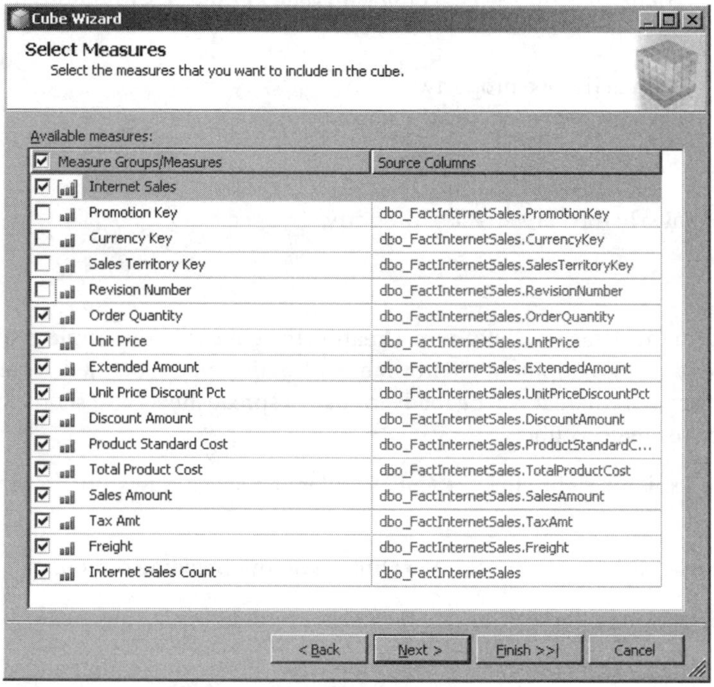

Figure 8-15. *Selecting measures*

11. Click the Next button.

12. On the Detecting Hierarchies screen, click the Next button.

13. On the Review New Dimensions screen, expand the Products node and the Attributes node. Uncheck the Large Photo attribute, because this field is so large it will have a negative impact on performance.

14. Click the Next button.

15. On the Completing the Wizard screen, click the Finish button.

16. Select Build ➤ DeployAWCube from the main menu.

Browsing the Cube in Excel

Once the cube is deployed, you can browse it with Excel. Excel will allow you to create a data connection to the cube using an Office Data Connection file. In this section, you will create an Office Data Connection file and use it to build a PivotTable against the deployed cube. This will give you an idea of how cubes work with Excel; however, you will not save this spreadsheet. This is because you will later upload the Office Data Connection file to SharePoint and recreate the spreadsheet to be deployed through Excel Services, which will allow the spreadsheet to appear in a SharePoint dashboard.

Follow these steps to browse the cube:

1. Log in to VSMOSS as a SharePoint administrator.

2. Select Start ➤ All Programs ➤ Microsoft Office ➤ Microsoft Office Excel 2007.

3. In Excel, click the Data tab.

4. Select From Other Sources ➤ From Analysis Services from the Data ribbon.

5. When the data connection wizard starts, enter **VSSQL** in the Server Name field and click the Next button.

6. In the Select Database and Table screen, select AWCube from the drop-down list and click the Next button.

7. On the Save Data Connection File and Finish screen, enter **AWCube.odc** in the File Name field.

8. Enter **AdventureWorks Cube** in the Friendly Name field.

9. Click the Finish button.

10. In the Import Data dialog, click the OK button.

11. In the PivotTable Field list pane, select Order Quantity and Sales Amount from the Internet Sales field list.

12. Select State Province Name – Geography from the Customer field list.

13. Select Model Name from the Product field list.

14. After browsing the data, close Excel. You do not have to save the spreadsheet because you will create a new one in the MOSS Report Center.

Adding the Data Connection

Once the Office Data Connection file is created, you can upload it to the data connection library associated with the Report Center. Connection files in the data connection library are trusted and can be used in spreadsheets and forms throughout SharePoint. Therefore, the best practice is to add connections to the data connection library rather than simply using them from a client machine.

Follow these steps to add the data connection file for the cube:

1. Open the home page of the intranet you created in Chapter 2.

2. Click the Reports tab to open the Report Center.

3. In the Report Center site, click the Data Connections link in the Quick Launch area.

4. In the data connection library, select New ➤ Office Data Connection File from the toolbar.

5. On the Upload Document page, click the Browse button.

6. In the Choose File dialog, navigate to My Document\My data Sources and locate the `AWCube.odc` file.

7. Select the `AWCube.odc` file and click the Open button.

8. On the Upload Document page, click the OK button.

9. On the Data Connections page, click the Check-In button.

10. In the data connection library, select Approve/Reject from the drop-down menu associated with the `AWCube.odc` file.

11. On the approval page, select the Approved option and click the OK button.

Creating a Report

After you have added the Office Data Connection file to the data connection library, you can use it to create a spreadsheet that is delivered through Excel Services. This will allow you to deliver the PivotTable through a web browser. Additionally, delivering the spreadsheet through the browser will make it possible to display it in a dashboard in the Report Center.

Follow these steps to create a new report:

1. In the Report Center site, click the Reports link in the Quick Launch area.

2. In the Reports Library, select New ➤ Report from the toolbar.

3. On the Reports Library page, enter **AWReport** in the Name field.

4. Enter **AdventureWorks Report** in the Title field.

5. Enter an owner for the report and click the OK button.

6. In the Reports Library, select Edit in Microsoft Office Excel from the drop-down menu associated with the new report.

7. In Microsoft Excel, click the Data tab.

8. In the Data ribbon, click the Connections button.

9. In the Workbook Connections dialog, click the Add button.

10. In the Existing Connections dialog, click the Browse for More button.

11. In the Select Data Source dialog, enter the URL for the data connection library in the Report Center (e.g., **http://vsmoss/Reports/Data%20Connections**).

12. Click the Open button.

13. Select the `AWCube.odc` file and click the Open button.

14. In the Workbook Connections dialog, click the Close button.

15. In the Data ribbon, click the Existing Connections button.

16. In the Existing Connections dialog, select the AdventureWorks Cube connection from the Connections in their Workbook section and click the Open button.

17. In the Import Data dialog, click the OK button.

18. In the PivotTable Field list pane, select Order Quantity and Sales Amount from the Internet Sales field list.

19. Select State Province Name – Geography from the Customer field list.

20. Select Model Name from the Product field list.

21. Save the spreadsheet and close Excel.

Building the Dashboard

The Report Center contains a library for creating dashboards. These dashboards are a combination of Excel Services spreadsheets and scorecards. In this section, you will create a new dashboard that uses the Excel spreadsheet you created earlier and creates a scorecard that displays KPIs.

Follow these steps to create a dashboard:

1. In the Report Center site, click the Dashboards link in the Quick Launch area.

2. In the Reports Library, select New ➤ Dashboard Page from the toolbar.

3. On the New Dashboard page, enter **AdventureWorks** in the File Name field.

4. Enter **AdventureWorks Dashboard** in the Page Title field.

5. In the Layout list, select One Column Vertical Layout.

6. Click the OK button.

Adding a Report

Reports are added to dashboards from Excel spreadsheets that can be deployed via Excel Services. In this section, you'll add the spreadsheet that you created earlier.

Follow these steps to add the report:

1. After the AdventureWorks dashboard is created, click the link titled Click Here to Open the Tool Pane under the Select a Workbook section.

2. In the tool pane, click the ellipsis next to the Workbook field.

3. In the Select a Link dialog, double-click the Reports Library.

4. Select the AWReport file and click the OK button.

5. In the tool pane, click the OK button.

Adding a KPI

KPIs are added to dashboards from any of several sources. You can add a KPI from a cube, a spreadsheet, or manually. In this section, you will add a KPI from the Excel spreadsheet you created earlier.

Follow these steps to add a KPI:

1. Select New ➤ Indicator Using Data in an Excel Workbook.

2. On the AdventureWorks KPI Definitions page, enter **Alberta Sales** in the Name field.

3. Click the Browse button next to the Workbook URL field.

4. In the Select a Link dialog, select the AWReport workbook and click the OK button.

5. Click the Select button next to the Cell Address field.

6. In the cell selection dialog, select the cell representing the total Alberta sales.

7. Click the Set button next to the field labeled Cell Address for Indicator Value.

8. Enter **35000** in the field labeled Cell Address for Indicator Goal.

9. Enter **20000** in the field labeled Cell Address for Indicator Warning.

10. Click the OK button.

11. On the AdventureWorks KPI Definitions page, click the OK button. Figure 8-16 shows the completed dashboard.

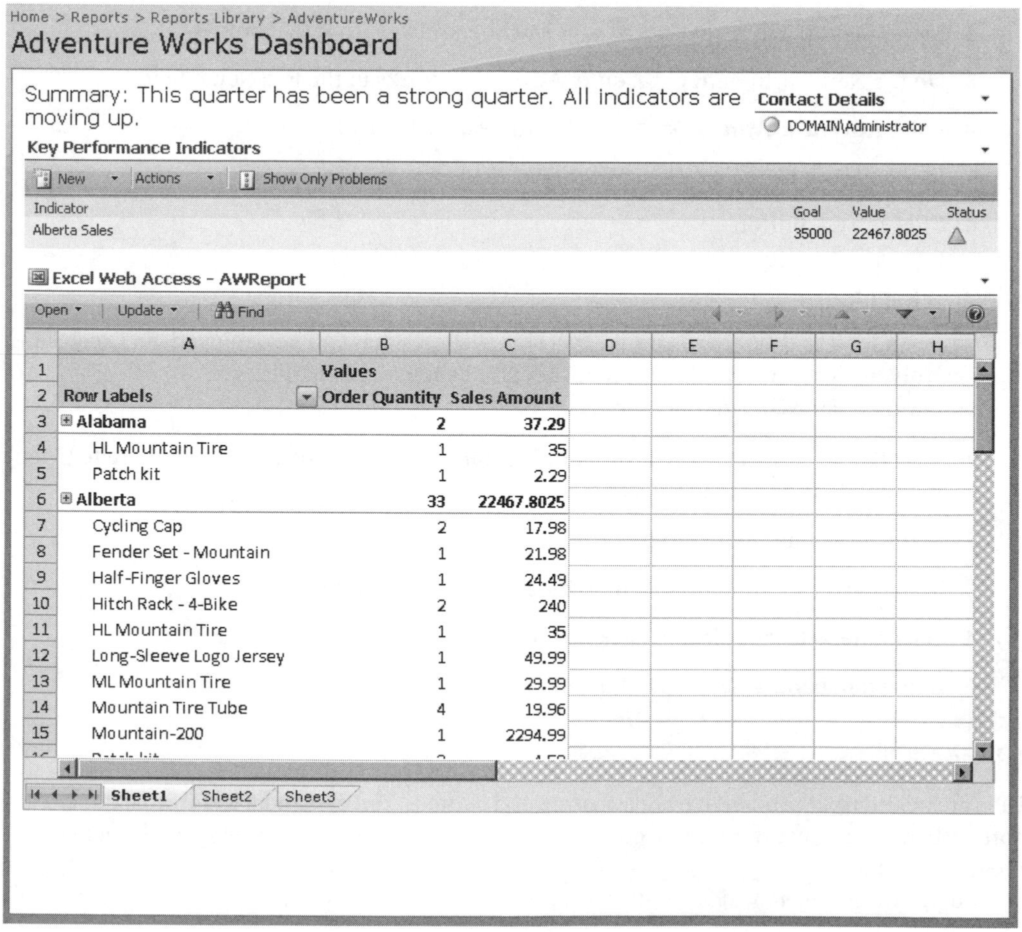

Figure 8-16. *The completed dashboard*

CHAPTER 9

SharePoint and Microsoft Office

Throughout this book, I have shown you the integration points between SharePoint and various Microsoft Office products. Generally, I have demonstrated integration points in context when those capabilities were related to the topic at hand. In this chapter, I will cover any additional integration points that have not been presented previously. I will also cover several aspects of custom development with Microsoft Office 2007 including the new open file formats and Visual Studio Tools for Office (VSTO). At the end of this chapter, you should have a strong understanding of all the techniques you can use to leverage Office in your SharePoint solutions.

Managing Document Information

At this point, you should be well-versed in the basic integration points between Office 2007 and SharePoint. You have seen and worked with both the Document Information Panel (DIP) and the Document Action Panel (DAP) in several places throughout the book. In this section, I cover some additional capabilities that you can use to enhance the integration between Office and SharePoint. I show you how to view related site data with the Document Management Information panel (which is different from the DIP), fill in document metadata values with Quick Parts, and customize the DIP with InfoPath.

Utilizing the Document Management Information Panel

The Document Management Information panel is a display present in Office 2003 that has been carried over to Office 2007. In Office 2003, this panel was called the Shared Workspace and presented information about the currently open document and the SharePoint site from which it originated. Although the panel has been renamed, it still presents the information as a series of five tabs named Status, Member, Tasks, Documents, and Links. Figure 9-1 shows a typical Document Management Information panel open in Word 2007.

The Status tab in the Document Management Information panel is used to present document status such as whether it is checked out and by whom. The Members tab lists all the users and groups that have access to the document. Additionally, if the members are running Microsoft Communicator or MSN Messenger, the tab will show *presence information*. Presence information indicates whether a user is online. Additionally, you can send e-mail and schedule meetings with members using the presence information interface. If a task list exists on the site, the Tasks tab will display the list. The Documents tab shows a list of documents that are in the same library as the currently open document. Finally, if there is a links list on the site, those links will appear in the Links tab.

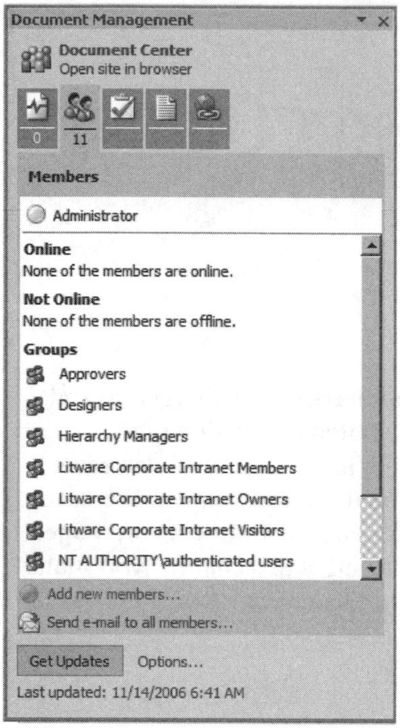

Figure 9-1. *A Document Management Information panel*

The Document Management Information panel does not open by default. If you want to see it, you can select Server ➤ Document Management Information from Word, Excel, or PowerPoint 2007. If you would like the panel to display every time you open a document that comes from a SharePoint library, you can configure it by clicking the Options link located on the Status tab.

Although the Document Management Information panel contains some useful information, you may be confused at first as to why you would see things such as tasks and links. These tabs appear primarily because the Document Management Information panel is actually designed to be used with a specific type of site called a Document Workspace. A Document Workspace is a site that is dedicated to the creation of a single document. You can create a Document Workspace directly from Word, Excel, or PowerPoint and then use it as a way to collaborate.

Follow these steps to create a Document Workspace:

1. Log in to VSCLIENT.

2. Select Start ➤ All Programs ➤ Microsoft Office ➤ Microsoft Office Word 2007.

3. In Word 2007, select Publish ➤ Create Document Workspace from the File menu. The Document Workspace creation panel will appear.

4. In the Document Workspace creation panel, select My Site from the drop-down list labeled Location for New Workspace.

5. Click the Create button.

6. When prompted, save the new document locally on VSCLIENT. You do not have to worry about the exact location because the document will be uploaded automatically to the new Document Workspace.

7. After the new Document Workspace is created, verify that the Document Management Information panel opens and click the link titled Open Site in Browser.

8. When the Site opens, verify that your document has been uploaded to the Shared Documents library. You can now invite others to this site to work on the document with you.

Using the Research Library

Using document workspaces through SharePoint helps end users assign tasks and assemble documents more easily when those documents are primarily built by teams. However, these collaboration features do not help the individual locate the actual information required to create the document. What is missing from the solution is a general tool that can bring back various types of information. This is where the Research Library comes into play. The Research Library is a general-purpose search tool that can search for information in reference books, line-of-business systems, the Internet, and even SharePoint. Out of the box, the Research Library provides access to several sources of information such as a dictionary and thesaurus.

The Research Library is accessible from the ribbon on the Review tab. On the Review tab, you'll find the Research button located in the Proofing group. Using the Research Library is straightforward regardless of the source you want to search. The end user simply selects a service and types a search string into the task pane. The Research Library then searches the selected service for responses to the search string. The responses vary depending upon the service. The Research Library might display definitions, alternative word choices, Internet hyperlinks, or any other kind of appropriate information. In many cases, you can then insert the information directly into your document.

The initial set of services that ship with Office 2003 are only moderately interesting, but the true value of the Research Library lies in the fact that you can extend the library to include SharePoint sites and other services. This is possible because the Research Library architecture is based on web services, and SharePoint web services can be used as a source for the Research Library.

To search a SharePoint Services site, follow these steps:

1. Open the Research Library in Microsoft Word by clicking the Review tab and then clicking the Research button.

2. At the bottom of the Research pane, click the Research Options link.

3. In the Research Options dialog, click the Add Services button.

4. In the Address box, type the URL **http://vsmoss/_vti_bin/search.asmx**.

5. Click Add.

6. In the Confirmation and Options dialog, click the Install button.

7. Close the Research Options dialog.

8. In the Research pane, select the SharePoint source from under the All Intranet Sites and Portals section of the drop-down list.

9. Type a search string into the Search For box and click the green arrow.

Working with Quick Parts

You have already seen in several examples how the DIP makes it easier for end users to fill in metadata for a document. The DIP presents the metadata fields in the document so that they can be filled in whenever the user knows the values. Additionally, the DIP can support elements such as lists to make it even easier to fill in valid data. While this approach is good, it certainly does not guarantee that good metadata is entered; after all, the end user could just simply type nonsense into the fields.

The solution to getting good metadata out of end users is to automatically populate the metadata from information in the document. This is where Quick Parts come into play. Quick Parts are a way to map the metadata fields in the DIP to text in the document template. In order to utilize Quick Parts, you should start with an existing content type for which you have already defined a template. Then you can enhance the content type with Quick Parts. As an example, you could take the Invoice content type you created in the exercise in Chapter 6 and enhance it to use Quick Parts.

If you completed Exercise 6-1, follow these steps to use Quick Parts:

1. Log in to VSCLIENT as a SharePoint administrator.

2. Navigate to the home page of the intranet site you created in Chapter 2.

3. Click the Document Center tab.

4. In the Document Center, click the Financial Documents library that you created in Exercise 6.1 in Chapter 6.

5. In the Financial Documents library, select New ➤ Invoice from the toolbar.

6. When the new Invoice document opens in Word, select the [Company Name] field in the body of the document and delete it.

7. Click the Insert tab.

8. On the Insert tab, select Quick Parts ➤ Document Property ➤ Client Name. A [Client Name] field should appear where the [Company Name] field was previously.

9. Click in the Job cell of the table in the Invoice document.

10. On the Insert tab, select Quick Parts ➤ Document Property ➤ Title. A [Title] field should now appear in the cell.

11. Select File ➤ Save As from the File menu and save the Enhanced Invoice document to your My Documents folder. You are going to use this as the template for a new content type.

12. Close Word and return to the home page of the intranet site you created in Chapter 2.

13. Select Site Settings ➤ Modify All Site Settings from the Site Action menu on the home page.

14. On the Site Settings page, click the Site Content Types link.

15. In the Site Content Type Gallery, click the Create link.

16. On the New Site Content Type page, enter **Enhanced Invoice** in the Name field.

17. Select Custom Financial Documents from the drop-down list labeled Select Parent Content Type From.

18. Select Invoice in the drop-down box labeled Parent Content Type.

19. Select Custom Financial Documents in the drop-down list labeled Existing Group.

20. Click the OK button to create the new content type.

21. In the Site Content Type Gallery, click the link for the new Enhanced Invoice.

22. On the Site Content Type page, click the Advanced Settings link.

23. On the Site Content Type Advanced Settings page, select the option to Upload a New Document Template and click the Browse button.

24. In the Choose File dialog, navigate to the My Documents folder and select the Enhanced Invoice template you saved earlier.

25. In the Choose File dialog, click the OK button.

26. On the Site Content Type Advanced Settings page, click the OK button.

27. Click the Document Center tab.

28. In the Document Center, click the Financial Documents library in the Quick Launch area.

29. Select Settings ➤ Document Library Settings from the toolbar.

30. On the Customize page, click the link titled Add from Existing Content Types.

31. On the Add Content Types page, select the Enhanced Invoice from the list labeled Available Site Content Types.

32. Click the OK button to add the content type to the Financial Documents library.

33. Return to the Financial Documents library and select New ➤ Enhanced Invoice from the toolbar.

34. When the new document opens, type a name in the Client Name metadata field in the Document Information Panel. Verify that the name appears in the document after you move the focus away.

35. Enter some text in the [Title] field in the Job cell of the document and verify that it appears in the Document Information Panel after you move the focus away.

Creating Custom Document Information Panels

Although SharePoint provides a default DIP for your content types, there may be times when you want to customize the DIP. Customizing the DIP is possible because the DIP is nothing more than an InfoPath form; therefore, you can add validation rules, format, graphics, or other elements to enhance the DIP. You may use any available InfoPath elements and functionality to create your custom DIP, but if you use elements that require full trust, the DIP must be signed just like any other InfoPath form.

Follow these steps to create a custom DIP:

1. Log in to VSCLIENT as a SharePoint administrator.

2. Navigate to the home page of the intranet site you created in Chapter 2.

3. Select Site Settings ➤ Modify All Site Settings from the Site Action menu on the home page.

4. On the Site Settings page, click the Site Content Types link.

5. In the Site Content Type Gallery, click the link for the Financial Document content type.

6. On the Site Content Type page, click the Document Information Panel Settings link.

7. On the Document Information Panel Settings page, click the link titled Create a New Custom Template.

8. When InfoPath starts, click the Finish button in the Data Source wizard.

9. When the DIP form appears, right-click the Amount field and select Text Box Properties from the context menu.

10. In the Text Box Properties dialog, click the Data Validation button.

11. In the Data Validation dialog, click the Add button.

12. In the Data Validation Condition dialog, select Is Less Than from the operator drop-down list.

13. Select Type a Number from the Argument list and enter **0**.

14. Enter **Value must be a positive number** in the Screen Tip field.

15. Click the OK button.

16. In the Data Validation dialog, click the OK button.

17. In the Text Box Properties dialog, click the Format button.

18. In the Decimal Format dialog, select 2 in the Decimal Places drop-down list.

19. Click the OK button.

20. In the Text Box Properties dialog, click the OK button.

21. Select File ➤ Save from the main menu.

22. In the Save As dialog, save the form as **CustomDIP.xsn** to the My Documents folder. The location is not critical because publishing the form will automatically upload it to SharePoint.

23. After the form is saved, click the Publish Form Template link in the Design Tasks pane.

24. In the Publishing Wizard, select to publish the form As a Document Information Panel Template for a SharePoint Site Content Type or List Content Type.

25. Click the Next button.

26. On the next screen, verify that the correct content type appears, and click the Publish button.

27. After the form is published, click the Close button and exit InfoPath.

28. In the browser, click the link titled Go Back to the Document Information Panel Settings Page.

29. On the Document Information Panel Settings page, click the OK button.

Now you should be able to return to the Financial Documents library, open any existing document, and see the custom DIP in action. Figure 9-2 shows the custom DIP identifying a validation error caused by a negative value and formatting the number to have two decimal places.

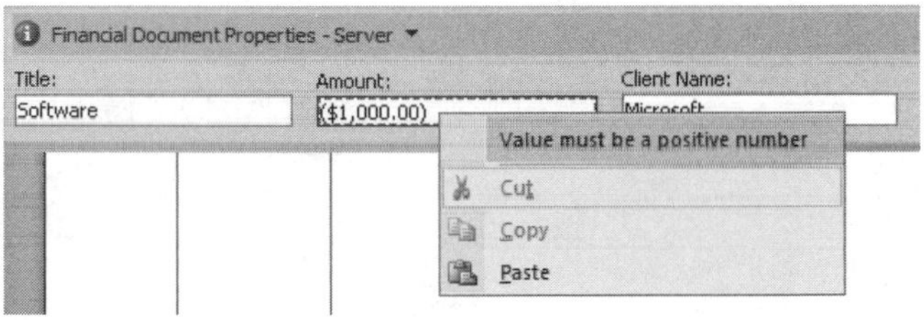

Figure 9-2. *A custom DIP*

Going Offline

Although the SharePoint interface could be used to access all manner of information and documents within an organization, most users still think of Microsoft Outlook as their "home base." Because the information in Outlook is personal in nature, it is the most logical choice to function as the center of a person's day. This means that many end users will want to leverage Outlook as much as possible for consuming information and only leave when it is absolutely necessary.

To this end, Outlook 2007 provides strong integration with SharePoint. In Chapter 3, I describe several of the key integration points between lists and Outlook. In particular, I show that you can synchronize lists with Outlook by selecting Actions ➤ Connect to Outlook from the drop-down menu on a list toolbar. This operation works not only for common lists such as tasks, contacts, and calendars, but also document libraries. In this way, a user can take documents offline from SharePoint, work on them locally, and upload them again at a later time.

When you take a document library offline, the list of available documents appears inside of Microsoft Outlook and is downloaded to an Outlook PST file named `SharePoint Lists.pst`. Outlook will allow you to preview the documents, but they are stored in the PST file as read-only copies. In order to make changes to the documents, they must be opened in the appropriate Office product and then edited offline.

Selecting to edit the document offline will save it into the folder My Documents\ SharePoint Drafts. Office keeps track of the fact that the document is being edited offline and allows you to synchronize it with SharePoint the next time you are online. Although you can check out a document before taking it offline, nothing prevents you from editing a document offline that you did not check out. In these cases, you may have several people making changes to the same document offline, resulting in conflicts that must be resolved during synchronization. Document conflicts such as these are handled by the Office product itself using the Document Updates pane. This pane allows you to merge conflicting changes, open both conflicting documents, and make manual changes, or simply write your changes over the saved changes. Figure 9-3 shows the Document Updates pane.

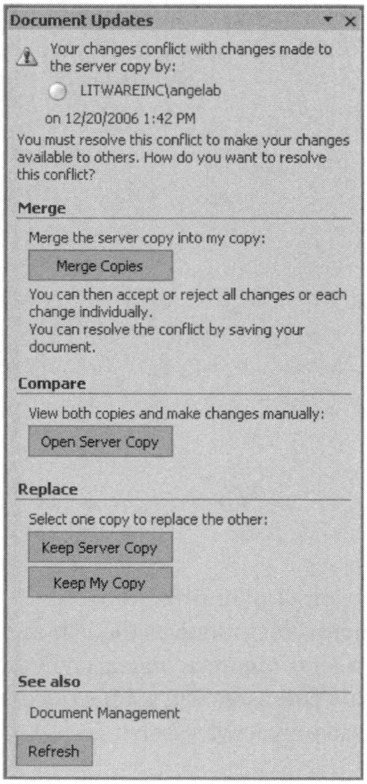

Figure 9-3. *Resolving document conflicts*

■**Note** There is no way to prevent Outlook from downloading all of the documents in a library when you go offline. While this makes it easy to grab a library and run, it also means that you can be downloading a significant amount of information. Documents that are candidates for offline use should be segregated into separate smaller libraries to make downloading efficient.

Going Mobile

Support for mobile devices is now built in to SharePoint through a set of pages located in the folder C:\Program Files\Common Files\Microsoft Shared\web server extensions\12\ TEMPLATE\LAYOUTS\MOBILE. The pages support a default mobile view for any site in SharePoint by simply navigating to the address of the home page with /_layouts/mobile/ default.aspx appended. For example, you can view the home page of your intranet by navigating to http://vsmoss/intranet/_layouts/mobile/default.aspx.

While you can certainly view the mobile pages in your desktop browser, it is much more useful to view them as they will actually appear in a device. In order to accomplish this, you can utilize the device emulator that is part of Visual Studio 2005. This emulator simulates several different devices on your desktop so you can target your development. In order to get the emulator working, however, you have to set it up as if you were synchronizing an actual mobile device.

Follow these steps to view your sites in the device emulator:

1. Log in to VSMOSS as a local administrator.

2. Download and install the ActiveSync 4.2 software from http://www.microsoft.com/ windowsmobile/downloads/activesync42.mspx. This software is used to connect mobile devices to your desktop.

3. Select Start ➤ All Programs ➤ Microsoft Visual Studio 2005.

4. Select Tools ➤ Device Emulator Manager from the main menu in Visual Studio.

5. In the Device Emulator Manager dialog, select Pocket PC 2003 SE Emulator.

6. Select Actions ➤ Connect. The emulator should appear in a new window.

7. Select Start ➤ All Programs ➤ Microsoft ActiveSync to start ActiveSync, which will now wait for a device to be cradled.

8. In the Device Emulator Manager dialog, make sure that the Pocket PC 2003 SE Emulator is selected. Select Actions ➤ Cradle from the menu. The New Partnership wizard should appear.

9. In the New Partnership wizard, select Guest Partnership and click the Next button.

10. When the Microsoft ActiveSync dialog indicates that the device is connected, select Start ➤ Internet Explorer in the Pocket PC 2003 Emulator.

11. Enter **http://vsmoss/intranet/_layouts/mobile/default.aspx** in the address bar and click the green arrow to open the page. You should now see the mobile version of the intranet home page.

When you first view a site through the emulator, you'll see a page with links to the standard lists and libraries such as Announcements, Tasks, and Shared Documents. If you want to add other lists to the mobile view, you must explicitly designate a list view as mobile. This is accomplished from the Edit View page associated with the view you want to display. The Mobile section contains options that you can select to make the view mobile as well as make it the default mobile view for the list. Figure 9-4 shows the Mobile section on the Edit View page.

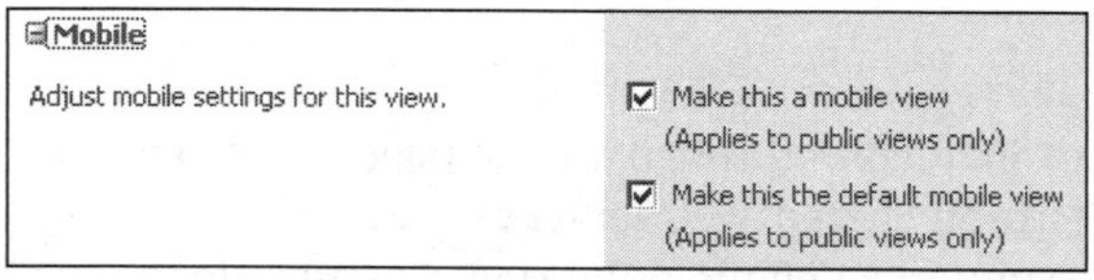

Figure 9-4. *Designating mobile views*

In addition to exposing lists for mobile consumption, you can also create your own custom pages for use with mobile devices. When you create your own custom pages, you can tailor them for display on a specific device. Additionally, you can utilize SharePoint object model code in the page. Developing for mobile devices is another broad category that goes beyond the scope of this book, but you can create some simple pages for mobile devices quite easily in Visual Studio.

Follow these steps to create a home page for a mobile device that displays all the sites in a collection:

1. With Visual Studio 2005 still open from the previous example, select File ➤ New ➤ Web Site from the main menu.

2. In the New Web Site dialog, select ASP.NET Web Site from the list of templates.

3. Select File System from the Location drop-down list.

4. Select Visual C# from the Language list.

5. Click the OK button.

6. When the new project opens, select the `Default.aspx` page in the Solution Explorer and delete it.

7. Right-click the project in the Solution Explorer and select Add New Item from the context menu.

8. In the Add New Item dialog, select Mobile Web Form.

9. Name the new form **Home.aspx**.

10. Make sure the box labeled Place Code in a Separate File is not checked. You cannot use code-behind in this solution.

11. Click the Add button.

12. When the new page opens, add the bolded code in Listing 9-1 to the page. This code adds references to the SharePoint object model and then uses the object model to get the address for each site in the collection. The address is then displayed in a new instance of a mobile `Link` control. I cover the SharePoint object model in detail in Chapter 11.

Listing 9-1. *A Mobile Home Page*

```
<%@ Page Language="C#" Inherits="System.Web.UI.MobileControls.MobilePage" %>
<%@ Assembly Name="Microsoft.SharePoint, Version=12.0.0.0,
            Culture=neutral, PublicKeyToken=71e9bce111e9429c"%>
<%@ Import Namespace="Microsoft.SharePoint" %>
<%@ Import Namespace="Microsoft.SharePoint.WebControls" %>
<%@ Import Namespace="System.Web.UI.MobileControls" %>
<%@ Register TagPrefix="mobile" Namespace="System.Web.UI.MobileControls"
    Assembly="System.Web.Mobile" %>

<script language="c#" runat="server">

    public void Page_Load()
    {
        SPSite site = SPControl.GetContextSite(Context);
        SPWebCollection webs = site.AllWebs;

        foreach (SPWeb web in webs)
        {
            Link webLink = new Link();
            webLink.NavigateUrl = web.Url +
              "/_layouts/mobile/default.aspx";
            webLink.Text = web.Title;
            welcomeForm.Controls.Add(webLink);

        }
    }

</script>

<html xmlns="http://www.w3.org/1999/xhtml" >
<body>
    <mobile:Form ID="welcomeForm" Runat="server">
        <mobile:Image ID="bannerImage" Runat="server"
        ImageUrl="../images/addtofavorites.gif">
        </mobile:Image>List of Sites<br />
    </mobile:Form>
</body>
</html>
```

13. Once you have edited the code, save your work.

14. Open the File Explorer and locate the `Home.aspx` page. Copy this page in to the LAYOUTS\MOBILE directory.

15. Using the mobile emulator that you opened earlier, navigate to the address `http://vsmoss/intranet/_layouts/mobile/home.aspx`. You should now see a list of available sites with links. Figure 9-5 shows the resulting page displaying various sites.

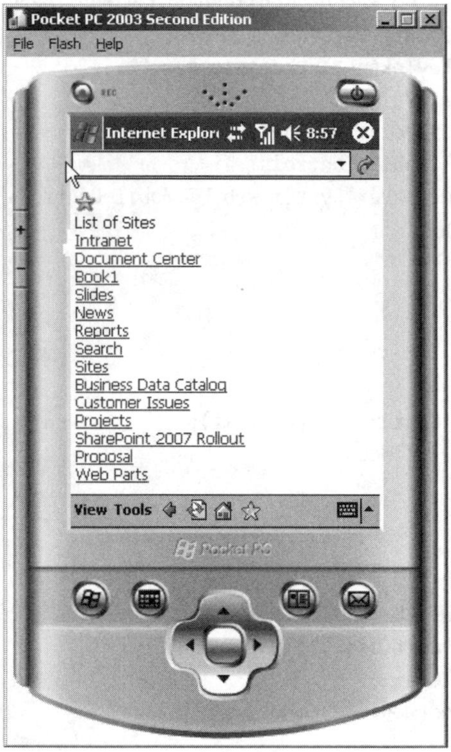

Figure 9-5. *A custom mobile welcome page*

Using the Office Open XML File Formats

Microsoft Word, Excel, and PowerPoint have new default XML file formats designed to make Office 2007 more extensible and interoperable. Throughout the book, you have made documents in these new formats, saved them to libraries, and used them for content types. As a user, you might not have even realized that a new file format was in use unless you noticed the new DOCX, XLSX, or PPTX file extensions.

The new file formats are based on the XML Paper Specification written by Microsoft. The idea is to create an open standard for document definitions so that they may be viewed in different tools and transformed between systems. All of this is intended to support interoperability between systems. Saving documents in the older format is still supported as an option, but you must explicitly select it in the Save dialog. As SharePoint developers, we care about these new file formats because they allow us to manipulate documents outside of Word, Excel, and PowerPoint.

In earlier versions of Office, the file format was a proprietary binary format that was completely undocumented. From a development perspective, the only way to manipulate a document was to use the object model through automation. This meant starting Word or Excel programmatically and then executing operations against it, such as creating new documents, importing data, or printing reports.

The problem with automating Word and Excel is that they were never intended to function as server products, but they were often deployed on servers to centralize the automation. Furthermore, the instances started in automation never really seemed to shut down. I have seen many Word and Excel automation applications that left countless copies running on the server. Generally, no one realized this was happening until the server ground to a crawl from lack of resources.

As Office moved forward, Microsoft tried to better this situation by introducing various levels of XML support and new ways to develop with Office applications. While these efforts improved some aspects of development, we were still never able to completely divorce ourselves from Word and Excel. The new XML file formats finally change that situation. Now we can write document-based applications without ever starting a copy of Word or Excel.

Understanding Document Packages

The new Office file formats consist of many different XML files all contained in a compressed ZIP file. This compressed ZIP file is called a *document package* and contains all of the content in a document including text, images, comments, change tracking, properties, and so on. Word, Excel, and PowerPoint all employ this same basic format but utilize different file extensions to designate documents, templates, and macros. Table 9-1 lists all of the file extensions for Word, Excel, and PowerPoint, and the associated document type.

Table 9-1. *Office 2007 File Extensions*

Extension	Document Type
DOCX	Word 2007 document
DOTX	Word 2007 template
DOCM	Word 2007 document containing macros
DOTM	Word 2007 template containing macros
XLSX	Excel 2007 document
XLTX	Excel 2007 template
XLSM	Excel 2007 document containing macros
XLTM	Excel 2007 template containing macros
PPTX	PowerPoint 2007 document
POTX	PowerPoint 2007 template
PPTM	PowerPoint 2007 document containing macros
POTM	PowerPoint 2007 template containing macros

The simplest way to become familiar with the file formats is to create a new document and then extract the package contents. This is possible because the package is simply a ZIP file. You can use standard ZIP utilities to open the package and view its contents.

Follow these steps to extract package contents:

1. Log in to VSCLIENT.

2. Select Start ➤ All Programs ➤ Microsoft Office ➤ Microsoft Office Word 2007.

3. In Word 2007, select New from the File menu.

4. In the New Document dialog, select memos from the Templates list.

5. Select Memo (Contemporary Design) from the Memos list view.

6. Click the Download button to download the new template from the Microsoft site.

7. When the new memo appears, click the Insert tab.

8. On the Insert tab, click the Picture button.

9. In the Insert Picture dialog, open the Sample Pictures folder.

10. Select a sample picture from the folder and click the Insert button.

11. Select Save from the File menu.

12. Save the document as `Memorandum.docx` to the My Documents folder.

13. Exit Word 2007.

14. Open the File Explorer and navigate to the My Documents folder.

15. In the My Documents folder, create a new folder named Package.

16. Right-click the `Memorandum.docx` file and select Rename from the context menu.

17. Rename the file to **Memorandum.docx.zip**.

18. Right-click the `Memorandum.docx.zip` file and select Open With ➤ Compressed (zipped) Folders.

19. Copy the contents from the open ZIP folder into the Package folder.

Once you have the file extracted, you will see that the package is made up of many files with XML extensions, one file with a JPEG extension, and several files with RELS extensions. Each of the XML files in the package is referred to as a *Part Item*. Resource files stored in the package, such as images, are referred to as *Content Type Items* (not to be confused with *content types* in SharePoint). The files with the RELS extensions are referred to as *Relationship Items* because they define the relationships between the Part Items and Content Type Items.

You'll also notice in the File Explorer that the package files have a certain folder structure. Initially, this may lead you to believe that the folder structure is specified as part of the package file format. However, this is not the case. The parts and content types are held together by the relationships, which are independent of any particular file folder structure.

Understanding the package structure begins by examining the `[Content_Types].xml` file. This file lists all of the parts in the package and their associated content type. If you examine this file, you'll see references to various parts of the document, including the document body, headers, footers, and styles. Listing 9-2 shows some sample entries from the `[Content_Types].xml` file.

Listing 9-2. *The [Content_Type].xml File*

```
<Override PartName="/word/document.xml"
ContentType="application/vnd.openxmlformats-➥
officedocument.wordprocessingml.document.main+xml"/>

<Override PartName="/word/styles.xml"
ContentType=
    "application/vnd.openxmlformats-officedocument.wordprocessingml.styles+xml"/>

<Override PartName="/word/settings.xml"
ContentType="application/vnd.openxmlformats-
officedocument.wordprocessingml.settings+xml"/>

<Override PartName="/word/footer2.xml"
ContentType="application/vnd.openxmlformats-
officedocument.wordprocessingml.footer+xml"/>
```

The entries in the `[Content_Types].xml` file define names for the parts using the `PartName` attribute. These entries could be changed to any name and are not related to the package structure. The `ContentType` attribute specifies the actual type of information that is found in the part item. The `+xml` suffix designates the part item as an XML file.

Because the part items are all XML files, you can open these and examine the contents as well. For example, the `document.xml` file contains the bulk of the content for the memorandum document. If you open this document in Visual Studio, you'll see that the XML file has text from the memo and a reference to the picture that you inserted into the body. Any changes made to this file will impact the document as it appears in Word.

Follow these steps to make a document change:

1. With the `Memorandum.docx.zip` file still open in the My Documents window, drag the `document.xml` file onto the desktop. Be sure to take this file from the compressed files and not the files you extracted earlier.

2. Right-click the `document.xml` file and select Open With ➤ Notepad from the context menu.

3. Select Edit ➤ Find from the menu.

4. In the Find dialog, type **How to Use This Memo Template** and click the Find Next button.

5. In the Find dialog, click the Cancel button to close it after the search text is located.

6. Change the selected text to read **How to Change the Text in a Document**.

7. Select File ➤ Save from the menu and close Notepad.

8. Carefully drag the `document.xml` file from your desktop back into the open `Memorandum.docx.zip` file.

9. In the File Explorer, rename the file `Memorandum.docx` and open it in Word 2007. You should now see your changes.

The structure of the package is defined by the relationship files. *Relationship* files are XML files that map content types to specific directories within the structure. This is what allows Word to assemble the document from the part items. Each entry in the file uses a `Type` attribute for a content type, and a `Target` attribute to reference a file. Listing 9-3 shows a relationship file from the sample in this chapter. Note how it maps the `document.xml` file you edited earlier.

Listing 9-3. *A Relationship File*

```
<?xml version="1.0" encoding="UTF-8" standalone="yes"?>
<Relationships
xmlns="http://schemas.openxmlformats.org/package/2006/relationships">

<Relationship Id="rId3"
Type="http://schemas.openxmlformats.org/officeDocument/2006/relationships➡
/extended-properties"
Target="docProps/app.xml"/>

<Relationship Id="rId2"
Type="http://schemas.openxmlformats.org/package/2006/relationships➡
/metadata/core-properties"
Target="docProps/core.xml"/>

<Relationship Id="rId1"
Type="http://schemas.openxmlformats.org/officeDocument/2006/relationships➡
/officeDocument"
Target="word/document.xml"/>

<Relationship Id="rId4"
Type="http://schemas.openxmlformats.org/officeDocument/2006/relationships➡
/custom-properties"
Target="docProps/custom.xml"/>

</Relationships>
```

Using System.IO.Packaging

While making changes to part items in a package is a neat trick, it's definitely not the way that you want to go about creating production applications with Office 2007. If you did, your application would have to parse countless lines of XML, searching for key elements to replace. That would be maddening to say the least. Fortunately, Microsoft has provided us with an additional layer of abstraction for working with packages in the form of the `System.IO.Packaging` namespace.

The Packaging namespace provides a set of classes that allow you to deal with the constituent parts of a package instead of the raw XML. The Package class represents the entire package file created by Word, Excel, or PowerPoint. You can use this class to open existing files or create new ones. The PackagePart class represents all of the part items inside the package file. You can use this class to add or edit part items. The PackageRelationship class represents all of the relationships in the package file. You can use this class to locate dependent parts.

The System.IO.Packaging namespace is part of the .NET Framework 3.0. You installed the .NET Framework 3.0 on VSMOSS (or VSWSS) when you created the development environment outlined in Chapter 2. In order to use the Packaging namespace, you must set a reference to it in Visual Studio 2005. However, the assembly containing the namespace is not easy to find initially. That's because it is located at C:\Program Files\Reference Assemblies\Microsoft\Framework\v3.0\WindowsBase.dll, which is an odd place to put an assembly. Nonetheless, you can browse there and set a reference.

Once you set a reference to the WindowsBase assembly, you can add some using statements to your code to make the appropriate namespaces available. You'll want to add not only the System.IO.Packaging namespace, but also the System.Xml namespace. Although the Packaging namespace makes development easier, it does not completely eliminate the need to deal with XML.

If you are going to read a file, the first thing you need to do is open it with the Package class. The Open method of the Package class allows you to open files for reading or writing. Listing 9-4 shows some simple code to open a file passed in as an argument to a console application.

Listing 9-4. *Opening an Office 2007 File*

```
using System;
using System.Collections.Generic;
using System.Text;
using System.IO;
using System.Xml;
using System.IO.Packaging;

namespace PackageItems
{
    class Program
    {
        private const string wordSpace =
            @"http://schemas.openxmlformats.org/wordprocessingml/2006/main";

        static void Main(string[] args)
        {
            try
            {
                using (Package package = Package.Open
                    (args[0], FileMode.Open, FileAccess.ReadWrite))
```

```
                {
                        //Work is done here on the file
                }
        }
        catch (Exception x)
        {
                Console.WriteLine(x.Message);
        }
    }
  }
}
```

Once the document is open, the next thing you want to do is locate the part items that you want to manipulate. In this example, I will simply print out all of the lines of text in the open document. In order to print out the text, I need to load the document.xml part into a stream and then use XPath to return all of the elements named <w:t> in the file, which is the element Word 2007 uses to mark text. Listing 9-5 shows the code that would be placed inside of Listing 9-4 as designated by the comment in that listing.

Listing 9-5. *Printing Out Text Elements from a Word File*

```
//Get the document part and load it into XML document
Uri uriDocument = new Uri("/word/document.xml", UriKind.Relative);
PackagePart documentPart = package.GetPart(uriDocument);

Stream partStream = package.GetPart(uriDocument).GetStream(
    FileMode.Open, FileAccess.ReadWrite);

NameTable nameTable = new NameTable();
XmlNamespaceManager manager = new XmlNamespaceManager(nameTable);
manager.AddNamespace("w", wordSpace);

XmlDocument document = new XmlDocument(nameTable);
document.Load(partStream);

XmlNodeList textNodes = document.SelectNodes("//w:t", manager);
foreach (XmlNode textNode in textNodes)
    {
        Console.WriteLine(textNode.InnerText);
    }
```

In Listing 9-5 notice that you can locate a part in the package by using the relative URI. You can obtain the URI by examining the relation parts in the package. Once you have a PackagePart object, you can open the XML file into a Stream object. Along with the Stream object, you'll want to create an XmlNamespaceManager object so that you can load the stream into an XmlDocument object and use XPath to access the elements. At that point, you simply process the XmlNode objects.

When you want to process all the nodes of a certain type, you can simply return them all through XPath. If you only want to process a single node, however, then you need some way to identify it in the file. Marking elements in the file can be accomplished by inserting a bookmark near the text of interest, using a field as a placeholder, or by superimposing your own XML schema over the Word document as you could do in Office 2003.

If you want to create a file from scratch, you have to create the part items, the relationships, and the package itself. This process is simple in concept but challenging and tedious in practice. This is because you must first create the part items in accordance with the proper schema for Word, Excel, or PowerPoint. Then you must create relationships for these parts. Finally, you create the package and place the parts and relationships inside.

Listing 9-6 shows a complete example of a console application that creates a Word document with a file name specified by the first argument and containing text specified in the second argument. There is also a complete exercise at the end of this chapter that uses the Open XML file formats to create a SharePoint feature that removes tracked changes and comments from a document.

■Tip To get help with schema documentation, visit the XML in Office Developer Portal at `http://msdn2.microsoft.com/en-us/office/aa905545.aspx`. Here you will find documentation, blogs, and video presentations about using the Open XML file formats.

Listing 9-6. *Creating a Word Document Programmatically*

```
using System;
using System.Collections.Generic;
using System.Text;
using System.IO;
using System.Xml;
using System.IO.Packaging;

namespace MakePackage
{
  class Program
  {
    private const string wordSpace =
    @"http://schemas.openxmlformats.org/wordprocessingml/2006/main";
    private const string partType = @"application/vnd.openxmlformats-➥
officedocument.wordprocessingml.document.main+xml";
    private const string partUri =
    @"http://schemas.openxmlformats.org/officeDocument/2006/relationships➥
/officeDocument";
    private const string partId = "rId1";

    static void Main(string[] args)
    {
```

```csharp
try
{
  using (Package package = Package.Open(
    args[0], FileMode.CreateNew, FileAccess.ReadWrite))
  {

    //Build the document.xml file with text in it
    XmlDocument documentXml = new XmlDocument();

    XmlElement documentElement = documentXml.CreateElement(
      "w:document", wordSpace);
    documentXml.AppendChild(documentElement);

    XmlElement bodyElement = documentXml.CreateElement(
      "w:body", wordSpace);
    documentElement.AppendChild(bodyElement);

    XmlElement pElement = documentXml.CreateElement("w:p", wordSpace);
    bodyElement.AppendChild(pElement);

    XmlElement rElement = documentXml.CreateElement("w:r", wordSpace);
    pElement.AppendChild(rElement);

    XmlElement tElement = documentXml.CreateElement("w:t", wordSpace);
    rElement.AppendChild(tElement);

    XmlNode tNode = documentXml.CreateNode(
      XmlNodeType.Text, "w:t", wordSpace);
    tNode.Value = args[1];
    tElement.AppendChild(tNode);

    //Create the part item for document.xml
    Uri Uri = new Uri("/word/document.xml", UriKind.Relative);
    PackagePart partDocumentXML = package.CreatePart(Uri,partType);
    StreamWriter stream = new
    StreamWriter(partDocumentXML.GetStream(
      FileMode.Create, FileAccess.Write));
    documentXml.Save(stream);
    stream.Close();
    package.Flush();

    //Create relationship for document.xml
    package.CreateRelationship(Uri, TargetMode.Internal, partUri, partId);
```

```
            package.Flush();
            package.Close();
        }
    }
    catch (Exception x)
    {
        Console.WriteLine(x.Message);
    }
}
}
}
```

Developing with Visual Studio Tools for Office

Although Office 2007 and SharePoint have many powerful integration points that require little or no effort on your part, if you want complete control over the appearance and functionality of Office 2007 products you should investigate the Visual Studio 2005 Tools for the 2007 Office System. This release of the Visual Studio Tools for Office is sometimes referred to as *Second Edition* to differentiate it from the first edition that primarily targeted Office 2003. Therefore, you'll often see the acronym VSTO 2005 SE associated with these tools.

VSTO 2005 SE is important because it brings the managed code development model to Office 2007 and lets you create add-ins, custom tabs, and custom task panes using Visual Studio as the development environment. Furthermore, you can deploy these customized documents as templates for content types in SharePoint. This experience stands in contrast to the Visual Basic for Applications (VBA) programming model, which is still available within Office products but does not support the .NET Framework. In this section, I show you how to get up and running with VSTO 2005 SE and give you some ideas of ways to use it with SharePoint.

Creating a Development Environment

In order to create VSTO 2005 SE solutions, you must install Microsoft Office 2007 on the machine where you will be developing. Additionally, you must be sure to install both Visual Basic for Applications (VBA) support and the Microsoft Office Primary Interop Assemblies (PIA). Installing VBA is required to support the development environment, while PIA are the COM assemblies required to integrate managed code with Office. Because your development environment was initially set up with a separate client, you'll need to install Microsoft Office on VSMOSS (or VSWSS) as part of the setup.

Follow these steps to install Microsoft Office 2007 in support of VSTO 2005 SE:

1. Log in to VSMOSS (or VSWSS) as a local administrator.

2. Start the installation for Microsoft Office 2007.

3. When prompted, enter your product key and accept the license agreement as normal.

4. On the Choose the Installation You Want screen, click the Customize button.

5. In the Installation Options, select to only install Microsoft Excel, InfoPath, Outlook, PowerPoint, and Word.

6. For each installed application, expand the options tree and ensure that the .NET Programmability Support option is enabled for installation. Figure 9-6 shows the Installation Options screen with the .NET Programmability option selected for Word.

7. Expand the Office Shared Features tree and ensure that Visual Basic for Applications is selected to install.

8. Click the Install Now button.

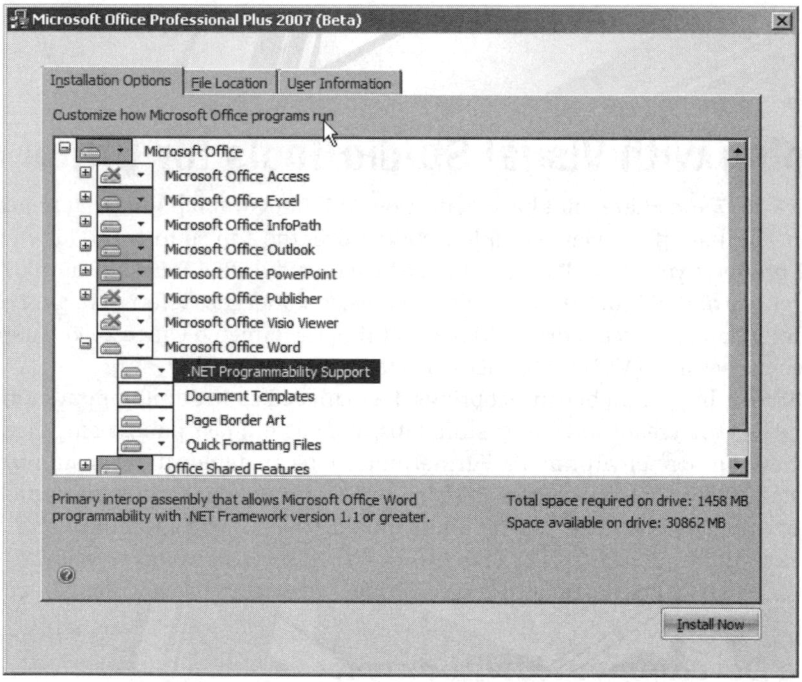

Figure 9-6. *Installing Office 2007 to support VSTO 2005 SE*

Once you have Microsoft Office 2007 installed, you can install VSTO 2005 SE. VSTO 2005 SE is available as a download from the Microsoft site. The simplest way to access the download is to visit the Visual Studio Tools for Office Developer Portal located at http://msdn2.microsoft.com/en-us/office/aa905543.aspx. Once you have the software downloaded, run the installation. The installation process is straightforward and requires no special configuration. Once you have completed the installation, you are ready to create projects.

All VSTO 2005 SE projects, whether they are add-ins, custom tabs, or custom task panes, are started in the same way. Inside of Visual Studio 2005, you select File ➤ New ➤ Project from the main menu. In the New Project dialog, you will see a project type named Office 2007 Add-Ins with templates corresponding to each of the Office applications you can target. You simply select the target application and create a new project. Figure 9-7 shows the New Project dialog in Visual Studio.

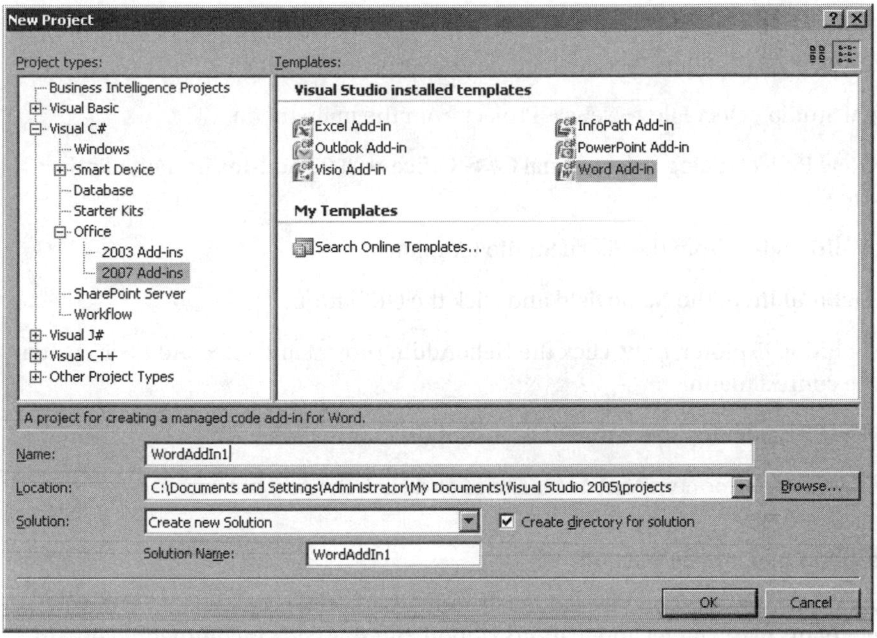

Figure 9-7. *Starting a VSTO 2005 SE project*

When you create a new project in VSTO 2005 SE, you get a new project template that has many of the components you need already stubbed out. The project itself comes with a class module that has several key namespaces referenced and some placeholders for code that should execute when the add-in starts up or shuts down. Additionally, the Add New Item dialog is populated with templates to support add-in development.

Along with the components and stubbed-out code, the new solution also contains a setup project. This setup project is suitable for deploying add-ins directly to client machines. Creating an add-in and making it available to clients using the project templates can be a fairly simple process.

Creating Office 2007 Add-Ins

Office 2007 supports the concept of an add-in that lets you add custom functionality to Office applications through the use of buttons that appear on the ribbon. Typically, add-ins are initiated by interacting with buttons on the ribbon that in turn exercise the application object model to achieve some functionality. For example, you could place a button on the Insert tab that adds a standard legal disclaimer to a document when it is pushed. The actual functionality of an add-in is limited only by what you can do with the .NET Framework and the object model of the targeted Office application.

Once you have started a new project in Visual Studio that targets a particular application, you can add buttons to the ribbon by using the Ribbon Support component. The Ribbon Support component is available in the Add New Item dialog. When you add this component, VSTO 2005 SE adds a new class to your project along with an XML file that holds button definitions.

Follow these steps to start a new add-in project:

1. Select Start ➤ All Programs ➤ Visual Studio 2005 ➤ Visual Studio 2005.

2. In Visual Studio, select File ➤ New ➤ Project from the main menu.

3. In the New Project dialog, select Visual C# ➤ Office ➤ 2007 Add-Ins from the Project Types tree.

4. Select Word Add-In from the Visual Studio templates.

5. Enter **HelloAddIn** in the Name field and click the OK button.

6. In the Solution Explorer, right-click the HelloAddIn project and select Add ➤ New Item from the context menu.

7. In the New Item dialog, select the Ribbon Support component.

8. Name the new component **MyAddInsTab.cs** and click the Add button.

Loading the Ribbon Support Component

When the Ribbon Support component is added, it comes with some code to automatically add the new elements to the target application's ribbon, but this code is commented out. In order to load your new elements, you simply have to uncomment this code, which overrides the RequestService method of the add-in. This is the method that is called when the Office application loads your Ribbon Support component. The code in Listing 9-7 shows the uncommented code from the MyAddInsTab.cs file.

Listing 9-7. *The RequestService Method*

```
public partial class ThisAddIn
{
    private MyAddInsTab ribbon;

    protected override object RequestService(Guid serviceGuid)
    {
        if (serviceGuid == typeof(Office.IRibbonExtensibility).GUID)
        {
            if (ribbon == null)
                ribbon = new MyAddInsTab();
            return ribbon;
        }

        return base.RequestService(serviceGuid);
    }
}
```

Adding Buttons to a Tab

Along with the code file, the Ribbon Support component also provides an XML file that defines what buttons appear in the ribbon. By default, this file comes with a toggle button defined. This type of button has two states: up and down. You could use this type of button to enable and disable parts of your add-in. However, you can also use many other controls such as buttons, check boxes, and lists.

As with all XML editing, it can be difficult to correctly define the elements. Therefore, you'll want to set a schema reference to the `CustomUI.xsd` schema, which contains the definitions for the control types. This schema can be found at C:\Program Files\Microsoft Visual Studio 8\Xml\Schemas\1033. In my example, I simply want to add a new button to the existing Insert tab. Therefore, I changed the `MyAddInsTab.xml` file to appear as shown in Listing 9-8.

Listing 9-8. *MyAddInsTab.xml Defining a Single Button*

```
<customUI xmlns=http://schemas.microsoft.com/office/2006/01/customui
  onLoad="OnLoad">
  <ribbon>
    <tabs>
      <tab idMso="TabInsert">
        <group id="HelloGroup" label="My Add-In">
          <button id="helloButton" label="Insert Hello,World!"
                  screentip="Say Hello" onAction="helloButton_Click"
                  supertip="Inserts Hello, World into the document."/>
        </group>
      </tab>
    </tabs>
  </ribbon>
</customUI>
```

The `customUI` element contains the entire definition for the groups and controls that will be added to the ribbon. The `onLoad` attribute of this element references a callback method in the associated code file that runs when the controls are loaded. The `ribbon` element contains a `tabs` element with multiple `tab` elements for customizing any tab within the application. Each `tab` element contains an `idMso` attribute for designating the target tab. This attribute is always the word `Tab` plus the name of the tab as it appears in the application. Additionally, you can specify a `tab` element with a custom `id` attribute and custom `label` attribute that will generate a new tab on the ribbon. Listing 9-9 shows how you would modify Listing 9-8 to show the button on a new tab named My Tab.

Listing 9-9. *Creating a New Tab*

```
<customUI xmlns=http://schemas.microsoft.com/office/2006/01/customui
  onLoad="OnLoad">
  <ribbon>
    <tabs>
      <tab id="MyTab" label="My Tab">
        <group id="HelloGroup" label="My Add-In">
          <button id="helloButton" label="Insert Hello,World!"
                  screentip="Say Hello" onAction="helloButton_Click"
                  supertip="Inserts Hello, World into the document."/>
```

```
        </group>
      </tab>
    </tabs>
  </ribbon>
</customUI>
```

The group element is used to create a new group within the targeted tab. Within the group, you can specify box, button, buttonGroup, checkbox, comboBox, control, dialogBoxLauncher, dropdown, dynamicMenu, editBox, label, labelControl, menu, separator, splitButton, or toggleButton, which all represent different UI elements. These elements support action attributes that let you specify a callback function to receive events for the element.

In my example, I defined a single button with a callback method named helloButton_Click. Therefore, I will need to define the callback function inside the code file of the Ribbon Support component. In the code file, you will find a region named Ribbon Callbacks. This is the region where the callback functions should be defined. By default, the region already contains a callback for OnLoad and a callback for the default toggle button that was defined in the template. You can simply delete the toggle button callback and add the code from Listing 9-10 to handle the button callback.

Listing 9-10. *The Button Callback Function*

```
public void helloButton_Click(Office.IRibbonControl control)
{
  Microsoft.Office.Interop.Word.Range currentRange =
  Globals.ThisAddIn.Application.Selection.Range;
  currentRange.Text = "Hello, World!";
}
```

Notice that the basic approach for the add-in is to access the object model for the target application from the callback function. The root of the object model is obtained through the Globals.ThisAddIn.Application object. From here, you can go on to manipulate the application as necessary. You're not limited to simply using the object model because now you have the full capability of the .NET Framework to integrate with databases, SharePoint sites, or anything else.

Once you have coded the callback, you should be able to run the add-in directly in Visual Studio. VSTO 2005 SE will start the target application and your add-in will be loaded. When you push the button, text should be added to the document. Figure 9-8 shows the final example.

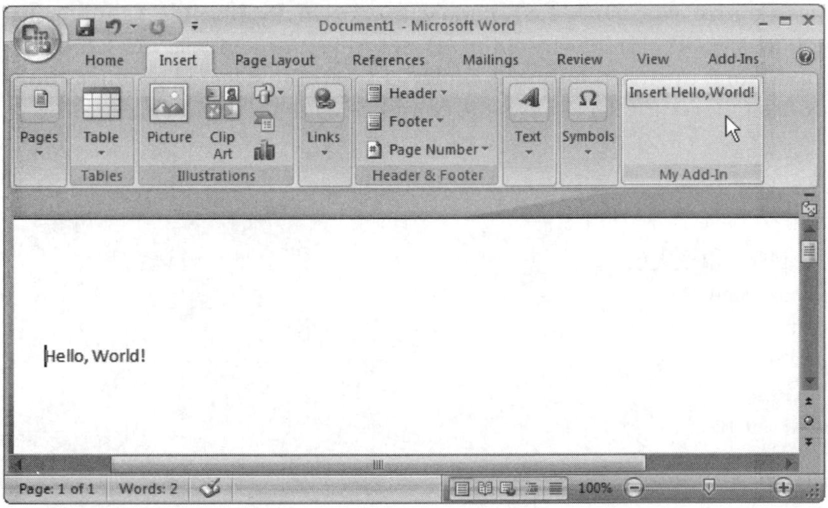

Figure 9-8. *The Hello, World! add-in*

Creating Office 2007 Task Panes

In addition to customizing the ribbon, you can also add custom task panes to Office 2007. Custom task panes allow you to create a completely custom user interface that can be displayed to the user. Custom task panes are an excellent way to integrate other systems with Office applications. To create a custom task pane, you begin with an add-in project just as you did before.

Custom task panes are designed and built through UserControls. Therefore, once you have a new project started, you must add a UserControl component to the project. On the UserControl, you can add any user interface elements you want from the toolbox. As an example, I created a simple UserControl with a ListBox and a Button. Using these controls, I will load a list of product names and numbers from a database and then use the button to insert them into a Word document. Figure 9-9 shows my UserControl in Visual Studio.

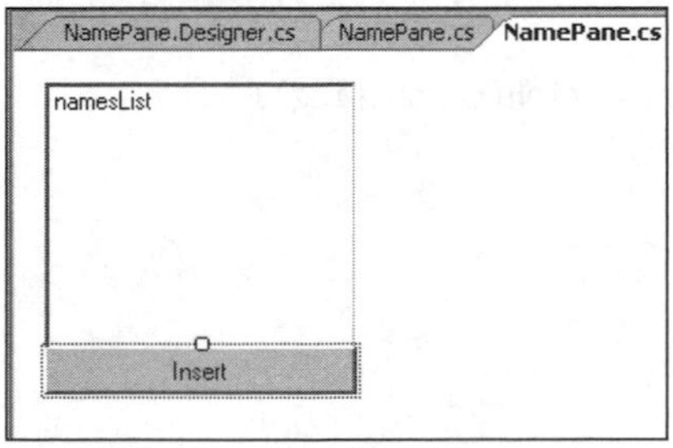

Figure 9-9. *A UserControl for a custom task pane*

Inside of the UserControl, you can add any code you want. In my example, I simply fill the list with product names and numbers from the AdventureWorks database when the UserControl is loaded. When the Insert button is clicked, I insert the selected product into the current Word document. Listing 9-11 shows the complete code for the UserControl.

Listing 9-11. *Code for the Custom UserControl*

```csharp
using System;
using System.Collections.Generic;
using System.ComponentModel;
using System.Drawing;
using System.Data;
using System.Text;
using System.Windows.Forms;
using System.Data.SqlClient;
using Word = Microsoft.Office.Interop.Word;

namespace Names
{
  public partial class NamePane : UserControl
  {
    public NamePane()
    {
      InitializeComponent();
    }

    private void NamePane_Load(object sender, EventArgs e)
    {
      try
      {
        string connString = "Data Source=win2k3template;➥
Initial Catalog=Adventureworks;Integrated Security=SSPI;";
        string sqlString = "Select Name + ', ' + ➥
          ProductNumber as FullProduct FROM Production.Product ORDER BY Name";

        using (SqlConnection connection = new SqlConnection(connString))
        {
          connection.Open();

          SqlCommand command = new SqlCommand();
          command.CommandText = sqlString;
          command.CommandType = CommandType.Text;
          command.Connection = connection;

          SqlDataReader reader = command.ExecuteReader();
```

```
            if (reader.HasRows)
            {
                while (reader.Read())
                {
                    namesList.Items.Add(reader.GetString(0));
                }
            }

            connection.Close();
        }
    }
    catch (Exception x)
    {
        MessageBox.Show(x.Message);
    }
}

private void insertButton_Click(object sender, EventArgs e)
{
    Word.Range currentRange = Globals.ThisAddIn.Application.Selection.Range;
    currentRange.Text = namesList.SelectedItem.ToString();
}

}
}
```

Once the UserControl is designed and coded, all you need to do is create a task pane from the UserControl at run time and display it. This is done in the startup event of the add-in. In this event, you must create a CustomTaskPane object and add your UserControl. Once this is done, you can run the add-in from Visual Studio. Listing 9-12 shows the code for loading the task pane, and Figure 9-10 shows a picture of the solution in action.

Listing 9-12. *Loading the New Task Pane*

```
using System;
using System.Windows.Forms;
using Microsoft.VisualStudio.Tools.Applications.Runtime;
using Word = Microsoft.Office.Interop.Word;
using Office = Microsoft.Office.Core;

namespace Names
{
  public partial class ThisAddIn
  {
    private NamePane namePane;
```

```csharp
private void ThisAddIn_Startup(object sender, System.EventArgs e)
{
    namePane = new NamePane();
    Microsoft.Office.Tools.CustomTaskPane newTaskPane =
        this.CustomTaskPanes.Add(namePane, "Names");
    newTaskPane.Visible = true;
}

private void ThisAddIn_Shutdown(object sender, System.EventArgs e)
{
}
}
}
```

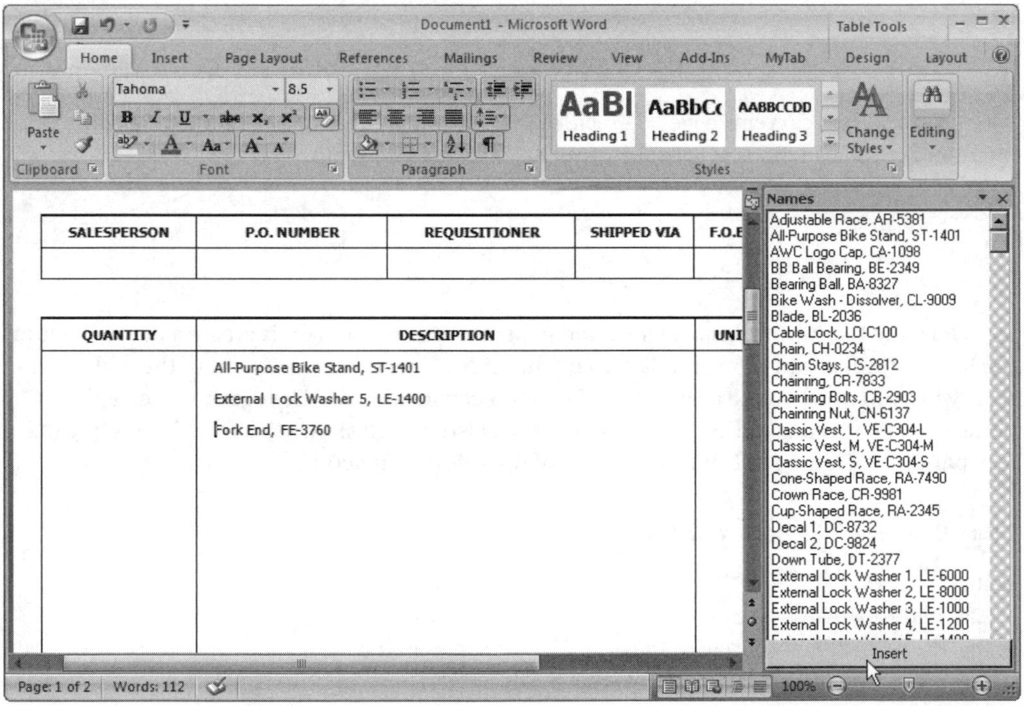

Figure 9-10. *The completed custom task pane*

Deploying VSTO 2005 SE Solutions

As I noted earlier, every VSTO 2005 SE solution template includes a setup project. This project can be used to deploy the solution directly to a client desktop. Additionally, you could deploy the solution from SharePoint library. In either case, there are several prerequisites that must be met on the client machine before the solution will run.

Follow these steps to prepare a client machine for VSTO solutions:

1. Log in to VSCLIENT as an administrator.

2. Download and install the .NET Framework 2.0 from `http://www.microsoft.com/` `downloads/details.aspx?FamilyID=0856eacb-4362-4b0d-8edd-aab15c5e04f5&` `displaylang=en`.

3. Ensure that you have installed the Primary Interop Assemblies and Visual Basic for Applications Support from the Office 2007 setup. If you did a complete install, these components should already be present.

4. Download and install the VSTO 2005 SE runtime from `http://go.microsoft.com/` `fwlink/?linkid=49612`.

Once you have the prerequisites on the client, you are ready to deploy the VSTO 2005 SE solution. If you are using the setup program created by the project, you can simply run the setup. If, however, you are deploying from SharePoint, the document and the assembly are going to be separated. The document will go into a document library or become the template for a content type while the associated assembly must be stored on a network location accessible through a UNC name. For example, you could create and share a directory on VSMOSS named Assemblies. In either case, the assemblies associated with the solution must be strongly named and you must explicitly trust them using the .NET Framework 2.0 Configuration utility.

Follow these steps to trust the solution assemblies:

1. On VSCLIENT, select Start ➤ Administrative Tools ➤ Microsoft .NET Framework 2.0 Configuration.

2. In the .NET Framework 2.0 Configuration dialog, expand the tree down the path Console Root ➤ .NET Framework 2.0 Configuration ➤ My Computer ➤ Runtime Security Policy ➤ Enterprise ➤ Code Groups ➤ All_Code.

3. Right-click the All_Code group and select New from the context menu.

4. Enter **VSTO Assemblies** in the Name field and click the Next button.

5. On the Choose a Condition Type screen, select URL from the drop-down list.

6. Enter the complete path to the location where you will deploy the assemblies (e.g., (\\VSMOSS\Assemblies).

7. Click the Next button.

8. On the Assign a Permission Set to the Code Group screen, select Full Trust from the drop-down list labeled Use Existing Permission Set.

9. Click the Next button.

10. Click the Finish button to complete the wizard.

11. In the .NET Framework 2.0 Configuration dialog, right-click the new VSTO Assemblies code group and select Properties from the context menu.

12. In the Properties dialog, check the box labeled Policy Levels Below This Level Will Not Be Evaluated. This ensures that the policy cannot be modified by any other policy.

13. Click the OK button.

Once you have trusted the assemblies, any project you install directly on the client computer using the setup project should run without trouble. However, if you intend to deploy the document into SharePoint, you must additionally trust the server location where the document will be stored. Trusting the documents is accomplished by creating another policy that is defined in the file MSOSEC.XML and contained in the assembly MSOSEC.DLL.

Follow these steps to trust a document location:

1. On VSCLIENT, open the File Explorer and navigate to C:\Program Files\ Microsoft Office\OFFICE12\ADDINS.

2. Drag the assembly MSOSEC.DLL from this directory and drop it in C:\Windows\ assembly to install it in the Global Assembly Cache.

3. Select Start ➤ Administrative Tools ➤ Microsoft .NET Framework 2.0 Configuration.

4. In the .NET Framework 2.0 Configuration dialog, expand the tree down the path Console Root ➤ . NET Framework 2.0 Configuration ➤ My Computer ➤ Runtime Security Policy ➤ Enterprise ➤ Code Groups ➤ All_Code.

5. Right-click the All_Code group and select New from the context menu.

6. Enter **VSTO Documents** in the Name field and click the Next button.

7. On the Choose a Condition Type screen, select (custom) from the drop-down list.

8. Click the Import button.

9. In the Import Custom Membership from XML dialog, navigate to the C:\Program Files\ Microsoft Office\OFFICE12\ADDINS directory.

10. Select the file MSOSEC.XML and click the Open button.

11. Click the Next button.

12. On the Assign a Permission Set to the Code Group screen, select Full Trust from the drop-down list labeled Use Existing Permission Set.

13. Click the Next button.

14. Click the Finish button to complete the wizard.

15. In the .NET Framework 2.0 Configuration dialog, right-click the new VSTO Documents code group and select Properties from the context menu.

16. In the Properties dialog, check the box labeled Policy Levels Below This Level Will Not Be Evaluated. This ensures that the policy cannot be modified by any other policy.

17. Click the OK button.

Once the assembly location is trusted and the documents are trusted, the last thing you have to do is modify the document so that it knows where the assembly is located. The document template created with a VSTO 2005 SE solution contains a deployment manifest that tells it where to find its associated assembly. Normally, the document simply looks in the same directory, but in the case of a SharePoint deployment, that is not possible. Fortunately, we can write a simple command-line application that modifies the deployment manifest. Listing 9-13 shows a complete command-line application that takes the document file name as the first argument and the assembly location as the second and updates the deployment manifest. Once that is done, you should be able to run the solution from a SharePoint library.

Listing 9-13. *Editing the Deployment Manifest*

```
using System;
using System.Collections.Generic;
using System.Text;
using Microsoft.VisualStudio.Tools.Applications.Runtime;

namespace DeploymentManifestEditor
{
    class Program
    {
        static void Main(string[] args)
        {
            ServerDocument document = null;

                document = new ServerDocument(args[0]);
                document.AppManifest.DeployManifestPath = args[1];
                document.Save();
                document.Close();

        }
    }
}
```

Exercise 9.1. Using the Office Open File Formats

The Office Open XML file formats allow you to create and edit Word, Excel, and PowerPoint documents programmatically. This is an ideal approach for working with documents in SharePoint solutions because you can process documents on the server while using SharePoint libraries as a storage mechanism. In this exercise, you will create a feature for SharePoint that uses the Open XML file formats to purge Word documents of review comments and tracked changes. This kind of functionality is perfect for preparing a document for delivery to a customer.

■**Caution** This exercise is for learning purposes only. The code has not been tested in a wide variety of situations and is not intended to be production-ready. Incorrectly manipulating Office documents can render them unreadable.

Starting the Project

This exercise will combine what you have learned about SharePoint features and the Office Open XML file formats. The feature will consist of an assembly designed to purge Word documents that is triggered through a new item on the document drop-down menu in SharePoint. To begin the exercise, you'll need to create a new project in Visual Studio.

Follow these steps to start the new project:

1. Log in to VSMOSS as a SharePoint administrator.

2. Select Start ➤ All Programs ➤ Visual Studio 2005 ➤ Visual Studio 2005.

3. When Visual Studio starts, select File ➤ New ➤ Project from the main menu.

4. In the New Project dialog, select Visual C# from the Project Types list.

5. Select Class Library from the Visual Studio Templates list.

6. Name the new project **WordCleaner** and click the OK button.

7. Right-click Class1.cs in the Solution Explorer and select Rename from the context menu.

8. Rename the file **Worker.cs** and hit the Enter key.

9. Select Project ➤ Add Reference from the main menu.

10. In the Add Reference dialog, click the Browse tab.

11. In the Browse tab, navigate to C:\Program Files\Reference Assemblies\Microsoft\Framework\v3.0.

12. Select the WindowsBase.dll assembly and click the OK button.

13. In the Worker.cs code window, add references to System.Xml, System.IO, and System.IO.Packaging. Listing 9-14 shows how your code should appear at this point.

Listing 9-14. *Starting the Project*

```
using System;
using System.Collections.Generic;
using System.Text;
using System.Xml;
using System.IO;
using System.IO.Packaging;

namespace WordCleaner
{
    public class Worker
    {
    }
}
```

Coding WordCleaner.Worker

After starting the project, the first thing to do is to create the assembly that will purge the Word documents. This is the part of the project that uses the Open XML file formats. This assembly will open the document to be purged, accept all of the changes made, and delete any comments. This will all be accomplished by manipulating the document part items and XML.

You'll start by creating a Sanitize and LogMessage method. The Sanitize method contains the main functionality, and you will code this over the next few sections. The LogMessage method is used to record errors in the event log. The code in Listing 9-15 shows the Sanitize method and the LogMessage method. Add the bolded code to your project as shown.

Listing 9-15. *The Sanitize and LogMessage Methods*

```
namespace WordCleaner
{
  public class Worker
  {
    //Namespace and URI constants
    private const string wordSpace =
      @"http://schemas.openxmlformats.org/wordprocessingml/2006/main";
    private const string docUri = @"/word/document.xml";

    public void Sanitize(string packagePath)
    {
      //Code here
    }

    static void LogMessage(string message, EventLogEntryType entry)
    {
      if (!EventLog.SourceExists("Word Cleaner"))
        EventLog.CreateEventSource("Word Cleaner", "Application");
      EventLog.WriteEntry("Word Cleaner", message, entry);
    }
  }
}
```

Opening the Package

The Sanitize method begins by opening the Word document file represented by the packagePath argument passed in to the method. Once the package is opened, the document part is loaded into a stream for editing. The document part represents the main body of the Word document and is stored in the package in the file document.xml. In order to purge the document of comments and changes, you must load the document.xml file into a stream and manipulate the XML. Add the code from Listing 9-16 to the Sanitize method to open the package and load the document part into a stream.

Listing 9-16. *Loading the Document Part into a Stream*

```
try
{
 //Open the package
 using (Package package = Package.Open(
                           packagePath, FileMode.Open, FileAccess.ReadWrite))
 {

    //Get the document part
    Uri uriDocument = new Uri(docUri, UriKind.Relative);
    PackagePart documentPart = package.GetPart(uriDocument);

    //Load the document part into a stream
    Stream partStream = documentPart.GetStream(
                          FileMode.Open, FileAccess.ReadWrite);

    //Add the namespace manager to reference the Word namespace
    NameTable nameTable = new NameTable();
    XmlNamespaceManager manager = new XmlNamespaceManager(nameTable);
    manager.AddNamespace("w", wordSpace);

    //Create a temporary XML document from the stream
    //so we can manipulate the XML elements
    XmlDocument tempDoc = new XmlDocument(nameTable);
    tempDoc.Load(partStream);

//More code will go here

  }
}
catch (Exception x)
{
    LogMessage(x.Message, EventLogEntryType.Error);
}
```

Removing Changes and Comments

Once the document part is loaded into a stream, you may use standard XML methods to manipulate the contents. In this exercise, you will remove all changed document text that is marked as deleted and all comments made during review. Additionally, you must promote inserted text changes so that they appear as accepted changes in the document. The whole process involves returning key nodes from the document part and deleting or modifying them.

Document text marked for deletion during a review is tracked in the document part with the element <w:del>. Inserted text is tracked with the element <w:ins>. Comments are tracked with three different elements: <w:commentRangeStart>, <w:commentRangeEnd>, and <w:commentReference>. Add the code from Listing 9-17 to the Sanitize method to manipulate the document elements.

Listing 9-17. *Modifying the Document Part*

```
//Remove deleted text from temporary XML document
XmlNodeList delNodes = tempDoc.SelectNodes("//w:del", manager);
foreach (XmlNode delNode in delNodes)
{
  delNode.ParentNode.RemoveChild(delNode);
}

//Promote the inserted text in temporary XMl document
//so it appears normally in the Word document
XmlNodeList insNodes = tempDoc.SelectNodes("//w:ins", manager);
foreach (XmlNode insNode in insNodes)
{
  foreach (XmlNode childNode in insNode.ChildNodes)
  {
    insNode.ParentNode.InsertBefore(childNode, insNode);
  }

  insNode.ParentNode.RemoveChild(insNode);
}

//Remove comments text from temporary XML document
//Must remove several different elements to accomplish this
XmlNodeList commentStartNodes = tempDoc.SelectNodes(
                          "//w:commentRangeStart", manager);
foreach (XmlNode commentStartNode in commentStartNodes)
{
  commentStartNode.ParentNode.RemoveChild(commentStartNode);
}

XmlNodeList commentEndNodes = tempDoc.SelectNodes(
                          "//w:commentRangeEnd", manager);
foreach (XmlNode commentEndNode in commentEndNodes)
{
  commentEndNode.ParentNode.RemoveChild(commentEndNode);
}

XmlNodeList commentRefNodes = tempDoc.SelectNodes(
                          "//w:commentReference", manager);
foreach (XmlNode commentRefNode in commentRefNodes)
{
  commentRefNode.ParentNode.RemoveChild(commentRefNode);
}

//Save the temporary XMl document changes back to the document part
documentPart.GetStream().SetLength(0);
tempDoc.Save(documentPart.GetStream());

//More code will follow
```

Deleting the Comments Part

To finish processing the file, you must remove the comment text from the package. The comment text is saved in the comments.xml file in the package. You must remove the comments.xml file from the package and delete the relationship between the document part and the comments part. Add the code from Listing 9-18 to remove the comment text from the package.

Listing 9-18. *Removing Comments and Relationships*

```
//delete the relationship with the comments part
Uri uriComments = new Uri("/word/comments.xml", UriKind.Relative);
PackagePart commentsPart = package.GetPart(uriComments);

PackageRelationshipCollection relationships = documentPart.GetRelationships();

foreach (PackageRelationship relationship in relationships)
{
  if (relationship.TargetUri.ToString() == "comments.xml")
  {
    documentPart.DeleteRelationship(relationship.Id);
    break;
  }
}

//Delete comments part from package
package.DeletePart(uriComments);

//Save the package changes
package.Flush();
package.Close();
```

Compiling the Assembly

Once the code is completed for the Worker class, it can be compiled. In this exercise, you will deploy the assembly to the Global Assembly Cache (GAC), so it must be digitally signed. Once signed, it can be built.

Follow these steps to build the assembly:

1. In the Solution Explorer, right-click the WordCleaner project and select Properties from the context menu.

2. In the Properties dialog, click the Signing tab.

3. On the Signing tab, check the box labeled Sign the Assembly.

4. Select <New…> from the drop-down list labeled Choose a Strong Name Key File.

5. In the Create Strong Name Key dialog, uncheck the box labeled Protect My Key File with a Password.

6. Enter **WordCleanerKey** in the Key File Name field.

7. Click the OK button.

8. Make sure that the configuration drop-down is set to release and select Build ➤ Build Word Cleaner from the main menu.

Creating the Worker.aspx Page

Although the basic purge functionality is contained in the assembly, we still need to create a mechanism for invoking the assembly. In this exercise, you'll invoke the assembly through an ASPX page that will be called from a new menu item in a document library. We could also have chosen to invoke the assembly as part of a workflow or in response to a list event. The point is that there are many options in SharePoint for implementing such functionality.

Follow these steps to create the ASPX page:

1. In the Solution Explorer, right-click the WordCleaner project and select Add ➤ New Item from the context menu.

2. In the Add New Item dialog, select Text File.

3. Name the Text File **Worker.aspx** and click the Add button. You are adding the ASPX page in this manner because we are not creating a web application and will simply deploy the file to the TEMPLATES directory later.

4. Add the code from Listing 9-19 to create the page. Notice that the page references both the `Microsoft.SharePoint` and the `WordCleaner` assemblies.

Listing 9-19. *The Worker.aspx Page*

```
<%@ Page Language="C#" Debug="true" %>
<%@ Assembly Name="WordCleaner,➥
        Version=1.0.0.0,➥
        Culture=neutral,➥
        PublicKeyToken=0e47d66474f01e8d" %>
<%@ Assembly Name="Microsoft.SharePoint,➥
        Version=12.0.0.0,➥
        Culture=neutral,➥
        PublicKeyToken=71e9bce111e9429c"%>
<%@ Import Namespace="WordCleaner" %>
<%@ Import Namespace="System.IO" %>
<%@ Import Namespace="Microsoft.SharePoint" %>
<%@ Import Namespace="Microsoft.SharePoint.WebControls" %>

<!DOCTYPE html PUBLIC "-//W3C//DTD XHTML 1.0 Transitional//EN"
  "http://www.w3.org/TR/xhtml1/DTD/xhtml1-transitional.dtd">
```

```
<html xmlns="http://www.w3.org/1999/xhtml">
<head id="Head1" runat="server">
  <title>Word Cleaner Worker Page</title>
</head>
<body>
  <form id="form1" runat="server">
    <div>
     <%

      try
      {
        //Code will go here
      }
      catch (Exception x)
      {
        Response.Write(x.Message + "\n");
      }

     %>
    </div>
  </form>
</body>
</html>
```

Coding the Worker.aspx Page

In order for the assembly to access a Word document, the document must be downloaded from SharePoint and manipulated locally. Once the changes are made, the document needs to be uploaded back to the document library. The Worker.aspx page performs the download of the file onto the server, invokes the cleaning assembly, and then uploads the file. After the page completes, it redirects back to the document library page. In this way, the user experiences a postback and then has a purged document in the library. Add the code from Listing 9-20 to the Worker.aspx page to download, purge, and upload the document.

Listing 9-20. *Downloading, Purging, and Uploading the Document*

```
//Get top-level site
SPSite site = SPControl.GetContextSite(Context);

//Build the destination path
string source = "http://" + site.HostName + Request.QueryString["Item"];
string cache =
   System.Environment.GetFolderPath(Environment.SpecialFolder.InternetCache);
string downPath = cache + "\\" + source.Substring(source.LastIndexOf("/") + 1);
string extension = source.Substring(source.LastIndexOf(".") + 1);
```

```
//Make sure it is a DOCX file
if(extension.ToUpper()!="DOCX")
  throw new Exception("Only DOCX files can be cleaned.");

//Download file
System.Net.WebClient client = new System.Net.WebClient();
client.Credentials = System.Net.CredentialCache.DefaultCredentials;
client.DownloadFile(source, downPath);

//Sanitize Document
WordCleaner.Worker worker = new WordCleaner.Worker();
worker.Sanitize(downPath);

//Upload File
FileStream stream = new FileStream(downPath, FileMode.Open, FileAccess.Read);
BinaryReader reader = new BinaryReader(stream);
byte[] bytes = reader.ReadBytes((int)stream.Length);
reader.Close();
stream.Close();
client.UploadData(source, "PUT", bytes);


//Redirect back to library
Response.Redirect(source.Substring(0,source.LastIndexOf("/"))
                  + "/Forms/AllItems.aspx");
```

Creating the Feature.xml File

As I stated earlier, the Worker.aspx page will be invoked from a new item on the document's drop-down menu. In order to create this new item, you'll have to create a Feature.xml file to represent the new feature. The Feature.xml file is straightforward and created in a manner that should be familiar to you by now.

Follow these steps to create a Feature.xml file:

1. In the Solution Explorer, right-click the WordCleaner project and select Add ➤ New Item from the context menu.

2. In the Add New Item dialog, select XML File.

3. Name the XML file **Feature.xml** and click the Add button.

4. Add the code from Listing 9-21 to create the Feature.xml file.

Listing 9-21. *The Feature.xml File*

```
<?xml version="1.0" encoding="utf-8" ?>
<Feature Title="Word Document Cleaner"
    Description="Accepts changes and removes comments from Word 2007 files."
    Scope="Site"
```

```
        Id="C67EBE69-0372-425f-A939-23F8A74418AF"
        xmlns="http://schemas.microsoft.com/sharepoint/">
    <ElementManifests>
        <ElementManifest Location="Elements.xml" />
    </ElementManifests>
</Feature>
```

Creating the Elements.xml File

The Elements.xml file is the manifest file for the new feature. This file is used to define the new menu item and link it to the Worker.aspx page. In this section, you will create the manifest file and code it to add a new item to the document's drop-down menu.

Follow these steps to create the Elements.xml file:

1. In the Solution Explorer, right-click the WordCleaner project and select Add ➤ New Item from the context menu.

2. In the Add New Item dialog, select XML File.

3. Name the XML file **Elements.xml** and click the Add button.

4. Add the code from Listing 9-22 to create the Elements.xml file.

Listing 9-22. *The Elements.xml File*

```
<?xml version="1.0" encoding="utf-8" ?>
<Elements xmlns="http://schemas.microsoft.com/sharepoint/">
    <CustomAction Id="UserInterfaceLightUp.ECBItemToolbar"
        RegistrationType="List"
        RegistrationId="101"
        Location="EditControlBlock"
        Sequence="106"
        Title="Cleanse Document"
        ImageUrl="/_layouts/images/AddToFavorites.gif">
        <UrlAction Url="/_layouts/Worker.aspx?Item={ItemUrl}" />
    </CustomAction>
</Elements>
```

Creating the Install.bat File

In order to install the new feature, you must create a folder in the TEMPLATES directory and copy the Feature.xml and Elements.xml files to this location. Additionally, you must copy the Worker.aspx file to the LAYOUTS directory. Finally, you must install the assembly in the GAC. You could certainly do all this by hand, but you'll create a batch file to automate the process instead.

Follow these steps to create the batch file:

1. In the Solution Explorer, right-click the WordCleaner project and select Add ➤ New Item from the context menu.

2. In the Add New Item dialog, select Text File.

3. Name the text file **Install.bat** and click the Add button.

4. Add the code from Listing 9-23 to create the Install.bat file. When you are done, run the batch file to install the feature.

Listing 9-23. *The Install.bat File*

```
@SET FEATUREDIR="c:\program files\common files\microsoft shared\➥
web server extensions\12\Template\Features"
@SET LAYOUTDIR="c:\program files\common files\microsoft shared\\➥
web server extensions\12\Template\Layouts"
@SET STSADM="c:\program files\common files\microsoft shared\\➥
web server extensions\12\bin\stsadm.exe"
@SET GACUTIL="C:\Program Files\Microsoft Visual Studio 8\\➥
SDK\v2.0\Bin\GacUtil.exe"

md %FEATUREDIR%\WordCleaner

xcopy /e /y Feature.xml %FEATUREDIR%\WordCleaner
xcopy /e /y Elements.xml %FEATUREDIR%\WordCleaner
xcopy /e /y Worker.aspx %LAYOUTDIR%

%GACUTIL% -if bin\release\WordCleaner.dll

%STSADM% -o installfeature -filename  WordCleaner\feature.xml -force

IISRESET

ECHO Finished

PAUSE
```

Activating and Using the Feature

Once the feature is installed, you may activate it. This feature is defined at the site collection level, so you will go to the Site Settings page for the site collection to activate it. Once activated, the new menu item should show up for all documents in the site collection.

Follow these steps to activate the feature:

1. Open the home page of the intranet site you created in Chapter 2.

2. Select Site Settings ➤ Modify All Site Settings from the Site Actions menu.

3. On the Site Settings page, click the link titled Site Collection Features under the Site Collection Administration section.

4. On the Site Collection Features page, click the Activate button associated with the Word Document Cleaner feature.

Once the feature is activated, navigate to any document library containing Word documents. If you drop the menu associated with a document, you should see the new Cleanse Document item. Before you select it, however, open the document in Word, turn on Track Changes, and add some comments. Then save the document and try purging it.

CHAPTER 10

■ ■ ■

SharePoint Web Parts

The power of SharePoint as a solution platform comes in no small measure from its support for web parts. The web parts framework built into Windows SharePoint Services (WSS) provides a consistent environment for both developer and user. Standard interfaces, attributes, and deployment models make web part construction straightforward, while standard interface elements to add, remove, and modify web parts make them easy to customize. Throughout our investigation of SharePoint, we have used web parts to integrate systems, customize functionality, and display information. Although WSS and MOSS ship with a number of useful web parts, you will inevitably want to create your own. In this chapter, I will examine the fundamental construction and deployment of web parts.

Web Part Basics

Creating a custom web part in SharePoint begins by inheriting from the `WebPart` class. Those who wrote web parts in the previous version of SharePoint will remember that those web parts also began by inheriting from the `WebPart` class. The big difference, however, is that the base class for web parts in SharePoint 2003 derives from `Microsoft.SharePoint.WebPartPages.WebPart`, whereas the base class for SharePoint 2007 web parts is `System.Web.UI.WebControls.WebParts.WebPart`. While this version of SharePoint provides full backward compatibility for web parts built on the `Microsoft.SharePoint` namespace, the best practice going forward is to use the `System.Web` namespace. Furthermore, the `Microsoft.SharePoint.WebPartPages.WebPart` class has been rebased in ASP.NET 2.0 so that it actually derives from the `System.Web.UI.WebControls.WebParts.WebPart` class anyway.

You begin the definition of a new web part by creating a new class library project in Visual Studio. After the project is created, you must set a reference to the `System.Web` namespace, which contains the `WebPart` base class. Once the reference is set, you may then set up the class to inherit from the base class. Listing 10-1 shows the foundational code for a web part.

Listing 10-1. *Starting a Web Part*

```
using System;
using System.Web.UI;
using System.Web.UI.WebControls.WebParts;
```

```
namespace myNamespace
{
    public class myWebPart:WebPart
    {

    }
}
```

Web Part Properties

Well-designed web parts function in a variety of different pages because they are configurable by an administrator or end user directly in the site. This configuration is possible because each web part supports a series of properties that can be set in the site and read by the web part at run time. In code, these properties are created in the same manner as any property for any class with the exception that they have special attributes that determine their behavior within SharePoint. The process of creating a property begins with a standard property construct.

Most properties are designed to be configured directly in the portal. Therefore, you must decorate the property with different attributes to define its behavior when a page is designed. These property values are subsequently serialized and saved when the page is processed so that the property values can be read later when an end user accesses the page. Each of the properties you define is decorated with the WebBrowsable, Personalizable, WebDisplayName, and WebDescription attributes.

The WebBrowsable attribute is a Boolean value that determines whether the built-in Share-Point property editing pane can access the property. You may set this value to either True or False. Although most of your properties will be browsable, you may have sensitive properties that should not be accessible by general users. Additionally, when you create a custom property editor later in the section titled "Custom Editor Parts," you will set this value to False.

The Personalizable attribute is an enumeration that determines whether the property values are saved for an individual or for all users of the page on which the web part sits. This attribute may be set to PersonalizationScope.User or PersonalizationScope.Shared. When the attribute is set to PersonalizationScope.User, the property value may be set for each user of a page. The web part infrastructure serializes and saves the values separately for each user. When the attribute is set to PersonalizationScope.Shared, the web part infrastructure saves only a single value of the property that is applied to all users of the page on which the web part sits.

Once you understand the property definition scheme, you can create as many as you need to properly configure the web part. Although they are easy to change, I recommend that you spend some time designing your web part before implementing the property set. If you think through the intended use of the web part, you will save yourself a lot of wasted time writing and rewriting property structures. Listing 10-2 shows a complete property definition for a database connections string that can be set by a user and then utilized by the web part.

Listing 10-2. *Creating a Property*

```
[Personalizable(PersonalizationScope.Shared),WebBrowsable(true),
WebDisplayName("Connection String"),
WebDescription("The connection string for the database")]
public string Connection
{
  get{return m_connection;}
  set{m_connection=value;}
}
```

Rendering Web Parts

Because the WebPart class inherits from System.Web.UI.Control, the entire user interface for a web part must be created through code. Although you can make use of ASP.NET controls in your web part, there is no drag-and-drop design capability in Visual Studio. This approach is definitely a drawback and can slow your ability to create web parts. Be that as it may, it becomes less of an issue once you have created a few web parts and learned the techniques for generating the user interface.

■**Note** It is popular among some developers to utilize a technique where a web part is made to load a user control at run time. Using this technique allows a developer to have a drag-and-drop experience at design time supported through the user control. I have written about this technique in my book *Advanced Share-Point Services Solutions* (Apress, 2004) but it is beyond the scope of this book. If you are interested in this approach, visit http://workspaces.gotdotnet.com/smartpart.

Properly rendering a web part requires that you first create any ASP.NET controls that you will need in code. The required ASP.NET controls are then added to the controls collection of the web part by overriding the CreateChildControls method of the base class. Finally, you can draw the output by overriding the RenderContents method. You may use any available ASP.NET control found in Visual Studio .NET or any ASP.NET control you have written to create the user interface for a web part. Remember though that these controls cannot be dragged onto a page. Instead, they must be declared in code. When you declare ASP.NET controls in code, be sure to set a reference to the appropriate namespace. Nearly all of the ASP.NET controls that you could want belong to the System.Web.UI.WebControls namespace.

Once the controls are declared, you can set their properties and add them to the Controls collection of the web part. You can do this by overriding the CreateChildControls method. In this method, set property values for each control and then add it to the Controls collection using the Controls.Add method. You can also utilize event handlers for the ASP.NET controls, which will be necessary to capture button clicks and the like. Listing 10-3 shows several controls being added to a web part.

Listing 10-3. *Adding ASP.NET Controls to a Web Part*

```
protected TextBox txtDisplay;
protected Button btnGo;

protected override void CreateChildControls()
{
    this.btnGo.Click += new System.EventHandler(this.btnGo_Click);
    this.Controls.Add(btnGo);

    txtDisplay.Width=Unit.Percentage(100);
    this.Controls.Add(txtDisplay);

}

private void btnGo_Click(object sender, System.EventArgs e)
{
    txtDisplay.Text=Text;
}
```

Once the controls are all configured and added to the web part, you are ready to draw the output. When rendering the user interface of the web part, you use the `HtmlTextWriter` class provided by the `RenderContents` method. This class allows you to create any manner of HTML output for the web part.

As a general rule, you should render your user interface within an HTML `<table>`. The reason for this is that you can never be sure what the web part page layout will look like. As you saw in Chapter 5, layouts and web part zones can take almost any form. Therefore, you should use the relative layout offered by the `<table>` tag to respect the width defined by the zone where the web part appears. Listing 10-4 shows how to render a table containing ASP.NET controls. You should take particular note of the `width` definition within the table.

■**Note** Style sheet purists may prefer to use a style class to control the layout of a web part. While you can certainly reference style sheet classes from a web part, SharePoint makes extensive use of layout tables, so I do not see much of an issue with using them in your web parts.

Listing 10-4. *Rendering ASP.NET Controls in an HTML Table*

```
protected override void RenderContents(HtmlTextWriter writer)
{
    writer.Write("<table border=\"0\" width=\"100%\">");
    writer.Write("<tr><td>");
    btnGo.RenderControl(writer);
    writer.Write("</td></tr>");
    writer.Write("<tr><td>");
```

```
txtDisplay.RenderControl(writer);
writer.Write("</td></tr>");
writer.Write("</table>");

}
```

The Web Part Life Cycle

Just like ASP.NET controls, web parts participate in a server-side request/response sequence
that loads a page in the portal each time it is requested, and unloads the page once it is sent
to the client. Web parts, therefore, follow the same control life cycle that ASP.NET controls
follow. You can see the events of this life cycle by creating a web part that generates output
in response to each key event. Listing 10-5 shows the code for a complete web part with all
of the major methods overridden to display the order in which they occur.

Listing 10-5. *Tracking the Web Part Life Cycle*

```
//The following are included in the project automatically
using System;
using System.Collections.Generic;
using System.Text;

//The following were added manually after setting a reference to System.Web
using System.Web.UI;
using System.Web.UI.WebControls;
using System.Web.UI.WebControls.WebParts;


namespace SPLifecycle
{
    public class Reporter:WebPart
    {
        //variable for reporting events
        private string m_report="";

        //variable for button and text
        private Button m_button;
        private TextBox m_text;

        protected override void OnInit(EventArgs e)
        {
            m_report += "OnInit<br/>";
            base.OnInit(e);
        }
```

```
protected override void LoadViewState(object savedState)
{
    m_report += "LoadViewState<br/>";

    object[] viewState = null;
    if (savedState != null)
    {
        viewState = (object[])savedState;
        base.LoadViewState(viewState[0]);
        m_report += (string)viewState[1] + "<br/>";
    }

}

protected override void CreateChildControls()
{
    m_report+="CreateChildControls<br/>";

    m_button = new Button();
    m_button.Text = "Push Me!";
    m_button.Click += new EventHandler(m_button_Click);
    Controls.Add(m_button);

    m_text = new TextBox();
    Controls.Add(m_text);
}

protected override void OnLoad(EventArgs e)
{
    m_report += "OnLoad<br/>";
    base.OnLoad(e);
}

void m_button_Click(object sender, EventArgs e)
{
    m_report+="Button Click<br/>";
}

protected override void OnPreRender(EventArgs e)
{
    m_report += "OnPreRender<br/>";
    base.OnPreRender(e);
}

protected override object SaveViewState()
{
    m_report += "SaveViewState<br/>";
```

```
            object[] viewState = new object[2];
            viewState[0] = base.SaveViewState();
            viewState[1] = "myData";

            return viewState;
        }

        protected override void RenderContents(HtmlTextWriter writer)
        {
            m_report += "RenderContents<br/>";
            writer.Write(m_report);
            m_text.RenderControl(writer);
            m_button.RenderControl(writer);
        }

        public override void Dispose()
        {
            base.Dispose();
        }

        protected override void OnUnload(EventArgs e)
        {
            base.OnUnload(e);
        }


    }
}
```

When a page from a WSS site that contains web parts is requested for the first time—or when it is submitted to the server—the web part life cycle begins. The first phase in this life cycle is marked by a call to the OnInit method of the WebPart class. During initialization, configuration values that were marked as WebBrowsable and set through the web part task pane are loaded into the web part.

After the web part is initialized, the ViewState of the web part is populated. ViewState is a property inherited from System.Web.UI.Control. The ViewState is filled from the state information that was previously serialized. Once the ViewState property is populated, the control returns to the same state it was in when it was last processed on the server. The ViewState is populated through a call to the LoadViewState method.

Although it is normally not necessary to override the LoadViewState method, it is useful if you would like to persist your own data within a web part. Overriding the LoadViewState method along with the corresponding SaveViewState method lets you store custom data within the web part's view state. In Listing 10-5, I use this technique to show how these methods fit into the overall web part life cycle.

When the viewstate becomes available, the web part's user interface may be created. As I showed earlier, this happens with a call to the CreateChildControls method. In this method, all of the constituent controls are created and added to the Controls collection. It is important to note that the CreateChildControls method does not always get called at the same point in the life cycle. When web parts are first rendered on the page, the method generally occurs after the OnLoad method. After a postback, however, the method is called before the OnLoad method. You can even force it to be called using the EnsureChildControls method. All this means that you must not make any hard assumptions about when this method will execute.

Once the web part interface has been created and the properties set from the viewstate, the server can make changes to the properties of the web part based on values that are posted by the client browser. Any new values that are posted during the request—such as text field values—are applied to the corresponding property of the web part. At this point, the web part has reached the state it was in just before the postback occurred.

After all of the new property values are applied to the web part, the page may begin using the information to process the end-user request. This begins through a call to the OnLoad method of the WebPart class. The OnLoad method fires for every web part regardless of how many properties have changed. Web part developers use the OnLoad method as the basis for the functionality embodied in the web part. During this event, web parts may obtain a connection to a database or other system to retrieve information for display. The key thing to remember about this method is that it always fires after the posted data has been applied to the web part.

Once the OnLoad method completes, any events triggered by the client interaction with the web part are fired. This includes all user-generated events such as the Click event associated with a button. It is critical for the web part developer to understand that the user-generated events happen after the OnLoad event. This means that you must be careful not to rely on the results of user-generated events when you write code for the OnLoad event.

Once the web part has finished handling the user-generated events, it is ready to create the output of the control. The web part begins creating this output with a call to the OnPreRender method of the WebPart class. The OnPreRender method gives the web part developer the opportunity to change any of the web part properties before the control output is drawn. This is the perfect place to run a database query that relies on several user-supplied values, because all of the values will be available at this point in the life cycle.

After the OnPreRender event is complete, the web part output may be drawn. Drawing begins through a call to the RenderContents method, which I discussed in the "Rendering Web Parts" section. In this method, the web part must programmatically generate its HTML output. This output will be rendered in the appropriate zone on the page in the portal.

The next step is to save the state of any controls on the page in the ViewState. The ViewState of the web part is serialized and saved to a hidden field in the web page. The ViewState is saved through a call to the SaveViewState event, which is inherited from the System.Web.UI.Control class.

Once the ViewState is saved, the control web part can be removed from the memory of the server. Web parts receive notification that they are about to be removed from memory through the Dispose event. This method allows the web part developer to release critical resources such as database connections before the web part is destroyed.

The web part life cycle ends when it is finally removed from memory. The last event to fire is the OnUnload event. This event notifies the web part that it is being removed from memory. Generally web part developers do not need access to this event because all cleanup should have been accomplished in the Dispose event.

Understanding the complete life cycle helps significantly when developing web parts. In particular, understanding when certain values are available to the web part will ensure that you create components with consistent behavior. Figure 10-1 shows the output of the life cycle web part.

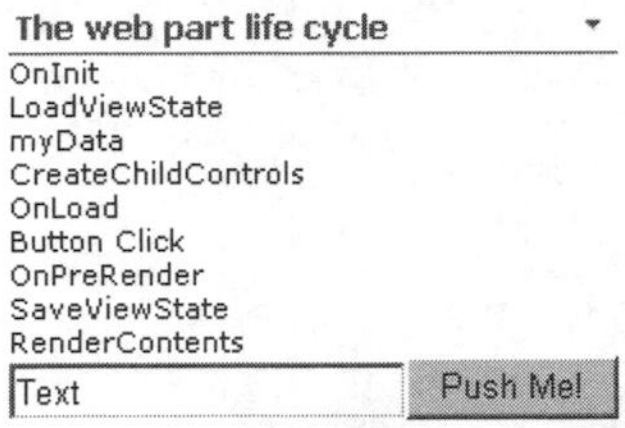

```
The web part life cycle        ▾
OnInit
LoadViewState
myData
CreateChildControls
OnLoad
Button Click
OnPreRender
SaveViewState
RenderContents
[Text                  ] [ Push Me! ]
```

Figure 10-1. *The web part life cycle*

Deploying Web Parts

After you have finished coding the web part, you are ready to begin the process of deploying it for use in WSS. To deploy a web part, you must make several decisions regarding its location and trust level within WSS. After it is deployed, you will then need to make it available to WSS sites through the Web Parts Gallery.

Understanding Deployment Options

Because SharePoint is a web-based application with potential ties to sensitive organizational information, web part security is a significant concern. These security concerns encompass not only access to information, but also potential malicious behavior by web parts. Imagine that a power user downloads and installs a free web part from the Internet. The web part has some nice site navigation that everyone likes, but in the background it is also crawling the network.

SharePoint web parts can be deployed with or without a strong name. Assemblies with a strong name may be deployed to the Global Assembly Cache (GAC) or the /bin directory of the targeted SharePoint site collection. Assemblies without a strong name may only be deployed to the /bin directory. The best practice, however, is to digitally sign web parts with a trusted certificate so that you can guarantee all of the web parts in your system are trustworthy. In my experience, however, most web parts are simply deployed using a strong name created by the developer at design time.

Before you can give your web part a strong name, you must generate a public/private key pair to use when signing the web part. You can create a key pair using the Strong Name tool (sn.exe) or have Visual Studio do it for you through the properties dialog. Figure 10-2 shows the Signing tab of the properties dialog in Visual Studio.

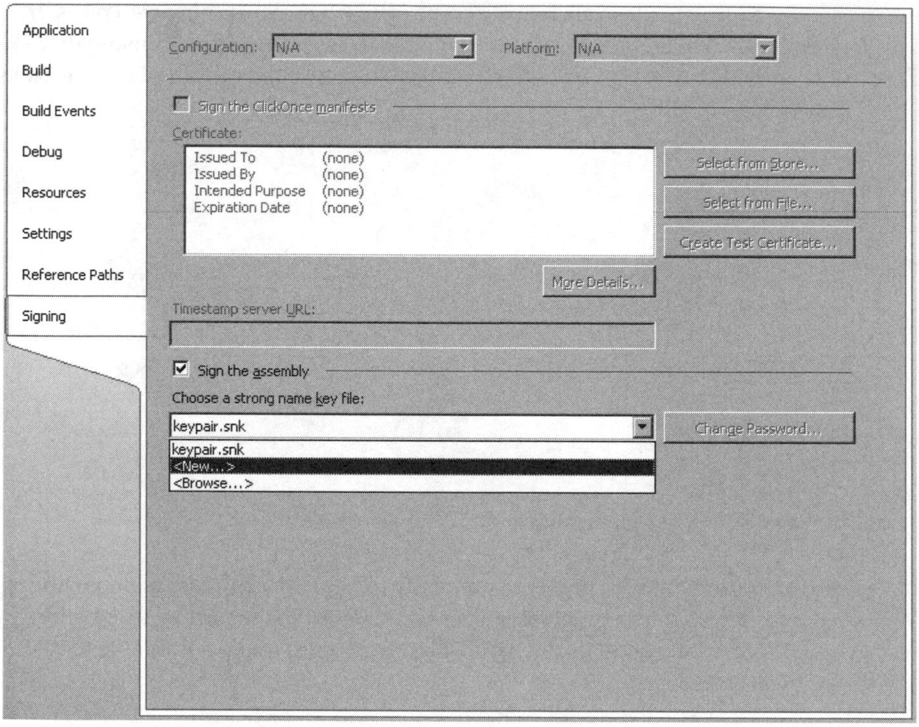

Figure 10-2. *Signing the web part*

If an organization already has a digital certificate, it may not be made generally available to developers who need to sign code. In this case, the developer may choose to delay signing the web part. When you delay signing, the web part space is reserved for the final signature, but you can still use the web part during development.

In order to delay signing the web part, you must set the `AssemblyDelaySign` attribute to `True`. You must then get the public key portion of the certificate and reference it using the `AssemblyKeyFile` attribute. Finally, you must instruct the .NET Framework to skip the strong name verification test for the web part by using the Strong Name tool with the following syntax:

```
sn -Vr [assembly.dll]
```

■**Caution** Skipping the strong name verification opens a security hole. Any web part that uses the same assembly name can spoof the genuine web part. Reserve this technique solely for development in organizations where the digital certificate is not provided to developers. Otherwise, always reference a valid key pair.

Regardless of how you choose to sign the web part, you should make sure that the version number specified in the `AssemblyInfo` file is absolute. Visual Studio .NET has the ability to autoincrement your project version using wildcards; however, this is not supported by strong naming. Therefore, you must specify an exact version for the web part. The following code fragment shows an example:

```
[assembly: AssemblyVersion("1.0.0.0")]
```

As I mentioned earlier, you can deploy a web part in either the GAC or the \bin directory of the associated web application. If you choose to deploy the web part in the \bin directory, you will also need to add the `AllowPartiallyTrustedCallers` attribute to the `AssemblyInfo` file. This is required because assemblies in the \bin directory will not operate with full trust. The `AllowPartiallyTrustedCallers` attribute is part of the `System.Security` namespace, so you must reference the namespace as shown in the following code fragment:

```
using System.Security;
[assembly: AllowPartiallyTrustedCallers]
```

Building the Web Part

After the assembly is signed, you can build the web part. Once the web part is built, you may either install it in the GAC or copy it to the \bin directory. Installing the web part in the GAC allows the web part to operate with full trust, whereas copying it to the \bin directory subjects it to the security policy defined in the associated web.config file. Generally, the best practice is to copy the web part to the \bin directory and adjust the security policy as required. I'll cover more on security policies in the section titled "Code Access Security."

If you are going to copy your web part to the \bin directory, you must locate the correct web application on the file system and create a \bin directory, because it does not exist by default. As I discussed earlier in the book, SharePoint creates folders for all of the web applications in the path \Inetpub\wwwroot\wss\VirtualDirectories. In this folder, you will find a folder for each web application that is generally named by port number. It is underneath this folder where you will create a \bin directory and copy the assembly. Figure 10-3 shows an example bin directory in the File Explorer.

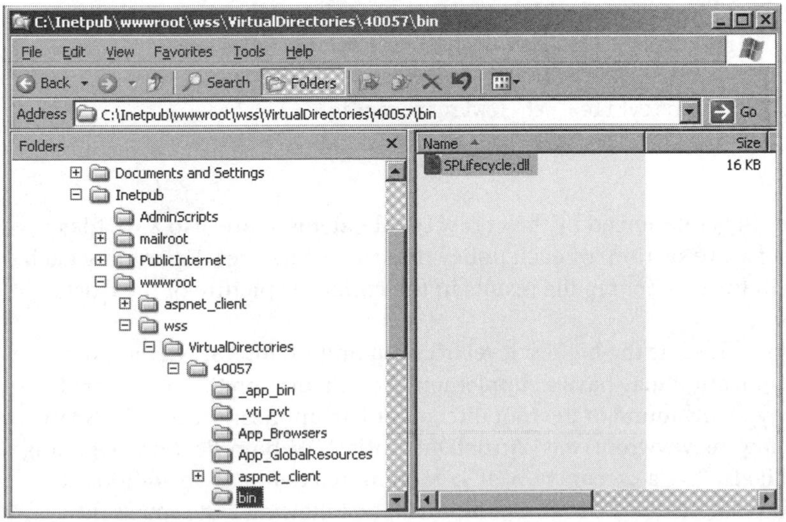

Figure 10-3. *Creating the \bin directory*

■**Caution** Do not deploy your web parts in the _app_bin directory. This is reserved for SharePoint.

Code Access Security

SharePoint is based on ASP.NET technology. As such, it is bound by the same security limitations that apply to any ASP.NET application. Practically speaking, this means that web parts are often restricted from accessing enterprise resources such as databases and web services unless you specifically configure SharePoint to allow such access. Managing how code can access enterprise resources is known as *code access security*.

Understanding Configuration Files

Code access security is implemented by a series of configuration files. The first configuration file of concern is web.config located in C:\Windows\Microsoft.NET\ Framework\v2.0.50727\ CONFIG. This file specifies master settings that will be inherited by all WSS sites that run on the server. This particular file is densely packed with information, and a complete discussion of the contents is beyond the scope of this book. However, one section—<securityPolicy>— is of immediate importance.

The <securityPolicy> section defines five levels of trust for ASP.NET applications: Full, High, Medium, Low, and Minimal. The trust level definitions allow you to assign partial permissions to an ASP.NET application that determine what resources the application can access. For example, applications with High levels of trust can read and write to files within their directory structure, whereas an application with a Low trust level can only read files. The permissions allotted by each level of trust are defined within a separate policy file designated by the <trustLevel> element. The following code shows the <securityPolicy> section for the machine.config file associated with an installation of WSS:

```
<securityPolicy>
    <trustLevel name="Full" policyFile="internal"/>
    <trustLevel name="High" policyFile="web_hightrust.config"/>
    <trustLevel name="Medium" policyFile="web_mediumtrust.config"/>
    <trustLevel name="Low" policyFile="web_lowtrust.config"/>
    <trustLevel name="Minimal" policyFile="web_minimaltrust.config"/>
</securityPolicy>
```

The security policy files referenced by the <trustLevel> element are also XML files. These files contain a separate section for each policy that the file defines. Examining each of the files referenced in the web.config file results in the complete picture of the trust levels and permissions.

The web.config file represents the highest level of configuration for ASP.NET applications; however, each application may have a supplemental configuration file also named web.config. This file is typically found in the root directory of an application, and for SharePoint it is located in \inetpub\wwwroot\wss\VirtualDirectories\[WebApplication]. Opening this file will reveal that it also has a <securityPolicy> section that defines two additional levels of trust known as WSS_Medium and WSS_Minimal. The following code shows the <securityPolicy> section from the file:

```
<securityPolicy>
  <trustLevel name="WSS_Medium"
  policyFile="C:\Program Files\Common Files\Microsoft Shared\
Web Server Extensions\12\config\wss_mediumtrust.config" />
  <trustLevel name="WSS_Minimal"
  policyFile="C:\Program Files\Common Files\Microsoft Shared\
Web Server Extensions\12\config\wss_minimaltrust.config" />
</securityPolicy>
```

The default installation of WSS defines a trust level of WSS_Minimal for all sites. Because web parts are deployed to the \bin directory, they are affected by the trust level set in the web.config file. This means that web parts associated with a SharePoint site have significant limitations. Most importantly, web parts running under WSS_Minimal cannot access any databases nor can they access the objects contained in the SharePoint object model. The Common Language Runtime (CLR) will throw an error if a web part attempts to access an unauthorized resource. Therefore, you must always implement appropriate error handling in a web part during attempts to access resources. Exception classes for these errors can be found in the Microsoft.SharePoint.Security namespace.

Customizing Policy Files

Because one of the major reasons to write a web part is to access data in other systems, you will undoubtedly want to raise the trust level under which certain web parts will run. You have three options for raising the trust level for assemblies in the \bin directory. All three have strengths and weaknesses you need to consider depending upon whether you are in a development, testing, or production environment.

The first option is simply to raise the trust level for all SharePoint Services sites by modifying the web.config file directly in a text editor. The trust level for SharePoint Services is set in the <system.web> section of the web.config file. To raise the level of trust, modify the <trust> tag to use any one of the seven defined levels. The following code shows an example with the trust level set to WSS_Medium:

```
<trust level="WSS_Medium" originUrl=""/>
```

Although making a global change to the trust level is simple, it should only be done in development environments. Generally, you should strive to limit access to resources to only essential web parts in a production environment. The default WSS_Minimal level is recommended for production.

The second option is to deploy all of your web parts into the GAC. The GAC grants the Full level of trust to web parts installed there without requiring a change to the web.config file. Once again, this is a fairly simple way to solve the problem, but it does make the web part available to all applications and servers. This is a potential problem, because a highly trusted component is now more widely accessible. Web parts can be added to the GAC using the command-line tool gacutil.exe with the following syntax:

```
gacutil -i [assembly.dll]
```

The final option for raising the trust level associated with a web part is to create your own custom policy file. Although this approach requires the most effort, it is easily the most secure. This approach should be considered the recommended best practice for production environments.

To create a custom policy file, follow these steps:

■**Note** If you are strictly following this text, you may not have developed your first web part yet. If this is the case, complete this series of steps after you finish the exercise at the end of the chapter.

---

1. Open the Windows File Explorer and navigate to \Program Files\Common Files\ Microsoft Shared\Web Server Extensions\12\config.

2. Copy wss_minimaltrust.config and paste it back to create a copy of the file.

3. Rename the copied file wss_sqltrust.config.

4. Open wss_sqltrust.config in Visual Studio for editing.

5. In the <SecurityClasses> section, add a reference to the SqlClientPermission class so web parts can access SQL databases:

```
<SecurityClass Name="SqlClientPermission"
Description="System.Data.SqlClient.SqlClientPermission, System.Data,
Version=1.0.53383.0, Culture=neutral,
PublicKeyToken=b77a5c561934e089"/>
```

6. In the <NamedPermissionSets> section, add a new permission set that grants all of the rights you want to define for your new policy, including access to SQL databases.

7. Extract the public key for the assembly from a web part you have developed by using the Security Utility tool with the following syntax:

```
secutil.exe -hex -s [assembly.dll]
```

8. Create a new <CodeGroup> section to apply the policy to the web part. This <CodeGroup> must precede the existing <CodeGroup> section defined for ASP.NET, because once a policy is assigned, processing stops. The following code shows an example:

```
<CodeGroup
    class="UnionCodeGroup"
    version="1"
    PermissionSetName="wss_sqltrust">
    <IMembershipCondition
        class="StrongNameMembershipCondition"
        version="1"
PublicKeyBlob="0x0024338300483383009433833338
306023383338324338305253413133834338300133833310
0936E3CD84B98E97825E63A7DBD7C15C10893315D16B5D9
8E7B7F38814BF0861D0BB5279A710EFFA
CA29A01BB745136FA2DDCAF8F5105C5F429DFF904A0B94
```

```
F0A4A8D27D3F8329CA4E7B44962D8764B8
D8A38D9F16859A035C23AC69D39D2969D03680C791C4D7
5B38BBE4D12C30467B6FE8F41131FC859E
D3B9B6F0D432478DC"
        Name="SPPivotalContacts"
/>
```

9. Save and close the file.

10. Open the `web.config` file in Visual Studio.

11. Edit the `<securityPolicy>` section to add a reference to the new policy as shown here:

```
<securityPolicy>
  <trustLevel name="WSS_Medium" policyFile="C:\Program Files\
Common Files\Microsoft Shared\Web Server
Extensions\12\config\wss_mediumtrust.config" />
  <trustLevel name="WSS_Minimal" policyFile="C:\Program Files\
Common Files\Microsoft Shared\Web Server
Extensions\12\config\wss_minimaltrust.config" />
  <trustLevel name="WSS_SQL" policyFile="C:\Program Files\
Common Files\Microsoft Shared\Web Server
Extensions\12\config\wss_sqltrust.config" />
</securityPolicy>
```

12. In the `<system.web>` section, modify the `<trust>` element to use the new policy as shown here:

```
<trust level="WSS_SQL" originUrl="" />
```

13. Save and close the file.

14. Restart IIS and the new policy will be in effect.

Listing 10-6 shows the final XML.

Listing 10-6. *Defining a New Policy*

```
<PermissionSet
    class="NamedPermissionSet"
    version="1"
    Name="wss_sqltrust">
        <IPermission
            class="AspNetHostingPermission"
            version="1"
            Level="Minimal"
        />
        <IPermission
            class="SecurityPermission"
            version="1"
            Flags="Execution"
        />
```

```
            <IPermission class="WebPartPermission"
                version="1"
                Connections="True"
            />
            <IPermission
                class="SqlClientPermission"
                version="1"
                Unrestricted="true"
            />
</PermissionSet>
```

The predefined security policies available to SharePoint lack templates for defining access to several key resources. These resources include the SharePoint object model and web services. Therefore, I will review the necessary modifications you must make to policy files in order to access these resources.

If you want your web part to be able to access the classes in the SharePoint namespace, you must define a new <IPermission> element in the policy file similar to what was done here for SQL access. The following code shows how to define the element:

```
<IPermission
    class="SharePointPermission"
    version="1"
    ObjectModel="true"
/>
```

Similarly, if you want your web part to be able to call a web service, you must also define a new <IPermission> element. In this element, you specify the Uniform Resource Identifier (URI) of the web service to access. This URI may be in the form of a regular expression, which means you can set it up to match more than one available web service. The following code shows how to define the element:

```
<IPermission class="WebPermission" version="1">
<ConnectAccess>
<URI uri="http://localhost/services/callreport.asmx?WSDL"/>
</ConnectAccess>
</IPermission>
```

Remember that in any case where a strongly named web part is in use, all of the other components must also be strongly named. This can cause problems when you are accessing web services or other libraries. In these cases, you must either install your web part to the GAC or implement a custom security policy.

Marking Web Parts As Safe

Adding a new web part to the \bin directory or the GAC handles the code access security issues for the part, but it is not sufficient to allow the part to be imported into SharePoint. In addition to permission to access resources, web parts also need permission to be imported into SharePoint. This permission is granted by marking the web part as Safe in the web.config file.

The web.config file contains not only the code access security policy but also the list of all assemblies allowed to run in a web part page. This information is kept in the <SafeControls> section of the file. Before a web part can be imported into SharePoint, it must be listed in the section. Listing 10-7 shows a truncated example of a <SafeControls> section.

Listing 10-7. *Controls Marked As Safe*

```
<SafeControls>
<SafeControl Assembly="SPMaskTool, Version=1.0.0.0, Culture=neutral,
PublicKeyToken=eb3e58846fb2ac2b" Namespace="SPMaskTool" TypeName="*" />
<SafeControl Assembly="SPPageView, Version=1.0.0.0, Culture=neutral,
PublicKeyToken=eb3e58846fb2ac2b" Namespace="SPPageView" TypeName="*" />
<SafeControl Assembly="SPDataList, Version=1.0.0.0, Culture=neutral,
PublicKeyToken=eb3e58846fb2ac2b" Namespace="SPDataList" TypeName="*" />
<SafeControl Assembly="SPDataSet, Version=1.0.0.0, Culture=neutral,
PublicKeyToken=eb3e58846fb2ac2b" Namespace="SPDataSet" TypeName="*" />
<SafeControl Assembly="SPPivotalContacts, Version=1.0.0.0, Culture=neutral,
PublicKeyToken=eb3e58846fb2ac2b"
Namespace="SPPivotalContacts" TypeName="*" />
<SafeControl Assembly="Citrix, Version=1.0.0.0, Culture=neutral,
PublicKeyToken=eb3e58846fb2ac2b" Namespace="Citrix" TypeName="*" />
</SafeControls>
```

In the <SafeControls> section, you must add a <SafeControl> element for each web part that you want to use in SharePoint. In the <SafeControl> element, you must specify several attributes:

- The Assembly attribute contains the fully qualified assembly name along with the Version, Culture, and PublicKeyToken attributes.

- The Version attribute contains the assembly version as it appears in the manifest file.

- The Culture attribute contains the culture designation, or "neutral" if none is provided.

- The PublicKeyToken attribute contains the token generated from the Strong Name tool.

- The Namespace attribute contains the namespace as defined in the web part project.

- The TypeName attribute contains the fully qualified name of the type or an asterisk to denote every web part in the assembly.

- Safe is an optional attribute that is normally set to True, but can be set to False to deny permission to a specific web part.

Creating Solution Packages

Setting the output path for the web part project to \bin or copying the assembly are simple ways to ensure that the final web part assembly is deployed to the right location; however, this technique is only useful in a development environment. For production environments, you will want to build a solution package that can be deployed independent of Visual Studio.

Creating solution packages is done inside Visual Studio .NET as a new cabinet project in the same solution where the web part project is located. When you create the cabinet, you need to create a solution manifest file and include the assembly file to successfully deploy the web part. SharePoint recognizes cabinet files with a WSP extension as solution packages. Solution packages can be used to deploy all manner of components.

Before you can create the solution package, you must create a manifest file to describe the solution. This file must be named `manifest.xml` and will include a reference to the assembly as well as an appropriate entry for the `SafeControls` section of the `web.config` file. The simplest way to make this file is to include it directly in the web part project. Listing 10-8 shows an example `manifest.xml` file that deploys a web part to the \bin directory.

Listing 10-8. *A Typical manifest.xml File*

```
<Solution xmlns=http://schemas.microsoft.com/sharepoint/
  SolutionId="997310BA-AB2E-4d97-87B4-4DABAB0EB796" >
  <Assemblies>
    <Assembly DeploymentTarget="WebApplication" Location="SPScript.dll">
      <SafeControls>
        <SafeControl
        Assembly="SPScript, Version=1.0.0.0, Culture=neutral,
        PublicKeyToken=689f1d0ba493bcce"
        Namespace="SPScript" Safe="True" TypeName="*"/>
      </SafeControls>
    </Assembly>
  </Assemblies>
</Solution>
```

The `Solution` element contains a `SolutionId` attribute that uses a `GUID` to uniquely identify the solution. The `Assembly` element contains a `DeploymentTarget` attribute that can be set to `WebApplication` or `GlobalAssemblyCache` to specify whether the assembly should be deployed to the \bin directory or the GAC, respectively. The `SafeControl` element is used to specify an entry in the `web.config` file for the assembly. Once you have the `manifest.xml` file created, you can create a deployment package for the web part.

Here are the steps to follow to create a deployment package:

■**Note** If you are strictly following this text, you may not have developed your first web part yet. If so, complete this series of steps after you finish the exercise at the end of the chapter.

---

1. Start Visual Studio.

2. Open a solution containing a web part project.

3. From the Visual Studio main menu, select File ➤ Add Project ➤ New Project to open the Add New Project dialog.

4. Click the Setup and Deployment Projects folder.

5. Select to create a new CAB project.

6. Name the project and click OK.

7. In the Solution Explorer, right-click the CAB project and select Add ➤ Project Output from the context menu.

8. In the Add Project Output Group dialog box, select the web part project you want to deploy from the Project drop-down list.

9. In the configuration drop-down list, select Release Any CPU.

10. In the Project list box, select Primary Output to include the assembly in the cabinet file.

11. Click OK.

12. In the Solution Explorer, right-click the CAB project again and select Add ➤ Project Output from the context menu.

13. In the Add Project Output Group dialog box, select the web part project you want to deploy.

14. In the configuration drop-down list, select Release Any CPU.

15. In the Project list box, select Content Files to include the `manifest.xml` file.

16. Click OK.

17. Build the cabinet project.

Once the cabinet file is created, you should rename it to have a WSP extension. Then you may add it to the *solution store*, which is a central location for deploying solutions to web applications. In order to add your solution to the store, you must use the administration tool StsAdm.exe. The tool is located in the directory \Program Files\Common Files\ Microsoft Shared\web server extensions\12\bin. Use the following command to add a solution to the solution store:

```
Stsadm.exe -o addsolution -filename mypart.wsp
```

Once your solution is added to the store, you can deploy it to any web application. Open the Central Administration web site and click the Solution Management link on the Operations tab. The Solution Management page displays all of the solutions in the store. Figure 10-4 shows the Solution Management page in the Central Administration web site.

Central Administration > Operations > Solution Management

Solution Management

This page has a list of the Solutions in the farm.

Name	Status	Deployed To
form-assets.wsp	Deployed	Globally deployed.
spscriptpackage.wsp	Not Deployed	None

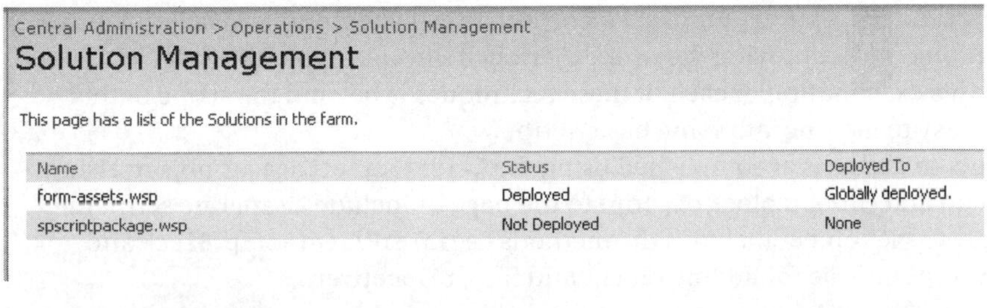

Figure 10-4. *The solution store*

From the Solution Management page, you can click any solution and then choose to deploy it. Deploying a solution from the solution store is much easier than copying the same files repeatedly to different web applications. Additionally, the Solution Management page can be used to remove a solution from a web application.

Using Custom Web Parts

Regardless of whether you edit the web.config file and copy the assembly by hand or use a solution package, a custom web part is not available for use until it is added to the Web Parts Gallery. You can access the Web Parts Gallery from the Site Settings page associated with the top-level site in a collection. This gallery shows all of the web parts that are available for use in the site collection.

You can add your custom web part to the gallery by clicking the New button, which will open the New Web Parts page. Any web part deployed manually or using a solution will appear on this page. You simply check the web parts that you want to add to the gallery, and then click the Populate Gallery button. After this, the selected web parts will be available for use on a web page. Figure 10-5 shows the New Web Parts page.

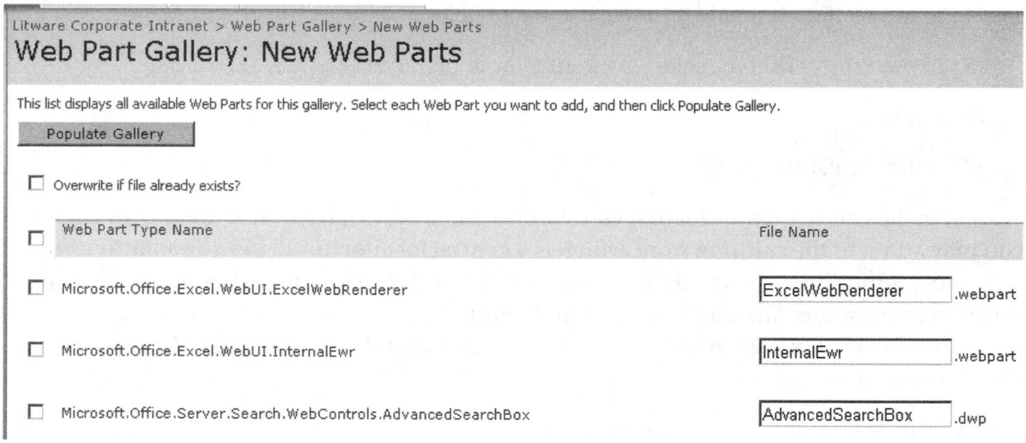

Litware Corporate Intranet > Web Part Gallery > New Web Parts
Web Part Gallery: New Web Parts

This list displays all available Web Parts for this gallery. Select each Web Part you want to add, and then click Populate Gallery.

| Populate Gallery |

☐ Overwrite if file already exists?

☐	Web Part Type Name	File Name
☐	Microsoft.Office.Excel.WebUI.ExcelWebRenderer	ExcelWebRenderer .webpart
☐	Microsoft.Office.Excel.WebUI.InternalEwr	InternalEwr .webpart
☐	Microsoft.Office.Server.Search.WebControls.AdvancedSearchBox	AdvancedSearchBox .dwp

Figure 10-5. *Adding web parts to the gallery*

Using Client-Side Script

Utilizing client-side script in a web part opens new development possibilities that include interacting with a rendered SharePoint page, incorporating Asynchronous JavaScript and XML (AJAX) solutions, and improving the user experience through dynamic HTML (DHTML). While an exhaustive examination of each of these techniques is beyond the scope of this book, it is pretty easy to incorporate some basic scripts.

Adding scripts to a page is accomplished using the ClientScriptManager object. Using this object, you can add either a block of script to the page or include a separate script file. The ClientScriptManager object includes the methods RegisterClientScriptBlock and RegisterClientScriptInclude for adding blocks and files, respectively.

You can use the ClientScriptManager object by getting a reference from the ClientScript property of the Page object. Typically, you will then call the IsClientScriptBlockRegistered method or the IsClientScriptIncludeRegistered method using a unique key for the script. If a script with that key has not already been registered, you proceed to register your own script.

When you register a script block, the code is inserted directly into the page. When you register a script file, on the other hand, a JavaScript include directive is created in the page. Listing 10-9 shows the code for two web parts; the first web part uses a script block, and the second web part uses an included file.

Listing 10-9. *Using Scripts*

```
//This web part generates a script block that looks like this
/*
<script type="text/javascript">
 <!--
  code
 // -->
</script>
 */

namespace SPScriptBlock
{
    public class Block:WebPart
    {
        string m_scriptBlock = "";
        string m_scriptKey = "scriptKey";

        //Key Property
        [Personalizable(PersonalizationScope.Shared), WebBrowsable(true),
        WebDisplayName("Script Key"),
        WebDescription("A unique key for the script.")]
        public string ScriptKey
        {
            get { return m_scriptKey; }
            set { m_scriptKey = value; }
        }

        //Script Property
        [Personalizable(PersonalizationScope.Shared), WebBrowsable(true),
        WebDisplayName("Script"),
        WebDescription("The JavaScript to insert in the page.")]
        public string Script
        {
            get { return m_scriptBlock; }
            set { m_scriptBlock = value; }
        }
```

```
            protected override void OnPreRender(EventArgs e)
            {
                base.OnPreRender(e);

                if (m_scriptBlock != "" &&
                   !Page.ClientScript.IsClientScriptBlockRegistered(m_scriptKey))
                     Page.ClientScript.RegisterClientScriptBlock(
                        typeof(string), m_scriptKey, m_scriptBlock, true);

            }

        }
    }

    //This part creates the include directive
    //<script src="{js file}" type="text/javascript"></script>

    namespace SPScriptInclude
    {
        public class Loader:WebPart
        {
            string m_scriptFile = "";
            string m_scriptKey = "scriptKey";

            //Key Property
            [Personalizable(PersonalizationScope.Shared), WebBrowsable(true),
            WebDisplayName("Script Key"),
            WebDescription("A unique key for the script.")]
            public string ScriptKey
            {
                get { return m_scriptKey; }
                set { m_scriptKey = value; }
            }

            //Script Property
            [Personalizable(PersonalizationScope.Shared), WebBrowsable(true),
            WebDisplayName("Script File"),
            WebDescription("The name of the JavaScript file to insert in the page.")]
            public string ScriptFile
            {
                get { return m_scriptFile; }
                set { m_scriptFile = value; }
            }


            protected override void OnPreRender(EventArgs e)
            {
```

```
        base.OnPreRender(e);

        if (m_scriptFile != "" &&
!Page.ClientScript.IsClientScriptIncludeRegistered(m_scriptKey))
            Page.ClientScript.RegisterClientScriptInclude(m_scriptKey,
Page.ResolveClientUrl(m_scriptFile));


    }

  }
}
```

Building Connectable Web Parts

The philosophy behind the use of web parts in SharePoint is that end users should be able to access information and assemble views without having to rely upon programmers to create custom web pages. One of the ways that this philosophy is put into action is through the use of web part *connections*. Connecting web parts in the portal allows a value from one web part to be used as an input, a sort, or a filter for the display of another web part. In Chapter 5, you saw this functionality from the end user perspective.

When you create connectable web parts, you can design them to use a custom interface of your own making or a standard set of interfaces provided by SharePoint. Using your own custom interfaces is significantly easier to implement than using the standard set of SharePoint interfaces. However, your own custom interfaces will be limited to connecting with other web parts that utilize the same interface. If you want to connect with existing SharePoint web parts, lists, and libraries, you must implement the standard set of SharePoint interfaces.

Building Custom Connection Interfaces

When you build custom connection interfaces, you start by defining an interface that returns the type of data that you want to pass from one part to another. There are no special requirements for this interface, and it looks like any you would define. The following code shows a simple interface defined to pass a string from one web part to another:

```
public interface IStringConnection
{
    string ProvidedString { get;}
}
```

The provider web part, which supplies the value to be passed, will implement the custom connection interface. Along with the implementation of the interface, the provider web part exposes a property that returns a reference to the connectable interface. The property must then be decorated with the ConnectionProvider attribute, which marks the interface as connectable within the web part infrastructure. Listing 10-10 shows how a web part class would implement an interface and expose it for connections.

Listing 10-10. *Implementing a Custom Interface*

```
public class StringProvider:WebPart,IStringConnection
{

    protected string m_string = "Test Data";

    [ConnectionProvider("String Provider")]
    public IStringConnection ConnectionInterface()
    {
        return this;
    }

    //The passed value
    public string ProvidedString
    {
        get { return m_string; }
    }
}
```

The consumer web part, which will receive the passed value, must contain a method for receiving the connection interface. This method is also decorated with the ConnectionProvider attribute. This attribute determines which web parts on a page are compatible for connections. Listing 10-11 shows how a web part class would obtain a reference to the connectable interface and receive the passed value.

Listing 10-11. *Receiving a Value*

```
public class SPStringConsumer : WebPart
{

    IStringConnection m_providerPart = null;

    [ConnectionConsumer("String Consumer")]
    public void GetConnectionInterface(IStringConnection providerPart)
    {
        m_providerPart = providerPart;
    }

    protected override void RenderContents(HtmlTextWriter writer)
    {
      try
      {
        writer.Write(m_providerPart.ProvidedString);
      }
      catch
```

```
    {
        writer.Write("No connection.");
    }
  }
}
```

Once you have created and deployed compatible web parts, you can add them to a page. After they are on the page, they can be connected using the web part menu associated with either the provider or the consumer. When compatible web parts are on the same page, a menu item titled Connections will be available for selecting a compatible web part. This menu item functions identically to the ones you have used previously in the book to connect out-of-the-box web parts.

Using Standard Connection Interfaces

While creating custom interfaces is a quick way to connect web parts, they cannot be used to connect to libraries, lists, or out-of-the box web parts. SharePoint provides a separate set of interfaces that constitute a standard mechanism for connecting web parts. These interfaces expose methods and events that allow the connection infrastructure to query your web parts for appropriate connection information and provide notification when another web part wants to connect. The available interfaces support passing a single piece of data, a row of data, or an entire list of data. Table 10-1 lists the available interfaces and their purposes.

Table 10-1. *Connection Interfaces*

Interface	Purpose
IWebPartField	Allows a web part to provide or consume a cell of data
IWebPartRow	Allows a web part to provide or consume a row of data
IWebPartTable	Allows a web part to provide or consume a recordset of data
IWebPartParameters	Allows a web part to provide or consume multiple cells of data that can be mapped to the data cells in another web part

If a provider web part and a consumer web part are exchanging similar data—such as a single cell—they may be connected directly using the web part menu associated with either part. Connection interfaces, however, can often allow connections that are not immediately obvious. For example, a web part that provides an entire row can be connected to a web part that only consumes a single field.

Determining which interfaces are compatible is handled by the web part infrastructure according to several rules. The first, and most obvious, rule is that web parts providing or consuming the same data structures are always compatible. For interfaces that use different data structures, extended connections—known as *transformers*—are allowed where they make sense. The web part infrastructure implements a selection dialog that allows end users to map fields from compatible interfaces when necessary. Figure 10-6 shows a typical field selection dialog in SharePoint.

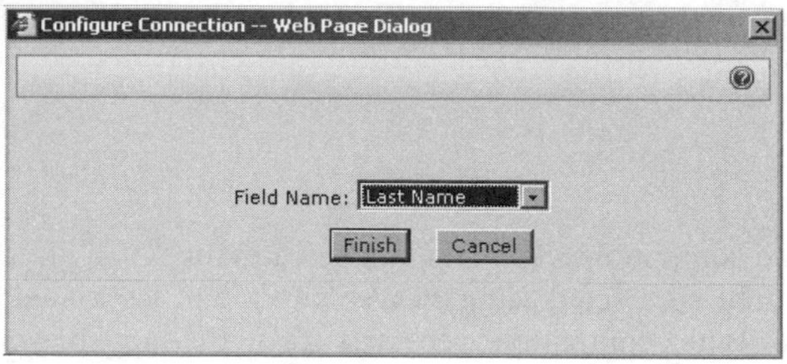

Figure 10-6. *Connecting web parts in SharePoint*

Building a Provider Web Part

You begin the process of creating a provider web part by deciding what kind of data it will expose. Based on this decision, your web part will implement the appropriate interface from Table 10-1. The code is very similar to creating your own custom interface except there are a couple of extra methods. Listing 10-12 shows the basic structure for stubbing out providers based on each of the available interfaces.

Listing 10-12. *Stubbing Out the Provider*

```
public class FieldProviderStub:WebPart,IWebPartField
{
    [ConnectionProvider("Data")]
    public IWebPartField ConnectionInterface()
    {
        return this;
    }

    public void GetFieldValue(FieldCallback callback)
    {
    }

    public PropertyDescriptor Schema
    {
        get {}
    }

}


public class RowProviderStub:WebPart,IWebPartRow
{
    [ConnectionProvider("Data")]
    public IWebPartRow ConnectionInterface()
    {
        return this;
    }
```

```csharp
    public void GetRowData(RowCallback callback)
    {
    }

    public PropertyDescriptorCollection Schema
    {
        get {}
    }

}


public class TableProviderStub:WebPart,IWebPartTable
{
    [ConnectionProvider("Data")]
    public IWebPartTable ConnectionInterface()
    {
        return this;
    }

    public void GetTableData(TableCallback callback)
    {
    }

    public PropertyDescriptorCollection Schema
    {
        get {}
    }

}


public class ParameterProviderStub:WebPart,IWebPartParameters
{
    [ConnectionProvider("Data")]
    public IWebPartParameters ConnectionInterface()
    {
        return this;
    }

    public void GetParametersData(ParametersCallback callback)
    {

    }
```

```
public PropertyDescriptorCollection Schema
{
    get {}
}

public void SetConsumerSchema(PropertyDescriptorCollection schema)
{
}

}
```

In just the same way as you did for custom interfaces, the provider must supply a reference to itself that is returned through a method decorated with the ConnectionProvider attribute. This reference is used by the web part infrastructure when connecting web parts.

Each provider must also implement a method for receiving a reference to the consumer web part. These methods are GetFieldValue, GetRowData, GetTableData, and GetParametersData, depending upon which interface you are implementing. During the connection process, the web part infrastructure will pass a callback reference in that you can use later to pass data to the consumer web part.

Each provider web part must also implement a method for exposing the schema for the data that will be returned. The method returns a System.ComponentModel.PropertyDescriptor if you are only passing a cell of data, or a System.ComponentModel. PropertyDescriptorCollection if you are passing a row, a table, or parameters. The returned schema can subsequently be used by the consumer to validate the passed data and ensure that it is meaningful.

The best way to implement these methods is to create a web part property for each piece of data that you want to make available. When you make a web part property, you can then use the System.ComponentModel.TypeDescriptor object to return information about the properties you want to expose. The following code shows how to return the schema for a LastName property.

```
public PropertyDescriptor Schema
{
    get { return TypeDescriptor.GetProperties(this)["LastName"];}
}
```

If you are implementing the IWebPartParameters interface, you will also have to create a SetConsumerSchema method. This method is called by the consumer web part during the connection process to pass the schema of the properties it has available for mapping. The provider can use this information to validate that the requested data is meaningful.

The data itself is transferred between the web parts on the server when the page is submitted. In the section "Understanding the Connection Life Cycle," I look in detail at the web part life cycle and how it is affected by connections. For now, examine Listing 10-13, which shows a complete provider web part that exposes a text value entered into a field.

Listing 10-13. *A Complete Provider Web Part*

```
public class TextProvider : WebPart, IWebPartField
{
    //Member variables
    protected Button button = null;
    protected TextBox text = null;
    string m_data = null;

    //Text Property
    [Personalizable(PersonalizationScope.Shared), WebBrowsable(false),
    WebDisplayName("Text"),
    WebDescription("The text to send")]
    public string Text
    {
        get { return m_data; }
        set { m_data = value; }
    }

    //Child controls
    protected override void CreateChildControls()
    {
        button = new Button();
        button.Text = "Send Data";
        button.Click += new EventHandler(button_Click);
        Controls.Add(button);

        text = new TextBox();
        Controls.Add(text);
    }

    //Show UI
    protected override void RenderContents(HtmlTextWriter writer)
    {
        button.RenderControl(writer);
        text.RenderControl(writer);
    }

    //The connection description
    [ConnectionProvider("Text")]
    public IWebPartField ConnectionInterface()
    {
        return this;
    }
```

```
        //Callback object
        public void GetFieldValue(FieldCallback callback)
        {
            //Send data to consumer
            callback.Invoke(text.Text);
        }

        //Publish schema
        public PropertyDescriptor Schema
        {
            get
            {return TypeDescriptor.GetProperties(this)["Text"];}
        }

        void button_Click(object sender, EventArgs e)
        {
            m_data = text.Text;
        }

}
```

Building a Consumer Web Part

When you create a consumer web part, you must first determine what kind of data structure
it will receive. However, you do not have to implement any specific interface to use the data
structure. Instead, you create a method decorated with the ConnectionProvider attribute to
receive a reference to the provider part. Additionally, you must register a callback method
with the provider part so the consumer can receive the data structure. This is done using del-
egates that are defined in the WebParts namespace. Listing 10-14 shows code stubbed out for
the different data structures that consumers can receive.

Listing 10-14. *Stubbing Out the Consumer*

```
public class FieldConsumerStub:WebPart
{

    [ConnectionConsumer("Field")]
    public void GetConnectionInterface(IWebPartField providerPart)
    {
        FieldCallback callback = new FieldCallback(ReceiveField);
        providerPart.GetFieldValue(callback);
    }

    public void ReceiveField(object field)
    {
    }

}
```

```
public class RowConsumerStub:WebPart
{
    [ConnectionConsumer("Row")]
    public void GetConnectionInterface(IWebPartRow providerPart)
    {
        RowCallback callback = new RowCallback(ReceiveRow);
        providerPart.GetRowData(callback);
    }

    public void ReceiveRow(object row)
    {
    }
}


public class TableConsumerStub:WebPart
{
    [ConnectionConsumer("Table")]
    public void GetConnectionInterface(IWebPartTable providerPart)
    {
        TableCallback callback = new TableCallback(ReceiveTable);
        providerPart.GetTableData(callback);
    }

    public void ReceiveTable(ICollection table)
    {
    }
}


public class ParametersConsumerStub:WebPart
{
    [ConnectionConsumer("Parameters")]
    public void GetConnectionInterface(IWebPartParameters providerPart)
    {
        //Specify what properties this part can map
        PropertyDescriptor[] property =
        {TypeDescriptor.GetProperties(this)["propertyName"]};
        PropertyDescriptorCollection schema =
        new PropertyDescriptorCollection(property);
        providerPart.SetConsumerSchema(schema);

        //Give provider reference to callback function
        ParametersCallback callback = new ParametersCallback(ReceiveParameters);
        providerPart.GetParametersData(callback);
    }
```

```
    public void ReceiveParameters(IDictionary parameters)
    {
    }
}
```

Understanding the Connection Life Cycle

The life cycle of parts involved in a connection follows the same events as an unconnected web part, with a few additions. The key new events occur when the connection interface is queried and the callback object is passed to the provider. The exact sequence of events that occurs during a connection is critical because certain values and objects may not exist until a specific time, and calling to them before they are created will result in errors.

The connection process begins when you choose to connect two web parts using the web part menu. When you make your selection, the current page is posted back and both the provider and the consumer execute the OnInit, LoadViewState, and OnLoad methods. So far, this is identical to the life cycle of an unconnected part.

After the web parts are loaded, the connection infrastructure queries the connection interfaces to get a reference to the provider web part and pass it to the consumer web part. The consumer web part then responds by sending the callback object to the provider. If the consumer expects to receive parameters, it may also publish its schema using the SetConsumerSchema method. At this point, the provider may immediately use the callback method to send a value.

Once references and data have been exchanged, the life cycle proceeds as normal. The CreateChildControls, OnPreRender, SaveViewState, RenderContents, OnUnload, and Dispose methods are executed. The consumer web part may use the passed data to affect its output as necessary.

After the connection is made, subsequent postbacks follow a slightly different sequence. Just like an unconnected web part, the connected web parts will execute OnInit, LoadViewState, CreateChildControls, and OnLoad. Now the sequence becomes interesting because the provider web part will proceed to execute any control events such as the Click method, but this will occur before the connection infrastructure provides the reference to the consumer web part.

It is important to understand that the references between the provider and the consumer are not persistent. They are reestablished by the connection infrastructure during each postback. Therefore, you cannot send data from provider to consumer until the reference is reestablished. This means that you cannot write code in control events to send data to the consumer, which is what you naturally want to do. Instead, use your control events to store data in the viewstate or another control. Then you can send the stored data as the source for the consumer. Listing 10-13 earlier shows this exact technique for a provider web part. At the end of this chapter, you will also find a complete exercise for creating connected web parts.

Custom Editor Parts

Throughout our investigation of web parts, you have used properties to configure the parts within SharePoint. The web parts you have created have supported fundamental types such as String and Boolean. The tool pane in SharePoint automatically creates the appropriate user interface element—called an *editor part*—for these basic properties in the tool pane. For example, the tool pane uses a text box editor part for String properties and a check box editor part for Boolean properties.

There may be times, however, when you want to create more complex properties. In these cases, you may need to create your own custom editor parts to allow the end user to set the properties of your web part. These custom editor parts allow you significant control over how your web parts are configured.

Creating an Editor Part

To create a custom editor part, you need to build a new class that inherits from the EditorPart class. Because an editor part is essentially a specialized web part that runs in the tool pane of SharePoint, you will find that you use many of the same skills to build an editor part that you used previously to build web parts.

Just like a standard web part, editor parts must override the CreateChildControls method to build a user interface. You draw the user interface by overriding the RenderContents method in the same way you would for a web part. When the user interface is drawn, the child controls show up in the property pane.

What makes an editor part different from a standard web part is that it has methods that allow it to receive events from the property pane in SharePoint. These events are fired whenever a user clicks Apply, OK, or Cancel in the tool pane. The EditorPart class allows your custom editor part to receive these events through the ApplyChanges and SyncChanges methods.

The ApplyChanges method is called by the web part infrastructure whenever a user clicks Apply or OK. In this method, you retrieve the new value of the property as it was entered into the property pane by the end user. You must in turn pass the property to the web part so that it can update its own display. In order to pass a value from the property pane to the web part, you must retrieve a reference to the web part using the WebPartToEdit property.

After any changes are made in the property pane, the web part infrastructure calls the SyncChanges method. This method is used to pass changes back from the web part to the property pane. This is necessary because the web part and the property pane can be out of sync if the user cancels an action or if there is a validation error you need to report to the user. Listing 10-15 shows a complete editor part for a custom phone number field that uses a regular expression to ensure the phone number is formatted correctly.

Listing 10-15. *A Custom Editor Part*

```
public class PhoneEditor:EditorPart
{
    TextBox property = null;
    Label messages = null;

    protected override void CreateChildControls()
    {
        property = new TextBox();
        Controls.Add(property);

        messages = new Label();
        Controls.Add(messages);
    }
```

```csharp
protected override void RenderContents(HtmlTextWriter writer)
{
    property.RenderControl(writer);
    writer.Write("<br/>");
    messages.RenderControl(writer);
}

public override bool ApplyChanges()
{
    try
    {
        Regex expression = new Regex(@"\(\d\d\d\)\s\d\d\d-\d\d\d\d");
        Match match = expression.Match(property.Text);
        if (match.Success == true)
        {
            ((PhoneLabel)WebPartToEdit).Phone = property.Text;
            messages.Text = "";
        }
        else
        {
            ((PhoneLabel)WebPartToEdit).Phone = "Invalid phone number";
        }
    }
    catch (Exception x)
    {
        messages.Text += x.Message;
    }
    return true;
}

public override void SyncChanges()
{
    try
    {
        property.Text = ((PhoneLabel)WebPartToEdit).Phone;
    }
    catch { }
}

}
```

Using an Editor Part

Once you have created a custom editor part, you must associate it with a web part. This is accomplished by overriding the CreateEditorParts method of the web part. When the CreateEditorParts method is called, you can create instances of any editor parts you want to load into the property pane. After the editor parts are created, you must add them to a new

EditorPartCollection and return the collection. Listing 10-16 shows a complete web part for displaying a phone number with a custom format.

Listing 10-16. *Using a Custom Editor Part*

```
public class PhoneLabel:WebPart
{
    protected string m_phone;

    [Personalizable(PersonalizationScope.Shared), WebBrowsable(false),
    WebDisplayName("Phone"),
    WebDescription("Phone number")]
    public string Phone
    {
        get { return m_phone; }
        set { m_phone = value; }
    }

    public override EditorPartCollection CreateEditorParts()
    {
        ArrayList partsArray = new ArrayList();

        PhoneEditor phonePart = new PhoneEditor();
        phonePart.ID = this.ID + "_editorPart1";
        phonePart.Title = "Phone Number";
        phonePart.GroupingText = "(xxx) xxx-xxxx";
        partsArray.Add(phonePart);

        EditorPartCollection parts = new EditorPartCollection(partsArray);
        return parts;
    }

    protected override void RenderContents(HtmlTextWriter writer)
    {
        writer.Write("<p>" + m_phone + "</p>");
    }
}
```

Exercise 10.1. A Complete Web Part

Throughout this chapter, you have examined all the aspects of creating custom web parts. In this exercise, you'll bring together several of the concepts into a complete web part. This web part will be used to access a database and display the results in a table.

Installing the AdventureWorks Database

You'll need a sample database for creating this web part. If you followed the setup instructions in Chapter 2, you should have SQL Server 2005 available to you. Unfortunately, SQL Server 2005 does not ship with a sample database. Therefore, you'll have to install a sample database before you can get started.

Follow these steps to install the sample database:

1. Log in to VSSQL as an administrator.

2. Open the browser and navigate to `http://go.microsoft.com/fwlink/?linkid=31046`.

3. Run the `AdventureWorksDB.msi` file.

4. Select Start ➤ All Programs ➤ Microsoft SQL Server 2005 ➤ SQL Server Management Studio.

5. Connect to the default instance of SQL Server running on VSSQL.

6. In SQL Server Management Studio, right-click the Databases folder and select Attach from the context menu.

7. In the Attach Databases dialog, click the Add button.

8. In the Locate Database Files dialog, select the `AdventureWorks_Data.mdf` file and click the OK button.

9. In the Attach Databases dialog, click the OK button.

10. Close SQL Server Management Studio.

Creating the New Project

Web parts are created as classes in Visual Studio 2005. In order to create the web part, you'll need to create a class and set some references to namespaces you will use. After creating the project, you'll import the referenced namespaces.

Follow these steps to create the new project:

1. Open Visual Studio .NET 2005.

2. Select File ➤ New ➤ Project from the menu.

3. In the New Project dialog, select the Visual C# folder.

4. From the project items, select Class Library.

5. Name the new project **SPDataPart**.

6. Click OK.

7. In the Solution Explorer, right-click the file `Class1.cs` and select Rename from the context menu.

8. Rename this file **Adventure.cs**.

9. In the source code, have the `Adventure` class inherit from the `WebPart` class as shown in the following code:

```
public class Adventure:WebPart
```

10. Select Project ➤ Add Reference from the main menu.

11. In the Add Reference dialog, select `System.Web` and `System.Drawing` from the component list.

12. Click the OK button.

13. Add the following statements to the top of the class definition to reference the required namespaces:

```
using System.Web.UI;
using System.Web.UI.WebControls;
using System.Web.UI.WebControls.WebParts;
using System.Data;
using System.Data.SqlClient;
using System.Drawing;
```

Coding the Web Part

Once you have the basic class stubbed out, you can proceed to code the web part. In this exercise, you'll add a property and some child controls to the web part. You'll use the properties and controls to query a database and display a result set.

Defining the Properties

The web part only requires a single property for defining the database connection string. Once deployed, you will have to set this string inside of SharePoint. Although we are using a connection string for simplicity, you should be careful about saving sensitive user and password information in a web part property. SharePoint has a single sign-on service that you'll learn about in Chapter 11, which is the appropriate place for storing credentials.

Add the following code to the `Adventure` class to define the `Connection` property:

```
//Member variables for properties
protected string m_connection;

//Connection Property
[Personalizable(PersonalizationScope.Shared),WebBrowsable(true),
WebDisplayName("Connection String"),
WebDescription("The connection string for the AdventureWorks database")]
public string Connection
{
    get{return m_connection;}
    set{m_connection=value;}
}
```

Defining the Child Controls

In order to use existing ASP.NET controls in your new web part, you must override the
CreateChildControls method. In this method, you programmatically create a new instance
of each child control, adjust its properties, and add it to the Controls set for the web part.
Listing 10-17 shows how to create the child controls for the web part.

Listing 10-17. *Defining the Child Controls*

```
DataGrid grid;
Label messages;

protected override void CreateChildControls()
{
    //Add grid
    grid = new DataGrid();
    grid.AutoGenerateColumns = false;
    grid.Width = Unit.Percentage(100);
    grid.GridLines = GridLines.Horizontal;
    grid.HeaderStyle.CssClass = "ms-vh2";
    grid.CellPadding = 2;

    //Grid columns
    BoundColumn column = new BoundColumn();
    column.DataField = "FullName";
    column.HeaderText = "Associate";
    grid.Columns.Add(column);
    column = new BoundColumn();
    column.DataField = "Title";
    column.HeaderText = "Title";
    grid.Columns.Add(column);

    column = new BoundColumn();
    column.DataField = "SalesTerritory";
    column.HeaderText = "Territory";
    grid.Columns.Add(column);

    column = new BoundColumn();
    column.DataField = "2002";
    column.HeaderText = "2002";
    column.DataFormatString = "{0:C}";
    column.ItemStyle.BackColor = Color.Wheat;
    grid.Columns.Add(column);

    column = new BoundColumn();
    column.DataField = "2003";
    column.HeaderText = "2003";
    column.DataFormatString = "{0:C}";
    grid.Columns.Add(column);
```

```
column = new BoundColumn();
column.DataField = "2004";
column.HeaderText = "2004";
column.DataFormatString = "{0:C}";
column.ItemStyle.BackColor = Color.Wheat;
grid.Columns.Add(column);

Controls.Add(grid);

//Add label
messages = new Label();
Controls.Add(messages);

}
```

Rendering the Web Part

Rendering the web part is done in the RenderContents method. In this exercise, you will create a layout table in HTML and then render the web part's constituent controls in the table. Layout tables are a good way to ensure that your web part looks good regardless of where it is positioned on the page.

Add the following code to the Adventure class to render the user interface:

```
protected override void RenderContents(HtmlTextWriter writer)
{
    DataSet dataSet = null;
    string sql = "SELECT    FullName, Title, SalesTerritory, " +
    "[2002], [2003], [2004] FROM Sales.vSalesPersonSalesByFiscalYears";

    //Get data
    using (SqlConnection conn = new SqlConnection(Connection))
    {
        try
        {
            conn.Open();
            SqlDataAdapter adapter = new SqlDataAdapter(sql, conn);
            dataSet = new DataSet("root");
            adapter.Fill(dataSet, "sales");

        }
        catch (SqlException x)
        {
            messages.Text = x.Message;
        }
        catch (Exception x)
        {
            messages.Text += x.Message;
        }
```

```
    }

    //Bind data
    try
    {
        grid.DataSource = dataSet;
        grid.DataMember = "sales";
        grid.DataBind();
    }
    catch (Exception x)
    {
        messages.Text += x.Message;
    }

    //Display data
    writer.Write("<table border=\"0\" width=\"100%\">");
    writer.Write("<tr><td>");
    grid.RenderControl(writer);
    writer.Write("</td></tr>");
    writer.Write("<tr><td>");
    messages.RenderControl(writer);
    writer.Write("</td></tr>");
    writer.Write("</table>");

    }
}
```

Deploying the Web Part

In order to deploy the web part, you must give it a strong name and allow partially trusted callers to access the web part. Additionally, you must create a solution package so that administrators can control which web applications will use the web part. In the next section you will create a strong name for the web part, but for now, open the AssemblyInfo.cs file and add the attribute [assembly: System.Security.AllowPartiallyTrustedCallers()].

Creating a Strong Name

Web parts should have a strong name when used with SharePoint. In order to give the web part a strong name, you have to create a key pair file using the Strong Name tool, sn.exe. Once the strong name is created, you must create a reference to it in the assembly file. Although you can also create a strong name in Visual Studio for your assembly, it's easier to use the same key pair file for all your testing and debugging.

Perform these steps to create a strong name:

1. Open a command window by selecting Start ➤ All Programs ➤ Microsoft Visual Studio 2005 ➤ Visual Studio 2005 Command Prompt.

2. In the command-line window, create a key file by executing the following line:

```
sn.exe -k c:\keypair.snk
```

3. In Visual Studio right-click the SPDataPart project and select Properties from the context menu.

4. In the Properties dialog, click the Signing tab.

5. Check the box labeled Sign the Assembly.

6. Select <Browse…> from the drop-down list on the Signing tab.

7. In the Select File dialog, navigate to c:\keypair.snk and select it.

8. Click the Open button.

Creating a Manifest File

Even though the web part has compiled successfully, it cannot run in SharePoint until it is deployed to the target web application and marked as safe. While you can certainly accomplish these tasks manually, the best way to deploy a web part is with a solution file. The solution file will make the web part available for deployment through the Central Administration web site, which will allow it to be deployed to multiple web applications from a single location. In order to create a solution, you must first add a manifest file to the web part project. The manifest file contains the information necessary to deploy the web part and update the web configuration file.

Follow these steps to create the manifest file:

1. In the Solution Explorer, right-click the project and select Add ➤ New Item from the context menu.

2. In the Add New Item dialog, select XML File.

3. Enter **manifest.xml** in the Name field and click the Add button.

4. When the new file opens, add the following code and save the file.

```xml
<?xml version="1.0" encoding="utf-8" ?>
<Solution xmlns="http://schemas.microsoft.com/sharepoint/"
  SolutionId="AF597DAB-65D7-4c1a-A012-D04184CA647E">
    <Assemblies>
      <Assembly DeploymentTarget="WebApplication"
      Location="SPDataPart.dll">
       <SafeControls>
        <SafeControl
         Assembly="SPDataPart, Version=1.0.0.0, Culture=neutral,
         PublicKeyToken=8c9fc716f38d08b2"
         Namespace="SPDataPart" TypeName="*"/>
       </SafeControls>
      </Assembly>
    </Assemblies>
</Solution>
```

Note Be sure to change the PublicKeyToken in the previous listing to match your assembly.

Creating a Solution Package

Once the manifest file is completed, you are ready to create a *solution package*. The solution package is essentially a cabinet file that contains the web part assembly and manifest file. Once created, you may add the solution to the Central Administration solution store where an administrator can determine which web applications can utilize the new web part.

Follow these steps to create the solution package:

1. From the Visual Studio main menu, select File ➤ Add Project ➤ New Project to open the Add New Project dialog.

2. Click the Setup and Deployment Projects folder.

3. Select to create a new CAB Project.

4. Name the project **SPDataPartSolution** and click OK.

5. In the Solution Explorer, right-click the CAB project and select Add ➤ Project Output from the context menu.

6. In the Add Project Output Group dialog box, select SPDataPart from the Project drop-down list.

7. In the configuration drop-down list, select (Active).

8. In the project list box, select Primary Output to include the assembly in the cabinet file.

9. Click OK.

10. In the Solution Explorer, right-click the CAB project again and select Add ➤ Project Output from the context menu.

11. In the Add Project Output Group dialog box, select SPDataPart from the Project drop-down list.

12. In the configuration drop-down list, select (Active).

13. In the Project list box, select Content Files to include the manifest.xml file.

14. Click OK.

15. Build the Cabinet project, which should also build the web part project for you automatically.

16. Once you have built the solution project, locate the SPDataPartSolution.CAB file and rename it to SPDataPartSolution.WSP.

17. Run the following command-line operation to add the solution package to the solution store:

```
Stsadm.exe -o addsolution -filename SPDataPartSolution.wsp
```

Deploying the Web Part to a Web Application

Once the solution package has been added to the solution store, you can access it from the Central Administration web site. From the Central Administration web site, you may select to deploy the solution to a web application. Once deployed to a web application, a site collection administrator can make the web part available through the Web Parts Gallery.

Follow these steps to deploy the web part:

1. Select Start ➤ All Programs ➤ Microsoft Office Server ➤ SharePoint 3.0 Central Administration.

2. In the Central Administration web site, click the Operations tab.

3. On the Operations page, click the Solution Management link under the Global Configuration section.

4. On the Solution Management page, click the link for the spdatapartsolution.wsp package to open the Solution Properties page.

5. On the Solution Properties page, click the Deploy Solution button.

6. On the Deploy Solution page, click the OK button.

Using the Web Part

Once the web part is properly deployed to a web application, it can be used in a page. To use the web part, it must be added to the Web Parts Gallery. Once it's added, it can drag it onto a page and have its properties set.

Perform these steps to use the web part:

1. Log In to the home page of a site collection as a site administrator.

2. Select Site Settings ➤ Modify All Site Settings from the Site Actions menu.

3. On the Site Settings page, click the Web Parts link under the Galleries section.

■**Note** If you do not see the Web Parts Gallery listed, you are not at the top-level site. Click the link titled Go to Top Level Site Settings.

---

4. On the Web Part Gallery page, click the New button.

5. On the New Web Parts page, check the box next to the SPDataPart.Adventure web part and click the Populate Gallery button.

6. Navigate to the site where you want to use the web part.

7. On the site, select Edit Page from the Site Actions menu.

8. Click the Add a Web Part link in any zone.

9. In the Add Web Parts dialog, check the Adventure web part and click the Add button.

10. When the web part appears on the page, drop the Edit menu and select Modify Shared Web Part.

11. Locate the Connection String property in the SPDataPart task pane and enter **Data Source=VSSQL;Initial Catalog=AdventureWorks;Integrated Security=SSPI;**. Figure 10-7 shows the final web part.

■**Note** Web parts that access databases require at least the WSS_Medium security policy in the `web.config` file. If you receive a security message from the web part, check the `trust` element in the `web.config` file.

SPAdventure ▾

Associate	Title	Territory	2002	2003	2004
Michael G Blythe	Sales Representative	Northeast	$1,951,086.83	$4,743,906.89	$4,557,045.05
Linda C Mitchell	Sales Representative	Southwest	$2,800,029.15	$4,647,225.44	$5,200,475.23
Jillian Carson	Sales Representative	Central	$3,308,895.85	$4,991,867.71	$3,857,163.63
Garrett R Vargas	Sales Representative	Canada	$1,135,639.26	$1,480,136.01	$1,764,938.99
Tsvi Michael Reiter	Sales Representative	Southeast	$3,242,697.01	$2,661,156.24	$2,811,012.72
Pamela O Ansman-Wolfe	Sales Representative	Northwest	$1,473,076.91	$900,368.58	$1,656,492.86
Shu K Ito	Sales Representative	Southwest	$2,040,118.62	$2,870,320.86	$3,018,725.49
José Edvaldo Saraiva	Sales Representative	Canada	$2,532,500.91	$1,488,793.34	$3,189,356.25
David R Campbell	Sales Representative	Northwest	$1,243,580.77	$1,377,431.33	$1,930,885.56
Jae B Pak	Sales Representative	United Kingdom		$5,287,044.31	$5,015,682.38
Ranjit R Varkey Chudukatil	Sales Representative	France		$1,677,652.44	$3,827,950.24
Tete A Mensa-Annan	Sales Representative	Northwest		$883,338.71	$1,931,620.18
Rachel B Valdez	Sales Representative	Germany			$2,241,204.04
Lynn N Tsoflias	Sales Representative	Australia			$1,758,385.93

Figure 10-7. *The completed web part*

Exercise 10.2. Connectable Web Parts

Connectable web parts allow you to use one web part to modify the behavior of another. A common use for connected web parts is for one web part to provide a filter value for the other. In this exercise, you will modify the web part from the previous exercise to consume a filter value. Then you will create a SharePoint contact list to filter the results by person. Because Exercise 10.1 is a prerequisite for this exercise, be sure you have it completed and running before you proceed.

Adding the Filter Property

After finishing Exercise 10.1, the Adventure web part will return an entire result set of information. In order to filter the results, you must add a property that can be used as a filter in the query. This property will filter by last name and be set by another web part. Therefore, the property will not be visible in the property pane.

Open the SPDataPart project and add the following code to the Adventure class to add the new LastName property for filtering:

```
//Filter value
string m_lastName = null;

//Filter Property
[Personalizable(PersonalizationScope.Shared), WebBrowsable(false),
WebDisplayName("Last Name"),
WebDescription("The last name to use as a filter")]
public string LastName
{
    get { return m_lastName; }
    set { m_lastName = value; }
}
```

Adding the Callback Method

Once the new property is added, you must add the code that will get a reference to the provider part and allow you to pass a reference to the callback function. Since this web part will only filter by last name, you will accept connections with providers that implement IWebPartField or an interface that can be transformed to provide a single value.

Add the following code to support these connections:

```
[ConnectionConsumer("Last Name")]
public void GetConnectionInterface(IWebPartField providerPart)
{
    FieldCallback callback = new FieldCallback(ReceiveField);
    providerPart.GetFieldValue(callback);
}

public void ReceiveField(object field)
{
    if(field!=null)
        LastName = field.ToString();
}
```

Modifying the SQL Statement

Once the web part connection is made, you will need to use the passed value to filter the SQL statement. In this exercise, you will simply change the SQL in the web part to use the passed value. Alter the SQL statement to appear as this:

```
string sql = "SELECT    FullName, Title, SalesTerritory, " +
"[2002], [2003], [2004] FROM Sales.vSalesPersonSalesByFiscalYears " +
"WHERE FullName LIKE '%" + LastName +"'";
```

Building and Deploying the Web Part

Once the web part modifications are made, build the part. If you followed the steps in the previous exercise, simply copy the new assembly into the \bin directory. There are no other steps required because you already gave it a strong name and modified the web configuration file.

Creating the Contact List

After the web part is deployed and functioning, you'll need to create a list to act as a filter. After you create the list, you'll connect it to the web part. Once connected, you can select items in the list and filter the data shown in the web part.

Follow these steps to create the list:

1. On the same site as the web part, select Create from the Site Actions menu.

2. On the Create page, click the Contacts link.

3. On the New page, enter **Sales Reps** in the Name field and click the Create button.

4. In the Quick Launch area of the site, click the Sales Reps link.

5. On the Sales Reps page, add a contact entry for **Michael Blythe**, **Jillian Carson**, and **Linda Mitchell**.

6. Return to the home page of the site and select Edit Page from the Site Actions menu.

7. Click the link to Add a Web Part in any zone.

8. In the Add Web Parts dialog, select the Sales Reps list and click the Add button.

9. Using the web part menu associated with the Adventure web part, select Connections ➤ Get Last Name From ➤ Sales Reps.

10. In the Configure Connection dialog, select Last Name from the drop-down list.

11. Click the Finish button.

12. Click the link titled Exit Edit Mode.

13. You should now be able to select contacts in the list and filter the results in the data grid. Figure 10-8 shows the final connected web parts.

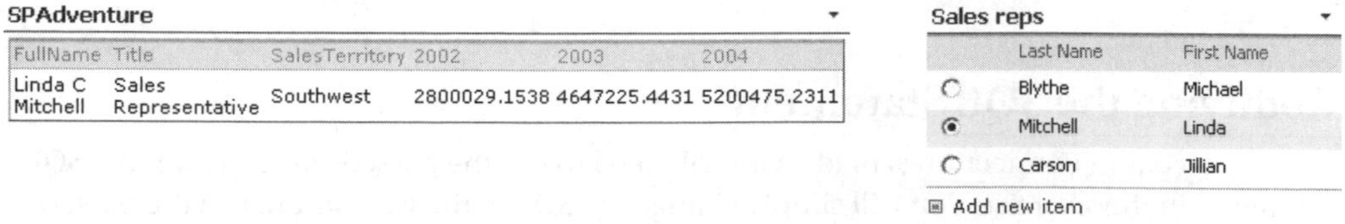

SPAdventure						▾
FullName	Title		SalesTerritory	2002	2003	2004
Linda C Mitchell	Sales Representative		Southwest	2800029.1538	4647225.4431	5200475.2311

Sales reps		▾
	Last Name	First Name
○	Blythe	Michael
◉	Mitchell	Linda
○	Carson	Jillian

▣ Add new item

Figure 10-8. *Connected web parts*

■ ■ ■

CHAPTER 11

Programming SharePoint Services

Throughout this book, I have presented many different techniques for configuring and customizing SharePoint. When discussing these techniques, I have focused on practical examples that solve common issues. There will be many times, however, when you want to go beyond the basics and create an advanced feature or solve a problem particular to your organization. In these situations, you will need a strong understanding of site definitions, the SharePoint object model, and the exposed web services. In this chapter, I will present these advanced programming interfaces so that you can make use of them in your solutions. All of these interfaces are fully documented in the WSS and MOSS SDKs available at http://msdn2.microsoft.com.

Understanding Site Definitions

Although I have presented many different ways to customize the look, navigation, and content of a SharePoint site, there are times when you will want to create your own site definition. Creating your own site definition has significant advantages because it represents a single template that can be used to create multiple sites. Furthermore, sites that are built from a site definition are always *uncustomized*, which means that changing the site definition will change all of the sites based on that template. I discussed the performance and maintenance issues surrounding customized and uncustomized pages in Chapter 5.

A site definition provides the fundamental structure of a site and specifies its initial feature set, available web parts, defined lists, navigational elements, and more. Site definitions are the underlying structures that result in the list of site templates that appear in SharePoint. As such, site definitions are the most fundamental building block of a SharePoint solution. A site definition consists of several files located in folders beneath the \Program Files\Common Files\Microsoft Shared\web server extensions\12\TEMPLATE\SiteTemplates directory. The key files are listed in Table 11-1, and I discuss them in detail throughout this section.

Table 11-1. *Key Site Definition Files*

File	Description
ONET.XML	This is the main site definition file. This file specifies various configurations available for a site including lists, web parts, navigation, and features.
Default.aspx	This is the file that will be used to render the home page of sites created from this definition. Each site definition may have its own Default.aspx file.
default.master	This is the default.master page for all site definitions. The same file is used for every site definition.
SCHEMA.XML	There are several files by this name that define the initial column set for lists and libraries in a site.
STDVIEW.XML	This file defines view information for a site. It should never be edited.
VWSTYLES.XML	This file defines view information for lists. It should never be edited.

Creating new site definitions is accomplished using the Collaborative Application Markup Language (CAML). CAML is a language based on XML elements that define all aspects of a SharePoint site, from link structure to available web parts. Each time you create a new SharePoint site, a CAML template is used to generate the pages associated with the site. By modifying these CAML structures, you can make small changes to a site layout or even create radically new site structures.

Creating a New Site Definition

While it is theoretically possible to create your own site definition from scratch, there really is no reason to attempt it. Instead, it is better to start off by copying one of the existing site definitions and modifying it. All of the site definitions can be found in the C:\Program Files\ Common Files\Microsoft Shared\web server extensions\12\TEMPLATE\Site Templates directory. In this directory, you will find a folder for each definition. Along with these specific site definitions, some common elements have been factored out into the separate directory C:\Program Files\Common Files\Microsoft Shared\web server extensions\12\TEMPLATE\ GLOBAL. This folder contains the definition for common lists and the default.master page.

■Note Once again, Microsoft has saddled us with some disappointing terminology by using the term *site template* in different ways. This term is sometimes used in SharePoint to refer to a site that has been saved as a *site template file (STP)*, but it is also used to refer to a *site definition*. This is unfortunate because there is a significant difference between these two mechanisms for creating new sites. Sites created from site definitions are always *uncustomized*, while sites created from STP files are always *customized*. As I discuss in Chapter 5, customizing sites can have a significant impact on maintenance. In order to avoid confusion, more precise terminology is required to make it clear which technique you are using to create a site.

In order to make your own site definition, all you have to do is copy one of the directories and give it a new name. When you create your new folder, make sure that it is located in the Site Templates directory. Copying an existing site definition folder will give you all of the elements necessary to render a new site template in SharePoint. As a simple example, I copied the STS folder—which defines a standard team site—and renamed it SOFTWARE. I want to use this site definition to create a new type of site for supporting software development projects. Figure 11-1 shows the new folder in the File Explorer.

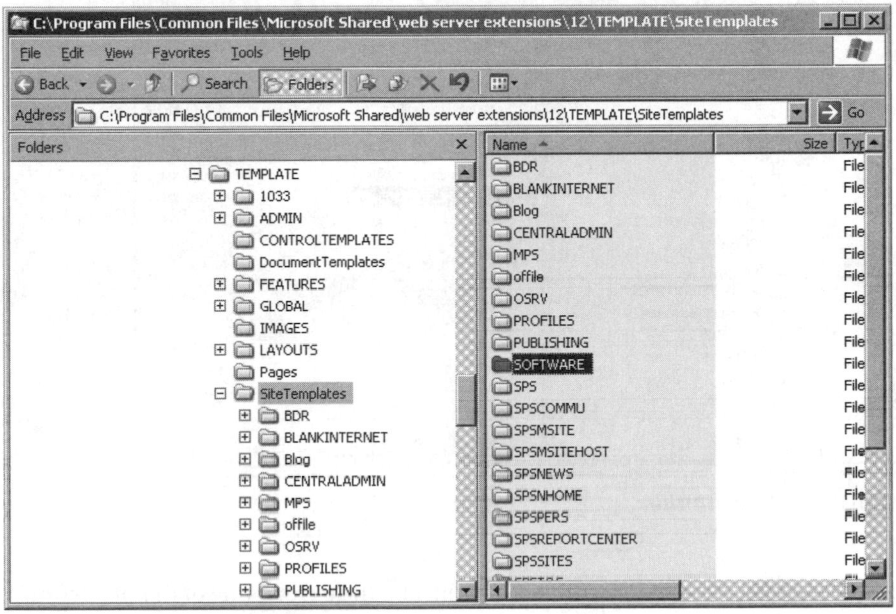

Figure 11-1. *Copying a site definition*

Copying a site definition folder is not enough to make the new site definition available for use within SharePoint. In order to make the template available, you must create a new *web template* file. A web template file is a listing of site definitions for SharePoint to load. The base web template file is named WEBTEMP.XML and is located in the *culture*\XML directory. This file contains the information about the basic site templates that are part of any SharePoint installation including team sites and Central Administration. If you also have MOSS installed alongside WSS, you will have several other files that contain all the templates that are specific to a MOSS installation. You can add information about your own site definitions by simply copying an existing web template file and appending a unique string at the end. This is because SharePoint combines all the template files that begin with WEBTEMP to create the complete set of site definitions. For my example, I copied the WEBTEMP.XML file and renamed it WEBTEMPSOFTWARE.XML. Figure 11-2 shows my new web template file in the File Explorer.

Once you have created your own web template file, you can simply open it in Visual Studio for editing. When you open the new template file, you'll see that it is made up of Template and Configuration elements. The Template elements reference the site definitions contained in the folders and the Configuration elements define one or more possible configurations for the site. These configurations determine, among other things, what web parts are displayed on the page by default. The STS template has, for example, three different configurations: Team Site, Blank Site, and Document Workspace.

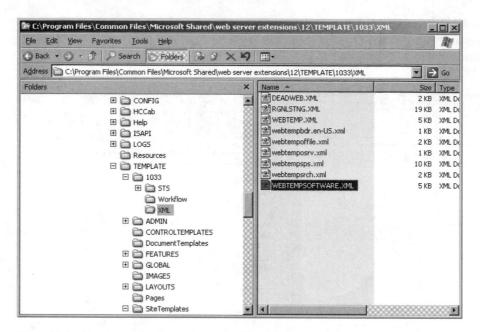

Figure 11-2. *Copying a site definition*

The Template element has a Name attribute that must be the exact name of the site definition folder you created. The ID attribute must contain a unique number that is greater than
10,000 because SharePoint reserves all smaller numbers for itself. In order to ensure that your
templates and configurations are consistent, you should be sure to use the Template element
that was originally associated with the site definition you copied. If you copied the STS definition, for example, then work with the STS template element in the XML file. Listing 11-1 shows
the WEBTEMPSOFTWARE.XML file from my example.

Listing 11-1. *A New Web Template File*

```xml
<?xml version="1.0" encoding="utf-8"?>
<!-- _lcid="1033" _version="12.0.4518" _dal="1" -->
<!-- _LocalBinding -->
<Templates xmlns:ows="Microsoft SharePoint">
 <Template Name="SOFTWARE" ID="10001">
    <Configuration
    ID="0"
    Title="Software Development"
    Hidden="FALSE"
    ImageUrl="/_layouts/images/stsprev.png"
    Description="A site for software projects."
    DisplayCategory="Collaboration" >
  </Configuration>
 </Template>
</Templates>
```

The Configuration element does not have to be changed in order to create your own site definition, but you may want to customize some of the text to make clear how your templates differ from the originals. You can give your templates titles and descriptions and associate an image with them. Table 11-2 explains each attribute of the Configuration element.

Table 11-2. *The Configuration Element*

Attribute	Type	Description
ID	Integer	The only required attribute. It must be a unique number.
Title	Text	A title for the configuration.
Description	Text	A description for the configuration.
Type	Text	An association between a configuration and a specific site definition.
Hidden	Boolean	A value that controls the visibility of the configuration. True hides the configuration and it is not available for use in SharePoint. False makes the configuration available.
ImageURL	Text	The URL of the preview image used in the template page. These are typically located in the directory \Program Files\Common Files\Microsoft Shared\ web server extensions\12\TEMPLATE\IMAGES.
DisplayCategory	Text	The tab under which the site definition will appear in SharePoint.
VisibilityFeatureDependency	GUID	The identifier of a feature that must be activated before this definition will be available in SharePoint.

Once you have copied a site definition folder and created a web template file, you must reset IIS. After that, your new site definition will appear in SharePoint. Of course, your new definition won't be any different than the old definition because you simply copied it. However, you do have the foundation in place for making the changes you want. Figure 11-3 shows the example site definition in the list of templates.

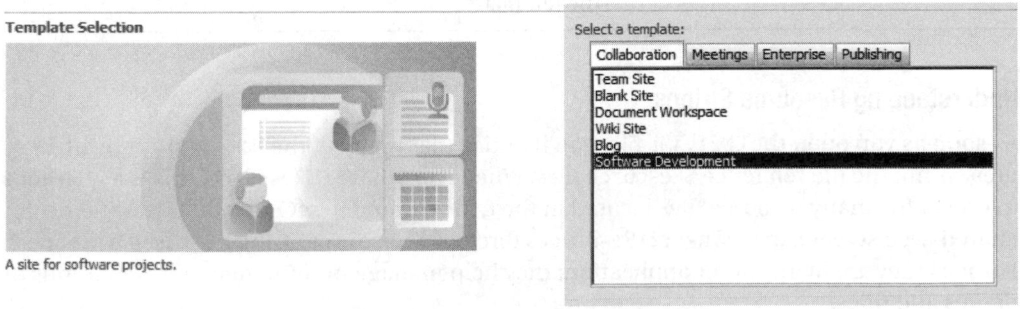

Figure 11-3. *A custom site definition in the SharePoint template list*

Customizing the Site Definition

In order to customize the configurations for your site definition, you will need to make changes to the ONET.XML file. ONET.XML is the backbone of the site definition in SharePoint. Each site definition folder contains its own ONET.XML file that describes all of the key aspects of the site. You can locate the ONET.XML file under your site definition folder in the XML directory.

The top-level element in ONET.XML is the Project element. This element is the container for all of the various configurations supported by the site definition. Most of the time, you will only see the Title and ListDir attributes specified, but there are several other attributes available. Table 11-3 lists all of the Project element attributes and their purpose.

Table 11-3. *The Project Element*

Attribute	Type	Description
AlternateCSS	Text	Allows you to specify a different Cascading Style Sheet (CSS) to use with your site definition.
AlternateHeader	Text	Allows you to specify an alternate header to use with your site definition. The header should be an ASPX file located in \Program Files\Common Files\Microsoft Shared\web server extensions\12\TEMPLATE\LAYOUTS\[culture].
CustomJSUrl	Text	Allows you to specify a custom JavaScript file that can be executed within your site's definition. These files should be located in \Program Files\Common Files\Microsoft Shared\web server extensions\12\TEMPLATE\LAYOUTS\[culture].
DisableWebDesignFeatures	Text	Allows you to specify that certain features in Microsoft SharePoint Designer cannot be used to edit your sites. This attribute is a semicolon-delimited list with any of the following values: wdfbackup; wdfrestore; wdfpackageimport; wdfpackageexport; wdfthemeweb; wdfthemepage; wdfnavigationbars; wdfnavigationview; wdfpublishview; wdfpublishselectedfile; wdfopensite; wdfnewsubsite.
ListDir	Text	Allows you to specify the subdirectory in your site definition folder where the list definitions are located. This is usually Lists. This is not required if you are not using any custom lists.
Title	Text	Allows you to specify the default title for sites built from the template.

Understanding Resource Strings

As soon as you open the ONET.XML file, you'll notice that many of the Name and Title attributes within the file reference $Resource files. Whenever you see $Resource, this is a reference to one of the many resource files located in the C:\Program Files\Common Files\Microsoft Shared\web server extensions\12\Resources directory. Resource strings are used in SharePoint as they are in any other application; they help manage multilingual representations of names and titles.

Customizing the Site Navigation

Once you have a working site definition, you'll want to make several changes to the final site structure. One of the most common changes you'll make is to the site navigation. By making changes to the NavBars element section in ONET.XML, you can alter the navigation elements in the SharePoint site. The NavBars element has no attributes but contains one or more NavBar elements that define the navigation elements in the site. A NavBar element in turn contains one or more NavBarLink elements that define a particular navigation link.

Opening ONET.XML in Visual Studio immediately exposes the NavBars element because it is near the top of the file. Within the NavBars element you'll see a NavBar element for the top navigation area and a separate NavBar element for each of the five Quick Launch areas defined for the basic SharePoint site. Within this element is defined the HTML that is used to display links added to the Quick Launch area. You can add a new NavBar to the Quick Launch area by simply copying an existing NavBar and changing the ID attribute to a unique value. Additionally, you can add links to the NavBar using the NavBarLink element. For my example, I added a new NavBar named Knowledge where I'll put links to the SharePoint software development kits. Listing 11-2 shows the definition for my new NavBar.

Listing 11-2. *A New NavBar*

```
<NavBar Name="Knowledge" Prefix="&lt;table border=0 cellpadding=4
        cellspacing=0&gt;"
        Body="&lt;tr&gt;&lt;td&gt;&lt;table border=0
        cellpadding=0 cellspacing=0&gt;&lt;tr&gt;&lt;
        td&gt;&lt;img src='/_layouts/images/blank.gif'
        ID='100' alt='' border=0&gt; &lt;/td&gt;&lt;td
        valign=top&gt;&lt;a ID=onetleftnavbar#LABEL_ID#
        href='#URL#'&gt;#LABEL#&lt;/td&gt;&lt;/tr&gt;&lt;/table&gt;
        &lt;/td&gt;&lt;/tr&gt;" Suffix="&lt;/table&gt;" ID="1028" >
<NavBarLink Name="MOSS SDK"
        Url="http://http://msdn2.microsoft.com/en-us/library/ms550992.aspx" />
  <NavBarLink Name="WSS SDK"
        Url="http://msdn2.microsoft.com/en-us/library/ms441339.aspx" />
  </NavBar>
```

Working with List and Document Templates

The ListTemplates element in ONET.XML contains the definitions for all of the lists that are part of the site definition. The ListTemplates element has no attributes but contains a set of ListTemplate elements. Each ListTemplate element references a list definition that is contained within the Lists directory of the site definition. Each list definition includes a SCHEMA.XML file for defining the list and several ASPX files for adding and editing list items. The lists that appear within the Lists directory are unique to the site definition, unlike the common lists that are defined in the GLOBAL directory.

The DocumentTemplates element in ONET.XML contains the definition for all of the document libraries that are part of the site definition. Just like the ListTemplates element, the DocumentTemplates element does not have any attributes. Instead it contains a set of

DocumentTemplate elements. Each DocumentTemplate element defines an available document library type that will appear on the Create page for the site.

Working with Configurations and Modules

The web template file contains a set of possible configurations for each site template. For example, the STS template, which defines the standard Team Site template in WSS, has three possible configurations. These are the Team Site, the Blank Site, and the Document Workspace configurations. Each of these configurations is also assigned a unique identifier. This unique identifier is the connection between the WEBTEMP.XML file and the ONET.XML file. Each configuration identifier contained in WEBTEMP.XML is referenced in the Configurations element of the ONET.XML file.

The Configurations element is used as a child of the Project element and contains the set of Configuration elements that relate to the configurations specified in the web template file. Each Configuration element in turn contains Lists, SiteFeatures, WebFeatures, and Modules elements that define the capabilities of the site.

The Lists element has no attributes, but contains a set of List elements that define the lists that will be initially created with the site. In my example, I didn't want a discussion list or an announcements list included by default, so I deleted these entries from ONET.XML. The SiteFeatures and Web Features elements define the features that will be deployed with the site definition by referencing the GUID of the feature.

The Modules element is used in two different places inside of the ONET.XML file. It can be a child element of either the Project element or the Configuration element. When used as a child of the Project element, the Modules element specifies components, such as web parts, to include in the site definition. When used as a child of the Configuration element, the Modules element ties a specific module to a site configuration.

The Modules element has no attributes but contains a set of Module elements. When used as a child of the Project element, the Module element contains a set of File elements that define external files that are part of the site definition. These external files are typically ASPX files such as the Default.aspx page that defines the appearance of the home page. When you include such files, they are stored directly under the site definition folder. Furthermore, you can edit these files in Visual Studio to change their appearance.

When you open the Default.aspx page, you'll notice that it is full of placeholders. This is exactly what you should expect based on what you've learned about SharePoint throughout the book. The Default.aspx page references the default.master page, which provides placeholders for content. It is the job of Default.aspx to define the content for the placeholders.

In my example, I wanted to add a third Web Part zone to the page, which normally only has two. My new Web Part zone will span the entire page and appear above the other two zones. The Web Part zones are defined as rows in a table within the PlaceHolderMain placeholder. By copying an existing zone and modifying it a bit, I was able to create the three zones. Listing 11-3 shows the code from my PlaceHolderMain placeholder.

Listing 11-3. *Adding a New Web Part Zone to Default.aspx*

```
<asp:Content ContentPlaceHolderId="PlaceHolderMain" runat="server">
  <table cellspacing="0" border="0" width="100%">
    <tr>
     <td class="ms-pagebreadcrumb">
        <asp:SiteMapPath SiteMapProvider="SPContentMapProvider" id="ContentMap"
        SkipLinkText="" NodeStyle-CssClass="ms-sitemapdirectional"
        runat="server"/>
      </td>
    </tr>
    <tr>
      <td class="ms-webpartpagedescription">
        <SharePoint:ProjectProperty Property="Description"
        runat="server"/></td>
    </tr>
    <tr>
      <td>
        <table width="100%" cellpadding=0 cellspacing=0
        style="padding: 5px 10px 10px 10px;">
      <tr>
      <td valign="top" width="100%">
      <WebPartPages:WebPartZone runat="server"
      FrameType="TitleBarOnly" ID="Top" Title="Top" />
       
      </td>
      </tr>
      <tr>
        <td valign="top" width="70%">
          <WebPartPages:WebPartZone runat="server"
          FrameType="TitleBarOnly" ID="Left" Title="loc:Left" />
           
        </td>
        <td> </td>
        <td valign="top" width="30%">
          <WebPartPages:WebPartZone runat="server" FrameType="TitleBarOnly"
          ID="Right" Title="loc:Right" />
           
        </td>
        <td> </td>
      </tr>
    </table>
</td>
</tr>
</table>
</asp:Content>
```

Within the File element, you may include several child elements such as View, AllUsersWebPart, and NavBarPage. The View element allows you to add a list to the page. The AllUsersWebPart element allows you to add a web part to the page, and the NavBarPage element is included if the file is the site home page. Using these elements, I have decided to remove the standard graphic that appears on the home page along with the calendar and announcements. Instead, I substituted a view of the document library. Listing 11-4 shows the code for the new default module and Figure 11-4 shows the final site in edit mode with the new links in the Quick Launch area, a new Web Part zone, and the document library displayed.

Listing 11-4. *Changing the Displayed Web Parts*

```
<Module Name="Default" Url="" Path="">
  <File Url="default.aspx" NavBarHome="True">
    <View List="$Resources:core,shareddocuments_Folder;"
      BaseViewID="6" WebPartZoneID="Left" />
    <View List="$Resources:core,lists_Folder;/$Resources:core,links_Folder;"
      BaseViewID="0" WebPartZoneID="Right" WebPartOrder="2" />
    <NavBarPage Name="$Resources:core,nav_Home;" ID="1002" Position="Start" />
    <NavBarPage Name="$Resources:core,nav_Home;" ID="0" Position="Start" />
  </File>
</Module>
```

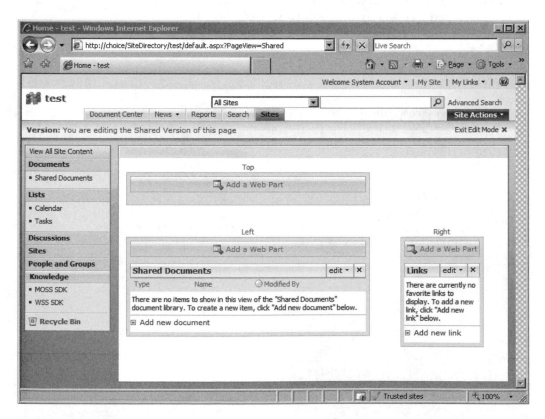

Figure 11-4. *The final site template in edit mode*

Understanding the SharePoint Object Model

Microsoft has spent a significant amount of time developing .NET namespaces for SharePoint. This comprehensive set of namespaces allows you programmatic access to a significant portion of WSS and MOSS. The SharePoint Services object model is extensive, to say the least. There are 30 namespaces within the object model and dozens of classes covering most of the features of SharePoint. The depth and breadth of the architecture makes it impractical to study the object model directly. Instead, it is better to use the object model to address broad categories of solutions that you can create. In this section, I cover the main portions of the object model that you will find useful.

Getting Started with the Object Model

In order to get started with the SharePoint object model, you must set a reference to the appropriate assemblies in Visual Studio. Generally, this means that you must have Visual Studio 2005 installed on the same machine as SharePoint. Opening the References dialog in Visual Studio will reveal several entries for both Windows SharePoint Services and Microsoft Office SharePoint Server. These references correspond to the different assemblies that make up a SharePoint installation. Figure 11-5 shows a view of the Global Assembly Cache (GAC) with some of the SharePoint assemblies visible. For most of the basic operations, you will generally need to set a reference to the `Microsoft.SharePoint.dll` assembly. This assembly appears as Windows SharePoint Services in the Visual Studio 2005 References dialog.

Assembly Name ▲	Version	Cul...	Public Key Token	Proces...
Microsoft.ReportViewer.WinForms	8.0.0.0		b03f5f7f11d50a3a	MSIL
Microsoft.SharePoint	12.0.0.0		71e9bce111e9429c	MSIL
Microsoft.SharePoint.AdministrationOperation	12.0.0.0		71e9bce111e9429c	MSIL
Microsoft.SharePoint.Diagnostics	12.0.0.0		71e9bce111e9429c	MSIL
Microsoft.SharePoint.Dsp	12.0.0.0		71e9bce111e9429c	MSIL
Microsoft.SharePoint.Dsp.OleDb	12.0.0.0		71e9bce111e9429c	MSIL
Microsoft.SharePoint.Dsp.SoapPT	12.0.0.0		71e9bce111e9429c	MSIL
Microsoft.SharePoint.Dsp.Sts	12.0.0.0		71e9bce111e9429c	MSIL
Microsoft.SharePoint.Dsp.XmlUrl	12.0.0.0		71e9bce111e9429c	MSIL
Microsoft.SharePoint.intl	12.0.0.0		71e9bce111e9429c	MSIL
Microsoft.SharePoint.Library	12.0.0.0		71e9bce111e9429c	MSIL
Microsoft.SharePoint.Portal	12.0.0.0		71e9bce111e9429c	MSIL
Microsoft.SharePoint.Portal.Intl	12.0.0.0		71e9bce111e9429c	MSIL
Microsoft.SharePoint.Portal.SingleSignon	12.0.0.0		71e9bce111e9429c	x86
Microsoft.SharePoint.Portal.SingleSignon.Security	12.0.0.0		71e9bce111e9429c	MSIL
Microsoft.SharePoint.Portal.Upgrade	12.0.0.0		71e9bce111e9429c	MSIL
Microsoft.SharePoint.Publishing	12.0.0.0		71e9bce111e9429c	MSIL
Microsoft.SharePoint.Publishing.Intl	12.0.0.0		71e9bce111e9429c	MSIL
Microsoft.SharePoint.Publishing.Intl.Resources	12.0.0.0	en-...	71e9bce111e9429c	MSIL
Microsoft.SharePoint.Search	12.0.0.0		71e9bce111e9429c	x86
Microsoft.SharePoint.Search.Intl	12.0.0.0		71e9bce111e9429c	MSIL
Microsoft.SharePoint.Search.Intl.Resources	12.0.0.0	en-...	71e9bce111e9429c	MSIL
Microsoft.SharePoint.Security	12.0.0.0		71e9bce111e9429c	MSIL
Microsoft.SharePoint.SetupConfiguration.Intl	12.0.0.0		71e9bce111e9429c	MSIL
Microsoft.SharePoint.WorkflowActions	12.0.0.0		71e9bce111e9429c	MSIL
Microsoft.SharePoint.WorkflowActions.intl	12.0.0.0		71e9bce111e9429c	MSIL
Microsoft.SharePoint.WorkflowActions.intl.resou...	12.0.0.0		71e9bce111e9429c	MSIL
Microsoft.SharePoint.Workflows	12.0.0.0		71e9bce111e9429c	MSIL

Figure 11-5. *SharePoint assemblies in the GAC*

Setting a reference to SharePoint assemblies is easy to do if you are creating a web part or writing an assembly as part of a feature. You simply use the References dialog and select the assembly as you have done countless times. Then just deploy the solution as I have outlined in previous chapters. When you are creating ASPX pages, however, the story is a bit different.

The simplest way to deploy ASPX pages is to create them in a single file and save them to the LAYOUTS directory. When you create ASPX files this way, however, the ASP.NET code must be written inline without the advantages of the normal code-behind model. Figure 11-6 shows the Add New Item dialog in Visual Studio. Note that the box labeled Place Code in Separate File is unchecked, which will create an ASPX page as a single file suitable for deployment into the LAYOUTS directory.

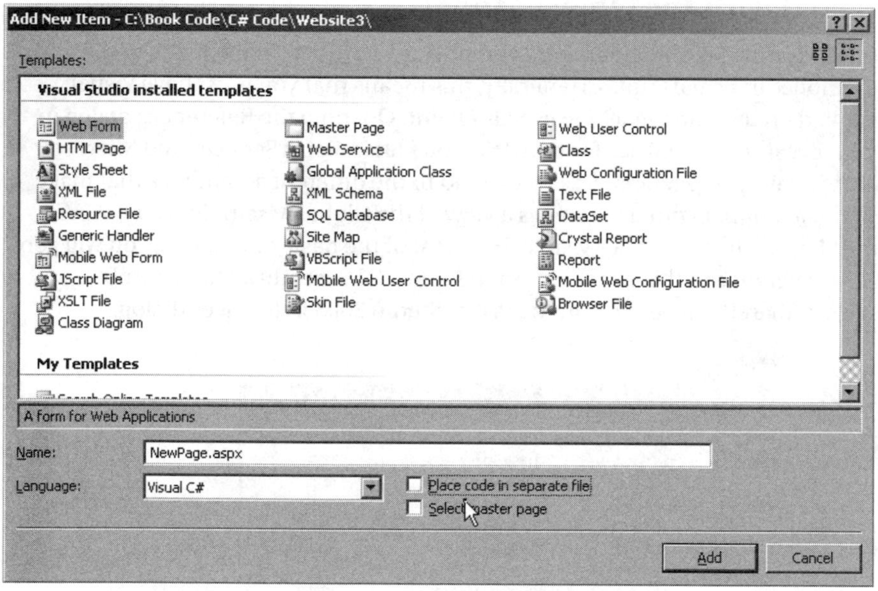

Figure 11-6. *Creating an ASPX file*

When you place all of your code in a single file, you must include the assembly references and namespaces imports at the top of the file. Additionally, you should reference the `application.master` or `default.master` file so that your pages take on the same look as other pages in SharePoint and you can make use of the content placeholders defined within the master page. Listing 11-5 shows how to set up a basic ASPX page with the proper references and the main content placeholder supported by the application master file.

Listing 11-5. *Setting Up an ASPX Page*

```
<%@ Page Language="C#" MasterPageFile="~/_layouts/application.master"%>
<%@ Assembly Name="Microsoft.SharePoint, Version=12.0.0.0,
            Culture=neutral, PublicKeyToken=71E9BCE111E9429C" %>
<%@ Import Namespace="Microsoft.SharePoint" %>
<%@ Import Namespace="Microsoft.SharePoint.WebControls" %>
```

```
<asp:Content ID="Content4" runat="server" ContentPlaceHolderID="PlaceHolderMain">
    //Page content goes here
</asp:Content>
```

■Note If you are interested in making use of the ASP code-behind model for developing SharePoint solutions, you can do it by creating a new web application in the LAYOUTS directory. However, this requires changes to the web configuration file and implementing the *form digest token*, which is part of the SharePoint page-level security model. Readers interested in this topic should reference the SDK.

Accessing Site Collections and Sites

Accessing objects in the SharePoint model is accomplished in a manner similar to any hierarchical object model you may have worked with in the past. The key to navigating such a model is to find the starting point for the model. In SharePoint, this is done through the ASP.NET Context object using the following code:

```
SPSite site = SPControl.GetContextSite(Context);
```

The SPControl class is a member of the `Microsoft.SharePoint.WebControls` namespace and is the base class from which all other WebControls in the namespace are created. You do not have to create an instance of the SPControl class to use it. Simply call the GetContextSite method and pass the Context property. The Context property comes from the `System.Web.UI.Page` object and is always available to web parts and ASPX pages that reside in the LAYOUTS directory. The GetContextSite method returns an SPSite object, which represents the site collection where the web part or ASPX page is currently running.

SPSite objects contain information about the site collection and the sites within it. In order to access any particular site in the collection, you must return a collection of SPWeb objects. You may then access the individual web sites by enumerating them or accessing one directly through an index. Listing 11-6 shows a code snippet that enumerates sites in a web part.

Listing 11-6. *Enumerating Sites in a Web Part*

```
protected override void RenderContents(HtmlTextWriter writer)
{
  SPSite siteCollection = SPControl.GetContextSite(Context);
  SPWebCollection sites = siteCollection.AllWebs;
  foreach (SPWeb site in sites)
  {
    writer.Write(site.Title + "<br/>");
  }
```

Note It is one of those oddities of naming conventions that a site collection is represented by an SPSite object, while a site is represented by an SPWeb object. This naming convention goes back to previous versions of SharePoint where site collections were sometimes called *sites* and sites were sometimes called *webs*. Over time, these naming conventions have lost favor, but the object model retains the names for consistency.

If you want to make use of object model code in an ASPX page, you must add the code to the PlaceHolderMain placeholder associated with the application master file. When you do this, you simply place the code directly in the ASPX page surrounded by the <% %> delimiters. Listing 11-7 shows an ASPX page that enumerates the sites in a collection using an ASPX page. You can take this page, save it to the LAYOUTS directory and access it through the browser with an address of the format http://[server]/[site]/_layouts/[pagename].aspx (e.g., http://vsmoss/sites/intranet/_layouts/SiteList.aspx).

Listing 11-7. *Enumerating Sites in a Web Page*

```
<%@ Page Language="C#" MasterPageFile="~/_layouts/application.master"%>
<%@ Assembly Name="Microsoft.SharePoint, Version=12.0.0.0,
            Culture=neutral, PublicKeyToken=71E9BCE111E9429C" %>
<%@ Import Namespace="Microsoft.SharePoint" %>
<%@ Import Namespace="Microsoft.SharePoint.WebControls" %>

<asp:Content ID="Content4" runat="server" ContentPlaceHolderID="PlaceHolderMain">
    <%
        SPSite siteCollection = SPControl.GetContextSite(Context);
        SPWebCollection sites = siteCollection.AllWebs;
        foreach (SPWeb site in sites)
        {
            Response.Write(site.Title + "<br/>");
        }
    %>
</asp:Content>
```

Elevating Permissions

Many of the operations you perform with the object model—even a simple listing—will require administrative permissions. This is because SharePoint applies security restrictions to the use of the object model. However, there are many times when you would like to display information—such as a site listing—to a user that does not have administrator rights. In these cases, you must utilize the SPSecurity class to temporarily run object model code with elevated permissions. These elevated permissions allow you to run code under the identity of the application pool account.

In order to run code with elevated permissions, you must encapsulate the code in a function that has no return value. You then create an instance of the CodeToRunElevated class using the name of the function as an argument. You can subsequently execute the code by calling the RunWithElevatedPrivileges method of the SPSecurity object and passing in the CodeToRunElevated object. Listing 11-8 shows an example that calls a method to list all of the available features in a farm.

Listing 11-8. *Running Code with Elevated Permissions*

```
<%@ Page Language="C#" MasterPageFile="~/_layouts/application.master"%>
<%@ Assembly Name="Microsoft.SharePoint, Version=12.0.0.0,
    Culture=neutral, PublicKeyToken=71E9BCE111E9429C" %>
<%@ Import Namespace="Microsoft.SharePoint" %>
<%@ Import Namespace="Microsoft.SharePoint.WebControls" %>

<asp:Content ID="Content4" runat="server"
    ContentPlaceHolderID="PlaceHolderMain">
<%

    SPSecurity.CodeToRunElevated myCode =
        new SPSecurity.CodeToRunElevated(ShowFeatures);
    SPSecurity.RunWithElevatedPrivileges(myCode);

%>
</asp:Content>

<script language="C#" runat="server">

    protected void ShowFeatures()
    {
        //Code goes here
    }
</script>
```

■**Caution** Running code with elevated permissions should be done only after careful consideration of the consequences. Obviously, you would not want to grant such permissions regularly. Additionally, this new capability should make you extremely wary of using third-party web parts from untrusted sources because they could easily be running with elevated privileges and you would not know it.

Accessing Lists and List Items

Along with site collections, you will access lists and list items frequently. Typically when dealing with lists, you are interested in a particular site rather than a site collection. You can get a reference to an individual site by using the GetContextWeb method of the SPControl object. Once a site is open, you may access all of the lists it contains through the SPListCollection object. The collection contains an SPList object for every list on the web site. The following code shows how to enumerate the lists for the current web site:

```
SPWeb site = SPControl.GetContextWeb(Context);
SPListCollection lists= site.Lists;

foreach(SPList list in lists)
{
    //add code here
}
```

It is important to understand that SharePoint considers almost everything to be a list. This includes not only obvious components such as task lists, but more subtle components such as document libraries and discussion forums. Therefore, you will find it useful to be able to differentiate between various lists that are returned in code. Each `SPList` object has a `BaseType` property that returns an `SPBaseType` enumeration specifying what kind of list is represented. Here is a list of the members of the `SPBaseType` enumeration:

- `SPBaseType.DiscussionBoard`

- `SPBaseType.DocumentLibrary`

- `SPBaseType.GenericList`

- `SPBaseType.Issue`

- `SPBaseType.Survey`

- `SPBaseType.UnspecifiedBaseType`

Once you have accessed a list of interest, you may subsequently access the items in the list. Each item in the list is represented by an `SPListItem` object contained in an `SPListItemCollection` object. Enumerating these list items follows the same pattern as you have already seen.

Regardless of whether you are accessing sites, lists, or items, each object has a set of properties and methods that are meaningful. Typically, this means returning the `Name`, `Title`, or `URL` associated with an object. Additionally, each object has some special properties and methods designed to return useful collections. For example, you can return just the webs associated with the current user by utilizing the `GetSubwebsForCurrentUser` method of the `SPWeb` class.

Accessing User Information

When iterating through sites and lists, you quite often want to know how they apply to the current user. You may be interested in knowing what role the current user has on a site or what items in a list are assigned to the current user. You can access this information using an `SPUser` object. The following code shows how to return the `SPUser` object that represents the current user:

```
SPSite siteCollection = SPControl.GetContextSite(Context);
SPWeb site = siteCollection.OpenWeb();
SPUser user = site.CurrentUser;
```

Once the `SPUser` object is returned, you can retrieve the logon name of the user through the `LoginName` property. You can also retrieve the display name for the user through the `Name` property. Because list assignments are made using these values, you can often determine which items in a list belong to the current user by comparing the Assign To field of a list item to these values. Listing 11-9 shows how to look through a collection of lists and display the tasks assigned to the current user in a web page.

Listing 11-9. *Determining List Item Ownership*

```csharp
<%@ Page Language="C#" MasterPageFile="~/_layouts/application.master"%>
<%@ Assembly Name="Microsoft.SharePoint, Version=12.0.0.0, Culture=neutral,
            PublicKeyToken=71E9BCE111E9429C" %>
<%@ Import Namespace="Microsoft.SharePoint" %>
<%@ Import Namespace="Microsoft.SharePoint.WebControls" %>

<asp:Content ID="Content4" runat="server"
 ContentPlaceHolderID="PlaceHolderMain">
<%
SPSite siteCollection = SPControl.GetContextSite(Context);
SPWeb site = siteCollection.OpenWeb();
SPUser user = site.CurrentUser;
SPListCollection lists = site.Lists;

Response.Write("Tasks for " + user.Name + "<br/>");

foreach (SPList list in lists)
{
  if (list.BaseType == SPBaseType.GenericList ||
      list.BaseType == SPBaseType.Issue)
  {
    for (int i = 0; i <= list.ItemCount - 1; i++)
    {

      try
      {
        SPListItem item = list.Items[i];
        string assignedTo = item["Assigned To"].ToString().ToUpper();
        if(assignedTo.IndexOf(user.LoginName.ToUpper()) > -1 ||
           assignedTo.IndexOf(user.Name.ToUpper()) > -1)
        {
            Response.Write(item.Title + "</br>");
        }
      }
      catch { }
    }
  }
}
site.Close();
siteCollection.Close();
%>
</asp:Content>
```

Using SharePoint Web Services

In addition to the object model, you can also access SharePoint information using web services. SharePoint exposes web services for a wide variety of data sources and administrative tasks. SharePoint web services are used in Visual Studio 2005 in the same way as any other web service. After starting a project, you must set a web reference to the web service. Table 11-4 lists all of the available web services for WSS and MOSS, describes each one, and lists the web reference address.

Table 11-4. *SharePoint Web Services*

Service	WSS/MOSS	Address	Description
Administration web service	Both	`http://[Central Administration site]/_vti_adm/Admin.asmx`	Provides services for creating, deleting, and managing site collections
Alerts web service	Both	`http://[Site Collection]/_vti_bin/alerts.asmx`	Provides services for managing alerts
Authentication web service	Both	`http://[Site Collection]/_vti_bin/authentication.asmx`	Provides services to authenticate users
Copy web service	Both	`http://[Site Collection]/_vti_bin/copy.asmx`	Provides services for copying files to or within a site
Document Workspace web service	Both	`http://[Site Collection]/_vti_bin/dws.asmx`	Provides services to interact with Document Workspaces
Forms web service	Both	`http://[Site Collection]/_vti_bin/forms.asmx`	Provides support for returning the forms that are used to manage lists
Imaging web service	Both	`http://[Site Collection]/_vti_bin/imaging.asmx`	Provides support for creating and managing image libraries
Lists web service	Both	`http://[Site Collection]/_vti_bin/lists.asmx`	Provides services to create, delete, and manage lists
Meetings web service	Both	`http://[Site Collection]/_vti_bin/meetings.asmx`	Provides services to create, delete, and manage Meeting Workspaces
People web service	Both	`http://[Site Collection]/_vti_bin/people.asmx`	Provides services to return information about people
Permissions web service	Both	`http://[Site Collection]/_vti_bin/permissions.asmx`	Provides support for managing site and list permissions
Site Data web service	Both	`http://[Site Collection]/_vti_bin/sitedata.asmx`	Provides services to return site and list data
Sites web service	Both	`http://[Site Collection]/_vti_bin/sites.asmx`	Provides support for returning data from sites
Search web service	Both	`http://[Site Collection]/_vti_bin/search.asmx`	Provides support for searching SharePoint
Users and Groups web service	Both	`http://[Site Collection]/_vti_bin/usergroup.asmx`	Provides support for working with SharePoint users and groups
Versions web service	Both	`http://[Site Collection]/_vti_bin/versions.asmx`	Provides support for working with file versions

Service	WSS/MOSS	Address	Description
Views web service	Both	http://[Site Collection]/_vti_bin/views.asmx	Provides support for working with list views
Web Part Pages web service	Both	http://[Site Collection]/_vti_bin/webpartpages.asmx	Provides support for managing web parts
Webs web service	Both	http://[Site Collection]/_vti_bin/webs.asmx	Provides support for creating, deleting, and managing sites and subsites
Official File web service	MOSS only	http://[Site Collection]/_vti_bin/officialfile.asmx	Provides support for sending files to a records repository
Published Links web service	MOSS only	http://[Site Collection]/_vti_bin/publishedlinks.asmx	Provides support for Office clients to receive links that are targeted at them by SharePoint
User Profile Change web service	MOSS only	http://[Site Collection]/_vti_bin/userprofilechangeservice.asmx	Provides support for changes to user profiles
User Profile web service	MOSS only	http://[Site Collection]/_vti_bin/userprofileservice.asmx	Provides support for returning information from user profiles
Workflow web service	MOSS only	http://[Site Collection]/_vti_bin/workflow.asmx	Provides support for managing workflows

Once the web service is referenced, you can use it in your project just like any other namespace. Values returned from the web service vary depending upon which service is called, but the calling technique is largely the same. Before calling the web service, you must authenticate the current user with the service. After authentication, you can make calls to the methods of the service. I'll go over the details necessary to accomplish this in the following sections.

Working with Site Data

An easy way to get started with SharePoint web services is to return some information about sites. Beginning with the site collection you are interested in, you can use the Webs web service to return the information for that particular collection. Using this web service, you can return all of the sites in the collection at once, or call methods recursively to build a hierarchy.

Once the web reference is made, it is a simple matter to return a collection of all webs in the referenced site collection. This can be done by calling the GetAllSubWebCollection method. Calling this method returns an XmlNode that contains the titles and addresses of every web in the current collection:

```
vsmoss.Webs service = new vsmoss.Webs();
service.Credentials=System.Net.CredentialCache.DefaultCredentials;
System.Xml.XmlNode node = service.GetAllSubWebCollection();
Console.WriteLine(node.OuterXml);
```

Working with List Data

Because many custom solutions involve list data, the Lists web service is used extensively by SharePoint developers. Therefore, it is a service with which you should be familiar. You can

access the Lists web service for the intranet you created in Chapter 2 at http://vsmoss/sites/
intranet/_vti_bin/lists.asmx. Figure 11-7 shows the resulting page in the browser, which
displays the available methods.

Figure 11-7. *Accessing a web service*

Once the Lists web service is referenced, you can authenticate against it and call methods.
The following code snippet shows how to authenticate the current user with the service and
return a set of lists as an XML fragment:

```
vsmoss.Lists service = new vsmoss.Lists();
service.Credentials=System.Net.CredentialCache.DefaultCredentials;
System.Xml.XmlNode node = service.GetListCollection();
Console.WriteLine(node.OuterXml);
```

The GetListCollection method is used to return a CAML fragment that defines all of the
lists available on a site. The return CAML fragment is a set of List elements. One List element
is returned for each list on the target site. Listing 11-10 shows a single List element of a return
CAML fragment.

Listing 11-10. *A Portion of the GetListCollection CAML Fragment*

```
<Lists xmlns="http://schemas.microsoft.com/sharepoint/soap/">
    <List
        DocTemplateUrl=""
        DefaultViewUrl="/sites/Test/Lists/Announcements/AllItems.aspx"
        ID="{970DF0FB-CC31-40C3-AF4C-6515C37CE582}"
        Title="Announcements"
        Description="Use the Announcements list to post messages on
        the home page of your site."
        ImageUrl="/_layouts/images/itann.gif"
        Name="{970DF0FB-CC31-40C3-AF4C-6515C37CE582}"
        BaseType="0"
        ServerTemplate="104"
        Created="20040603 16:00:26"
        Modified="20040603 16:00:26"
        LastDeleted="20040603 16:00:26"
        Version="0"
        Direction="none"
        ThumbnailSize=""
        WebImageWidth=""
        WebImageHeight=""
        Flags="4096"
        ItemCount="1"
        AnonymousPermMask=""
        RootFolder=""
        ReadSecurity="1"
        WriteSecurity="1"
        Author="1"
        EventSinkAssembly="" EventSinkClass="" EventSinkData=""
        EmailInsertsFolder=""
        AllowDeletion="True"
        AllowMultiResponses="False"
        EnableAttachments="True"
        EnableModeration="False"
        EnableVersioning="False"
        Hidden="False"
        MultipleDataList="False"
        Ordered="False"
        ShowUser="True" />
    .
    .
    .
</Lists>
```

You can access the fields associated with a list by calling the GetList method. The GetList method takes the title or GUID of the list as an argument and returns a CAML fragment that contains a single `List` element along with a collection of `Field` elements that provide information about each field in the list. The CAML fragment returned from the `GetList` method can be quite long, depending on how many fields are defined in the list. Listing 11-11 only shows the first `Field` element of a CAML fragment associated with a standard document library.

Listing 11-11. *A Portion of the Returned GetList CAML Fragment*

```
<List ...>
   <Fields>
      <Field ColName="tp_ID" ReadOnly="TRUE" Type="Counter" Name="ID"
DisplayName="ID" FromBaseType="TRUE" /><Field ColName="tp_Created"
Hidden="TRUE" ReadOnly="TRUE" Type="DateTime" Name="Created"
DisplayName="Created Date" StorageTZ="TRUE" FromBaseType="TRUE" />
.
.
.
   <Fields>
   <RegionalSettings>
      <Language>1033</Language>
      <Locale>1033</Locale>
      <AdvanceHijri>0</AdvanceHijri>
      <CalendarType>1</CalendarType>
      <Time24>False</Time24>
      <TimeZone>300</TimeZone>
      <SortOrder>2070</SortOrder>
      <Presence>True</Presence>
   </RegionalSettings>
</List>
```

Once you understand the fields associated with a list, you will want to return specific items from the list. Returning items from a list is accomplished using the `GetListItems` method of the web service. Like all the other method calls I have presented, the return value from the `GetListItems` method is a CAML fragment. The set of items returned is enclosed within a data element and each item is defined using a `row` element. The attributes of the `row` element will vary based on how you construct the method call, but you should note the `ID`, `Title`, and `FileRef` attributes because these will be critical later when working with the returned items. Listing 11-12 shows a typical returned CAML fragment containing the information for a single document.

Listing 11-12. *Returned GetListItems CAML Fragment*

```
<listitems xmlns:s="uuid:BDC6E3F0-6DA3-11d1-A2A3-00AA00C14882"
   xmlns:dt="uuid:C2F41010-65B3-11d1-A29F-00AA00C14882"
   xmlns:rs="urn:schemas-microsoft-com:rowset" xmlns:z="#RowsetSchema"
    xmlns="http://schemas.microsoft.com/sharepoint/soap/">
```

```
  <rs:data ItemCount="1">
    <z:row ows_FileRef="1;#sites/Test/Shared Documents/Document1.doc"
    ows_Title="New Document"
    ows_Customer="DataLan"
    ows_Last_x0020_Modified="1;#2004-06-03 17:54:01"
    ows_ID="1"
    ows_owshiddenversion="8" ows_FSObjType="1;#0"
    ows_FileLeafRef="1;#Document1.doc"
    ows_Modified="2004-06-03 17:54:01"
    ows_Editor="1;#SPS\administrator"
    ows_DocIcon="doc" />
  </rs:data>
</listitems>
```

The GetListItems method takes several arguments and requires some additional effort to call because several of the parameters are actually CAML fragments themselves. These parameters must be constructed in code before the method call is made. Specifically, the GetListItems method requires the following parameters: listName, viewName, query, viewFields, rowLimit, and queryOptions.

The listName parameter is either the list name (e. g., Shared Documents) or the GUID of the target list from which items are to be returned. This is the same parameter that is used throughout the various methods of the Lists web service. This parameter is required.

The viewName parameter is the GUID of the view to be used when determining what fields to return. This parameter is optional and can be replaced with the keyword null in C#. When no view is specified, the method will return the fields contained in the default list view unless you override this behavior by specifying different fields. Generally, it is easier not to supply this parameter and specify the desired fields later.

The query parameter is a properly formatted CAML Query element that specifies what items to return from the list. This parameter is optional and can be replaced with the keyword null in C#. When provided, the defined query overrides the query normally associated with the default view.

The viewFields parameter is a properly formatted CAML ViewFields element that specifies what fields are to be returned with each item. This parameter is optional and can be replaced with the keyword or null in C#. When provided, the defined field set overrides the field set normally associated with the default view.

The rowLimit parameter is a string representing the number of items to return from the method call. This parameter is optional and can be replaced with the keyword null in C#. When provided, the rowLimit overrides the limits associated with the default view. The rowLimit parameter can also be used to set up a paging when used in conjunction with the queryOptions parameter.

The queryOptions parameter is a properly formatted QueryOptions element. This parameter is optional and can be replaced with the keyword null in C#. The QueryOptions element acts as a container for other elements that specify the options for the method call.

In the same way that we parsed the returned CAML fragment from previous method calls, we can do this to display the information returned from the GetListItems method; however, you should note that the field names returned from this method call are prefixed with ows_, which must be taken into consideration when writing the code. Listing 11-13 shows a complete example that returns all the documents from a library and displays their titles in a list.

Listing 11-13. *Returning Documents from a Library*

```
MyService.Lists objService = new MyService.Lists();
objService.Url = "http://Server_Name/Site_Path/_vti_bin/Lists.asmx";
objService.Credentials = System.Net.CredentialCache.DefaultCredentials;
XmlDocument objDocument = new XmlDocument();
XmlNode objQuery;
objQuery = objDocument.CreateNode(XmlNodeType.Element, "Query", "");
objQuery.InnerXml = "<OrderBy><FieldRef Name='Title'></FieldRef></OrderBy>";
XmlNode objFields;
objFields = objDocument.CreateNode(XmlNodeType.Element, "ViewFields", "");
objFields.InnerXml = "<FieldRef Name='Title'/>";
XmlNode objCAML;
objCAML = objService.GetListItems(MylstLists.SelectedItem.ToString, null,
          objQuery, objFields, null, null);
foreach (XmlNode objNode in objCAML.ChildNodes(1).ChildNodes) {
 if (!((objNode.Attributes == null)) &&
    !((objNode.Attributes("ows_Title") == null))) {
   MyDocs.Items.Add(objNode.Attributes("ows_Title").Value);
 }
}
```

After you have identified the fields for a given document, you may want to update them and save those changes back to the list. You can update any field associated with a list using the UpdateListItems method of the Lists web service. This method takes as parameters the title or GUID of the list and a CAML Batch element that defines the operations to be performed on the list items.

The CAML Batch element is a container for one or more Method elements that define the individual operations to be performed as a single batch. This structure allows you to perform multiple insert, update, and delete operations with a single call to the UpdateListItems method of the web service. The Method element provides an identifier attribute for the individual operation and a command attribute to specify an insert, update, or delete operation. Each Method element in turn contains a set of Field elements that provide data for the method and identify the item to receive the operation. As an example, the following code shows a Batch element that defines an update to the Title field of the document associated with ID=3:

```
<Batch>
    <Method ID='MyIdentifier' Cmd='Update'>
        <Field Name='ID'>3</Field>
        <Field Name='FileRef'>
            http://MyServer/MySite/MyDocs/Document1.doc
        </Field>
        <Field Name='Title'>My New Title</Field>
    </Method>
</Batch>
```

Using the Single Sign-On Service

The Single Sign-On (SSO) service is a combination of a Windows 2003 service, a SQL Server data store, and web-based administration tools that provide credential storage and retrieval services to your web parts, applications, and the business data catalog. Using the service allows your solutions to programmatically log in to external systems using credentials specifi-cally provided for that purpose. For example, you could write a web part that retrieves creden-tials from SSO to access a database and display information. SSO is installed by default along with MOSS; however, the service is stopped and set to manual startup. In order to begin work-ing with SSO, you must configure and start the service.

Setting Up SSO

Before the SSO service can be started, you must create a new global security group that will contain an account used to run the service. This same group will contain the accounts that are authorized to administer the SSO service. The account used to run the SSO service will also be a member of this group. This group must meet several requirements:

- Belong to the local administrators group on the application server.

- Belong to the local administrators group on the server running the configuration database.

- Belong to the WSS_ADMIN_WPG group on every server in the farm where SharePoint is installed.

- Have db_owner and public rights for the SharePoint configuration database.

- Belong to the Server Administrators role for the SQL Server instance where the SSO database is located.

Once you have defined a security group with an account, you can configure the SSO serv-ice to run under the specified account. Additionally, you can add users to the security group so that they can define credentials in the data store. Designated users may then define sets of applications and credentials for enterprise applications.

To set up the required SSO accounts, follow these steps:

1. Log in to VSPDC as the domain administrator.

2. Select Start ➤ Administrative Tools ➤ Active Directory Users and Computers.

3. In the Active Directory Users and Computers dialog, right-click the Users folder and select New ➤ Group from the context menu.

4. In the New Object dialog, type **SSOAdmins** in the Group Name. Any member of this group will be allowed to administer the SSO service.

5. Click OK.

6. In the Active Directory Users and Computers dialog, right-click the Users folder and select New ➤ User from the pop-up menu.

7. In the New Object dialog, type **SSOService** in the Full Name and User Logon Name boxes.

8. Click Next.

9. Type a password for the account.

10. Uncheck the User Must Change Password at Next Logon box.

11. Check the User Cannot Change Password box.

12. Check the Password Never Expires box.

13. Click Next.

14. On the next screen, click Finish.

15. Right-click the SSOService account and select Properties from the pop-up menu.

16. On the Member Of tab, click Add.

17. Type in the account name **DOMAIN\SSOAdmins** and click the Check Names button.

18. Once the account name is validated, click OK.

19. Click OK again.

After the required accounts are created, you must give them permissions on the local servers where SharePoint is running. This means adding the SSO administrator group to the local administrators account and the WSS_ADMIN_WPG.

To add the SSO administrators to the local groups, follow these steps:

1. Log in to VSMOSS as the local administrator.

2. Select Start ➤ Administrative Tools ➤ Computer Management.

3. In the Computer Management dialog, expand the Local Users and Groups node and open the Groups folder.

4. In the Groups folder, right-click Administrators and select Add to Group from the context menu.

5. In the Administrators Properties dialog, click Add.

6. Type in the account name **DOMAIN\SSOAdmins** and click the Check Names button.

7. Once the account name is validated, click OK.

8. In the Administrators Properties dialog, click OK.

9. In the Groups folder, right-click WSS_ADMIN_WPG and select Add to Group from the context menu.

10. In the WSS_ADMIN_WPG Properties dialog, click Add.

11. Type in the account name **DOMAIN\SSOAdmins** and click the Check Names button.

12. Once the account name is validated, click OK.

In addition to having access to the local machine where SharePoint runs, the SSO administrator group must also have access to the SQL Server installation. This will allow the group to read and write credentials. SSO uses SQL Server as its credential store.

To set up SQL Server permissions, follow these steps:

1. Log in to VSSQL as the local administrator.

2. Select All Programs ➤ Microsoft SQL Server 2005 ➤ SQL Server Management Studio.

3. In the Connect to Server dialog, select VSSQL from the Server Name drop-down list and click the Connect button.

4. Expand the Security folder in the Object Explorer tree.

5. Right-click the Logins node and select New Login from the context menu.

6. In the Login dialog, type **DOMAIN\SSOAdmins** in the Login Name field.

7. Click the User Mapping page.

8. On the User Mapping page, check the box associated with the MOSS configuration database (e.g., MOSS_Config).

9. In the list of database roles, check db_owner and Public.

10. Click the Server Roles page.

11. On the Server Roles page, check the Serveradmin box.

12. Click OK.

13. Right-click the Logins node and select New Login from the context menu.

14. In the Login dialog, type **DOMAIN\SSOService** in the Login Name field.

15. Click the Server Roles page.

16. On the Server Roles page, check the Securityadmin and Dbcreator boxes.

17. Click OK.

Once the SSO administrator account has all the required permission sets, you can start the SSO service. The SSO service must be set up to run under the account you created earlier. Once the correct identity is added, the service should be configured to start automatically.

Follow these steps to start the SSO service:

1. Log in to VSMOSS as the local administrator.

2. Select Start ➤ Administrative Tools ➤ Services.

3. In the Services dialog, right-click the Microsoft Single Sign-On Service and select Properties from the context menu.

4. On the Log On tab, select the option This Account, and type **DOMAIN\SSOService**.

5. Enter the password you set for this account.

6. Click Apply.

7. On the General tab, change the Startup Type to Automatic.

8. Click Start to start the service.

Before you can access credentials using SSO, an application definition must be created for the credentials. *Application definitions* consist of a unique name for the application and the definition of the logon fields to accept. SSO is capable of managing a number of fields beyond username and password. In fact, you can define any custom field for the service, such as domain or database name. The exact fields that you define will depend upon what fields are expected by the target application.

SSO administration is done through the Central Administration site by clicking the link titled Manage Settings for Single Sign-On located on the Operations tab. When you first access the administration pages, only one option is available. You must complete the setup by logging in as the SSO Service account and clicking the Manage Server Settings link. The server settings require you to specify the accounts that will be used to manage the SSO service and define new applications. Until these settings are complete, you cannot define new applications. Figure 11-8 shows what the page should look like the first time you access it.

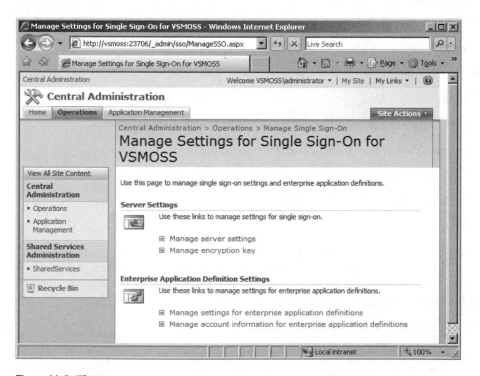

Figure 11-8. *The manage server settings page*

Follow these steps to complete the configuration of SSO:

1. Log in to VSMOSS as DOMAIN\SSOService.

2. Select Start ➤ All Programs ➤ Microsoft Office Server ➤ SharePoint 3.0 Central Administration.

3. When the Central Administration site opens, click the Operations tab.

4. Click the link titled Manage Settings for Single Sign-On.

5. On the Manage Settings for Single Sign-On page, enter **DOMAIN\SSOAdmins** in both of the Account Name fields.

6. Click the OK button.

Once the initial settings are entered, you may return to the Manage Settings for Single Sign-On page where the additional hyperlinks will be available. Clicking Manage Settings for Enterprise Application Definitions opens a page where you may define new applications. This page allows you to name the application, define the fields that should be managed, and determine whether the application will use a group or an individual login.

You should use a group login when you want a single set of credentials to be used by your code, regardless of what user is accessing the system. This design is often associated with read-only information, where users do not normally need separate identification. An organization might use this, for example, to give employees access to public information regarding corporate performance. In this scenario, it is not important which employee is accessing the system, because the read-only information will not change.

Where you are more concerned about access and permissions you should use an individual login. Applications defined with an individual login will require that each end user have his or her own set of credentials. SSO is capable of prompting individuals for credentials the first time they use a solution; after this, the service automatically stores the credentials for future use.

To create an enterprise application definition, follow these steps:

1. Log in to VSMOSS as a member of the DOMAIN\SSOAdmins group.

2. Select Start ➤ All Programs ➤ Microsoft Office Server ➤ SharePoint 3.0 Central Administration.

3. When the Central Administration site opens, click the Operations tab.

4. Click the link titled Manage Settings for Single Sign-On.

5. On the Manage Settings for Single Sign-On page, click Manage Settings for Enterprise Application Definitions.

6. On the Manage Enterprise Application Definitions page, click the New Item link.

7. On the Create Enterprise Application Definition page, type **My Application** into the Display Name box.

8. Type **MyApp** into the Application Name box.

9. Type **administrator@domain.local** into the Contact E-mail Address box.

10. Change the Account Type to Individual.

11. Type **Username** into the Field 1: Display Name box.

12. Type **Password** into the Field 2: Display Name box.

13. Choose the Yes option for Mask under Field 2 to mask the password when it is entered.

14. Click OK.

Although SSO is capable of prompting users for credentials, you can set them up ahead of time by using the administrative web pages. Because you will not know individual login information, this capability is clearly most useful when an application is defined to utilize a group login. Individual logins will generally prompt users for credentials when they first use your application.

Here is what you need to do to define login credentials:

1. Log in to VSMOSS as a member of the DOMAIN\SSOAdmins group.

2. Select Start ➤ All Programs ➤ Microsoft Office Server ➤ SharePoint 3.0 Central Administration.

3. When the Central Administration site opens, click the Operations tab.

4. Click the link titled Manage Settings for Single Sign-On.

5. On the Manage Settings for Single Sign-On page, click Manage Account Information for Enterprise Application Definitions.

6. In the User Account Name box, enter **DOMAIN\Administrator**.

7. Click OK.

8. On the Account Information page, type **MyUsername** into the User Name box.

9. Type **MyPassword** into the Password box.

10. Click OK.

Using SSO in Code

One of the most common uses for SSO is to allow web parts to access external systems. As I discussed in Chapter 2, SSO is a good alternative to Kerberos because it will allow a web part to authenticate to an external source regardless of how many "hops" are between it and the SharePoint server. Additionally, SSO can work across the Internet between domains. In order to use the Microsoft SSO service in code, you must first set a reference to the `SingleSignOn` assembly in Visual Studio which is contained in the namespace `Microsoft.SharePoint.Portal.SingleSignon`.

The `Microsoft.SharePoint.Portal.SingleSignon` namespace provides several classes that provide complete access to all of the administration functions of SSO. You can use these classes not only to access enterprise systems, but also to create your own separate administration interface. You can even go so far as to build a web part that allows portal users to perform self-service on their own credentials.

When code needs to access an external system, it calls the GetCredentials method. Any user is allowed to call GetCredentials; however, the active security policy determines the level of access allowed. If the credentials exist in the data store, they are returned as an array of strings. The order of the data returned in the array is the same as the order in which the application fields are defined by the administrator. The following code shows the basic technique:

Note The policies WSS_Minimal and WSS_Medium do not allow access to SSO functionality. In order to grant access, you must modify the web configuration file or create a custom policy file.

```
string user = null; ;
string password = null; ;
string[] credentials = null;

Credentials.GetCredentials(1, "MyApp", ref credentials);

user = credentials[0];
password = credentials[1];
```

If the code attempts to retrieve credentials and fails, the GetCredentials method throws a SingleSignonCredsNotFoundException. Any other SSO error is thrown as a SingleSignonException. The exact reason for the failure is subsequently determined by examining the LastErrorCode property of the SingleSignonException object. You should not be concerned that the credentials do not exist when you attempt to retrieve them. This situation can happen frequently with application definitions that contain an individual login. In fact, it is almost guaranteed to happen the first time a user invokes a code that accesses a new application definition.

Because an administrator will not know individual credentials, your web part should expect to handle the SingleSignonCredsNotFoundException the first time any user accesses your code. In response, you must help the user enter the correct credentials into the data store for future use. SSO supports the user by providing a web page where the user can enter their credentials if they are not found.

Users access the logon form provided by the SSO by clicking a hyperlink that you build in code. The hyperlink is generated by the SingleSignonLocator class. This class supports the GetCredentialEntryUrl method, which takes the application name as an argument. Listing 11-14 shows a complete example of an ASPX page that accesses the credentials for the application you created earlier and creates a sign-in link if the credentials are not found.

Caution The GetCredentialEntryUrl method will fail if the current user has no account information in the SSO database. Talk about a catch-22! The workaround is to first define dummy credentials for each user and then delete them. This will associate the user with an application definition while ensuring that the SingleSignonCredsNotFoundException exception occurs when the code is first accessed.

Listing 11-14. *Using SSO in Code*

```
<%@ Page Language="C#" MasterPageFile="~/_layouts/application.master"%>
<%@ Assembly Name="Microsoft.SharePoint, Version=12.0.0.0,
    Culture=neutral, PublicKeyToken=71E9BCE111E9429C" %>
<%@ Assembly Name="Microsoft.SharePoint.Portal, Version=12.0.0.0,
    Culture=neutral, PublicKeyToken=71E9BCE111E9429C" %>
<%@ Assembly Name="Microsoft.SharePoint.Portal.SingleSignon, Version=12.0.0.0,
    Culture=neutral, PublicKeyToken=71E9BCE111E9429C" %>
<%@ Import Namespace="Microsoft.SharePoint" %>
<%@ Import Namespace="Microsoft.SharePoint.WebControls" %>
<%@ Import Namespace="Microsoft.SharePoint.Portal" %>
<%@ Import Namespace="Microsoft.SharePoint.Portal.SingleSignon" %>

<asp:Content ID="Content4" runat="server"
    ContentPlaceHolderID="PlaceHolderMain">
<%

    try
    {
        string user = null; ;
        string password = null; ;
        string[] credentials = null;

        Credentials.GetCredentials(1, "MyApp", ref credentials);

        user = credentials[0];
        password = credentials[1];

        Response.Write(user);
        Response.Write("<br/>");
        Response.Write(password);
    }
    catch (SingleSignonCredsNotFoundException x)
    {
        Response.Write("<a href=\"" +
           SingleSignonLocator.GetCredentialEntryUrl("MyApp")
           + "\"> Please sign in </a>");
    }
    catch (SingleSignonException x)
    {
        Response.Write("<p>" + x.Message + "</p>");
    }
    catch (Exception x)
    {
        Response.Write("<p>" + x.Message + "</p>");
    }

%>
</asp:Content>
```

Exercise 11.1. Creating a Site Definition

Creating custom site definitions allows you to tightly control the capabilities and features that are deployed when a site is created. This is a useful approach when you intend to create many copies of the same site and you want to maintain the connection between the sites and the definition to simplify maintenance. In this exercise, you will create a custom site definition for a blank site with publishing features enabled. This type of site is valuable because it allows you to start with no predefined content while still having publishing enabled. This is a good way to build up a site because you can start with this definition and then add your own page layouts as I discuss in Chapter 5. Figure 11-9 shows a site built from the definition in this exercise.

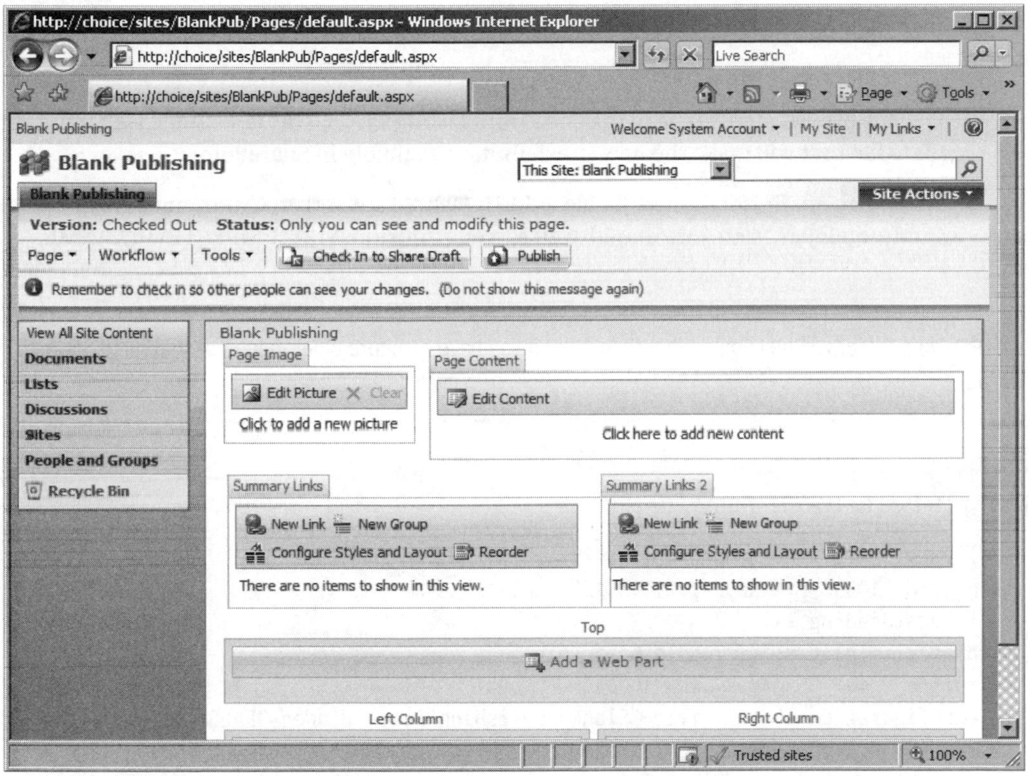

Figure 11-9. *Editing a blank publishing site*

Copying the Site Definition

In this exercise, you will start with the standard team site definition and customize it to create the blank publishing site. To begin this process, you will create a copy of the STS site definition and rename it BLANKPUB. Then you will create a web template file for the new definition.

Follow these steps to get started:

1. Log in to VSMOSS as a SharePoint administrator.

2. Open the File Explorer and navigate to the directory C:\Program Files\Common Files\ Microsoft Shared\web server extensions\12\TEMPLATE\Site Templates.

3. In the File Explorer, right-click the STS folder and select Copy from the context menu.

4. Right-click the File Explorer area inside of the Site Templates folder and select Paste from the context menu. A copy of the STS folder will be created.

5. Right-click the copy of the STS folder and select Rename from the context menu.

6. Rename the folder BLANKPUB.

7. Select Start ➤ All Programs ➤ Accessories ➤ Notepad.

8. When Notepad starts, type in the code from Listing 11-15. This is a simple web template file that will make the new site definition available in SharePoint.

9. When you are finished, save the file as WEBTEMPBLANKPUB.XML to C:\Program Files\ Common Files\Microsoft Shared\web server extensions\12\TEMPLATE\1033\XML.

■**Note** Your folder will be named other than 1033 if you have a culture other than English–United States (en-us).

Listing 11-15. *The Web Template File*

```
<?xml version="1.0" encoding="utf-8"?>
<!-- _lcid="1033" _version="12.0.4518" _dal="1" -->
<!-- _LocalBinding -->
<Templates xmlns:ows="Microsoft SharePoint">
 <Template Name="BLANKPUB" ID="10005">
    <Configuration ID="0" Title="Blank Publishing Site" Hidden="FALSE"
  ImageUrl="/_layouts/images/blankprev.png" Description="A blank publishing site."
  DisplayCategory="Publishing" AllowGlobalFeatureAssociations="False" />
 </Template>
</Templates>
```

Modifying the Configurations Section

Once the site definition is copied, you must make several modifications to create the blank publishing site definition. Most of these changes will be made in the ONET.XML file, but you'll also delete an extra file. Creating a blank site is a bit easier because you'll mostly be removing information from the site definition. In this section, you'll create the proper configuration for the site definition.

Follow these steps to make the required changes:

1. Open the File Explorer and navigate to C:\Program Files\Common Files\Microsoft Shared\web server extensions\12\TEMPLATE\Site Templates\BLANKPUB.

2. In the BLANKPUB folder, delete the file `DEFAULTDWS.ASPX`. This file is used for the Document Workspace configuration of the team site. You will not need it for your definition.

3. In the File Explorer, open the XML folder.

4. In the XML folder, right-click `ONET.XML` and select Open With ➤ Microsoft Visual Studio 2005.

5. In the `ONET.XML` file, you will keep all of the `NavBars`, `ListTemplate`, and `DocumentTemplate` elements.

6. Scroll down to the `Configurations` element. Here you will find four configurations named `NewWeb`, `Default`, `Blank`, and `DWS`.

7. The blank publishing site most resembles the blank team site. Therefore, you can delete the entire configuration for the `Default` and `DWS` configurations. Don't delete the `NewWeb` configuration—it is for internal use—and keep the `Blank` configuration to build on.

8. Then change the `ID` for the `Blank` configuration from 1 to 0. The 0 identifier matches the value in `WEBTEMPBLANKPUB.XML`.

9. Now you'll modify the configuration to include the publishing features in the site definition. Reference Listing 11-16 and edit the `Configurations` section of `ONET.XML`.

Listing 11-16. *The Configurations Section*

```
<Configurations>
  <Configuration ID="-1" Name="NewWeb" />
  <Configuration ID="0" Name="Default">
    <Lists />
    <Modules>
      <Module Name="Default" />
    </Modules>
    <SiteFeatures>
        <!-- BasicWebParts Feature -->
        <Feature ID="00BFEA71-1C5E-4A24-B310-BA51C3EB7A57" />
          <!-- PublishingPrerequisites -->
          <Feature ID="A392DA98-270B-4e85-9769-04C0FDE267AA" />
          <!-- Office SharePoint Server Publishing -->
          <Feature ID="F6924D36-2FA8-4f0b-B16D-06B7250180FA" />
          </SiteFeatures>
      <WebFeatures>
        <!-- TeamCollab Feature -->
        <Feature ID="00BFEA71-4EA5-48D4-A4AD-7EA5C011ABE5" />
        <!-- MobilityRedirect -->
```

```
          <Feature ID="F41CC668-37E5-4743-B4A8-74D1DB3FD8A4" />
          <!-- Office SharePoint Server Publishing -->
          <Feature ID="94C94CA6-B32F-4da9-A9E3-1F3D343D7ECB" />
        </WebFeatures>
      </Configuration>
    </Configurations>
```

Modifying the Modules Section

After you have the Configurations section edited, you'll need to make changes to the Modules section. The Modules section defines the ASPX files that are part of the definition and the web parts that will appear on the page. In this case, you'll be removing everything except the home page and it will be rendered with no web parts.

Follow these steps to make the required changes:

1. Scroll down to the Modules section of the ONET.XML file.

2. In the Modules section, delete the Default and DWS Module elements. These modules are associated with the configurations that you deleted earlier.

3. When you are done, you should only have the DefaultBlank Module remaining. Rename this module Default to keep it in sync with the changes you made earlier.

4. When you have made the changes, carefully edit the remaining module to look like Listing 11-17.

Listing 11-17. *The Modules Section*

```
<Modules>
  <Module Name="Default" Url="" Path="">
    <File Url="default.aspx" NavBarHome="True" Type="Ghostable">
      <NavBarPage Name="$Resources:core,nav_Home;" ID="1002" Position="Start" />
      <NavBarPage Name="$Resources:core,nav_Home;" ID="0" Position="Start" />
    </File>
  </Module>
</Modules>
```

Using the Site Definition

After you have completed the site definition, reset Internet Information Server so that your new definition will be loaded by SharePoint. After the server is reset, you can create a new site collection from the Central Administration web site in the usual way. This time, however, the blank publishing site should appear in the list of available templates.

Exercise 11.2. Building a Site Explorer

Displaying all of the sites that make up a SharePoint farm is a common programming task. Because of all of the different ways to retrieve data from SharePoint, there are actually several approaches to producing such a view. You could use the object model to get the information on site collections and sites, but this would require your application to reside on the Share-Point server or to create your own web service. In this project, you will use a combination of direct calls to the database and the Webs web service to create a hierarchical listing of all sites and webs in a given SharePoint installation. This approach allows you to get such information remotely.

To start the project, follow these steps:

1. Start Visual Studio 2005.

2. In Visual Studio, select File ➤ New ➤ Project from the main menu.

3. In the Project Types window of the New Project dialog, click the Visual C# node.

4. In the Templates window, select Windows Application.

5. Name the new project **Site Explorer** and press the OK button.

6. When the new project is open, drop a `TreeView` control onto Form1.

7. Open the code window for `Form1.cs` and add the following statements:

```
using System.Data.SqlClient;
using System.Net;
using System.Xml;
```

Adding the Web Reference

This project makes use of the Webs web service to return information about sites and webs. In this section, you will set a reference to this web service. It does not matter which site you reference when setting up the service, because we will change it in code later.

Follow these steps to set the web reference:

1. In Visual Studio, select Project ➤ Add Web Reference from the menu.

2. In the Add Web Reference dialog, type **http://vsmoss/sites/intranet/_vti_bin/ Webs.asmx?WSDL** and press the Go arrow.

3. When the Webs web service is located, type **MOSSService** in the Web Reference Name box and push the Add Reference button.

Returning All Sites

Before we can create the hierarchical view of the SharePoint installation, we must return the set of all sites that are contained in the installation. In this exercise, you will retrieve this information directly from the SharePoint configuration database. Going directly against the SharePoint databases can be a dangerous technique if you are doing more than reading data; however, it's handy to know that you can do it safely to retrieve information. Add the code from Listing 11-18 to return the top-level sites and add them to the tree.

Listing 11-18. *Returning Top-Level Sites*

```
private void Form1_Load(object sender, EventArgs e)
{
    string conn =
    "Integrated Security=SSPI;" +
    "Initial Catalog=WSS_Content" +
    ";Data Source=VSSQL";

    string sql = "SELECT Title, FullUrl " +
    "FROM dbo.Webs " +
    "WHERE (ParentWebId IS NULL) AND (FullUrl <> '') " +
    "AND (FullUrl IS NOT NULL) " +
    "ORDER BY Title";

    try
    {
        //Return the sites
        using (SqlConnection connection = new SqlConnection(conn))
        {
            SqlDataAdapter adapter = new SqlDataAdapter();

            DataSet dataSet = new DataSet("root");
            adapter.SelectCommand = new SqlCommand(sql, connection);
            adapter.Fill(dataSet, "Sites");

            //Put top-level sites in tree
            DataRowCollection siteRows = dataSet.Tables["Sites"].Rows;

            foreach (DataRow siteRow in siteRows)
            {
                TreeNode treeNode = new TreeNode();
                treeNode.Text = siteRow["Title"].ToString();
                treeNode.Tag = "http://CHOICE/" +
                siteRow["FullUrl"].ToString();
                treeView1.Nodes.Add(treeNode);
                fillTree(treeNode);
            }
        }
    }
    catch (Exception x)
    {
        MessageBox.Show(x.Message);
    }

}
```

Adding Child Sites

Once the top-level sites are returned, you can use the Webs web service to return all of the child webs beneath each site. This is done through a recursive call to the web service. These calls are made until each branch is filled out to the leaf. Add the code from Listing 11-19 to build out the tree.

Listing 11-19. *Adding Child Webs*

```
private void fillTree(TreeNode parent)
{
    //Redirect web service
    SPSService.Webs service = new SPSService.Webs();
    service.Url = parent.Tag.ToString() + "/_vti_bin/Webs.asmx";
    service.Credentials = CredentialCache.DefaultCredentials;

    //Get child webs
    XmlNode nodes = service.GetWebCollection();

    //Add child webs to tree
    foreach(XmlNode node in nodes)
    {
        TreeNode child = new TreeNode();
        child.Text = node.Attributes["Title"].Value;
        child.Tag = node.Attributes["Url"].Value;
        parent.Nodes.Add(child);
        fillTree(child);

    }
}
```

Running the Sample

After you have all the code entered, simply run the project. The tree view should return with a complete listing of all sites and webs in the target installation. If you have trouble, check to be sure that you are referencing the correct server and that your account has permission to access the content database.

CHAPTER 12

■ ■ ■

SharePoint Operations and Administration

Throughout this book, you have used the Central Administration web site to manage web applications, site collections, and users. However, administration and maintenance in Share-Point go beyond simply creating new web sites. Just like any other critical business system in your organization, SharePoint requires a comprehensive maintenance plan to protect corporate data and ensure optimal performance. In this chapter, I will examine the major administrative tasks you must perform to keep a SharePoint installation healthy.

Using Backup and Restore

One of the first things that you will want to configure in a production environment is proper backup of the SharePoint installation. Backup and recovery is performed manually through the Central Administration interface via the Operations tab. Here you will find a Backup and Restore section with several links. You can also create a script to automate the backup process using the command-line utility STSADM.EXE. You'll find a brief discussion of STSADM.EXE in the section titled "Using the Command-Line Utility" later in the chapter. In this section, I present the process for performing a manual backup and restore.

Creating a Target Folder

When backups are performed, SharePoint saves the configuration and content information as a series of files. These files are saved to a target directory, which must have appropriate permissions established for the backup to succeed. Therefore, you should create a network location for backup data before beginning your first backup operation. Generally this means creating a folder and granting rights to the following key accounts:

- The account under which SQL Server 2005 is running

- The account under which you will log in to manually run backup jobs

- The server from where you will access the Central Administration site

- The account running the Shared Services pool

- The account running the Central Administration application pool

---

■Note If you are running SQL Server 2005 under the Local System account, which is the configuration described in Chapter 2, you'll need to grant the computer running SQL Server access to the folder.

Follow these steps to create a network backup location:

1. Log in to VSSQL as a domain administrator.

2. Open the File Explorer and create a new directory at the location C:\SharePointBackups.

3. Right-click the SharePointBackups folder and select Properties from the context menu.

4. In the Properties dialog, click the Sharing tab.

5. On the Sharing tab, select the option labeled Share This Folder.

6. Click the Security tab.

7. Click the Add button.

8. In the Select Users, Computers, or Groups dialog, click the Object Types button.

9. In the Object Types dialog, check the Computers box and click the OK button.

10. In the Select Users, Computers, or Groups dialog, type **VSSQL;VSMOSS; Administrator;SPConfigAcct;SPSharedServicesPool** and click the Check Names button.

11. When the names are resolved, click the OK button.

12. Select the VSSQL account and grant the Modify, Read & Execute, List Folder Contents, Read, and Write permissions.

13. Grant these same permissions to the VSMOSS and Administrator accounts.

14. Click the Sharing tab.

15. Click the Permissions button.

16. In the Permissions dialog, click the Add button.

17. In the Select Users, Computers, or Groups dialog, click the Object Types button.

18. In the Object Types dialog, check the Computers box and click the OK button.

19. In the Select Users, Computers, or Groups dialog, type **VSSQL;VSMOSS; Administrator;SPConfigAcct;SPSharedServicesPool** and click the Check Names button.

20. When the names are resolved, click the OK button.

21. Select the VSSQL account and grant the Change and Read permissions.

22. Grant these same permissions to the VSMOSS and Administrator accounts.

23. In the Properties dialog, click the OK button.

Performing a Backup

Once the network folder is set up with the proper permissions, you can initiate a backup. The backup and recovery utility is primarily focused on information contained in the content database. The backup utility does not back up the configuration database, external files such as web part assemblies, or custom features you deployed. Therefore, you should also have a plan to back up all of the servers in the farm and all SQL Server databases.

Follow these steps to back up your farm:

1. Log in to VSMOSS as a farm administrator.

2. Select Start ➤ All Programs ➤ Microsoft Office Server ➤ SharePoint 3.0 Central Administration.

3. When the Central Administration site opens, click the Operations tab.

4. On the Operations tab, click the link titled Perform a Backup.

5. On the Perform a Backup page, check the box next to the Farm item. This selects the entire farm for backup.

6. Click the link titled Continue to Backup Options.

7. On the Start Backup page, enter **\\VSSQL\SharePointBackups** in the Backup Location field. Figure 12-1 shows this page.

8. Click the OK button.

When you initiate a backup, SharePoint schedules the job for execution by the Windows SharePoint Services Timer service. Therefore, the job may not start for a couple of minutes after you initiate it. The Timer service runs under the same account as the Central Administration site pool and is responsible for executing all scheduled jobs. You can see a list of scheduled jobs by clicking the link titled Timer Job Definitions on the Operations tab.

While the backup is executing, the status will be shown as the page is periodically refreshed. If the job runs successfully, you will see each part of the backup indicate completion. If the job fails, the page will reflect the error and abort the backup. In order to start a new backup, you must delete the failed backup job from the list of job definitions.

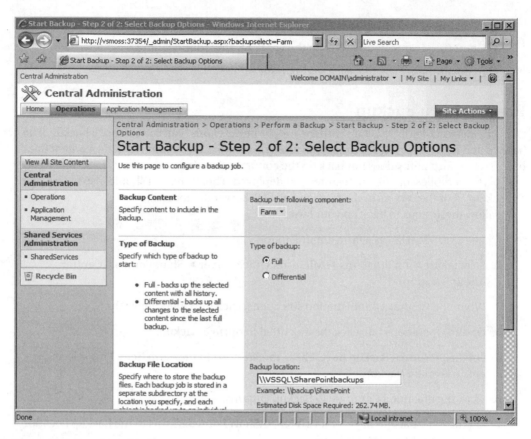

Figure 12-1. *Starting a backup*

Performing a Restore

Once you have a backup package, you may use it to restore all or part of a SharePoint farm. Clicking the link titled Restore from Backup on the Operations tab will take you through a series of pages where you can select the backup package that you want to restore and the portions of the farm to restore. You can use the backup package to restore to the same farm or a different farm, which is an excellent way to move content from a development environment into a production environment.

Using Logs and Reports

SharePoint utilizes logs to track key events, errors, and usage for the farm, site collections, and sites. SharePoint logs are an excellent tool for troubleshooting operations and identifying problems with your own custom applications. SharePoint logs can also be enabled to track usage data in the farm so that you can analyze the traffic for sites. In this section, I explain how to enable and configure the different logging and reporting mechanisms in SharePoint.

Working with the Unified Logging Service

When you are working with a SharePoint installation, you will undoubtedly experience errors on pages or issues with configurations that you do not immediately understand. For example, you may find that your profile imports are not running as expected or your search index is not being properly built. If you have a custom feature involved, the situation may be even more complicated. In all of these cases, you'll need good logging information to sort out the problem.

Oftentimes, SharePoint components will make entries in the Application, System, or Security event logs. In fact, I have recommended that your components do the same. This information can be invaluable in troubleshooting a problem. However, SharePoint also maintains a separate logging system called the Unified Logging Service (ULS).

The ULS is a farmwide logging service that can be used by every SharePoint component. It consists of a series of text files located in the path C:\Program Files\Common Files\Microsoft Shared\web server extensions\12\LOGS. Here you will find many text files with a LOG extension that contain entries from the mundane to the critical. When things go wrong with SharePoint, the answer can often be found in these logs.

The Central Administration site provides configuration settings for the ULS that you can change to help provide better information when troubleshooting. You can access the ULS configuration settings from the Operations tab by clicking the Diagnostic Logging link. Figure 12-2 shows the settings page.

On the Diagnostic Logging page, you will see settings that allow you to participate in the Microsoft Customer Experience Improvement Program and collect error reports for delivery to Microsoft. The Customer Experience Improvement Program is a way for you to provide usage information anonymously to Microsoft. This data is used to determine what parts of the product are used most often and for direct development of the next version. The error reports are used by Microsoft to help identify and correct common problems. These programs are similar to ones that you may have seen for other products such as Office.

The last two sections of the Diagnostic Logging page are used to configure the ULS. The Event Throttling section is used to limit the entries that are made to the ULS, and the Trace Log section is used to determine the maximum number of log files to create and how long an individual log should be kept in use. These settings are important because the log files can become quite large if left unchecked.

The log files are created as tab-delimited text and contain the fields Timestamp, Process, TID, Area, Category, EventID, Level, Message, and Correlation. You can start to troubleshoot issues by looking for entries around the time that an issue occurred. However, if you have not throttled the logs, you will see many entries, so the time stamp may not be that useful. The category information is more useful because it contains specific identifiers for SharePoint components, such as Business Data for the BDC. You can also search for messages with a High or Critical level, which are often associated with operational problems.

Unfortunately, SharePoint does not come with a viewer for the ULS. Therefore, the only way to view the logs is to open them in Notepad or import them into Excel. At the end of this chapter, I have included an exercise that you can do to build a ULS viewer feature. This feature allows you to view and filter the ULS from within the Central Administration site.

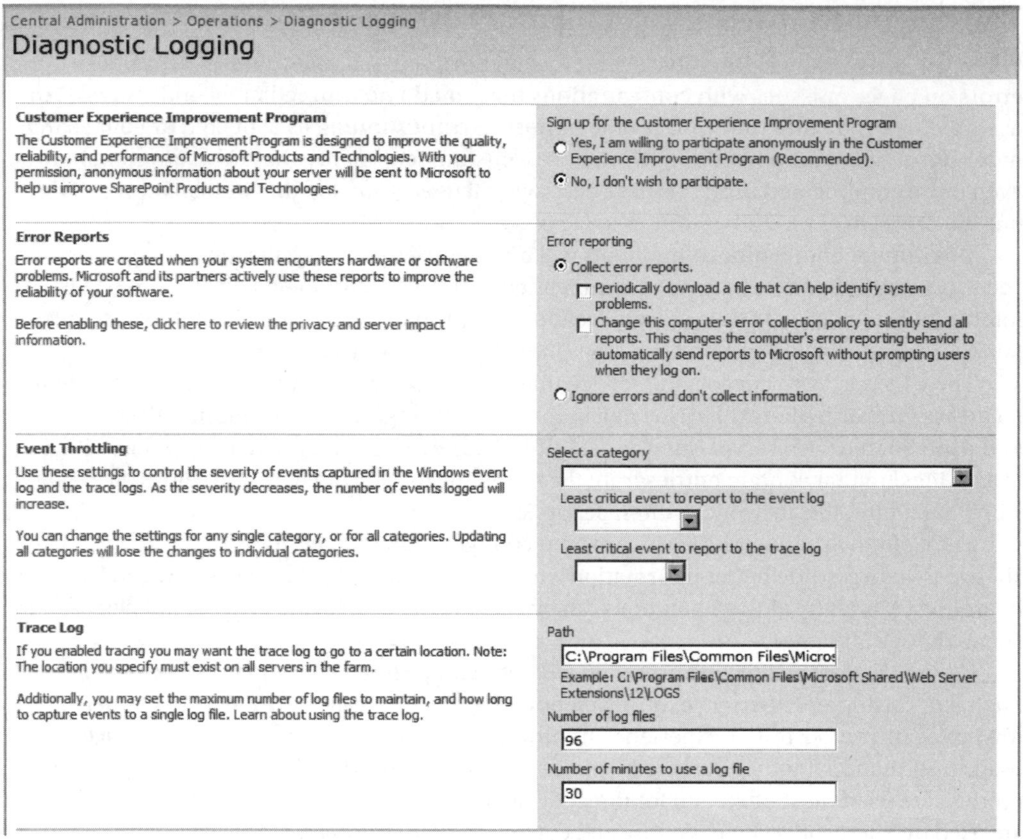

Figure 12-2. *Configuring the Unified Logging Service*

Working with Portal Usage Reporting

Portal usage reporting is a service that logs statistics about site activity in a SharePoint farm. Before you start the service, you should recognize that gathering usage information can have a negative impact on the performance of the farm. If you do enable usage logging, be sure to schedule the log processing outside of normal business hours. In order to use the service, it must first be enabled in the Central Administration site. For a MOSS installation, you must also configure processing in the Shared Services Provider.

Follow these steps to configure usage reporting in MOSS:

1. Log in to VSMOSS as a farm administrator.

2. Select Start ➤ All Programs ➤ Microsoft Office Server ➤ SharePoint 3.0 Central Administration.

3. When the Central Administration site opens, click the Operations tab.

4. Under the Logging and Reporting section, click the link titled Usage Analysis Processing.

5. On the Usage Analysis Processing page, check the box labeled Enable Logging.

6. Check the box labeled Enable Usage Analysis Processing.

7. Click the OK button.

8. In the Central Administration site, click the link in the Quick Launch area to open the Shared Services Administration site.

9. On the home page of the Shared Services Administration site, click the Usage Reporting link.

10. On the Configure Advanced Usage Analysis Processing page, check the box labeled Enable Advanced Usage Analysis Processing.

11. Click the OK button.

12. Open the home page of the intranet site you created in Chapter 2 (e. g., `http://vsmoss/sites/intranet/pages/default.aspx`).

13. On the home page, select Site Settings ➤ Modify All Site Settings from the Site Actions menu.

14. On the Site Settings page, click the link titled Site Collection Usage Reports.

After you enable usage processing, it may take several minutes before you can view the usage page in a site collection. Additionally, no usage data will initially be available because the data is created when the scheduled usage processing job runs. Figure 12-3 shows a usage report for the intranet site collection shortly after setting up the service.

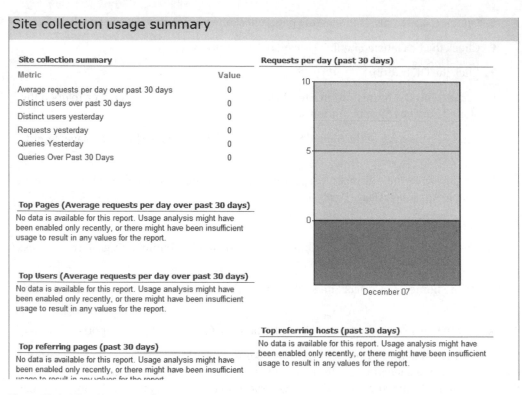

Figure 12-3. *Viewing usage data*

Working with Information Management Policy Usage Reports

In Chapter 6, I discussed information policies and how to apply them to documents within SharePoint. Once policies are in place, you can set up to generate reports that show how many items are using each policy across the farm. These reports are generated as Excel spreadsheets with a pivot table, a description of each active policy, and a list of sites where the policy is in use. Regular policy reporting is designed to help organizations evaluate the effectiveness of the active policies.

Follow these steps to set up policy usage reporting:

1. Open the home page of the intranet site you created in Chapter 2 (e. g., `http://vsmoss/sites/intranet/pages/default.aspx`).

2. Click the Reports tab to open the Report Center.

3. Click the link titled View All Site Content in the Quick Launch area.

4. On the All Site Content page, click the Create link.

5. On the Create page, click the Document Library link.

6. On the New page, enter **Policy Usage Reports** in the Name field.

7. Select Microsoft Office Excel spreadsheet from the Document Template drop-down list.

8. Click the Create button.

9. Select Start ➤ All Programs ➤ Microsoft Office Server ➤ SharePoint 3.0 Central Administration.

10. When the Central Administration site opens, click the Operations tab.

11. Under the Logging and Reporting section, click the link titled Information Management Policy Usage Reports.

12. On the Information Management Policy Usage Reports page, click the Web Application drop-down and select Change Web Application.

13. In the Select Web Application dialog, select the Intranet web application.

14. On the Information Management Policy Usage Reports page, check the box labeled Enable Recurring Policy Usage Reports.

15. Enter **/Reports/Policy%20/Usage%20/Reports** in the Report File Location field.

16. Click the Check URL button to verify the entered location refers to the document library you created earlier.

17. Click the Create Reports Now button.

18. Click the OK button. A new report should be generated in the document library you created earlier.

Configuring Caching Options

MOSS supports several caching options that can be used to improve the performance of sites in the farm. The caching options in MOSS are built on top of the ASP.NET 2.0 caching options with some additional functionality. Caching in SharePoint can be set up for site pages and binary large objects (BLOB) such as image files. Complete pages are cached using the output cache while individual items are cached using the object cache.

Caching elements of a SharePoint site collection can result in significant performance increases. Once an element is rendered, SharePoint does not have to make additional round-trips to the database for content or reload web parts into memory until the cached elements time-out. Because of the decreased load, caching helps the farm scale easier as well.

Caching is not without drawbacks, however. Caching uses additional memory for storing the cached elements. In a web farm, caching can also lead to discrepancies in the viewed content. If different versions of a page are cached on each web front end, and the load balancer is set up to send client requests to any available server, it would be possible for a user to see different versions of a page with each postback. If caching is implemented properly, such issues are unlikely to cause major problems so you should consider caching a net positive overall.

Understanding Cache Profiles

One of the improvements MOSS makes over ASP.NET 2.0 caching is the implementation of *cache profiles*. A cache profile is a group of cache settings that you can create and then specifically use with output caching. Using cache profiles, you can control the degree of caching and tune the performance of the farm.

Cache profiles are generally created for a specific zone. Because a group of users in a given zone will see the same elements, it makes sense to group cache profiles in this way. Out of the box, SharePoint defines profiles for the zones you create within a web application, but you can customize them or create your own. Before you enable output caching, you should configure the cache profiles.

Follow these steps to configure cache profiles:

1. Open the home page of the intranet site you created in Chapter 2 (e. g., `http://vsmoss/sites/intranet/pages/default.aspx`).

2. On the home page, select Site Settings ➤ Modify All Site Settings from the Site Actions menu.

3. On the Site Settings page, click the link titled Site Collection Cache Profiles.

4. In the Cache Profiles list, click on the Intranet (Collaboration Site) link. Figure 12-4 shows the Intranet cache profile.

Intranet > Cache Profiles > Intranet (Collaboration Site)

Cache Profiles: Intranet (Collaboration Site)

Close

🗐 New Item | 📝 Edit Item | ✖ Delete Item | 📇 Manage Permissions | Alert Me

Title	Intranet (Collaboration Site)
Display Name	
Display Description	Optimized for collaboration sites where authoring, web part cusomization, and minor version are enabled.
Perform ACL Check	Yes
Enabled	Yes
Duration	180
Check for Changes	Yes
Vary by Custom Parameter	
Vary by HTTP Header	Browser
Vary by Query String Parameters	
Vary by User Rights	Yes
Cacheability	ServerAndPrivate
Safe for Authenticated Use	Yes
Allow writers to view cached content	

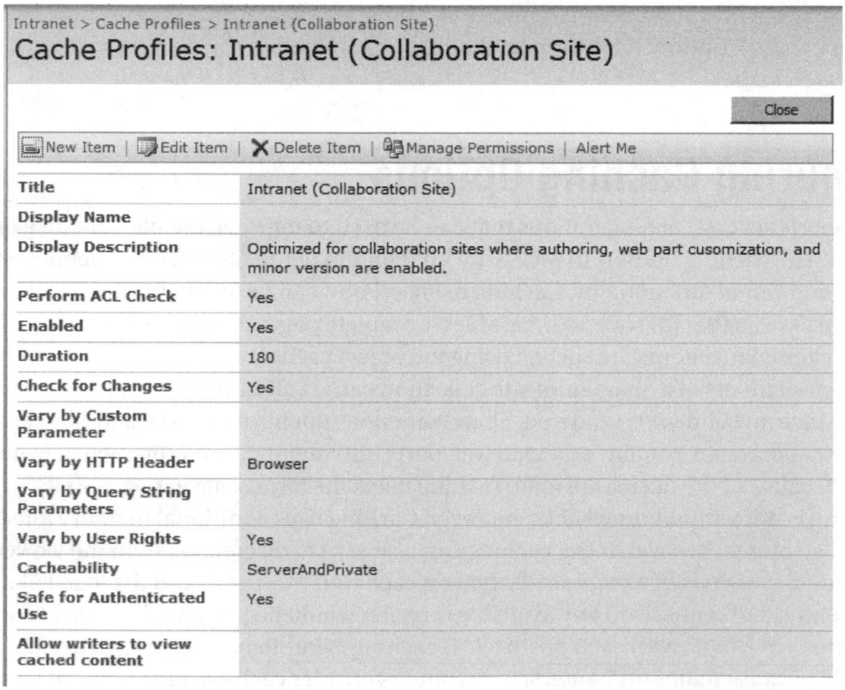

Figure 12-4. *Viewing cache profiles*

The fields in the cache profile represent different settings that are applied to the output cache of a site collection or site. You can change any of these settings or create a new profile with unique settings. Table 12-1 lists all of the available settings and describes their functions.

Table 12-1. *Cache Profile Settings*

Setting	Values	Description
Allow Writers to View Cached Content	Check/Uncheck	When enabled, content authors will have their pages cached even if they are in draft form.
Cacheability	NoCache, Private, Public, Server, ServerAndNoCache, ServerAndPrivate	NoCache denies caching; Private caches on the web client; Public caches on the client, proxy server, and web server; Server caches on the server; ServerAndNoCache caches on the server and specifically denies client caching; ServerAndPrivate caches at the client and server.
Check for Changes	Check/Uncheck	When enabled, this checks for changes to the content and flushes the cache if the associated site content has changed.
Duration	Number	This sets the number of seconds to keep output cached before it expires.
Enabled	Check/Uncheck	This turns on caching for this profile.
Perform ACL Check	Check/Uncheck	When enabled, this setting ensures that all content in the output cache is security trimmed. When disabled, performance is better, but no security trimming occurs. Therefore, this option should only be disabled when security trimming is not required.
Safe for Authenticated Use	Check/Uncheck	This setting marks the policy as safe for use by authenticated users.
Vary by Custom Parameter	Text	This setting specifies a string that represents a header by which to vary the output cache. For example, setting this to Accept-Charset varies the output for each browser's character set.
Vary by HTTP Header	Text	This setting specifies a list of HTTP headers by which to vary the output cache. Requests with these headers will receive the same output.
Vary by Query String Parameters	Text	This setting specifies a list of QueryString parameters by which to vary the output cache. Requests with the same parameters will receive the same output.
Vary by Rights	Check/Uncheck	When enabled, this provides the same cached output to users with identical rights.

Configuring Output Caching

Once you are satisfied with the cache profiles, you can enable output caching. Output caching may be managed at the site collection, and all sites within the collection will inherit these settings. When you enable output caching, you must specify the profiles to use for both authenticated and anonymous users.

Follow these steps to enable caching:

1. Open the home page of the intranet site you created in Chapter 2 (e. g., `http://vsmoss/sites/intranet/pages/default.aspx`).

2. On the home page, select Site Settings ➤ Modify All Site Settings from the Site Actions menu.

3. On the Site Settings page, click the link titled Site Collection Output Cache.

4. On the Site Collection Output Cache page, check the box labeled Enable Output Cache.

5. In the Authenticated Cache Profile, select Intranet (Collaboration Site) from the drop-down list.

6. Click the OK button.

7. On the Site Settings page, click the link titled Site Output Cache.

8. On the Site Output Cache page, verify that the site is inheriting its settings from the site collection.

9. Click the OK button.

Configuring Object and Disk Caching

Object caching is a mechanism used by SharePoint to cache site, page, and page layout properties. *Disk caching* is used to cache BLOBs so that they do not have to be retrieved from the database. Object and disk caching are extremely fast and can significantly improve performance of sites, especially when large media files are involved. By default, object caching is always on, and disk caching is turned off. In order to enable disk caching, you must edit the `web.config` file for the web application where you want to use it. The `BlobCache` element controls disk caching and is shown in the following code:

```
<BlobCache location="C:\blobCache" path="\.(gif|jpg|png|css|js)$"
        maxSize="10" max-age="86400" enabled="false"/>
```

Changing the value of the `enabled` attribute to `True` will enable disk caching. The attributes associated with the `BlobCache` element control the configuration of the object cache. These are set to generally acceptable values, but may be changed. Table 12-2 lists the attributes and their effects on the object cache.

Table 12-2. *The BlobCache Elements*

Attribute	Description
location	The directory where the cached files will be stored
path	A regular expression that matches file extensions to determine which files are cached
maxSize	The maximum size of the disk-based cache in gigabytes
max-age	The amount of time in seconds that the client browser caches BLOBs
enabled	A value to enable or disable the object cache

You can manage the object and disk cache through SharePoint. Each site collection has access to cache management through the Site Settings page. On the Site Settings page, you can click the link titled Site Collection Object Cache to access a page that will let you change the maximum size, flush a cache, or change attributes. Figure 12-5 shows the page.

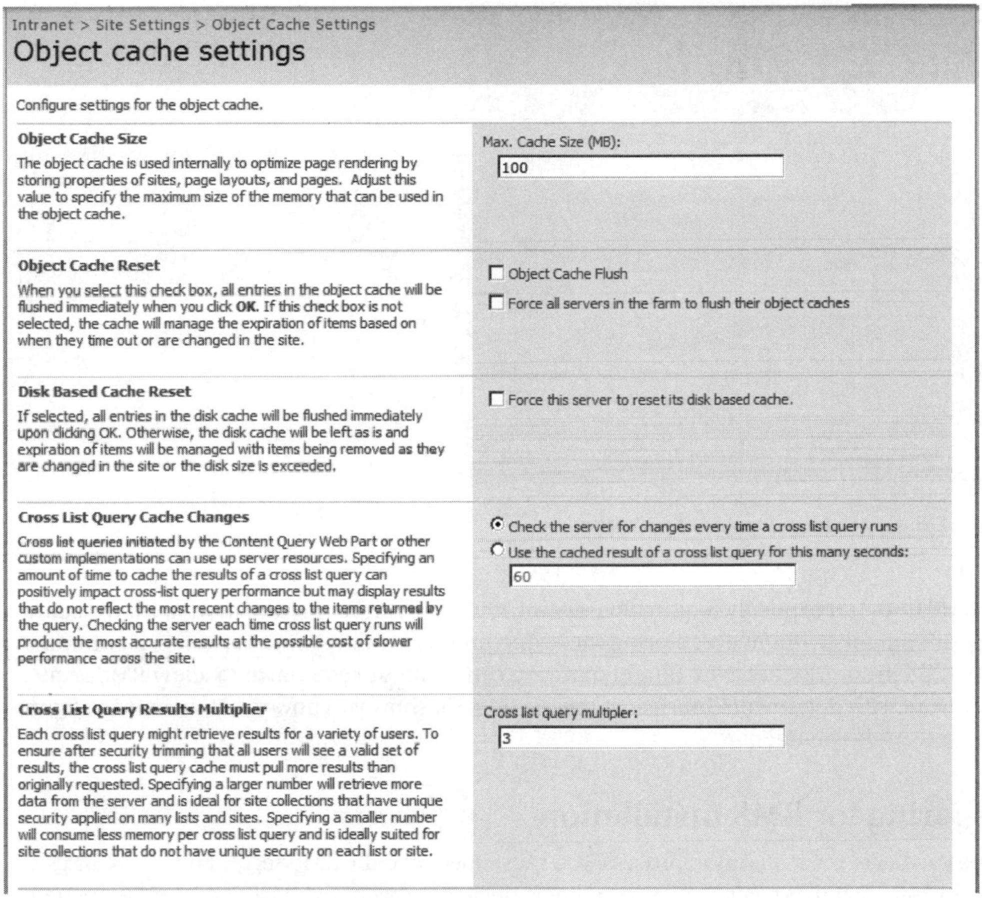

Intranet > Site Settings > Object Cache Settings

Object cache settings

Configure settings for the object cache.

Object Cache Size

The object cache is used internally to optimize page rendering by storing properties of sites, page layouts, and pages. Adjust this value to specify the maximum size of the memory that can be used in the object cache.

Max. Cache Size (MB):

100

Object Cache Reset

When you select this check box, all entries in the object cache will be flushed immediately when you click **OK**. If this check box is not selected, the cache will manage the expiration of items based on when they time out or are changed in the site.

☐ Object Cache Flush

☐ Force all servers in the farm to flush their object caches

Disk Based Cache Reset

If selected, all entries in the disk cache will be flushed immediately upon clicking OK. Otherwise, the disk cache will be left as is and expiration of items will be managed with items being removed as they are changed in the site or the disk size is exceeded.

☐ Force this server to reset its disk based cache.

Cross List Query Cache Changes

Cross list queries initiated by the Content Query Web Part or other custom implementations can use up server resources. Specifying an amount of time to cache the results of a cross list query can positively impact cross-list query performance but may display results that do not reflect the most recent changes to the items returned by the query. Checking the server each time cross list query runs will produce the most accurate results at the possible cost of slower performance across the site.

◉ Check the server for changes every time a cross list query runs

○ Use the cached result of a cross list query for this many seconds:

60

Cross List Query Results Multiplier

Each cross list query might retrieve results for a variety of users. To ensure after security trimming that all users will see a valid set of results, the cross list query cache must pull more results than originally requested. Specifying a larger number will retrieve more data from the server and is ideal for site collections that have unique security applied on many lists and sites. Specifying a smaller number will consume less memory per cross list query and is ideally suited for site collections that do not have unique security on each list or site.

Cross list query multipler:

3

Figure 12-5. *Managing the object and disk caches*

Using Windows Rights Management

Windows Rights Management Services (RMS) is a technology that allows you to control granular permissions associated with documents. RMS is an enhancement to typical file-level permissions and allows you to control who can view, edit, copy, print, or e-mail your documents. RMS is useful for ensuring that highly sensitive documents are not printed, copied, or mailed outside of the organization.

Document restrictions can be put in place either by an author or by policy on a document library. Document authors can implement restrictions by selecting Prepare ➤ Restrict Permission ➤ Restricted Access from the menu in Microsoft Office 2007, which displays a dialog allowing you to assign users either read or change permissions. *Read permissions* allow the document to be viewed but prevents changing, printing, or copying content. *Change permissions* allow reading, editing, and saving but not printing. Figure 12-6 shows the Permission dialog in Word 2007.

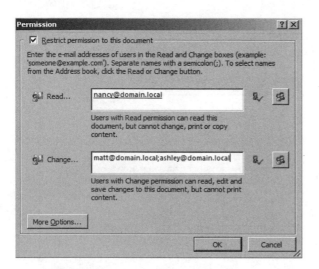

Figure 12-6. *Restricting document permissions*

RMS does not explicitly require SharePoint 2007. You can set up RMS and use it to secure Office documents without ever storing those documents in SharePoint. However, if you want to use RMS in conjunction with SharePoint, you can configure your farm to allow RMS security to work with document libraries. In this section, I'll show you how to set up and configure RMS for use with SharePoint.

Preparing for RMS Installation

Before you begin the installation process, you must download the RMS server and client. RMS works by establishing a centralized server that verifies permissions when a document is opened. Each person wishing to use RMS documents must have the RMS client installed on their machine as well. Additionally, the SharePoint server requires the RMS client to be installed so that document libraries can be configured to support RMS. Table 12-3 lists the required software and the location from which it can be downloaded.

Table 12-3. *Required Software*

Software	Location
RMS server	`http://www.microsoft.com/downloads/details.aspx?FamilyId=5794538F-E572-4542-A5BD-901B2720F068&displaylang=en`
RMS client	`http://www.microsoft.com/downloads/details.aspx?FamilyId=02DA5107-2919-414B-A5A3-3102C7447838&displaylang=en`

After you have downloaded the required software, you can prepare the server for RMS installation. In this example, I will use the VSSQL server from the development environment to host the RMS server. The server running RMS must be an application server with Message Queuing and .NET Framework 1.1 installed.

Follow these steps to prepare for RMS installation:

1. Log in to VSSQL as a domain administrator.

2. Select Start ➤ Control Panel ➤ Add or Remove Programs.

3. In the Add or Remove Programs dialog, click the Add/Remove Windows Components button.

4. In the Windows Components Wizard, select Application Server and click the Details button.

5. In the Application Server dialog, check the box associated with Message Queuing and click the OK button.

6. In the Windows Components Wizard, click the Next button.

7. When Message Queuing installation is complete, close the Add/Remove Programs dialog.

8. Select Start ➤ Administrative Tools ➤ Internet Information Services (IIS) Manager.

9. In the IIS Manager, expand the tree until the Web Service Extensions folder is visible.

10. If ASP.NET v1.1.4322 is not visible, click the link titled Add a New Web Service Extension.

11. In the New Web Service Extension dialog, click the Add button.

12. In the Add File dialog, click the Browse button.

13. Browse to the file located at C:\Windows \Microsoft .NET\Framework\v1.1.4322\ aspnet_isapi.dll and click the Open button.

14. In the Add File dialog, click the OK button.

15. In the New Web Service Extension dialog, enter **ASP.NET v1.1.4322** in the Extension Name field.

16. Check the box labeled Set Extension Status to Allowed.

17. Click the OK button.

Installing the RMS Server

The RMS server software installation is straightforward, but you must perform a few configuration steps after the installation. Specifically, you must provision the RMS server on to an IIS web site and register RMS in Active Directory so that client machines can find it.

Follow these steps to install and configure the RMS server:

1. Launch the Windows Rights Management server installation and follow the steps.

2. When the installation is complete, select Start ➤ All Programs ➤ Windows RMS ➤ Windows RMS Administration.

3. In the Windows RMS Global Administration site, click the link titled Provision RMS on this Web Site.

4. On the Provision the RMS Root Certification Server page, select the Remote Database option under the Configuration Database section.

5. Under the RMS Service Account section, enter DOMAIN\SPConfigAcct in the User Name field.

6. Enter the appropriate password in the Password field.

7. Under the Private Key Protection and Enrollment section, enter a strong password in the RMS Private Key Password field.

8. Enter a contact name in the Administrative Contact field.

9. Under the RMS Proxy Settings section, clear the box labeled This Computer Uses a Proxy Server to Connect to the Internet.

10. Click the Submit button.

11. When provisioning is complete, select Start ➤ All Programs ➤ Windows RMS ➤ Windows RMS Administration.

12. In the Windows RMS Global Administration site, click the link titled Administer RMS on This Web Site.

13. On the Administration for Default Web Site page, click the link titled RMS Service Connection Point.

14. On the RMS Service Connection Point page, click the Register URL button.

15. Open the Windows File Explorer and navigate to the file C:\Inetpub\wwwroot\WRM_wmcs\Certification\ServerCertification.asmx.

16. Right-click the `ServerCertification.asmx` file and select Properties from the context menu.

17. Click the Security tab.

18. On the Security tab, click the Add button.

19. In the Select Users, Computers, or Groups dialog, type **Authenticated Users** and click the Check Names button. This step is required so that the Central Administration web site can utilize the RMS client when configuring RMS for the SharePoint farm.

20. Click the OK button.

21. In the `ServerCertification.asmx` Properties dialog, click the OK button.

Configuring RMS in the SharePoint Farm

Once the RMS server is installed, you may set up RMS for SharePoint. SharePoint uses the Central Administration web site to enable the use of RMS on document libraries in the farm. In order to work with RMS, the RMS client must be installed on the SharePoint server before configuring the farm.

Follow these steps to configure RMS for the SharePoint farm:

1. Log in to VSMOSS as a domain administrator.

2. Launch the Windows Rights Management client installation and follow the steps.

3. When the installation is complete, select Start ➤ All Programs ➤ Microsoft Office Server ➤ SharePoint 3.0 Central Administration.

4. When the Central Administration site opens, click the Operations tab.

5. Under the Security Configuration section, click the link titled Information Rights Management.

6. On the Information Rights Management page, click the option labeled Use the Default RMS Server Specified in Active Directory.

7. Click the OK button.

8. Open the home page of the intranet site you created in Chapter 2 (e. g., `http://vsmoss/sites/intranet/pages/default.aspx`).

9. Click the Document Center tab.

10. In the Document Center, click the Documents library.

11. In the Documents library, select Settings ➤ Document Library Settings.

12. On the Customize page, click the link titled Information Rights Management.

13. Check the box labeled Restrict Permission to Documents in This Library on Download.

14. Enter **Restricted** in the Permission Policy Title field.

15. Enter **Secured documents** in the Permission Policy Description field.

16. Click the OK button.

Using RMS with Documents

Once RMS is configured on the farm and you have established a policy for a document library, you can test it from a client machine. Each client must have the RMS client software installed before they can access protected documents. Once installed, clients may use RMS to protect their own documents as well as work with documents protected by SharePoint.

Follow these steps to use RMS from a client:

1. Log in to VSCLIENT as a local administrator.

2. Launch the Windows Rights Management client installation and follow the steps.

3. Open the home page of the intranet site you created in Chapter 2 as someone other than the author of documents in the library.

4. Click the Document Center tab.

5. In the Document Center, click the Documents library and open a document from the library.

6. Verify that the Print button is disabled in Word. Figure 12-7 shows the menu in Word 2007 with the Print command disabled.

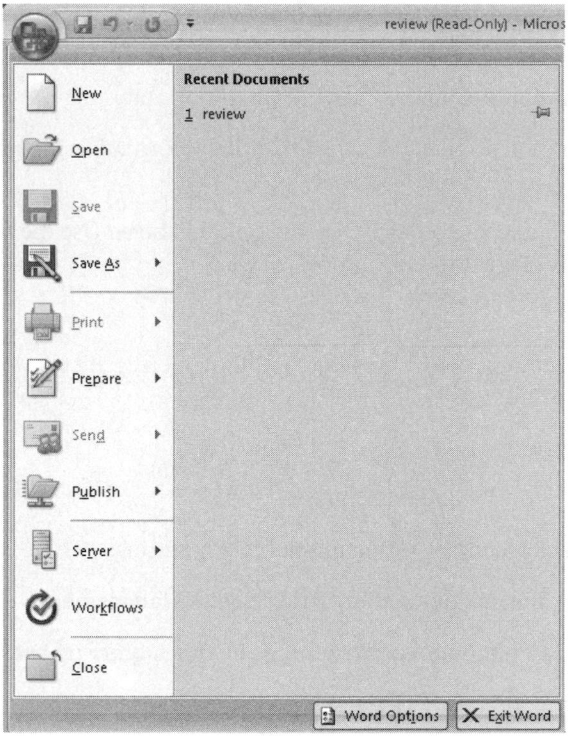

Figure 12-7. *The File menu in Word 2007*

Configuring Antivirus Protection

SharePoint 2007 supports antivirus scanning of documents when they are uploaded into a document library or opened by a user. In order to perform the scanning, however, you must purchase a commercial antivirus program and install it on each front-end web server in the farm. Most of the big-name vendors have product offerings specifically for SharePoint. Once installed, you may configure antivirus support by clicking the Antivirus link on the Operations page. Figure 12-8 shows the Anitvirus page in the Central Administration site.

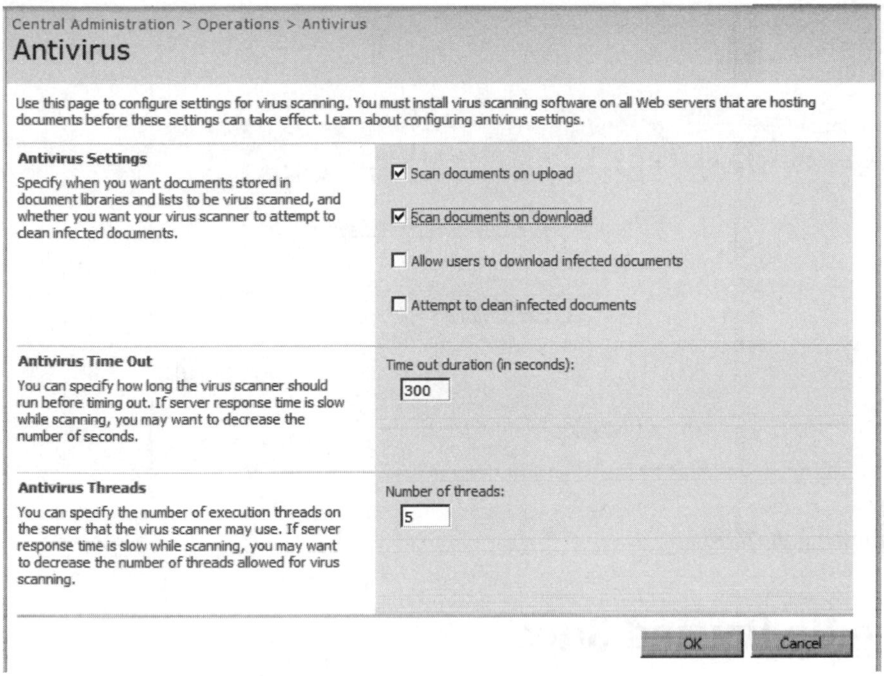

Figure 12-8. *Configuring antivirus support*

Quiescing the Farm

SharePoint 2007 introduces a new word into the technical lexicon to describe taking a farm out of service. *Quiesce* is defined as the act of going to rest. Interestingly, this word is not even present in the references contained within the Word 2007 Research pane, but you will see it on the Operations tab under the Global Configuration section.

When you quiesce a farm, you cause it to shut down slowly so that it can finish processing pending requests. Although the farm will immediately stop accepting new requests, it will try to complete all existing requests so that users do not experience a sudden service interruption. This is in stark contrast to a simple IIS reset, which will simply drop all requests. When you quiesce the farm, you specify a duration over which to complete the operation. While the farm is quiescing, it will continue to process any pending requests. If the specified duration is exceeded, these requests will subsequently be dropped. Figure 12-9 shows the options for quiescing the farm.

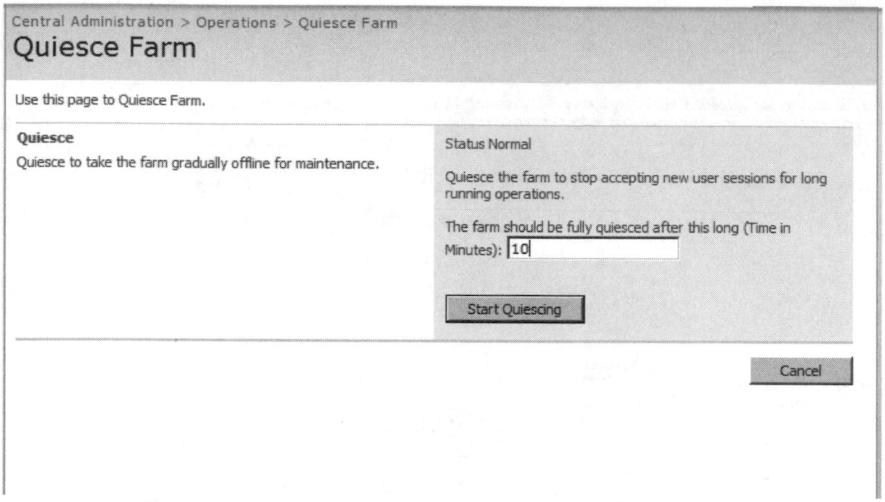

Central Administration > Operations > Quiesce Farm
Quiesce Farm

Use this page to Quiesce Farm.

Quiesce
Quiesce to take the farm gradually offline for maintenance.

Status Normal

Quiesce the farm to stop accepting new user sessions for long running operations.

The farm should be fully quiesced after this long (Time in Minutes): [10]

[Start Quiescing]

[Cancel]

Figure 12-9. *Quiescing the farm*

Cleaning Up Unused Sites

If your SharePoint infrastructure is successful, you may find that you have a proliferation of team and departmental sites. The problem with site proliferation is that there is really no motivation for any user to delete a site after it has served its purpose. If a user creates a site for the annual company sales meeting, for example, he or she is unlikely to care about the site after the meeting is over. This can lead to many dead sites in the farm.

The solution in SharePoint is to implement site-use confirmation and deletion. This facility allows SharePoint to query site owners and determine whether a site is still in use. The owners confirm sites that are still in use, whereas sites that are no longer useful may be deleted. If you want, you can even set up SharePoint to automatically delete sites that have not been confirmed over a period of time.

Site use and confirmation is configured to send e-mail notifications to the owner of a site collection that has not been used for a specified period of time. When the e-mail is received, the owner will have a set of hyperlinks in the e-mail that will allow the owner to confirm that the site is in use or delete the site. If you have enabled automatic site deletion, the site will automatically be deleted if the site collection owner fails to respond to the request after a configured number of notifications. Figure 12-10 shows the configuration page, which is accessible from the Application Management tab in the Central Administration site.

Enabling automatic site deletion ensures that unneeded sites are always removed from the farm. However, automatically deleting sites can result in the removal of sites that are seldom used but contain valuable information. For this reason, you should always set reasonable notification intervals that give plenty of opportunity for site collection owners to respond. Finally, you should require that all site collections have a designated secondary owner who can respond to the notifications if the primary owner is unavailable.

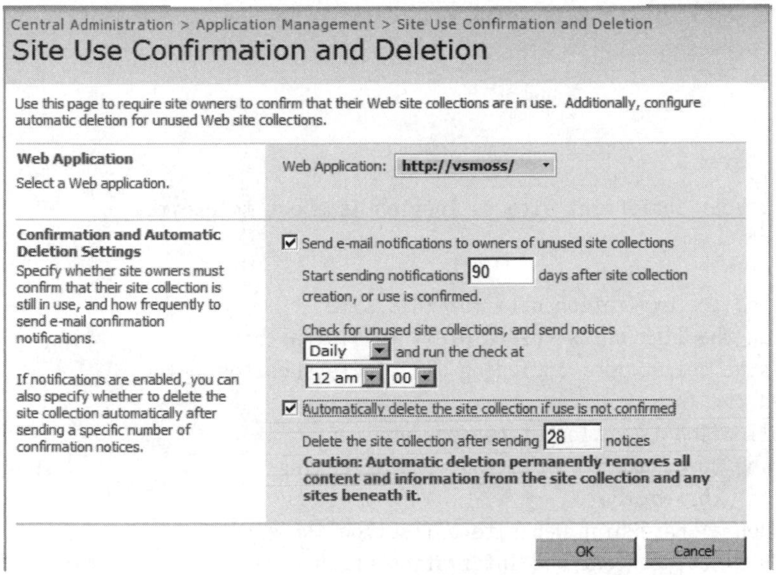

Figure 12-10. *Configuring site-use confirmation and deletion*

The site use confirmation and deletion system uses two different message texts to send notifications: one text is used when you enable site confirmation, while the other text is used if you have also enabled automatic deletion. Administrators may customize these notices, which are located in C:\Program Files\Common Files\Microsoft Shared\Web Server Extensions\12\TEMPLATE\1033\XML\DeadWeb.xml. Listing 12-1 shows the contents of the notification file.

Listing 12-1. *The Site Notification Message*

```
<?xml version="1.0" encoding="utf-8"?>
<!-- _lcid="1033" _version="12.0.4518" _dal="1" -->
<!-- _LocalBinding -->
<Email>
  <Confirmation>
    <ConfirmationSubject>
      Confirm SharePoint Web site in use
    </ConfirmationSubject>
    <ConfirmationBody>
      <![CDATA[Please follow the link below
      to your SharePoint Web site to confirm that it is still in use.
      <br><a href="|0">|0</a><br><br>
      If the site is not being used, please go to <a href="|1">|1</a>,
      and select "Delete This Site" to remove the Web site.
      <br><br>
```

```
        You will receive reminders of this until you confirm the
        site is in use, or delete it.]]>
      </ConfirmationBody>
    </Confirmation>
    <AutoDeleteWarning>
      <AutoDeleteSubject>
        ACTION REQUIRED: Your SharePoint site collection is about to expire
      </AutoDeleteSubject>
      <AutoDeleteBody>
        <![CDATA[To extend the expiration date for this site
        collection, click the link below:<br><a href="|0">|0</a><br><br>
        Otherwise this site collection, including all of its subsites,
        might be deleted.<br><br>
        If this site collection is no longer needed, you can
        delete it by going to <a href="|1">|1</a>, and selecting
        "Delete this site".<br><br>
        Please note - When a SharePoint Web site collection is
        deleted, all Web sites, content and information which
        were part of the site collection are completely erased.
        The site can only be restored if a backup exists.]]>
      </AutoDeleteBody>
    </AutoDeleteWarning>
  </Email>
```

Implementing Quotas and Locks

When you create SharePoint sites, there is really no limit to the amount of information that users may store there. In some cases, this can lead to very large sites that take up a significant amount of storage space. If you would like to limit the size of sites, you can implement a quota template that defines the storage limits.

Quota templates are created by clicking the link found on the Application Management page. Quota templates define a maximum allowed storage limit and a point at which a warning e-mail should be sent to the site administrator. When you open the Quota Templates page, you'll see that SharePoint has defined some templates for you, but you can easily create your own.

Quota templates are applied to sites by clicking the link titled Site Collection Quotas and Locks on the Application Management tab. On this page, you may select the site collection to which you want to apply a quota. Then you may select the quota template to implement.

Along with specifying a quota, you may also use this page to lock a site collection. Locking a site collection allows you to specify various levels of access to a site collection while preserving the existing data. This is an excellent way to archive a site collection that is not in use but has valuable information within it. Figure 12-11 shows the Site Collection Quota and Locks page.

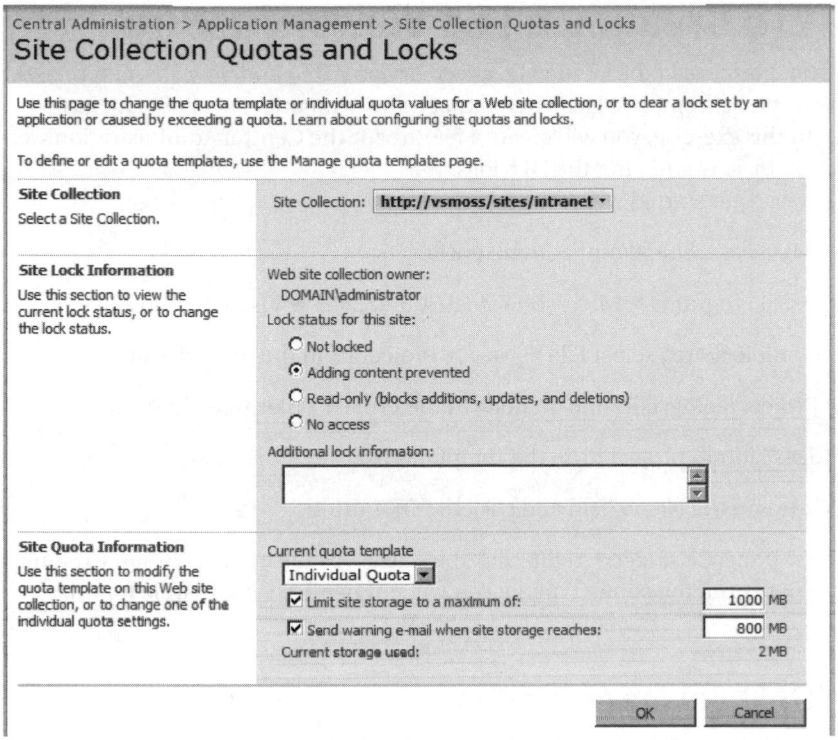

Central Administration > Application Management > Site Collection Quotas and Locks

Site Collection Quotas and Locks

Use this page to change the quota template or individual quota values for a Web site collection, or to clear a lock set by an application or caused by exceeding a quota. Learn about configuring site quotas and locks.

To define or edit a quota templates, use the Manage quota templates page.

Site Collection Select a Site Collection.	Site Collection: **http://vsmoss/sites/intranet** ▾
Site Lock Information Use this section to view the current lock status, or to change the lock status.	Web site collection owner: DOMAIN\administrator Lock status for this site: ○ Not locked ● Adding content prevented ○ Read-only (blocks additions, updates, and deletions) ○ No access Additional lock information:
Site Quota Information Use this section to modify the quota template on this Web site collection, or to change one of the individual quota settings.	Current quota template Individual Quota ▾ ☑ Limit site storage to a maximum of: 1000 MB ☑ Send warning e-mail when site storage reaches: 800 MB Current storage used: 2 MB

OK   Cancel

Figure 12-11. *Manging quotas and locks*

Using the Command-Line Utility

This chapter has covered several key administrative tasks that you can perform through the Central Administration web site. However, you can perform these tasks and many others through the command-line utility STSADM.EXE, which is located in the folder C:\Program Files\Common Files\Microsoft Shared\web server extensions\12\bin. I have mentioned STSADM.EXE in previous chapters for such things as installing features, but this utility is capable of performing a wide variety of tasks. Typically, you'll use the –o parameter to specify the operation to perform followed by a series of values to use with the operation. The following code shows an example operation that installs the NewButton feature.

```
STSADM.EXE –o installfeature –filename NewButton\Feature.xml
```

STSADM.EXE supports a few dozen operations. Executing STSADM.EXE -help will list all of the possible operations you can perform with the utility. Executing the help command followed by the name of an operation will display the proper format for the operation and the required parameters.

Exercise 12.1. Creating a Log Viewer Feature

Earlier in this chapter, I discussed the Unified Logging Service (ULS) and how SharePoint uses it to record key events and exceptions. I also noted that there is no utility available for easily viewing these logs. In this exercise, you will create a feature for the Central Administration web site that will allow you to view and filter the ULS logs.

Follow these steps to get started with the project:

1. Log in to VSMOSS as a SharePoint administrator.

2. Select Start ➤ All Programs ➤ Microsoft Visual Studio 2005 ➤ Visual Studio 2005.

3. When Visual Studio starts, select File ➤ New ➤ Project from the main menu.

4. In the New Project dialog, click the C# node in the Project Types tree.

5. Select the Class Library project from the Templates list.

6. Enter **LogViewer** in the Name field and click the OK button.

7. When the new project is created, right-click the `Class1.cs` file in the Solution Explorer and select Delete from the context menu. You will not need a class module for this project.

Creating the ULSLogViewer Page

The heart of this project is the `ULSLogViewer.aspx` page. This page will be deployed so that it becomes part of the Central Administration web site. The goal is to create a page that fits in with the site and looks like it was part of the original product. In order to make this happen, you will create the ASPX page as a single file and deploy it into the folder C:\Program Files\ Common Files\web server extensions\12\TEMPLATE\ADMIN folder. This folder is similar to the LAYOUTS folder you used when you created features for site collections. Pages placed in the ADMIN folder can use the `admin.master` file, which defines the look and feel for the Central Administration web site.

Follow these steps to create the `ULSLogViewer.aspx` page:

1. In Visual Studio, select Project ➤ Add New Item from the main menu.

2. In the Add New Item dialog, select to add a text file to the project. You must select a text file because web forms are not available to this project type.

3. Enter **ULSLogViewer.aspx** in the Name field.

4. Click the OK button.

Adding Required References

Once the new blank page is open in Visual Studio, you must begin the process of coding the page. Creating a page that can successfully run inside the Central Administration web site requires careful attention to detail. Although you will have IntelliSense available, you do not have a visual development environment or access to all of the project elements such as the `admin.master`. Therefore, you may see some errors during design that will not impact the page when it is properly deployed. In any case, you must start by adding the appropriate references to the admin.master page, the control templates, and the required assemblies. Add the code from Listing 12-2 to the page to add these references.

Listing 12-2. *Required References*

```
<%@ Page Language="C#" MasterPageFile="~/_admin/admin.master" %>

<%@ Assembly Name="Microsoft.SharePoint, Version=12.0.0.0,
    Culture=neutral,PublicKeyToken=71e9bce111e9429c" %>
<%@ Assembly Name="Microsoft.SharePoint.ApplicationPages.Administration,
    Version=12.0.0.0, Culture=neutral, PublicKeyToken=71e9bce111e9429c" %>
<%@ Assembly Name="System.Web, Version=2.0.0.0, Culture=neutral,
    PublicKeyToken=b03f5f7f11d50a3a" %>
<%@ Import Namespace="Microsoft.SharePoint.ApplicationPages" %>
<%@ Import Namespace="Microsoft.SharePoint" %>
<%@ Import Namespace="Microsoft.SharePoint" %>
<%@ Import Namespace="Microsoft.SharePoint.Administration" %>
<%@ Import Namespace="System.IO" %>
<%@ Import Namespace="System.Web.UI" %>
<%@ Import Namespace="System.Data" %>
<%@ Register TagPrefix="SharePoint"
    Namespace="Microsoft.SharePoint.WebControls" %>
<%@ Register TagPrefix="Utilities"
    Namespace="Microsoft.SharePoint.Utilities"
    Assembly="Microsoft.SharePoint, Version=12.0.0.0,
    Culture=neutral, PublicKeyToken=71e9bce111e9429c" %>
<%@ Register TagPrefix="wssuc" TagName="InputFormSection"
    Src="~/_controltemplates/InputFormSection.ascx" %>
<%@ Register TagPrefix="wssuc" TagName="InputFormControl"
    Src="~/_controltemplates/InputFormControl.ascx" %>
<%@ Register TagPrefix="wssuc" TagName="ButtonSection"
    Src="~/_controltemplates/ButtonSection.ascx" %>
```

Coding Placeholders

Once you have the required references at the top of the page, you may begin to add content to the placeholders. The available placeholders are defined by the admin.master page and include placeholders for the page title and description. Add the code from Listing 12-3 to define these content placeholders.

Listing 12-3. *Placeholders Code*

```
<asp:Content ID="Content2" runat="server"
    ContentPlaceHolderID="PlaceHolderPageTitleInTitleArea">
    Unified Logging Service (ULS) Logs
</asp:Content>
```

```
<asp:Content ID="Content3" runat="server"
    ContentPlaceHolderID="PlaceHolderPageDescription">
    This page allows you to browse the Unified Logging Service logs
</asp:Content>
```

Coding the Main Placeholder

The most complicated part of the page is the code for the main placeholder. The main place-holder represents the body of the page. Here you will define drop-down lists to select the log file for viewing as well as parameters for filtering the logs. The layout of this page is controlled by the user controls InputFormSection and InputFormControl. These user controls were created specifically for the Central Administration site and give it that familiar two-column look with explanations on the left and controls on the right. There is some effort involved in working through this code, but it is an excellent way to learn how a SharePoint page is laid out. Add the code from Listing 12-4 to create the main body of the page.

Listing 12-4. *The Main Placeholder Code*

```
<asp:Content ID="Content4" runat="server"
    ContentPlaceHolderID="PlaceHolderMain">
  <table border="0" cellspacing="0" cellpadding="0"
  class="ms-propertysheet" width="100%">
    <tr><td>
      <!-- This section lists the log files that are on the server -->
      <wssuc:InputFormSection Title="Available log files" runat="server">
        <template_description>
          <asp:Literal Id="Literal1" runat="server"
          text="These are the available log files that you can view."/>
        </template_description>
        <template_inputformcontrols>
          <wssuc:InputFormControl runat="server"
          LabelText="Select a log file to view">
            <Template_control>
              <asp:DropDownList ID="listFiles" runat="server"
              EnableViewState="true" Width="100%"/>
            </Template_control>
          </wssuc:InputFormControl>
        </template_inputformcontrols>
      </wssuc:InputFormSection>

      <!-- This section filters the logs by category and severity -->
      <wssuc:InputFormSection Title="Log Filtering" runat="server">
        <template_description>
          <asp:Literal runat="server"
          text="Select the keywords to use when filtering the logs"/>
        </template_description>
```

```
<template_inputformcontrols>
  <TABLE border="0" cellspacing="0" cellpadding="0" width="100%">
    <tr><td>
      <wssuc:InputFormControl runat="server"
      LabelText="This category..."
      LabelAssociatedControlId="listCategories">
      <Template_control>
        <asp:DropDownList Id="listCategories" runat="server"
        EnableViewState="true">
          <asp:ListItem value="empty" Text=""/>
          <asp:ListItem value="Administration" Text="Administration"/>
          <asp:ListItem value="Backup and Restore"
          Text="Backup and Restore"/>
          <asp:ListItem value="Backward Compatible"
          Text="Backward Compatible Administration and Object Model"/>
          <asp:ListItem value="Business Data"
          Text="Business Data Catalog"/>
          <asp:ListItem value="Communication" Text="Communication"/>
          <asp:ListItem value="Content Deployment"
          Text="Content Deployment"/>
          <asp:ListItem value="Database" Text="Database"/>
          <asp:ListItem value="Document Management"
          Text="Document Management"/>
          <asp:ListItem value="E-Mail" Text="E-Mail" />
          <asp:ListItem value="Excel" Text="Excel Services"/>
          <asp:ListItem value="Feature Infrastructure"
          Text="Feature Infrastructure"/>
          <asp:ListItem value="Fields" Text="Fields"/>
          <asp:ListItem value="Forms Services" Text="Forms Services"/>
          <asp:ListItem value="General" Text="General"/>
          <asp:ListItem value="Information Policy Management"
          Text="Information Policy Management"/>
          <asp:ListItem value="IRM"
          Text="Information Rights Management"/>
          <asp:ListItem value="Knowledge Network Server"
          Text="Knowledge Network Server"/>
          <asp:ListItem value="Launcher Service"
          Text="Launcher Service"/>
          <asp:ListItem value="Load Balancer Service"
          Text="Load Balancer Service"/>
          <asp:ListItem value="Long running operation infrastructure"
          Text="Long running operation infrastructure"/>
          <asp:ListItem value="MCMS 2002 Migration"
          Text="MCMS 2002 Migration"/>
          <asp:ListItem value="Office Server" Text="MOSS General"/>
          <asp:ListItem value="Shared Services"
          Text="MOSS Shared Services"/>
```

```
            <asp:ListItem value="MS Search" Text="MS Search"/>
            <asp:ListItem value="Project Server" Text="Project Server"/>
            <asp:ListItem value="Publishing" Text="Publishing Features"/>
            <asp:ListItem value="Records Center" Text="Records Center"/>
            <asp:ListItem value="Runtime" Text="Runtime"/>
            <asp:ListItem value="Server Help" Text="Server Help"/>
            <asp:ListItem value="Session State Service"
            Text="Session State Service"/>
            <asp:ListItem value="Setup and Upgrade"
            Text="Setup and Upgrade"/>
            <asp:ListItem value="SharePoint Services"
            Text="SharePoint Services"/>
            <asp:ListItem value="Site Directory" Text="Site Directory"/>
            <asp:ListItem value="Site Management" Text="Site Management"/>
            <asp:ListItem value="SSO" Text="SSO"/>
            <asp:ListItem value="Timer" Text="Timer"/>
            <asp:ListItem value="Topology" Text="Topology"/>
            <asp:ListItem value="Unified Logging Service"
            Text="Unified Logging Service"/>
            <asp:ListItem value="Upgrade" Text="Upgrade"/>
            <asp:ListItem value="User Profiles" Text="User Profiles"/>
            <asp:ListItem value="Web Controls" Text="Web Controls"/>
            <asp:ListItem value="Web Parts" Text="Web Parts"/>
            <asp:ListItem value="WebParts" Text="WebParts"/>
            <asp:ListItem value="Workflow" Text="Workflow"/>
        </asp:DropDownList>
      </Template_control>
    </wssuc:InputFormControl>
  </td></tr>
  <tr><td>
    <wssuc:InputFormControl runat="server"
    LabelText="AND this event severity..."
    LabelAssociatedControlId="listEvent" >
      <Template_control>
        <asp:DropDownList id="listEvent" runat="server"
          EnableViewState="true">
        <asp:ListItem Value="empty" Text=""/>
        <asp:ListItem Value="Error" Text="Error"/>
        <asp:ListItem Value="Warning" Text="Warning"/>
        <asp:ListItem Value="Failure" Text="Failure"/>
        <asp:ListItem Value="Critical" Text="Critical"/>
        <asp:ListItem Value="Success" Text="Success"/>
        <asp:ListItem Value="Information" Text="Information"/>
        </asp:DropDownList>
      </Template_control>
    </wssuc:InputFormControl>
  </td></tr>
```

```
  <tr><td>
    <wssuc:InputFormControl runat="server"
    LabelText="OR this trace severity"
    LabelAssociatedControlId="listTrace" >
      <Template_control>
        <asp:DropDownList id="listTrace" runat="server"
        EnableViewState="true">
          <asp:ListItem Value="empty" Text=""/>
          <asp:ListItem Value="Unexpected" Text="Unexpected"/>
          <asp:ListItem Value="Monitorable" Text="Monitorable"/>
          <asp:ListItem Value="High" Text="High"/>
          <asp:ListItem Value="Medium" Text="Medium"/>
          <asp:ListItem Value="Verbose" Text="Verbose"/>
        </asp:DropDownList>
      </Template_control>
    </wssuc:InputFormControl>
  </td></tr>
</TABLE>
</template_inputformcontrols>
</wssuc:InputFormSection>
<!-- This section contains a button to show the logs -->
<wssuc:InputFormSection Title="Show the log" runat="server">
  <template_description>
    <asp:Literal Id="Literal3" runat="server"
    text="Press the button to view the selected log."/><br />
      <asp:Literal Id="Literal2" runat="server"
      text="Note: Logs can take some time to process and display."/>
        </template_description>
          <template_inputformcontrols>
            <wssuc:InputFormControl runat="server" LabelText="">
              <Template_control>
                <asp:Button Id="buttonGo" Text="Go" Width="60px"
                runat="server" onclick="FillGrid"/>
              </Template_control>
            </wssuc:InputFormControl>
          </template_inputformcontrols>
        </wssuc:InputFormSection>
      </td></tr>
    </table>
  <!-- This table shows the selected log entries -->
  <table border="0" cellspacing="0" cellpadding="0"
  class="ms-propertysheet" width="100%">
    <tr><td>
      <asp:Label runat="server" ID="message" class="ms-error" />
    </td></tr>
```

```
        <tr><td>
          asp:DataGrid runat="server" ID="gridLog" Width="100%"
          class="ms-descriptionText" GridLines="Horizontal" />
        </td></tr>
    </table>
</asp:Content>
```

Adding Required Script

The last part of the page involves writing the code to parse the logs and display them in a grid. This code is reasonably straightforward. It simply opens the selected log file, separates it into columns, and loads a custom DataTable with the information. The DataTable is then bound to a DataGrid for display. Add the code from Listing 12-5 to finish the page.

■**Note** Be sure the connection string in the following code is correct for your environment.

Listing 12-5. *Processing the Logs*

```
<script runat="server">


  protected void Page_Load(object sender, EventArgs e)
  {

    if (!Page.IsPostBack)
    {
      try
      {
        //Open the farm
        SPFarm farm = SPFarm.Open
        ("Data Source=VSSQL;Initial Catalog=MOSS_Config;➥
        Integrated Security=SSPI");

        //Get reference to ULS
        SPDiagnosticsService diagnostics = new SPDiagnosticsService("log", farm);
        string[] files = Directory.GetFiles(diagnostics.LogLocation,"*.log");

        //Show list of logs
        DataTable lines = new DataTable("Lines");
        lines.Columns.Add("Name", typeof(string));
        lines.Columns.Add("Path", typeof(string));
```

```
      for (int i = files.Length - 1; i>-1; i--)
      {
        if (files[i].IndexOf("Diagnostics") == -1)
        {
          string[] line = { files[i].Substring(files[i].LastIndexOf("\\") + 1),
          files[i] };
          lines.Rows.Add(line);
        }
      }

      listFiles.DataSource = lines;
      listFiles.DataTextField = "Name";
      listFiles.DataValueField = "Path";
      listFiles.DataBind();
      listFiles.Items.Insert(0, "Select a file...");


    }
    catch (Exception x)
    {
      message.Text = x.Message;
    }
  }
}

protected void FillGrid(object sender, EventArgs e)
{

  try
  {
    message.Text = "";

    //Create table
    DataTable entries = new DataTable("Entries");
    entries.Columns.Add("Timestamp", typeof(string));
    entries.Columns.Add("Process", typeof(string));
    entries.Columns.Add("TID", typeof(string));
    entries.Columns.Add("Area", typeof(string));
    entries.Columns.Add("Category", typeof(string));
    entries.Columns.Add("EventID", typeof(string));
    entries.Columns.Add("Level", typeof(string));
    entries.Columns.Add("Message", typeof(string));
    entries.Columns.Add("Correlation", typeof(string));
```

```
//Fill table
StreamReader reader = new StreamReader(listFiles.SelectedValue);
reader.ReadLine().Split(new char[] { '\t' });

while (!reader.EndOfStream)
{
  string[] fields = reader.ReadLine().Split(new char[] { '\t' });

 //Category selected
  if(listCategories.Text != "empty")
  {
    //Category and Level selected
    if(listEvent.Text != "empty" || listTrace.Text != "empty")
    {
      if(fields[4].IndexOf(listCategories.Text) >= 0
         &&
         (fields[6].IndexOf(listEvent.Text) >= 0
         ||
         fields[6].IndexOf(listTrace.Text) >= 0))
         {
           entries.Rows.Add(fields);
         }

         }
         //Category, but no Level selected
         else
         {
         if(fields[4].IndexOf(listCategories.Text) >= 0)
         {
           entries.Rows.Add(fields);
         }
       }
     }

    //Category not selected
    else
    {
      //Level selected
      if(listEvent.Text != "empty" || listTrace.Text != "empty")
      {
        if(fields[6].IndexOf(listEvent.Text) >= 0
           ||
           fields[6].IndexOf(listTrace.Text) >= 0)
           {
             entries.Rows.Add(fields);
           }
         }
```

```
                    //Nothing selected
                    else
                    {
                        entries.Rows.Add(fields);
                    }
                }
            }

        //Show in grid
        gridLog.DataSource = entries;
        gridLog.DataBind();
    }

    catch (Exception x)
    {
        message.Text = x.Message;
    }
}

</script>
```

Creating the Feature File

Once the log viewing page is written, you must create a feature to add a new section to the Central Administration site that contains a link to the new page. This feature will be created just as you created other features in Chapter 7. First, you must create a Feature.xml file, then you must create a manifest file to implement the new link. Add a new XML file named Feature.xml to your project and add the code from Listing 12-6.

Listing 12-6. *The Feature File*

```
<?xml version="1.0" encoding="utf-8" ?>
<Feature xmlns=http://schemas.microsoft.com/sharepoint/
  Id="7B636574-FF78-4103-9791-879614CF6D1D"
  Scope="Farm"
  Title="Unified Logging Service (ULS) viewer"
  Description="Allows you to view ULS logs">
  <ElementManifests>
    <ElementManifest Location="Elements.xml" />
  </ElementManifests>
</Feature>
```

Creating the Manifest File

The manifest file describes the new section and link to be added to the Central Administration web site. The new section is created through a CustomActionGroup element. The link is created with a CustomAction element. Add a new XML file named Elements.xml to your project and add the code from Listing 12-7.

Listing 12-7. *The Manifest File*

```
<Elements xmlns="http://schemas.microsoft.com/sharepoint/">
  <CustomActionGroup Id="BDDBB947-CBC6-47f7-B57A-6C8BEB0E19D7"
    Location="Microsoft.SharePoint.Administration.Operations"
    Title="Utilities"
    Sequence="1000" />
  <CustomAction
    Id="E57ECD33-91FD-4fc3-A4E8-E1B932178CB4"
    GroupId="BDDBB947-CBC6-47f7-B57A-6C8BEB0E19D7"
    Location="Microsoft.SharePoint.Administration.Operations"
    Sequence="10"
    Title="View Unified Logging Service"
    Description="Displays Unified Logging Service (ULS) logs.">
      <UrlAction Url="_admin/ULSLogViewer.aspx" />
  </CustomAction>
</Elements>
```

Deploying the Feature

Deploying the feature is accomplished by creating a new folder under the Features directory and copying the Feature.xml and Elements.xml files into the folder. You must also copy the ULSLogViewer.aspx file into the ADMIN directory. Once the files are copied, you can install the feature and then access it from the Operations tab of the Central Administration site. To make deployment easier, Listing 12-8 shows a batch file you can use to accomplish the required steps. Figure 12-12 shows the resulting page in the Central Administration web site.

Listing 12-8. *The Batch Installation File*

```
@SET TEMPLATEDIR=
"c:\program files\common files\microsoft shared\web server extensions\12\Template"
@SET ADMINDIR=
"c:\program files\common files\microsoft shared\web server extensions\12\Template"
@SET STSADM=
"c:\program files\common files\microsoft shared\web server extensions\12\bin\stsadm"


MKDIR %TEMPLATEDIR%\FEATURES\LogViewer
XCOPY Feature.xml %TEMPLATEDIR%\FEATURES\LogViewer
XCOPY Elements.xml %TEMPLATEDIR%\FEATURES\LogViewer
XCOPY ULSLogViewer.aspx  %TEMPLATEDIR%\Admin
%STSADM% -o installfeature -filename  LogViewer\Feature.xml
IISRESET

ECHO "Installation Complete"
PAUSE
```

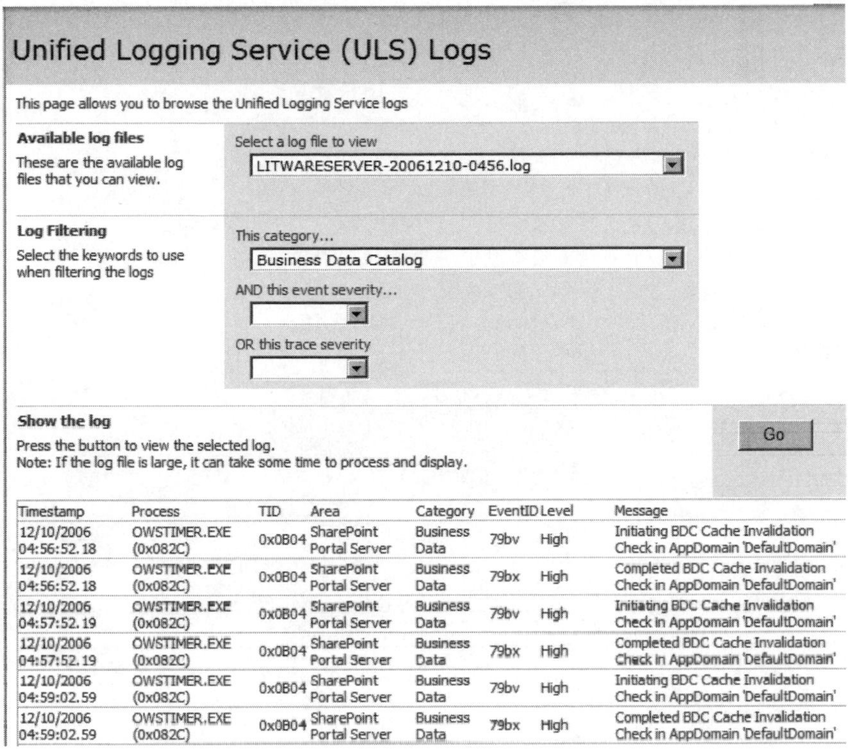

Unified Logging Service (ULS) Logs

This page allows you to browse the Unified Logging Service logs

Available log files

These are the available log files that you can view.

Select a log file to view

LITWARESERVER-20061210-0456.log

Log Filtering

Select the keywords to use when filtering the logs

This category...

Business Data Catalog

AND this event severity...

OR this trace severity

Show the log

Press the button to view the selected log.
Note: If the log file is large, it can take some time to process and display.

Go

Timestamp	Process	TID	Area	Category	EventID	Level	Message
12/10/2006 04:56:52.18	OWSTIMER.EXE (0x082C)	0x0B04	SharePoint Portal Server	Business Data	79bv	High	Initiating BDC Cache Invalidation Check in AppDomain 'DefaultDomain'
12/10/2006 04:56:52.18	OWSTIMER.EXE (0x082C)	0x0B04	SharePoint Portal Server	Business Data	79bx	High	Completed BDC Cache Invalidation Check in AppDomain 'DefaultDomain'
12/10/2006 04:57:52.19	OWSTIMER.EXE (0x082C)	0x0B04	SharePoint Portal Server	Business Data	79bv	High	Initiating BDC Cache Invalidation Check in AppDomain 'DefaultDomain'
12/10/2006 04:57:52.19	OWSTIMER.EXE (0x082C)	0x0B04	SharePoint Portal Server	Business Data	79bx	High	Completed BDC Cache Invalidation Check in AppDomain 'DefaultDomain'
12/10/2006 04:59:02.59	OWSTIMER.EXE (0x082C)	0x0B04	SharePoint Portal Server	Business Data	79bv	High	Initiating BDC Cache Invalidation Check in AppDomain 'DefaultDomain'
12/10/2006 04:59:02.59	OWSTIMER.EXE (0x082C)	0x0B04	SharePoint Portal Server	Business Data	79bx	High	Completed BDC Cache Invalidation Check in AppDomain 'DefaultDomain'

Figure 12-12. *The ULS log viewer*

Index

■T

You Need the Companion eBook

Your purchase of this book entitles you to buy the companion PDF-version eBook for only $10. Take the weightless companion with you anywhere.

We believe this Apress title will prove so indispensable that you'll want to carry it with you everywhere, which is why we are offering the companion eBook (in PDF format) for $10 to customers who purchase this book now. Convenient and fully searchable, the PDF version of any content-rich, page-heavy Apress book makes a valuable addition to your programming library. You can easily find and copy code—or perform examples by quickly toggling between instructions and the application. Even simultaneously tackling a donut, diet soda, and complex code becomes simplified with hands-free eBooks!

Once you purchase your book, getting the $10 companion eBook is simple:

❶ Visit **www.apress.com/promo/tendollars/**.

❷ Complete a basic registration form to receive a randomly generated question about this title.

❸ Answer the question correctly in 60 seconds, and you will receive a promotional code to redeem for the $10.00 eBook.

2560 Ninth Street • Suite 219 • Berkeley, CA 94710

eBookshop

Offer valid through 8/07.